A Variorum Commentary on the
Poems of John Milton
Volume 5, Part 4 [*Paradise Lost*, Book 4]

A Variorum Commentary on the Poems of John Milton

GENERAL EDITOR:

P. J. Klemp

CONTRIBUTING EDITORS:

Archie Burnett
W. Gardner Campbell
Claudia Champagne
Stephen B. Dobranski
Richard J. DuRocher
Cheryl Fresch
Edward Jones
Jameela Lares
John Leonard
John Mulryan
Stella Revard
Louis Schwartz

A Variorum Commentary on the Poems of John Milton

VOLUME 5, PART 4

Paradise Lost, Book 4

By

Cheryl H. Fresch

Edited by

P. J. Klemp

Duquesne University Press

Pittsburgh, Pennsylvania

Published in the United States of America by
DUQUESNE UNIVERSITY PRESS
600 Forbes Avenue
Pittsburgh, Pennsylvania 15282

LCCN 70129962
ISBN 978-0-8207-0442-5

∞ Printed on acid-free paper.

This volume is supported, in part, by a grant from the Calgon Corporation.

For Susan Joy Fresch,
beloved sister

Contents

Abbreviations of Milton's Writings

Animad	*Animadversions upon the Remonstrants Defence*
Apol	*An Apology against a Pamphlet*
Arc	*Arcades*
Areop	*Areopagitica*
Circum	"Upon the Circumcision"
Colas	*Colasterion*
DDD	*The Doctrine and Discipline of Divorce*
Def 2	*Pro populo anglicano defensio secunda* (*The Second Defence*)
DocCh	*De doctrina Christiana*
Educ	*Of Education*
Eikon	*Eikonoklastes*
El	*Elegy*
Eli	*In obitum Praesulis Eliensis*
EpDam	*Epitaphium Damonis*
FInf	"On the Death of a Fair Infant Dying of a Cough"
Hirelings	*Considerations Touching the Likeliest Means to Remove Hirelings Out of the Church*
HistBr	*The History of Britain*
Idea	"De Idea Platonica"
IlPen	*Il Penseroso*
L'All	*L'Allegro*
Lyc	*Lycidas*
Mask	*A Mask Presented at Ludlow Castle* (*Comus*)

Nat	"On the Morning of Christ's Nativity"
Naturam	"Naturam non pati senium"
Passion	"The Passion"
Patrem	*Ad Patrem*
PL	*Paradise Lost*
PR	*Paradise Regained*
Procan	*In obitum Procancellarii medici*
Prol	*Prolusions*
QNov	*In quintum Novembris*
RCG	*The Reason of Church-Government*
Ref	*Of Reformation*
SA	*Samson Agonistes*
Tetr	*Tetrachordon*
Time	"On Time"
Vac	"At a Vacation Exercise"

Preface

P. J. KLEMP

A Variorum Commentary on the Poems of John Milton has been a work in progress for over half a century. Another step in bringing closure to that monumental work, this volume on Book 4 of *Paradise Lost*, like the volume on *Samson Agonistes* published by Duquesne University Press in 2009, is a tangible sign of the scholarly continuity that exists between a new generation of Miltonists and our esteemed predecessors. Commentary about Milton's poems extends back to his own century, and the first variorum edition of *Paradise Lost* appeared in 1749 and that of *Paradise Regained*, *Samson Agonistes*, and many of the shorter poems in 1752, both edited by Thomas Newton. While this current volume looks back to those landmarks of scholarship, our main goal is to continue and complete the *Variorum Commentary* published between 1970 and 1975 by Columbia University Press.

Although the *Variorum Commentary* appeared in the 1970s, its inception occurred fully two decades earlier, in 1949. Merritt Y. Hughes, the *Variorum Commentary*'s first general editor, explains the process by which that scholarly project took shape. Following a survey of the Modern Language Association's members conducted by J. Milton French, in December 1949 the "interested section" of that organization "commissioned" the new *Variorum Commentary*. The editors selected were some of the twentieth century's finest Milton scholars, starting with French, who conducted the initial survey and declined the offer to become general editor. The rest of the participants were of the same stature, many of them joining French in being named Honored Scholars of the Milton Society of America: Merritt Y. Hughes (assigned to annotate *Paradise Lost*), Walter MacKellar (*Paradise Regained*), William Riley Parker (*Samson Agonistes*), A. S. P. Woodhouse (the so-called minor English poems), Douglas Bush (the Latin and Greek poems), and James E. Shaw (the Italian poems). If this epic catalog of scholars shines so brightly as to intimidate future generations who toil in the variorum's fields, it soon grew shorter.

For this generation of Milton scholars faced mortality, some well before their time. The opening volume of the Columbia University Press *Variorum Commentary* refers to the deaths of James E. Shaw, whose work on the Italian poems was updated by A. Bartlett Giamatti, and of William Riley Parker, whose work on *Samson Agonistes* would be carried on by John Steadman and, decades later, by Stephen B. Dobranski and Archie Burnett. The second volume refers to more departures—including that of A. S. P. Woodhouse, whose commentary on the minor English poems was completed by Douglas Bush. In his preface to that volume, Bush expresses his grief over the death of Merritt Y. Hughes, the annotator of *Paradise Lost*, which would mark perhaps the greatest impediment to the completion of the *Variorum Commentary*. If some of the variorum's charter members left scholarly work for others to complete almost immediately, Hughes's work on *Paradise Lost* and Parker's on *Samson Agonistes* would need to wait for future generations.

Since no one except John Steadman had expressed any interest in completing the *Variorum Commentary*, the indefatigable Albert C. Labriola stepped in as general editor, prompted by his respect for the labors of Hughes and Parker, a respect that also motivates the new contributing editors. Having seen the *Variorum Commentary* languish in an unfinished state, Al first located the typescripts that had been collecting dust in boxes. With the help of John Steadman, who held the draft of Hughes's annotations to *Paradise Lost* (and had done some minor revising of them) as well as Parker's introduction and annotations to *Samson Agonistes*, Al gathered up these typescripts, facilitated the transfer of the publishing rights, recruited a new group of esteemed Miltonists to take over the research and compilation, and secured funding to allow the project to get underway. In mid-1997, the editorial process officially began when a delivery van brought seven boxes of this material to my doorstep. Fortunately, just before his death in early 2009, Al was able to see the appearance of the first volume of the new *Variorum Commentary* that he had initiated.

Because more than three centuries of scholarship have accumulated about Milton's poems, much of that scholarship rich and perceptive, no variorum commentary could synthesize and present all, or even the bulk, of it. The term *variorum,* as demonstrated by the original Columbia University Press volumes and *"Paradise Lost," 1668–1968: Three Centuries of Commentary* (2004), by Earl Miner, William Moeck, and Stephen Jablonski, does not imply exhaustive coverage of scholarship. Indeed, by overwhelming readers and blurring key studies with exceedingly minor ones, such a goal would make the variorum unwieldy, unusable. Scholars working on the older volumes, like their counterparts working on the Duquesne University Press volumes devoted to *Paradise Lost* and *Samson Agonistes*, encountered the problem of making selections from a mountain of riches. In the preface to the first volume of the *Variorum Commentary*, Merritt Y. Hughes remarks that he had to look back almost two centuries to find his *Variorum*'s immediate predecessor, which was Todd's *Poetical Works* from 1801. In the world of Miltonic scholarship, those had been two busy centuries, as Hughes explains: "The bulk of Miltonic scholarship and criticism has grown so enormously since Todd . . . that his successors . . . are beset with problems of selection and annotation" (1:vi). Working to complete the *Variorum Commentary*, the current *Variorum*'s 12 contributing editors — all of whom have been attempting to locate and synthesize the most significant Milton scholarship about *Paradise Lost* before 1970 (the cutoff date determined by the year when the original volumes started to appear) — face precisely the same problems that Hughes mentions.

As today's contributing editors work with material left behind by Merritt Y. Hughes and William Riley Parker, they deal with many other issues that the original compilers also had to address. When he inherited the "minor" English poems following A. S. P. Woodhouse's death, Douglas Bush found himself in the position that the new contributing editors occupy with respect to their predecessors, Hughes and Parker. Bush notes that Woodhouse "left a large but far from complete manuscript which was given to me to revise and finish. The work he had done was, as we should expect, substantial, precise, and judicious." However, "The manuscript was a first draft, ranging in various parts from approximately finished form to pencilled notes" (Hughes, *Variorum* 2:1:ix). The current *Variorum Commentary*'s contributing editors inherited something quite similar: a draft of Hughes's annotations (about 5,000 pages, many containing only one sentence) to *Paradise Lost*, up to Book 11, line 613, with some revisions by John Steadman (Hughes did not begin work on an introduction), and Parker's annotations (about 2,000 pages) and nearly complete introduction (208 pages) to *Samson Agonistes*. The current contributing editors, who in the late 1990s received lightly edited versions of Hughes's annotations to *Paradise Lost* and Parker's introduction and annotations to *Samson Agonistes*, understand what it means to work in someone's shadow. Even Douglas Bush expressed uneasiness about this role in handling Woodhouse's manuscript:

> There has...been much to add in various places.... Most small additions...have been made silently.... While I have been very reluctant to change what he wrote, it has often seemed necessary, as the manuscript grew in bulk, to omit, condense, or otherwise alter.... In general, the effort to revise and complete the work of another man...has involved endless difficulties. I cannot claim to have resolved them without various kinds and degrees of awkwardness; but I hope that my editorial operations have not blurred or misrepresented Woodhouse's insights and opinions. (Hughes, *Variorum* 2:1.ix–x)

Part of the current *Variorum Commentary*'s methodology, an act of historical reconstruction that is analogous to Bush's treatment of Woodhouse's manuscript, is to use as much of Hughes's and Parker's material as future readers will find valuable, incorporating it into the new material.

The *Variorum Commentary* on *Paradise Lost*, besides continuing the *Variorum*'s philosophy about selective coverage, cutoff date, and respect for the work of departed Milton scholars, also shares its view about presenting a text of the poetry. If Hughes judged that it was "neither necessary nor feasible to include another text" in 1970 (Hughes, *Variorum* 1:v), the recent proliferation of editions of Milton's writings makes such an undertaking even less necessary as part of our *Variorum Commentary*. Nevertheless, because the use of the *Variorum Commentary* on *Paradise Lost* will inevitably result in closer scrutiny of the books of Genesis and Revelation, for example, and of Milton's poems, it is recommended that readers keep these texts at hand.

Although the goals of a variorum commentary are largely consistent from generation to generation, the scholarly environment of the 1970s differs in many ways from the one we inhabit in a new millennium. In his prefatory remarks, Hughes articulated the goals of the *Variorum Commentary*:

> While the chief end is interpretative criticism, the larger part of a variorum commentary must necessarily be given to supplying information of all kinds, from the history and meaning of words to the history and meaning of ideas. Our object in this work is to furnish a body of variorum notes and discussions uniting all available scholarly illuminations [*sic*] of the texts on all levels from the semantic and syntactical to those of deliberate or unconscious echoes of other works in all the languages known to Milton. In notes on the longer passages we have considered their inner rhetorical organization and involvements in the design of the poem as a whole, in the backgrounds of the

literary traditions of which they themselves are outstanding developments, and in the many aspects of Milton's interests—theological, cosmological, hexameral, historical, psychological, and so on. (1.vi–vii)

Today's contributing editors grew up with the *Variorum Commentary*'s values and assumptions in their consciousness, and with the volumes at their side. Whether or not the contributing editors fully endorse that volume's foundational values, it is worth noting that those unspoken assumptions include more than a hint of new critical interest in formal matters of poetic design, which would make poststructuralists uncomfortable; a thorough old historical privileging of Milton's text over any context (historical, literary, theological, and so forth), a hierarchy that new historicists would qualify; the veneration of Milton, his verse, and the canon in general, a view interrogated by those who work in multicultural studies or engage in debates about the canon; and a perspective that advances the significance of notes, marginal material that appears on the bottom of the page in most editions, but that *is* a variorum commentary from cover to cover. Those scholars working on the history of the book and those bibliographers interested in the material conditions under which texts are produced, exchanged, and consumed would grasp the scope of a Milton variorum, new or old, but only after its assumptions were thoroughly examined. Perhaps nothing better characterizes the difference in Hughes's scholarly environment and our own than this emphasis on continuous reflection, particularly about privileging and, to use the title of Adrian Johns's study, *The Nature of the Book*, which forms part of the new *Variorum Commentary*'s foundation.

After we have completed the *Variorum Commentary* on *"Paradise Lost,"* we hope to turn to an even more ambitious project, updating the entire *Variorum Commentary*—on the shorter English poems, Latin and Greek poems, Italian poems, *Paradise Lost*, *Paradise Regained*, and *Samson Agonistes*—to cover scholarship published from 1970 to 2000.

Acknowledgments

I most gratefully acknowledge the advice, encouragement, and support of those colleagues and friends who have helped to make this publication possible. Several research grants awarded by the Research Allocation Committee at the University of New Mexico permitted me to undertake the early work on this book at the Huntington Library in San Marino, California, and the Folger Shakespeare Library in Washington, D.C. In addition to the staffs at those splendid research institutions, I am deeply indebted to the Zimmerman Library staff at the University of New Mexico. Most fondly, however, I acknowledge my debt to the librarians of Pattee Library and Paterno Library at the Pennsylvania State University and the librarians of Olin Library at Cornell University.

With 80 pages of annotations on *Paradise Lost*, Book 4, Merritt Y. Hughes firmly set in place the foundation for this volume and established a place to begin, but he also provided an impressive critical standard to seek to maintain. To pursue the variorum project that Hughes, along with J. Milton French, A. S. P. Woodhouse, Douglas Bush, James E. Shaw, William Riley Parker, and Walter MacKellar first undertook in 1949 has been both humbling and inspiring. I thank the associate general editor, and then general editor, Paul J. Klemp, at the University of Wisconsin—Oshkosh for his unfailingly perceptive editorial oversight throughout the years we have worked together on this book. So too I am grateful to Kathleen Meyer and the editorial staff at Duquesne University Press. Working with the other current contributing editors of the *Variorum Commentary on the Poems of John Milton* has been an honor and a pleasure. I am indebted to Archie Burnett, W. Gardner Campbell, Claudia Champagne, Stephen B. Dobranski, Edward Jones, Jameela Lares, John Leonard, John Mulryan, Stella Revard, and Louis Schwartz for all their help along the way, and with them I mourn the untimely passing of our dear colleague Richard J. DuRocher in 2010.

Finally, any effort to acknowledge the extent of my debt to Albert C. Labriola, who determined to complete the project begun by that earlier generation of Miltonists, will forever remain inadequate. Professor Labriola's firm, quiet support throughout my academic life has sustained it. The memory of his dignity, integrity, and dedication will endure for all of us who admired him and miss him.

A Note on the Annotations

The annotations in this volume mirror the organizational pattern established in the earlier volumes of *A Variorum Commentary on the Poems of John Milton*. Proceeding line by line through Book 4 of *Paradise Lost,* the annotations may be as brief as a few words, or may extend over several pages, as do the annotations on the garden of Eden or the annotations on the marriage of Adam and Eve. Annotations on longer passages often subsume annotations on lines within the longer passage, and the subsumed annotations are subsequently presented. All of my quotations from or citations to Milton's writings refer to the Columbia edition of *The Works of John Milton* (1931–38). In the preface to the first volume of the *Variorum Commentary,* Merritt Y. Hughes sets out the critical rationale that shaped the content of the annotations in that volume. Paul Klemp qoutes that statement in the preceding preface to this volume on *Paradise Lost,* Book 4, and in the "Commentary" I have been guided by Merritt Hughes's remarks.

Introducing the reference list for "The Latin and Greek Poems" in that first volume of *A Variorum Commentary on the Poems of John Milton,* Douglas Bush explains, "The nature of the material forbids anything like a complete bibliography or index and this one represents a very limited fusion of the two purposes" (341). Subsequent editors of the *Variorum Commentary* have followed a variety of formats for listing sources. In the Works Cited, I have combined modern scholarly and critical studies of Milton's poetry with the primary sources referenced by editors and critics, as well as those referenced by Milton. I have included classical Greek and Latin authors in that list, usually referencing the Loeb Classical Library, and, unless otherwise indicated, the translations of those authors are the Loeb translations.

Cross-references to commentaries identified with bold numbers are to the line-by-line entries in this book; numbers not in bold refer to pages within the scholarly writing there cited.

Paradise Lost, Book 4

1–12. Book 4 opens with the narrator invoking the voice of John the Divine in the book of Revelation, and that association has received sustained critical attention. While Patrick Hume (131) explains that John the Divine and John the writer of the Gospel are one and the same, and although he lays out the etymology of *Apocalyps,* Hume does not actually refer Revelation to the opening of Book 4. The eighteenth century commentator James Paterson (294) first comments on the echo from Rev. 12: "Our *Divine Poet* judiciously introduces this Book in Imitation of St. *John,* who in a *Vision* saw *Satan* descending to the *Earth,* Rev. 12.12." H. Stebbing brings attention not to the apocalyptic Satan's desire for revenge but to the prophecy of "the overthrow of Satan, whose first attempts upon Man's purity and happiness form the ground-work of this part of the poem" (88). John Upton (411) and Thomas Newton (227) register Shakespearean echoes here ("O, for a falc'ner's voice" in *Romeo and Juliet* 2.2.159, and "O for a Muse of fire," in the prologue to *Henry V,* respectively), but the association with Revelation remains dominant. Newton stresses that Milton's purpose is "to raise the horror and attention of his reader . . . by wishing that the same warning voice had been utter'd now at Satan's first coming, that St. John, who in a vision saw the *Apocalyps* or Revelation of the most remarkable events which were to befall the Christian Church to the end of the world, heard" (227, qtd. in Todd [1842], 2:51). Shifting the visionary terminology a bit, John Keats relates that an unidentified friend "says this Book has the finest opening of any. The point of time is gigantically critical—the wax is melted, the seal is about to be applied—and Milton breaks out 'O for that warning voice,' &c. There is moreover an opportunity for a Grandeur of Tenderness. The opportunity is not lost. Nothing can be higher—nothing so more than Delphic" (3:263). Several twentieth century critics continue to consider the echo with Revelation. Noting that the "momentary voice of the poet at the beginning of Book IV" serves "to bridge time periods," Rosalie L. Colie explains, "In IV, the brief reference to the Apocalypse recalls both John's act of foreseeing and the sight he foresaw, the end of the world and the ultimate destruction of Satan." In short, she concludes, "The reference to Revelations also makes all well: the fall implies salvation" (137). Jon S. Lawry explains that Satan's destructive designs and God's creative designs on Eden intersecting at this point prompt the call for a "warning voice" (169). Drawing attention to the description of Uriel in *PL* 3.622–23, James H. Sims points out that Uriel "will, in Milton's scheme, have the privilege of announcing the destruction of Satan's power over the earth when anti-Christ is defeated at Armageddon" (*Bible* 143–44).

Several modern critics draw attention to Raphael's upcoming visit and the narrator's cry "O for that warning voice." William Empson believes, "Milton wishes very lyrically that Adam and Eve could have been warned by himself," because, according to Empson, Milton "felt there was something inadequate about the warning of Raphael, though he avoids directly claiming that he himself would have done better" (*Milton's God* 61). John S. Diekhoff contends that Raphael comes to Eden "in answer to the foreshadowing appeal that Milton prefixes to Book IV in his own person" (*Milton's* Paradise Lost 91), whereas Lawry, describing Milton as "almost a 'first' John of Patmos," explains that "the poem in itself, with Milton as hierophant, will supply a 'warning voice' from Raphael across the entire center of the epic" (169). Finding great power in the voice of the speaker who opens Book 4 "thrusting off" the Fall, Irene Samuel explains, "A warning voice will in fact come in Book V and converse with Adam through Book VIII, making the event of Book IX all but impossible, while never letting us forget that it is coming" ("*Paradise Lost*" 20). Also see Samuel in **1013–15**.

Grant McColley and Allan H. Gilbert look at the association between Raphael's visit and the bard's cry as they study the epic's development out of Milton's early drafts for a drama on the Fall. McColley reports that in the notes for the third act of draft 3, the "Chorus fears for Adam" (*"Paradise Lost": An Account* 284), and in the description of the third act of draft 4, "Adam Unparadiz'd," "Lucifer appears, after his overthrow; bemoans himself; seeks revenge upon man. The chorus prepares resistance at his first approach. At last, after discourse of enmity on either side, he departs" (286). Also see McColley in **827–30**. Gilbert acknowledges that the bard's stated "hope for man's escape is out of harmony with the Almighty's assertion that Satan 'shall pervert' man (III.92), and also disregards Raphael's mission" (*On the Composition* 66). Gilbert resolves this difficulty by arguing that the bard's wish "was written before the visit of Raphael was planned" and he suggests, "It is as if Milton planned a warning with detailed explanation, then rejected it for the long [war-in-heaven] narratives" (67). Also see Gilbert in **125** and McColley in **124–30**.

Finally, in this "slight" (*Milton* 210) prologue, E. M. W. Tillyard hears the pessimism that he later finds "implicit in the description of *Paradise*" (241). For George Wesley Whiting, the epic's "pessimissm is more profound and more poignant than that of Evangelical Christianity; it has a bitter personal note which is the deliberate expression of Milton's character and experience" (*Milton's Literary Milieu* 175).

3–9. Several recent critics have drawn attention to the theme and image of descent in the opening of Book 4. Developing the metaphoric and structural significance of rising and falling throughout the epic, Jackson I. Cope (110) draws particular attention to "came down" in this sequence: "As Book Four opens, Milton associates Satan with 'the Dragon' of Revelations who 'Came furious down,' even as '*Satan,* now first inflamed with rage, came down' (IV, 3–9). The verb is scriptural, but it inaugurates a subtle shift, an emphasis upon willed swooping descent rather than retributive falling" (40). As he discusses the balanced structure of *PL,* John T. Shawcross draws attention to the parallels between Books 4 and 9, explaining that Satan's descent to paradise parallels in reverse his descent to hell in Book 9. Furthermore, Shawcross writes, "Book IV shows Satan confronting Paradise and observing the love of Adam and Eve, chaste and beautiful; Uriel descends to warn the watch to intercept an evil spirit escaped from Hell. Approaching Eve in a dream, Satan is driven off by Ithuriel and Zephon to Gabriel, and from thence by a Sign in Heaven. Book IX parallels in reverse and in opposing terms this previous book: now the angelic guard leaves Paradise and the judgment of God is given; Sin and Death ascend to build a bridge from Hell to Earth, intercepting the stairs to Heaven. As they have succumbed to the temptation Adam and Eve fall to quarreling, to remorse, to 'weeping and gnashing of teeth'" ("Balanced Structure" 699–700). Referring to the 1667 edition, Shawcross also considers numerological relationships: "Four and eight, as feminine and thus weak numbers, require that the assault and fall of Eve take place in those books of the epic" (710).

3.   *Then when:* A. W. Verity points to 4.838 and 970 as he notes that Milton often uses this emphatic phrase (453).

Dragon: "Dragon; Sax. Fr. Sp. Lat. Gr. i. e. Sharp-sighted; watchful, and causing Pain. A dreadful and venomous Serpent, with great Eyes, a narrow Mouth, and very quick Sight. It differs only from other Serpents in this, that it is an old, large and over-grown one" (Paterson 295).

Verity (453) cross-references "old Dragon" in *Nat* 168.

As he seeks to refute A. J. A. Waldock's charge that there are two Satans in *PL*, Davis P. Harding finds special significance in Milton's here alluding to Satan as "the Dragon." Noting that Milton first refers to Satan as "th' Infernal Serpent" at 4.34, but between that opening reference and this allusion, which immediately precedes Satan's soliloquy, that Milton "never once directly and openly identifies Satan as the Serpent," Harding contends that "if it is the Lucifer-in-Satan which, in the beginning, is allowed to engage our attention, it is also true that Milton never lets us forget for long that the qualities of the Serpent coexist in Satan along with those of Lucifer, poised and ready, when the right time comes, to perform their work of fraud and destruction" (*Club* 63). See Waldock 93.

6–10.   The relationship between an ordinary and a prophetic sense of time becomes a critical issue here. Bentley argues that the verbs in this sequence should be in the present tense (105). Rejecting Bentley's tense changes, Zachary Pearce (106), however, also ignores the prophetic nature of the bard's view of the action, which James Paterson (294) notes when he comments on the narrator's reference to Revelation. Several twentieth century scholars clarify the temporal involvement of prelapsarian and postlapsarian humanity here. Focusing on the adverb *now* in 8–9, Jon S. Lawry explains that, as Book 4 proceeds, "Time at once shifts toward the present, engaging the woe as ours," and reinforcing the understanding of *PL* as a methexis, Lawry writes, "Because his [Milton's] Christian subject is assumed to be true and because both author and audience are directly involved in it, his works open into a participative enactment, as *methexis*" (V). Alastair Fowler hears the echo of Rev. 12.12 ("but a short time") in "While time was" (6) and finds an implied "analogy between the end of the prelapsarian world and the end of M[ilton]'s own world" (608).

8. *Haply:* Stanley Fish brings attention to the word *haply* in conjunction with the warning motif: "The assumption is of a causal relationship between Satan's presence in Paradise and the Fall, and of a corresponding relationship between the availability of a warning voice and the hope of escape. But the narrator corrects himself by adding a qualification, 'Haply so scap'd,' *perhaps* they would have escaped, admitting in effect that warning or no warning, with or without Satan, escape still depends on the exercise of their wills" (*Surprised* 234).

9. *inflam'd with rage:* identifying the fundamentally conventional nature of the theology of *PL,* and cross-referencing 4.105–13 and 502–04, as well as 1.106–08, 1.661–62, and 2.832–44, Grant McColley describes as "well-known" the notion that Satan, as evil, hated God and both hated and envied man (*"Paradise Lost"* 205).

After he points out that in Book 2 the same phrase is applied to Phlegethon (581), and to Death as he pursues Sin (791), Edward S. Le Comte explains that, in his three uses of this phrase, "Milton passes from the literal to the figurative" (*Yet Once More* 39).

10. *Tempter…Accuser:* Satan's identity as the "Accuser of man-kind" is first underscored when Newton (228) refers this line to Rev. 12.10 (qtd. in Todd [1842], 2:51). David Masson more completely fits this point into the poem's total context: "In the passage in the Apocalypse just cited, describing Satan's 'second rout' from Heaven, he comes to Earth as 'the accuser of the brethren' (Rev. xii. 10); but in the action of the poem he is the Tempter. The word Devil, from the Greek *Diabolos,* means 'Slanderer' or 'Accuser'" (*Poetical Works* 3:167). Acknowledging that Satan's identity spans from tempter of Eve in Genesis to "the accuser of our brethren" in Revelation, Merritt Y. Hughes (*Complete Poems* 277) adds Satan's appearance as the accuser of Job before God (Job 1.6–12, 2.1–6). Robert H. West, examining the "casual yet association-packed way" that Milton responds to the long and rich tradition of angelology, notes that, "When Milton calls Satan *Accuser* and *Tempter*…and when by intimation, at least, he lets us know that the devils are *Aerial Powers* and *False Gods,* he has touched directly a much-repeated classification of evil spirits into nine orders designated by these and similar terms" (156). As he examines literary renditions of Christian divine history, Frank S. Kastor situates Satan's tempter identity within a broad range of Satanic characterizations, including the rebel general in the heavenly war and the leader of the demonic council ("Milton's Tempter" 383).

11–12. A. W. Verity (452) notes that the intent to "avenge himself for his loss" is Satan's reason for acting against man, but while arguing against C. S. Lewis's reading of Satan, by seeking to establish the sublimity of Satan's courage, endurance, and determination, G. Rostrevor Hamilton admits that there is "nothing heroic" (26) in Satan's seeking revenge against God by attacking Adam and Eve. See Lewis and Hamilton in **32–112**.

11. *innocent frail man:* John Peter (94) insists that the innocence and frailty of Adam and Eve draw us to them: "They are less like 'our two first Parents' than like our children, unblemished and defenceless replicas of ourselves, and we feel some of the protectiveness towards them that we feel towards a son and daughter."

Listing this bardic epithet for Adam, along with those found at 144, 323–24, 408, and 495, as well as yet others scattered throughout the epic, Kester Svendsen points out that the narrator's epithets "outnumber those applied to Adam by any character in the poem, and they reveal also something of Milton's practice of ringing changes on a central idea. He uses most frequently an epithet indicative of Adam's paternity of the human race" ("Epic Address" 192).

innocent: Leland Ryken explains how words such as *innocent* describe the conceptual background of the apocalyptic state, a state frequently alluded to throughout the paradisal scenes of Book 4, as "one of complete goodness, perfection, and innocence" (60).

13. From the nineteenth through the twentieth century, editorial controversy has surrounded the comma at the end of this line and its effect upon the understanding of Satan's state of mind as he approaches Eden. Quoting a note from Robert Thyer, who associates the line with 3.740–41 to emphasize that Satan was not moved by joy as he approached Eden, Todd in his 1801 edition supplies Newton's argument (228) for omitting the comma that appears in both the 1667 and 1674 editions: "Satan was bold *far off and fearless;* and, as he drew nearer, was pleased with *hop'd success:* But, now he is come to earth *to begin his dire attempt,* he does not *rejoice* in it; his heart misgives him; *horrour and doubt distract* him. This is all very natural." Todd's support for Thyer's reading is withdrawn from subsequent editions, however ([1801], 2:248; [1826], 2:272; [1842], 2:41). In the twentieth century, Verity also omits the comma, explaining, "The nearer Satan approaches to the scene of his task the more he realises its enormity and peril, and the less his confidence becomes" (452), while Hughes, who keeps the comma, reasons that omitting it "would turn the statement into a clearer slur upon Satan's courage" ("Variorum"). Also maintaining the comma, Alastair Fowler describes Satan's state of mind: "the imminence of the actual aggression—*nigh the birth*—causes him to shrink in horror" (609).

16. *rowling:* Fowler notes the *OED*'s definition of the intransitive verb *roll* (II.14) in reference to "time, and especially of cyclic periods"; "moving on" (609).

17. As notes accumulate on "a devillish Engine," the phrase's commonplace nature becomes evident. Writing in 1748, John Upton (412) first associates the simile with a similar one in *Macbeth* 5.2.22–25. Mitford (110) provides more literary antecedents for the simile, pointing to Edmund Spenser's *The Faerie Queene* 1.7.13, John Russell's *The Two Famous Pitcht Battles of Lypsich and Lutzen* 15, *Hamlet* 3.4.206–07, Francis Beaumont's *Fair Maid of the Inn* 2.1.59–62, and Ausonius's Epigram 72. Merritt Y. Hughes cross-references the invention of the cannon in *PL* 6.518 (*Complete Poems* 277) and notes, "The proverbial recoil of the cannon was commonplace when Hamlet said ''tis sport, to have the engineer / Hoist with his own petar'" ("Variorum"). Edward S. Le Comte emphasizes Milton's personal fondness for this metaphor, tracing the repetition of "back recoils" and "back recoiled" throughout *PL* (4.17, 9.172, 6.194, 2.759) but adding that "the circumstance of defeat" described by the phrase "had been prophesied" in line 593 of Milton's *Mask*, "But evil on itself shall back recoil," and concluding that "it is interesting to see the abstract turning into the concrete, evil back recoiling becoming the reeling Satan" (*Yet Once More* 59). Noting that the Father in 3.84–86 predicts that Satan's evil will recoil upon him, James H. Sims (*Bible* 18) establishes the notion of evil recoiling upon the evildoer as a biblical commonplace, listing 1 Sam. 25.39; 2 Chron. 6.23; Neh. 4.4; Esth. 9.25; Ps. 7.16; Ezek. 9.10, 11.21; Joel 3.4; and Judg. 9.57. Finally, as he summarizes these points and contributes yet another cross-reference within *PL* ("Engins" in 1.750), Alastair Fowler (609) adds that Milton is "playing also on *engine* = 'plot' (*OED* 3)."

18. *horror and doubt distract:* Hume's annotation here reveals one of the admirable features of his contribution to Milton criticism. Keenly sensitive to etymological matters, Hume highlights the Latinate root of *distract*, which enhances the reference to Satan's psychological suffering: "The amazement of his Guilt, and the uncertain success of new Mischiefs undertaken, which how much they may add more to his Punishment than Revenge, confounds all Consideration. *Distracts his Thoughts;* Put him upon a Rack, where all his Resolutions against th' Almighty, vain and frivolous, are rent to pieces. *Distracts,* of *distrahere,* Lat. To pull in pieces" (131).

Empson brings great emphasis to this line, insisting that "until Satan is in sight of Paradise he is convinced that God is not omnipotent" (*Milton's God* 37). Also see Empson in **32–113**.

20–26. Identifying the literary and theological parallels for the concept of the hell within has dominated criticism on these lines. Todd ([1842], 2:52) supplies specific references to Fairfax's translation of Tasso's *Gerusalemme Liberata,* titled *Godfrey of Bulloigne* 12.77; Cristoforo Landino's commentary on canto 34 of Dante's *Inferno* sigs. cxxi^v–cxxxiii; Bede's *Ecclesiastical History* 5.13; and Shakespeare's *King John* 5.7.46. Masson notes, "The idea here is an old one" and credits Todd for tracing it to various authors (*Poetical Works* 3:167). Twentieth century critics have mined the theological depths of the hell-within concept. In 1925, Marjorie H. Nicolson glosses this sequence, as well as 4.846–49, with Henry More's explanation in *The Immortality of the Soul* (208) that a damned soul that endeavored to stay in hell and "to endure that hideous pain of destroying the vital congruity of her vehicle by that sulphureous fire" would nevertheless—upon release—"catch life again in the Air, and all the former troubles and vexations would return, besides the overplus of these pangs of death. *For Memory would return, and an ill Conscience would return,* and all those busie Furies, those disordered Passions which follow it" ("Spirit World" 445–46 and n14). Grant McColley ("*Paradise Lost*" 206–07; Paradise Lost: *An Account* 140–41) traces a variety of Scholastic versions of the hell-within concept to Thomas Aquinas. In the *Summa Theologica* 1.64.4, for example, Aquinas provides the following gloss on James 3.6: "They carry the fire of hell with them wherever they go." Associating this episode in *PL* with passages such as those found in part 1, section 51, of Sir Thomas Browne's *Religio Medici* (*Works* 1:62–63) and Christopher Marlowe's *Dr. Faustus* 1.3.304–10, McColley continues to indicate the theologically conventional quality of Satan's admission ("*Paradise Lost*" 206–07). Robert H. West, Merritt Y. Hughes, J. M. Evans, and Alastair Fowler maintain McColley's understanding of the conventional and widespread notion of "The Hell within," although George Coffin Taylor insists that

Milton is indebted to one modern source. West states, "Milton is giving his reader a widely acknowledged fact about angels, which the great angelologists had worked out in all its paradoxical details" (104). While he, like McColley, tacks Bonaventure (*Sentences* II, d, vi, 2,2 [*opera* 2:157–59]) onto the list of theologians referring to the hell within, Hughes (*Complete Poems* 277–78) stresses that there were many assertions of the doctrine, the "most famous" being Marlowe's. Cf. Hughes in **75–78**. Evans points out that, to the minds of "medieval poets and artists, Satan and his followers changed from angels into demons even as they fell. Milton's point seems to be that the floor of Hell does not mark the limit of the Devil's descent; his pictorial and physical fall is followed by a still heavier one in the 'Hell within him' " (231). Like McColley, Fowler (609) references both the passage from *Doctor Faustus* and the passage from *Religio Medici*, but he also points to Milton's own *DDD* (Patterson, *Works* 3:442), as does Hughes in his gloss on 75–77. George Coffin Taylor (339–40), however, argues for a specific connection between Milton's presentation of the hell-within motif and Sylvester's translation of Du Bartas's *The Divine Weeks and Works* 2.1.2.37–56. As does Elbert N. S. Thompson before him, Robert Martin Adams (154–57) rejects Taylor's claim. Both Thompson and Adams maintain that the idea of the hell within is conventional, and both insist, as Thompson puts it, "With all the richest store of the world's literature to inspire him, Milton could not have felt the need of assistance from a poet so inartistic and eccentric" (*Essays* 163).

The cross-referencing that a number of twentieth century scholars in addition to Fowler and Hughes have presented evidences the strong appeal to Milton of the hell-within notion. Verity (452), for example, cross-references *PL* 1.254–55 and 4.75–78; Le Comte (*Yet Once More* 8–9) points to "his own dungeon" in *Mask* 384 and "Dungeon of thyself" in *SA* 156, whereas Hughes (*Complete Poems* 277–78) adds *PL* 6.181. As he, too, notes the cross-reference with *PL* 4.75, where Satan himself admits that "My self am Hell," J. B. Broadbent designates both as "devices" by which Milton is able to "express what is really a spiritual or psychological experience, the insinuation of evil into good, in terms of epic action" (*Some Graver Subject* 169).

Michael Lieb considers the concept of the hell within as he discusses the dialectics by which Milton develops the theme of creation: "The aberration or 'breach' of the holy union results in a complete loss of security and an enforced subjection to the distraction of 'horror and doubt.' Satan undergoes the Chaos of a world bound to an utter loss of sublime creativity. His own person of Chaos is conceived of as a Hell, and he remains as a result of his 'breach' an uncreated personality" (89). Recalling the figure of Sin's children incessantly returning to rape her, and the concept of return as it figures in Milton's theme of creation, Lieb also focuses critical attention on the imagery of return introducing and recurring within Satan's first soliloquy, especially in lines 15–18, 42–42, and 46–48 (164).

23–26. C. A. Patrides (*Milton and the Christian Tradition* 112) understands this episode in Satan's career as a "crisis of conscience" and juxtaposes it to the conclusion of Adam's postlapsarian soliloquy, "O Conscience, into what Abyss of fears / And horrors hast thou driv'n me" (10.842–43), as well as the Father's promise to give fallen humanity his "Umpire *Conscience*" (3.195) as a guide.

24–27. Insisting that the "rhymes in *Paradise Lost* are not mere accident," John S. Diekhoff ("Rhyme" 543) here identifies two of the epic's 17 couplets, and, he notes, adding these two back-to-back couplets to the couplets in lines 204–05 and 956–57 gives Book 4, along with Book 9, the highest number of couplets in the epic ("Rhyme" 539–40). Also see S. Ernest Sprott in **28–37.**

24–26. Bentley (106), puzzling over the *memory* of the future, suggests "theory," but Pearce's explanation, "Memory is *recordatio,* or the thinking and reflecting upon any thing" (107) begins to gather together classical uses of *recordatio* that support Milton's link between *memory* and "what must be." Other early editors strengthen Pearce's argument, with the Richardsons (137) adding a reference to Horace's *Odes* 4.12.26 and *Satires* 2.6.31, Newton (228) adding Virgil's *Georgics* 4.156, and Todd ([1842], 2:52) adding Ovid's *Tristia* 4.1.99. Twentieth century editors have extended this growing list of literary parallels. After he cross-references Samson's painful memory of "Times past, what once I was, and what am now" in *SA* 22, Verity (452–53), for one, associates both Samson's and Satan's words with Francesca's cry in Dante's *Inferno* 5.121–23. Verity then acknowledges Dante's debt to Boethius's *The Consolation of Philosophy* 2.4.3–6 and points out that in his *Troilus and Criseyde* 3.1625–28 (*Major Poetry* 151), Chaucer also echoed Dante. In addition, Verity references Sir Thomas Browne's *Christian Morals* 2.10 (*Works* 1:265–66). To Verity's list, Merritt Y. Hughes (*Complete Poetry* 278) tacks on Aquinas's *Summa Theologica,* suppl. 3.98.7. Although Alastair Fowler (609) believes that Milton "primarily means 'recollect' (cp. *memento mori*)," he adds, "The passage seems also, however, to echo St Augustine's deep meditation on time in *Confessions* xi.28, so that M[ilton] may

imply that Satan *can* only remember—there is for him, as we say, no future."
Most recently, Arnold Stein has fully elaborated the classical understanding
of *memorie* that Pearce first presents. Identifying the first 31 lines of Book 4
as a "brief invocation-prologue," Stein discusses the "figurative" meaning of
memorie as that "which can be awakened to the past; or even to the present
(through the agency of conscience–understanding), the real present that seems
part of the past because it unhappily is (it was no dream), and because one has
been awakened to it; or awakened even to the future, because the future that
can be anticipated and yet is accepted as inevitable has become a conscious part
of the past, and so, fitly, part of the torture of memory. The paradox is a witty
exploration of the level of consciousness that lies under the joyless speed" (55).
Finally, Helen Darbishire once more glances back at Bentley's complaint, finding in it evidence of the early editor's "failure in poetic imagination," but also
stating that such comments from Bentley "awaken us to a boldness, a violence,
a tendency to paradox in Milton's imaginative phrasing which the splendour and
sustained majesty of his style in *Paradise Lost* tend to mask" (*Milton's "Paradise
Lost"* 17).

27–29. Arnold Stein, Joseph H. Summers, and James H. Sims develop the appropriateness of this setting, in both a temporal sense and a physical sense. Stein sees
that Satan's turning from "Sometimes towards Eden" to "Sometimes towards
Heav'n," underscored by the phrase "Then much revolving," provides "a brilliant setting" for Satan's first soliloquy (55). Also see Stein in **24–26.** Summers
finds that Satan's first soliloquy "dramatizes his sterility and self-destructiveness
just before we approach, in his company, the 'fertile ground' of the Garden"
(94). Sims also much approves Milton's setting, because it provides Satan a view
of both heaven, "where he attempted to lead the angels in revolt against God
(with partial success), and Earth, into which he is now planning to bring upon
man disobedience and death" (*Bible* 75).

27–28. Todd ([1842], 2:53) credits Benjamin Stillingfleet for an unpublished
note referencing Homer's *Odyssey* 13.197 which describes Odysseus, unaware
that he has awakened on the shore of Ithaca, about to express his uncertainty
and fear in a soliloquy.

27. *Eden:* both Verity (453) and Sims (*Bible* 75) report that the literal meaning
of Eden is "pleasant, pleasure, delight." Cf. **132, 214–15.**

30. *Meridian Towre:* although eighteenth and nineteenth century editors gather together a number of literary antecedents for the tower image, several twentieth century critics consider the significance of the precise time that it establishes. The Richardsons (137–38) refer Milton's phrase to Virgil's similar tower image in *Culex* 41 and to Spenser's translation in "Virgil's Gnat" 65–66 (*Poetical Works* 487). Cf. Newton 229; Todd ([1842], 2:53). The precise time established by this metaphor draws the attention of Alastair Fowler and Laurence Stapleton. Asserting, "Noon, when the sun crosses the *meridian,* is throughout *PL* a critical time of judgment," Fowler (610) adds Mal. 4.1 to the Virgilian reference the early editors note. Fowler, explaining that the biblical "Son of righteousness" metaphor was often read in astronomical terms, concludes, "The point is of thematic importance, in view of M[ilton]'s structural positioning of Christ the Sun of righteousness at the numerological centre of the whole poem." Fowler also points to "symbolic noon" at 3.616–17, 9.739–43. Stapleton, developing the importance of the contrast between specific and indefinite time in the epic points out that, "until he lands in the sun, Satan himself is never in the light. Then—and this is a surprising virtuoso transition from vague to specific time, by means of the continued sun image—Satan after his steep flight lands on Mt. Niphates.... From now until the end of the poem, the chronology is definitely established" (739–40).

31. *revolving:* Hume (131) offers the first etymological note that continues to characterize the commentary on this word. Hume's extended gloss, however, also anticipates Stein's earlier one on 27–29: "Tossing and turning over many direful Thoughts, risen from Conscience waking of despair that slumber'd, &c. An admirable Description of tormenting Guilt, discovered when too late to be discharged. *Revolving, of revolvere,* Lat. To roll to and fro, then to think and in *Virgil* to relate. *Sed quid ego haec autem, nequicquam ingrata revolvo. Aen*[*eid*]. 2[.101]." Although he, like Verity (453), defines *revolving* as "pondering," Fowler (610) also cross-references *PR* 1.185–86. The *OED* quotes *PR* 1.185–86 to exemplify the meaning "To turn over (something) in the mind, breast, thoughts, etc." (1.4), whereas it defines *revolve* as "To consider, think over, ponder or meditate upon (something)" in the subsequent entry, 1.4.b.

32–113. This is the first of Satan's three soliloquies in Book 4, the other two occurring at 358–92 and 505–35. The earliest important comment on this first soliloquy is a remark by Edward Phillips in his *Life of John Milton*. Mentioning his uncle's plans for a tragedy on the Fall, Phillips reports that the soliloquy's first ten lines had been composed "several Years before the Poem was begun," having been "designed for the very beginning of the said Tragedy" (qtd. in Darbishire, *Early Lives* 72). Although Phillips does not suggest any difference between Satan's characterization in this soliloquy and his characterization in the earlier books, one of the major critical controversies of the twentieth century swirls about Milton's presentation of Satan as he moves from hell into Eden. Often referring back to the nineteenth century Romantic view of Satan, some critics charge that Milton degrades Satan by means such as the soliloquies in Book 4, whereas other modern critics contend that Satan is rather revealed as degenerate in this and subsequent soliloquies.

The earliest critics are not unaware that Satan in Book 4 is different from Satan in Books 1 and 2, but that difference apparently does not strike them as problematic, for what distinguishes their commentary here is great praise, and often great praise for the naturalness of the change in Satan's characterization. John Dennis's intense admiration of the speech finds expression throughout his writings. Condemning Richard Blackmore's 1697 presentation of devils in *King Arthur* (see, e.g., Books 3, 6, and 11), Dennis discusses the goodness still revealed in Milton's Satan as he "shows Remorse upon the Top of Niphates in that Speech…which begins with that wonderful Apostrophe to the Sun." Advising writers like Blackmore to heed Milton's handling of devils, Dennis also anticipates the great debates about Satan that later blossom: "*Milton,* to introduce his Devils with success, saw that it was necessary to give them something that was allied to Goodness. Upon which he very dextrously feign'd, that the Change which was caus'd by their Fall, was not wrought in them all at once; and that there was not an entire Alteration work'd in them, till they had a second time provok'd their Creatour by succeeding in their attempt upon Man" (1:107–08). In *The Grounds of Criticism in Poetry,* Dennis returns to Satan's apostrophe to the sun as exemplifying "the Enthusiasm of Admiration," which passion, Dennis explains, is produced by "the great Phaenomena of the Material World; because they too lead the Soul to its Maker." Dennis also points to 605–09 as an example of "Enthusiasm of Admiration" (1:348). Finally, in the "Letters on Milton and Wycherley" (1721–22), Dennis describes not only the speech itself but also the entire epic as sublime, insisting that Milton had "carried away the Prize of Sublimity from both Ancients and Moderns" (2:221). Newton's enthusiastic approval of the soliloquy is involved with his recognition that Milton chose this particular place—and not another—for the soliloquy: "And what a noble opening of a play would this have been! The lines were certainly too good to be lost, and the author has done well to employ them here, they could not have been better employ'd any where" (2:230). Also extremely impressed by the speech, which he declares "the finest that is ascribed to *Satan* in the whole Poem," Joseph Addison more clearly moves toward identifying the critical flash point of the future controversy as he considers the changes in Satan's character: "*Satan* being now within Prospect of *Eden,* and looking round upon the Glories of the Creation, is filled with Sentiments different from those which he discovered whilst he was in Hell. The Place inspires him with Thoughts more adapted to it: He reflects upon the happy Condition from whence he fell, and breaks forth into a Speech that is softened with several transient Touches of Remorse and Self-accusation: But at length he confirms himself in Impenitence, and in his design of drawing Man into his own State of Guilt and Misery" (*Spectator* 3:171). Cf. Newton 230.

Although the dynamic difference between Satan in Eden and Satan in hell dominates Addison's reading, the Romantics who understood Satan as the hero of *PL* insist upon his unyielding perseverance in Eden, as well as in hell. Hazlitt, declaring Satan "the most heroic subject that ever was chosen for a poem" (121), praises many of the characteristics expressed in his first soliloquy, but especially the intensity of Satan's thought: "Satan is not the principle of malignity, or of the abstract love of evil, but of the abstract love of power, of pride, of self-will personified, to which last principle all other good and evil, and even his own, are subordinate" (123). For the Romantics, it is Satan's "confirm[ing] himself in Impenitence," as Addison (*Spectator* 3:171) puts it, which elevates him to sublime, if not heroic, status. Shelley insists, "Milton's Devil as a moral being is as far superior to his God" ("Defence" 129; cf. Shelley's "On the Devil" 90). With William Blake's declaration that Milton was "of the Devils party without knowing it" (*Marriage* 35), the issue of Milton's artistic control of Satan is most famously expressed, and another element in the slowly brewing controversy is firmly stated. Although Addison praises the "great deal of Art" with which Milton shapes Satan's "Conflict of Passions" (*Spectator* 3:171), the Romantics believe that Milton's Satan had escaped his creator's control.

In Verity's remarks at the turn of the century, the terms of the twentieth century controversy about Milton's handling of Satan begin to present themselves. Verity writes, "One of the most powerful features of *Paradise Lost* is the presentment of the gradual debasement and decline of Satan as the evil he works against man masters himself" (453). But where Verity speaks of Satan's decline because of his inherent evil, Walter Raleigh soon speaks of Milton's degrading Satan, and Raleigh's reading quickly triggers heated debate. Sharing the Romantics' view of God as "a whimsical Tyrant" (129), Raleigh recalls Blake, albeit in terms of the new psychology of the unconscious, when he claims that Milton "was not fully conscious…of what he was doing" (133). Comparing Satan to Prometheus, as another "fearless antagonist of Omnipotence," Raleigh reasons that Satan is therefore either a fool or a hero, "and Milton is far indeed from permitting us to think him a fool" (133). Narrowing his attention to Book 4, and finding the Satan who soliloquizes on Mt. Niphates admirable, "a lover of beauty reluctantly compelled to shatter it," Raleigh concludes that "by the time he had completed the Fourth Book, Milton became uneasy as to the effect he was producing. Up to that point magnanimity and courage had been almost the monopoly of Satan" (138). From the narration of the war in heaven onward, Raleigh contends, Milton therefore sought to regain control of Satan, "to right the balance" (138). Although Raleigh concludes that other critics therefore see a "degradation" of Satan throughout *PL,* he believes that his "original" concept of Satan "lived on in the imagination and memory of Milton, and was revived, with an added pathos, in *Paradise Regained*" (139). Tillyard's *Milton* (1930) broadly echoes Raleigh's opinion—"I do not see how one can avoid admitting that Milton did partly ally himself with Satan" (234)—but Elmer Edgar Stoll's 1933 article, "From the Superhuman to the Human," importantly counters the enduring Romantic view of Satan. Stoll also most significantly answers the idea of degradation with the idea of degeneration: "Satan degenerates and gradually loses our sympathy. As he surveys the new world and then approaches the couple in Paradise, he falls more and more a prey to envy and hatred, jeers and sneers instead of breathing defiance and melancholy, and stoops to flattery and deceit" (6).

 C. S. Lewis's *Preface to "Paradise Lost"* (1942) most sharply focuses this roiling debate. Lewis, like those critics he sets out to answer, finds "Satan is the best drawn of Milton's characters" (100), but, unlike Raleigh, Lewis believes Satan is indeed more a fool than a hero. Lewis dismisses the theory that Milton came to realize that Satan looked too attractive and that he needed "to right the balance." Rejecting the possibility of Milton creating Satan "by blundering and accident," Lewis asserts, "We need not doubt that it was the poet's intention to be fair to evil, to give it a run for its money—to show it *first* at the height, with all its rants and melodrama and 'Godlike imitated state' about it, and *then* to trace what actually becomes of such self-intoxication when it encounters reality. Fortunately we happen to know that the terrible soliloquy in Book IV (32–113) was conceived and in part composed before the first two books. It was from this conception that Milton started" (100). Lewis's argument quickly drew fire from Elmer Edgar Stoll and G. Rostrevor Hamilton and, a few years later, A. J. A. Waldock. Stoll, who in 1933 had plotted Satan's "degeneration," in 1944 echoes Raleigh on Milton's effort to "right the balance," specifically glancing at the "disparaging moral comments" that Milton as narrator periodically applies to Satan ("Give the Devil" 119–20). As does Stoll, Hamilton sees a divided Milton. While Stoll, arguing against Lewis, focuses on l.110, Hamilton considers the soliloquy in its entirety as he rejects Lewis's emphasis on Satan's absurdity to claim instead that Satan's "conscience tears rents in his blindness. He sees that his pride and ingratitude have been beyond excuse, that he has only himself to upbraid. He realizes the vanity of his boast against Omnipotence, and knows that disdain of subjection has been his ruin" (25). So, too, a decade later, Robert Martin Adams attacks Lewis's sweeping remark: "Satan may be a fool, as Mr. Lewis asserts…, but a good deal of Miltonic ingenuity was expended in a great many areas of the poem to keep us from thinking so" (152). The most powerful voice to answer Lewis, however, is Waldock, who echoes Raleigh as he contends that Milton degrades Satan. Waldock argues that Satan's soliloquizing on Mt. Niphates is "not a development from the old, he is not a changed Satan, he is a new Satan." Waldock insists, "Satan, in short, does not degenerate: *he is degraded*" by changes that "do not generate themselves from within" but "are imposed from without" (93). R. J. Zwi Werblowsky (6) similarly understands Satan's first soliloquy and its role in the characterization of Satan throughout the epic.

   With *Lucifer and Prometheus* (1952), Werblowsky moves to head up a group of modern critics who associate Milton's Satan with the Greek hero Prometheus. Besides Raleigh, for example, Maud Bodkin finds Milton's Satan Promethean: "We have seen the Promethean hero defying a God identified with superseded values—with a parental rule from which liberation must be achieved, with an established order in face of which new ways of life must be devised and asserted. In his rebellion the hero falls under the devil-pattern, destroyer of values felt as supreme. Thus Milton condemns his hero, who yet, within the experience conveyed, is found akin to the Prometheus figure" (269). So too, contending in *God without Thunder* that "the Hebrew Lucifer is equated in Milton to the Greek Prometheus" (131), John Crowe Ransom reasons that "eventually Milton, after nearly making out of Lucifer a heroic champion of mankind, returns to the orthodox tradition and repudiates his dangerous if specious services" (133). While he brings more prominent development to those earlier assertions about Milton's Satan as a Promethean hero, and while he agrees, "Prometheus, the sinner and culture-hero, can be detected in the Satan of *Paradise Lost*," Werblowsky carefully qualifies that claim: "This does not mean that there are identifiable literary connections between Prometheus and Satan, nor do I claim any influence of Aeschylos on Milton. All the argument wants to show is that the unconscious archetypal meaning or mythological contents of the Prometheus figure, is so near to that of Satan, that it could easily be absorbed by the latter, and that this absorption has in fact taken place to a remarkable degree in Milton's *Paradise Lost*" (xix).

The claim that Satan is heroic—Promethean or otherwise—is answered by a steady stream of critical commentary appearing through the middle decades of the twentieth century. Common to the majority of these readings of Satan's first soliloquy is the insistence that the speech be located within the context of the entire epic. For example, a number of critics who reject the heroic understanding of Satan, as well as the charge that Milton is degrading him, draw attention to the setting—alone and in Eden—within which Satan delivers his first soliloquy. One might first note, however, that in adapting Milton's epic for his opera *The State of Innocence, and Fall of Man,* John Dryden, who sets the first of Lucifer's soliloquies on the sun, rather than on Earth, opens that speech (2.2.1–21) with Lucifer's admission that he is "monstrous" and "disfigur'd" (*Works* 12:108). Conceding that Satan's first soliloquy offers "ammunition for romantic quotation," and also finding the Satan of Book 4 a startling contrast to the Satan of Books 1–2, S. Musgrove describes the setting as the "face of light, the noonday sun," and finds that the first soliloquy reveals Satan for what he is. Disclosing "more self-knowledge than any of the great speeches in I and II," Satan, according to Musgrove, is "disintegrating" (306–07). Very similar is the opinion of Balachandra Rajan, who insists, "It is only in the speech on Mount Niphates, when the external magnificence surrounding Satan is stripped away, that we find his stature visibly reduced and his heroic grandeur battered and corroded by the endless siege of contraries within him.... It is one of the functions of the Niphates speech to effect this reduction in scale for by doing so it helps to link two conceptions of Satan which might otherwise by harassingly opposed" (*"Paradise Lost" and the Seventeenth Century Reader* 96–97). Tillyard agrees with Rajan "that what side of his character Satan shows depends on the circumstances," and certainly as Satan stands on Niphates, Tillyard reasons, he "lacks the support of his fellows, the soothing illusion of strength through mere numbers, and the pride of leadership. Moreover he has left his realm of darkness. He is alone and in the more alien realm of light. No wonder if he changes his tone" (*Studies* 58). Arnold Stein maintains this critical approach: "There seems reason for believing that the main difference between the Satan of the first two books and the later Satan is the difference between a leader making a public appearance and a leader on a solitary mission. That Satan is less magnificent away from his followers hardly proves a falling-off in Milton's creative powers, or a sudden realization that his villain has been getting the best lines. The paradox is true to life: the leader has greater stature when he is before his millions, but partly through being forced to deny his essential solitary self (even while taking self as the standard of measure)" (5). William Empson also draws attention to Satan's isolation when he enters this vigorous discussion about Satan in *Milton's God*. Acknowledging the claims of inconsistency in Satan's characterization, but alluding also to Phillips's comment on the opening lines of the first soliloquy, Empson insists, "Surely it is only fair to the author to interpret the words so as to make the character consistent, when this is found to be quite possible. The sharpness of the jolt does rather suggest that Milton was fitting in some old material; but he might have judged that the sudden change in Satan's beliefs needed to be expressed by a jolt. On the other hand, it is often confidently asserted that this speech admits his previous speeches to have all been lies; a view which makes the character consistent by making him ridiculous, though I think some critics combine it with complaining that he has become a quite different character. We have not had Satan alone before—he has always been either negotiating with rival powers or encouraging his followers, so this is the first time he could have told us that he regards lying to his followers as a painful duty. I think Milton would realize that the words could be taken like that, but would regard it as a crude interpretation" (64–65).

Focusing on epic structure more than the isolated setting of Satan's soliloquy, critics such as Arthur Barker, Robert Martin Adams, John Peter, and J. Martin Evans also reject the charge that Milton is degrading Satan. Barker discusses the effects of seeing the epic's 12 books as three sets of four books: each unit of four books, he explains, "pauses and turns, as do Virgil's upon its centre. It is not merely the direction of Satan's actual flight which changes between books III and IV; the apparent revival which has brought him to the verge of heaven's light now becomes a clear process of degeneration marked by God's comments,

Satan's soliloquy, and his discomfiture in the garden" ("Structural Pattern" 26).
In *Ikon: John Milton and the Modern Critics,* Adams considers Satan's decline
from Books 1–2 to Book 4 as a feature of the direction of the entire epic story:
"One of the main directions which the whole story takes is away from the fabulous
and mythical into the prosaic and everyday. The conventional, much-described
decline of Satan is paralleled by a decline of God from the miraculous to the legal
and then to the episodic level, a decline of man from a princely to a schoolboy
figure, a narrowing of the theater and the issues from cosmic to psychological
scope. The myth is brought down in the last books to its practical application,
as Michael offers Adam a series of enlightened aphorisms to guide him through
life" (125). Adams specifically answers Waldock's charge that Milton as narrator
degrades Satan: "Professor Waldock objects to all the editorial restrictions with
which Milton has attempted to control that [Satan's] energy. But the nature
of things requires that any epic poem involving Satan treat him as a malignant
power; and the more power he has of his own, the more malignant he must be
presumed" (56). John Peter also acknowledges the consequences of the epic's
thematic structure: "A better account of Satan's progress in the poem would
be to say that he is progressively simplified." Peter continues, "Dramatic intensity, once located within the figure of Satan, has shifted elsewhere [to Adam
and Eve], and Milton's artistry has shifted with it" (62). Evans focuses on the
motives assigned to Satan's rebellion and temptation of Adam and Eve, noting
that the motives become "more ignoble" as the epic develops: "What is more,
they are organized in such a way that the proud antagonist of God soon gives
way to the jealous rival of the Son, and ultimately to the envious tempter of
Man. This progressive degeneration, so pungently summarized by C. S. Lewis,
may of course be quite accidental, but the kind of manipulation I have described
strongly suggests that it was very carefully calculated" (231).

Evidencing a variety of critical strategies, a number of critics at the mid-
twentieth century seem to share William Empson's views as they pursue the
consistency of Satan's characterization throughout *PL.* Somewhat anticipatory
of this critical approach is Kester Svendsen's 1949 study of the epithets applied
to Satan: "the close exercise of poetic decorum in the epithets and the repetition
of key titles for Satan tend to unify his characterization. It is hardly possible to
believe in a perfectly calculated progressive deterioration; but instead of seeing
two Satans in the poem, one may, on the basis of the epithets, see two sides
(among many) of Satan's nature" ("Epic Address" 198). Rather than the epithets,
Davis P. Harding examines the allusions, specifically the "veiled allusions" in

Books 1–3. "In these books [1–3] there are two kinds of veiled allusions which perform the task of systematic disparagement, allusions to the deformed giants who warred on Jove and allusions to serpents or dragons" (*Club* 52). J. B. Broadbent finds Satan "true to life," as he "represents man struggling against God. Disdain (82), fear of mockery from his fellows, and distrust of his own motives (93[–97]) prevent repentance. God cannot be denied, but at least the world may be shared with him" (*Some Graver Subject* 170).

The claim that Satan is a Promethean hero is perhaps most vigorously rejected by Robert Martin Adams. Asserting that Werblowsky thoroughly misrepresents Prometheus, Adams counters that Prometheus "is the wise counselor and the son of Themis, who is the goddess of Justice; Zeus, on the other hand is the usurper and tyrant, the raw new king whose rule is maintained only by force" (46). Adams argues that "if one looks at the matter distinctly, it will be apparent that the similarities between Satan and Prometheus do not amount to much more than this, that they are antagonists of the reigning deity who excite a measure of admiration. Their enmity for the deity is founded on different motives and expressed in different ways. Satan is active, causing others to suffer, Prometheus is passive, suffering himself" (47).

John M. Steadman presents the most sweeping and sustained series of essays arguing against the old—and new—Romantic views of Satan. In "Image and Idol" (1960), he employs Renaissance poetic theory to support Lewis's charge that Satan is consistently a liar: "Any detail which Milton might invent to describe the Archfiend's activities before or after the temptation must—according to Renaissance poetic theory—be consistent with his role as tempter in Book IX" (645). In "Ethos and Dianoia" (1967), Steadman employs rhetorical theory: "Though there is indeed a striking difference in tone between Satan's orations in the first book and his soliloquy on Mount Niphates, this does not spring (as critics have often argued) from inconsistency in character, but rather from different rhetorical functions. The dissimilarity is, on the whole, less ethical than rhetorical" (223). Also see Steadman's "Milton's Rhetoric." In *Milton and the Renaissance Hero* (1967), Steadman analyzes Satan's first soliloquy as it develops the epic formulas of sapience and magnanimity to reveal Satan as an idol or false image of both moral virtues: "The 'technique of degradation,' which Waldock has wrongly censured in Milton's treatment of Satan, has its roots in the conventions of poetic justice." Steadman continues: "The devil's soliloquy on Mount Niphates fills a basic requirement of poetic justice—to display the misery of sin" (180). In *Milton's Epic Characters* (1968), Steadman develops the contrast between Satan's role in the war in heaven and his role in the garden once again to deny his heroism: "Though this change in tactics involved a comparable shift in epic prototypes—a partial substitution of the Ulysses-pattern for that of Achilles or Turnus—it did not violate heroic decorum or the conventional *ethos* of an epic hero. The heroic idol is just as specious in the fallen commander who glories in his strength as in the cunning dissembler who prosecutes his enterprise by guile. In either case the defeated Archangel embodies only the 'semblance' rather than the 'substance' of heroism" (311).

Perhaps one might see Stanley Fish as having the final word on the degeneration-versus-degradation debate. In an appendix to *Surprised by Sin* (1967), Fish declares, "It follows, then, that between Books I and VI Satan does not change at all. His degradation is a critical myth" (345). Also see Fish, "Discovery" 1, 5.

While the debate about the degeneration or degradation of Satan dominates the criticism evoked by the soliloquy on Mt. Niphates, Edward Phillips's remarks about Satan's soliloquy and Milton's early plans for a tragedy on the Fall also figure importantly in the critical discourse of the first half of the twentieth century. In 1947, not only was Waldock's *"Paradise Lost" and Its Critics* published but so was Allan H. Gilbert's *On the Composition of "Paradise Lost."* Gilbert traces the difference between the voice of Satan and the narrator's characterization of him to the stages of the epic's composition and its derivation from Milton's early plans for a tragedy on the Fall. Developing his argument for the influence of the early dramatic drafts, Gilbert (18–19) insists, "The fourth book has much affinity with tragedy." Helen Gardner, Alastair Fowler, and J. Martin Evans also look back to Milton's early dramatic plans when reading Satan's first soliloquy. Gardner recalls that in "Adam Unparadiz'd" Satan is assigned two soliloquies: "in the first he was to 'bemoan himself' and 'seek revenge upon man'" ("Milton's 'Satan'" 65), but Gardner argues that Satan is best understood in relation to the heroes of Elizabethan tragedy, figures such as Macbeth and Faustus. In his soliloquies, Gardner insists, "the quality which makes Satan a tragic figure appears most strikingly, and it is the quality that Mr. Lewis makes weightiest against him: his egoism" (49). Cf. Gardner *A Reading* 113. Fowler (192) writes in accord with Gardner, describing the speech as "an interior duologue between Satan's better and worse selves," and comparing it to "the repartee" between Marlowe's good and evil angels in *Doctor Faustus* 1.1.97–104, 2.1.403–10, 2.2.563–64, and 2.2.630–33. Fowler adds, "At the same time, the self-dramatising of despair is for M[ilton] itself satanic," and he quotes Broadbent's remark: "The characters of *Paradise Lost* do not soliloquise until they have fallen." See Broadbent, *Some Graver Subject* 80. For his part, Evans stresses the influence on *PL* of Hugo Grotius's *Adamus Exul*: "*Adamus Exul* begins in precisely the same way, so if Phillips's evidence is accepted it would seem that Milton produced a fifth draft which began, like the Dutch play, with Satan's soliloquy as he arrives within sight of Eden at dawn" (214). Todd ([1842], 2:53) had earlier presented a few other dramatic parallels for Satan's first soliloquy. While Todd finds resemblances to Prometheus's first speech in Aeschylus's tragedy (*Prometheus Bound* 88–126), he reports that John Warton in an unpublished note associates Satan's first soliloquy with the opening of Euripides's *The Phoenician Maidens*, as Benjamin Stillingfleet does to Euripides's *Hippolytus* 355.

Cross-referencing with other speeches within *PL* has also illuminated Satan's first soliloquy. S. Musgrove cross-references it with Satan's final soliloquy (9.99–178), describing each as "a speech made in, and largely to, light," but while the first is "a sunlight speech," the other is "a starlight speech," and therefore "One could say that the lights are going out for Satan" (312). The bard's invocation of light opening Book 3 also juxtaposes Satan's address to the sun, but, Musgrove explains, Satan's speech "is the damned soul's cry to the lesser light that is, none the less, a type of the eternal beam" (307). A. S. P. Woodhouse describes the contrast between the two speeches as the contrast between a curse and a prayer for divine illumination (113), and Jackson I. Cope makes similar associations as he discusses the structural import of light and dark within the epic (117–18). Marjorie H. Nicolson follows a similar line of thought, suggesting that Satan's first soliloquy, set alongside the openings of Books 1, 3, 7, and 9, might be considered a prologue, but she notes that, "if so, it is deliberately in reverse to the plan of the others, all of which follow a pattern established in the general prologue" (*John Milton* 183). William G. Riggs explains that "the comparable addresses to light serve emphatically to demonstrate the difference between the poet and the Apostate. While the poet asks for assistance, humbles himself before holy Light, prays, Satan hurls envious defiance at a lesser luminary" (68).

Sacvan Bercovitch (249) associates Satan's hateful words to the sun with the ironic description of him as the "radiant Sun" in 2.492.

32–35. Edward Bysshe presents this passage under "Sun" in the "Collection" section of *The Art of English Poetry* (389).

33–34. Todd cites William Drummond's *Song* 1.46, which describes the sun at noon as "*Most princely looking.*" Crediting a private note from Charles Dunster, Todd ([1842], 2:53) refers the lines to Orpheus's description in his hymn "To the Sun" 16, while he also compares the lines to "lordly eye" in 3.578. Fowler notes that the Neoplatonists had developed Orphic and Platonic theories of the sun as a divine image "into a full-scale solar theology" (610).

33. *like the God:* Patrick Hume (132) acknowledges Satan's subsequent success in persuading mankind to worship the sun and points out that God therefore "by *Moses* so strictly forewarn'd his People of Idolatry, *Lest thou lift up thy Eyes unto Heaven, and when thou seest the Sun and Moon, and the Stars, even all the Host of Heaven, thou shouldst be seduced to serve and worship them,* Deut. 4. Vers. 19." Newton's thoughts recall Hume's: "Satan is made to address the sun, as it was the most conspicuous part of the creation; and the thought is very natural of addressing it like the God of this world, when so many of the Heathen nations have worshipped and adored it as such" (230).

34–35. Source study is brought to bear on these lines. Todd ([1842], 2:53) acknowledges Bowle's reference to Sir John Harington's translation of Ariosto's *Orlando Furioso* 4.55.1–2, where the stars are said "*their heads to hide.*" Mary Steward Leather (404) and A. W. Verity (453) consider Milton's lines as a source for Pope's *Epistle* 3.282 (*Poems* 3.2:113), and Leather also cites Pope's *Iliad* 15.170 (*Poems* 8:203).

John Dryden's Lucifer, soliloquizing as *The State of Innocence, and Fall of Man* 2.2 opens, converts the claim voiced by Milton's Satan that the stars hide before the splendor of the sun. As "the body of the Sun," according to Dryden's stage directions, "is dark'ned," Lucifer laments, "Am I become so monstrous? So disfigur'd, / That nature cannot suffer my approach, / Or look me in the face? But stands agast; / And that fair light which gilds this new made Orb, / Shorn of his beams, shrinks in?" (*Works* 12:108).

B. A. Wright sees evidence here that refutes the opinion that Milton was unable to express feelings or sensations: "Having come from journeying among the stars Satan would be impressed by the unbroken sun-filled sky. It is one of those dramatic strokes that set the scene, and give interest and life to a narrative" (*Milton's "Paradise Lost"* 126).

Leland Ryken here locates evidence of Milton's technique of expressing apocalypse through distance. One of Milton's strategies for presenting God as other is to distance him as a disembodied voice or presence, and therefore, Ryken explains, "our glimpse of God's glory and power is suggested indirectly by being conveyed to us through the response of God's creation to his presence" (158).

37–39. Isabel Gamble MacCaffrey, examining the incorporation of temporal processes into the structural patterns of *PL,* explains that the concept of comparison enters Satan's world after his fall, as it enters Adam and Eve's world after their fall. Consequently, she notes, "Satan's awareness of time reaches a climax when the sight of Paradise presses contrast on him" (78). Citing Rev. 2.5, "Remember therefore from whence thou are fallen, and repent," Alastair Fowler supports MacCaffrey's reading (611).

37. Several modern critics have pursued the basis of Satan's hatred of the sun. Kester Svendsen considers its origins in legend. With respect to Satan, identified as the "Dragon" (4.3), Svendsen explains that "in the old legend, the sun which engendered the python killed it; and Satan suffers a kind of death at the height of his triumph when, 'Now Dragon grown' [10.529] literally, he merges with his symbol" (*Milton and Science* 145). James H. Sims (*Bible* 176) establishes the biblical associations between the Son and the sun that provide the theological basis for Satan's hatred of the sun. Directing attention to such Old Testament texts as Mal. 4.2 and such New Testament texts as John 9.5 and Rev. 1.16 and 2.5, Sims concludes, "The Biblical allusions of the beginning of Satan's soliloquy emphasize the parallel between his hatred of the Son and of the sun and indicate the reason for his hatred; he 'that doeth evill, hateth the light' (John 3:20)." Mario A. DiCesare understands Satan's hatred of the sun as a matter of recognition: "Recognizing God in the symbolism of the Sun, Satan is also perversely recognizing himself as an empty parody of the Godhead." When Satan announces his hatred of the sun, DiCesare writes, he "totally rejects the Other" (" 'Advent'rous' " 6).

39. *above thy Spheare:* David Masson notes that this phrase is to be read by reference to the Ptolemaic universe, in which the sun is situated in the fourth sphere around the earth (*Poetical Works* 3:167).

40–47. Both Frank Allen Patterson (*Student's Milton* 82n32) and Sir H. J. C. Grierson associate Satan's lament with Claudius's speech in *Hamlet* 3.3.36–72, when, Grierson explains, Claudius "pours forth the agitation of his tormented conscience; and Milton's the more impressive because of the loftier character of Satan…and his more terrible situation" (126–27).

40. *Till Pride and worse Ambition:* Hume draws a fine theological distinction here: "Pride is a kind of excessive and vicious Self-esteem, that raises Men in their own Opinions above what is just and right: But Ambition is that which adds Fewel to this Flame, and claps Spurs to these furious and inordinate Desires that break forth into the most execrable Acts to accomplish their haughty Designs; which makes our Author stigmatize Ambition as a worse Sin than Pride" (132). Rejecting Bentley's change of "worse" to "curs'd" (107), Pearce (108) reasons much as does Hume and notes that Satan "always lays the blame on his *Ambition,* as in v. 61 and 92." Newton (231) and Todd ([1842], 2:53–54) quote both Hume and Pearce. In the soliloquy that opens *The State of Innocence, and Fall of Man* 2.2.11–14, John Dryden's Lucifer describes ambition as "Accurst" (5) and, when he later prepares to deceive Uriel, apostrophizes pride: "Down, my pride, / And all my swelling thoughts; I must forget, / A while, I am a Devil; and put on / A smooth, submissive face" (*Works* 12:108).

41. *matchless:* as B. A. Wright notes, Edward Phillips, in his *Life of Milton,* misquotes his uncle's text, writing "glorious" for "matchless" (*Milton's Poems* 580). Fowler suggests that Phillips may not have been misquoting, but quoting rather from an earlier version (611). See Darbishire, *Early Lives* 73.

In his 1795 edition of *PR* Charles Dunster associates this *matchless* with *PR* 1.233, "By matchless Deeds express thy matchless Sire," noting that there is "considerable resemblance, both in the *rythm* [*sic*] and in the *repetition*" (28).

John T. Shawcross's gloss is "both 'unequaled' and 'not to be contested'" (*Complete Poetry* 318).

42–53. James H. Sims and later William A. McQueen note the irony in this sequence in which Satan's voice echoes God's voice or the voices of those through whom God speaks. When he remarks that God created him as he "was," rather than as he currently "is," Satan, Sims explains, "is corroborating God's word (through Ezekiel) to himself: 'thou was perfect in thy wayes, from the day that thou wast created, till inequity was found in thee' (Ezek. 28:15). In the same Biblical context, Satan was told, 'thou hast corrupted thy wisedome by reason of thy brightnesse' (Ezek. 28:17). Satan's words also allude to the promise of James that 'God...giveth to al *men* liberally, and upbraideth not' (Jas. 1:5) and to John's definition of the love of God as keeping God's commandments 'and his commandments are not grievous' (I John 5:3)" (*Bible* 176–77). McQueen more broadly argues, "Satan momentarily becomes a spokesman for the official 'argument' of the poem—a function quite similar to that performed by God and the Narrator in the first three books and the angelic spokesmen in later books" (61).

In his first soliloquy in paradise, which opens the third act of Dryden's *The State of Innocence, and Fall of Man* (*Works* 12:113), Lucifer, admitting that God "bounteously bestow'd unenvy'd good" (9) on him, similarly admits his own ungratefulness.

42–44. Verity (453) cross-references 1.116–17 and 5.860. Referring to the second of these associations, John S. Diekhoff reasons, "The admission of the present soliloquy brands the claim [to be 'self-begot'] a lie when we meet it chronologically earlier although actually later in the poem" (*Milton's "Paradise Lost": A Commentary* 36).

47. *easiest recompence:* Edward S. Le Comte points to the recurrence of this phrase in *PR* 3.122–29 and explains, "In the two epics Milton proceeds to ask what God's own glory is. The Creator's glory comes from the gratitude of the created, he says in two passages of identical import linked by the phrase "easiest recompense" (*Yet Once More* 52).

50. *sdeind:* Hume identifies the word as "an Italian Imitation of *sdegnare,* It. *dedignari,* to contemn, to despise" (132). Newton (231) points to Spenser's use of "sdayned" in *The Faerie Queene* 5.5.44, and Todd ([1842], 2:54) adds Michael Drayton's *Moses His Birth and Miracles* 1.394 (*Works* 3:367) and Fairfax's translation of Tasso's *Gerusalemme Liberata,* titled *Godfrey of Bulloigne* 20.128. Supplying the etymological information and the definition that Hume first presents, the *OED* 1 cites both Spenser's use and Milton's.

51–52. As he defines *quit,* "pay off, settle," Verity glances at Edmund Burke who, according to him, "quotes Milton much" (453). Verity quotes from "On Moving His Resolutions for Conciliation with the Colonies, March 22, 1775" in which Burke talks of "the immense, ever-growing, eternal debt, which is due to generous Government from protected freedom" (1:248). Also see Verity on Burke in **96–97** and **291–95**.

52. *gratitude:* in his remarks on the reasons traditionally assigned to Satan's rebellion, C. A. Patrides (*Milton and the Christian Tradition* 93–94) brings attention to ingratitude: "Given the all-inclusive nature of pride ('there is no sinne almost but pride doth participate with it' [Miles Smith, *Sermon Preached at Worcester* 15]), Milton variously analysed Lucifer's disobedience and mentioned the fallen archangel's ingratitude towards the Creator (IV.42–57). The reiterated censure of ingratitude during the Renaissance as a marble-hearted fiend, as 'worse then *Heathenish;* yea more then *Brutish*' [Nehemiah Rogers, *The Penitent Citizen* 88], reveals the kind of response the poet was expecting of his readers. In Donne's reminder [*Sermons* 6:42], 'No book of Ethics, of morall doctrine, is come to us, wherein there is not, almost in every leafe, some detestation, some Anathema against ingratitude.'"

53. *still paying:* John Mitford (112) quotes Edward Benlowe's *Theophila* 29, "Still paying, ne-er discharged."

55–56. While complaining about the syntax of these lines, Bentley (107) notices that Satan's words recall Cicero's sentiment in *De Officiis* 2.20. Newton (231) clarifies Milton's syntax: "This verb is to be connected with the other verbs in v. 50, I *sdein'd* and *thought.*"

58–72. Verity (454) associates the sequence with God's assertion in 3.102, "Freely they stood who stood, and fell who fell," as do Merritt Y. Hughes and Alastair Fowler. Hughes also refers to "Raphael's insistence on the free obedience of the good angels (V, 535)" (*Complete Poems* 279). Furthermore, he concludes, "Satan's confession which does not end in repentance is the justification of God's indictment of him and his followers in 3.98–130" ("Variorum"). Reasoning that God's love granted the angels free will because "his love desired a free response from them," Fowler continues, "This divine love can be represented as ultimately responsible for Satan's fall, since it occasioned the freedom of his will" (612).

Francis Peck (181) refers Satan's catechism on free will to Basil's *Quod Deus Non Est Auctor. Malorum,* cols. 345–48.

59. *stood:* Alastair Fowler (612) refers Milton's use here to a combination of two meanings quoted by the *OED:* "remained" (15.e) and "stood firm and not fallen" (9.b).

67. Explaining that Milton's prosody is syllabic rather than accentual, S. Ernest Sprott establishes the principles of elision in *PL.* In this line, Sprott finds a "w-glide" (85) in the first of two consecutive vowels between words ("to accuse"), where neither vowel is stressed.

73–75. Bringing Faustus's outcry "Whither should I fly? / If unto God, he'll throw me down to Hell" from Marlowe's *Doctor Faustus* 2.1.66–67 into association with Satan's cry, James H. Sims refers both voices to the Psalmist's in Ps. 139.7–8 and explains, "The allusion increases the reader's awareness that each speaker is condemned in his own self-will" (*Bible* 105).

73. *Me miserable:* A. W. Verity (454) provides the Latin expression *me miserum,* which Latinism *OED* 7.b registers as it quotes *PL* 2.73–74. Alastair Fowler (612) also notes the Latinism here but reports, "A similar exclamatory use of 'me' was common in Elizabethan dramatic contexts," which *OED* 7.a indicates in citing Robert Greene's *Menaphon* sig. H4. See Robert Bridges's comment on prosody in **138.**

75–78. The nature of hell is the focus of criticism on these lines, and that criticism most often engages with the fact that, while it is a geophysical place, hell in *PL* is also a psychological state. A number of the critics contributing to the debate about Satan's degeneration or his degradation stress this understanding of hell, as do critics commenting on the narrator's earlier reference to the "Hell within" Satan. See earlier discussions in **20–26, 32–112.**

While his note on 20–26 links Satan's psychological suffering with that of Marlowe's Mephistophilis, as expressed in *Doctor Faustus* 1.3.304–10, Merritt Y. Hughes nevertheless cautions that this association can be misleading if it neglects the reality of hell as a place. In Bishop Joseph Hall's *Heaven upon Earth* 92, Hughes finds expressed a "perfect parallel to the assumption in *Paradise Lost* that, while Satan himself *is* hell, his 'evil mansion' is at the same time truly and unmetaphorically extant somewhere in the remote fastnesses of Chaos" ("'Myself am Hell'" 87). Cf. Hughes in 1.252–63, 4.20–26, 9.119–23, and 10.837–44n. Hughes (*Complete Poems* 279) also glosses this sequence with a passage from Milton's own *DDD* (Patterson, *Works* 3:442). Ernest Schanzer's reading invokes the language of place change to describe Satan's mental torment: "the movement from the mental Heaven or Paradise to the mental Hell is an outward-going movement, or movement from the centre to the periphery, from God to the Self" (136). Satan's soliloquies, Schanzer argues, present "the incessant conflict between two directly opposite states" (137), the angelic and the diabolic. Like Schanzer, Balachandra Rajan also understands that Satan's hellish mental torment is "the diabolic perversion of the paradise within" (*Lofty Rhyme* 93). "In man's world," Albert W. Fields notes, "Satan comes as near as he can to knowing self. His self-awareness is elicited by the sun's brilliance, an external that not only recalls a lost paradise but intensifies the darkness of his inner being" (396).

Rather than the location of hell—within a mental or a geographical place—the terribly dynamic nature of hell focuses several other critics' comments. The Richardsons first remark on Satan's tormented understanding of the dynamics of hell: "the Lowest Hell he found was a Heaven to that Torment he felt from the dread of Worse, the Hell of Hells was in his own Terrify'd Mind. Hell Has, Fear Can have no Bounds" (138). In 1949, Ruth Mohl elaborates on this much earlier understanding. Just as Milton believed in human perfectibility not as a state of static completion, as in Dante, but as "a gradual progress towards an infinite excellence," so, she argues, Milton believed with "evil there is likewise no end," for "evil increases step by step but is never completed" (124). Ernest Schanzer also refers this point about the dynamics of hell to Dante but asserts, "in one respect the Hell in Satan's mind seems more like Dante's abode of Hell than like Milton's. It consists of many circles of every increasing torment, as Satan tells us in his great soliloquy" (144). Michael Lieb focuses attention on the dynamic imagery of swallowing that describes Milton's hell, pointing out that Satan here "characterizes the feeling of being swallowed and devoured in a hole just before he penetrates the confines of Eden." Lieb cross-references *PL* 6.874–75, as he notes, "Here the satanic crew undergoes the experience that it attributes both to Hell and the Abyss. The metaphor of being devoured is fused with the idea of being swallowed up in a womb. The 'yawning' mouth opens as wide as possible to chew and swallow its food" (24–25).

79–87. Satan's attitude to language is revealed here, argues Anne Davidson Ferry, who contends that in his private, as in his public speech, Satan disconnects words from meanings: "Characteristically he thinks of the 'word' as if it were separable from its meaning: 'submission' is a name which he can arbitrarily use or refuse in describing his relationship to God, and indeed 'submission' has no meaning that he can understand, nor do words referring to any other moral or theological qualities or states" (*Milton and the Miltonic Dryden* 53).

79–82. Patrick Hume's annotation at first appears to be one of his primarily etymological notes, but the annotation also glances at Satan's understanding of the theology of salvation, which is the issue subsequent critics most doggedly pursue. From an introductory paraphrase, "Quit thy harden'd Obstinacy, and melt into Repentance," Hume proceeds, "*Relent*, of *Ralentir*, Fr. to grow soft again, of *re* and *lentesceere*, Lat. to soften, to melt, as tough viscous and fat things do at Fire" (132). While both Newton and Todd consider changing *relent* to "repent" in anticipation of *Repentance* in 80, they also engage with the theology of repentance. Newton (232) suggests changing *relent* to "repent," as he cross-references 93 ("say I could repent"), glances at Claudius's soliloquy in *Hamlet* 3.4.36–72, but concludes that *relent* is correct: "Satan could not at first bring himself to say *repent*, and therefore makes use of the softer term *relent*." Todd's vexed attention to this line is remarkable. In 1801, Todd (23) adds biblical support to Newton's note; crediting a note from John Gillies, he refers to Heb. 12.17, and then also adds his own reference to Wisd. of Sol. 12.10. In 1809, Todd (3:83) drops the reference to Wisdom, and introduces the Gillies reference by remarking, "*Relent* is the true reading. See the observation on Addison's Criticism, in this edition, vol. ii. p. 43. *Relent* indeed refers, in which opinion Mr. Dunster concurs with me, to Satan's *fix'd mind, &c.* And to his *unconquerable will*, &c. B. i. 97, 106." In his observation on Addison's criticism in the second volume of the 1809 edition, Todd (2:44) tracks additional support for "relent" to Sylvester's translation of Du Bartas's *Divine Weeks and Works.* In 1826, Todd (2:277) strengthens his argument for *relent* as he agrees with Charles Dunster's cross-referencing of *PL* 1.97 and 106. Even more support is added in 1842 (2:55) with a reference to Sophocles's *Philoctetes* 1302. Dryden's dramatic adaptation of Lucifer's soliloquy, which opens the third act of *The State of Innocence, and Fall of Man,* uniquely contributes to this discussion, as Lucifer assertively coordinates his inability to repent with God's inability to relent: "I mourn it now, unable to repent, / As he, who knows my hatred, to relent, / Jealous of pow'r once question'd" (*Works* 12:113). Several early twentieth century scholars trace specific theological underpinnings for Satan's refusal to relent and seek repentance. In "Variorum," Merritt Y. Hughes, for example, quotes Augustine's *The City of God* 14.27, where Satan is described as "the wicked angel who, in punishment for his first wicked volition, was doomed to an obduracy which prevents him now from willing the good." Helen Gardner looks at Aquinas's *Summa Theologica* (suppl. 16.3), reporting, "Aquinas decides that the fallen angels cannot repent, since, though they know the beginnings of penitence in fear, their free-will is perverted" ("Milton's 'Satan'" 48). William McQueen juxtaposes Satan's words and Milton's own statements on the doctrine of salvation in *DocCh* 1.19 (Patterson, *Works* 15:378–92), as well as Adam's lament in 10.841–44. Satan, unlike Adam, moves not to contrition, but to despair and damnation (62). Broadening the theological focus a bit, several additional modern critics nevertheless maintain the point that Satan rejects salvation. Arthur E. Barker contends that throughout *PL* Satan willfully refuses to respond to the call to be saved: "His meditations at the beginning of Book IV sufficiently illustrate the refusal to believe of those who are called without the Law or the Gospel, and who in consequence have no one to blame but themselves" ("Structural and Doctrinal Pattern" 186). J. B. Broadbent writes, "Whatever the technical causes, Satan is presented as undergoing a series of reactions which progressively extinguish his own gleams of self-knowledge and other-pity and block the angelic impulses that might have saved him; so that by Book IV and Book IX he embodies irredeemable despair more than absolute evil" (*Some Graver Subject* 76). P. T. Forsyth explains that, when Satan rejects the thought of submission, "he contemplates only submission to Omnipotent power, not to Infinite Holy love" (458). James H. Sims follows up on the biblical reference that Todd credits to Gillies, Heb. 12.16–17, which names Esau as a profane person. For Sims, Satan's sorrow resembles Esau's because it "is a self-pitying sorrow which is concerned not with his sin but with his loss" (*Bible* 175).

James Holly Hanford sets Satan's consideration of repentance against a dramatic, not only a theological, background, pointing, as so many have, to the links between Milton's Satan and Marlowe's Mephistophilis in *Doctor Faustus* 1.3.304–10, and between Satan's first soliloquy and Claudius's soliloquy in *Hamlet* 3.4.36–72 ("Dramatic Element" 190). Cf. Grierson in **40–57** and Patrides in **93–104**.

82–85. With attribution to Benjamin Stillingfleet, Todd ([1842], 2:55) associates these lines with Hector's soliloquy in Homer's *Iliad* 22.99–108 deploring his having drawn the Trojans into a battle that they lost and dreading his shame should he confess his miscalculation. Davis P. Harding develops that connection: "Recklessness, bred of despair, is the prevailing mood of both Hector and Satan. Each contemplates submission and each rejects it for the same reason: their fear of that disgrace in the eyes of their followers which, in the heroic code, is far worse than death or defeat. Hector then thinks of the possibility of a negotiated peace with Achilles as Satan debates the possibility of reconcilement with God. Both in the end decide to pursue a positive course of action—positive without hope." Harding also points to the serpent simile that Homer uses to describe Hector immediately before he soliloquizes (*Club* 66).

82. *Disdain:* acknowledging that *Disdain* is italicized in the first and second editions, while *submission* (81) is not, Bentley (108) reverses the typography. Newton (232) and Todd ([1842], 2:55) italicize neither word. Like the Columbia editors, Merritt Y. Hughes (*Complete Poems* 279) and John T. Shawcross (*Complete Poetry* 319) restore the italicization of the first editions, whereas Verity (101) and Alastair Fowler (613) delete the italicization.

84. *other…other:* A. W. Verity (454) cross-references this formula's appearance in 10.861–62, and in his notes on that passage, he describes it as "a favorite form of emphasis" (612) in Milton, citing its occurrence in *Mask* 612–13, as well as in *Lyc* 174. To Verity's gloss, Fowler (613) adds that the construction also occurs in Dante's *Inferno* 3.91–92 and 3.88–89.

86. *Th' Omnipotent:* Kester Svendsen examines epic reference as a function of decorum in *PL* and sets Satan's epithet for God here against his usual type of reference for God, pointing out that Satan "concedes in his epithet on Mount

Niphates that the Father is supreme in the universe, but not often does he make this admission" ("Epic Address" 204).

87. *abide:* Hume (132) supports his definition, "to sustain, to endure," by reference to Virgil's *Aeneid* 6.95. The explanatory notes in William Dodd's 1762 edition gloss *abide* with Samuel Johnson's definition 6, "To bear or support the consequences of a thing," which Johnson illustrates by quoting this very line in his *Dictionary*.

89–92. Isabel Gamble MacCaffrey, who argues that each of the principal places in *PL* carries moral meaning, explains that when Satan arrives in the garden, his earlier claim, "The mind is its own place" (1.254), "has here acquired a terrible and unexpected meaning. Satan's arguments about place have, therefore, a kind of truth—though it is a truth that recoils on the speaker and proves itself in a direction opposite from the one intended" (72).

In these lines, "the dialectical counterpart of the divine state of 'reduction'" is revealed, according to Michael Lieb, who explains, "On the sublime or deific level, God himself is paradoxically 'reduced' to the condition of the angels through the glorification of his angelic offspring (V, 842–845). That is, the result of the angels' adoring God is the 'reduction' of God as a ruler to the state of those who obey. The antithesis of the sublime experience is the degenerate experience: Satan also is 'reduced' through the glorification of his host. He laments rather than celebrates the fact" (8).

89. *adore:* Satan's tone here is variously understood. William Empson sees a certain discomfort in Satan's admission that "he has at times accepted for himself what he had disapproved of giving to the Son. But this would be hard to avoid, and to worry about it only proves that he is a deeply conscientious republican" (*Milton's God* 76). Alastair Fowler disagrees with Empson, finding that "'adore' is sufficiently explained as an amplification of the contrast between outward supremacy and inward torment. Satan says that his advancement is made hollow by his misery, not that it is excessive. Apparently either his remorse or his political education is insufficient for qualms about the class structure of hell" (613).

92. Frank Allen Patterson notes Satan's "satire against himself" as he acknowledges that his ambition has won him the "joy of miserie" (*Student's Milton* 82).

93–104. *Grace:* A. W. Verity and C. A. Patrides place Satan's remarks on grace in a theological context, whereas Alastair Fowler provides a nodding reference to a political context. Verity (454) briefly comments that *Act of Grace* in 94 means "doing penance, asking pardon." In "The Salvation of Satan," Patrides establishes the theological controversy complicating Satan's reflections by examining the notion of *apocatastasis,* which Origen's commentator Jean Daniélou explains as follows: "in the end God's patient love will succeed in making all his creatures weary of their unfaithfulness. The most stubborn will eventually give in and consent to love him, and at last even his enemy death will be overcome" (287). While *apocatastasis* gained some support in the Eastern church, Patrides explains, it was basically and sometimes vehemently rejected in the Western church. Finally, Patrides notes, Satan's decision in this soliloquy not to seek Grace "coincides with the decree pronounced by God the Father before the rebellion in Heaven that disobedient angels would be confined to Hell 'without redemption, without end' (V, 615)" (472–73). Fowler (613) turns to the *OED,* where, he reports, *Grace* II.6 means "by concession of favour, not of right." Fowler adds, "The phrase was often used in political contexts, in the special sense 'free pardon by formal act of Parliament' (*OED* II 15 b)."

96–97. Verity (454) points out that in his speech "On Moving His Resolutions for Conciliation with the Colonies, March 22, 1775," Edmund Burke quotes these lines. Also see Verity on Burke and Milton in **51–52** and **291–95**.

105–10. On Satan's hatred and envy, see McColley in **9**.

108–10. Modern critics energetically argue the heroism or the foolishness of Satan's vaunt here, usually in conjunction with the larger issue of Satan's characterization. Setting Milton's Satan against the heroes of earlier epics, Lascelles Abercrombie asserts, "The epic hero has always represented humanity by being superhuman; in Satan he has grown into the supernatural" (83). As he considers Satan's vow, "Evil be thou my Good," Abercrombie explains, "We may see what a change has come over epic poetry, if we compare this supernatural imagination of Milton's with the supernatural machinery of any previous epic poet. Virgil is the most scrupulous in this respect; and towards the inevitable change, which Milton completed and perfected from Camoens and Tasso, Virgil took a great step in making Jupiter professedly almighty. But compare Virgil's

'Tantaene animis celestibus irae?' [*Aeneid* 1.11; 'Is anger so great in celestial spirits?'] with Milton's 'Evil, be thou my good!' It is the difference between an accidental device and essential substance" (82). James H. Sims later develops the reference to Camoens, arguing that allusions to Camoens's questioning of Portuguese heroism enhance Milton's presentation of Satan's voyage into the garden ("Camoens' Lusiads" 46n21). Sims also cross-references Satan's vaunt with earlier imagery in *PL* 2.632–43, concluding, "Satan can now be said to have rounded his spiritual Cape of Hope" (41). Sims brings additional development to these associations in **159–65**.

C. S. Lewis's feisty reading of this sequence triggers the most animated responses in the middle decades of the twentieth century. Lewis finds contradiction, rather than heroic passion, in Satan's words: "What we see in Satan is the horrible co-existence of a subtle and incessant intellectual activity with an incapacity to understand anything.... He says 'Evil be thou my good' (which includes 'Nonsense be thou my sense') and his prayer is granted" (99). Energetic replies to Lewis's reading follow from Elmer Edgar Stoll, R. J. Zwi Werblowsky, and Arnold Stein, among others. In "Give the Devil His Due," Stoll insists that Satan's vaunt is neither foolish nor nonsensical but rather movingly, dramatically resolute: "In the world as we know it, such an outcry is...neither logic nor psychology" (112). Aligning Satan's words with Iago's "Hell and night / Must bring this monstrous birth to the world's light" in *Othello* 1.3.409–10, Stoll suggests, "A 'motiveless malignity' in the villain, as Coleridge and Lamb rightly call it, may not only provoke a bigger, more unmingled emotion, but also relieve the hero of responsibility for the villain's misdoing" (113). Years later, Werblowsky takes direct aim at Lewis's reading: "I wonder whether Mr. Lewis has ever thought of expounding *Isaiah* V.20: 'Woe unto them that call evil good, and good evil; that put darkness for light, and light for darkness; that put bitter for sweet, and sweet for bitter!' in a similar way, to wit that the prophet reproached the Israelites with sinning against logic as their only perversion" (8). Also see Sims, *Bible* 178. Arnold Stein similarly finds Lewis's criticism of limited value: "Should we apply strict logic to Satan, as though he were a philosophical position instead of a dramatic character, then of course he could not escape absurdity." Stein contends that Satan "is partly aware of his absurdity, but he is unaware of the total situation, and he cannot master it by means of glib irony. Yet to dismiss him as ridiculous is also to dismiss him as a dramatic character, without allowing ourselves to experience his failure. That is to substitute logical judgment for dramatic experience" (4).

By the early 1960s, Lewis's provocative reading of Satan's vow seems less central to the critical discussion. As he denies Waldock's understanding of Satan's characterization, John M. Steadman explains that, soliloquizing on Mt. Niphates, Satan "reveals essentially the same moral purpose as beside the burning lake" (*Milton's Epic Characters* 312). B. A. Wright's reading carries much the same emphasis: "Satan and his fellows are evil—remembering it not as a doctrinal point but as a fact determining their whole situation, their actions and words at every stage. They differ from men in that they are incapable of repentance; they are lost souls 'to whom hope never comes, that comes to all.' It is summed up at the end of Satan's opening soliloquy in Book IV: 'Evil be thou my Good'" (*Milton's "Paradise Lost"* 53). As the degeneration-degradation debate fades, Harold E. Toliver offers a reading of Satan's vow that embraces earlier views while also establishing a focus on Satan's use of language, a focus similar to Anne Davidson Ferry's. While Toliver describes Satan's voice here as "authentic," rather than "simulated," as in Books 1–2, he also describes it as "ultimately meaningless: evil cannot be good, though it may ironically be Satan's good. The pronouncement is at once Satan's most absurd and most heroic moment, a definition of self by defiance. It is an attempt to create meaning where there can be none, and into it are funneled all of the paradoxes of the Satanic position and infernal linguistics" (162). See Ferry in **79–87**.

108. Todd ([1842], 2:56) cites a parallel in Medea's speech from Apollonius Rhodius's *Argonautica* 3.785 and Spenser's *The Faerie Queene* 1.5.43.

110–13. A long consideration of punctuation and diction is set off by Bentley (108), who, describing the "Pointing and Reading" of the entire sequence as "vitious," puts a semicolon at the end of 111, changes "I hold" to "I'll hold," replaces *and* in 112 with "o'ER," and is very disappointed by the repetition of "By Thee." Pearce (109–10) accepts only Bentley's semicolon, which the Richardsons (139) change to a comma, explaining that it strengthens the effect of the repetition of "By thee." Newton (234) keeps the comma, and declaring that the passage "may easily be understood," reasons as follows: "*Evil, be thou my good;* be thou all my delight, all my happiness; *by thee I hold at least divided empire with Heaven's King* at present, I ruling in Hell as God in Heaven: *by thee* I say; he is made to repeat it with emphasis, to add the greater force to his diabolical sentiment, and to mark it more strongly to the reader: *and* in a short time *will reign perhaps more than half,* in this new world as well as in Hell: *as* *man ere long, and this new world shall know*. And he is very properly made to conclude his speech with this, as this was now his main business and the end of his coming hither." Maintaining the comma at the end of 111, and repeating Newton's reading, Todd ([1842], 2:56–57) also presents Dunster's suggestion that Satan's reasoning here recalls the reasoning of the Devil in lines 418–21 of Avitus's *De Originali Peccato*, the second book of the five-book *Poematum de Mosaicae Historiae Gestis*. With less emphasis, Todd also refers Satan's speech to Allecto's speech to Satan in Richard Crashaw's *Sospetto d'Herode* 34 (*Poems* 118). Masson (*Poetical Works* 3:167) understands Satan's reasoning about "more than half" as do Newton and Todd, adding Greenwood's reference to a line attributed to Virgil, "Divisum imperium cum Jove Caesar habet." Fowler moves beyond Newton's remark on the emphasis achieved by the repetition of "by thee" to suggest that the doubling may be "to render the divisive, dyadic character of the evil addressed" (614).

110. A. W. Verity (454) juxtaposes Satan's declaration here to his confession in 9.122–23, "all good to me becomes / Bane."

114–23. For the most part there is consensus about the actual visual changes described as crossing Satan's face here, and literary precedents help focus the description, but discord about Milton's overall presentation of Satan as he moves from hell to the garden splinters the critical reading of the significance of those changes. On that critical discord, see **32–113**.

each passion dimm'd his face: although Hawkey ("Various Readings"), cross-referencing 10.1009, insists that *pale* (115) is a noun, he and the Richardsons (140) share the understanding, reported by Newton (234–35), that Satan's face "was thrice chang'd with pale through the successive agitations of these three passions." This early understanding that "Satan's face grew pale three times—first with ire, then with envy, then with despair," David Masson rejects, and offers that "a shadow or dim scowl of each of these passions in succession passed over his face, followed by paleness" (*Poetical Works* 3:167). Verity, however, agrees with the early editors (454). Assuming that Satan remains disguised as a cherub, and that his face therefore ought to be red, Alastair Fowler contends that Milton is here punning "visually on red the cherubic colour, and red the ordinary ruddiness of a sanguine human complexion unaffected by passion" (614). However the changes crossing Satan's face may appear, the changing itself has been traced to earlier literary sources and parallels. Todd ([1842],

2:57) refers to *The Faerie Queene* 1.9.16, where Arthur attempts to conceal the show of passion on his face as he speaks with Una and Redcross. Irene Samuel argues that Satan's "passions, each with its distinctive pallor, correspond to the three variously colored heads of Dante's Lucifer" in *Inferno* 34.7–45, and, referencing the commentary of Bernardino Daniello 151, for whom each color corresponds with one of the humors, she concludes, "*Ira, Invidia, Accidia* are equivalent to the anger, envy, despair by which Milton repeatedly characterizes Satan" (*Dante* 123). Merritt Y. Hughes (*Complete Poems* 280) advances the association between the humors and Satan's passions by quoting from Timothy Bright's *A Treatise of Melancholie* 97.

The degeneration-degradation debate presented in **32–113** bears upon the critical reception given the description of Satan's "dimm'd...face." John Peter, describing Satan's behavior on Mt. Niphates as "unheroic," for example, claims that Satan's complexity here is "decomposing," but Peter also faults Milton for the change (54). John Steadman insists upon Satan's heroism but specifies that it is an "Odysseus-type" of heroism, "characterized by wiles, ruses, disguises and deceptions" ("Image" 648). Continuing, Steadman argues, "The soliloquy on Mount Niphates revealed the emptiness of Satan's vaunts in Hell and at the same time betrayed to Uriel the spurious nature of his angelic disguise. Ithuriel's spear unmasked him in a subsequent disguise, and Gabriel's interrogations forced him to contradict himself" (649). Anne Davidson Ferry and Frank Kermode further elaborate the sense of division discussed by Peter and Steadman. Ferry writes, "The diction here, with its emphasis on deep artifice and false creation (recalling Spenser's descriptions of the magician, Archimago), implies that the division which characterizes fallen beings is a violation of nature, that unity of being is the original state of all creatures as it was of Adam and Eve in Eden, Satan once in Heaven" (*Milton's Epic Voice* 121). Similarly, Kermode, noting that "the theme of physiological perturbation" returns to paradise in Book 9, concludes that "the effect of the Fall in Book ix can be measured by the degree to which the humours of the lovers are distempered by the fruit" (115). Marjorie H. Nicolson succinctly presents a similar reading: "Further changes in his physical appearance [revealed in 4.115] reflect the moral descent" (*John Milton* 236). Allan H. Gilbert suggests that the contradictory presentation of Satan here results from Milton's effort to adapt earlier dramatic plans for the epic (*On the Composition* 18–19). See Gilbert in **32–113**.

dimm'd: tracing this word's etymology to Old English for "dark," James Paterson (296–97) explains, "*Satan's devilish* Passions took off the Disguise, which he put on before *Uriel,* and discovered himself to be a mere *Devil* indeed." A. Bartlett Giamatti, who notes the contrast between 110 and 114, expands on Paterson's point: "The deceiver is perceived in his deceit as Satan, forced to convert his fallen situation to his advantage ('Evil be thou my good,' IV, 110), cannot escape the massive irony of the universe whereby good from evil will come. But the point is made: falsity and illusion are about to enter the garden" (331).

115. *ire:* The Richardsons (140) comment that "Fear" instead of "Ire" appears in the Argument to Book 4, and explain, "Fear" is "Warranted by *v.* 14 and 18."

118–19. The Richardsons exclaim, "This Short Reflection admirably heightens the Accursed Character of *Satan* by being Oppos'd to it, Set by it. what Reader feels it not!" (141), whereas A. W. Verity (454) considers the statement's literary parallels, noting that it may refer to the *Aeneid* 1.11, as 6.788 and 9.729 certainly do. Verity also points to *The Faerie Queene* 2.8.1.

121. *Artificer of fraud:* in *Spectator* 321, Addison explains that Satan's transformations and stratagems at this point "are Circumstances that give an agreeable Surprize to the Reader, and are devised with great Art, to connect that Series of Adventures in which the Poet has engaged this great Artificer of Fraud" (3:172). Kester Svendsen makes a similar point. Establishing that "Artificer of fraud" is one of the many epic epithets for Satan, Svendsen explains, "Milton as narrator capitalizes upon and signalizes nearly every change of scene or situation by changing the epithet for Satan. It will be seen that the epithets reveal Milton's attitude toward Satan as a character in an epic poem, and that they epitomize Milton's understanding of the psychological and philosophical as well as the narrative functions of the antagonist" ("Epic Address" 196). Also see Svendsen in **32–113.**

Todd ([1842], 2:57; 4:455) first cross-references "fraudumque magister" in *QNov* 17 and points out that Gregory Nazianzen's designation for the old dragon in *Christus Patiens* is *fraudis artifex* (col. 137). David Masson (*Poetical Works* 3:167), Edward S. Le Comte (*Yet Once More* 8–9), and Merritt Y. Hughes (*Complete Poems* 280) repeat that cross-reference, and Hughes ("Variorum") also points to the concept of Satan as the "father of lies" in 3.93, 3.683, 5.709, and *PR* 1.407.

122. *under saintly shew:* Hume (132) directs readers to 2 Cor. 11.14: "Transforming himself into an Angel of Light."

123. *couch't with:* glossing the phrase as "Lodg'd," and deriving it from the French "Couche," the Richardsons (141) cross-reference *coucht* at 876. Verity (454) offers this gloss, "united with; it implies lying hid (Fr. *couche*)," and Hughes (*Complete Poems* 280) brings even more emphasis to the notion of hiding in his note, "lying concealed." Alastair Fowler draws together these definitions and finds, "The intricacy of the line is mimetic" (615).

124–30. Two minor critical controversies grow out of this passage, one about physical geography and one about angelology. The Richardsons (141) quickly dismiss Bentley's claim (109) that "Armenian," not "*Assyrian*" is the correct reference, and Todd's note supplies the geographical explanation behind the controversy: "Niphates divides Armenia from Assyria; and from this mountain the river Tigris, that is, 'Hiddekel, which goeth toward the *east of Assyria*,' takes its rise" ([1842], 2:58). David Masson similarly clarifies the geography: "Niphates, in Armenia, near the border of Assyria proper, but within the general region often named Assyria" (*Poetical Works* 3:167). Cross-referencing "this *Assyrian* Garden" at 285, Allan H. Gilbert supports Todd and Masson, as he observes that Assyria, "sometimes in the Old Testament called Ashur," is a district "in the upper part of Mesopotamia, along the shores of the Tigris. The chief city was Ninevah. The word is also used in a wider sense, as applied to the whole Assyrian Empire" (*Geographical Dictionary* 26). Gilbert (210) associates this sequence with *PL* 4.569 and 11.381, as well as with *PR* 3.252, 3.253, 3.265, 4.26, and 4.236 as he quotes Strabo, who identifies "th' *Assyrian* mount" as Niphates in his *Geography* 11.12.4.

In the angelological dispute, Grant McColley takes issue with Harris Francis Fletcher (243–44), who contends that Milton's concept of Uriel as the "Angel of the Sun" derives from the Midrash on Num. 2.10 (*Midrash* 3:39). McColley instead points to Enoch 20.2, 33.2–4, 72.1–82.8 where "Uriel is the first named of the seven archangels who watch" ("The Book of Enoch" 26).

125. *once warnd:* Grant McColley, studying the chronology of the composition of *PL,* and recognizing that Uriel had not previously been warned, assumes that lines 124–30 are an "interpolation," which is also "partially incompatible with the verses which precede it." He therefore assigns the sequence to what he determines to be the earliest of Milton's three periods of composition, 1652–53 (*"Paradise Lost": An Account* 321). Similarly puzzled by this phrase, and noting that Uriel does not appear in the early dramatic plans, Gilbert concludes that Uriel's role "was devised when Milton was working on the heroic form. But it must have been early in the composition of that form, early enough at least to permit of subsequent revision in the course of which the scene of warning disappeared, leaving behind some puzzling vestiges" (*On the Composition* 42). Verity (454) points the passage forward to Uriel's warning Gabriel at 564–75.

126–27. John Keats claims that Milton "is not content with simple description, he must station," and offers as evidence Eve's recollection of first seeing Adam (4.477–78), as well as Uriel's seeing Satan on Niphates: "This last with all its accompaniments, and keeping in mind the Theory of Spirits' eyes and the simile of Galileo, has a dramatic vastness and solemnity fit and worthy to hold one amazed in the midst of this *Paradise Lost*" (265). John R. Knott returns to the notion of Milton stationing the eye of the viewer in his commentary on the expansive description of the garden in **205–87** ("Symbolic" 42).

127. *disfigur'd:* Alastair Fowler (615) reports in *The Immortality of the Soul* 3.10.5 that Henry More explains that spirits cannot for long conceal their true selves.

128–29. F. T. Prince identifies as evidence of the Italian element in Milton's verse the separation of associated substantives combined with adjectives in these lines (*Italian Element* 116). Such separation suspends or interrupts the sense of the statement, as Prince, focusing on these lines, goes on to explain that "rhetoric, which seeks to reproduce the vividness or impressions, or to give the emphasis of passion, is entirely justified in placing the 'gestures' first. And while it might then seem more logical to say 'His gestures fierce and mad demeanour, then alone, he marked,' this would also bring about a loss of vividness and emphasis: the expression would decline into flatness and heaviness" (122).

130–33. In this sequence, John S. Diekhoff finds one of the 52 instances "of rhyming lines enclosing two not rhyming" ("Rhyme" 541). The other such separated rhymes in Book 4 are in 247–50, 307, 308–10, 311, and 751–54.

131–83. Editors and critics from 1695 well into the first half of the twentieth century principally consider the literary and geographic references and allusions in this extended description of Satan's movement from Mt. Niphates up the paradisal mountain, over the wall, and into the garden. Several of the most provocative phrases, such as "woodie Theatre" (141), and a few of the longer segments, such as the "*Sabean* Odours" segment (162–71), elicit sustained discussion and debate. To be sure, Stopford Augustus Brooke's 1879 discussion of "expectation" in a much longer sequence (153–268) is a most remarkable and sensitive reading of Satan's approach to and entrance into the garden, but C. S. Lewis's treatment of the topic in *A Preface to "Paradise Lost"* has become most influential. Understanding the sequence as a vision of the archetypal journey home, Lewis influences much of the subsequent criticism on these lines.

Lewis explains that the visual descriptions are "archetypal" (48) and therefore not definite and authorial, but evocative: "While seeming to describe his own imagination he must actually arouse ours, and arouse it not to make definite pictures, but to find again in our own depth the Paradisal light of which all explicit images are only the momentary reflection. We are his organ: when he appears to be describing Paradise he is in fact drawing out the Paradisal Stop in us" (49). The poetic device that Lewis calls "vertical serialism" (49), as well as the device of surprise and reversal, significantly serve to establish the slowly unfolding "dream landscape" (49) he discusses. Emphasizing the difficulty of the ascent to the walled garden, Lewis explains that, at about 137, Milton "begins playing on the note of progression—upward progression, a vertical serialism. *Overhead* is *insuperable height* of trees (138). But that is not enough. The trees are ladder-like or serial trees (cedar, pine, and fir) with one traditionally eastern and triumphal tree (the palm) thrown in (139). They stand like a stage set (140) where Milton is thinking of *silvis scaena coruscis*. They go up in tiers like a theatre (140–142).... Above all these trees, *yet higher* (142) springs up the green, living wall of Paradise. And now a moment's rest from our looking upward; at a wave of the wand we are seeing the whole thing reversed—we are Adam, King of Earth, looking *down* from that green rampart into this lower world (144–145)—and, of course, when we return it seems loftier still. For even that wall was not the real top.... Above the wall—yes, at last, almost beyond belief, we see for once with mortal eyes the trees of Paradise itself" (49–50).

For the next several decades, C. S. Lewis establishes the point of departure for innumerable critics commenting on this episode, and Arnold Stein's reading perhaps most notably reveals Lewis's influence. Echoing Lewis, Stein writes that "the dream [descriptive of Satan's entering paradise] has qualities reminiscent of an archetypal return" (56). For Stein, the slow and difficult approach up the mountain is crucial to the reader's experience of paradise remembered: "We first approach the happy garden from the Fall. Immediately outside this 'happy rural seat of various view' is the impassable wilderness—steep, hairy, overgrown, grotesque, wild, denying access; the trees that rise in ascent are of insuperable height; beneath them all is steep and savage, entwined, tangling, perplexing.... It has become so much a part of the experience of entering the Garden that it enters with us; we bring the outside, at least as vivid memory, into the more vivid inside. And if the entrance into Paradise is—as it must be for fallen man—a return, then we bring a recent immediate memory of the outside into our ancient memory of the inside" (52).

The subsequent vision of paradise, Stein explains, is therefore "not a pure mystic vision in which identity is lost, for a sense of doubleness is permitted, and surprise, and even deception" (56). While Stein's concept of doubleness is fully developed by reference to paradise itself (4.205–87), the approach to the garden establishes the doubleness, and that the "verdurous wall" between the garden and the fallen world outside is so easily bounded points to the relationship between the approach up the mountain and the paradise atop the mountain, a relationship emphasized by both Lewis and Stein, and richly developed by many later critics. Frank Kermode, for example, points out that "the difficulty of access to Eden" does not apply to Satan who easily leaps the wall, but to us; "we are stumbling, disorientated, with Satan into an unintelligible purity" (107).

In "The Devil and Doctor Jung," the second chapter of his 1955 publication *Ikon,* Robert Martin Adams delivers a major critical attack on the readings developed by Lewis and Stein, however, faulting both for the "use or abuse of Jungian ideas which consists of borrowing nothing more than a vocabulary and not even a total vocabulary at that but just a favorite word, probably 'archetype' or 'archetypal'" (36). While Adams approves the critical directness of the "full-blown Jungian" Maud Bodkin, he sees confusion in the "charming circularities" of Lewis and Stein. Adams recalls that Lewis "mentions rising tiers of trees, and adds incautiously that 'as in dream landscapes, we find that what seemed the top is not the top.' For Stein this observation imports 'that the sequence of Satan's entering Paradise resembles a dream' and not only so, but 'the dream has qualities reminiscent of an archetypal return,' partly because of the 'hairy sides' of IV, 135, and partly because the experience described is 'real-unreal' like a dream" (37). Adams also forcefully objects to Lewis's notion of Milton "drawing out the Paradisal Stop." It is as if, Adams explains, "readers were so many Hammond Electric Organs" (38).

131–66. Indicative of early eighteenth century poetic taste, this sequence is the sole item under "Paradise" in the "Collection of…Descriptions…in the best *English* Poets" in Edward Bysshe's *The Art of English Poetry* 298. As he does frequently, Bysshe fuses a few lines from another location in *PL*, in this case 5.377–79, to the beginning of the quotation. Passages from *PL* also dominate the entries on "The Garden of Eden" and "Adam and Eve in Paradise" in Bysshe's *Art*. See Bysshe in **216–68, 300–51**.

131–48. While the garden in Genesis is not situated atop a mountain, Milton's garden is described not only here as "the champain head / Of a steep wilderness" (134–35) but later as situated atop "a Rock / Of Alablaster" (4.543–44), and those two different mountain locations have long elicited critical attention. The basic mountaintop location has been authorized with biblical and literary references other than Genesis. Through all his editions, Todd, for example, refers it to Dante's earthly Paradise atop Mt. Purgatory in *Purgatorio* 28, adding that in Book 4 Milton "appears indeed to have repeatedly consulted his [Dante's] fine canto" ([1801], 256–57; [1809], 3:85; [1826], 2:281; [1842], 2:58). Thomas Keightley (*Poems* 1:339) finds biblical authority for the location of Milton's Paradise in Ezek. 28.13–14 while also referencing Dante's mountain paradise, as well as Ariosto's in *Orlando Furioso* 34.50. Verity (455) points out that when Dante's Adam talks with Dante in Paradise, he says that God had put him "in the uplifted Garden." In addition, Verity notes the allusion to Milton's mountaintop garden developed through the third stanza of William Collins's 1747 publication "Ode on the Poetical Character" (*Works* 33–34). Grant McColley suggests that an analogue for Milton's heavily wooded mountaintop location is Spenser's Garden of Adonis in *The Faerie Queene* 3.6.29–45 ("Milton's Technique" 71). McColley draws a similar conclusion in **239–68**.

That the mountain is here described as heavily wooded but is later described as "a Rock / Of Alablaster" (4.543–44) is yet another crux challenging Grant McColley and other twentieth century Milton scholars. McColley admits that Milton actually "went so far as to locate the Garden upon two radically different mountains" (*"Paradise Lost": An Account* 143). In another study (*"Paradise Lost"* 208), McColley argues that the second hill (4.543–48; 11.118–19,

376–84; 12.638–40), which he asserts is "the setting for both the first and second temptations, was the famous Mount Amara." McColley explains: "Since Milton had, in keeping with other writers [Tasso, *Il Mondo Creato* 7.759; Thomas Peyton, *The Glasse of Time* 41], rejected Amara as the true place of Paradise and had located the Garden in the accepted region, there was nothing heterodox in making use of physical characteristics ascribed to the Abyssinian mountain [4.280–85]." Surveying earlier pseudepigraphic, midrashic, patristic, medieval, and Renaissance descriptions, Sister Mary Irma Corcoran widens the focus on sources that may have contributed to Milton's two different descriptions of the mountain: "These passages reflect the 'delicious Land' and the 'natural Amphitheatre' of 'woodie hils' described by Purchas [*Purchas His Pilgrimage* 699] and pictured in Blaeu's atlas [*Le Theatre*], the single ascent of Heylyn's Amara [*Microcosmos* 728], the plateaus crowning the peaks described by Purchas, Heylyn, and others, the insuperable mounts of Ceylon and Amara, the 'precipitous crags,' 'overhanging lofty rock,' and 'unapproachable cliffs' of Diodorus [*The Library of History* 3.20] and the plots of Ortelius [*Theatrum Orbis Terrarum*], the alabaster gate of Heylyn's Meroe, and the exotic fruit and evergreen trees that ornamented every description of a distant Paradise" (20). In Milton's two different paradisal mountains, Gilbert finds support for his views on the stages in which Milton composed his epic. Gilbert also associates this crux with the angelic guard: "So long as Eden is a 'shaggie Hill' (IV.224), there is no hint of angelic guardians, but when the craggie, overhanging cliff of Mt. Amara is adopted, they are present (IV.549)." Gilbert finds it probable that "the two conceptions indicate different times of composition. Mt. Amara...is perhaps the earlier" (*On the Composition* 39–40).

Broader, more abstract concerns with Milton's description of the garden's mountaintop location figure importantly in the responses of a number of other twentieth century critics. Making a distinction between realism and familiarity that anticipates critical discussions of the garden itself in 205–87, and recalling C. S. Lewis's remarks on the approach to Eden at 131–83, J. B. Broadbent develops the fanciful quality in Milton's description by contrasting it with Edmund Waller's description of the gardenlike setting of the Bermudas in "The Battle of the Summer Islands." Milton's tone, Broadbent contends, "has entirely changed the significance of these things. Waller's Bermudas are familiar and real; realism was one necessary element in Milton's Paradise; familiarity was not" ("Milton's Paradise" 162). As Jackson I. Cope discusses the symbolic dimension of time and space in *PL,* he refers to Eden as "an encased jewel" located atop the steep wilderness and explains that "there is a consistent connotative antithesis throughout the poem between circumscription and spaciousness" (58), with circumscription symbolizing order and spaciousness symbolizing "the natural milieu of disorder and evil" (59). In the following year, 1963, Roy Daniells applies aesthetic theory to the topic of the garden's geographical location: "The garden paradise of Adam and Eve is contained by a wall, within and above which can be seen 'a circling row of goodliest Trees.' While this circular place of worship is in one sense self-contained, it is also part of a larger whole which invites an axial vista" (*Milton, Mannerism* 95). Daniells then explains the effect of this distinction as the difference between living "in a state of perfect and stable felicity within the circle of the garden under the dome of heaven" and living "in Eden, which as their 'nether Empire,' calls for penetration and into Eden and the wide world the future will take them" (95–96). In a later article, labeling the garden a *hortus conclusus,* Daniells notices that, because Adam "never approaches the wall, never leans out like the Blessed Damozel...he never seems bounded or limited in his movements" ("Happy Rural Seat" 4). Leland Ryken understands the unfamiliar and removed quality of the mountaintop location as another element of Milton's apocalyptic vision (180). Also see Ryken in **205–355**.

131–42. Davis P. Harding and Louis L. Martz discuss Milton's poetic strategies as he describes Satan's viewing of the paradisal mountain. Acknowledging the parallel between Virgil and Milton that Hume identifies in his note on "Silvan Scene" (140), Harding is most concerned with the way both Virgil and Milton describe looking up at such a site: "By holding back his main verbs, 'suspending' them, as critics have termed the process, Milton like Virgil is able to throw the emphasis where he wants it, in this case on the descriptive details, the garden's 'Insuperable highth.' The ascending structure here has an obvious relevance. Satan is at the foot of Paradise, and we actually see the Mount as Satan sees it; our eyes follow his upwards. This perspective intensifies our awareness of the awful proximity of Evil to Good and of the crisis in human affairs soon to come" (*Club* 126). Cf. Lewis on "vertical serialism" in **131–83**. As does Harding, Martz also notes the Virgilian phrase, but as he brings attention to **131–42**, Martz's wider focus is on the style of Book 4 as "a development out of the highly wrought style of Book 1" (*Paradise Within* 119). Contending, "The 'purer air' of Paradise demands a purer style moving out of the high epic manner toward something that at times comes close to a pastoral simplicity, though always enfolded within the epic mode" (119), Martz finds that 131–42 "represents in little the manner of Milton's presentation of Paradise: with a generous infiltration of epic similes and classical allusions, though widely spaced, and not so frequent by half as in the opening book" (118).

131–37. Tense shifting throughout these lines ("fares…deni'd"), as well as in subsequent lines, prompts Anne Davidson Ferry to clarify the temporal point of view of Milton's speaker, as opposed to Satan's. For Satan, "the setting is physically present; the events are happening to him in the present time, or belong to his immediate past or future," while the fallen speaker "shares our previous history, but as a blind bard inspired with supernatural vision, he miraculously experiences the events and places of pre-history in the present and miraculously sees into the future. His manipulations of tenses therefore transcend our experience of time, logic, grammar" (*Milton's Epic Voice* 53).

131. *fares:* "*Fares* from *Faran,* an old French-Teutonic word signifying to go on a Journey. also from the Saxon *Faer,* a Step. Thus we say Fare ye well, or Fare well, wishing a Good Journey; and a Coach-man, or Water-man is paid his Fare when he is paid his Journey" (Richardson, *Explanatory* 141).

132. *Eden:* Patrick Hume's assertion that Eden is the "Name of a Country, and particularly of *Mesopotamia*" endures without refutation, but later critics never repeat his attack on St. Jerome's translation of *Eden.* Hume (137) chides St. Jerome for "very erroneously" translating *Eden* as "Pleasure" in the Vulgate version of Gen. 2.8 ("Plantaverat autem Dominus Deus Paradisum voluptatis a principio"). Hume pursues this error into the Vulgate's Gen. 2.10 ("Et Fluvius egrediebatur de loco voluptatis"). With Gen. 4.16, Hume claims, Jerome "was ashamed to say that *Cain* dwelt on the East of Pleasure, but has there used the proper Name of the Region *Eden, Ad Orientalem Plagam Eden.*" Twentieth century Miltonists with a focus on the poet's handling of biblical materials accept the soundness of Jerome's translation and celebrate its contribution to Milton's presentation of the garden. Corcoran writes: "Within this secluded garden, all was beauty and delight. Some versions of Scripture translated the *Eden* of the Hebrew to 'a place of pleasure.' In his epic, Milton echoed the 'delicious Land' of Purchas [*Purchas His Pilgrimage* 699] and the *paradisum deliciarum* of the [Brian] Walton translation of the Septuagint [*S. S. Biblia Polyglotta*] when he wrote of 'delicious Paradise' (IV, 132), and he combined the two concepts of

Eden in the further lines [208–10]" (20–21). Sims reasserts Hume's point that "the Garden is not identical with Eden, it is *in* Eden," but then associates the sensuous element in Milton's description of the garden with his recognition that "the meaning of the Hebrew word transliterated 'Eden' is 'pleasant'" (*Bible* 22). Frank Kermode (103) similarly refers the sensuous joy of Milton's paradise to the Vulgate versions of Gen. 2.8, "in paradisum voluptatis," and Gen. 2.15, "in paradisum deliciarum." Also see **27, 214–15**.

Paradise: J. B. Broadbent argues that the garden's "traditional location and shape were based ultimately on the Zend word *pairidaeza,* a pleasure-garden elaborated in Persia from the oasis (Diodorus Siculus [*Library of History* 3.46] describes one of them)" (*Some Graver Subject* 173). On Diodorus's garden see **159–65**.

133. *enclosure green:* surveying other references to mountaintop gardens, both biblical and nonbiblical, Alastair Fowler (616) adds that the *hortus conclusus* of the Song of Sol. 4.12 also bears upon Milton's description of the garden.

134. *champain head:* "an open, level summit of open land" (Verity 454). Also see Verity in **131–48**.

135. *steep:* following the *OED* 1, Merritt Y. Hughes assigns this word the obsolete meaning of "lofty" ("Variorum").

hairie: while Patrick Hume's annotation tracing this metaphor to a number of classical literary antecedents prompts no reaction, and remains unnoticed even by Hughes, who provides a similar gloss, C. S. Lewis's brief remark on *hairie* in *A Preface to "Paradise Lost"* not only has become one of those popularly known bits of literary criticism but also has been thoroughly developed by a number of other twentieth century scholars. "Leaves," Hume asserts, "by a frequent Metaphor, are called the Honour, and the Hair of the Trees" (133), and he cites Virgil's *Georgics* 4.137, as well as Horace's *Odes* 4.7.1–2 and *Epodes* 11.5–6. Several hundred years later, Lewis orders Milton's reader: "Do not overlook *hairy.* The Freudian idea that the happy garden is an image of the human body would not have frightened Milton in the least" (49). Subsequent critics maintain and develop Lewis's point. Arnold Stein, for example, refers his archetypal reading of 131–83 to it (see **131–83**). Robert Martin Adams develops the point as he responds to Lewis and Stein: "the physiological overtones of 'hairie sides' do not disturb Mr. Lewis…and they please Mr. Stein by providing a sort of justification for the adjective 'archetypal.' Paradise, though both gentlemen are too nice to say so right out, is evidently a womb" (37). Cross-referencing the paradisal mountain's "hairie sides" with the prelapsarian serpent's "hairie Main terrific" (7.497), Michael Lieb sees that hairiness, in both cases, is "the imagery of a fallen environment where desires are untempered and libidinous" (155). Lieb develops the point that Milton's garden "becomes a living organism that takes on characteristics of bodily functions" by considering Satan's role as he ascends the paradisal mountain: "Sexually, Satan assumes the posture of an assault: he is about to attempt to penetrate and thereby defile a pure, unfallen, womb-like area that shelters and sustains what exists within. Psychologically, Satan represents the upsurge of the subconscious or chaotic forces that are attempting to overwhelm the bliss of the innocent personality. Indeed, the implication of Chaos is in the very description: the 'overgrown' or untempered 'thicket,' the 'grotesque and wild' 'wilderness' are integral parts of the scenery" (69). Finding Milton's efforts to present Adam and Eve's prelapsarian sexuality "not wholly successful," J. B. Broadbent ("Milton's Paradise" 172) also recalls Lewis's views and suggests that "it is possible to take the whole description as an allegory of the human body—e.g., 'Access deni'd' (IV, 317)," and that this reading "does soften the hardness complained of by Mr. Wilson Knight" (see **205–87**). Finally, echoing Hume, Hughes qualifies the emphasis on the physical meaning of "hairie sides" when he notes that *hairie* "is equivalent to Latin *hirsutus* in the sense of 'bristling' in which Virgil used it" ("Variorum").

136. *grottesque and wilde:* Brooks and Hardy point out that *grottesque* "appears here for the first time in English, some hundred years ahead of its next recorded appearance" (274). See *OED* 1.b. Of *grottesque*, Hughes writes that "the form is French though the word comes from Italian *grotto*, a cave. In Milton's time it referred to painting or sculpture in which foliage was prominent" (*Complete Poems* 281). Hughes also suggests that, as synonyms, *grottesque and wilde* "seem to be simply objective epithets influenced by the contemporary taste for the 'natural wildness' which Bacon valued in his essay 'Of Gardens' [*Works* 12:242]. Contrast the different sense in which 'wilde' applies to the 'lower World, to this obscure / And wilde' (11.283–84), where Adam and Eve face banishment" ("Variorum"). Alastair Fowler (616) suggests that Milton's picturing of paradise recalls Spenser's remarks to Gabriel Harvey before *The Shepheardes Calender:* "In most exquisite pictures they use to blaze and portraict not only the daintie lineaments of beautye, but also rounde about it to shadow the rude thickets and craggy clifts, that by the basenesse of such parts, more excellency may accrew to the principall" (*Poetical Works* 417).

137–42. From the early editors, the trees on the paradisal mountain prompt richly detailed commentary about their literary pedigrees, practical values, and sensuous appeal. The cedar (139) Hume describes as "a tall growing Tree of a sweet smell," which is "useful and ornamental in Building...expressive of the highest Extravagance," and the sap of which "was esteemed an admirable Preservative against the Worms and Rottenness" (133–34). Hume then refers the cedar to Pss. 29.5 and 16.104, and 1 Kings 6.18–36; *Aeneid* 7.13; Horace's *The Art of Poetry* 331–32; and Persius's *Satires* 1.42. Pine, "firr," and palm (139) Hume annotates along similar lines, tracing the pine to Virgil's *Aeneid* 11.136; the fir to Virgil's *Eclogues* 7.66 and *Aeneid* 8.91; and the palm to Virgil's *Georgics* 2.67–68 and 3.49, as well as to Horace's *Odes* 1.1.5–6. Besides care in tracing classical antecedents, a genuine feeling for the symbolic values of these trees pervades Hume's commentary, as when he remarks that the palm is "A celebrated Tree of a tall and strong Body, rising against all impediment and opposition, and therefore made the Reward and Crown of Conquerors," and that the fir is "another Montaneer, raising his Gigantick Arms towards Heaven" (133–34). James Paterson also offers detailed notes on Milton's trees, but while he provides fewer classical citations than does Hume, he instead intersperses the remarks of a naturalist among his extensive biblical references. On *Cedar,* for example, Paterson reports, "It grows chiefly on M. *Lebanon,* and in the *Woods of America,* was much in Esteem of Old, and highly celebrated in Scripture, but now are very much decreased" (297–98). While A. W. Verity (455) wonders whether thoughts of Vallombrosa, visited by the young Milton during his Italian journey, shaped Milton's description of the ranks of trees, Fowler locates the tree-enclosed garden in literature. Fowler (616–17) points to several similarly treed Spenserian gardens in *The Faerie Queene:* Mt. Acidale (6.10.6), the home of Belphoebe (3.5.39), and the "second paradise" enclosing the Temple of Venus (4.10.22–23). Describing the *Palm* (139) as "the only unconventional tree" in the catalog of trees surrounding Milton's garden, Fowler suggests that its appearance may be connected with Ps. 92.12. Fowler also directs attention to Sylvester's translation of Du Bartas's *The Divine Weeks and Works* 2.1.1.527–30 and 2.4.2.658, where the palm symbolizes chastity or marital loyalty. While

J. B. Broadbent acknowledges the conventional symbolism attached to trees, he stresses that Milton, unlike his poetic predecessors, "simply names the trees" (*Some Graver Subject* 182). Also see Broadbent on the trees of the "blissful Bower" in **694**.

137. *Access deni'd:* Hume (133) locates a parallel in Virgil's description of Circe's grove in *Aeneid* 7.11.

138. *Insuperable highth:* what the Richardsons see as a possible logic problem because of "Yet higher" at 142, Leland Ryken sees as a feature of Milton's apocalyptic vision. The Richardsons explain that this description of the trees' height on the sides of the paradisal mountain "does not contradict what is said *v.* 142. Other Trees might be planted higher, but None on the same Ground could Surmount them; as These were the Loftyest Kinds of Trees, These were Highest of their Kind" (142). Ryken here identifies the poetic device of "apocalypse through negation," whereby empirical qualities are denied "to suggest a realm where only transcendental qualities exist" (100).

In his study of Milton's prosody, specifically Milton's third rule of pure *L,* which leads to terminal and internal elisions, Robert Bridges explains that when adjectives ending in *–ble* occur first in a line, as does *Insuperable,* that placement gives every syllable "full value" (31). Also see Bridges in **73, 250,** and **596**.

shade: both B. A. Wright and Anne Davidson Ferry draw attention to the word *shade,* not only in this passage (138, 141) but also throughout Book 4. Wright believes that Milton regards *shade* as "tree," an "imitation of 'umbra' for 'arbor' in Latin poetic use," and such usage "naturally occurs most frequently in the description of Paradise in Book IV" (*Milton's "Paradise Lost"* 70), but seeking to answer those critics who condemn the so-called Latinisms in Milton's verse, Wright explains that such words "were current in educated speech of the Elizabethan and Stuart periods, when all literate people were versed in Latin" (69). Also see Wright's expanded study of *shade* in " 'Shade.' " While she acknowledges that *shade* "in its variety of forms occurs throughout *Paradise Lost,*" Anne Davidson Ferry finds that the word so frequently and so emphatically appears in the descriptions of Eden that "it grows in meanings with the effect of a sacred metaphor" (*Milton's Epic Voice* 169). While *shade* is especially apropos of the nuptial bower, Ferry continues, the entire garden eventually shares in the values associated with shade: "it is a region holy, refreshing, benevolent, protected. The same associations accumulate around unfallen man, appropriately, since Eden is a 'state' of innocence, both a place and a condition" (171). Also see Ferry and Wright in **572**, and Ferry in **1013–15**.

140. *A Silvan Scene:* Hume (134) identifies the parallel in Virgil's *Aeneid* 1.164– 65, which a number of later editors repeat. See Harding and Martz in **131–42**. Merritt Y. Hughes notes that *Silvan* means "Abounding in trees or woods" (*OED* 3) and cross-references *Silvan Lodge* in 5.377 ("Variorum"). Although it cites *PL* 4.140 to exemplify definition 3, *OED* cites *PL* 5.377 to exemplify definition 2, "Consisting of or formed by woods or trees."

141. *a woodie Theatre:* here, as with "Silvan Scene" in the preceding line, Hume (124) establishes a parallel with the *Aeneid* 5.288–89 that many subsequent editors repeat. Todd reedits his notes on *woodie Theatre* with every new edition of *Poetical Works*. In 1801 (4:253), he credits George Steevens for an unpublished reference to a theater of trees in Sidney's *The New Arcadia* 111, and he points to a grove of "theatrick fashion" in Sir John Harington's *The History of Polindor and Flostella* 5 and quotes Oliver Goldsmith's *The Traveller, or a Prospect of Society* 107–8 (*Works* 4:253). In closing, Todd reminds readers, "It must not be forgotten that Virgil, in his fifth *Aeneid,* describes a natural theatre" (257). In 1809 (3:86), Todd adds to the 1801 list *The Faerie Queene* 6.10.6, Lycophron's *Cassandra* 600, and part 2, sig. L.b, of Abraham Fraunce's *Countesse of Pembroke's Ivychurch.* In the editions of 1826 (2:281–82) and 1842 (2:58), Todd drops the Goldsmith reference but retains all else. Mitford (115) contributes references to Seneca's *Troades* 112, and Solinus's *Polyhistor* 38.

Revealing no interest in tracking analogs or sources, but concerned rather with chiding Addison and Johnson for considering Milton a pedant, De Quincey argues that the *woodie Theatre* exemplifies Milton's use of the "principle of subtle and lurking antagonism," a principle that A. Bartlett Giamatti also develops in his reading of the phrase. De Quincey explains that, "As a place of rest, it was necessary that it [the garden] should be placed in close collision with the unresting strife of cities" (*On Milton* 403–04). Giamatti broadens this principle of antagonism, identifying it as "the old garden theme of the relation between the real and the good, the illusory and the evil" (331). With the theater metaphor, Giamatti argues, Milton "makes the garden a setting for illusion, just as in Elizabethan drama the world was a stage, where poets played with the serious idea of playing. Yet here, as we will see, the image of the theatre has a double function. The garden is not only the scene for Satan's artifice which means corruption and brings death; as we will see it is also the stage for God's art which is life, those divine illusions which are reality" (331–32).

Davis P. Harding and Merritt Y. Hughes variously refer to dictionaries in their notes on this phrase. Drawing *Scene* (140) into conjunction with *Theatre*, Harding (*Club* 126n17) reports that the Latin *scaena* means "the background or scene or the stage of a theater." Hughes points out that the *OED*, defining *ranks* as "rows or lines of things placed at different levels" (7) and *Theatre* as "a natural formation or place suggesting such a structure" (1.c) quotes Milton's lines 140 and 141 ("Variorum").

142. *Of stateliest view:* Leland Ryken (51) explains that one of Milton's many strategies for establishing the apocalyptic state of paradise is the superlative contrast as in this phrase, and he also points to 4.147 ("fairest Fruit"), 217 ("Trees of noblest kind"), and 321 ("the lovliest pair").

143. *The verduous wall:* while the Richardsons (142) cross-reference "enclosure green" of 4.133, Evert Mordecai Clark (145–46) suggests that this description "may hark back to that of [John] Mandeville's Ethiopian Paradise [*The Voiage and Travaile* 303]...which was 'enclosed all about with a wall,...all covered with mosse.'"

Establishing the elements of Milton's syllabic prosody, S. Ernest Sprott argues that *verdurous* here exemplifies the principle of elision before a vocalic *r* within a word (96). Also see Sprott in **260.**

144. *our general Sire:* "We are therefore taken into the scene while Satan is still excluded from it. We are included in its physical bounds and in its moral history; Adam is the 'general Sire' of reader and narrator but not of Satan" (Ferry, *Milton's Epic Voice* 52).

145. *neather Empire:* Edward S. Le Comte (*Yet Once More* 39) sets this against *nether Empire* in 2.296.

147–49. At this point, several mid-twentieth-century critics consider how Milton's description of the trees of paradise is involved with the issue of time. Alastair

Fowler (617) points to the conventional simultaneity of "Blossoms and Fruits at once" in earthly paradises such as those presented in Ariosto's *Orlando Furioso* 34.50; Fairfax's 1600 translation of Tasso's *Gerusalemme Liberata,* titled *Godfrey of Bulloigne,* 16.10; and Spenser's *The Faerie Queene* 3.6.42. Fowler notes, however, that Milton, unlike these earlier authors, indicates the reason for that simultaneity in 10.651–706. Fowler also sets Gen. 1.12 as Milton's biblical authority. While similarly acknowledging the conventionality of "Blossoms and Fruits at once," John R. Knott finds that Milton does not declare such conventions "in the manner of someone proving the authenticity of his version of the myth by trotting out the familiar properties." Milton's presentation is "never static, or simply pictorial," Knott argues: "We know that the trees of the Garden bear golden fruit and are perpetually in flower because we see them as they actually appear to Satan" ("Symbolic Landscape" 40). Developing his reading of the approach to paradise, C. S. Lewis notes that this sequence is the "first bit of direct description" of the trees of paradise. Satan has not bounded over the "verdurous wall," but both the "goodliest Trees" and the "fairest Fruit" within are visible to those without. Lewis explains, "*Of course,* the trees have golden fruit. We always knew they would." Lewis then glances ahead to the simile of the rainbow at 4.150–52 as he observes that "at once our glimpse of Paradise recedes to the rainbow's end" (50). Also see Lewis in **131–48**. Isabel Gamble MacCaffrey also suggests that although the trees and fruits are paradisal, the reader's view is complicated by the Fall: "The goodliest trees and fairest fruits of Paradise are invested with the associations surrounding their descendants in the world of time; Milton reconstructs the 'eternal causes' from his knowledge of the generations that have passed since they were first planted in Paradise" (116). Similarly considering Milton's efforts to prevent the problem of process from corrupting his prelapsarian garden, Roy Daniells celebrates the appropriateness of Milton's choice of one particular tree: "But how unerringly Milton has singled out the orange tree, which is a tree for all seasons" ("Happy Rural Seat" 13).

147. *loaden with fairest Fruit:* Edward S. Le Comte (*Yet Once More* 51) associates this phrasing with "loaden with stormy blasts" in *PR* 4.418.

   Fruit: Bentley (15) draws from this sequence yet another critical discussion that carries through the centuries when he proposes to change *Fruit* to *Fruits,* to parallel *Fruits* in 148. Cross-referencing 4.249, 4.422, 5.341, 8.307, and *Mask* 396, Pearce (112) rejects the change: "when Milton speaks of what is hanging on the trees, he calls it *fruit* in the singular number (when gathered, in the plural)." Newton (237) joins the debate, and later, Todd ([1842], 2:59) dutifully reports all. In the late nineteenth century, Masson (*Poetical Works* 3:168) resurrects the controversy: "Milton, when he thinks of a mass of fruit, or of one piece of fruit, uses the singular, but, when he thinks of many individual fruits, or of various kinds of fruits, whether hanging or plucked, the plural. For example, in this very passage, the 'fruits' of line 148 are the same as the 'fruit' of line 147, still unplucked, but only thought of distributively." For support, Masson refers to 5.87, 8.44, 8.147, 9.745, 9.996, 10.565, 10.603, 10.687, and *Mask* 712.

149. *enameld:* focusing on metallurgy as he reports that enamel is "two parts Lead and one Tin, well calcined in an Oven of Reverberation," Patrick Hume (134) indicates no discomfort with Milton's applying such a word to the garden's trees, but a number of modern critics do object, and, indeed, some fervently object. Like "vegetable Gold" (4.220), *enameld* provokes strong condemnation from such critics as G. Wilson Knight and F. R. Leavis, who find Milton's paradise hard and unnatural. See Knight and Leavis in **220**. Responding to such criticism, Broadbent brings particular attention to *enameld*, explaining that while today the word "suggests the hard whiteness of bathrooms and saucepans," in the seventeenth century it meant "the brilliant color used in miniatures and jewelry—it was the color rather than the hardness which took effect" ("Milton's Paradise" 165). Fowler glosses *enameld* as "fresh, lustrous, bright; variegated. With no suggestion of hardness" (617). Giamatti (142n10) similarly argues that the seventeenth century meaning of *enameld* must be restored for Milton's reader, but Giamatti also focuses on the word's seventeenth century literary pedigree. Giamatti lists Ariosto's *Orlando Furioso* 6.20–25; Dante's *Inferno* 4.118 and *Purgatorio* 8.114; Camoens's *The Lusiads* 9.21.4; and Ronsard's *La Franciade* 3.544. Moreover, Giamatti points out that Milton had earlier used *enameld* in *Lyc* 139 and *Arc* 84 while Andrew Marvell in lines 13–14 of "Bermudas" (*Poems* 1:18) made the conventional descriptive term into "a process." The *OED* 3 quotes Milton's use in *Arc* to exemplify the meaning "Beautified with various colours." Leland Ryken recalls Broadbent's response to G. Wilson Knight, and acknowledges the conventional meaning of *enameld,* but Ryken also argues for the word's apocalyptic significance (77). This enameled imagery, Ryken continues, "consists of a whole complex of images naming jewels, minerals, and qualities of human artifice" (79), and while typical of Milton's heaven, such images, occurring "along with the lush vegetation and profuse life of Eden," also characterize Milton's paradise (82).

150. *impress'd:* Walter Clyde Curry (135) tentatively considers an association between Milton's *impress'd* and the Cartesian concept of pression. He quotes E. T. Whittaker on the Cartesian hypothesis: "According to the Cartesian philosophy, all space...is a plenum, so that a particle can move only by taking the place of other particles which are themselves displaced. Light was imagined to be essentially a pressure transmitted through this dense mass of particles" (xiii).

151–52. Examining Milton's methods of compounding and distributing similes against the methods of his epic predecessors, James Whaler ("Compounding" 315) writes that here, as at 707–8 and 987, Milton presents "simple and rapid...examples of compounding similes."

151. *in:* Hume has it *on* (134), with which only Bentley (110) agrees.
   Evening: explaining her plan for a "reformed text" of *PL*, Helen Darbishire draws attention to this word, which in her 1952 edition is spelled *Eevning*, a spelling not adopted by other editors: "*Evening*, always a disyllable in *Paradise Lost*, may be spelt *ev'ning*, *eev'ning*, or *eevning*, but should not be spelt *evening*, which according to Milton's notation would represent a trisyllable" (*Poetical Works* 1:xxvii). S. Ernest Sprott (140) registers his uncertainty with Darbishire's argument: "On a broad view, the spelling is in confusion; but it is certain that Milton distinguished between a dissyllabic *even* (adjective) and a monosyllabic *ev'n* (substantive and adverb)." A few years later, Robert Martin Adams rejects all of Darbishire's assertions about Milton's editorial principles, vigorously denying what he sees as her image of Milton as an "exacting corrector of the proofs of *Paradise Lost*" (60).
   humid Bow: Verity (455) cross-references *Mask* 992.

153–268. Writing in 1879, Stopford Augustus Brooke carefully considers Milton's lengthy and complicated description of the approach to and entrance into the garden, a topic to which twentieth century critics give much attention: "Expectation, in Milton's manner, is kept on tiptoe; touch after touch is added to enhance what is coming, as when 'of pure now purer air meets his approach.' A splendid simile of the odorous winds wafted from Paradise lifts still higher our imagination, but it is somewhat spoiled, also in Milton's way, by a far-fetched allusion to the story of Tobit, and still more, by a reversion to the controversial cry of Lycidas against hireling wolves when Satan overleaps the wall. But we do not even then get to Paradise. There is still a pause of expectation, and Milton moralizes, and makes the map of Eden. Then at last is Paradise; and the lines he gives to it—in metrical weight and balance perfect—(how beautiful the sound of this—'Rolling on orient pearls and sands of gold;' and of this the thought and sound—'Flowers of all hue, and without thorn the rose;') are equal to the height of loveliness he seeks to hold, and rise at the close, when one would think music and loveliness could be no more—into fuller beauty and more enchanted music" (102–03). See **153–71**.

153–71. This passage brings detailed and diverse attention to the scents of paradise, and, like the entire sequence describing Satan's approach to the garden, introduces many topics that will continue to develop in the forthcoming description (**205–87**). As Brooke indicates in the preceding note, Milton's paradise is sensuously experienced even before it is entered; the scents of paradise, fanned by "gentle gales" (156), are first smelled, as the "goodliest Trees loaden with fairest Fruit" (147) are first seen, by those still outside the "verdurous wall" (143). Introducing his analysis of this three-part presentation of the garden's scents, Arnold Stein (58) describes it as "the marvelous outdoing itself" as "Paradise comes to meet" Satan. The three parts of this sequence are as follows: 153–59 (a description of the "pure now purer aire"), 159–65 (a metaphor involving realistic geographic and nautical references), and 166–71 (a comparison with the apocryphal story of Tobias and Asmodeus).

153–59. With admiration for Milton's achievement, Newton (238) identifies a handful of literary parallels or sources for the "pure now purer aire" (153) of paradise, the first being *Twelfth Night* 1.1.5–7. In addition to presenting Robert Thyer's reference to the *dolce aura* of Ariosto's Paradise in *Orlando Furioso* 34.51, Newton also asserts that the figure of "the air's stealing and dispersing the sweets of flowers, is very common in the best Italian poets," and he references Marino's *L'Adone* 1.131. Tacking Newton's note onto the end of his, Todd ([1842], 2:59) refers "of pure now purer aire" to Dante's *Purgatorio* 28.7–9. Todd also traces the mountaintop location of Milton's paradise to *Purgatorio* 28. See **131–48**.

While these earlier editors focus attention on the literary anticipations of Milton's "pure now purer aire," modern critics look to the reactions evoked in both Satan and the reader by the air of paradise. C. S. Lewis (50), for example, points out that the serialism shaping the presentation of the trees on the paradisal mountain recurs in conjunction with the air of paradise: "the air is growing purer every minute (153); and this idea (*Quan la douss aura venta*) at once passes into a 19-line exploitation of the most evocative of the senses, suddenly countered by the stench of Satan" (167). To similar effect, Ryken explains that, with the opening phrase "of pure now purer aire," Milton develops his apocalyptic vision through the technique of contrasts (48). Ryken adds that "once Paradise has been established so fully as a place of fragrance we need only be reminded of its odors in subsequent passages in order for its fragrance to remain in our minds as one of the garden's dominant characteristics" (222). Even G. Wilson Knight, one of the major critics condemning what he considers the "deliberating aestheticism" of Milton's efforts to visualize paradise, nevertheless writes that in this episode Milton "engages the reader deeply in the allurements of exquisite smell and appeal to the taste" (83). Knight declares the description of Satan's arrival Milton's "best scent-passage" and concludes, "Whatever the limitations of Milton's impressionism, his use of smell and taste is probably more abundant than that of any English poet but Keats, who directly follows, while revitalizing, the Miltonic emphasis" (85). See Knight on Milton's "deliberating aestheticism" in **205–87**. About 15 years after Knight praises Milton's achievement here, Arnold Stein presents his detailed analysis of that achievement. This first of the three sections, 153–59, Stein contends, "never ceases to explore the drama of Satan's consciousness. The 'joy' is a small echo of the speed he has not been rejoicing in. The air that can 'drive' any sadness except 'despair' reawakens the echo of the 'conscience' that awoke slumbering despair" (58). Aware of those who find Milton's garden unnatural, Stein brings special attention to *dispense* in 157, a word that is "perhaps excessive for a mere natural act" but a word that also "may suggest the larger dispensation of Providence which this act reflects (as the lordly eye 'Dispenses Light from farr' [3.579])" (58–59). While Sacvan Bercovitch does not mention the "pure now purer aire," his understanding of Satan at this point is much the same as Stein's: "The goodness of creation gives Satan, momentarily, a realistic perspective. The 'delight and joy' before him resemble what he has lost, so that although the prospect of release from Hell drives off his sorrow, the sense of reality remains" (247). In his study of the overwhelming sensuous appeal of Milton's paradise, Knott ("Symbolic Landscape"

40–41) focuses his remarks on the garden's scents by responding to Thomas Greene, who contends that "the spices of the Garden contribute to a 'lulling heaviness' in its atmosphere and offer an 'invitation to indolence'" (396). Also see Greene in **166–71**. Disagreeing, Knott explains that "this should be true only for someone not acclimatized to such a special atmosphere: Satan, or the fallen reader with his dulled senses" (41).

153. *Lantskip:* this is the spelling in both the first and second editions, and is accepted by the Columbia editors, as well as by Merritt Y. Hughes (*Complete Poems* 281) and Helen Darbishire (*Poetical Works* 1:77), although Bentley (110) and Verity (103) print *landskip,* and Fowler (618) *landscape.* Cross-referencing the word's recurrence at 2.491, Fowler acknowledges that in the early editions the spelling is *Lantskip,* but finds "no phonetic difference between the two forms" (530).

of pure now purer: Verity (455), like R. C. Browne (1:348), asserts that this idiom, where *of* expresses transformation, has classical precedent, and offers the support of Sophocles's *Oedipus the King* 454, as well as Horace's *Odes* 3.30.13. In addition, Verity lists Milton's other uses of the same idiom in *PL* 8.433, 10.720, 10.723, and 12.167. Fowler (618) rejects any nod to classical precedent here, as he points to the *OED* VIII.20.b, "where examples from English authors as venerable as Bede are cited."

155–56. Todd ([1842], 2:59–60) refers readers to Milton's *Educ* (Patterson, *Works* 4:290).

155. *drive:* Keightley explains that Milton, following the example of the Latin poets, simplifies the compound "drive away" to the simple *drive,* as in *PL* 1.783, he simplifies "wheel to" to *wheel* (*Account* 437).

156–59. *gales:* in *Ref,* Edward S. Le Comte locates Milton's first association of gales with gentle, wings, and fanning: "God…sent out a gentle gale and message of peace from the wings of those his cherubims that fan his mercy seat" (Patterson, *Works* 3:60). In the poetry (*PL* 4.156–57 and 8.515–18, and *PR* 2.363–65), Le Comte notes that *odours* is added to that cluster (*Yet Once More* 97). Fowler ponders the unusualness of Milton's use of *gales,* reporting, as does Verity (455), that while the word came to mean "gentle breeze" in conventional eighteenth century poetic diction, in the seventeenth century, the word ordinarily meant something "very near to Mod. Eng. 'wind'" (618). In addition to the meanings Fowler presents, the *OED* also records eighteenth century usages in which a *gale* was "regarded as the vehicle of odours" (1.c), as well as Old French and Italian roots that support the definition of gale as "merriment, mirth" (1). The larger context for Milton's *gales* suggests that these understandings may also have figured in his word choice.

158. *Native perfumes:* is Hume glosses this phrase as "Natural Sweets; such as grow, *Nativus,* Lat." (135), but his annotation seems to go unnoticed by his successors. Bentley's reaction to Milton's phrase anticipates the enduring controversy about art and nature in Milton's garden that is presented in **205–87**. "Perfumes around" is Bentley's emendation, offering this explanation for the change: "*Native perfumes* seems here an improper Epithet: for who could suspect, there were already, as afterwards, *Artificial* ones? Besides, if they were *native not only to Paradise, but to the gentle Gales,* how came they to be *stoln* ones?" (110). Pearce dismisses Bentley's objections, advancing that "*native* signifies natural; perfumes which were not artificial, but came from the flours and sweet shrubs: they were *native* to Paradise, but not to the *Gales;* and therefore the *Gales* are justly said to have *stolen* them" (112). Pearce then insightfully considers the narrator's effect on the presentation of paradise: "Tho' there were no Artificial Perfumes then, yet in a Poet, who writes when there are such, it is a beauty to use an Epithet, which expresses the excellency of the Perfumes of Paradise, by saying that they were natural" (112–13). Pearce (113) concludes by cross-referencing "native Honor clad" in 4.289. The Richardsons also take up Bentley's point: "the Winds dispens'd Native perfumes which they had Stoln. This may seem Non-sense, but *Native* Here is not meant as being So to the Winds but as These Perfumes arose Naturally from the Flowers, Spices, *&c.* and were not produc'd by Art. there is another Sense to be given to this Epithet; Native, that is to say, Arising in the place where those Winds were also born. and This is the more likely to be *Milton's* Meaning because he has had it Elsewhere, as in those two Gentile Lines in his Juvenile Poems. Eleg. 3" (143). Thomas Keightley (*Poems* 1:341) associates Milton's phrase with Ariosto's wording in *Orlando Furioso* 34.51 and Dante's wording in *Purgatorio* 24.145–57. R. C. Browne, pointing to *Twelfth Night* 1.1.7, identifies the theft image as "common" (1:348), and Alastair Fowler concurs (618).

159–71. Examining Milton's methods of compounding, varying, and distributing similes against the methods of his epic predecessors, James Whaler draws attention to negation in this passage: "Milton first declares what the delightful fragrance of Paradise is like, and then suggests the very opposite" ("Compounding" 314).

159–65. This second of the three parts in the sequence describing the garden's scents (153–71) consists of literary and geographical or historical references, and a number of the topics of critical concern here resurface in the forthcoming description of paradise in **205–87**. Todd ([1842], 2:60–61) firmly establishes the foundation for the critical discussion of literary sources when, crediting "Mr. Wakefield" for an unpublished note, he quotes Diodorus Siculus's *The Library of History* 3.46, where the plants of Sabea, or Arabia Felix, are described as yielding "inexpressible fragrance to the senses; not unenjoyed even by the navigator, though he sails by at a great distance from the shore." Although Milton may very well have consulted Purchas and other travel writers, as well as Pliny, both critics and editors steadily acknowledge the significance of his overwhelming debt to Diodorus (Keightley, *Poems* 1:341; Thompson, "Milton's Knowledge" 162; Gilbert, *Geographical Dictionary* 27–28; Verity 455–56; Whiting, *Milton's Literary Milieu* 68, 118–19; Hughes, *Complete Poems* 280–81). As is true for his responses to all of his so-called sources, however, Milton adapts the material from Diodorus. Grant McColley points out, for example, that "the idea that sailors paused to enjoy the exquisite perfume, the poet may well have added, for Diodorus made no mention of it" (*"Paradise Lost": An Account* 144). Yet Robert Ralston Cawley explains (71–72) that Milton does not "modernize" Diodorus, as he often modernizes his classical sources, by adding to them information provided by modern geographers such as Peter Heylyn who, while repeating the centuries-old comment about the fragrance of "*Arabie* the blest" (*Cosmography* 3:117), also stresses "the thieving nature of its inhabitants" (3:118), a commonplace Milton never mentions. Difficulties with the geography of Milton's adaptation of Diodorus, however, were rather quickly identified. The Richardsons (144) only quietly glance at the problem as they comment on *delay* in 163: "the North-East Winds are Contrary to Those whose Course is from the Cape to *Mozambic,* and So On; but they bring the *Arabian* Perfumes with them, which well Recompence the Forc'd Delay." But Thomas Keightley firmly confronts—and also explains—the problem: "What is here asserted is an impossibility. Any one who will look on a map of the world will see that when a vessel going to India has passed Mozambic, the coast of Arabia is due north to her, and at an immense distance, with a portion of the east coast of Africa interposed. In no case then, and in no part, could those who had sailed by the Cape of Hope and Mozambic meet with Sabean odours wafted by north-east winds. Milton's blindness amply excuses this mistake" (*Account* 430). While Verity opens his note quoting Keightley, and while he suggests that "*north,* according to modern geography," probably ought to replace *North-East* in 161, he also implies that geographical accuracy may not have been Milton's principal concern. Concluding, Verity quotes Diodorus and reasons that Milton "had this special description in mind, as it is removed only a few chapters from that account of Ammon and Amalthea which was the undoubted source of 275–79" (455–56). The concern with the accuracy of Milton's geographical references continues to elicit attention into the mid-twentieth century. Rehearsing Keightley's discussion, Masson suggests, "Milton seems, in his blindness, to have forgotten geographical distances and bearings," and offers another explanation: "In the maps of Africa in Milton's days, . . . the east side of Africa trends away west from Cape Guardafui to the Cape of Good Hope so much more rapidly than in our present maps, that a vessel off Mozambique in *them* would not be due south, but rather south-west of Arabia Felix. Hence, in the matter of bearing, Milton's recollection of his maps was not so incorrect as it must be admitted to have been in the matter of distance" (*Poetical Works* 3:169). Elbert N. S. Thompson also turns to the old maps, as well as the description of Arabia in Diodorus as he supports Masson's refutation of Keightley ("Milton's Knowledge" 162). Decades later, Robert Ralston Cawley similarly backs Masson (72).

The accuracy of the geographical references does not concern Hilaire Belloc as much as Milton's love of maps and place-names such as *Mozambic* and *Arabie.* For Belloc, the "harmony, the concord, the spell of place-names" here, as well as in 211–14 and 280–85, is "that one of Milton's excellences which is almost personal to himself" (256), and, he continues, "it may be said that if a man has become too poor to travel he can still replace that pastime by reading to himself the fourth book of 'Paradise Lost'" (258). On the evocative quality of Milton's place-names, also see Anne Davidson Ferry in **162**.

Not geographical reference but Satan's association with heroic explorers of new worlds prompts the notes of several later critics. Brooks and Hardy focus on words such as *wilderness, grottesque,* and *wilde,* and they cross-reference

9.1115–18 as they explain, "Satan has to see himself as the explorer about to penetrate the country of the aborigines" (274). B. A. Wright develops a similar understanding: "Nowadays trading may not strike us as romantic or heroic, but in the sixteenth and seventeenth centuries the great voyages of discovery...were undertaken by merchant adventurers in pursuit of trade. Milton uses these voyages magnificently to describe Satan's hazardous voyage to Earth." Wright contends that Milton believed heroism on the battlefield was less glorious than the heroism demanded by "the struggle with nature, the search for knowledge, the exploration of the world" (*Milton's "Paradise Lost"* 109). Michael Wilding argues that, by locating Satan in this context of the voyages of discovery, Milton is "both showing his courage as an intrepid sea-traveller, and showing in Satan activities of mankind in the fallen world" (36). Wilding, however, also sees the more ironic and far-reaching results of Satan's voyage: "Eden is an undeveloped land found for the first time by Satan the explorer-trader. He expects, of course, to find mankind easy to exploit—primitive savages. But the irony is that he sees...not 'naked' savages or savage 'natives' inferior to Satan, but possessors of a primitive innocence much superior. Satan's scheme has recoiled. Yet it recoils again with a further irony; for despite their innocence and 'Majestie,' Satan does succeed" (36).

159. *balmie spoiles:* Hume's earlier detailed attention to the trees on the paradisal mountain is sustained here (135): "Those Spicy Spoils. *Balmy,* sweet delicious....the Balm-Tree preferable for its smell to all other Odours, growing only in *Judea,* and near to Destruction by the Malice of the *Jews,* at the sacking of their chief City, as *Pliny* relates [*Natural History* 4:81]." Hume concludes with a supporting quotation from Virgil's *Georgics* 2.119. See Hume on the paradisal trees in **137–42**. For Frank Kermode, *balmie* "is a key-word in the life-asserting part of the poem, being used in the sense in which Donne uses it in the 'Nocturnall [upon S. Lucies Day, being the shortest day' 6 (*Elegies* 84)], as referring to the whole principle of life and growth" (108). Milton's *spoiles* is the first example cited by the *OED* I.1.b for the figurative application of the following meaning: "Goods, esp. such as are valuable, taken from an enemy or captured city in time of war; the possessions of which a defeated enemy is deprived or stripped by the victor; in more general sense, any goods, property, territory, etc., seized by force, acquired by confiscation, or obtained by similar means; booty, loot, plunder."

160. *the Cape of Hope:* J. B. Broadbent, Arnold Stein, and James H. Sims see irony coloring the simile comparing Satan to "them who sail / Beyond the Cape of Hope." Broadbent explains that the simile "returns us to the beginning of Satan's voyage when flying up through Hell he looked like the mirage of an East Indian merchant fleet trading for spice. But the heroic idyll is smashed with a grim recital of the plot of *Tobit* as if Satan's sensibility were corrupting the balms of Paradise into the sexual reek of 'the fishie fume'" (*Some Graver Subject* 170). Acknowledging that the "surface impression" of the epic simile appears conventional, Stein probes beneath that surface to where "biting relevance wittily plays. First, there is the mischievous pun on Satan's having voyaged beyond the Cape of Hope. The remote and inaccessible joys of Mozambique and Saba and Arabia Felix (Englished 'the blest') are carried by winds from the east; Satan, we remember, has approached Paradise from the west, so the 'gentle gales' are also from the east. The voyagers *slack* their course with *such* delay; Satan has lost the impetus of his joyless speed and slacked in the duty he invented and accepted; when we return to him directly again it is to note that he has been journeying on 'pensive and slow'" (59). Sims attends to the Cape of Hope reference as he develops the larger specific associations between Satan's voyage and the voyages of the Portuguese presented in Camoens's *Lusiads*. Recalling the ship imagery describing Satan's voyage from hell to paradise, this sequence, Sims explains, "ironically associates Satan with the Portuguese voyagers who first rounded the Cape and opened a new door of hope to European commerce; of course, the result of Satan's voyage is his own repudiation of hope [4.108–10] and his attempt to doom man in hopelessness. Camoens's description of the steady deterioration of hope among Gama and his men as they rounded the Cape but found no navigational help from either the strange ports or the strange stars may have influenced Milton's portrayal of Satan's valediction to hope" ("Camoens' *Lusiads*" 42). As do Broadbent and Sims, Allan H. Gilbert (*Geographical Dictionary* 72) cross-references *the Cape of Hope* with 2.641. Gilbert later explains, "That part of the circumfluent ocean south of the known world was in antiquity called the Ethiopian Sea" (118).

161. *Mozambic:* while James Paterson (298) notes that the island "is barren and unhealthful, but populous: because of the great *Trade* with the *Portuguese,* who possess it now," Allan H. Gilbert (*Geographical Dictionary* 199), identifying the island as a "district of Portuguese East Africa, and its chief town, situated on a coral island," establishes its famous fertility by quoting from

Samuel Purchas's *Hakluytus Posthumus, or Purchas His Pilgrimes* 2:1023 (*Geographical Dictionary* 200). In addition to quoting from Purchas (*Complete Poems* 281), Merritt Y. Hughes refers to Camoens's *Lusiads* 1.54–106, where the conquest of Mozambic by Vasco da Gama's fleet is the first military episode and the beginning of its history as the capital of Portuguese East Africa ("Variorum").

162. *Sabean Odours:* several critical discussions of the Miltonic simile are anchored to this geographical reference. Walter Raleigh, for example, contrasts this type of simile with Milton's more rustic ones, asserting that Milton "prefers to maintain dignity and distance by choosing comparisons from ancient history and mythology" (234). Both Rosalie L. Colie and Anne Davidson Ferry consider Milton's treatment of time in this simile, and his "techniques," as Colie explains, "to deal across the barriers of time and eternity" (136). She contends that Milton "uses not only the geographical revelations of European expansion but the functions of men of that time as well…to remind readers of the reality of the experiences of supernatural beings" (136–37). Of the referential particularity in such similes, Ferry writes: "The attention to particular times of day or season or weather, like the insistence on the names of particular places and figures, reflects the quality of experience which the narrator and the reader share. As human beings we are always bound by time and space, and as fallen men we are ruled by change" (*Milton's Epic Voice* 78). While the names so abundant in Milton's similes "reflect the shattering of unity, like the proliferation of tongues in the story of Babel," Ferry reminds readers that the names also "have their own beauty…and they evoke all the wealth of learning and feeling, the glamor and sympathy we associate with the world of poetry" (80). On Milton's fondness for place-names, also see Hilaire Belloc in 159–65. Helen Gardner argues that epic similes like the "*Sabean* Odors" simile permit Milton "to convey imaginatively what 'surmounts the reach of human sense,'…to describe without describing and to preserve in us the sense that what he tells us is both true and a fiction. The simile says at the same time 'like' and 'not like.' Or, in the form that Milton made particularly his own, the negative simile, it says 'not like' but yet 'not wholly unlike'" (*Reading* 50–51).

Thomas Greene maintains that the "*Sabean* Odours" meeting Satan look forward to the description of paradise where "scented air and tangled flowers are not calculated to permit hard work much relevance." Therefore, in both Milton's garden and Arabia Felix, Greene concludes, "the fragrance seems an invitation to indolence. It even suggests an incipient sexuality" (401). See Greene in **257–66**. Also see John R. Knott's response to Greene in **153–59**.

Sabean: Gilbert explains that the adjective *Sabean* pertains to "Sheba, the land of the Sabeans, in Arabia Felix, usually identified with Yemen, in southeast Arabia. For the fame of its spices see 2 Chronicles 9.9" (*Geographical Dictionary* 250). Hughes (*Complete Poems* 281) adds Philemon Holland's 1634 translation of Pliny's note that *Sabean* "in the Greeke tongue signifieth a secret mysterie" (1:366). Hughes continues, "It was in *Araby the blest* or *Arabia Felix,* the land described by Diodorus (III, xlv) as swept by winds that 'waft the air from off that land, perfumed with sweet odours of myrrh and other odoriferous plants, to the adjacent parts of the sea.'"

163. Presenting the standard editorial gloss on the commonplace notion of the fragrances and spices associated with "*Arabie* the blest" (see **159–65, 160, 162**), A. W. Verity (456) also recalls Lady Macbeth's lament in *Macbeth* 5.1.55–56.

165. *old Ocean smiles:* "Old Ocean," explains Hume, because "the Ancients, both Poets and Philosophers, reputed the Ocean the eldest of the Gods, meaning thereby that without Humidity there could neither be any Generation or Corruption, and so consequently no World" (135). Cf. Paterson 299. Hughes ("Variorum") shares the suggestion made by the nineteenth century editor R. C. Browne (1:349) that Milton may here be echoing Aeschylus's *Prometheus Bound* 89–90.

166–71. This closing segment of the three-part sequence (153–71) dedicated to describing the scents of paradise refers to the story of Tobias, from the apocryphal book of Tobit, which most of the early editors rehearse (e.g., Hume 135, Richardson 144), and which Hughes succinctly paraphrases, concluding with the passage describing the demon Asmodeus's flight from the foul smell of the fish liver that Tobias, instructed by Raphael, burned in his wedding chamber (*Complete Poems* 281). Specifying Reginald Scot's *Discoverie of Witchcraft* 15.28, Dante's *Paradiso* 4.48, and Sir Thomas Browne's *Vulgar Errors* 1.10 (*Works* 2:63–70), Verity's note also acknowledges the popularity of the story of Tobias and Raphael (456).

Milton's evocation of the story of Tobias has long puzzled editors and critics, however, striking some as inappropriate. Todd ([1842], 2: 61) reports Charles

Dunster's unpublished objections, as well as Bannister's: "Surely the closing this beautiful description with this history of Asmodeus, has by no means a good effect. Mr. Bannister observes, that it seems to give an air of burlesque very unsuitable to its sublime dignity." Thomas Keightley notes that he agrees with Bannister and Dunster "in not admiring this passage" (*Poems* 1:342). In the twentieth century, C. S. Lewis (44) finds pointless the narrator's claim that Satan was "better pleas'd" than Asmodeus was with "fishy fume," and John Peter echoes Lewis: "it is inconceivable that Satan would be otherwise than 'better pleas'd' with the odours of the Garden. All that the allusion does is to establish a random connexion betwen two evil spirits" (57). Defending Milton's reference to the Tobias narrative are Frank Kermode, Arnold Stein, and James H. Sims, Kermode explains that Milton's "principle intention is simply to get into the context a bad smell. The simile offers as an excuse for its existence a perfunctory logical connection with what is being said; but it is used to achieve a purely sensuous effect. As soon as we approach Eden there is a mingling of the good actual odour with a bad one; of Life with Death" (108–09). Stein (59) also thinks that Milton's comparison-contrast works: "besides the deliberate incongruity of the fishy perfume and the anticipatory suggestion of Satan's potential love for Eve, [the Asmodeus reference] provides an ironic contrast in tempo: 'From Media post to Egypt, there fast bound.' (The irony of 'fast bound' is more than verbal: it looks at Satan's present lingering pace, at the driving external compulsion that Satan and Asmodeus finally share, like final fast imprisonment, and at Satan's punning bound over all bound into the Garden)." Also see Robert Martin Adams in **171**. Sims reasons that the connection between Satan and Asmodeus is much more a contrast than a comparison: "The reference to Tobit 8:1–4 emphasizes by contrasting Satan and Asmodeus, the similarity between Satan and the sailors of the preceding simile. They have struggled against the forces of God's world (he even wishes to destroy the world and man) and against God Himself. Yet within sight and smell of the abode he hates, he finds himself entertained by the very sweets of which he has come to be the 'bane' (1.167), the destroyer (from Old English *bana*, 'slayer'). Asmodeus came to the bridal chamber of Sara 'enamourd,' but found himself hating the smell of her chamber because of the burning heart and liver of the fish. Therefore, although Satan came to destroy the sweets, he is pleased with them; Asmodeus came to love Sara and, displeased by the stink, was driven away. Satan was 'better pleas'd' because he stayed to carry out his mission whereas Asmodeus fled. Satan's hate is a far stronger motive than Asmodeus' love because Satan will stay to destroy that which pleases him, while Asmodeus allowed that which displeased him to cause him to leave what he loved. The 'better' (which seems so illogical on the surface) is simply Miltonic irony" (*Bible* 229).

Several recent studies develop thematic connections between Milton's reference to the Asmodeus-Tobit story and episodes involving the descent of a spiritual being in *PL*. John T. Shawcross, for example, considers the Asmodeus-Tobit story, which "emphasizes sexuality and lustfulness," as "an obverse example of the poet's nightly visitation" by his muse: "The nature of these opposing nightly visits is echoed in Satan's visit to Eve as she sleeps in IV (related in V) and in God's presence in Eve's dream in XII." Shawcross points out that Milton also alludes to the story of Tobias in 5.221–23 and 6.362–68 ("Metaphor of Inspiration" 82). Verity (456) had earlier cross-referenced 5.221–23. Supported by their shared references to the story of Tobias, Thomas Greene contends, "Milton is implicitly comparing" Satan's approach to the garden and the descent of Raphael in 5.291–97: "Asmodeus or Satan has sexual designs upon Sara, the spouse of Tobias, just as Satan designs to seduce Eve. Raphael appears in Tobit as the protector of a marriage" (396). Also see Jackson I. Cope on the Raphael-Satan comparison in **194–204**.

166. *So:* cross-referencing 4.192 and 3.440, Verity identifies *so* as Milton's "favourite completion of a simile" (456).

168. *Asmodeus:* A. W. Verity (456–57) cross-references *Asmadai* in *PL* 6.363 and *Asmodai* in *PR* 2.151 as "forms closer to the Heb. *Aschmedai*, 'the destroyer.' He is thought to be connected with the *Aeshma Daeva* (an evil demon) of the ancient Persian religion. He is sometimes taken as a type of lust, perhaps through the story in the Book of Tobit." Verity also quotes Tennyson's *St. Simeon Stylites* 169 (*Poems* 1:602). Regarding the cross-reference to 6.363, John E. Parish explains that Milton has cleverly foreshadowed in the demon's heavenly defeat his future defeat by Raphael. Alastair Fowler (619) reports the Scholastic tradition of the nine orders of devils, "of which Asmodeus led the fourth, the 'malicious revenging devils,'" according to Robert Burton in *Anatomy of Melancholy* 1.2.1.2.

170. *with a vengeance:* Verity (457) identifies this as "an intensive phrase, used here with a certain grim humour = 'in all speed.' Cf. *Coriolanus*, II. 2. 6, 'he's vengeance proud,' i.e. intensely; but there the use is more colloquial."

171. *Media…Ægypt:* Allan H. Gilbert comments on both places, glossing *Media* as "Now the northwest part of Persia, south of the Caspian Sea and the River Araxes" (*Geographical Dictionary* 185), and noting, "Milton's references to Egypt are almost all dependent on the Bible, and many of them figurative. He refers most often to the sojourn of the children of Israel in the land, and their escape from it" (111).

    there fast bound: discussing punning in *PL,* Robert Martin Adams disagrees with Arnold Stein's reading and concludes that "it does not seem likely that he [Milton] wanted to have the last three words ['there fast bound'] bear two meanings, 'there tied securely' or 'hastening in that direction'" (86). See Stein on "fast bound" in **166–71**. Also see *bound* in **181**.

172. *savage:* controversy about the identity of the viewer to whom the paradisal hill appears *savage* marks the twentieth century critical response to this word, but that uncertainty leads toward the much wider controversy about Milton's visualization of Eden, especially in **205–87**. Defining *savage* as "wild," and offering the support of *PR* 3.23, Verity traces the word "through the French from Lat. *silvaticus,* 'woody'" (457). Similarly, Hughes traces *savage* to the Italian *selvaggio,* from the Latin *silvaticum* for "woody," to conclude tentatively that *savage* "may mean simply that the hill was covered with trees" (*Complete Poems* 281). A few years earlier, Brooks and Hardy anticipate Hughes's reading only to reject it, as they argue that Milton "presents the Hill as *Satan* saw it (or as fallen man would have to see it), and the adjectives 'savage,' 'wilde,' and 'grottesque' hold in suspension Satan's conflicting attitudes towards its 'wildness'—feelings of repulsion as well as attraction" (274). Fowler's note is "wild, rugged" (620). Countering this reading is Margaret Giovannini, who insists that the image of the "savage Hill" is not "a figment of Satan's imagination," and although seen "through Satan's jaundiced eye," it "provides effective contrast between the Garden and its near surroundings." Anne Davidson Ferry enters the debate to explain that "the speaker places us at a geographical distance from the character and his setting by showing us the outlines of the mountain Satan wishes to climb (IV, 172). This is not the way the hill looks to Satan 'Now' trying to ascend it but how it is envisioned by the narrator" (*Milton's Epic Voice* 52).

176. *perplext:* Verity notes "made difficult (or entangled)" (457).

177. Early editors and critics struggle with this line's syntax and logic. Bentley faults Milton's wandering attention: "There was no MAN yet, to endeavour to pass that way: and if *Beasts pass'd* it, and made a *Path;* the Shrubs and Bushes were not *perplex'd* enough" (111). The Richardsons explain, "neither Man nor Beast who should Travel This way could get Forward" (144). Hawkey ("Various Readings"), maintaining the line as Milton printed it, notes Bentley's objections, as well as Pearce's suggested *"none pass'd that way."* Acknowledging that this is "a remarkable manner of speaking," and paraphrasing the second half of the line as "that would have pass'd that way," Newton (240) authorizes Milton's syntax and logic by reference to Virgil (*Aeneid* 6.467) and Euripides (*Ion* 1326), but also with a cross-reference to *PL* 2.642. Todd variously quotes Newton ([1801], 262; [1809], 3:90; [1826], 286; [1842], 2:61). Paraphrasing the line "that should now or hereafter endeavour to pass that way," John Upton (344) refers it to Shakespeare's *Measure for Measure* 3.1.6–8. The critical discussion appears to end with Masson's admission that, while the phrase "that passed" is "a peculiar construction," it may be understood as "that should have tried to pass" (*Poetical Works* 3:169).

178–83. Satan's entry into the garden by leaping over the wall opposite the eastern gate has provoked commentary about the garden's architecture, as well as about the intruder who so contemptuously encounters it. The gate's eastern location is variously explained, but the authority of Genesis is foremost in these critical notes. Gen. 2.8 locates the garden itself "eastward in Eden," and to support the eastern location of the gate in *PL,* David Masson cross-references 208–11 (*Poetical Works* 3:169). Like Masson, Hughes refers the gate's location to Gen. 2.8 but also points to Gen. 3.24, which establishes that the cherubs preventing the expelled Adam and Eve from returning to the garden are posted "east of the Garden of Eden" (*Complete Poems* 282). Also see *PL* 12.638. In addition, Hughes ("Variorum") turns to Sister Mary Irma Corcoran's response. Corcoran explains that the garden "was said to have been situated in the East because that region was 'the right hand of the heavens' and the source of light and of learning" (31). Developing this topic to consider the significance of direction throughout *PL,* H. F. Robins offers an analogy with the heavenly gate, which, like this one, "is designed to allow only the passage of the upright" (100). Like Robins, Roy Daniells also understands that the civility of life in the garden is evident as visitors like Uriel and Raphael arrive at the eastern gate: "Arrivals are carefully controlled, a superb sense of order reigns, and the privacy of the human pair is never invaded" ("Happy Rural Seat" 4). Cf. 542–50.

Satan, of course, is not an "upright" visitor to the garden but initially invades and violates it by avoiding its gate and leaping its western wall. The manner of his entry elicits commentary on both him and the wall that so strikingly fails to preserve Adam and Eve's privacy. Citing the *Aeneid* 6.260 and 292, the Richardsons identify a Virgilian parallel for the wall: "the Fortifications made about Paradise to no purpose are of the Same Kind as the Sword the Sybil bids *Aeneas* draw to defend himself against the Ghosts in his Descent into Hell; but when he was presently after going to make use of it she tells him it would be to no purpose" (144–45). More recently, Barbara Kiefer Lewalski returns to the problem: "This perilous exposure of Eden in the midst of apparent security is the emblem of a moral reality which Milton sees as perpetual. . . . For Adam and Eve the external paradise can be secure only so long as they cultivate and enhance the paradise within" (96). Satan's coming from "th' other side" (179), over the western wall, squarely reveals him as evil, according to H. F. Robins: "From the evil west has come evil to mankind" (100). Cf. 579–81. John M. Steadman, however, reminds us of the heroism that complicates the impropriety of Satan's entrance. Noting that Rodomonte in Ariosto's *Orlando Furioso* 14 enters Paris in much the same way, Steadman explains that, "In their combination of valor and impiety, both [Satan and Rodomonte] display a marked resemblance to the *contemptor divum* of classical epic" ("Milton-Ariosto" 515). Robert Martin Adams brings the figure of the garden as a womb to bear upon his reading of Satan's impious entry: "There was only one entry 'on th' other side' [4.179], but this did not bother Satan; 'due entrance he disdain'd,' jumped over the wall, and landed on his feet within. If we are not yet rid of the womb overtone, some of the more sensitive of us are going to be slightly queasy at this point. 'Que diable allait-il faire dans *cette* galere?'" (37). Adams develops "the womb overtone" with his remarks on *hairie* in **135**.

179. *th' arch-fellon:* as so often, Hume follows etymology to explain Milton's word choice, while several twentieth century critics focus their attention on the compound nature of this epithet. Hume traces *fellon* to "the Sax. *Felle,* cruel; and *Felonia,* (in our Law-Books) Ideo dicta est, quia fieri *debet felleo anim,* Cooke, Inst. Lib. 4. Others derive it of *Fehl,* Sax. A Fault, of the Lat. *falli,* to be deceived, and in this sense Satan is the chief Felon, the Arch-Sinner and Deceiver" (136).

The *OED* expands on this uncertainty about the etymology of *fellon* but finds "most probable" a derivation from the Latin *fell*, "gall," adding: "the original sense being 'one who, or something which, is full of bitterness' (or 'venom')." Kester Svendsen brings attention to all the compounds of *arch* as "a special feature of the decorum in the treatment of Satan" ("Epic Address" 198). Merritt Y. Hughes, in whose edition the spelling is *arch-felon*, notes that although the word is "compounded like 'Archfiend' in 1.156 and 209, *arch-felon* means the "archetypal felon rather than the ruler of all felons. Cf. 'First grand Thief' in 4.192" ("Variorum").

Endeavoring to answer those modern critics who contend that with such pejorative epithets Milton degrades Satan, Stein argues that *arch-fellon* is not "external commentary" but rather "anticipation of the imagery. From contempt and ease to hunger and ease, to the vague itch of 'bent to unhoord' and mere skulking trickery: Satan diminishes in the images" (12).

181.   *bound . . . bound:* while Milton's punning, here his punning on *bound*, disturbs and disappoints a number of eighteenth and nineteenth century editors and critics, twentieth century critics almost celebrate such wordplay. In *Spectator* 297, Addison (3:63) strongly objects to the "Jingle" of *bound* as he discusses the "Faults" of *PL*, and Bentley soon echoes that condemnation (112). Endeavoring to excuse the pun, Todd ([1842], 2:61) borrows George Steevens's strategy of citing Milton's wordplay "in order to keep Shakespeare in countenance" (*The Plays* 10:34n20) and offers Shakespeare's punning in *Romeo and Juliet* 1.4.19–21 to keep Milton in countenance. Landor's Southey declares the pun "unpardonable," proceeds to condemn the metaphors that follow, and then admits that he "would gladly have seen omitted all between verses 160 and 205" (20).

Within the context of a discussion of Milton's diction, Walter Raleigh brings a new approach to Milton's punning, seeking more to understand than to condemn or defend it. Raleigh explains that Milton "is often not satisfied with one meaning from a word, but will make it do double duty" (208). Raleigh continues: "It was this habit of 'verbal curiosity' and condensation which seduced Milton into punning. Some of his puns are very bad. There is a modern idea that a pun is a thing to laugh at. Milton's puns, like Shakespeare's, give no smallest countenance to this theory. Sometimes he plays with what is merely a chance identity of sound as when Satan, entering Paradise 'At one slight bound high overleapt all bound.' But in most of these cases it seems likely that he believed in an etymological relation between the two words" (210–11). With the twentieth century, the critical distress over Milton's punning largely disappears, and praise often colors the commentary on *bound*. For example, see Verity 457 and 394, and Frank Allen Patterson, *Student's Milton* 83. At midcentury, E. M. W. Tillyard situates the pun at the core of a critical reading celebrating the humor in Milton's description of Satan's approach to paradise. Tillyard argues that Milton turns to humor to ease the transition from Satan's tragically heroic speech on Mt. Niphates to his undignified disguise as a cormorant, and he contends that the pun on *bound* "serves to lower the tension of the passage" (*Studies in Milton* 74). Rather than humor, James H. Sims finds prophetic meaning in Milton's emphasis on *bound*, tracing the word to Rev. 20.2 and 10 and noting that it is the "ultimate fate of Satan to be bound and cast into the lake of fire forever" (*Bible* 230). Cf. Stein in **166–71** and Adams in **171**. F. T. Prince also praises such puns, conceits, and other forms of verbal wit in *PL* as evidence of Milton's "extreme intellectual energy," from which the success of the entire poem derives (*Italian Element* 123). To some extent, Alastair Fowler agrees, identifying the "subdued pun or paronomasia" as "an instance of M[ilton]'s reenlivening awareness of language," but Fowler nevertheless finds the wordplay on *bound* "not particularly successful. There is no comic implication, despite Tillyard" (620). J. B. Broadbent more firmly condemns the play on *bound*. See Broadbent in **183–93**.

183–93. This series of similes has received considerable attention from later twentieth century critics who find here revealed both Satan and the narrator, and the heated debate about the degeneration or degradation of Satan in Book 4 is glimpsed beneath that commentary. Balachandra Rajan initiates the discussion, noting that after Satan's soliloquy on Mt. Niphates exposes Satan, "The imagery accordingly becomes more and more homilectical [*sic*]; it is addressed to Everyman in the familiar traditions of the pulpit, in figures [the *Wolfe* and the *Thief*] whose content is plain and unmistakable and whose moral meaning is insistently asserted" (*"Paradise Lost" and the Seventeenth Century Reader* 98). What Rajan describes as a "homilectical [*sic*]" revelation of Satan, Tillyard, extending his point on 181, discusses as a humorous belittling of the "rich Burgher" figure by "the ingenuity of a cat-burglar. The passage thus understood, *or o're the tiles* is a perfect touch of deliberate comedy" (*Studies* 74). Also see Le Comte, "Milton as Satirist" 48–51. Contending that the heroic similes applied to Satan after Book 2 reveal a "loss of poetic energy or resonance" (55), John Peter focuses on this series of similes. He finds the wolf simile "humdrum," and the burglar simile, "with its suggestion of smug incompetence on the part of the householder, tends to reflect adversely on Gabriel, Adam, and even God. Nor can one make more of it by pretending, in the teeth of the evidence, that it is humorous, as Dr. Tillyard does" (57). Although his objections are different from Peter's, J. B. Broadbent is also disappointed as he reads this passage. He recognizes Satan's bounding over the wall as "an emblem of transgression itself," but he finds it "not very successful for its seriousness is spoilt by the pun" (*Some Graver Subject* 169). Countering such critiques as Broadbent's and Peter's is Anne Davidson Ferry's reading. With the understanding that similes "are one of the most important marks of the speaker's style," Ferry moves the focus of the discussion from Satan to the narrator as she explains that the similes "remind us that he is a poet familiar with the literary conventions of epic and a man familiar with a life infinitely remote from the fallen world of innocence destroyed, of petty viciousness, of corruption even in God's Church. Yet his familiarity with mortal verse and his experience of mortal vice do not destroy his understanding of the archetypal world" (*Milton's Epic Voice* 54). Complementing Ferry's remarks is an earlier study of Milton's similes by James Whaler, who identifies this series, consisting of three similes (183–87, 188–91, and 193) as one of the "instances in which one or more members are complex" ("Compounding" 315) and looks to Homer and Virgil, among others, for epic precedents. Homer, Whaler reports, offers only ten simile groups and only four of them have more than two members. In the *Aeneid,* "no more than two similes ever occur together, no individual simile in any group ever runs to the extent of three full lines, and only 16 groups occur. (Milton has 30 groups, of which seven contain three or more similes)" (315–16). Whaler also considers the irregular distribution of Milton's similes, especially their "massing" in *PL* 1–4 (327).

The literary antecedents—classical and biblical—for the wolf and thief imagery have been steadily pursued from the eighteenth century onward. Acknowledging that while wolf similes are not uncommon in Homer and Virgil, Newton points out that the associated simile of the thief casts a new light on the figure of the wolf, and he traces that light to John 10.1: "He that entereth not by the door into the sheepfold, but climbeth up some other way, the same is a thief and a robber" (240). Todd ([1842], 2:62) repeats Newton's note and suggests a source in Tasso's *Gerusalemme Liberata* 19.35. Mitford (117) glosses the wolf with "Keen as the evening wolf" from Edward Benlowe's *Theophila* 44 and the thief who climbs in the window with *The Faerie Queene* 1.3.17. In his specialized study of the topic, James Whaler reports that Milton in *PL* virtually renounces animal similes, but this, his only wolf simile, "carries with it at least twice as much associative force as any wolf-simile in Vergil. For Vergil can do little more than adapt from Homer and Apollonius. But Milton is persuaded to employ such a Homero-Vergilian image only when it carries to his audience a world of Scriptural conviction" ("Animal Simile" 543). Merritt Y. Hughes adds two more biblical parallels to the John 10.1 reference, Acts 20.29 and Ezek. 22.27 ("Variorum"). Hughes (*Complete Poems* 282) also cross-references the wolf simile in *Lyc* 115. Asserting that the wolf and thief images "emphasize the outrageous disdain connected with the Devil's intrusion into God's world and man's Garden," James H. Sims (*Bible* 231) cross-references *PL* 12.508 and *PR* 4.604, where the angels identify Satan as the "Thief of Paradise." Finally, Sims explains, "And the images being taken from the discourse of Jesus on himself as the Good Shepherd brings a suggestion, which does not need to be stated, that no matter what evil the 'first grand Thief' may accomplish, the Good Shepherd, who 'giveth his life for the sheepe' (John 10:11), will overrule it and bring out of it good for the sheep to the glory of the Father" (*Bible* 232). Alastair Fowler (620) associates the thief image with Joel 2.3–9: "The land is as the garden of Eden before them...they shall climb up upon the houses; they shall enter in at the windows like a thief." While both George Coffin Taylor (73) and Grant McColley (*"Paradise Lost": An Account* 145) note that Du Bartas also compares Satan to a thief invading the garden, Robert Martin Adams finds unconvincing many of their efforts to associate Milton and Du Bartas (156–57).

183–87. Edward Bysshe includes this passage under "Wolf" in *The Art of English Poetry* 426.

183. *prowling:* "to Prole, or Prowle is to Look out in order to Pilfer, from the old French word *Proyeler,* to go upon the Prey" (Richardson, *Explanatory Notes* 145). The *OED* cites 183–84 to exemplify *prowling* as "That prowls, in various senses" (b).

186. *secure:* Verity, Fowler, and the *OED* bring varying degrees of emphasis to the notion of overconfidence as they define this adjective. Verity's gloss is "implying a false sense of security; cf. Lat. *securus*" (457), and in his edition's "Glossary"

(717), Verity emphasizes this point by explaining that Elizabethan writers often suggest the Latin meaning of *securus,* "free from anxiety, unconcerned," as they use *secure* "to indicate a false feeling rather than actual state of safety." Supporting this understanding, Verity cross-references *PL* 5.238, 9.371, and 10.779, and *Eikon* 18 (Patterson, *Works* 5:236). Fowler (620) understands "over-confident" as the meaning of *secure.* The *OED* A.1 identifies as archaic the meaning "Without care, careless; free from care, apprehension or anxiety, or alarm; over-confident." Also see *secure* in 791.

187. With his reading of this line, James Whaler offers to exemplify his claim that Milton creates rhythmic line patterns that "ring true to thought, image, or situation in his fable" (*Counterpoint* 18), a reading that Christopher Ricks firmly rejects. "The initial spondee," for Whaler, "is the crouch before the spring. The constricted front vowel in 'leaps' is the muscular tension at the moment of leaping. The open back vowel in 'o'er' eases that tension as the brute body attains mid-flight in its vault" (18). For Ricks, however, "All the ringing phrases [in Whaler's reading] seem…pure imagination—the brute body, quivering with success, the agile arc, and so on. And how can it be true that 'the initial spondee is the crouch before the spring' when the meaning of the words insists that the wolf *leaps* with the very first syllable?" (26).

188. *unhoord:* Fowler (620) observes that the *OED* shows this as the earliest use of *unhoard* meaning "take out of hoard."

190. *Cross-barrd:* studying Milton's prosody, S. Ernest Sprott (14) explains, "In the later poems there is some evidence that Milton was attempting to methodize his use of the hyphen, so that when a word whose first syllable coincides with the second of a verse foot is joined by a hyphen to a directly preceding monosyllabic adjective, or to an adjective which acts as an adverb, the accent and stress will fall on the adjective, and the foot will become inverted." Sprott points to the same phenomenon with "Hell-doomd" (2.697) and "Skie-tinctur'd" (5.285) but also acknowledges the inconsistency of "Heav'n Star-pav'd" at 976.

192–93. This thief metaphor recurs in a number of Milton's works, both prose and poetry, as several editors indicate. In addition to *PR* 4.604, which James H.

Sims notes (*Bible* 231), as does Charles Dunster (263), Verity (457) refers Milton's image of the thief to *Hirelings* (Patterson, *Works* 6:72), as well as *PL* 12.507–11. Edward S. Le Comte (*Yet Once More* 89) identifies Milton's first use of this metaphor in *Apol* (Patterson, *Works* 3:360), and Fowler (620) contributes a cross-reference to the ending of Milton's sonnet on Cromwell.

192. In the striking series of monosyllables in this line, Balachandra Rajan hears the sounds once described by John Bailey in *Milton* 166 as "a bell tolling into the silence of midnight," the sounds that, for Rajan, "rivet our attention to the doom which they predict" (*"Paradise Lost" and the Seventeenth Century Reader* 126).

193. *lewd Hirelings:* unpacking etymological matters, for which he is often condemned, Patrick Hume reveals, but does not develop, a fine point of irony in Milton's word choice: "Wicked Mercenary Priests, Avaritious greedy Hirelings, of the Sax. *Hira,* a Mercenary Servant. *Lewd,* is a word expressing general Wickedness, of *Laerede,* signifying a *Laick,* one of the common People, and therefore more Flagitious generally than the Clergy, a dissolute Person, as the word *Laxus,* Lat.... seems to signifie" (136). Subsequent editors annotate the term, but the irony that Hume recognizes appears to be lost, until Thomas Keightley's edition of 1859. The Richardsons (145) define *lewd* as "Profane, Impious"; Newton (240), as "wicked, vicious, as well as wanton"; and Todd ([1842], 2:62), as "profligate or ignorant," even after quoting from Acts 17.5. Stebbing's gloss is "impious or wicked" (93). Eventually, Keightley's note recovers Hume's point: "of the laity. As these were ignorant as compared with the clergy, it came to signify ignorant, and then got its present meaning, like *villain, churl,* etc." (*Poems* 1:343). David Masson maintains and Alastair Fowler develops Hume's initial point involving the laity and the clergy. Masson notes, "*Lewd* meant originally 'laic,' or belonging to the laity as distinct from the clergy (A.-S. *laewede*): hence 'ignorant' or 'illiterate;' hence 'low,' 'base,' 'dissolute'" (*Poetical Works* 3:169–70). Fowler first defines *lewd* as "wicked, vile," and then adds "Or more probably 'untrained, ignorant'—M[ilton] thought ministers ought to support themselves (as many Sectarians in fact did) by learning a trade or profession" (621). The *OED* 5 cites Milton's line as an example of the following obsolete meaning: "Of persons, their actions, etc.: Bad, vile, evil, wicked, base; unprincipled, ill-conditioned; good-for-nothing, worthless, 'naughty.'"

194–204. In Milton's presentation of Satan perching like a cormorant in the Tree of Life, the cormorant comparison usually produces notes on literary sources that are repeated from one commentary to another. How to understand the *vertue* (198) of the Tree of Life as "the pledge / Of immortality" (200–01) has been far from settled, however. Is the *vertue* of "that life-giving Plant," to quote Fowler's terminology, "effectual" or "significative" (621)? Also troubling for critics from Hume onward are the narrator's remarks about Satan's use of the tree, and heatedly controversial for mid-twentieth-century critics is the poet's rationale for creating the scene in the first place.

Understanding the Tree of Life as both a tree and "the pledge / Of immortality," Hume (136) associates Milton's *middle* (195) with "in the midst" (Gen. 2.9): "*In the midst*, is a Hebrew Phrase, expressing not only the Local Situation of this enlivening Tree, but denoting its Excellency." To this reading Hume brings the authority of Rev. 2.7. Hume more provocatively comments on the Tree of Life as the "pledge / Of immortality," asserting that its "hidden mystick Power" is as "the Type and Figure of the *Son of God*, Saviour of Mankind, whose Fruit is *Life and Immortality*" (137). While Newton (241) and Todd ([1842], 2:62) repeat Hume's initial note, they do not offer his reading of "pledge / Of immortality," and the Richardsons blunt Hume's emphasis on typology in that reading when they gloss *pledge* as "The Token, the Gage, the Warrant of Immortality" (146). Twentieth century critical commentary lays bare the thorny theological issue suggested by the differences between Hume's annotation and the annotations of the Richardsons, Newton, and Todd. Basil Willey contends that, as Milton assigns to Satan in his third soliloquy the analysis of the "magical properties of the forbidden tree" (256), which Milton rejects for a more rational understanding as expressed in *Areop* (Patterson, *Works* 4:310–11) and *DocCh* (Patterson, *Works* 15:115), so he shows no interest in the Tree of Life, and "dismisses the offending text with a nonchalant sophism" (260) expressed by the Father following the Fall when he explains the need to expel Adam from the garden lest he eat from the Tree of Life "And live for ever, *dream at least to live / For ever*" (261). George Wesley Whiting (*Milton's Literary Milieu* 51) points out that Walter Ralegh shared Milton's understanding that both the Tree of Knowledge and the Tree of Life were "actual, not allegorical," were, to quote Ralegh's *The History of the World* 1.4.1, "material Trees." Whiting notes that Ralegh also immediately describes the two trees as "Figures of the Law and of the Gospel," which, of course, recalls Hume's terminology on the Tree of Life. Within the following 15 or so years, scholars such as Sister

Mary Irma Corcoran, Arnold Williams, Merritt Y. Hughes, and Alastair Fowler reveal the complications of the theological responses to the Tree of Life, bringing into focus the problem of how—literally or symbolically—to understand its power to give life. Corcoran emphasizes the Christian tradition that the tree "had intrinsic power to confer bodily immortality outright or to prolong life for a very long time" (27). Williams moves from that view of the tree as he sets Milton's text in *PL* against *DocCh* (Patterson, *Works* 15:115), noting that, in the treatise, Milton opines that the tree should be recognized as a "symbol," not a "sacrament" ("Milton" 273), the term preferred by Augustinian commentators on Genesis: "It seems likely that Milton intended the 'pledge' of *Paradise Lost* as a loose translation of the 'symbol' (*symbolum*) of *Christian doctrine*" (274). Returning to the point opening Hume's commentary, Hughes notes that the Tree of Life in Gen. 2.9 shares its central eminence in Eden with the Tree of Knowledge, as it does not in Rev. 2.7. While Corcoran had reported the tradition that the Tree of Life "had power to confer bodily immortality outright," Hughes presents the topic with less certitude, noting that the *virtue* of the Tree of Life "is implied in the possibility [considered in Gen. 3.22] that Adam might after his sin, 'put forth his hand, and take also of the tree of life, and eat, and live forever.'" Hughes also cross-references *pledge* in *PL* 8.325 (*Complete Poems* 282; "Variorum"). Fowler (621) covers much the same territory as do Hughes and Williams, finally aligning Milton with Andrew Willet, whose *Hexapla in Genesin* 28, according to Fowler, "fixed in popular form the Augustinian view that the tree of life was not effectual but significative."

Ann Gossman and John M. Steadman continue to consider the theological traditions giving meaning to the Tree of Life. Gossman firmly recovers the patristic authority associating the Tree of Life with Christ or life eternal, and conjectures "that if Adam and Eve had abstained from the Tree of Knowledge in the face of temptation, the Tree of Life might have been used to spiritualize them for immortality in Heaven" (686), whereas Steadman brings the theological issues attending the meaning of the Tree of Life in *PL* to bear on the "Fruits fetcht from the tree of life," which the angels serve to Christ at the end of *PR* ("The 'Tree of Life'" 386–87). Finally, less concerned with theological fine points, Evert Mordecai Clark argues that comparable to Milton's Tree of Life is the Cubayo tree described as "pleasant, beyond all comparison, in taste, and whereunto for the vertue is imputed the health and long life of the Inhabitants" in *Purchas His Pilgrimage* 566. Clark concludes, "Here Milton, like Purchas, is dwelling upon the *virtue* of a 'life-giving Plant,' the means of health and longevity in the one, and in the other the mystic symbol of immortality" (147). See additional commentary on the Tree of Life and the Tree of Knowledge in **218–22, 513–27**.

Satan's sitting "like a Cormorant" in the Tree of Life leads to the pursuit of literary parallels. While Patrick Hume identifies the cormorant as "A very Voracious Sea-Fowl, and a great Devourer of Fish" whose "Name is the Corruption of *Corvus Marinus,* Lat. the Sea-crow" (136), Addison initiates the inquiry into literary parallels, comparing Satan to Ulysses, and remarking that Satan "makes a much longer Voyage than *Ulysses,* puts in practice many more Wiles and Stratagems, and hides himself under a greater variety of Shapes and Appearances" (*Spectator* 2:564). In a subsequent *Spectator,* Addison suggests that Satan's cormorant disguise "seems raised upon that Passage in the *Iliad* [7.58–60], where two Deities [Athena and Apollo] are described, as perching on the Top of an Oak in the Shape of Vulturs" (3:172). In his footnotes on the Mt. Ida episode in the *Iliad* 14, Pope (*Poems* 8:181n395) claims that Milton's presentation of Satan as a cormorant on the Tree of Life adapts Homer's presentation of Sleep sitting on a fir tree in the *Iliad* 14.290–91. In his first edition of Milton, Todd, crediting Bowle, quotes lines 63–64 of Avitus's *De Originali Peccato,* the second part of the five-book *Poematum de Mosaicae Historiae Gestis,* as a possible source for the bird transformation ([1801], 263–64). In subsequent editions, Todd also refers to Addison's remark ([1809], 3:92; [1826], 2:288; [1842], 2:62–63). Thomas Keightley (*Poems* 1:343) cites Isa. 34.11. Verity (457), also directing readers to consider Isa. 34.11, but asserting that " 'pelican' is the correct rendering," adds *Richard II* 2.1.38 and *Coriolanus* 1.1.125 to the growing list of literary parallels or sources. James H. Sims (*Bible* 263) and Alastair Fowler (621) acknowledge the Isaiah reference as foreshadowing the judgment of Satan. Fowler and Sister Mary Irma Corcoran also investigate the cormorant as a symbol for corrupt clergy. Fowler quotes from Thomas Nashe's *Anatomie of Absurditie* 36: "The cormorants of our age, who...have alwaies their mouthes open to aske, and...gape after Colledge living." In addition Fowler reports that living across from St. James's Park, Milton would have heard the cries of actual—not figurative—cormorants (621). Corcoran (37) reports a "striking resemblance" between Milton's Satan and the cormorant who symbolized "Law-State-Church Pyrats" in Thomas Scot's *Philomythie,* sig. F4v. Corcoran (38) also refers Satan's subsequent behavior "among the sportful herd" (4.396) to Scot's allegory of the cormorant.

Satan as cormorant not only has been compared to other literary cormorants but also has been contrasted with yet other bird figures. Merritt Y. Hughes, for example, cross-references the vulture simile in 3.431 (*Complete Poems* 282). Jackson I. Cope (115–16) contrasts Satan's entrance into the garden with Raphael's. Cf. Thomas Greene on the Raphael-Satan relationship in **166–71**. Underscoring the dialectics between divine and demonic creation, Michael Lieb develops the contrast between Satan as a cormorant "devising Death" and God as a dove creating life (138). While these critics juxtapose Satan as cormorant to other bird figures, Allan H. Gilbert juxtaposes Satan as serpent to Satan as cormorant. Until one recalls the dramatic roots of Milton's epic, it may be puzzling, Gilbert admits, that Satan laments in 9.164–65 that he is "now constrain'd / Into a beast," when in Book 4 he assumes several animal disguises, including the cormorant. Gilbert concludes that all of the nonserpent disguises "may be of later date than Satan's expression of disgust at imbruiting the essence that aspired to deity" (94).

As noted previously, troublesome to Hume and the majority of those editors and critics who immediately follow him is the narrator's comment about Satan's using the Tree of Life "For prospect, what well us'd had bin the pledge / Of immortality" (200–01). Without much assurance, Hume (137) suggests, "Our Author must in this have respect to some Allegorick sense, for 'tis unconceivable that Satan could have better'd his sad estate by eating of the *Tree of Life,* for he was already immortal *a parte post,* to his cost and everlasting misery." Hume reports that Rupert of Deutz believed that neither Adam nor Satan knew about the Tree of Life, for, Hume translates Rupert, "if he [Satan] had understood there had been a Tree of that vivifying Vertue, he would never have persued his Malice by halves, but as he perswaded him to eat of the forbidden Tree, and thereby to sin and become miserable, so he would doubtless have incited him to have tasted of this Tree of Life, to have made him Immortal in Immutable Misery. *Cap. 30. Lib. 3. Comment. In Genes*" (138). Like Hume, Bentley, too, is puzzled, declaring Milton's narrative remark "a strange Sentiment, no way reconcileable to the rest of the Poem or the Poet's Notions. He [the narrator] seems to blame and censure *Satan,* that he made no better use of the *Tree of Life,* than for Prospect: that with a wise use of it, he might have *regain'd true Life and Immortality.* What could he mean by this?" (112–13) Pearce rather doggedly maintains that Milton believed there was indeed something better for Satan to make of the Tree of Life, "a Virtue, which he might have received from it, but did not." Pearce concedes, however, that it is a something better "which we cannot readily find out in his [the narrator's] words" (115). While the Richardsons greatly appreciate the "Picture" of Satan on the Tree of Life, they talk about the situation in broadly logical and ethical terms, and thereby skirt the theological conundrum so perplexing to other readers (146–47). The nagging uncertainty about Milton's meaning when he refers to Satan's failure better to use the Tree of Life returns with Newton's questions: "But what use then would our author have had Satan to have made of the tree of life? Would eating of it have alter'd his condition, or have render'd him more immortal than he was already? What other use then could he have made of it, unless he had taken occasion from thence to reflect duly on life and immortality, and thereby had put himself in a condition to regain true life and a happy immortality? If the poet had not some such meaning as this, it is not easy to say what is the sense of the passage" (241–42). Todd repeats Newton's puzzled response ([1842], 2:63).

While modern critics do not struggle so vigorously with the puzzle of how Satan might have used the Tree of Life, they, too, offer no compelling readings. More placid than perturbed by the problem, David Masson, who does admit that the meaning of 200–01 is "supersubtle," settles for saying, "there may be something in it. Milton may have meant that Satan sat like a cormorant on the Tree of Life, using it for the mean purpose of prospect only, and little aware of its mysterious virtue, and of the higher uses to which it might have been turned even by himself" (*Poetical Works* 3:170). A. W. Verity dares to suggest what the better use might have been: "Perhaps M[ilton] means that if Satan had eaten of the tree's fruit its saving power might have given him *true life*—a regeneration of spirit that, leading to repentance, would have enabled him to regain his true archangelic immortality" (457). Both Merritt Y. Hughes and John Peter respond to the topic by focusing attention on the notion of *immortality*. Hughes reasons, "By willfully cutting himself off from the beatific vision Satan has lost understanding of *what well us'd had been the pledge / Of immortality*" ("Variorum"). John Peter, however, denies that such a negotiation of meaning is possible, as he points out that the assumption here that Satan is mortal is "seemingly without regard to other passages [1.53, 116–17, 138–39, 318, 622, and 2.553] with which this view conflicts" (34). Finally, Alastair Fowler responds to the question of how Satan could better have used the tree: "The answer is that if he had thought on the *virtue* (secret property) of the tree, and had been obedient, he might have *true life . . . regained*" (621).

Geoffrey Bullough refers the picture of Satan sitting in the Tree of Life to a suggestion in Jacob Cats's *Trou-Ringh* 4 that in the "deep mystery" of the Tree of Knowledge "a bad spirit oft could there be found" (108), but rather than some type of source, it is Milton's purpose in creating this scene that has provoked the most critical attention. While the Richardsons appreciate the picture of Satan atop the Tree of Life, A. J. A. Waldock exclaims against it as another example of Milton's degradation of Satan: "Satan perched on his bough, neglecting his opportunities, put to incidental, momentary use as a sort of illustration to a trivial homily! This is Sunday-school-motto technique. It was mean of Milton to use his Satan so" (87). John Peter similarly complains that "we are expected to relish the irony of his [Satan's] nescience regarding its fruit" (34).

While these modern critics condemn, others praise. Waldock's "trivial homily" becomes something quite different for Louis L. Martz, who sees the pedagogical value of the scene: "Far from manipulating his readers, the bard himself seems rather to be guided by the revelations of the action as he explores the way toward Eden" (*Paradise Within* 109). Isabel Gamble MacCaffrey also sees a valuable lesson in the picture of Satan in the Tree of Life: "Milton includes in these lines a hint to more fortunate pilgrims that God's gifts, 'well us'd,' *can* lead to Paradise regained. Unregenerate, Satan brings his Hell with him" (194–95). Like Martz, Helen Gardner, Arnold Stein, and Anne Davidson Ferry are clearly seeking to counter Waldock's reading of this episode, as they focus on Milton's role as commentator. Identifying this passage as "a commentary that extends (in anticipation) to the Garden too...[and] emphasizes the fallen viewpoint, the loss of the misused Garden already hanging over man," Stein continues: "we move from the regaining of true life which concerns only Satan, to the pledge of immortality, which more nearly concerns Adam" (60–61). Gardner explains that *PL* "has a dramatic concentration unprecedented in epic," but because Milton's voice "is heard in constant comment," as here, "one has then to say that the universe of *Paradise Lost* is wholly undramatic, because the dramatist himself defies the first rule of dramatic presentation by being himself present throughout, as actor in his own play" (*Reading* 35). Ferry's remarks on these lines anticipate the forthcoming description of paradise and the critical debate about Milton's ability to make paradise visible. Sharing Stein's understanding that the blind bard has a double point of view, Ferry insists, "This is not 'Milton' suddenly intervening between Satan's point of view and the reader in order to speak out on his favorite theme, misused freedom. This is the same narrator who has described the hill, the undergrowth, and Satan's actions, who has uncovered his dissembling and told us his hidden schemes. It is the same narrator who will describe to us what 'To all delight of human sense' (IV, 206)—his, our own, and Adam's—is exposed but not to Satan's who 'Saw undelighted all delight' (IV, 286)" (*Milton's Epic Voice* 55).

195. F. T. Prince points to this line as he discusses the Italian element in Milton's epic: "A common usage in Italian poetry from Dante and Petrarch onwards is the addition of a second adjective, as an interjection or afterthought, to an already qualified substantive" (*Italian Element* 112). Attaching qualifiers to that second adjectival phrase, and widening the separation between the adjectival phrase and the substantive, brings even more desirable complexity to the verse, Prince explains, and may be seen in Milton's construction of this passage (115).

202. R. C. Browne (1:349) refers this line to Juvenal's *Satires* 10.2.

204–05. John S. Diekhoff notes the rhyme ("Rhyme" 543).

205–87. This lengthy description of the garden, flowing out of the earlier description of the mountain on which the garden sits (131–83) and flowing into the subsequent description of Adam and Eve (288–355), is the focus of a critical debate among early critics that develops into one of the most fervent discussions in twentieth century literary criticism. Indeed, at the center of this description, the narrator himself calls for the debate, uncertain "if Art could tell" (236) about this garden, where "not nice Art / In Beds and curious Knots, but Nature boon / Powrd forth profuse on Hill and Dale and Plaine" (241–43). Adapting the classic art-versus-nature topos, as he slides from "Art" to "not nice Art," and settling that complication at the core of his description, Milton himself, that is, provokes the debate about the success or failure of his description of the garden.

    Sharing none of the narrator's stated uncertainty about his "Art," Addison praises Milton's description, celebrating its particularity: "the Description of *Paradise* would have been faulty, had not the Poet been very particular in it, not only as it is the Scene of the Principal Action, but as it is requisite to give us an Idea of that Happiness from which our first Parents fell." Milton's imagination, or, more exactly, Milton's "Exuberance of Imagination," Addison most energetically celebrates, claiming it "has pour'd forth such a redundancy of Ornaments on this Seat of Happiness and Innocence, that it would be endless to point out each Particular" (*Spectator* 3:170–71). Samuel Johnson, however, faults Milton's description of paradise, criticizing its lack of particularity, and the imagination Addison praises is the fancy Johnson condemns: "The appearances of nature, and the occurrences of life, did not satiate his [Milton's] appetite of greatness. To paint things as they are, requires a minute attention, and employs the memory rather than the fancy. Milton's delight was to sport in the wide regions of possibility; reality was a scene too narrow for his mind" (*Milton* 1:287). Moving from condemnation to praise within a 30-year period, Joseph Warton's critical responses mirror both Addison's and Johnson's. The "redundancy of Ornaments" that Addison praises, Warton finds objectionably fanciful in 1753. In *The Adventurer,* of October 23, 1753, "Palaeophilus" soundly criticizes the unnaturalness of Milton's description of the garden. Conceding that the description is usually praised as a striking example of "a florid and vigorous imagination," Warton argues that "it requires much greater strength of mind, to form an assemblage of natural objects, and range with propriety and beauty, than to bring together the greatest variety of the most splendid images, without any regard to their use or congruity." Sharpening his focus to specific images in Milton's description, he finds, " 'Saphire fountains that rolling over orient PEARL run NECTAR, roses without thorns, trees that bear fruit of VEGETABLE GOLD, and weep odorous gums and balms,' are easily feigned; but having no relative beauty as pictures of nature, nor any absolute excellence as derived from truth, they can only please those, who when they read exercise no faculty but fancy, and admire because they do not think" (182). In 1782, however, in *An Essay on the Writings and Genius of Pope,* Warton praises Milton's garden: "it was the vigorous and creative imagination of MILTON, superior to the prejudice of his times, that exhibited in his EDEN, the first hints and outlines of what a beautiful garden should be; for even his beloved ARIOSTO and TASSO, in their luxuriant pictures of the gardens of ALCINA [*Orlando Furioso* 6.20–24] and ARMIDA [*Gerusalemme Liberata* 16.9–16], shewed they were not free from the unnatural and *narrow* taste of their countrymen; and even his master, SPENSER, has an *artificial fountain* in the midst of his *bowre of bliss* [*The Faerie Queene* 2.12.60]" (2:178). The Richardsons' admiration for the description of the garden in *PL* 4 is at times rhapsodic. Most enthusiastically, they praise its fusion of art and nature: "Then back again to *Eden* to describe the River which supply'd the Garden with Water, whose Course is shown with great Beauty of Invention and Fancy. Now he no longer Delays his Impatient Reader, but Pours forth a Rapid Stream of Exquisite Beauties, Again and Again. Inanimate, Natural, Beauties"

(149). The literary references that others condemn as artificial, the Richardsons commend. Looking at Milton's juxtaposing the Edenic garden with the negative catalog of literary gardens in 268–85, for example, the Richardsons argue, "This Description is Improv'd and Enforc'd by Comparing Paradise with What the most Admired Writers of the Antients have given us the most Exalted Ideas of" (149). Finally, the Richardsons insist that Milton's 242 lines of description "give an Idea of Earthly Beauty and Happiness beyond what can be found in any Other Humane Writer, are Themselves the Utmost that Poetry can do; they have Told if not what the Artist Conceiv'd, All that Art Can Tell" (149–50). In these closing remarks, as they continue ardently to praise Milton's vision of the garden, the Richardsons nevertheless glance at the limitations of art that may not be adequate to the artist's conception, and doing so, they echo the narrator, who interrupts his description of the garden to wonder "if Art could tell" (236). Indeed, that subjunctive clause is the point of departure for the Richardsons' entire commentary on the description of the garden: "*Milton's* Imagination had a picture which He Dispairs of Communicating to his Readers in its full Beauty, but does what he Can for them; They, if they are Equally Expert at This Kind of Painting may have One, but not in All respects the same, as Fine: 'tis worth their Utmost Endeavours to Try. Paradise and it's Inhabitants, and How they are Employ'd! 'Tis Enchanting! 'Tis Beyond Expression!" (148). As the Richardsons explain that the limitations of the artist's art requires the readers' "Utmost Endeavours" if the "Painting" is to be seen, they once again anticipate an element that will figure in some of the twentieth century critical responses to Milton's garden.

    As the nineteenth century turned into the twentieth, the critical appreciation of Milton's description of the garden usually echoes that of Tennyson, who is charmed by "all that bowery loneliness" (2:652). Surveying Milton's use of classical mythology in 1900, Charles Grosvenor Osgood explains the basis of the beauty in Milton's "pictures of nature." Implicit in Osgood's analysis is the assumption that Milton is a poet, not a naturalist. Rather like the Richardsons, Osgood acknowledges the literary density of the descriptions of nature, finding classical allusions sometimes piled "four or five deep," and, like the Richardsons, Osgood praises the result, "an effect of great richness" (xiv). Addressing the art-versus-nature topos, Osgood argues that Milton's succeeds because he presents nature "in terms of human life." Indeed, for Osgood, "The best art therefore personifies the forces of nature" (xvi).

    In that same year, 1900, Walter Raleigh, however, registers a quite different opinion about Milton's garden: "We cannot settle down in the midst of this 'enormous bliss'; we wander through the place, open-mouthed with wonder, like country visitors admiring the Crown jewels, and then—we long to be at home" (122–23). Finally, in the very influential article announcing that the "true theme" of *PL* "is Paradise itself," Paul Elmer More declares Milton's description "one perfect picture of Eden" (280). Within a few decades the perfection of Milton's picture, however, is more vigorously contested than ever before.

In the late 1930s, the major detractors of Milton's description of the garden speak most forcefully, beginning in 1935, with T. S. Eliot's first essay on Milton, in which he asserts, "At no period is the visual imagination conspicuous in Milton's poetry" (33). From the sweeping claim that Milton's sensuousness "had been withered early by book-learning" (33), Eliot, contrasting Milton and Shakespeare, concludes that Milton's images lack particularity and are "*artificial* and *conventional*" (34). Milton's verse is aural, not visual, for Eliot: "Indeed, I find, in reading *Paradise Lost,* that I am happiest where there is least to visualize. The eye is not shocked in his twilit Hell as it is in the Garden of Eden, where I for one can get pleasure from the verse only by the deliberate effort not to visualize Adam and Eve and their surroundings" (37). Within a year of Eliot's tremendously influential first essay, F. R. Leavis vigorously condemns Milton's vague or generalized descriptions, and the key terms of his remarks echo Eliot's. Leavis labels Milton's diction "laboured, pedantic artifice," suggesting, "Milton seems here to be focussing rather upon words than upon perceptions, sensations or things" (49). Milton's "Grand Style," writes Leavis, "compels us to recognize it as an impressive stylization" (50). Closing ranks with Eliot and Leavis are G. Wilson Knight in 1939 and L. C. Knights in 1942. G. Wilson Knight contends that Milton's method "tends to harden and solidify what is more properly flexible and yielding. The divine profusion is supposed to go beyond nature (IV.207–08) but instead falls short of it. A certain deliberating aestheticism insists on translating the natural into terms of human artistry, and you have excessive luxuriance side by side with a stony, carven immobility" (83). It should here be pointed out, however, that Knight admires and praises other descriptive sequences; see **598–609** and **690–705**. L. C. Knights expresses similar views as he argues that Milton's paradise "is not deeply felt" and its imagery is "often inappropriate" (147). Finally, T. S. Eliot speaks once more about Milton's visual description of the garden in his 1947 essay on Milton, in which he still describes Milton's vision as general and vague, rather than particular, but in this second essay, Eliot explains that such a vision is necessary in an epic: "a more vivid picture of the earthly Paradise would have been less paradisiacal. For a greater definiteness, a more detailed account of flora and fauna, could only have assimilated Eden to the landscapes of earth with which we are familiar. As it is, the impression of Eden which we retain...has a supernatural glory unexperienced by men of normal vision" ("Milton" 71–72).

The major critical voices answering the detractors of Milton's description of the garden are immediately heard in the mid-1930s, until a veritable chorus of voices defends, analyzes, and celebrates Milton's presentation of the garden in the criticism of the 1960s. In her 1935 *Milton,* Rose Macaulay, for example, deftly considers the adverse criticism of the earlier critics: "Milton has been charged with not being a realistic nature-observer; his answer might be, what did he want with actual nature, when he could imagine a garden of such luxuriant curious loveliness of detail, such steep magnificence of design?" (130–31). In that same year, William Empson's *Some Versions of Pastoral* presents a reading of Milton's garden that focuses on feeling rather than visual detail and sensuous particularity. Empson explains that "somewhere in his mind," Milton believed "that the human creature is essentially out of place in the world and needed no fall in time to make him so. This very complete ambivalence of feeling is then thrown out and attached to Nature in the garden" (178). For Empson, Milton's garden is most significantly sad: "The whole beauty of the thing is a rich nostalgia, but not simply for a lost Eden; sorrow is inherent in Eden itself" (179). A few years previous, Empson's reaction is anticipated by E. M. W. Tillyard, who finds the loss of Eden "is implicit in the description of Paradise, which has in it the hopeless ache for the unattainable" (*Milton* 241). Toward the end of the 1930s, Tillyard directly engages with the claim that Milton's garden lacks sensuous particularity by invoking William James's theories of "potential forms of consciousness" in *The Varieties of Religious Experience* 378. Quoting James, "lyric poetry and music are alive and significant only in proportion as they fetch these vague vistas of a life continuous with our own, beckoning and inviting, yet ever eluding our pursuit" (375), Tillyard continues, "Thus Milton's description of Paradise in book four of *Paradise Lost* represents one of these 'other forms of consciousness,' one of 'these vague vistas of a life continuous with our own'" (*Miltonic Setting* 49). Tillyard concludes his analysis of Milton's description of paradise by aligning his views with Maud Bodkin's in *Archetypal Patterns in Poetry*. C. S. Lewis (50) also sets out to counter the charges leveled against Milton's description of the garden, explaining the appropriateness of Milton's so-called vagueness. Recalling the Richardsons' views on the cooperation between the artist and the reader if the picture of paradise is to be glimpsed, Lewis contends that with the line "In narrow room Natures whole wealth" (207), "We are in at last, and now the poet has to do something in the way of description; well for him that the Paradise-complex in us is now thoroughly awake and that almost any particular image he gives us will be caught up and assimilated. But he does not begin with a particular image, rather with an idea—*in narrow room Nature's whole wealth.* The 'narrow room,' the sense of a small guarded place, of sweetness rolled into a ball, is essential. God had *planted* it all" (210). George Wesley Whiting situates the richness of Milton's description of the garden within a seventeenth century literary context and quotes heavily from Book 1, Chapter 3, "Of the place of paradise," in Sir Walter Ralegh's *The History of the World.* Whiting insists, however, that while the beauty of Milton's garden probably reveals some debt to the earlier historian, "Raleigh's extended exposition completely fails to achieve the artistic unity and the objectivity of Milton's superb word picture" (*Milton's Literary Milieu* 48). Another of the most influential voices countering critics like Leavis is Douglas Bush: "While wrong-headed on the main point, Mr. Leavis has a glimmer of the truth in his vague sense of opulence. Milton knew quite as well as his critic that he was assembling the stock properties of traditional earthly paradises. Far from trying to render the sensation of being in a garden, he was suggesting, through conventional symbols, a golden age more perfect than even the classical poets had imagined" (*"Paradise Lost" in Our Time* 96). Elsewhere, Bush insists that Milton's "vast stage and superhuman action demand...the constant use of the general and suggestive" (*English Literature* 406). Again very much recalling and developing the Richardsons' emphasis on the cooperation necessary between the poet and the reader, Don Cameron Allen argues, "All visual imagery depends on words suggesting color, shape, and motion. The transference of the image from the bare words of the text to the imaginative faculty of the reader demands almost as much nervous energy as was expended by the poet in the original conception of the words. By selecting words of a more stimulating and precise quality and by setting them down in an extraordinary but not unnatural sequence, the poet performs the greater task, but the reader must exhaust an almost equal amount of mental tissue in completing what the poet has begun" ("Description" 96).

J. B. Broadbent's initial response to the critical controversy is to propose "new grounds for a criticism of Milton's descriptive method, which has been attacked with special reference to Paradise" ("Milton's Paradise" 160), and for Broadbent the new ground is travel literature. Contending that, in describing paradise, Milton combines literary tradition with seventeenth century travel literature, Broadbent explains that "places actually like this were being discovered and settled to east and west throughout the sixteenth and seventeenth centuries; when they came across such fertile districts the explorers often described them as 'paradises' " (160). Broadbent also directly engages with G. Wilson Knight's earlier remarks: "Mr. Knight complains that this 'divine profusion is supposed to go beyond nature but instead falls short of it' in being artificial—that is, *un*natural. But the supernatural is to us unnatural; and Milton tries to suggest the power of unfallen Nature by making her provide not only raw but finished products as well—damascene work, mosaic, and so on. Yet he insists that even these strange glories are entirely natural, for they are the miracles of prelapsarian Nature" (166). Later, in *Some Graver Subject,* Broadbent much more forcefully turns to the ongoing debate, and again, as in Allen's remarks, echoes of the Richardsons are heard: "Milton's description of Paradise has been used to exemplify 'composition' as inferior to 'imaginative creation' in an aesthetic argument conducted by Ruskin, and subsequently by Leavis and Knight. But the virtue of the writing in its context has to be judged by more specific criteria" (172). What Broadbent sees as Milton presents his vision of prelapsarian life is dynamic balancing: "The poet's reverence for his materials—art and nature, man and woman, Man and God—catches us up into a phase of reciprocating humility and dignity that is an apotheosis of humanity" (172). So, too, the realities of nature in the prelapsarian garden do not "stream away into idealism, allegory or wish-fulfilment" (182) but rather dynamically play against each other: "The balance between nature and art lies in 'odorous Gumms and Balme' against and within 'fruit burnisht with Golden Rinde' " (184).

By the 1960s, critical defensiveness in response to G. Wilson Knight's condemnation of the "excessive luxurience" of Milton's garden yields to critical celebrations of its sensuousness. In *The Muse's Method,* Joseph Summers declares that the lengthy and uninterrupted description of paradise is "one of the most shocking and most brilliant effects in the poem. After the perversions of Hell and the transcendence of Heaven, we are introduced to the vision of perfect human fulfilment, 'enormous bliss' " (94). For David Daiches in *Milton,* literary beauty and natural beauty combine to produce Milton's vision of nature idealized: "All human longings for an ideal garden are suggested by Milton's employment of many different mythological elements together with contemporary notions of garden beauty (though Eden represented natural, not artificial, beauty, with no sign of 'nice Art / In Beds and curious Knots' but only profuse Nature), keeping on and on, sustaining and varying image and reference until the picture of ideal nature almost bursts with its own richness" (187). Helen Gardner also invokes the notion of the ideal as she discusses Milton's garden: "This garden is not something opposed to nature. It is nature idealized and in perfection. It is the new conception of a garden as nature in miniature, where trees, bowers, and fountains, lakes and waterfalls make up a landscape, a conception that comes to perfection in eighteenth century garden parks, and that spread all over Europe as *le jardin anglais*. Milton is of his age in thus picturing the Garden of Eden as a landscape garden" (*Reading* 79).

During the 1960s, those examining Milton's picture of the garden also move to develop the significance of the garden's sensuousness as a challenge within the wholeness of prelapsarian human experience. William G. Madsen squarely focuses attention on such phrases as "Nature's whole wealth" (207) and "Nature boon / Powrd forth profuse" (242–43). Quoting Maynard Mack's *Milton* 20, Madsen argues, "The Garden is 'the great imaginative image of perfection' in *Paradise Lost*, and in its luxuriance on the one hand and its need of cultivation on the other we may see, I think, an analogy to the relation of passion and reason in the mind of man" ("Idea" 244). Ten years later, in *From Shadowy Types to Truth: Studies in Milton's Symbolism*, Madsen recalls Louis Martz as he insists that "the Garden is the symbolic center of the poem in the sense that from it the chief metaphors of the spiritual life are drawn" (83). From that premise, he concludes, "the Garden is a fleshly type of the future 'Paradise within,' which is the image of Christ in man" (84). See Martz's *Paradise Within* 105–67. Marjorie H. Nicolson writes that Milton held two different views of nature: one that "taught restraint and limitation, and one that expressed herself in profusion and superabundance" (*Breaking* 182). The garden, which God directed prelapsarian humanity to tend and keep, Nicolson characterizes as "wild, luxuriant, excessive, profuse. Upon it Adam and Eve imposed limitation and restraint, pruning its luxuriance, improving not only upon Nature but presumably upon God" (186). Dennis H. Burden maintains a similar emphasis, understanding the "Garden's wildness as an aspect of its enormous fertility, and hence as an exemplification of the profusion of God's goodness. The common enough distinction between art and nature, between control and abundance, helped to carry him [Milton] across this problem of the Garden that, though innocent, needed to be subdued" (44–45). Barbara Kiefer Lewalski most firmly draws the point that Milton's garden is presented as the arena for human growth toward perfection. While acknowledging its conventional features, Lewalski argues that Milton's paradise presents "a mode of life steadily increasing in complexity and challenge and difficulty but at the same time and by that very fact, in perfection" (88).

The garden's "surprising tendency to excess and disorder, to overprofuseness and languid softness" (89) challenges the growth of Adam and Eve, making their work "not merely the expected ritual gesture, but a necessary and immense task" (90). Marking something of a formal conclusion to the controversy about Milton's visualization of the garden is John R. Knott's 1970 essay "Symbolic Landscape in *Paradise Lost*." Echoing the opinion of many other scholars, Knott writes that "while this walled, mountaintop garden is traditional, Milton reshaped the tradition of the earthly paradise" (38). The "narrow literalism" that the poet shunned, Knott explains, "would have defeated Milton's purpose of exposing the reader to a condition of life that is more nearly mythic than historic. He knew that we must shake off our bondage to the familiar, and temporarily forget our normal sense of time, if we are to respond fully to a prelapsarian world" (38). According to Knott, the challenge that Milton answered with his vision of the garden "was to show nature perfected without making it unbelievable. We are asked to take some things on faith: thornless roses, an unvarying climate, fruit of 'golden rind.' Yet these features are part of an idealized scene that can stand for a heightened version of the nature we know" (38).

While Knott's 1970 essay might be seen to mark the subsiding of the critical argument about the success or failure of Milton's vision of the garden, it also brings into focus another aspect of the intensely visual quality of Book 4. Setting Milton's visualization of paradise against Spenser's visualization of the Bower of Bliss in *The Faerie Queene* 2.12.42–83, Knott contends, "Milton directs the reader's vision over the landscape . . . without violating the illusion of reality. The scene has spatial depth, as Spenser's does not, largely because it is presented as a prospect. Milton brings Satan, and thus the reader, into the scene by stationing him on the Tree of Life, whereas Spenser simply sets Guyon aside before embarking on his *descriptio*. Moreover, Milton indicates the relationship of features to one another by continually shifting his perspective, providing what Eisenstein [59] has called 'cinematographic instructions' in commenting on other passages from *Paradise Lost*" (42). See Keats on "stationing" in **126–27**. Broadbent also glances at this topic when he notes that in the description of the garden "we are led from actuality to myth," and he writes that the " 'happy rural seat' is almost laughably the England of Penshurst [see Ben Jonson's *To Penshurst* (*Ben Jonson* 8:93–96)], Cooper's Hill [see Sir John Denham's *Cooper's Hill*] and Appleton House [see Andrew Marvell's *Upon Appleton House* (*Poems* 1:62–86)]" (*Some Graver Subject* 184). The point is that the mythic referents in the description of the garden, to which the narrator's words direct the reader's eye, would not be seen by Satan's eye as he surveys the garden. The larger critical point, then, is through whose eye is this complex idealized scene seen, and, as commentary on 285–99 will indicate, that scene also soon includes the first glimpse of Adam and Eve. By far the majority of twentieth century critics assert that the garden is seen through the eye of Satan. Grant McColley, considering the associations between Milton's early dramatic drafts of the Fall story and *PL*, notes that, in "Adam Unparadiz'd," Gabriel is to describe the garden, whereas in *PL* "it is through his [Satan's] eyes that we first glimpse the heavenly spot known as the Garden of Eden" (*"Paradise Lost": An Account* 288). William Empson agrees: "We first see Paradise through the eyes of the entering Satan" (*Some Versions* 181–82). This opinion is also shared by Don Cameron Allen ("Description" 104), Frank Kermode (106), and Knott ("Symbolic Landscape" 38), among others. For Arnold Stein, though, it is the reader's eye that sees the garden, and there is "a sense of doubleness" (56) in all it sees. Stein emphasizes that entering the garden, we come from "outside . . . from the Fall," and "it enters with us; we bring the outside, at least as vivid memory, into the more vivid inside. And if the entrance into Paradise is—as it must be for fallen man—a return, then we bring a recent immediate memory of the outside into our ancient memory of the inside" (52). Also see Stein in **131–83**. Jacques Blondel similarly speaks of a double vision: "Milton made his reader share in the creating of that dramatic double vision inasmuch as we precede Adam and Eve in Eden, along with the 'Father of Lies' for our guide. That double vision should prevent the critic from asserting that we should be from the very beginning *after* the Fall as Millicent Bell perhaps uncautiously claimed" (263). See Bell's "The Fallacy of the Fall." Roy Daniells moves beyond the notion of the reader's double vision as he glances ahead to 247, where the garden is identified as "A happy rural seat of various view." Daniells writes, "Though we view it through the eyes of God, the Son, Raphael, Uriel, Gabriel, Michael, Adam, Eve, Satan, and Milton, we cannot draw its lines. We finally agree to see it variously" ("Happy Rural Seat" 5). For some critics, it is the future redemption of the past that complicates the eye that sees, as well as the vision seen, within Milton's garden. Louis L. Martz argues, for example, that the "central theme" of Milton's epic is seeing paradise as Adam saw it, but Martz speaks in terms of "a renewal of human vision," and, recalling the Richardsons' attention to the reader's "Endeavours" (148), Martz also discusses that vision as one that lies within the reader (*Paradise Within* 105). Leland Ryken identifies Milton's vision as apocalyptic, accepting the characterization of it as vague or generalizing but recognizing that as a necessary feature of the apocalyptic vision rather than a failure in pictorial vision (213). Sacvan Bercovitch and John Halkett suggest additional challenges regarding the effort to identify the eye whose perception establishes this first description of the garden. For both, the one who sees is Satan, but also for both critics, Satan's consciousness is as much the object as the subject of the vision. Bercovitch argues that Satan's pride and despair alternate as "complementary and interrelated points of view following from the denial of reality" (248). Halkett (101) states, "Satan's consciousness" is the "instrument through which the reader first glimpses 'Heaven on Earth' (IV. 208)." That the identity of the eye viewing and making visible the garden is far from insignificant is clarified by Anne Davidson Ferry in 1963 as she also considers the verbal complication of the vision: "We see the earthly Paradise for the first time on the occasion of Satan's entrance into it," but insists, "we do not see it as he [Satan] does" (*Milton's Epic Voice* 51). She argues that the language describing what Satan sees is "the language of the narrator, not the language of the fallen Archangel, so that our interpretation of the scene we are made to imagine is the speaker's" (52).

206. Arguing that "a direct and unifying intercourse exists between unfallen man and unfallen Nature, in which the functions of one are reflected in the functions of the other," Michael Lieb explains that as a result, "Eden becomes a timeless world of perpetuated bliss, where every action has creative possibilities" (71).

   all: Knott draws attention to this word's contribution to Milton's presentation of paradise: "Once we are within the Garden the limiting wall disappears. Here are '*All* Trees of noblest kind for sight, smell, taste' [217], 'Flours of *all* hue' [256]; as we are told at the very beginning of the description, Satan is 'To *all* delight of human sense expos'd'" ("Symbolic Landscape" 43). William Empson's remarks on *all,* specifically Satan's use of it in his second soliloquy, constitute the most famous consideration of this word (*Structure* 103). See Empson in **383**.

207–09. While Sister Mary Irma Corcoran contrasts Milton's garden with earlier allegorical understandings to insist that its meaning is rooted in its role as home to Adam and Eve, several critics, including Alastair Fowler and Leland Ryken, find that its meaning is also involved with Platonic Ideas. Corcoran reports that, "Among pre-Reformation Christian writers, the garden was interpreted allegorically as the Church or the Blessed Virgin Mary. To some, it was the presence of God. According to a less exalted non-literal interpretation, the garden represented Adam" (31). Corcoran also believes, however, that Milton was indifferent to these interpretations: "If the garden was a sacred place to him, it was so only because of the holiness of its inhabitants" (32). Fowler (622) points to the Platonic underpinnings of "A Heav'n on Earth" (208) as he cross-references 5.574–75, where he notes, "It was a fundamental doctrine of Platonism that the phenomenal world bears to the heavenly world of Ideas the same relation as shadow to reality" (711). Establishing the foundations of Milton's apocalyptic vision, Leland Ryken also comments on the Platonic influence here: "The most accurate conclusion would seem to be that the Platonic theory of Ideas fitted well with Milton's doctrine of accommodation, and that he used it to supplement that doctrine instead of insisting on it as the basic principle of his apocalyptic poetics" (32–33).

207–08. Fowler (622) identifies the "tradition, based on *Gen.* ii 5 and 9, that creation was instantaneous and that Paradise comprehended the potentiality of all future life," a tradition extending from St. Augustine's *The Literal Meaning of Genesis* 5.3 to Spenser's Garden of Adonis (*The Faerie Queene* 3.6.30).

208. *Heav'n:* studying Milton's prosody, S. Ernest Sprott points out that, "Within the line, monosyllabic *Heav'n* is wrongly spelt as a dissyllable only six times (P.L., II, 1004; III, 261, 503; IV, 208; V, 240; IX, 933), and the 1674 edition emended the second last of these to a monosyllable" (144).

209–14. Fowler describes the effort to fix the geographical location of the garden as a "furious controversy," the broad lines of which he summarizes: "Among those who believed in a local terrestrial Paradise, as many placed it S. of modern Persia, in Chaldea, at the fertile confluence of the Tigris and the Euphrates, as N., at the source of these rivers, near Mt Niphates" (622). From Hume forward to Fowler, Milton's readers have endeavored to determine how Milton responded to this controversy, and this sequence in Book 4 focuses those critical efforts. Hume (137) points to all of the biblical texts that subsequent editors and critics will continue to cite: Gen. 2.8, 2.10, 4.16, 10.22, and 11.31; Isa. 37.12; Ezek. 27.23; and Acts 7.4. Hume locates Milton's Eden in Mesopotamia, but his description of Mesopotamia is blurry. Newton, Paterson, and Todd survey much the same geographical, historical, and biblical territory that Hume covers without bringing any more clarity to the topic. Revealingly, however, while Newton clarifies the location of Telassar as "upon the common stream of Tigris and Euphrates" (242), Paterson locates Seleucia at that confluence (301). Also see Todd ([1842], 2:63). Further complicating Hume's effort to locate Eden, as well as the efforts of some of his successors, is Isa. 37.12 ("the children of Eden which were at Telassar"), the biblical text that echoes in 213–14, but while the geography of Eden may thereby be more blurred, made intriguingly clear is Hume's belief not only in the historical and geographical reality of the garden in Genesis but also in the possibility that the garden may have been reinhabited after the Flood. Considering a passage in Ralegh's 1614 *The History of the World* 1.3.10 in conjunction with Isa. 37.12, Hume ponders the relationship between Eden and Telassar: "That the *Eden* in these Texts, was not the same with that where Gods Garden *Paradise* was planted, *Cajetan* would infer, from its being so populous, when the Flaming Sword rendered the other both uninhabitable and inaccessible; which was true before the Deluge, but *Paradise* being by that defaced, as our Poet supposes [*PL* 11.829–35].... What might hinder it from being inhabited, and from either regaining, or retaining the Name of *Eden,* as the most pleasant, rich, best watered, and thence the most fruitful Country imaginable?" (137). To Thomas Keightley in 1859, the quest to locate the site of Eden looks quaint at best: "it is utterly vain for us to seek for Eden in the mountains of Armenia, or, with Milton, in the plains of Mesopotamia." Considering the geography involved in Milton's description, Keightley concludes that Milton had been misled "by those passages of Scripture in which Eden occurs as a proper name [Isa. 37.12], and he too precipitately concluded that they must be the same with the original region of that name." Keightley suggests that Milton gathered together those scriptural passages, and "extend[ed] the region of Eden from the Hauran (*Auronitis*), a district south of Damascus, to Seleucia on the Tigris, his imagination bestowing antediluvian verdure and fertility on the sandy wastes between Damascus and the Euphrates" (*Poems* 4:64). While Keightley acknowledges the role of Milton's imagination as he situates Eden in what is actually an area of "sandy wastes," David Masson, just a few decades later, does not consider that particular geographical reality as he directs readers literally to map Milton's geographical references—and even to plot Satan's approach to the garden: "What may be called the most orthodox hypothesis is that which Milton follows. It places Eden in Syria and Mesopotamia. Milton gives his own notion of the exact limits in one direction as being from Auran on the west...to Seleucia on the east." Masson continues, "If the reader will refer to our present maps, he will find that the region thus indicated is about 450 miles wide from west to east, and that it was so situated with respect to Mount Niphates, or Nimroud-Tagh, in Armenia; that Satan, approaching it from that mountain, must have come upon its northern frontier, but at a spot much nearer to its eastern extremity." After even more detailed plotting, however, Masson admits that Milton "still leaves the geography of Eden partly indefinite," and Masson reasons the cause as "a haze in the poet's recollections of his maps" (*Poetical Works* 3:170–71). A. W. Verity locates Seleucia on the Tigris, and cross-referencing "great *Seleucia*" in *PR* 3.291, cautions, "M[ilton] terms it 'great Seleucia' to distinguish it from other cities of the same name, such as the Seleucia near Antioch." Moving to gloss Telassar at 214, which he locates "on the east bank of the Euphrates," Verity brings attention to the *Or* of 213, which connects Seleucia and Telassar. Verity cites 2 Kings 19.12 and Isa. 37.12 when identifying the Telassar reference as a "second description of the site of Eden" (458). Elbert N. S. Thompson declares, "No scholar of the seventeenth century felt a keener interest in geography than did John Milton," and takes exception to Masson's closing remark about the probable source of the "partly indefinite" geography of Eden. Thompson seems, rather, to share Keightley's reservations about the effort to plot the location of paradise: "Milton...took the theory that seemed most plausible, but used only so much of it as was needed for the poet's work and left to others all useless speculation.... The noticeable absence of dogmatism in his description was due, not to the clouded memory of the blind poet, but to his realization of the insufficiency of the evidence at hand" ("Milton's Knowledge" 158). As aware of Milton's passion for geography as were Masson and Thompson, a number of other critics continue to respond to this sequence by situating its place-names against the maps of the period. Allan H. Gilbert (*Geographical Dictionary* 40) looks at Samuel Bochart's *Geographiae Sacrae* 1; George Wesley Whiting refers to the maps published in Bibles (*Milton's Literary Milieu* 45, 108); and Merritt Y. Hughes (*Complete Poems* 283) glances at Willem Blaeu's map of Mesopotamia, as well as his verbal description of the location of Telassar in *Geographie Blaviane* 11.33. While all more or less establish the traditional nature of Milton's presentation, they do not arrive at the same point, for the ever-evolving tradition was a complicated intermingling of the imaginative and the actual, as J. B. Broadbent makes clear when identifying the three stages in the quest to realize the garden's location. The first stage is the description in Genesis. The second stage Broadbent associates with writers like John Mandeville (*The Voiage and Travaile* 304), who, while "admitting he had never been there, reported that in the river Pison or Ganges 'ben manye preciouse stones, and mochel of lignu Aloes, and moche gravelle of Gold.' The third, Renaissance stage is found in Purchas [*Hakluytus Posthumus or Purchas His Pilgrimes* 6:108)], who reported truthfully that in the Persian Gulf, 'they found sand mingled with Gold.'" Broadbent concludes, "This coming true of dreams lies behind the hesperianising of Lyly and Greene, Marlowe, Jonson and Drayton, and Milton" (*Some Graver Subject* 174). The long and arduous struggle to arrive at a concise reading of the geographical referents in Milton's lines has therefore appeared to yield to the acceptance of a consensus reading, as the remarks of Arnold Williams, Alastair Fowler, and Marjorie H. Nicolson indicate. Eden was probably located, Williams concludes, "somewhere between Palestine and Persia," and Mesopotamia, he continues, "was by all odds the favorite location" (*Common Expositor* 99). Identifying the northern and then the southern options mentioned at the beginning of this note on **209–14**, Fowler says that Milton "contrives to include both views" (622; Fowler also refers to a third possibility in 9.64n). Finally, having herself surveyed the controversy about the garden's location, Nicolson (*John Milton* 237) flatly concludes, "Milton's Garden is clearly a circumscribed portion of the earth, geographically located within limits which he defines in lines 208–215." Nicolson continues to insist, however, that the environment qualifying that geographical locale is an imaginative environment that bestows "antediluvian verdure...on the sandy wastes," and she suggests the influence of those gardens surrounded by forests that Milton knew from Dante and Spenser. Also see Sister Mary Irma Corcoran in **131–48**.

209–11. James H. Sims stresses Milton's attention to his biblical source, Gen. 2.8: "The poet, giving careful attention to the text, makes a distinction that many preachers did not (and do not) make: the Garden is not identical with Eden, it is *in* Eden" (*Bible* 22).

210–12. Roy Daniells notes, "The 'general panorama' established in 4.144–5... becomes an axial vista down the valley of the Tigris-Euphrates toward the Persian Gulf, but it is the reader, not Adam, who looks where Milton points" ("Happy Rural Seat" 5). Cf. **590–92**.

211–14. See Hilaire Belloc in **159–65**.

211. *Auran:* Hume (137) establishes Haran, Harran, and Charran as synonymous with Auran, and he locates the city in Mesopotamia. Referencing Gen. 11.31 and Acts 7.4, Hume reports that the city is "memorable for the remove of Abraham to it from Ur in Chaldea," and quoting Lucan's *The Civil War* 1.104–05, he also notes the city's association with the overthrow of Crassus by the Parthians. About 50 years later, James Paterson (301) defines *Auran* as "wrath," and, by reference to Gen. 29.4, identifies it as Haran.

212. *Seleucia:* Hume identifies this as a famous city of Mesopotamia, situated on the Tigris, and—from Appianus of Alexandria's *Roman History* 2:213–15—he reports that it was "anciently called *Chalne* and *Chalaune.*" Afterward, Hume continues, Coche, Alexandria, Seleucia, and now, "*Bachad, Bagdad* and *Bagdett,* a great, rich, and populous City, the Seat of the *Califs,* often mistaken for *Babylon,* forty Miles distant from it, and situated on *Euphrates*" (137). As Allan Gilbert reports (*Geographical Dictionary* 259), Pliny (*Natural History* 2:431) supplies a fuller account of the intricate relationship between Babylon and Seleucia. As with *Auran* (211), Paterson offers a definition rather than a geographical location: "a glaring light" (301).

213–14. Hume first clarifies Milton's allusion to Isa. 37.12, adding that the "Edenites" were garrisoned there to resist the Assyrians, and then he recalls the description of Telassar as an island stronghold in the Tigris in Sir Walter Ralegh's *The History of the World* 1.3.10, though Hume later locates Telassar in the Euphrates (137). As noted previously (**209–14**), other editors establish the identity of Seleucia and Telassar, although as Allan H. Gilbert (*Geographical Dictionary* 289) admits, Telassar is "A place in Mesopotamia not exactly identified. Milton's reference depends on 2 Kings 19.12 and Isaiah 37.12, and he puts the place on the eastern border of Eden, apparently identifying it with Seleucia on the Tigris. This is in accord with Tremellius and Junius, who write of Telessar: 'Quae postea Seleucia dicta est, Hhedenis metropolis' (*Biblia Sacra,* London, 1585, note on 2 Kings 19.12)."

Alastair Fowler finds the mention of Telassar "another dramatic irony, for it prophesies war in Eden. The allusion is to 2 Kings xix 11[–12] or Is. xxxvii 11[–12], where Telassar is an instance of lands destroyed utterly" (622).

214–15. Todd presents a note contributed by Sir W. Jones on the meaning of Eden: "It is observable that *Aden,* in the Eastern dialects, is precisely the same word with *Eden,* which we apply to the garden of Paradise: It has two senses, according to a slight difference in its pronunciation; its first meaning is *a settled abode,* its second, *delight, softness,* or *tranquillity:* The word *Eden* had, probably, one of these senses in the sacred text, though we use it as a proper name" ([1842], 2:64). Cf. *PL* 4.27, 4.132. James H. Sims develops the second of these meanings: "Milton's description of sensations felt by a person in Eden is as much in accord with the literal meaning of *Eden,* 'pleasure,' 'delight,' as poetry can make it" (*Bible* 76).

216–68. Stitching 5.292–97 onto its beginning, Edward Bysshe presents this passage under "Garden of Eden" in *The Art of English Poetry* (298–99). Also see Bysshe in **131–66, 300–51**.

216–22. This sequence is positioned between the earlier description of the trees within the garden, glimpsed from without and described as the "goodliest Trees loaden with fairest Fruit" (147), and the subsequent description of the trees within the garden weeping "odorous Gumms and Balme" (248) and bearing fruit "burnisht with Golden Rinde" (249). With 216–22, the only trees particularized are the "Tree of Life" and the "Tree of Knowledge." As with Milton's entire presentation of paradise, source studies occupy some critics' attention. Evert Mordecai Clark (146), for example, acknowledges the possibility of Milton's being indebted to ancient and modern historians and travel writers, but insists here upon his debt to *Purchas His Pilgrimage* 566. Hume's note manages an interesting variation on the typical quest for sources. Broadly referencing his *Apologia Secunda pro Christianis,* Hume (137–38) develops Justin Martyr's argument that in their fictions the classical poets imitated biblical truth, declaring that nectar, ambrosia, nepenthe, and moly are "imitations of this wonderful Tree." David P. Harding (*Milton and the Renaissance Ovid* 80) specifically juxtaposes Ovid's Hesperian garden and Milton's paradise, and draws pointed attention to the parallel between Milton's Tree of Life bearing fruit of "vegetable gold" and Ovid's "tree of golden foliage and crackling branches of yellow gold" in *Metamorphoses* 10.648. Merritt Y. Hughes also attends to the influence of the Hesperian garden, reporting that, in *The History of the World* 1.6.4, "Raleigh said that the dragon of the Hesperides was 'taken from the

Serpent, which tempted Evah: so was Paradise it selfe transported out of Asia into Africa' " (*Complete Poems* 283).

217. Although both Arnold Stein and J. B. Broadbent invoke Edmund Waller's description of the Bermudas in "The Battle of the Summer Islands" (1645) as they discuss Milton's garden, the two critics arrive at different evaluations. Focusing on this line, Stein is puzzled by what appears to him to be the brusqueness of Milton's verse, as opposed to the richness of Waller's, and to Stein, that "kind of intermittent brusqueness, is one of the strangest qualities of his description of Paradise" (73). A few years later, Broadbent argues that within the richness of Waller's description sounds a note of mockery: "In mocking the heroic manner Waller has secularised its materials" (*Some Graver Subject* 175–76). Milton, Broadbent contends, "holds his realism under his poem's ethic" (176).

218–22. While the Tree of Life in which Satan earlier sat like a cormorant was then identified as "The middle Tree" (195) without reference to the Tree of Knowledge, now the two are set side by side, and at this point, the Tree of Knowledge draws more critical attention. Patrick Hume's annotations (138) rely heavily on biblical texts that bring a certainty to his commentary not often revealed by later editors and critics. With Gen. 2.9 in mind, for example, Hume identifies the phrase "of Good and Evil," which does not actually here appear in Milton's verse, as a "Hebraism," by which "is meant the Knowledge of all things," and Hume then explains that the name indicates "that sad Experimental Knowledge that our first Father found by eating its forbidden Fruit: Of *Good*, the Favour of *God*, and happy Innocence lost; and the *Evil* of Sin, and his Makers *Displeasure and Wrath*." Subtly glancing at the idea of touching the forbidden tree, a stipulation in neither Gen. 2.17 nor in this passage in Milton's text, but a stipulation that Eve mentions in both Gen. 3.3 and *PL* 9.647–54, Hume quickly points out that there was only one such tree "that it might be more remarkable, and that *Adam* by no mistake might pretend ignorantly so much as to touch it" (138). While the source of the tree's name intrigues Hume, and he reports that some authorities suggest that either "deceived" Adam or Moses named the tree, Hume (138) continues to rely on Genesis as he considers the forbidden tree's meaning "as an everlasting Monument of the Glozing Lyes of the Tempter" who had assured Eve that she and Adam "shall be as gods, knowing good and evil" (Gen. 3.5). Finally, in Satan's promise to Eve, Hume hears the note of irony later heard in God's voice in Gen. 3.22, which, he notes, Rupert of Deutz (*Commentari-orum in Genesim* 3.22) and Benedictus Pererius (*Commentariorum* 272–73) also considered ironical. By reference to *Areop* (Patterson, *Works* 4:311), Todd more tentatively suggests, "Perhaps this is that doom which Adam fell into, of knowing good and evil; that is to say, of knowing good by evil" ([1842], 2:64). Both Hume and Todd present their major comments on the Tree of Life in 194 when it is first mentioned, but at this point Francis Peck (182) comments on both trees. His reading of the Tree of Life presents the controversial association with Christ, first aired by Hume (**194–204**) and traced by Peck to Guillaume Bucanus's *Institutions of Christian Religion* 111, and while Hume and Todd ponder the meaning of the name of the Tree of Knowledge, Peck, turning to Basil (*Quod Deus Non est Auctor,* cols. 339–42), seeks rather to justify the ways of God, who set the tree in the garden. Twentieth century critics such as Sister Mary Irma Corcoran and C. A. Patrides also continue to clarify the nature of the forbidden tree. Corcoran reports that the tree's "mixed nature appeared in both Christian and Jewish works. The most detailed development of this idea was that of St. Gregory of Nyssa [*De Hominis Opificio,* col. 198], who sug-gested that this was a tree in which there was mixed knowledge of good and evil, ornamented with the delights anticipated by the senses" (25). Corcoran then points out the theological complications of such an understanding: "In all orthodox Christian exegesis, this theory is the only intimation of anything even remotely evil in Paradise before the fall. The mixed coloring of the tree, how-ever, was described by various writers" (26). Finally, while Corcoran concludes that Milton presents the tree "as attractively as possible," she concedes that he nonetheless "compromised with the *Anglo-Saxon Genesis* [*Genesis B* 207] when he referred to it as "our Death, the Tree of Knowledge" (26). Cf. Geoffrey Bullough on Cats in **194–204**. Patrides ("Tree" 241) establishes the theological conventionality of both the raison d'être and the name of the forbidden tree in *PL,* explaining that the prohibition for Milton was a pledge, a sign or symbol of Adam's obedience, and for theologians from Augustine (*The Literal Meaning of Genesis* 8.15–16) through such popular English Reformers as William Alley, from whose *Ptochomuseion* 110v Patrides ("Tree" 241) quotes: the tree "was called the tree of knowledge of good and evill *Ab eventu,* that is, of that which followed the eatyng thereof, for although man dyd know before *Speculative,* what was ill, yet he dyd not know it *practice,* by experience." By reference to *DocCh* 1.10, where Milton states that the Tree of the Knowledge of Good and Evil came to be so called because "since Adam tasted it, we not only know evil, but we know good only by means of evil" (Patterson, *Works* 15:115), Alastair Fowler (623) supports Patrides.

219. Describing the elements of Milton's syllabic prosody, S. Ernest Sprott points to this line, and 342, as he discusses the inversion of feet: "The rule, generally, is that in order that inversion may take place there must be a diaeresis [the end of a foot coincides with the end of a word] between the inverting and the preceding foot ['eminent, blooming'], and the stress syllable of the preceding foot must be strongly accented or followed by a definite compensatory" (100). Also see Sprott in **342**.

blooming: Hughes notes that this line is quoted in the *OED* 3 to illustrate *bloom* in its obsolete, transitive sense: to "bring into bloom" or "cause to flourish" ("Variorum").

220–22. Dennis Burden (126–27) contrasts the brevity of this reference to the forbidden tree with the much more extended treatment of all the other trees, as at 246–51, and adds that this contrast also shows in Adam's remarks about the trees in 421–27.

220. S. Ernest Sprott points to this entire line as he argues that Milton "does in fact preserve the secondary accent on the *a* of *–able* words." Sprott locates other "instances in which such words occur with full syllabic value and cannot be elided without leaving less than ten syllables in the line" (91). Also see Sprott in **250** and **843**.

vegetable Gold: this phrase is one of several most famously shaping much of the mid-twentieth century debate about Milton's description of the garden. See **205–87**. In "vegetable Gold," F. R. Leavis (50) locates what he considers the deficiencies of Milton's style: its unnaturalness, its hardness, its stylization, its sensuous poverty. Recalling a phrase from the younger Milton's *Mask* 715, Leavis comments, "It would be of no use to try and argue with any one who contended that 'vegetable Gold' exemplified the same kind of fusion [of nature and art] as 'green shops'" (50). Douglas Bush's response to Leavis is one of the most sustained: "While the critic seems to think the Tree of Life should have been presented in terms acceptable to the horticulturist, Milton wishes, with an oblique glance at the apples of the Hesperides, to suggest a mysterious growth hardly to be approached in words. In the paradoxical phrase 'vegetable

Gold,' which Mr. Leavis especially scorns, each word is altered and quickened by the other" (*"Paradise Lost" in Our Time* 95). Also among those rejecting Leavis's reading are J. B. Broadbent, David Daiches, and Fowler. For Broadbent, what Milton means by "vegetable Gold" is "not cabbagey, but the essence of cabbages—life, vigor, growth, increase" ("Milton's Paradise" 175). Daiches declares that "vegetable Gold" is "perfect in its generalized suggestion of natural beauty" (176). Following the course of the controversy, Fowler sets forth an alchemic understanding of "vegetable Gold" that, however, first appears in 1695 in Hume's annotation. Hume writes, "Of Vegetable Gold, of growing Gold, according to the conceit of the Chymists, that their *Aurum Potabile,* their *Liquid Gold,* is the highest Preservative, able to cure all Diseases, and to postpone Old Age and Death for a long time. *Vegetable, Vegetabilis,* Lat. any thing that grows, encreaseth and flourisheth, and is productive of its kind, as Plants and Trees, that have a *Vegetative* Being" (137–38). Like Hume, Fowler considers the Latin root of "vegetable" (*OED* s.v. *Vegetable* a.I.d), as he explains, " 'Vegetable stone' and 'potable gold'...were both varieties of the philosophers' stone that preserved health." Like Bush, Fowler then also associates Milton's golden fruit with the Hesperian fruit gathered by Atalanta, as both "were often used to symbolize the alchemical *Magnum Opus*" (623).

Isabel Gamble MacCaffrey also glances at the medieval traditions adhering to the notion of gold, but while she asserts Milton usually saw gold "with medieval eyes, as something unfruitful, and so belonging to death," she also admits, "He was not immune to traditional accounts of golden pavements in Heaven; but when placed in a favorable light in *Paradise Lost,* gold is usually (not always) modified into an adjective, *golden,* or surrounded by organic imagery—or even made organic itself, as in the famous 'vegetable gold' " (161). Somewhat like MacCaffrey, William G. Madsen and A. Bartlett Giamatti step out of the mainstream of the controversy about the naturalness or unnaturalness of Milton's description of the garden to consider the ambiguous moral values evoked by the phrasing here. Associating the gold of the Tree of Life with Eve's golden hair (495–97) and bringing 201–04 to bear on both, Madsen ("Idea" 233) develops his contention that Milton, espousing the orthodox Christian view, believes in the goodness of matter, precisely as does Augustine (*The City of God* 15.22). Giamatti, too, does not so much condemn or commend Milton's formulation "vegetable Gold," as he rather insists that the phrase suggests "something sinister...unnatural and unhealthy" that "seems to taint all the fruit in the garden" (308). Aware of the critical controversy, Giamatti explains:

"While I agree with Bush's hint and Broadbent's statement that in the phrase 'vegetable Gold' (and 'burnisht with Golden Rind') we find a harmonious and innocent balance between art and nature, I would also suggest that, as usual, Milton is having it both ways at once. For because of the context in which those golden grapes appear in Spenser—the Bower of Bliss [*The Faerie Queene* 2.12.55]—Milton is perhaps also exploiting the darker side of the traditional Art-Nature theme" (310).

Leland Ryken's reading of "vegetable Gold" uniquely contributes to the debate. He describes the phrase as a "mystic oxymoron" establishing Milton's apocalyptic vision: "The greatest number of mystic oxymorons in *Paradise Lost* involve a fusion of a solid, enameled image with a vegetative image" (90).

222–24. Arguing that rhyming is far from accidental in Milton's epic, John S. Diekhoff lists this sequence as of one the 45 instances in *PL* "of rhymes separated by but a single line." Diekhoff notes that the *ill-hill* rhyme also echoes with *rill*, four lines later. Identifying the same rhyme pattern in seven other sequences in Book 4 (288–90, 393–95, 469–71, 529–31, 678–80, 702–04, and 898–900), Diekhoff shows that Book 4 has more such rhyming patterns than any other book in the epic ("Rhyme" 540).

223–40. The quest to locate Eden and the Edenic garden has always involved the critical effort to plot its river system, as the notes on 209–14 reveal. While Gen. 2.10–14 names the Pison, Gihon, Hiddekel, and Euphrates as the four rivers that derive from the one that "went out of Eden to water the garden," none of the "four main Streams" (233) in Milton's account is ever named. Also unnamed in Book 4 is the primary river that passes beneath the "shaggie hill" (224) of paradise, later to divide into those "four main Streams." Perhaps as a consequence, much of the commentary on the rivers of Eden and the irrigation of paradise has split into an opposition between a literal and a figurative response to Milton's text: while some critics look to locate Eden's streams and river on a map, others read them allegorically; and similarly, while some critics compare the garden's irrigation system with actual horticultural practice, others see the irrigation system metaphorically.

Eighteenth century editors ponder the literal geography of Mesopotamia, but almost to a person, they acknowledge the imprecision of Milton's presentation. True, Hume (138) and Paterson (302) gloss the primary river flowing

"Southward through *Eden*" (223) as the Euphrates, but Hume then cheerfully admits his own uncertainty about the later "four main Streams." Suggesting that Sir Walter Ralegh's reference to the Tigris and Euphrates in *The History of the World* 1.3.11 may be ill founded, Hume also cites Lucan's reference to the two rivers in *The Civil War* 3.256–58, but as for himself, he writes, "I will not enter on the inextricable difficulty, but leave the Rivers to wander their own way." Newton notes Milton's reference to the Tigris at *PL* 9.71 as Satan returns to the garden, and in an extended comment endeavors to deal with the river system, only finally to admit that Milton himself was uncertain (244–45). While he repeats Newton's note, Todd ([1842], 2:64–65) also presents an opposing view of the matter, directing readers to the fourth chapter ("Explication du dixieme verset [Gen. 2]") of Pierre Daniel Huet's *Traitte de la Situation du Paradis Terrestre,* one of the more popular treatises that literally fix the location of the garden. Todd then suggests a source for Milton's elaborate river and irrigation system—including its fountain—in Niccolai Caussini's *De Eloquentia Sacra et Humana* 724. One of those modern critics pursuing Milton's love of maps, David Masson also ponders issues of physical geography in looking at this passage, immediately admitting, however, "It is impossible to identify this river-system of the Scriptural Eden with the existing river-system of the Syrian and Mesopotamian region supposed to be Eden in the poem. Much ingenuity has been spent on the attempt to do so; but many commentators have been content to suppose an alteration of the river-system of Western Asia by the Deluge. Milton, it will be seen, gets rid of the difficulty by adhering to the Scriptural account and yet adapting it to his own description of Paradise without naming the rivers." Cross-referencing *PL* 9.71, as does Newton, Masson identifies the river flowing south through Eden as the Tigris, points out that Milton cuts short his description of Eden at large to detail the garden itself, and Masson cautions that "the reader must not forget the great river underneath it, and the concealed gulf through which it flows, as these are of importance afterwards" (*Poetical Works* 3:171–72). While Verity (458) and Hughes ("Variorum"), referencing 9.71–73, and John T. Shawcross (*Complete Poetry* 323n15), referencing 4.210–12, also think the river flowing south through Eden is probably the Tigris, Allan H. Gilbert references 1.419–21, as well as *PR* 3.384 and Gen. 15.18, when he identifies the "River large" (223) as the Euphrates (*Geographical Dictionary* 119). Shawcross glosses the "four main Streams" (233) as "traditionally the Nile, Euphrates, Tigris, and Indus" (*Complete Poetry* 323n16).

If the rivers of Milton's Eden slip away from precise identification, the paradisal irrigation system has seemed more easily realized for several mid-twentieth-century critics. Evert Mordecai Clark (147) associates the complex but natural irrigation system in Milton's garden with the one Samuel Purchas describes in Amara (*Purchas His Pilgrimage* 566). Vigorously confronting those who condemn Milton's garden as more mythic than real, J. B. Broadbent points to the paradisal irrigation system for support: "Milton suggests by rhythm and personification, an emblematic value for the legend; confirms the fact by reference to osmotic pressure; and brings the whole thing under the direct creativity of God" (*Some Graver Subject* 175). Several years earlier, in "Milton's Paradise" 162, Broadbent supports his emphasis on reality in Milton's garden by associating its irrigation system with "real horticulture," quoting a description of a similar irrigation system in John Leo Africanus's *A Geographical Historie of Africa* 2:443. Also see Broadbent in **205–87**. While Alastair Fowler dismisses the notion that capillary action could account for the fountain's flow, he, too, develops the physical reality of the garden's irrigation system as he discusses Milton's awareness of hydromechanics (623–24).

Attention to the more figurative elements in Milton's description of the Edenic rivers and the garden's irrigation system joyfully begins with Patrick Hume and is emphasized and clarified by James Paterson. Hume explains that the "rapid current" was "drawn up by gentle heat through the Veins of the hollow Earth, rose like a sweet Spring, and water'd the lovely Garden. *Porous,* of the Greek . . . a Passage and Way, whence those small and imperceptible passages through the Skin in Human Bodies, by which any thing is received or ejected, as Sweat and other Excrementitious Matters" (138). In what is perhaps a more scientific voice, Paterson makes the same point: "*Pores* are very small *Holes* in the Skins of *Men, Beasts, Vegetables, Minerals,* and every Thing else, not discernable by the naked Eye, thro' which the *Sweat, Juice, Nourishment,* &c. are received and discharged; And without those *Pores* we could not live. . . . Here, the Water of the *Euphrates,* which ran thro' the *Pores* or *Veins* of the *Earth,* as the *Poet* supposes, as a *Fig.* of *Rhet.*" (302).

In the twentieth century, Freudian and Jungian psychology reshapes critical attention to the anthropomorphic elements in Milton's description of the garden and its irrigation system. In *Archetypal Patterns in Poetry,* Maud Bodkin, with Jungian theory as a point of departure, discusses the fountain, the mountain paradise, and the watery depths beneath it in *PL* in conjunction with similar complexes in Greek and Hebrew literature, as well as in Coleridge's "Kubla Khan," and concludes that "the image of the watered garden and the mountain height show some persistent affinity with the desire and imaginative enjoyment of supreme well-being, or divine bliss while the cavern depth appears as the objectification of an imaginative fear" (114). Within ten years of *Archetypal Patterns*, C. S. Lewis's highly influential *A Preface to "Paradise Lost"* appeared, and the metaphoric association between Milton's paradise and the human body, as well as the human experience, gained prominence as a topic of critical discourse. Like Bodkin, Lewis (51) compares the "River large" of 223 with Coleridge's Alph, as both "plunge into darkness." Closely noting the description of the water rising from the darkness "through *pores* at the bidding of *kindly thirst* (228)," Lewis writes, "Paradise again reminds us of a human body; and in contrast with this organic dark we have *crisped brooks* above (237) and the hard, bright suggestions of *pearl* and *gold* (238)." Isabel Gamble MacCaffrey moves from the parallel between the human circulatory system and the "veins / Of porous Earth" to the respiratory parallel of 805–06 as she argues, "This river, with its variety and unity, is the backbone of Milton's description in the fourth book. . . . The importance of fountains, rivers, and 'rills' for Milton, and their contrast with the destructive salt sea has been noted; their freshening power is here traced to its source in the veins that nourish Eden. The vital spirits, too, become the 'breath' of the body's rivers, the blood [805]; for Milton's microcosm/macrocosm relation works in both directions" (151). Michael Lieb (70) recalls MacCaffrey's reading as he, too, draws attention to the physiological vocabulary in Milton's description of the garden's river system, adding that the "river recalls the life-giving waters of Heaven, for, as Don Cameron Allen ["Description" 99] reminds us, 'here is life without end, the eventual awakening to life' that sustains not only the womb world itself but the inhabitants of the womb as well." Louis L. Martz, Michael Wilding, and Arnold Stein, celebrating the order symbolized by Milton's paradisal river system, see in the anthropomorphic presentation of that system an important device intimating the close bond between man and nature, between Milton's gardeners and his garden. Martz explains that the style of Book 4, "moving with a clear design, conveys the underlying order of idyllic life. Everywhere, within the wild, luxuriant growth of Paradise, lies the clear evidence of a basic plan, as in that orderly, conical hill which meets the view at first, or in the flexible manner of its watering" (*Paradise Within* 120). For Wilding, "The anthropomorphic suggestions mark nature's closeness to prelapsarian man—a closeness in function that creates a closeness of sympathy. The thirst, hence, is 'kindly'—and the pun emphasizes Milton's idea of unfallen Eden: 'kindly' means 'benevolent' and also 'natural.' Because the thirst is natural, part of a natural process, it is also benevolent; in the unfallen world nature is benevolent" (79). Arnold Stein sees "an image of perfect order, with the Garden in the center being served by the waters that separate, then further separate, then partly unite, then finally unite. The underground stream is 'with kindly thirst up drawn' through *veins* of *porous* earth—nature in the Garden is, like man, a symbol of the macrocosm" (65). Scrutinizing the Jungian elements in Stein's reading of *PL*, specifically those elements implying that the garden is a womb, Robert Martin Adams registers his reservations: "If we have no womb overtones to reckon with, the situation is pleasantly representative of a turnip patch, though not much more exalted than that. But if we start with one big dark river which later divides into four and try to work the details in with certain elementary features of the uro-genitary system in the human female—if we find ourselves trying to imagine what Gabriel is perched on [at the 'Ivorie Port' (778)], supposing Paradise to be a womb—I think we will soon find ourselves regretting the whole concept of an 'archetypal return' and be happy to drop it" (37–38).

While philosophy, rather than human physiology, had dominated the traditional figurative readings of the Edenic river system that would have been available to Milton, scholars have usually argued that his garden shows little evidence of that philosophical influence. Alastair Fowler notes the reading associated with Ambrose (*De Paradiso* 1.3) and Philo (*Allegorical Interpretation of Genesis* 1.19) who understood the four rivers of Eden as metaphors of "the four cardinal virtues, the single source as the fountain of grace on which these depend" (624), while Sister Mary Irma Corcoran details the patristic readings to which Fowler points. Corcoran also states her opinion, however, that, "Although Milton mentioned the pleasant sound of the streams (V, 5[−7]) and the water scooped in rinds for the evening meal (IV, 335[−36]), he gave no real warrant for attaching spiritual meaning to any of the passages" (33–34). Conceding probable spiritual significance to Milton's mention of the Tigris (9.71), "anciently associated with the virtue of temperance," only in 237–41 does Corcoran glimpse what "may be a remote echo of patristic and medieval descriptions of grace or bliss from God nourishing the plants, which are virtues" (34). William G. Madsen is similarly wary of both Platonic and patristic readings of Milton's river system. While acknowledging that Milton's paradise "teems with symbols," Madsen insists that those symbols are "paradoxically typological and prophetic, not Platonic; they speak of what lies ahead, not what lies above; they are a shadow of things to come. The rivers of Paradise, for example, do not stand for the four cardinal virtues, as they do in Henry More's allegorical interpretation [*Conjectura Cabbalistica* 23, 35], which is in the Platonizing manner of Philo Judaeus, but in their movements they foreshadow the Fall and man's subsequent wandering" (*From Shadowy Types* 102). Catching a note also heard in Maud Bodkin's reading of the "cavern depth" beneath the paradisal mountain, Madsen's point about the rivers' foreshadowing of the Fall is a figurative understanding a number of other mid-twentieth-century critics share. Michael Wilding, for example, also finds ominous Milton's description of the river system of paradise: "The four rivers parallel with a tragic irony the four rivers of Hell; the 'wandring' suggests fallen man—the 'wandring steps' of Adam and Eve leaving Paradise after the Fall; and hell is suggested further by 'the nether Flood' which the united rills of Paradise 'fell' to meet—just as Adam and Eve will fall to meet the Hellish rivers. Man will leave Paradise and wander like the divided rivers, through a fallen world of famous realms—the fallen world already imaged in Hell" (78–79).

223. H. F. Robins draws attention to the river's southern flow as he associates it with the delineation of Satan's return to the garden in Book 9: "When Satan re-enters the Garden to effect the actual temptation, he comes with perfect consistency from the north." Traditionally, Robins asserts, the north was "the most ominous of directions" (101).

224. *shaggie:* cross-referencing "the shaggy top of *Mona* high" in *Lyc* 54, as well as *PL* 6.645, where the warring angels seize the "seated Hills" of heaven "by the shaggy tops," Allan H. Gilbert assumes that the adjective in all three cases refers to the forests covering these sites (*Geographical Dictionary* 23). Also see Wilding in **225–27**. In "Variorum," Hughes points out that the *OED* 1.f quotes this verse "to exemplify the transference of the primary meaning of *shaggie* ('covered with long, coarse bushy hair'). Cf. 'Hairie' in 4.135." Also see the consideration of the two mountains of paradise in **131–48**.

Verity brings unique attention to the visual point of view here, insisting that the "wood-covered hill" would have to be "seen sideways" to appear *shaggie* (458).

225–27. Michael Wilding argues that the mountain of paradise recalls the "mountains thrown in the war—as if it is one flung down to Earth: indeed creation is a result of the evil of the war. But if it has been 'thrown' once, it can be moved again easily — as it is after the Fall (XI.829ff.). From its first mention, then, the mount of Paradise is shown as vulnerable" (78). Also see Wilding in **223–40**, and compare Gilbert in **224**.

226. *mould:* "A more pure Earth as properest for Such a Garden. This Mountain is the same described, 132, *&c.* See the Word Mould us'd in the same Sense, V.321" (Richardson, *Explanatory* 148). The Richardsons' reference to 5.321, where Eve describes Adam as "earths hallowd mould," is not cited to illustrate the *OED* 4, "Earth regarded as the material of the human body," but instead *Nat* 138 is quoted: "And leprous sin will melt from earthly mould." Hughes notes the *OED* 3, "The upper soil of cultivated land; garden-soil" ("Variorum").

228–30. The *Fountain* from which "many a rill / Waterd the Garden" in *PL* seems opposed to Gen. 2.6 in the Authorized Version, "But there went up a mist from the earth, and watered the whole face of the ground," prompting a series of editors and critics to pursue the authority for Milton's *Fountain.* Todd ([1842], 2:64) appears to be the first to comment on the difference, as he directs readers to compare Dante's *Purgatorio* 28.121–24. Also cf. Todd's reference to Caussini in **223–40**. Thomas Keightley and Arnold Williams point out that the Hebrew text of Gen. 2.6 has *fountain,* not *mist.* While Keightley therefore claims it "likely" that Milton derived the idea of the fountain from the Septuagint (*Account* 465), Williams points to the Vulgate translation, which translated the Hebrew word as *fountain* or *spring,* and concludes, "This translation is doubtless the origin of the literary and poetic descriptions of Paradise which, like Milton's, have a fountain or a well in the midst of Paradise" (*Common Expositor* 94). Acknowledging the fountain in the Vulgate and Dante, Fowler (623–24) nevertheless claims that Milton's "principal model" is Philo's description of the irrigation system of the garden in *Questions and Answers on Genesis* 1.12.

228. *kindly:* Hughes ("Variorum") glosses this as "natural" and explains, "Milton implies a natural cause for the irrigation at a time when 'the Lord God had not caused it to rain upon the earth' (Gen. 2.5)."

231–32. "The River here is said to *fall down the steep Glade,* by washing down all that stood in its way, and overbearing the Trees that opposed its precipitate fall from the steep side of *Paradise*" (Hume 138).

233–39. The *wandring* (234) of the *Streams* (233) and the "Rowling…With mazie error" (238–39) of the "crisped Brooks" (237) draw no commentary from the earliest editors, and while Verity (459) later briefly cautions that the word *error* is to be taken in the literal sense of the Latin *error*, "wandering," it is not until the 1950s and 1960s that sustained critical attention is brought to the ambiguity of these words, which, to some, seem to compromise the nature of the garden before the Fall. To be sure, Arnold Stein (62) agrees with Verity's reading. However, Stein soon admits, "Back of the phrase are the echoes from hell, Belial's precious thoughts that wander, and the debates of the philosophical angels 'in wandring mazes lost'" (66–67). Developing the argument that Milton uses "outer nature to reflect the inner natures of the men who inhabit it," and quoting Stein with approval, William G. Madsen turns to this sequence as a continuing description of the course of the "nether Flood, / Which from his darksom passage now appears" (231–32): "'Darksome,' 'wand'ring,' and 'mazy error' do not imply that Nature is already fallen; they speak, paradoxically, of a Nature that is innocent but capable of falling" ("Idea" 282). Christopher Ricks develops the implications of Madsen's and Stein's readings. "With the Fall of Man, language falls too," Ricks (109) argues, and therefore, he explains, the meaning of *error* is not "simply 'wandering,' it is 'wandering (not error).' Certainly the word is a reminder of the Fall, in that it takes us back to a time when there were no infected words because there were no infected actions." Pointing to *error* in its fallen meaning (9.1048–49, 1178, 1180–81), Ricks also notes its prelapsarian presentation in 7.302, where the waters are described "with Serpent errour wandring," at which point, he reasons, "It is surely easier to believe in a slightly ingenious Milton than in one who could be so strangely absent-minded as to use both 'serpent' and 'error' without in some way invoking the Fall" (110). A. Bartlett Giamatti presents a very similar argument. In "mazie error," Giamatti sees an example of what he describes as Milton's Satanic style, the "sinuosity, complexity, ambiguity of Milton's language" (297), which, while employed in describing the unfallen garden and its gardeners, also permits Milton to "describe perfection while…preparing for sin" (299). Giamatti cross-references *mazie* in descriptions of the serpent in 9.161–62 and 183, as well as in 9.499–500, and concludes, "there is in paradise something potentially wrong which is directly linked to what is actively evil" (305). Finally, Stanley Fish turns to this topic of prelapsarian and postlapsarian language, but he also looks ahead to the redemption of language: "Paradise is that place and time where roses are without thorns and fables are true…and language is perfect, no redundancy, no equivocals, and above all no ambiguities. But ambiguity is the attribute most easily attached to 'wand'ring' on the basis of its previous occurrences" (*Surprised* 134–35). Asserting, "Evil exists only in the fallen mind which makes a naturally good universe the reflection of its own corruption" (136), Fish traces Milton's provocative manipulations of *wand'ring* through Book 11 and finally into the last lines of Book 12, where, he points out, "it is now the movement of faith, the sign of one's willingness to go out at the command of God" (138). Fish concludes: "Under Providence, through the medium of faith, the word is able to include all its meanings, even those which are literally contradictory, and is thus returned, after many permutations, to its original purity and innocence. Its ambiguity, like all other refractions of the divine unity, has been an illusion, *our* illusion" (138).

233. Verity (458) associates this line with Dante's description in *Purgatorio* 33.112–14: "Euphrates and Tigris welling up from one spring, and parting like friends that linger" (trans. Verity). Verity also supplies the following lines from Tennyson's *Geraint and Enid* 762–65 (*Poems* 3:370): "And never yet, since high in Paradise / O'er the four rivers the first roses blew, / Came purer pleasure unto mortal kind / Than lived thro' her."

236. *if Art could tell:* questioning the meaning of the word *Art*, Bentley initiates a discussion that fits into the larger debate about art versus nature in Milton's description of the garden, a debate surveyed in **205–87**. As so often, Bentley blames "a mistake of the Printer"; this time the mistake has changed *Aught* to *Art*, prompting Bentley to ask, "What can *Art* mean here? the Art of *Gardening*, or rather the Art of *Poetry?*" And to Bentley's mind, "Both are improper" (114). Taking up Bentley's question, Pearce opts for the art of poetry (115–16), while Todd ([1842], 2:65) allows a note from Charles Dunster to speak for him: "Bentley asks whether the poet means here the art of poetry, or the art of gardening? Both, he adds, are improper. It is indeed awkwardly expressed; but, I apprehend, it includes both. It is an apology for the poet's attempting, on such slight ground as the brief account of Paradise in Scripture, to fabricate in his imagination, and describe in his poem, an extensively varied scene of sequestered beauty, fertility, and delight." J. B. Broadbent's reading of "if Art could tell" locates it at the conclusion of a sequence beginning with "thence united fell" at 230: "That art could tell of such things is ground for hubris, yet all hubris drains away in the fluent rhythms, the wondering tone; but the humility remaining is humility in the face of what man himself has created" (*Some Graver Subject* 173).

237. *Saphire Fount:* offering Philo's understanding that sapphire, such as that on Aaron's breastplate, symbolizes "the man who exercises good sense" (*Allegorical Interpretation of Genesis* 1.26), Fowler (625) concludes, "M[ilton]'s *sapphire fount* would appear to be more than an image of natural beauty: to symbolize, indeed, the wisdom underlying all the virtues. Delicate as it is, this touch seems to imply a more or less moralized landscape. Cf. also Ezek. xxviii 13–15."

Fount: Verity (458) glosses this as "source," and cross-references 3.535, while the *OED* 1, defining the word as "A spring, source, FOUNTAIN," cites *PL* 3.357 ("And flours aloft shading the Fount of Life").

crisped: naturalizing what might strike the twentieth century reader as an artificial term, Hume defines *crisped* as "Curled, wrinkled, as Water is by the Wind, or little purling Brooks by opposition of Stones" (139). Paterson makes almost the same point (302). Supplying a parallel from Andrew Ramsey's *Poemata Sacra* 3, Mitford (119) is the first of several later editors who gloss Milton's *crisped* with examples of similar usage by other poets. Verity (459), for example, quotes Lord Byron's *Childe Harold* 4.474 (*Complete Poetical Works* 2:142) and cross-references *Mask* 984: "Along the crisped shades and bowres." Also cf. *PL* 11.843. Fowler (625) notes Ben Jonson's *crisped* in *The Vision of Delight* 186–87 (*Ben Jonson* 7:469). The *OED* 4 also cites *Mask* 984 to exemplify "Applied to trees: sense uncertain." In responding to G. Wilson Knight's objections to the "deliberating aestheticism" and "hard" quality of Milton's paradise, Broadbent considers the meaning of *crisped* that these editors establish. Broadbent similarly considers the meaning of *enameld* at 149 ("Milton's Paradise" 165).

238. *Orient Pearl and sands of Gold:* from Hume to Broadbent, editors and critics have tracked down literary locations for these features of the brooks in Milton's garden. Hume quotes Lucan (*The Civil War* 3.209–10) and Virgil (*Aeneid* 11.142; *Georgics* 2.137), who refer such sands to the Tagus, Pactolus, and Hermus (139). Newton (245–46) names the same rivers, cross-references the "orient Gemmes" in heaven's gate (*PL* 3.507), and points to "orient pearl" in Shakespeare's *Richard III* 4.4.322 and in John Fletcher's *The Faithful Shepherdess* 3.1.385 (*Dramatic Works* 3:543). Todd ([1842], 2:65) credits Newton with a third reference, *Volpone* 3.7.191 (*Ben Jonson* 5:83), and he supplies a description of paradise in John Davies's *Wittes Pilgrimage* sig. T2, where "Rivers of nectar ran on golden sand." To the growing list, Mitford (119) adds a reference to *Antony and Cleopatra* 1.5.40 as well as *Don Quixote* 4.64. Broadbent ("Milton's Paradise" 161; *Some Graver Subject* 174) finds descriptive parallels for Milton's "Orient Pearl and sands of Gold" in sixteenth and seventeenth century travel literature: the Ganges in John Mandeville's *Voiage and Travaile* 304, and the Gulf of Arabia in Samuel Purchas's *Hakluytus Posthumus, or, Purchas His Pilgrimes* 10:23. Fowler (625), however, claims that the riches on the bottoms of Milton's "crisped Brooks" (237) "have little to do with his reading of travel books." Instead, Fowler refers those riches to Gen. 2.11–12, describing Pison, "which compasseth... Havilah, where there is gold; And the gold of that land is good: there is bdellium and the onyx stone," *bdellium* being understood as a type of pearl. Fowler reports that Philo, following the Septuagint version of the Bible, specifies ruby and greenstone, rather than bdellium and onyx, and identifies the greenstone, symbolic of "the man who exercises good sense" (*Allegorical Interpretation of Genesis* 1.26), with the sapphire of Aaron's breastplate.

239–68. As he studies Milton's technique of source adaptation, Grant McColley refers this descriptive sequence to Spenser's *The Faerie Queene* 3.6.42–44. Asserting that "the similarities... are almost too patent for comment," McColley finds here the same pattern that he identifies in the earlier sequence in 131–48: "the backward sequential order of his [Spenser's] ideas is the forward sequential order of the comparable ideas in Milton" ("Milton's Technique" 71).

239. *mazie error:* for twentieth century readers, the critical concern here is the negative, or postlapsarian, connotations that have accrued to *mazie error*. Rejecting those fallen connotations, Verity (459) understands *error* in its literal Latin sense of "a wandering" and points to Tennyson's similar use in *Gareth and Lynette* 1184 (*Poems* 3:318): "The damsel's headlong error through the wood." Fowler, however, brings the negative connotations to bear when he defines *error* as "devious wandering course," and, quoting from the remarks of Arnold Stein and Christopher Ricks, declares that *error* is "One of the most resonant key words in the poem" (625). See Verity, Stein, and Ricks in **233–39**. In his study of Milton's techniques for establishing his apocalyptic vision, Leland Ryken echoes Stein's view on the fall of language presented in **233–39**. Ryken sees "mazie error" as "an example of how words which were originally positive in meaning but eventually acquired negative connotations can be used to reflect a parallel contrast between unfallen and fallen moral states" (234–35).

pendant shades: Hume (139) offers Virgil's *Eclogues* 9.20 as he explains, "Trees hanging over the Streams, or growing on that Ground the Brooks past under. The Shadow, for the Tree that casts it, frequent with the Poets."

240. *Ran Nectar:* the nectar flowing in the "crisped Brooks" (237) is one of the many descriptive details associating Milton's vision of the garden and classical visions of paradisal settings, and commentators from Hume forward have traced those associations. Hume, providing quotations from Virgil's *Eclogues* 5.71 and *Georgics* 4.163–64, identifies nectar and ambrosia as the drink and meat of the gods, which preserved "their Mirth and Immortality" (139). Charles Grosvenor Osgood (6) references Homer's *Iliad* 1.598 and *Odyssey* 5.92–94. Davis P. Harding looks to Ovid: "Milton's account of Paradise is full of details which are strongly reminiscent of Ovid's Golden Age," but the most precise parallels between the two, according to Harding, are that spring is eternal and the rivers run nectar (*Milton and the Renaissance Ovid* 79). Hughes cites *Metamorphoses* 1.111 and, repeating Todd's reference to John Davies's *Wittes Pilgrimage* sig. T2 in his note on 238, insists that Ovid's "nectarian rivers" had been established as a natural feature of paradise in earlier English poetry ("Variorum").

241–43. Concentrated into the commentary on these lines are additional considerations of the art-versus-nature topos that dominates criticism on the entire sequence describing the garden (**205–87**). Balachandra Rajan establishes the webbed associations between these lines and those again juxtaposing art and nature in 5.294–97, as well as those describing Eve and Adam after the Fall (9.792–94, 1013–15), as exemplifying the style of *PL:* "By insistently changing the shape of things the poem obliges us to see all things in their context; and as part of the same effort it insistently changes the shape of words" (*Lofty Rhyme* 108). Also see Rajan on **990–1004**. John R. Knott, Grant McColley, and A. Bartlett Giamatti place Milton's garden against other idealized gardens as they consider the art-versus-nature topos. Knott comments broadly on the "Flours worthy of Paradise" (241): "Even the flowers seem alive and not static or decorative. In most ideal landscapes flowers are said to enamel, or paint, meadows and fields; comparisons with tapestry are frequent. But Milton makes his flowers a manifestation of the abundance of paradise and thus another proof of God's bounty" ("Symbolic Landscape" 40–41). In their remarks, both McColley and Giamatti associate Milton's garden with Spenser's gardens. McColley (*"Paradise Lost": An Account* 146–47) identifies here one of the many links between Milton's paradise and Spenser's Garden of Adonis in *The Faerie Queene* 3.6.44, noting, "Spenser wrote of an arbor 'not by art, but of the tree's own inclination made,... knitting their rank branches... with wanton ivy twine entrailed.'" Giamatti concludes, "Milton is obviously communicating the benign magnificence and munificence of Nature, the 'natural' quality of paradise where art in some constricting deadening sense seems to be superseded or absent. But while he does this, Milton also obliquely recalls a garden [Spenser's Bower of Bliss in *The Faerie Queene* 2.12.42–82] where precisely what seems to be absent here was very much present" (310–11). While Knott, Giamatti, and McColley understand art as disapprovingly contrasted with nature in this passage, Dennis Burden and Alastair Fowler develop very different views. Burden reads these lines with Gen. 1.28 in mind, where God directs Adam to "Be fruitful, and multiply, and replenish the earth, and subdue it." Acknowledging that *subdue* "might seem to suggest some wildness on the Garden's part, some possible misrule, Milton has to make it clear that this represents no threat to Man. His first tactic is to read the garden's wildness as an aspect of its enormous fertility, and hence as an exemplification of the profusion of God's goodness. The common enough distinction between art and nature, between control and abundance, helped to carry him across this problem of the Garden that, though innocent, needed to be subdued.... His second tactic is to link the wildness of the garden with God's command to the human pair to multiply...so that God's promise of children is remedial, providing assistance for their work" (44–45). Also considering the directive to man in Gen. 1.28, and noting Burden's commentary on *subdue*, Fowler writes, "This was a difficult notion, which in the poem is at first given the most innocent explanation possible: namely, that the earth has to be subdued only in the sense that art will be needed to put profuse nature in order" (625).

241. *nice*: Merritt Y. Hughes ("Variorum") glosses *nice* as "delicate, expert," loosely combining several entries in the *OED*, which does not cite *nice* in *PL* 4.241 but does cite *Mask* 139, "The nice Morn on th' Indian steep," to exemplify meaning 5: "Coy, shy, (affectedly) modest, reserved," and it cites *PL* 6.584–86 ("All at once thir Reeds / Put forth, and to a narrow vent appli'd /

With nicest touch") to exemplify meaning 13: "Minutely or carefully accurate." Among the additional meanings of *nice* listed in the *OED* are "Foolish, stupid, senseless" (1); "Wanton, loose-mannered; lascivious" (2); "Critical, doubtful, full of danger or uncertainty" (11.a); "Agreeable" (15); and "Not obvious or readily apprehended" (9). Before surveying meaning, the *OED* acknowledges, "The precise development of the very divergent senses which this word has acquired in English is not altogether clear. In many examples from the 16th and 17th centuries it is difficult to say in what particular sense the writer intended it to be taken." Cf. *nice* in *PL* 5.433, 8.399; *PR* 4.157.

242. *Knots:* the notion of flower beds laid out in intricate or elaborate designs is common to the glosses of Shawcross (*Complete* 323), Hughes ("Variorum"), and Fowler (626). Fowler quotes Henry Peacham's *The Complete Gentleman* 166 describing the walks in Europe where trees "are placed in curious knots, as we use to set our herbes in gardens." Fowler adds, "In M[ilton]'s time such formal, artificial arrangements could already seem insipid" (626).

    boon: Shawcross (*Complete* 323) glosses this as "bountiful," Hughes ("Variorum") as "good (in the sense of 'generous' or 'liberal')." Defining *boon* as "Gracious, bounteous, benign," the *OED* A.3 quotes Milton's line and suggests that, used in this sense, the adjective, derived from French, probably carried associations with the English noun *boon* meaning "favour, benefaction, good gift."

243–45. Arnold Stein (70) considers these lines "a miracle of imaginative sensuousness" and explains: "We seem to be witnessing the miracle in action—the pouring forth is exploded outward rhythmically by the *profuse,* which springs out of the first two words, out of their important consonants, and out of the meaning. *Profuse,* which modifies and means one thing, also retains its verbal force and means *poured forth.* It is as if what was being described then happened, by a kind of imaginative fiat: the first statement saying what the second does." Stein also finds this "extravagant trick with language" at work in 223–25, as well as 260–61. Also see *PL* 8.286.

243. *Powrd forth profuse:* echoing Stein in **243–45**, Michael Wilding writes, "In its reduplicative alliterative pattern, the phrase suggests teeming fertility. The profusion is a fertility of procreation, suggestive of human birth" (80).

244–46. See Anne Davidson Ferry's comment on *shade* in **137–42.**

244. *smote:* from Robert Thyer, Todd notes references to the sun's smoting the field in Ariosto's *Orlando Furioso* 8.20 and 10.35. In his 1826 edition, Todd (2:292) adds a note from Bowles pointing to *The Faerie Queene* 2.12.63, "The sunny beames, which on the billowes bett," and 3.5.49, "When the bright sunne his beams theron doth beat"; to George Chapman's *Ovid's Banquet of Sense* 3, "When with right beams the Sun her bosom beat" (22); and to John Fletcher's *The Faithful Shepherdess* 1.3.188–89 (*Dramatic Works* 3:517). In his 1842 edition, Todd (2:65–66) refers to Richard Niccols's line "While heaven's light the earth's broade face shall smite," in *The Mirror for Magistrates* 875 and "The sun shall not smite thee by day" in Ps. 121.6. To Todd's list, Mitford (120) adds Valerius Flaccus's *Argonautica* 1.495–96.

245. *unpierc't shade:* Todd ([1842], 2:66) points to Song 7.34 in Drayton's *Poly-olbion:* "*Shades not pierc't* with sommer's sunne" (*Works* 4:128).

246. *Imbround:* Todd ([1842], 2:66) reports Robert Thyer's observation, "a person must be acquainted with the Italian language to discern the force and exact propriety of this term: it is a word which their poets make use of to describe any thing shaded." The *OED* 1 defines *Embrown* as "To darken, make dusky," and the first citation is *PL* 4.246, as Hughes (*Complete Poetry* 283) notes, also cross-referencing 9.1088. In "Variorum," Hughes quotes Dante's description of the streams flowing darkly in the shady forest of the earthly paradise in *Purgatorio* 28.31–32. Fowler adds, "In M[ilton]'s time shadows were in fact for some reason regularly painted brown" (626).

    Bowrs: quoting 246, the *OED* 3 exemplifies the meaning "A place closed in or overarched with branches of trees, shrubs, or other plants; a shady recess, leafy covert, arbour."

247–50. John S. Diekhoff notes the rhyming in this sequence ("Rhyme" 541). See Diekhoff in **130–33.**

247. *happy rural seat:* Joseph H. Summers and Michael Wilding pursue the main element creating the happiness that characterizes Milton's "rural seat."

For Summers, the garden's "various view" is key to that happiness: "No static vision would fulfil 'all delight of human sense' (IV.206) as well as soul, and perfect fulfilment is exactly what 'A Heaven on Earth' (IV.208) implies" (73). For Wilding, happiness is involved with the garden's similarity to "an idealized country mansion...in the landscaped grounds and in the rural domestic security and in the contentment evoked." Wilding finds: "The formal implications of the country 'seat' are qualified in Book IV by the complete simplicity, by the innocence of emotion, evoked by 'happie.' It is a simplicity forming a fine alliance with the formal pomp of 'rural seat'" (81).

248–49. William Empson and A. Bartlett Giamatti associate this description of the trees in the "Groves" (248) of the garden with the earlier references to the Tree of Life (218) and the Tree of Knowledge (221). Empson asserts, "The trees that glitter with unheeding beauty and the trees that weep with prescience are alike associated with the tree of knowledge; the same Nature produced the *balm* of healing and the fatal *fruit;* they cannot convey to Adam either its knowledge or the knowledge that it is to be avoided, and by their own nature foretell the necessity of the Fall. The melancholy of our feeling that Eden must be lost so soon, once attached to its vegetation, makes us feel that it is inherently melancholy" (*Some Versions* 179). Empson's reading is questioned by Fowler, however, who insists, "M[ilton] would hardly have agreed...that the trees 'by their own nature foretell the necessity of the Fall.' He seems to imply quite a different thought—that Nature's balm precedes the 'wound' of Nature in the same way that Election to salvation precedes the Fall" (626). Giamatti (313) takes the "Golden Rinde" (249) of the trees in the garden's groves back to the earlier phrase "vegetable Gold" (220) describing the Tree of Life, but Giamatti believes that the association between these references to the trees is fulfilled in the much later description of the tempting serpent's "burnisht Neck of verdant Gold" (9.501). Although his principal concern is identifying classical literary parallels for Milton's phrase "burnisht with Golden Rinde," Patrick Hume glances at the negative connotation that Giamatti develops. Supplying quotes from Virgil's *Eclogues* 6.61 and Ovid's *Metamorphoses* 10.648–50, Hume glosses Milton's phrase "Whose shining outside glittered like polish'd Gold, the *Mala Aurea* & *Citrea* of the Poets" (139).

248. *wept:* early editors bring sustained attention to the traditional nature of this metaphor. Explaining that from "*Myrrhe* and *Balm*...Gum is distill'd, a sort of sweet and odoriferous Sweat, styled in Lat. *Lacrymae,* the Tears of those Trees," Hume (139) supplies supporting quotations from Ovid's *Metamorphoses* 10.500 and Virgil's *Georgics* 2.118–19. Newton (246) repeats the Ovid reference, as does Todd, who, mentioning Pope and Shakespeare, also acknowledges, "Many instances of this metaphor might be added from our old and modern poets" ([1842], 2:66). The late nineteenth century editor R. C. Browne (1:350) recalls *Othello* 5.2.350–51, where Othello compares his tears to the "medicinal gum" of the Arabian trees. Citing this line to exemplify the definition "To shed (moisture or water) in drops; to exude (a liquid, etc.)," the *OED* 9 also quotes *PL* 9.1002–03: "Skie lowr'd, and muttering Thunder, some sad drops / Wept at compleating of the mortal Sin."

rich: following his comment on *wept,* Newton brings a postlapsarian connotation to *rich,* noting that the adjective describes the trees but not the fruits, because "*odorous gums and balm* carry usually a higher price than fruit" (246).

Twentieth century critics develop the conventionality of the garden's fragrance. Allan H. Gilbert, for example, explains that the attention to fragrance is a feature in the many travel books' descriptions of exotic locales. Gilbert (*Geographical Dictionary* 156) quotes from Purchas's *Hakluytus Posthumus* 4.1308: "Cabueriba is very great and esteemed for the Balme that it hath; to get this Balme they prick the barke of the tree, and lay a little Cotton wooll to the cuts, and from certaine to certaine dayes they goe to gather the Oyle that it hath distilled. The Portugals calle it Balme, because it is very like to the true Balme of the Vineyeards of Engedi; it serveth for greene wounds, and taketh away the scarre; it smelleth very well, and of it, and of the barke of the tree they make Beades, and other smelling things." Returning to Gilbert's acknowledgment, Cawley describes Purchas's remarks on balm as "*e pluribus unum*" (99). John R. Knott cross-references a number of other passages describing the fragrance of paradise, contending, however, that Milton's presentation moves beyond the conventional: "The fragrance of the Garden more than any other traditional feature communicates a sense of intense and inescapable sensuous delight. Milton goes far beyond the customary brief reference to rich odors." With such attention to the fragrances of the garden, Milton creates, in Knott's words, "an active nature, gratifying the sense of smell with an irresistible profusion of odors" ("Symbolic Landscape" 41).

249–51. *Fables:* Bentley first brings critical attention to the question of the truth of *Fables,* and the discussion he initiates draws in both early and modern editors and twentieth century critics. Accusing Milton's "Editor, whoever he was, our Author's Acquaintance," of changing "Apples" to *Fables,* Bentley ponders, "Fables, says he, if true, here only true. Very quaint: but pray you, Sir, how can *Fables* be true *anywhere?* a Contradiction in the very Terms." Bentley also recognizes, however, that his answer is unsatisfactory for Hesperian apples, reputed to be of solid gold, could not have been "of delicious taste," and he therefore decides to delete "Hesperian Fables true, / If true, here only." What remains, "Burnish'd with golden Rind Hung amiable, and of delicious taste," then serves to support Bentley's claims about the editor's meddling with Milton's text: "the very pat joining of the Verse betrays the [editor's] Insertion" (114). Pearce responds to Bentley's concerns by noting that if Milton understood *Fable* as *fabula,* which means "something commonly talked of, whether true or false,...the sense is clear of the objection." To sidestep the practical problem of tasting apples of solid gold, Pearce more conservatively replaces Bentley's radical excision of the text with parentheses: "Others, whose fruit burnish'd with golden rind / Hung amiable, (Hesperian fables true, / If true, here only) and of delicious taste" (116–17). In the Richardsons' response appears the understanding that modern critics develop in more detail: "What is said of the *Hesperian* gardens is true here only; if all is not pure invention, this garden was meant: And moreover these fruits have a delicious taste; those there had none" (150). While he does not comment on the truth of "*Hesperian* Fables," Thomas Warton underscores their enduring appeal to Milton. In *Observations on the "Fairy Queen,"* Warton cross-references this passage with *PL* 3.568 and 8.631, *PR* 2.357, and *Mask* 393, 981–83, concluding, "The fable of the garden of the Hesperides seems to have affected the imagination of Milton in a very particular manner, as his allusions to it are remarkably frequent" (2:26). Sustaining the critical dispute about the truth of fables, Todd ([1842], 2:66–67) nevertheless seems to try to equivocate, quoting Pearce but also adding the Richardsons' note. In the mid-twentieth century, Arnold Williams and Isabel Gamble MacCaffrey elaborate upon the Richardsons' sense of the truth of "*Hesperian* Fables" in their work with Renaissance commentaries on Genesis and Renaissance mythographers. Williams points out that it "was commonplace for the [Renaissance] commentaries [on Genesis] to quote Ovid, Lucan, and other classical poets who wrote of the golden age." When commenting on the Garden of Eden, Williams reports, "Many of the commentators say that Paradise excelled the gardens of Semeramis, Alcinous, Lydia, Gordius, Hesperides, or whatever other famous gardens they could collect from classical myth and history" (*Common Expositor* 108). MacCaffrey (5) more fully contextualizes the Richardsons' point, arguing that Milton, like Renaissance mythographers, saw parallels, rather than distortions of Christian mythology, in the myths of other cultures. MacCaffrey quotes from *Mythomystes* 76, for example, in which Henry Reynolds explains that both ancient poets and philosophers meant paradise or Eden when they referred to their *horti Hesperidum*. Also see Osgood in **605, 705–08**, and Empson in **705–08**. Jacques Blondel speaks in similar terms, and referring to the entire description of Eden in Book 4, explains, "The hymn of praise is thus sung in the language of mythological fiction so as to enhance the beauty and make Eden no creation of the heated brain, no illusion, but so as to show how fiction itself exemplifies the actuality" (260).

The issue of the naturalness of Milton's garden that prominently figures in **205–87** also predictably resurfaces here. While forcefully commending the method by which Milton unites the fanciful with the realistic as he describes the Garden of Eden, J. B. Broadbent glances at that which first concerned Richard Bentley, the impossibility of actually tasting apples of gold. Broadbent believes that Milton did not succeed in establishing the sensuousness of nature in *PL* and acknowledges the perceptiveness of F. R. Leavis on this point. Cf. Leavis in **205–87**. Glancing at **251, 257–58**, and **265**, Broadbent explains that, "although the senses are offered satisfaction, we are not sensuously satisfied as we read. Smell, touch, taste, have their objects in odorous sweets...; but we are left to turn these words into sensations, for the poet does not communicate the experience itself" ("Milton's Paradise" 170). Broadbent concedes, however, that "surely in Paradise the details are not so sensuously rich because sensuousness would have been out of place: these are the riches of God" (171). In *Some Graver Subject* several years later, he returns to this topic, this time contrasting the sensuousness of *PL* and Milton's earlier *Mask*. In *PL*, Broadbent believes that the poet offers only "the objects of sense-experience—'the smell of field and grove,' 'Grots and Caves of cool recess,' fruits 'of delicious taste'—at one syntactical remove; Comus tempts our greed with the imagined sensations of them" (176). Looking at *Mask* 393–94, where the Second Brother describes "beauty, like the fair Hesperian Tree / Laden with blooming gold," Edward S. Le Comte explains that the repetition reveals Milton's "evolution as a poet. The principal weight of theme shifts from classical to Biblical, but the poet never ceases to be remarkably mobile, so that, whether in youth or in maturity...he gets the best of both worlds: has his forbidden fruit and eats the apples of the Hesperides, too." Like MacCaffrey and Williams, Le Comte also points out that the association between Eden and the Hesperides was typical of the Renaissance (*Yet Once More* 56).

Anne Davidson Ferry argues that the complex identity of the blind bard, as well as the fallen audience, is poignantly and most importantly revealed by such references to pagan fables: "throughout *Paradise Lost*, the allusions to the fables feigned by pagan poets evoke a sense of all the wealth of knowledge and feeling which has entered the world since Adam's Fall. By his disobedience we lost our original simplicity and innocence, but we gained a multiplicity of choices; we gained the beauty, the poignancy and the variety of mortal experience" (*Milton's Epic Voice* 37).

250. Establishing the principles of Milton's syllabic prosody, S. Ernest Sprott points to "amiable, *Hesperian*" in this line to exemplify the following: "The semivowels also may suffer elision of their preceding vowels before the aspirate" (87), later adding, "It seems generally better to elide *–able* words externally rather than internally" (92). Also see Sprott in **220**. Robert Bridges earlier makes a similar determination (12). Also see Bridges in **73**, **138**, and **596**.

   amiable: Verity (459) repeats R. C. Browne's reference (1:350) to Bottom's "amiable cheeks" in *A Midsummer Night's Dream* 4.1.2 and adds a reference to Ps. 84.1.

251. In *Rambler* 88, Samuel Johnson identifies the "great peculiarity of Milton's versification" as "the elision of one vowel before another, or the suppression of the last syllable of a word ending with a vowel, when a vowel begins the following word," and this "elision of vowels, however graceful it may seem to other nations," Johnson suggests, "may be very unsuitable to the genius of the English tongue" (4:102). For Johnson, such "abscision of a vowel is undoubtedly vicious when it is strongly sounded, and makes, with its associate consonant, a full and audible syllable," and quoting 4.251, as well as 5.407, 5.628, 12.168, 7.236, and 10.766, Johnson insists that in these passages "the music is injured, and in some the meaning obscured" (4:103).

252–68. The critical language praising this descriptive sequence is rather obviously aimed at answering such critics as T. S. Eliot and F. R. Leavis, who find Milton's presentation of the garden as hard, vague, artificial, and lacking sensuous appeal. See Eliot and Leavis in **205–87**. Of this sequence, for example, Arnold

Stein writes, "The generalized sensuous excitement in language and rhythm (which are made to bear a major burden) serves more than the argument of any single or focused detail. It is a frankly 'literary' demonstration of Paradise, the expected gorgeousness of nature wantoning. The archetypal pattern of order is still the theme, but these are bravura variations on the theme." The rhythm, Stein describes as "an extraordinary metaphor of order; it does not wanton, but is at once sensuously exciting and controlling" (69). Michael Wilding argues, "Nature is for man's service and so supplies him—'spred her store' [255]. This is not a Romantic nature rampaging wild for its own sake, expressing itself as nature; nature here serves man" (81). John R. Knott writes, "Milton suggests the actuality of the Garden without allowing its contours to harden. Groves and bowers are not located precisely, nor are 'Hill and Dale and Plaine' [243]." For Knott, the connective *or* in this sequence "makes the parts of the landscape seem interchangeable, as if to suggest that all views are equally pleasant" ("Symbolic Landscape" 43).

252. *Lawns:* Hume defines this as "Uncultivated, rude, shrubby Plains, of the Fr. *Lande,* a Plain in a Park." The *OED* sb. 2.1 cites *Lyc* 25 to illustrate "An open space between woods; a glade."

level Downs: "The *Downs* have their Name of Saxon original of *Dune,* a Mountain, they being Plains spread on the tops of Hills" (Hume 140).

255. *irriguous:* Hume (140), defining the term as "well-water'd," "full of Springs and Rills," points out that while Horace applies the adjective to a garden in *Satires* 2.4.16, Virgil applies it to a fountain in *Georgics* 4.32.

In "Variorum," Merritt Y. Hughes records that the *OED* 1 cites Milton's line to illustrate the following meaning: "Irrigated; moistened, bedewed, wet; *esp.* of a region or tract of land: Well-watered, moist, watery."

256. *without Thorn the Rose:* until Todd recalls Robert Herrick's "The Rose" (*Poems* 396), early editors appear uncertain about the theological legitimacy of the thornless rose in Milton's paradise. Hume contrasts the thornless rose with the curse laid upon the earth in Gen. 3.18, then cautiously adds, "whether the charming Rose had not its Guard about it originally, that every rude Hand might not sully and prostitute its blushing Beauties, is not determinable" (140). While Bentley declares the thornless rose a "puerile Fancy" (215), Newton,

like Hume, recalls the curse in Gen. 3.18 as he concludes, "the general opinion has prevailed that there were no thorns before" (247). In *European Magazine and London Review,* November 1795, "E" corroborates Newton's claim by quoting from Basil's Homily 5, cols. 105–06, as well as his Third Oration, *De Paradiso,* col. 66. "E" concludes his brief note: "The Father and the Poet have with equal seriousness asserted, that the rose was originally without a thorn" (296). Todd's notes most authoritatively settle the patristic background; initially, Todd offers Hurd's assertion that the thornless rose originated with Tasso's *Il Mondo Creato* 3.1156–64, but then downplays that reference by quoting Herrick's "The Rose" 1–2: "Before Mans fall, the Rose was born / (*S. Ambrose* sayes) without the Thorn." Acknowledging that St. Basil (*Hexameron* 3.11) shares Ambrose's opinion, Todd then concludes, "Milton, in his description of Paradise particularly, appears to have consulted the Fathers" ([1842], 2:67). More than a hundred years later, George Wesley Whiting, rehearsing the development of the eighteenth century discussion, arrives at the same conclusion: "The commentaries of St. Basil and St. Ambrose provide a firm theological basis for Milton's statement. There is thus no warrant whatever for the theory that the line embodies an Italian conceit. Milton had long ago rejected such ornaments. The thornless rose is a symbol of the sinless state of man before the Fall" ("'And Without Thorn'" 62). Arnold Williams (*Common Expositor* 108–09) reports, however, that the more realistic Renaissance commentators on Genesis had reservations about Basil's well-known understanding of the paradisal rose, as well as Basil's view that there were no noxious plants in paradise: "Pererius, who reports it [*Commentariorum* 53, 136], is not convinced that the noxious plants were created after the fall, since that implies an incompleteness in the first creation, nor can he accept a thornless rose. Thorns belong to the nature of the rose. However, Pererius gladly admits that the noxious plants had no power to harm man, nor the thorns to prick him."

Unconcerned with theological sources or poetic analogues, John Peter explains how this phrase anchors Milton's description of the garden, which offers "a lavishness of language and suggestion seldom surpassed in the entire poem. The glitter and richness of the scene would be outlandish . . . but it is beautifully clinched by the simplest of phrases: 'and without Thorn the Rose'" (88). Just the opposite view, however, is asserted by Knott, who reads the phrase as "an aside" that "adds the final touch to a line that subtly lifts the description into the realm of the miraculous" ("Symbolic Landscape" 40).

Robert Bridges and B. A. Wright comment on accent in this famous phrase. Bridges explains that "when a disyllable accented on the last was followed immediately by another strongly accented syllable, the accent of the former was sometimes in speaking shifted back." While Bridges, therefore, believes that "recession is possible" here, he concludes that it is "evidently not intended" (74). Also rather uncertain about Milton's intention with the phrase, Wright concludes that the entire line "is poignant or trite according as one reads it or not with this unusual stressing" ("Stressing" 203). Also see Wright **654–56**.

As he discusses Milton's lengthy description of the garden, and responds to the heated debate about its naturalness or its artificiality, J. B. Broadbent points to the very succinct balancing of aesthetic values in this line: "'Flours of all hue' (256) is confident of the actual; 'without thorn the rose' reverently asserts the ideal" (*Some Graver Subject* 172). For the full presentation of the debate about the garden's naturalness versus its artificiality, see **205–87**.

257–66. Thomas Greene contrasts nature within the garden and nature outside the garden: "One understands the artistic logic of this drowsiness. The loveliest paradise of our deepest fancy is of its essence dreamy. But Milton's nature as a whole, the nature without the garden, is not dreamy, before the fall or after it. The nature is vital, energetic, robust, dynamic, possessed of a Baroque joy in living movement" (402).

257. *Another:* Bentley's concern (115) about the logical difficulty of *Another* when Milton had not earlier referred to a former side to the garden stirs Pearce (118) to point out, "It is not unusual with *Milton* to say *on the other side,* when he had not mention'd *one side* before, as in *v.* 985. *On th' other side.* See also II.706." Newton (247) follows Pearce's lead, supplying references to 2.108, 4.985, and 9.888, as well as to *Aeneid* 1.474, 8.682, and 9.521.

258. *mantling:* the richness of meaning in this adjective is impressively developed in the notes provided by Hume and Paterson. With his typical attention to etymology, Hume (140) lays the foundation: "The spreading Vine exposes to the Sun her Purple Fruit, and by degrees creeps up, wantoning and extravagant. *Mantling,* of *Mantle,* and this of the Fr. *Manteau,* of the Lat. *Mantelum,* used by Plautus [*Captivi* 520] for a Cloak; so the Mantling Vine from its covering any thing it grows against, or overspreads." Hume also includes a cross-reference to Raphael's mantling wings at *PL* 5.279. To Hume's cross-reference, the Richardsons (150) add the swan's mantling wings at *PL* 7.439, and Verity (459) points to "mantling vine" in *Mask* 294. Tracing the meaning of *mantling* exactly as Hume does, James Paterson develops the metaphor by linking *mantling* with *fringed* in 262, which he glosses as "A Lace on the Edge or Border of a Garment" (303).

260–61. Arnold Stein praises Milton's "extravagant trick with language" here, as well as in 243: "The leisurely and melodious movement of water falling is abruptly changed to the immediate crashing fall. The rhythmic effect is perhaps at the imaginative center, but Milton has also cunningly released the verbal force of *disperst,* and the original Latin meaning, which becomes a fresh metaphor when it is the oneness of water that is being dispersed. Technically the device is rather close to the one illustrated by *profuse.* So, one may add, is the way the consonants are marshaled for the sudden release—the p-r-f of 'Powrd forth' and the p-r-f of 'profuse,' the d-s-p of 'Down the slope hills' and the d-s-p of 'disperst'" (70–71).

260. *Luxuriant:* Hume (140) defines the term as "growing rank, and running out into Leaves and curling Tendrils, of the Lat. *Luxuriare,* to grow rank," and refers Milton's understanding of the term to Virgil's *Georgics* 1.191 and 3.81.

    murmuring: again cross-referencing Virgil's *Georgics* 1, this time lines 108–10, Hume traces the word through the Latin *murmurare* to the Greek and defines it as "a word made in imitation of the sound of Running Streams, when troubled with the Stone or Gravel" (140).

    Studying the principles guiding Milton's syllabic prosody, S. Ernest Sprott points to *murmuring* as an example of the principle of elision before a vocalic *r* within a word (96). Also see Sprott on *verdurous* in **143**.

262–66. Fowler (627) finds the conventions associated with the gardens of Venus throughout this passage, but, he continues, "Venus is present not only in her capacity as goddess of gardens, but also as the form-giver, presiding over the generative cycle unfolded in the Graces and the Hours [4.267]." To exemplify his assertion, "Paradises were commonly portrayed as gardens of Venus," Fowler points to the Garden of Adonis in *The Faerie Queene* 3.6.39–42 and the garden enclosing the Temple of Venus in *The Faerie Queene* 4.10.21–25. Fowler explains that Milton's "mantling vine" (258) is involved in "the same complex of associations" and directs readers to Ovid's *Art of Love* 1.244 and Euripides's *The Bacchanals* 773. Specifying Tasso's garden of Armida in *Gerusalemme Liberata* 16.12, and Spenser's Bower of Bliss in *The Faerie Queene* 2.12.70–71, he adds, "The harmony of bird song, rustling leaves and *murmuring waters* (l. 260) was a usual feature of gardens of Venus."

262. *fringed:* defining *fringe* as "An ornamental bordering" (sb. 1) and "Anything resembling this" (sb. 2), the *OED* cites this line, as well as Shakespeare's *The Tempest* 1.2.408, to illustrate the past participial meaning "Furnished with a fringe." Mitford (120) provides examples of Thomas Carew's similar use of the term in *Coelum Britannicum* 906–07 (*Poems* 177) and "To My Friend G. N. from Wrest" 89 (*Poems* 88). Also see Paterson on *fringed* in **258**.

    Myrtle: as so often, Hume's gloss (140) reflects the editor's day-to-day encounters with nature as well as his scholarship. He notes the plant's small size, its "pleasing Fragrancy," and its "perpetual Verdure," as well as Virgil's reference in *Georgics* 4.124.

263. *Her chrystal mirror:* insisting that 263 should read "ITS *crystal mirror holds,*" Bentley objects to the personification of the lake: "The Lake holds a Mirror to the Bank. Why must this Lake then be made a Person?" (115) Newton responds, in part, to Bentley: "He makes the lake we may observe a person, and a critic like Dr. Bentley may find fault with it; but it is usual with the poets to personify lakes and rivers, as Homer does the river Scamander [*Iliad* 21.212–21] and Virgil the Tiber [*Aeneid* 8.31–65], and Milton himself makes a person of the river of bliss, and a female person too, III.359, as he does here of the lake" (247–48).

264–75. Charles Grosvenor Osgood develops his argument about the role of mythology in Milton's personification of nature as he responds to this sequence: "in the comparisons occurring here Milton has not stopped with mere allusions to myths…but has outlined in his concise and significant way the stories of Proserpina and Amalthea, and has suggested the voice heard in the Castalian spring sacred to the Apollo and Daphne of the Orient, thus furnishing appropriate personal types to reflect the natural beauty previously described" (xvi). Considerably later in the twentieth century, David Daiches speaks in much the same voice: "There is a tremulous glory in this description of ideal Nature fully realized, and repetitions such as 'airs, vernal airs,' and 'Proserpin gathring flowr's / Her self a fairer Flowre' help to give the proper emotional quality to the verse. The classical imagery is neither purely decorative nor as solidly grounded in reality as the biblical groundwork of the story: Milton uses myth for what it is, the imaginative projection of all men's deepest hopes and fears" (151–52).

264–68. While John Peter finds that the first part of Milton's description of the garden (131–235) "occasions some disappointment" and justifies L. C. Knights's assertion that it "is not deeply felt," from about 235 onward, Peter finds Milton's verse "almost faultless, and richly evocative" (88). Extending the accumulating and multiple associations of scene and sound discussed by other critics responding to 264–66, Peter focuses on this five-line sequence: "After the mention of birdsong 'aires' are all but 'tunes,' but 'vernal aires' brings in the suggestion of scent, and this, after the ambiguous 'Breathing,' is at once confirmed by 'the smell of field and grove.' The word 'attune' revives the idea of music, but 'trembling' maintains the counter-suggestion of the 'aires' as 'breezes,' so that when the music really emerges, with the 'dance,' it keeps the enrichments of scent it has been gathering from phrase to phrase. The technique in lines like these is wonderfully assured" (89).

264–66. Hume initially comments on the dynamic sensuousness of this sequence and recognizes Milton's play with *aires,* but—except for James Paterson in 1744—subsequent critics and editors give little attention to this passage until 1935, when William Empson explains that Milton's punning on *aires* makes for its remarkable success. Hume (140) glosses "vernal aires" as "Soft Breaths and gentle Gales, perfumed by Flowry Fields and Orange Groves," which, he explains, "move the Trees trembling Leaves into a Tune, consorting with the Feather'd Quire. *Aires* seem here to be meant of Musical Airs, sweet and yet brisk…for all Musick, either Vocal or Instrumental, is but the beating and breaking of the Air, according to various Measure and Modulations." Hume closes with a quotation from Virgil's *Georgics* 2.328. Bentley notes, "Airs signify Tunes," but he nonetheless argues to change "aires" to the singular "air," more clearly to refer to the element (115). Pearce (119) argues to retain the plural, signifying "Gales or breaths of wind," and, like Bentley, seems unaware of the associations of meaning presented by Hume. In his 1744 *Commentary,* Paterson immediately identifies "*aires*" as a musical term and notes: "Gentle Gales or Breaths or the sweet *Air*. Here, *Musical Tunes,* the Notes of Birds in the Spring. The word is doubled, to add the greater *Force* and *Beauty,* by a *Fig.* of *Rhet.*" Paterson carries through with Milton's wordplay as he then proceeds to *attune:* "To *join in Tune.* Here, to put the *Trees* and *Leaves* into a regular and delightful Motion, which causeth a *whistling Tune* or *Sound,* by a *Fig.* of *Rhet.*" (304). In his 1801 edition, Todd, crediting a note contributed by John Bowle, quotes Spenser's *The Faerie Queene* 3.1.40: "sweet birds thereto *applide* / Their dainty layes and dulcet melody." In later editions, Todd aligns 264–66 with 156 ("now gentle gales"), as well as with Dante's *Purgatorio* 28.15, but never directly responds to the earlier editors' remarks on *aires* ([1842], 2:67). Empson returns attention to *aires* as he discusses Bentley's edition of *PL* in *Some Versions of Pastoral.* Finding it strange that Bentley misses Milton's punning, Empson explains, "The airs attune the leaves because the air itself is as enlivening as an air; the trees and wild flowers that are smelt on the air match, as if they caused, as if they were caused by, the birds and leaves that are heard on the air; nature, because of a pun, becomes a single organism." Glancing back at Bentley, Empson concludes, "A critical theory is powerful indeed when it can blind its holders to so much beauty" (149). Cf. Bentley, Pearce, and Empson in **555**. Merritt Y. Hughes ("Variorum") associates Empson's sense of a pun in this sequence with Pope's "Let Vernal Aires thro' trembling Osiers play" in *Spring, The First Pastoral, or Damon* 5 (*Poems* 1:60). Perhaps the first major critic to look at Empson looking at Bentley looking at Milton is John Crowe Ransom, who, like a number of later critics, does not accept that there is a pun at work in Milton's lines: "I cannot see that Milton requires a pun in order to be intelligible, or is improved when we read the pun into his meaning. This one would be a very disagreeable pun." Ransom then firmly faults Empson for overreading ("Mr. Empson" 326). Isabel Gamble MacCaffrey recalls Empson's reference to the "secret pun" in these lines, but, like Ransom, has reservations about that emphasis, preferring to explain that the lines "contain, in marvelously telescoped though not very secret form, three different image-strands, all important for Milton's larger picture. One is organic, again: taking *airs* as the winds that are actually the breath of the Garden. Another is music, and a third, the sweet smell that seemed to come into Milton's imagination at once when he thought of Paradise" (150). Christopher Ricks is similarly not so sure about punning here: "*Airs* does not present us with two meanings both of which make literal sense, and so it is not perhaps a pun. But it offers a main meaning—breezes—while at the same time anticipating the music, lending to the breezes an enhancing suggestion. The effect is one of tincture or reflection, not of fusion. A prose paraphrase would have to offer breezes as the sense; but such a paraphrase would lose the beautiful suggestion that in Paradise the airs were magically musical. In essence, the beauty is one of anticipation—*prolepsis* is surely the key-figure throughout *Paradise Lost,* in the fable itself, in allusion, in simile, and even in syntax and word-play" (105). In his study of Milton and the modern critics, Robert Martin Adams brings some detailed attention to punning throughout *PL.* On the wordplay in these two lines, he admits that Milton "may have wanted 'aires, vernal airs'... to suggest both tunes and breezes" (86), and Adams suggests that "one might establish a spectrum of Miltonic puns and ambiguities, ranging down from the most to the least functional" (88).

264. C. S. Lewis draws attention to this line as it triggers the climax of Milton's description of paradise: "The representation begins swelling and trembling at 264 with the nervous reiteration of *airs* in order that it may *burst* in the following lines—may flow into a riot of mythology where we are so to speak, drenched. That is the real climax; and then, having been emparadised, we are ready at line 288 to meet at last the white, erect, severe, voluptuous forms of our first parents" (51).

   quire: this is the obsolete form of *choir.* The *OED* 3 illustrates the meaning "A company of singers; *spec.* an organized body of singers who perform at concerts" when transferred and used figuratively "of angels, birds, echoes, etc." by citing 12.366 ("They...by a Quire / Of squadrond Angels hear his Carol sung").

   apply: A. W. Verity (459) defines *apply* as either "practice" or "add," but Hughes ("Variorum") points out that the *OED* 16 quotes the line to illustrate *apply* in its obsolete sense of "To devote one's energy to, to handle vigorously; to wield, practise."

265. *attune:* in his annotation on 264–66, Patrick Hume never really defines this word but does assert that *attune* is "a word of our Authors Coinage, of *Tune*" (140). Actually, as the *OED* 1 points out, *attune* meaning "To bring into musical accord" first appears in *The Faerie Queene* 2.12.76, where it, like Milton's *attune,* appears in conjunction with *quire:* "then gan all the quire of birdes / Their diverse notes t'attune unto his lay." More suggestive of the

OED's definition 3, "To make tuneful or melodious," is Paterson's gloss: "To *join in Tune*" (304). The *OED* cites Milton's line to exemplify neither of these definitions, however, but to exemplify definition 2, "To bring (a musical instrument) to the right pitch; to tune. Also *fig.*" Ransom's commentary seems most sensitive to these three variations of meaning: "The birds make tunes but do not need an external apparatus, they furnish their own choir; then the breezes follow suit, but they have to do it by attuning the leaves, just as it might be said that Pan makes music by attuning the reed" ("Mr. Empson" 326).

266–94. J. B. Broadbent presents a very close reading of this sequence as he explains that Adam and Eve "do not walk on to the stage but emerge from already-innocent Paradise." In the description of Pan dancing with the Hours, Broadbent sees Spenser and Botticelli, but then, "in the middle of a line the tone drops and Persephone gently presages the Fall but also, in the pain which it cost Ceres 'To seek her through the world,' the salvation of man. Then the *expeditio* of the Nyseian Isle and Mount Amara kaleidoscopes glittering patterns so that it is with a shock that the vision steadies, we are returned to the eyes of Satan who 'Saw undelighted all delight' and out of the confusion of vegetation, myth, geography, emerge 'Two of far nobler shape…'" (*Some Graver Subject* 185). See Broadbent in **288–1015** for his views on prelapsarian innocence.

266–68. The content of Hume's annotations on Pan, the Graces, and the Hours, linking Milton's presentation to classical literary texts, recurs nearly without question until 1900. Newton (248), for example, quotes most of Hume, contributing only a few missing line numbers, whereas Todd ([1842], 2:67–68) merely condenses, but also similarly credits, Hume. In bringing additional material to bear on Milton's references to Pan, the Graces, and the Hours, Charles Grosvenor Osgood's *The Classical Mythology of Milton's English Poems* (1900) not only adds to Hume's early readings but also occasionally denies them.

Pan: Hume repeats Macrobius's understanding that Pan is "Universae substantiae Materialis Dominator"; "the ruler of all material substance" (*Saturnalia* 1.22.2), and, Hume concludes, "Exactly well therefore does our Poet give him the Title of Universal *Pan*, and joyn him with the dancing Hours and Graces" (140). In his lengthier commentary on Pan, Osgood most obviously develops his overriding thesis on Milton's use of classical mythology to personify nature. Quoting from both the Homeric and the Orphic ("To Pan" 1–3) hymns that

Hume also references, Osgood shifts the interpretation of Pan away from Pan as "Universal Nature" to personify him as going "hither and thither through the dense thickets." In *Homeric Hymn* 19.24 (*The Homeric Hymns* 444–45), Osgood points out that Pan is described "delighting his mind with sweet lays in the soft meadow," and Osgood finds this description comparable not only to 266 but also to "Milton's more elaborate description of Eden preceding" (67). Merritt Y. Hughes (*Complete Poems* 284) adds to the critical understanding of Milton's Pan, referencing Natale Conti's *Mythologiae* 5.6, where Conti identifies Pan "with nature itself, proceeding from and created by the divine mind." In "Variorum," Hughes adds that Conti takes Pan's "horns, hoofs, and goatskin as signifying all nature from the stars to the forests on the hills and the herds on the plains. Pan was the leader of the chorus of rural gods, and as the god of nature he was enthroned with the Hours attending him. But Conti also interpreted the myths of Pan as signifying that from the moment of its creation nature was filled with movement in every part."

Graces and the *Hours:* these Hume (141) identifies as "the Flowers and fruitful Seasons," and adds that "the beautiful Seasons, in which all things seem to dance and smile, in an Universal Joy, is plain from Horace: 'Diffugere nives; Redeunt jam Gramina Campis, &c. / Gratia cum Nymphis, Geminisque sororibus audet / Ducere nuda Chorus'; 'The snow has fled; already the grass is returning to the fields, &c. / The Grace, with the Nymphs and her twin sisters, ventures unrobed to lead her bands'" (*Odes* 4.7.1). Hume also discusses the Hours by reference to the *Homeric Hymn to Pythian Apollo* 195–98 (*The Homeric Hymns* 338–39) in which the poet "joyns both the Graces and the Hours Hand in Hand, with Harmony, Youth and Venus, three Charming Companions." While he notes that Hesiod's understanding of the genealogy of the Graces (*Theogony* 906–11), which Hume presents via Horace, "was the commonest," Osgood adds that Homer refers to "an indefinite number of Graces" in the *Iliad* 14.267. Osgood also cross-references Milton's two opposing genealogies for the Graces in *L'All* 12–24. Like Hume, Osgood cites the *Homeric Hymn to Pythian Apollo* for the association between the Graces and the Hours, but Osgood also points to Pausanius's *Description of Greece* 2.17.4, 5.11.7 as well as Ovid's *Fasti* 5.200–20. Contradicting Horace's comment on the Graces, as presented by Hume, Osgood adds that "the Graces have nothing to do with the coming of Spring, though their name often suggested flowers, especially roses. . . . The association of the Graces with Pan . . . seems to be Pindaric" (38–39). Moving forward from Hume's reference to Homer and Aratus, which establishes that the Hours stand for all seasons, Osgood (44) explains, "Milton, with later classical writers, associates them with Spring and the flowers," and he quotes from Pindar's Fragment 75.13–16, "For the Athenians" (*Odes* 554–55). A. W. Verity understands that there are three Graces—Euphrosyne, Aglaia, and Thalia—but, like Osgood, he dissociates them from the seasons, asserting that they "personified the refinements and elevated joys of life" (460). This is one of the passages by which Evert Mordecai Clark (139) links Milton's garden with the Abyssinian paradise of Amara, where, according to Samuel Purchas in *Purchas His Pilgrimage* 565, "the Graces and Muses are Actors."

Beyond the challenge of pursuing parallels or sources for Milton's presentation of the classical deities in this passage is the basic consideration of how these mythological references serve the purposes of the poem. While the early nineteenth century editor H. Stebbing insists, "The graces of mythological allusion were never more beautifully employed than in the whole of this passage" (95), J. B. Broadbent expresses some doubt about its success. Reflecting on G. Wilson Knight's objections to the description of the garden, Broadbent concedes that fancy and allegory "do intrude with the dance of Pan with the Hours and Graces..., and we feel it to be out of place, like cherubs in a portrait. And Mr. Knight is perhaps fair so far as he complains that the artifice outweighs the nature. But the balance appears to be struck more evenly when we know about the geographical background; and the final result is more justly appreciated when we recognize the problems involved" ("Milton's Paradise" 170). See G. Wilson Knight in **205–87**. Also see John R. Knott in **267**.

267. *dance:* Hume, understanding the Graces and Hours as "beautiful Seasons," diminishes the image of the dance in his annotation, "all things seem to dance" (140), but later editors and critics sharpen the image. In his 1795 edition of *PR*, Charles Dunster (10) associates this dance with "the circling hours" in *PR* 1.57. Oscar Kuhns (3) finds a parallel in Dante's *Purgatorio* 29.4, while Verity (459) suggests a connection with the dance of the Virtues in *Purgatorio* 29.121–29. In addition to referring this sequence to the visual arts, specifically Botticelli's *Primavera,* Verity (460) cross-references "While the jolly hours lead on propitious *May*" in Milton's first sonnet, and points to William Collins's similar figure in "Eclogue the Third. Abra; or, the Georgian Sultana" 3.39–50 (*Works* 11). For Knott, the dance that unites and animates the mythological figures makes the passage remarkably successful: "Most references to eternal spring in accounts of the earthly paradise or the golden age are only slightly more elaborate than the Ovidian assertion, '*Ver erat aeternum*' ['spring was everlasting' (*Metamorphoses* 1.107)]. But Milton has 'Universal Pan / Knit with the Graces and the Hours' (IV, 266–67) lead on 'Eternal Spring' in a graceful dance that complements the harmony of trembling leaves and the song of the birds and is an expression of the vibrant life of the Garden as well as an emblem of order" ("Symbolic Landscape" 40). Hughes (*Complete Poems* 284) refers to the dance of "The Graces and the rosy-bosom'd Hours" in *Mask* 986.

268–85. This catalog of pastoral places that can compare only negatively to the Edenic garden consists of either four or five sections, depending on how one reads the *and* of 273. Those five sections are 268–72 ("Not that faire field / Of *Enna*"), 272–73 ("nor that sweet Grove / Of *Daphne*"), 273–74 ("and th' inspir'd / *Castalian* Spring"), 275–79 ("nor that *Nyseian* Ile"), and 280–84 ("nor…Mount *Amara*"). The overall structure of this extended series of similes has drawn the attention of James Whaler and Alastair Fowler, both of whom cross-reference similar constructions in *PL*. Fowler contends that the four streams mentioned in this sequence are "corresponding to, and as it were replacing, the four undescribed rivers of Paradise (233). Indeed, the two sets have a member in common: the Nile, which was almost invariably identified with Gihon, the second Biblical river." Fowler also explains, "the first comparison introduces a lunar deity, the second solar and lunar deities together…and the third a solar deity; while the fourth comparison refers to the equinoctial line, and thus to the just balancing of the domains of sun and moon, day and night" (628). For Whaler ("Compounding" 315), this block of similes is comparable to those at 159–71 and 183–93, "in which one or more members are complex"; furthermore, Whaler points out in a later footnote (317n1), that this is one of only two simile groups in *PL* that begin with a negative, the other being 11.213–15 and 216–20. Both scholars also survey earlier epics for structural precedents, Fowler (628) comparing this list of "dismissive comparisons" with a similar one in Spenser's *The Faerie Queene* 2.12.52. Attention to the complex development of the similes more tightly restricts Whaler's search for precedents, however. While finding that neither Homer nor Virgil offered a model for Milton, Whaler locates "something of the richness in grouping" (318) demonstrated in 268–85 in Lucan's *The Civil War* 10.474–77, which describes the plot to assassinate Caesar in Alexandria: "Neither the land of Thessaly, nor the barren realm of Juba, nor Pontus with the unnatural warfare of Pharnaces, nor the region round which cold Hiberus flows, nor the savage Syrtis—no country has ventured on such crimes as Egypt, with all her luxury, has committed."

Much earlier, not the form but the content of this series of similes earns Richard Bentley's disapproval, but the eighteenth century editor's view has gained few supporters, for nearly all other critics have variously praised this passage. To Milton's extended denial that any mythic garden could compare with the biblical garden, Bentley inquires, "Why, sir, who would suspect they could; though you had never told us of it?" (115). Pearce dismisses Bentley's remark as "of small weight" (120), but Empson two centuries later answers the early editor's mocking question: "A man who had given his life to the classics might easily have suspected it; it is to Milton that the pagan beauty of these gardens has appealed more richly than the perfection of the garden of God" (*Some Versions* 165). See Robert Martin Adams (114) on Empson on Bentley. Two of the first to admire the entire catalog of negative comparisons as a unit are the Richardsons, who explain that the place-names are "Places Celebrated by the Ancients for their Great Beauty, the Idea of which adds to the Pleasure of the Reader at the same time as it more Strongly Paints the Paradise the Poet has an idea of, and endeavours to Communicate" (151). Among the twentieth century critics, both Arnold Stein, who, like the Richardsons, praises Milton's entire description of the garden in Book 4, and John Peter, who, like L. C. Knights, finds that same description "not deeply felt" (147), speak admiringly of the effect produced by the threat contained within this celebration of paradisal beauty. Stein sees the series of negative comparisons as a reminder of the inevitability of the Fall: "We are never allowed to rest with the beauties of the sensuous paradise, for they, like the self-consciousness, are only a necessary part of the whole image. There is always the pressure of time and the larger plan. That fair field of Enna is not introduced with reluctant coyness, for the sake of the fine lines alone—not with Satan watching, ready to act out the archetype of the myth" (71). Furthermore, Stein explains, "Milton is no more committed to keeping the Garden pure of these invasions from time than Adam is, to whom the prospect of Paradise without Eve seems living 'again in these wilde Woods forlorn'" (72). John Peter's dissatisfaction with Milton's efforts to present the garden in 131–235 evaporates here: "Even when the Proserpine metaphor has passed, and the analogies are scaled back to a more formal level, with encrustations of proper nouns, the undertones in the verse continue faintly but audibly. The '*Nyseian* Ile' and 'Mount *Amara*' (275, 281), for example, are not merely colourful place-names; they denote localities of refuge or retirement, havens of safety, and thus preserve the air of menace that Satan's presence and the reference to 'gloomie *Dis*' have both aroused" (89). C. S. Lewis similarly responds to what Peter refers to as "the undertones" in this sequence. Downplaying both the geographical details and the mythological fine points, Lewis finds that the catalog of place-names is fundamentally evocative: "Unlearned readers may reassure themselves. In order to get the good out of this simile it is not at all necessary to look up these places in the notes, nor has pedantry any share in the poet's motives for selecting them. All that we need to know the poet tells us. The one was a river island and the other a high mountain, and both were *hiding places*. If only we will read on, asking no questions, the sense of Eden's secrecy…will come out of that simile and enrich what Milton is all the time trying to evoke in each reader—the consciousness of Paradise" (43). Robert Martin Adams develops a similar understanding, arguing that such lists are "a part of Milton's poetical equipment and not by any means a minor part" (186).

Triggering Lewis's declaration that "it is not at all necessary to look up these places in the notes" is the number of studies that have focused on glossing the place-names in 268–85. Indeed, such scholarship has dominated the criticism prompted by this sequence, and the sources identified are involved with geography—both ancient and early modern, and both cartographical and literary—as well as with mythology, for as Arnold Williams reports of the Renaissance commentaries on Genesis regarding the location of the garden, "Commentators of the Renaissance wanted some location of which they could draw a map, some country about which they knew or could learn something" (*Common Expositor* 98). Hume (142), for example, not only cites dozens of classical literary texts as he annotates what John Peter later describes as the "encrustations of proper nouns" (89) in each of the five sections but also refers "that sweet Grove / Of *Daphne*" (272–73) to a map by Abraham Ortelius, and Hume's appreciation for the authority of such nonliterary sources is vigorously embraced by a number of those twentieth century critics who also bring maps to bear on the question of the garden's location as delineated in 209–14. One such scholar is George Wesley Whiting who, like Hume, reports that in Ortelius's *Theatrum Orbis Terrarum* are to be located all of the sites named in this passage (*Milton's Literary Milieu* 108). Also see Hilaire Belloc on Milton's use of place-names in **159–65**.

268–72. Recalling that Proserpine, the daughter of Jupiter and Ceres, was "carried away by *Pluto* the Subterranean God, as she was gathering Flowers on the top of *Enna*, a beauteous Plain, on an Hill not far from a City of the same Name in the middle of the island of Sicily," Hume (141–42) begins the work of identifying analogs or sources, citing the key Ovidian passage, *Metamorphoses* 5.391–571; quoting Claudian's *Rape of Proserpine* 1.101–03; and referring to Cicero's version of the story in his "Against Verres" 2.4.48.106 and 2.4.50.111. While Newton (249), glancing at the reference to "Proserpine's wrath" in Spenser's *The Faerie Queene* 1.2.2, emphasizes that the stress should be on the second syllable of *Proserpine,* Todd ([1842], 2:68) adds Euripides's *Ion* 889 to Hume's Ovidian reference. Twentieth century scholars have vigorously maintained the pursuit of Milton's sources. At the century's beginning, Charles Grosvenor Osgood (20) places the *Homeric Hymn to Demeter* (*The Homeric Hymns* 288–325) behind Hume's reference to Ovid's *Metamorphoses,* and also points to Ovid's *Fasti* 4.421 and Hesiod's *Theogony* 453, 912. In addition, Osgood cross-references *Proserpin* with 9.396. Allan Gilbert (*Geographical Dictionary* 115) quotes or cites Diodorus's *The Library of History* 5.3 and Claudian, in addition to Ovid and Cicero. George W. Whiting (*Milton's Literary Milieu* 108–09), as pointed out in **268–85**, brings cartography and travel literature to bear on the "faire field / Of *Enna*" passage, pointing to Ortelius's map of Sicily in his *Theatrum Orbis Terrarum* fol. xxiii, where a lake surrounded by trees bears a legend identifying it as the "umbilicus Siciliae" ("navel of Sicily"), where Proserpine was raped by Pluto. Whiting also quotes from a description of the island and lake in George Sandys's *A Relation of a Journey,* which identifies Sicily as the home of Ceres and Proserpine. Robert Ralston Cawley concedes that Ortelius "may have played his part," but argues that here, as in 2.1019–22, "Homer so dominates the passage that there seems scarcely to be room for anyone else" (108). In his edition of Milton (*Complete Poems* 284), Merritt Y. Hughes repeats the earlier references to Ovid's *Metamorphoses* and the Homeric *Hymn to Demeter,* but also reminds readers of Milton's reference to the myth in a letter to Charles Diodati in 1637: "Ceres never sought her daughter Proserpina...with greater ardor than I do this idea of Beauty" (Patterson, *Works* 12:26). Also see Le Comte in **271**. In "Variorum," however, Hughes recalls Oscar Kuhns's earlier study of Dante's influence on Milton to claim that "the key to Milton's allusion here is Dante's exclamation to Mathilde [*Purgatorio* 28.49–51] when he meets her with her arms full of the flowers of a symbolic spring in the Earthly Paradise and compares her to Proserpine when she lost her flowers of spring and at the same time was lost to her mother." See Kuhns 3. Starnes and Talbert, who express reservations about *Metamorphoses* 5 as a source because "in Ovid Proserpina is gathering lilies in a beautiful 'grove'; no field is mentioned," contend that the opening remarks about Proserpine in Carolus Stephanus's (Charles Estienne's) *Dictionarum Historicum, Geographicum, Poeticum* 367 are "more suggestive of the content and phrasing in Milton's allusion" (276).

Samuel Johnson does not contribute to this growing list of the sources or allusions involved in Milton's "faire field / Of *Enna*" passage but rather takes the occasion to condemn Milton's pedantry in one of the best-known sections in "Milton." Granting that "sublimity" is the "characteristic quality" (286) of *PL,* Johnson finds that "reality was a scene too narrow for his [Milton's] mind" (287) and that Milton is consequently more indebted to literature than to nature as he describes Eden: "his images and descriptions of the scenes and operations of Nature do not seem to be always copied from original form, nor to have the freshness, raciness, and energy of immediate observation. He saw Nature, as Dryden expresses it, *through the spectacles of books;* and on most occasions calls learning to his assistance. The garden of Eden brings to his mind the vale of *Enna,* where Proserpine was gathering flowers" (287). In *Of Dramatick Poesie,* Dryden, of course, makes no reference to Milton, but, comparing Shakespeare and Ben Jonson, praises Shakespeare because "he was naturally learn'd; he needed not the spectacles of Books to read Nature; he look'd inwards, and found her there" (*Works* 17:55). Dryden's memorable phrasing and Johnson's appropriation of it recur to Southey and Landor as they discuss Milton, and they as soundly condemn Dryden as they condemn Johnson. Southey appeals to Landor: "You will not countenance the critic, nor Dryden whom he quotes, in saying that Milton 'saw Nature through the spectacles of books.'" Landor replies: "Unhappily both he and Dryden saw Nature from between the houses of Fleet-street. If ever there was a poet who knew her well, and described her in all her loveliness, it was Milton" (4:51). At the end of the nineteenth century, Mary Steward Leather (407) aims all her dismay at Dryden, recalling the lament of the blind Milton in *Sonnet* 19, and accusing Dryden of having "forgotten those lines which tell of the approach of Satan to Eden, that glorious description of evening in the fourth book, and those scattered similes pregnant with observation" (407).

Johnson's passing disapproval of Milton's "Not that faire field / Of *Enna*" has gathered no substantial support from later critics; in fact, a rare critical consensus lavishes praise instead on this sequence. Keats, for example, identifies the Ceres passage as one of "very extraordinary beauty in the Paradise Lost . . . unexampled elsewhere." It is Keats's opinion that this passage, as well as *Lyc* 57–59, is "exclusively Miltonic without the shadow of another mind ancient or Modern"

(264). Perhaps better known is Matthew Arnold's designation of 270–71 as one of the "touchstones" of English poetry, a passage that "possesses the very highest poetical quality" (20). In the twentieth century, David Daiches, recalling Arnold's comment, is one of many modern critics to ponder the quality of the power of these few lines: "It is in the combined suggestion of infinite beauty and of foreboding and loss that Milton manages to capture the plangent sense of transience which accompanies all postlapsarian response to beauty, and thus even while describing a prelapsarian scene he introduces overtones of the Fall. And more than that—these overtones emphasize a paradox that lies at the very heart of *Paradise Lost*, namely that only after one has lost something ideally lovely can its true worth be known, so that the Fall is necessary that we may pursue the ideal, in the teeth of all the obstacles that now confront us, with a deeper sense of its desirability" (152–53). Daiches's analysis resounds in the remarks of others. Claiming that the association between Eden and Enna is "the most beautiful and famous of all Milton's similes," Douglas Bush points to "the pathos of familiarity in 'all that pain,' the implied likeness between the beauty and the fate of Proserpine and motherless Eve, and the pervasive and suggestive economy and understatement" (*"Paradise Lost" in Our Time* 101). Cf. Bush, *English Literature* 406–07. In *Mythology and the Renaissance Tradition,* Bush again discusses this passage, identifying the association between Eden and Enna as the "supreme example" of "Milton's compression of a whole Ovidian tale into an epic simile," and Bush contends that, while such mythological allusions "suggest grandeur, or remoteness, or both," they also "often achieve at the same time the opposite effect; in a poem depicting heaven and hell and earth and infinite space even bookish associations may relate the unknown and indescribable to the familiar and accepted" (282). For Christopher Ricks, Milton's lines create one of the two descriptions of paradise that "soar above all Milton's other accounts of it; and what they have in common is that neither directly confronts Paradise" (148). Ricks explains: "It is, I believe, the very fact that Milton's gaze is not directly on Paradise which makes these lines among the most haunting he ever wrote. And the *not* of 'Not that faire field…' is itself an opportunity for Milton to release his full feelings while still gaining all the advantages of the oblique. It seems to me similarly remarkable that if asked to point to the most moving account of Eve in the poem, it is once again these lines that I would quote. Eve is never more powerfully and tragically herself than when Milton glimpses her as Proserpin" (148–49). Elmer Edgar Stoll expresses his sense of the quality of this sequence by adapting Tennyson's metaphor identifying Milton as "the organ voice of England." Stoll claims that in these lines, as well as 256, 730–31, "The organ becomes the flute, or rather, it is the same instrument, played with the softer stops" ("From the Superhuman" 9). See Tennyson's "Milton" (*Poems* 2:651–52) and Tennyson in **205–87**.

As the "faire field / Of *Enna*" reference hauntingly casts the postlapsarian world like a shadow over paradise, a number of critics have pursued the point Ricks and Bush mention, the way Eve's inevitable association with Proserpine affects Milton's presentation of her. A. W. Verity suggests this line of thought by cross-referencing 9.432: "Her self, thought fairest unsupported Flour." Balachandra Rajan notes, "When Eve is compared to Proserpine we know that she will be gathered by Satan as Proserpine was gathered by Dis" (*"Paradise Lost" and the Seventeenth Century Reader* 124). Isabel Gamble MacCaffrey cross-references the association between Eve and Ceres in 9.395–96, as well as the description of Eve as "fairest unsupported Flour" (432), and explains that both the Christian and the Greek myths "record the death of innocence at the hands of Hell's forces" (122). Maud Bodkin focuses on the archetypal pattern whereby Satan "struggle[s] upwards from his tremendous cavern below the realm of Chaos, to waylay the flower-like Eve in her walled Paradise and make her an inmate of his Hell, even as Pluto rose from beneath the earth to carry off Proserpine from her flowery meadow" (97–98). Glancing at Tillyard's reading of Eve's fall, Bodkin also solidly acknowledges, however, that Milton's Eve is not simply flowerlike innocence, but "a responsible being, duly warned of danger, and in her act illustrating not so much the pathos of human destiny as the culpable 'levity and shallowness' of the human mind. It is true that this view of Eve is present in the poem, emphasized by certain passages, and logically inconsistent with the image elsewhere communicated of the helpless victim, piteous as Proserpine or Adonis. Yet such inconsistency in poetry will not surprise us—where feeling, not logic, dictates the blending and alternation of the many meanings latent in the theme to which the poet's sensibility responds" (166). William Empson also develops the complications in the Eve-Proserpine association, finding in it "implications against Eve," who, like Proserpine, "was captured by the king of Hell, but she then became queen of it, became Sin, then, on Milton's scheme; Eve, we are to remember, becomes an ally of Satan when she tempts Adam to eat with her. Daphne was not seduced by Apollo as Eve was by Satan (both affairs involve desire, a devil, and a tree); Eve might really have done better than a mere pagan nymph; one must class her with the consenting Amalthea. And all the references to guarding children remind us that children were the result of the fall" (*Some Versions* 165–66). Robert Martin Adams, however, rejects this, along with other Empsonian readings, insisting, "Proserpina did not become Sin in any sense Milton would have recognized, because she could still come back to earth for six of the 12 months, and when she came, she brought summer-time and the flowering of the earth; because she is never associated with the active seduction or punishment of sinners, but only with alleviating their misfortunes as a fellow victim; and because if she became Sin, there would be no reason for Ceres to look for her so long and so hard" (119). Adams then glances ahead to Milton's mention of "*Daphne* by *Orontes*" (4.273): "Empson suggests that because she resisted Apollo, Milton introduced her to the detriment of Eve, who fell to Satan. But note how this argument trips over the preceding one regarding Proserpina. Eve is like Proserpina, to whom something terrible happened; she is worse than Daphne, who came off fairly well. The interpretations could just as easily be reversed. Eve is better than Proserpina because at least she never had to marry Satan, and she is like Daphne in that, saved by divine favor, she was not really, irrevocably seduced" (120). Finally, Adams points out, "Milton is really comparing groves, not people" (120). Continuing the scholarly exercise of source study, A. Bartlett Giamatti develops the complications of the Eve-Prosperpine association. Giamatti recognizes that Milton employs two different versions of the Proserpine story to two different effects. "Milton establishes the superiority of this garden over Henna, and other places, and obliquely compares Eve to Proserpine, the flower among flowers snatched away by the King of the Underworld. It is the ancient conceit . . . which goes back originally to the *Hymn to Demeter.* Here the veiled allusion, developed fully in Book IX, is sad rather than sinister. The classical Proserpine casts a shadow on Eve's fate, rather than her character, while the suspicious Proserpine echoes derive from Spenser's Garden of Proserpina [*The Faerie Queene* 2.7.51–55]. . . . But it is interesting to see how Milton uses all the Proserpines of other gardens for his portrait of this woman in the garden in Eden" (319).

Finally, Thomas Kranidas refers the Proserpine image to the imminent entrance of both Adam and Eve: "There is an extraordinary exercise of 'practical' myth in creating the immediate perspective for the first sight of Adam and Eve. The sensuousness is super-biological, a tightening of the richness of God's gifts which separates the pre-lapsarian garden from gardens. But biology glimmers through in 'Grazing the tender herb' [253] or in the lovely reminiscence of Proserpina: 'Her self a faire Flowre by gloomie *Dis* / Was gatherd, which cost *Ceres* all that pain' (IV, 270–71). This is the most broadly relevant of the classical allusions, but all of them contribute to the perspective of richness and distance from which the reader first views the couple. And the last-minute reminder of Satan's framing eye contributes further to the objectifying of our first view of our parents" (138).

268.   *Eternal Spring:* citing Virgil's *Georgics* 2.338–42 and Ovid's *Metamorphoses* 1.107–08, Patrick Hume asserts, "All the Poets favour the opinion of the Worlds Creation in the Spring" (140–41), and later critics continue to extend that list of poets. In his study of Dante's influence on Milton, Oscar Kuhns (3) refers the notion of spring being the only season before the biblical Fall to Dante's *Purgatorio* 28.143, a parallel that A. W. Verity (459) mentions, as he also notices the eternal spring notion in Milton's youthful *El* 5. Allan H. Gilbert ("Milton and the *Aminta* 97) associates Milton's "Eternal Spring" with "primavera eterna" from the chorus ending act 1 of Tasso's *Aminta*. While Merritt Y. Hughes (*Complete Poems* 284) points to Spenser's Garden of Adonis, described in *The Faerie Queene* 3.6.42, as a place of eternal spring, and John R. Knott agrees, Knott also brings Spenser's Bower of Bliss, *The Faerie Queene* 2.12.42–82, to bear upon Milton's presentation of paradise ("Symbolic Landscape" 39). Also see Knott in **205–87**.

Several twentieth century critics pursue the theological, rather than the poetic, underpinnings of the eternal-spring topos. Arnold Williams (*Common Expositor* 63) comments on the famous rabbinical debate about the season of the creation of the world: Rabbi Eliezer arguing for spring, and Rabbi Josuah for fall. "One encounters this topic fairly frequently in Renaissance literature, sometimes as an example of fruitless search, as by Browne [*Pseudodoxia Epidemica* 6.2 (*Works* 2:410–12)]." Alastair Fowler claims Christian tradition for the notion of the world being created in the spring, explaining, "It was supported by typological argument ('Christ was crucified the same day that Adam was created'); by appeal to tradition (when Moses instituted the custom of reckoning Nisan—March / April—the 'first' month, he was returning to primitive usage; see *Exod.* xii 2); and by numerical calculations based on literalistic applications of Scripture" (628–29). Leland Ryken develops his understanding of Milton's apocalyptic vision by reference to the mystic oxymoron of the paradisal seasons: "The entire contradictory fusion of spring and harvest is best understood as an attempt to portray apocalyptic reality through a technique of mystic oxymoron" (93).

271. Edward S. Le Comte (*Yet Once More* 117) finds this line "foreshadowed with remarkable closeness" in Milton's September 23, 1637, letter to Diodati: "Ceres never sought her daughter Proserpina…with greater ardor than I do this idea of Beauty" (Patterson, *Works* 12:26). Also see Merritt Y. Hughes in **268–72**.

272–74. More broadly indicated in **268–85**, Milton's poetry intersects with geography in this second of the three similes within this extended series of similes. The place-names are identified and located by means of literary sources, as well as maps, but the *and* that links the "*Castalian* Spring" to the "sweet Grove / Of *Daphne*" creates some uncertainty about their geographical relationship. As so often, Patrick Hume does the spadework. Crediting Sozomen's *Ecclesiastical History* 19.5, Hume explains, "*Daphne* was the most celebrated and delicious Suburbs of *Antioch,* the Capital of *Syria,* or rather of the East, seated on both the Banks of *Orontes:* It was a vast Grove of Lawrels…intermixt with tall Cypress-Trees, defying the Suns piercing Rays, under whose thick Shade nevertheless, the Earth was Luxuriant in Flowers, it was full of Fountains, and had one supposed to derive its Waters from the *Castalian* Spring, and endued with the same Power of promoting the Spirit of Divination in its Drinkers, as well as that at *Delphos.*" Anticipating George Wesley Whiting by a couple of centuries, Hume points out that Abraham Ortelius "has an exact Delineation of this bounteous Grove in the end of his Maps." See *Theatrum Orbis Terrarum* fol. xxxvii. Then, as he quotes Juvenal's *Satires* 3.62 and Lucan's *The Civil War* 6.51, Hume describes *Orontes* as "a beautiful River of *Syria,* springing out of Mount *Libanus,* and running to *Antioch.*" With Virgil's *Georgics* 3.292–93 and Horace's *Odes* 3.4.61 as his authorities, Hume proceeds to locate the "*Castalian* Spring" at the foot of Parnassus, and explains that it was "so named of Castalia, a Virgin Mistress of Apollo, turned into this cold Stream, for refusing his Flames." Finally, Hume reports that the fountain bestowed the power of inspiration on those who washed their eyes in it, as well as those who drank of it (142). While Hume writes that one of the fountains in the grove of Daphne by Orontes was "supposed to derive its Waters from the Castalian Spring," the Richardsons, drawing attention to the connective between them, the *and* of 273, insist that the "*Castalian* Spring" is "Not that known One at the Foot of *Parnassus,* but that of the Grove of *Daphne,*" which most famously "Foretold *Hadrian's* Advancement to the Empire." The Richardsons firmly explain that, "if *Milton* had meant the Other *Castalian* Spring, he would have said *Nor* instead of *And;* besides it would have been opposing Paradise to a Spring, whereas the water'd Garden is oppos'd to a Grove and Spring together" (151–52). Paterson obviously accepts that understanding, but while Hume explains that washing one's eyes at the "*Castalian* Spring" or drinking of it promoted "the Spirit of Divination," Paterson attributes the power of inspiration to the spring's sound: "Because the pleasant Sound of it gliding down that Hill, elevated the Imagination, [it] was said to inspire the *Poets* of Old. Here is another of this *Name* by the grove of *Daphne* at *Antioch,* which foretold *Hadrian's* Advancement to the *Empire. Milton* seems to mean this *Spring*" (306–07). Among the moderns, Charles Grosvenor Osgood refers the story of Daphne and Apollo to Ovid's *Metamorphoses* 1.452–567 but, citing Pausanius's *Description of Greece* 8.20.2, notes that the legend was relocated on the banks of the Orontes and the gardens of Daphne at Antioch. Osgood traces exquisite descriptions of the gardens to a variety of ancient writers but follows Hume to Sozomen, and similarly reports that the prophetic powers of the "*Castalian* Spring" were equated with those at Delphi. Osgood brings even more complication to the procedure to be followed by those seeking divine help at the spring: "on one occasion a prophecy was obtained by dipping in the spring a laurel-leaf, which came forth bearing a prophetic inscription. Accounts seem generally to point to an utterance of some sort from the spring itself, rather than from a priest of the spring" (9). In addition to Sozomen, quoted at length by Hume, Allan H. Gilbert (*Geographical Dictionary* 98–99) identifies the "sweet Grove / Of *Daphne* by *Orontes*" by citing Samuel Purchas's *Purchas His Pilgrimage* 71, and by quoting Libanius, Oration 11.235. Cross-referencing 9.80, Gilbert identifies the Orontes as "The chief river of Syria, rising in the Anti-Lebanons, and flowing into the Mediterranean" (221). Cross-referencing *El* 4.32 and 5.9, Gilbert identifies the "*Castalian* Spring" as "a fountain at Delphi, the water of which was used for purification in connection with the worship of Apollo there. It was supposed to impart poetic inspiration to those who drank its waters" (*Geographical Dictionary* 76). Like Gilbert, also returning to territory covered by Hume, George Wesley Whiting refers the "sweet Grove / Of *Daphne* by *Orontes*" to Ortelius xxxvii who not only presents a chart of the grove, but also describes it, detailing its trees, as does Sozomen (*Milton's Literary Milieu* 110).

275–79. For these geographical and mythological references, DeWitt T. Starnes and Ernest William Talbert (237) suggest that Milton first consulted a Renaissance dictionary and then proceeded to the primary sources there cited, but centuries earlier, Patrick Hume establishes Diodorus Siculus as that original source, and Hume's emphasis on Diodorus is maintained by most later editors and critics, as are the topics of discussion that Hume emphasizes: the "*Nyseian* Ile," the mythological pedigree of "old *Cham*," and the lineage of "Young *Bacchus*."

that Nyseian Ile: referring to descriptions of the island in the *Homeric Hymn to Dionysus* 8–9 (*The Homeric Hymns* 450–51), Ovid's *Metamorphoses* 3.314–15, Sir Walter Ralegh's *The History of the World* 1.6.5, as well as Diodorus, Hume is more dedicated to setting forth the island's pastoral beauties than plotting its geographical location, which becomes the stronger interest for the early twentieth century critics. Crediting Diodorus's *Library of History* 2.5 as his source, Hume explains that from the river Triton, "*Pallas took her Name Tritonia, of her appearing first on its Banks.*" The island itself, Hume reports, "for its Fertility, the Goodness of the Air and Soil, and for the Production of the choicest and most delicious Fruits, the coolest Fountains and most delightful Shades, as well as for abundance of the choicest Vines naturally growing there, was extreamly celebrated." Hume also relates that "in recompence of her Favours, her beloved *Jupiter* made [Amalthea] Queen of a fruitful Country, which lying in the shape of a Bulls Horn, gave occasion to the Proverb *Amaltheae Cornu*" (143). David Masson brings more attention to issues of geography, and later critics such as Elbert N. S. Thompson, Allan H. Gilbert, and George Wesley Whiting maintain his focus. Masson points out, "There were not a few places named Nysa in the ancient world; but the particular Nyseian isle here meant seems to be the island in the lake Tritonis about the middle of the northern coast of Africa, where the river Triton flows from the lake into the lesser Syrtis. Here, according to the account adopted in the text—but, according to other accounts, at Nysa in Ethiopia, to the south of Egypt—the infant Bacchus (*Dionysos*) was educated" (*Poetical Works* 3:173). Laura E. Lockwood points to Abraham Ortelius's 1624 edition of *Theatrum Orbis Terrarum* xxxvi, where, on a map titled "Africae Propriae Tabula" and dated 1590, she finds "the river Triton with the Isle of Nysa clearly marked" (86). Elbert N. S. Thompson's study of the old maps and the old geographers supports Masson's and Lockwood's conclusions (163–64).

Gilbert (*Geographical Dictionary* 214–15) follows Hume and others to reproduce the lengthy description of the "*Nyseian* Ile" from Diodorus, but commenting on "the River *Triton*," Gilbert brings together modern and ancient geography: "The River Triton is at present represented by a salt lake, not connected with the sea, known as the Chott el-Djerid, in modern Tunis. Its outlet has been blocked, perhaps by an upheaval of the coast. It should be noted, however, that the ancients (*e. g.*, Dionysius Periegetes, line 267) sometimes refer to it as a lake rather than a river." Gilbert (*Geographical Dictionary* 303–04) also describes Ortelius's map *Africae Propriae* earlier referenced by Lockwood. Rehearsing all the details on "that *Nyseian* Ile," Whiting adds his voice to the claim echoing down from Hume into the mid-twentieth century that Milton "esteemed and used Diodorus's *Library of History*." Whiting also supports the thesis first offered by Lockwood and then supported by Thompson and Gilbert: "All the evidence indicates that Milton was familiar with the maps in Ortelius" (Milton's *Literary Milieu* 64; also see 101, 118–19).

old Cham: as Starnes and Talbert (237) point out, Diodorus does not mention this character, although he does figure large in Ralegh's account in *History of the World* 1.6, and it is following Ralegh's similar effort that Hume tries to clarify the mingling of biblical and classical mythology in this sequence: "*Cham* or *Ham*, the second Son of *Noah*, (therefore styled Old) Peopled *Egypt* and *Lybia*, and was the most Ancient and Renowned of all the *Jupiters;* He of the *Grecians* and *Romans*, being an Upstart in Comparison, living not long before the *Trojan* War, as is evident by his Sons, *Castor, Pollux, Hercules, Sarpedon*, and others employed in it" (143). Cf. Bush, *Mythology* 278–79. James Paterson's note (307) on Amalthea's horn brings the history of Job, as well as the history of Noah, into the mix of biblical and classical references here: "*Jupiter* gave her a Horn of Plenty, which supplied every Thing. This *Fable* is taken from the Name of one of *Job's* three Daughters, called *Keren-Happuch, Heb*. The *Horn of Plenty;* whose Name the LXX translate, the *Horn* of *Amalthea*. See *Job*. 42.14." Charles Grosvenor Osgood (7) adds to the Cham-Ammon topic a discussion of the same in Samuel Bochart's *Geographiae Sacrae* 1.1, 2.1, while Robert Martin Adams, developing the wordplay Ralegh first recognizes, looks at the Cham-Ammon parallel as a pun: "As for Cham, as it is a more striking departure from the conventional forms, so it gets a line of explanation to soften, if not to obliterate the effect of a pun." Adams explains that such a pun was intended to bring out the "mythological parallel between the sons of Noah and some classical deities or heroes" (85). Also see Adams in **717**.

Young Bacchus: Hume points to the uncommon lineage of Milton's "Young *Bacchus.*" While Bacchus's parents are usually identified as Jupiter and Semele, presented, for example, in Hesiod's *Theogony* 940–41, Milton and Diodorus report that Amalthea was his mother. Furthermore, as Hume understands, Rhea is commonly known as the mother, not the wife, of Jupiter (143). Like Hume, the Richardsons realize that Bacchus "is commonly said not to be the Son of *Amalthea* but *Semele,* but *Milton* follows *Diodorus Siculus* in This, who quotes a most Ancient Poet as his Authority" (152). Keightley notes that in Diodorus's narrative, Amalthea and her son are not reported to have been hidden (*Account* 432). Masson also acknowledges that Milton follows Diodorus here (*Poetical Works* 3:173). William Empson brings his own complication to this family tree, believing that because Milton "wanted a mixed notion for demigod of the glory and fertility of the earth, because of his pagan feelings about Paradise," he therefore "adopted Bacchus in such a way as to make us confuse him with Jupiter" (*Some Versions* 166). While Merritt Y. Hughes appreciates the rationale Empson attributes to Milton, he corrects Empson (*Complete Poems* 284).

Hilaire Belloc registers no interest in Milton's sources for any of the mythological or geographical references in this entire sequence but rather labels the passage another of Milton's "frailties," explaining, "when he is giving examples of his knowledge he cannot refrain from displaying it even at the expense of his verse, putting in little asides to let the reader know that he is learned enough to gloss a bald statement" (253). Belloc also considers 344–47 and "superior" in 499 as "frailties."

277. *Lybian Jove:* Gilbert reports, "Among the ancients Libya was the name for the continent of Africa, so far as it was known, excluding Egypt. In the time of Milton it was applied to the Sahara" (*Geographical Dictionary* 173). Gilbert contends, "Milton refers to 'Libyan Jove' ('Libyc Hammon') because of the famous temple of Jupiter Ammon in the desert west of Egypt" (174).

278–79. *Florid Son / Young Bacchus:* while Hume condemns Bacchus, the "God of Wine," as "too well known all over the World, and too much worshipp'd" (143), the Richardsons acknowledge the charms of the ancient god so differently represented by the moderns: "Bacchus is here said to be *Florid, Gay,* and *Beautiful;* He is always Such with the ancients. a Fat Beast across a Tun is Modern and Barbarous" (152). Verity (460) glosses *Florid* as "ruddy, being the god of wine," and refers to Dryden's *Alexander's Feast* 42 (*Works* 7:4).

280–85. Concerns with topography and geography mark most of the critical commentary on this sequence, with early modern—rather than classical—sources providing the support for that commentary. While Todd clearly cites Purchas and Heylyn, whom twentieth century critics also agree are Milton's principal sources, Hume mentions neither, although his description of the paradisal garden atop Mt. Amara echoes that found in both early modern travel writers. Hume establishes the "*Abassin* Kings" as "the Kings of *Ethiopia*" and explains that they "kept under sweet retirement their Royal Sons on Mount *Amara,* encompass'd round with Alabaster Rocks a whole Days Journey high; though this by some was taken to be *Paradise* under the burning Line, by *Niles* long-hidden Head, but distant far from this fair *Syrian* Garden, &c. The Upper *Ethiopia,* (the Dominion of *Prester John*) was anciently called *Abassine,* of its chief River *Abas,* and *Abissinia* is the Name of one of its Kingdoms." Hume then describes Amara as "a Province about the middle of the higher *Ethiopia,* and one of the 70 petty Kingdoms formerly Tributary, and now annext to the *Abassin* Empire: In it there is a Mountain of the same name (*Hambar*), about 90 Miles in compass, and a Days Journey high, with one only access, and that impregnably fortified: The Summit of this shining Rock is adorned with many beautiful Palaces, a most delightful Place, and charming Prospect, where the Emperours Sons are carefully guarded, and as diligently educated" (143). Defining *Abassin* as "*Arab.* A *scattered People;* an antient People of *Arabia,* near *Sabaea,*" Paterson identifies these people as "the Posterity of *Joktan,* who settled afterwards in *Ethiopia Superior,* and there erected a vast Empire of 26 or 30 distinct Kingdoms." Directing readers to Gen. 10.26 and 1 Chron. 1.8, Paterson then slips from the biblical reference to modern history: "The *Portuguese* discovered this Empire to the *Europeans.* A.D. 1500. And the *Dutch* call it the Country of *Prester John,* from *Unchan Jahannan,* one of the *Emperors* of it, about A.D. 1200." In conclusion, Paterson notes, "The Inhabitants are all black, and for the most Part *Christians*" (307). Similarly identifying this geographical locale as "upper Ethiopia, or *Abyssinia,*" Todd ([1842], 2:69) firmly and specifically credits *Purchas His Pilgrimage* 743 as he quotes Samuel Purchas's description of the beautiful garden that nevertheless falls short of Milton's Edenic garden.

From Peter Heylyn's *Microcosmos* 728, however, Todd also quotes details that reappear in Milton's text: "The hill of Amara is *a dayes journey high:* on the toppe whereof are 34 pallaces, *in which the yonger sonnes of the emperour are continuallie inclosed,* to avoide sedition. They injoy there whatsoever is fit for delight or princely education, &c. This mountaine hath but one ascent up, which is *impregnablie fortified,* and was destinate to this use anno 470, or thereabouts" ([1842], 2:68–69). While several bring early modern cartography to bear on Milton's geographical details in this sequence, twentieth century critics confirm Purchas and Heylyn as Milton's principal sources. A. W. Verity, for one, writes that Heylyn "seems to have been his [Milton's] chief authority in matters relating to the customs of foreign nations and geography." Verity also points out that Amara "is rather a range of hills than a single 'mount'" (460–61). Quoting generously from both Purchas and Heylyn in his detailed study "Milton's Abyssinian Paradise," Evert Mordecai Clark concludes that, "in comparing the description of Paradise in the fourth Book of *Paradise Lost* with earlier descriptions of its Amaran predecessor, one becomes convinced that Milton, though he must have been acquainted with Abyssinian literary backgrounds extending back to the Old Testament and Homer, went no further afield for much of his descriptive material than the convenient contemporary geographers Purchas and Heylyn" (142). Not only does Verity come down for Heylyn as Milton's "chief authority" (460), but precisely juxtaposing Milton's reference to Mt. Amara with Heylyn's description, as does Todd, Robert Ralston Cawley also insists, "surely Todd was right in his original conjecture that here [280–85] we have Heylyn" (69). With Heylyn's maps, Cawley proffers even more evidence of Milton's debt to the early modern travel writer (70). George Wesley Whiting and Allan H. Gilbert also bring contemporary maps to bear on Milton's text. Whiting (*Milton's Literary Milieu* 110) reports that Mt. Amara appears on most contemporary maps of the region, including Ortelius's map of Africa, while Gilbert (*Geographical Dictionary* 208) looks at Mercator's *Atlas* 623, and also reveals that Prester John figures not only in Ortelius's map of Africa but also in his verbal account of Abyssinia (205). Grant McColley (*"Paradise Lost": An Account* 322–23) adds Heylyn's *Cosmographie* 4.53 to his *Microcosmos,* and Allan H. Gilbert (*Geographical Dictionary* 18) quotes from Elisee Reclus's *The Universal Geography* 10.175, making Cawley's conclusion that in 280–85 "Milton is reflecting primarily the work of a modern traveler" (69) seem irrefutable. Also see Elbert Thompson, "Milton's Knowledge" 164. Unconcerned with the details of the Heylyn-versus-Purchas discussion conducted by such scholars as Cawley, Gilbert, Whiting, and McColley, William Empson nevertheless shares their basic understanding of the influences at work in this sequence: "the appeal of the lines is to an idea opposite to that of seclusion. They fling into the scale against Paradise, only still to be outweighed, what many beside Milton would have thought worthy to be put to such a use; the Elizabethan excitement about distant travel and trading, about the discovery of luxury and the sources of the Nile" (*Some Versions* 166).

In conclusion, the Richardsons' (151) understanding of the many places named in 268–85 as "Places Celebrated by the Ancients for their Great Beauty, the Idea of which adds to the Pleasure of the Reader at the same time as it more Strongly Paints the Paradise the Poet has an idea of, and endeavours to Communicate," reverberates in Robert Ralston Cawley's remarks on what he calls Milton's strategy of objectification in this sequence. By *objectification*, Cawley means "the mention of some highly specific place which has the effect of bringing out the picture often with the magic of a stereoscope." To be specific, Cawley explains, "when the poet sought places to compare with his own 'Paradise of Eden,' he chose as one, 'Mount *Amara*, though this by some suppos'd true Paradise.' The very mention of little-known Amara, together with such impressive details as the Abassin Kings' issue, the shining rock and the 'whole dayes journy high,' serves to bring the picture forward in a way that makes it memorable" (129). Also see Hilaire Belloc in **159–65**.

280. *Abassin Kings:* Evert Mordecai Clark notes that in *The Principall Navigations* 7:129, Richard Hakluyt prints a letter from the queen, dated 1597, addressed to "the Emperour of Aethiopia," and thus, says Clark, "Milton's later phrase 'Abassin kings' had royal precedent" (133).

Masson (*Poetical Works* 3:173) and Verity recall Samuel Johnson's *The History of Rasselas, Prince of Abyssinia,* Verity (461) noting that Johnson, however, locates Abyssinia in a "Happy Valley" (11), not atop a mountain.

282. *under the Ethiop Line:* the *OED* B.1, quoting Milton's phrase, tenders the attributive meaning of "the equator," but it does so with a question mark. From Hume forward, however, "equator" has been the gloss of most editors and critics. Opening his annotations on 280–85 by noting that Mt. Amara "by some was taken to be *Paradise* under the burning Line," Hume again refers to the "burning Line" as he annotates this phrase: "Under the *Equinoctial* Line, the Fertility and wonderful Pleasantness of the Country, giving occasion to . . . place

Paradise under this Burning Line, formerly thought uninhabitable, though by Experience found to be fanned daily by a Cool Eastern Breeze, the Nights being temperate by the entire Interposition of the Earth, that no place is to be found on Earth that approaches nearer to the Nature, Beauty, and Abundance of *Paradise,* than this Climate. This Country of the *Abissins* lies under the Torrid Zone, stretching from the Tropick of *Cancer* beyond the *Equator. Ethiop* . . . Gr. scorch'd, and thence black and burnt, according to the Complexions of its discoloured Inhabitants" (143–44). Samuel Purchas's *Purchas His Pilgrimage* 743, as quoted by Todd, locates Mt. Amara "under the Equinoctiall line" ([1842], 2:69). According to Evert Mordecai Clark (140), Heylyn similarly locates Amara, "not much distant from the Æquator, if not plainly under it" (*Cosmographie* 4:64). Masson, who locates Mt. Amara "about half-way between the Tropic of Cancer and the Equator," concludes that "it may be said to be 'under the Ethiop line'" (*Poetical Works* 3:173). Allan H. Gilbert (*Geographical Dictionary* 118) firmly identifies "the *Ethiop* Line" as the equator. Gilbert (116) cross-references 9.64 and 10.672, although he suggests that the latter may refer to "the celestial equator," as does 3.617. Finally, Evert Mordecai Clark points out, "In locating Mount Amara on the equator, both Milton and Purchas, though wrong, were in exact accord with the best maps available up to the year of the completion of *Paradise Lost*" (144).

283. *By Nilus head:* with this detail, geography again controls criticism, although both Hume and Todd reveal more than a bit of uncertainty about that geography. Quoting Lucan's *The Civil War* 10.282–85, Hume notes that Sostric, Cambyses, Alexander the Great, and others had unsuccessfully sought the "Fountains of the *Nile.*" Hume then follows these classical references with Jean de Thevenot's narrative (1.240) about the Ethiopian ambassador he had met at Grand Cairo who reported that the "*Nile* has his Head in a great Well, casting up its Water very high out of the Ground in a large Plain called *Ovembromma* in the Province of *Ago.*" (Thevenot actually reports that the "Well" or "Fountain," not the "Plain," is called Ovembromma.) Citing P. Joannes Baptista Scortia's *De Natura et Incremento Nili* 133–42, Hume adds, "It is on all Hands confirmed, that the Cause of the *Niles* Annual Inundation, is from the excessive Rains that fall in *Ethiopia* for three Months together in their Winter, but the *Egyptian* Summer. . . . Of *Ethiopia* being the Native Country of the *Nile,* and of its rising by Rains, the Ancients were of Opinion, though not well assured"

(144). Samuel Purchas, whose *Purchas His Pilgrimage* 743 Todd quotes, colors his geography with poetry as he presents a different understanding of the relationship between the Nile and Mt. Amara. Purchas explains that the plain on top of Mt. Amara yields "a pleasant spring which passeth through all that plaine, paying his tributes to every garden that will exact it, and making a lake, whence issueth a river, which, having from these tops espied *Nilus,* never leaves seeking to find him, whom he cannot leave both to seeke and finde, that by his direction and conveyance hee may together with him present himselfe before the father and great king of waters, the Sea" ([1842] 2:69). With David Masson (*Poetical Works* 3:173), Allan H. Gilbert (*Geographical Dictionary* 208), and Evert Mordecai Clark (144), the geography is clarified; each explains that it is the Blue Nile that has its head near Mt. Amara, although the older belief was that the true Nile did. Referencing the *Aeneid* 6.800, which celebrates the river's seven mouths, Gilbert points out that "only within the last century has the geography of the Nile become known. Knowledge of it in the time of Milton is represented by the following from Purchas [*Purchas His Pilgrimage* 852]: 'There are many fish in Nilius in the end of the Province of Goyama [in Abyssinia], where is a bottomless Lake . . . whence continually springs abundance of water, being the head of that River.' " Gilbert adds, "The map-makers of the time (e.g., Mercator, p. 623) represent the Nile as rising not in Abyssinia, but in lakes far to the south, much farther than those in which the Nile is now known to rise" (*Geographical Dictionary* 208).

enclosd with shining Rock: this description of Mt. Amara recalls the discussion about the two different mountains of paradise in 131–48, but the overriding concern to identify Milton's source has dominated critical attention. Describing the "shining Rock" as "Alabaster," Hume, however, rather obviously associates this description of Mt. Amara with 543–44 describing the Edenic garden's gate as "a Rock / Of Alablaster" (143). Grant McColley, considering Milton's sources as he attempts to date the epic's composition, reports that both Samuel Purchas in *Purchas His Pilgrimage* 565–66 and Peter Heylin in *Cosmographie* 4:64 similarly describe the rockiness of Mt. Amara, but McColley leans toward Heylin as Milton's source (*"Paradise Lost": An Account* 322–23). Developing McColley's acknowledgment, Evert Mordecai Clark (139) quotes extensively from both Purchas and Heylin, including Purchas's report that Mt. Amara "is situate in a great Plaine, largely extending it selfe every way, without other hill in the same for the space of 30. leagues, the forme thereof round and circular, the height such, that it is a daies work to ascend from the foot to the top; round about the rocke is cut so smooth, and even, without any unequall swellings, that it seemeth to him that stands beneath, like a high wall, whereon the heaven is as it were propped: & at the top it is over-hanged with rocks, jutting forth of the sides the space of a mile, bearing out like mushromes, so that it is impossible to ascend it, or by ramming with earth, battering with canon, scaling, or otherwise to winn it." While Robert Ralston Cawley rules the controversy about sources as "perhaps unnecessary" (69), he includes the shining quality of the rock that is Mt. Amara as one of a number of elements that make it more likely that Heylyn, rather than Purchas, is Milton's source here (70).

284. *A whole days journy high:* this is an element of the description of Mt. Amara in both Purchas (*Purchas His Pilgrimage* 565–66) and Heylyn (*Microcosmos* 728; *Cosmographie* 4:64). Todd quotes Heylyn ([1842], 2:69), and Evert Mordecai Clark (139) provides the passage from Purchas. Like "shining Rock" (283), this phrase is considered by Grant McColley as he attempts to date the epic's composition. McColley writes that both phrases "apparently were drawn from a work published in 1652, the *Cosmography* of Peter Heylyn." But, McColley acknowledges, Heylyn's reference to Amara being "a day's journey high" had earlier appeared in Heylyn's *Microcosmos,* and the "shining Rock" item "conceivably, although improbably, could have been developed from Purchas. In any event, Milton had sufficient time to have used the *Cosmography* in the 1652–53 period." McColley, it seems, overlooks "it is a daies work to ascend from the foot to the top" in Purchas's 1613 *Pilgrimage* (*"Paradise Lost": An Account* 322–23). Robert Ralston Cawley, similarly deciding for Heylyn as Milton's principal source, focuses attention on this phrase (69–70).

    but wide remote: "Far removed: *Remotus,* Lat. *Assyrian* Garden, planted in *Eden,* afterwards call'd *Assyria,* bordering on *Mesopotamia*" (Hume 144).

285–99. The topic of visualizing Eden is reintroduced with the entrance of Adam and Eve, and again there is an intriguing uncertainty as to the identity of the seeing eye. See **205–87.** Irene Samuel insists that we "behold it [Eden], not through the distorting lenses of Satan's eyes—that would be to mar the place fatally in advance—but over his shoulder. We see what is there to behold as he cannot; he sees 'undelighted all delight' (IV, 286); we can allow ourselves delight alloyed only by our sense of what lies ahead because of his presence. Among the poetic achievements of this Eden is that it almost makes us forget the danger" ("*Paradise Lost* as Mimesis" 20). Insisting that "we are seeing Eden through Satan's eyes," Michael Wilding, however, explains, "We never do—and never could—see innocence unimpinged by evil" (81). James H. Sims (*Bible* 24) focuses more on the identity of the eye visualizing Adam and Eve than the identity of the eye visualizing the garden: "The repetition of 'seemd' (ll. 290, 291, 296) keeps the reader conscious that Satan is the observer; the 'seemd' is then dropped and the poet himself speaks of the difference in the outward appearance of the pair, a difference which symbolizes man's superior nature: 'Hee for God only, shee for God in him.'" Stanley Fish notes, "Milton warns us of what is to come even before we see our first parents, although the warning goes unrecognized and unheeded." Fish, drawing attention to *nobler* (288), *new*, and *strange* (287), asks, "Nobler than what or whom? Strange and new to whom? The questions may seem unnecessary in view of the narrative situation: the creatures are new to Satan, and among them Adam and Eve stand out 'erect and tall.' But in fact it is the reader in addition to Satan who is the stranger in Paradise, although he may not realize it until the description of Eve presents a problem he can solve only at his own expense" (*Surprised* 100–01). Douglas Bush does not try to identify the eye first glimpsing Adam and Eve but speaks rather of the "tragic irony" through which they are glimpsed: "Readers who find Adam and Eve somewhat stodgy in their idyllic pastoral happiness must have missed the tragic irony through which the pair are viewed.... [We see] primeval beauty, harmony, love, and joy...after Satan has entered the garden; the contrast between present and future indeed draws expressions of pity not only from the poet but from the malignant tempter" ("*Paradise Lost*" in Our *Time* 75–76). Also see Bush, "Ironic and Ambiguous Allusion" 637.

285. *Assyrian Garden:* Newton (250) and Todd ([1842] 2:69) repeat the Richardsons' (152) claim that Milton here accepts Strabo in whose *Geography* 16.1.1 Mesopotamia is located in ancient Assyria. Hume makes a similar point explaining that Eden was "afterwards call'd *Assyria*, bordering on *Mesopotamia*" (144). Sister Mary Irma Corcoran points out that while borrowing from numerous hexameral writings, "Milton nevertheless accepted the traditional site of Paradise, the Tigris-Euphrates region, describing it as 'this Assyrian garden'" (20).

286. *kind:* "A natural group having the same origin" (*OED* 10). Cf. *kind* in 6.73.

288–1015. Milton's description of prelapsarian human life begins at this point, and the terms of the critical controversy swirling about this topic mirror those swirling about the description of the prelapsarian garden: at issue is the naturalness of Adam and Eve. Early eighteenth century critics insist upon the happiness of the first couple, but by the end of the century, Samuel Johnson is equally insistent that Adam and Eve "are without human feeling," and a similar division characterizes twentieth century responses to the topic.

The Richardsons exuberantly praise Milton's paradise (**205–87**), and that tone also marks their response to the initial presentation of prelapsarian Adam and Eve, with whom they assert that Milton establishes "an Idea of Earthly Beauty and Happiness beyond what can be found in any Other Humane Writer" (150). Similarly, Addison, having celebrated the "Exuberance of Imagination" in Milton's description of paradise (**205–87**), turns to Adam and Eve within that paradise: "there is scarce a Speech of *Adam* or *Eve* in the whole Poem, wherein the Sentiments and Allusions are not taken from this their delightful Habitation. The Reader, during their whole Course of Action, always finds himself in the Walks of *Paradise*" (*Spectator* 3:171). Insisting that Adam and Eve "seldom lose Sight of their happy Station in any thing they speak or do; and . . . their Thoughts are always *Paradisiacal*," Addison concludes that they are "exquisitely drawn, and sufficient to make the fallen Angel gaze upon them with all that Astonishment, and those Emotions of Envy, in which he is represented" (*Spectator* 3:174). Samuel Johnson, however, most soundly condemns Milton's prelapsarian Adam and Eve. In *Milton,* Johnson argues that the first man and woman are human only after they fall. Conceding they are "venerable before their fall for dignity and innocence," and "their affection is tender without weakness, and their piety sublime without presumption" (288), Johnson also asserts that Adam and Eve are without human feeling: "As human passions did not enter the world before the Fall, there is in the *Paradise Lost* little opportunity for the pathetic" (288). What Johnson considers the "inconvenience" of the "plan of *Paradise Lost*" is "that it comprises neither human actions nor human manners. The man and woman who act and suffer, are in a state which no other man or woman can ever know. The reader finds no transaction in which he can be engaged; beholds no condition in which he can by any effort of imagination place himself; he has, therefore, little natural curiosity or sympathy" (289). Finally, Johnson concludes, "The want of human interest is always felt" (290).

Early in the nineteenth century, Hazlitt registers his disagreement with Johnson, comparing Adam and Eve to the lilies of the field from Matt. 6:28, and asserting, "All things seem to acquire fresh sweetness, and to be clothed with fresh beauty in their sight" (129), but Johnson's view held sway, by the end of the century even acquiring the tinge of ridicule in H. A. Taine's condemnation of prelapsarian Adam and Eve. Noting that Milton's human figures are sometimes viewed as imitations of Raphael's figures, "glorious, strong voluptuous children, naked in the light of heaven, motionless and absorbed before grand landscapes," Taine moves beyond Adam and Eve's statuesque appearance to argue that their "bright vacant eyes [express]...no more thought than the bull or the horse on the grass beside them." Furthermore, writes Taine, "I listen, and I hear an English household, two reasoners of the period—Colonel Hutchinson and his wife" (2.2.297). Opposed to Taine's reaction, though, is that of Stopford Augustus Brooke who exclaims that the introduction of Adam and Eve is "worthy of the long preparation!" (103). See Brooke on the approach to Eden in **153–268**. As Brooke also declares that Book 4 is "the most varied of all [the books] in interest and beauty," he understands that its fulcrum is the presentation of man: "As before in thought, so here in action, all Hell, in the person of Satan; and all Heaven, in the archangelic interest of Uriel and Gabriel, and in the vision of the scales of God, are collected round Man" (102).

During the first few decades of the twentieth century, the humorous disapproval of Milton's presentation of human life continues, as Adam and Eve are labeled "nut-eaters" by Walter Raleigh and "Old Age Pensioners" by E. M. W. Tillyard, but also developing is an awareness of the significance of Johnson's recognition that prelapsarian and postlapsarian human natures are not the same. While calling Adam and Eve "nut-eaters," and ridiculing Adam as being "from the depth of his inexperience...lavishly sententious," Walter Raleigh explains that Adam and Eve's lifestyle reveals "the sad truth that we are dependent, not only for the pleasure of our life, but even for many of the dearest pleasures of our imagination, on the devices introduced by the necessities of sin" (122). Tillyard asserts that Milton "fails to convince us that Adam and Eve are happy" and that disapproval rests upon his argument that Milton "can find no adequate scope for their active natures" (*Milton* 239). To Tillyard, Adam and Eve are therefore "Old Age Pensioners enjoying perpetual youth" (239). Basil Willey similarly rejects the notion of prelapsarian happiness that Addison and the Richardsons so celebrate, charging that Milton fails "to convince us that the prelapsarian life of Adam and Eve in the 'happy garden' was genuinely happy" (247). Douglas Bush, while granting, "Milton's ethical scheme is always rational," also finds it "not always equally human and humane" and, recalling Johnson, contends, "Adam and Eve are at first artificial beings in an artificial world, but they are human-ized by sin and suffering" (*Renaissance* 120). In *A Preface to "Paradise Lost"* 117, C. S. Lewis endeavors to illuminate Milton's presentation of prelapsarian human life with theological authority, specifically by comparing Milton's Adam to the conceptions of Adam held by Ambrose and Augustine. For Ambrose, Lewis explains, Adam was " 'a heavenly being' " (*In Ps[almum]* 118), and for Augustine, Adam was a man whose " 'mental powers…surpassed those of the most brilliant philosopher as much as the speed of a bird surpasses that of a tortoise' (*Op[us] Imperf[ectum] C[ontra] Iulian* 5.1 [*Contra Secundam Juliani,* col. 1432])." Consequently, Lewis argues, "No useful criticism of the Miltonic Adam is possible until the last trace of the *naif,* simple, childlike Adam has been removed from our imaginations. The task of a Christian poet presenting the unfallen first of men is not that of recovering the freshness and simplicity of mere nature, but of drawing someone who, in his solitude and nakedness, shall *really* be what Solomon and Charlemagne and Haroun-al-Raschid and Louis XIV lamely and unsuccessfully strove to imitate on thrones of ivory between lanes of drawn swords and under jewelled baldachins. And from the very first sight we have of the human pair Milton begins doing so" (118). A. J. A. Waldock surveys the differences between Raleigh's and Lewis's views on Adam, and finds Raleigh's Adam closer to the truth of the poem, but for Waldock, Milton's difficulties presenting prelapsarian man may be attributed to his not believing in "primal happiness. What, after all has Milton—…who could not praise a fugitive and cloistered virtue unexercised and unbreathed—to do with effortless innocence, the 'blank' virtue, of prelapsarian man? It is another of the paradoxes of the poem" (22).

Through the next several decades, most of the critics who write about Milton's Adam and Eve are involved in the effort to try to understand "primal happiness," to clarify prelapsarian life by loosening the strands of the paradox of prelapsarian virtue that Waldock identifies. J. B. Broadbent, for example, attempts to clarify the meaning of prelapsarian innocence: "Their innocence is a moment of poten-tial: it must change: either develop into something richer or be lost." Taking a somewhat different approach, Broadbent continues, "Adam and Eve are not innocent for they have no nocence, intellectual or sexual, to transcend; so he has to present them as unconsciously transcending what we know to be evil. He mitigates the difficulty by embedding them in the innocence of their habitation. They do not walk on to the stage but emerge from already-innocent Paradise as its phenomenal 'Master work, the end Of all yet don' (VII. 505)" (*Some Graver*

Subject 185; cf. Broadbent, "Milton's Paradise" 169–70). Broadbent's close reading of 266–94 brings detailed support to his understanding of how Adam and Eve "walk on to the stage." While Helen Darbishire accepts Johnson's claim that Adam and Eve "act and suffer…in a state which no other man or woman can ever know," she also insists that Milton "somehow brings to life this man and woman, Eve more fully than Adam. Eve as we first know her is a triumph of poetic creation of the same order as Shakespeare's Miranda" (*Milton's "Paradise Lost"* 39). As Davis P. Harding engages with the difficulties of presenting prelapsarian life to readers who know only postlapsarian life, he shifts attention to the role Milton shapes for those postlapsarian readers: "To accomplish by artifice what could not be accomplished in fact, Milton sought to implant in the minds of his readers a secret, furtive tentative uneasiness about Adam and Eve—not so much doubts as the shadows of doubts—while simultaneously maintaining the illusion of their entire sinlessness" (*Club* 69). As he stresses their youthfulness, John Peter somewhat similarly implies how Milton involves the fallen reader's awareness in his presentation of Adam and Eve: "being young, they are also in some degree defenceless, inexperienced. There is something fragile about their innocence and their devotion to each other" (91). Also considering the effect of the gap between prelapsarian and postlapsarian human natures, Marjorie H. Nicolson writes, "In the earlier books of *Paradise Lost,* Milton deliberately stresses the idyllic and generic qualities of Man and Woman before the Fall, very different from the man and woman we shall find later when they are reduced to our own level. The first Adam and Eve are prototypes of what Man might have been, as far removed from us in their perfection as they seem in time and place. Beautiful moving and speaking statues, they are like the angels who did not fall, models of a great impassivity" (*John Milton* 239). Writing toward the end of the 1960s, J. M. Evans and Louis L. Martz underscore the importance of much of this critical controversy about the nature of prelapsarian human life. Evans declares, "The interpretation of the whole poem, then, ultimately hinges on the view taken of Adam and Eve's condition before the Fall, on the significance we give to the word 'perfection' in this context" (245). Dismissing Tillyard's charge that Milton is "faking" (*Studies* 10), and that Adam and Eve are fallen before they fall, Martz presents a more detailed understanding of the dynamic nature of Adam and Eve's prelapsarian nature. Martz explains that it is Milton's insistence on their unfallen freedom of will that establishes Adam and Eve as "a couple *perfectly human* before the Fall, truly the 'human pair'" (*"Paradise Lost:* The Power" 46). Life in Milton's prelapsarian garden "is never static or passive," Martz concludes, stressing that "man's dignity depends upon the power of choice, which inevitably includes the right to err as well as the right to make amends for error. To Milton man's 'perfection' lies in man's ability to grow, however painfully, in wisdom and understanding" (47).

Finally, as the critical effort to understand Milton's description of prelapsarian human nature develops through the middle decades of the twentieth century, it does so in tandem with the critical effort to understand his description of paradise. Most certainly, critics looking at Milton's garden paradise set atop its "shaggie hill" (224) are increasingly sensitive to the complications of Milton's presentation of prelapsarian nature, but so, too, are they increasingly sensitive to the prelapsarian man and woman living and working within that garden paradise for, as Evans expresses it, "Adam and Eve's physical relationship to the garden is in fact an image of their psychological relationship both to their own passions and to each other" (250). See the discussion of prelapsarian labor in **610–33**.

288–311. Considering the difference between the more general versus the more detailed descriptions of the creations of the first couple in Gen. 1 and Gen. 2, James H. Sims detects a similar pattern in this sequence: "as in the Genesis account where the general statement of the creation of mankind as male and female is followed by a detailed account of the creation of Adam and Eve, Milton follows the general statement that the image of God shone on both Adam and Eve by a detailed explanation of the person of each" (*Bible* 24).

288–95. Critics have always noted that as Adam and Eve enter the scene, they are initially described in terms of their moral qualities rather than their particular physical characteristics, but critics have also always acknowledged that the physical beauty of Adam and Eve visually expresses their moral beauty. Patrick Hume develops the first explanation of the connection between the moral qualities and the naked bodies of Adam and Eve: "A glorious Nakedness, heightned and set off by spotless Innocence.... For in the State of Innocence, there was such an Agreement between Soul and Body, so exact an Obedience paid by the Sensual to the Rational and Sovereign part, that no audacious, unbecoming thought could with a guilty Blush have stain'd the Cheek of *Adam*, Majestick even in Nakedness" (144). To Hume's argument, James Paterson adds etymological support, tracing *naked* (290) to the Hebrew for "*Pure, clean, innocent;* unclothed" (308). In their exultant celebration of Milton's "Painting" of paradise, the Richardsons succinctly catch the manner of the visualization of Adam and Eve, which they designate Milton's "far more Noble Picture" of "the Outward and the Inward Man" (150), and Addison writes, "We see Man and Woman in the highest Innocence and Perfection, and in the most abject State of Guilt and Infirmity" (*Spectator* 2:563). William Hazlitt, finding the "figures" of Adam and Eve "very prominent" in *PL,* reasons, "As there is little action in it, the interest is constantly kept up by the beauty and grandeur of the images" (335). In the early twentieth century, Walter Raleigh identifies Milton's visualization of Adam and Eve as "Classic" (220), and a number of subsequent critics variously define that term. Raleigh believes that Milton intends Adam's and Eve's "physical delineation is to be accommodated by the imagination of the reader to this long catalogue of moral qualities—nobility, honour, majesty, lordliness, worth, divinity, glory, brightness, truth, wisdom, sanctitude, severity, and purity" (222). Raleigh also reasons about the effect of Milton's blindness on his visual imagination: "Since the veil had fallen he had lived with the luminous shapes that he could picture against the dark. The human face had lost, in his recollection of it, something of its minuter delineation, but nothing of its radiance. On the other hand, the human figure, in its most significant gestures and larger movements, haunted his visions" (153). For Raleigh, Milton's Adam and Eve have on their first appearance "the same shining quality [as Milton's dead wife in Sonnet 23], the same vagueness of beauty expressing itself in purely emotional terms" (154). In his first essay on Milton, "A Note on the Verse of John Milton," T. S. Eliot announces his now-famous opinion, "Milton may be said never to have seen anything" and specifically complains about Milton's presentation of Adam and Eve within their garden: "I for one can get pleasure from the verse only by the deliberate effort not to visualize Adam and Eve and their surroundings" (37). Qualifying those views in his 1947 essay, Eliot adds, however, that in addition to his "weakness of visual observation" (71), Milton had "little interest in, or understanding of, individual human beings," reasoning that "such an interest in human beings was not required—indeed its *absence* was a necessary condition—for the creation of his figures of Adam and Eve" (70). If the figures of Adam and Eve had been "more particularized," Eliot insists, "they would be false" (70). Eliot's remarks on Milton's description of Adam and Eve, like his remarks on the garden, stirred the inevitable responses, and William Empson's reply is among the most powerful. "So long as you gave Mr. Eliot images of someone being tortured his nerves were at peace," charges Empson, "but if you gave him an image of two people making each other happy he screamed."

Empson opines, "The naked figures of Paradise, by the way, strike me as of the Venetian school" (*Milton's God* 30). Invoking the term *classic,* as had Raleigh, Isabel Gamble MacCaffrey specifies that Milton's figures of Adam and Eve reveal the "classicism of the Renaissance." Comparing them to Michelangelo's figures, she explains, "Both poet and painter were striving to combine physical and abstract qualities into single, luminous shapes" (98). Davis P. Harding also points to Milton's "strong classicizing tendency." Adam and Eve's "moral perfection is reflected in a transcendent physical beauty," Harding writes, adding that Milton "has secured his effects without particularizing" (*Club* 69). Like MacCaffrey, J. B. Broadbent refers Milton's naked Adam and Eve to Michelangelo's figures: "Adam and Eve are still Michelangelic figures; their flesh has that massiveness which expresses an interest not in secondary sexual characteristics as such, but in physical form as the object of aesthetic contemplation" ("Milton's Paradise" 172). Broadbent explains that Adam and Eve's "majesty is insisted on, but it is independent of man-made pomp and accouterments; just as they are 'with native Honour clad In naked Majesty' (*PL*, IV, 289), so their dwelling place, and especially their bower, are sumptuously adorned by Nature. What is to fallen man the essential inconsistency of Paradise is precisely indicated by those oxymorons of 'naked Majesty' and 'native Honour'" (166). Wayne Shumaker contends, however, that our first glimpse of Adam and Eve is actually not at all visual: "Although we seem to be contemplating human beings, we are in fact being instructed about how we should react to images which will be offered later" (*Unpremeditated Verse* 49). Shumaker continues, "We are informed about the conclusions—rather affective than cortical—to be drawn from the visual image but are not, for the moment, given the image itself. Yet we *seem* to be looking, to have an object before our eyes" (50). John M. Steadman considers the relationship Milton creates between the physical and the moral qualities of the naked Adam and Eve by reference to the traditional opposition between romantic and marital love: "By placing the motif of romantic love within the context of matrimony, Milton gives it a moral elevation notably lacking in most of his predecessors." Furthermore, Steadman explains, "The same moral gravity characterizes the description of Eve's physical charms. As Milton develops it, this motif too is emblematic of original purity and the state of innocence. In the romance tradition nakedness is not uncommonly associated with lust or shame" (*Milton* 122). Understanding the description of Adam and Eve as apocalyptic, rather than classical, Leland Ryken explains Milton's use of the technique of conceptual imagery, which Ryken defines as any physical or abstract phenomenon. Milton's initial description of Adam and Eve, Ryken notes, is remarkable for its "heavy reliance on conceptual images. No fewer than 14 conceptual terms comprise the poetic texture of the description: nobleness, God-likeness, honor, majesty, lordship, worthiness, glory, truth, wisdom, sanctitude, severity, purity, freedom, and authority. Each of the terms names a quality which is no less real and distinct than a tangible object perceived through the senses, and although many modern critics would deny the statement, such conceptual images possess all the multiplicity of associations and complexity of connotations that a concrete physical image does" (194). Ryken finds such conceptual imagery "consistently complementing the sensory descriptions of the human pair" throughout the epic's middle books (194).

288–90. John S. Diekhoff notes the rhyme in this passage ("Rhyme" 540). See Diekhoff in **222–24**.

288–89. *erect and tall, / Godlike erect:* setting Milton's words against the classical reading of man's uprightness, from Ovid's *Metamorphoses* 1.85–86 ("Os homini sublime dedit, Coelumque [videre] / Jussi, & erectos ad sidera tollere vultus"; "he gave to man an up-lifted face and bade him stand erect and turn his eyes to heaven"), Patrick Hume concludes, "Well may he [Milton] term our first Parents *Godlike,* the Originals of Mankind, made by God himself, after his own Image, it better suiting the Protoplast than . . . any of the *Homerick* Heroes. *Erectus,* Lat. Upright" (144). A. W. Verity notes, "The repetition of 'erect' is important, since M[ilton] treats man's stature as a symbol of his sovereignty over the 'prone' beast-creation" (461). Sister Mary Irma Corcoran and C. A. Patrides bring more depth and breadth to the reading Hume first announces. Quoting from Aristotle's *De Partibus Animalium* 4.10.686B and Aquinas's *Summa Theologica* 4.268–71, Corcoran explains, "Even more significant than the beauty of Adam was his erect posture" (47). She also notes (48) that Adam's "first conscious movement" in *PL*—standing up and looking up (8.258–61)—is similarly the first conscious movement ascribed to Adam in *Pirke de Rabbi Eliezer* 78 and in Giambattista Andreini's *L'Adamo* 1.1. In "Renaissance Ideas on Man's Upright Form," Patrides, adding to Hume's glance at Ovid, references Aristotle's *De Partibus Animalium* 686A, Cicero's *De Natura Deorum* 2.56, and Plato's *Cratylus* 399C. Patrides presents Christian theologians as well as Renaissance poets and philosophers who, also celebrating the significance of man's erect form, sound much like John Donne in "Meditation 3" of *Devotions upon Emergent Occasions* 10: "*Man* in his naturall forme, is carried to the contemplation of that place, which is his *home, Heaven*" (256). Jackson I. Cope reads the emphasis on humanity's erect form in association with the preceding description of Eden, where "the topography builds upward in lavish detail," and he finds that "Adam and Eve, first seen, image the aspiring pattern" (111). On the anthropomorphic description of paradise see **131–83**.

289. *native Honour:* Alastair Fowler, labeling this phrase "A striking oxymoron," explains that "the Golden Age was more usually portrayed as free from the restraints and falsities of honour," as expressed in the first chorus, ending act 1, of Torquato Tasso's *Aminta.* Fowler points out that Milton's "ideal of natural honour—contrasted with fallen *honour dishonourable* (l. 314)" was nevertheless anticipated by earlier writers such as Battista Guarini in his moralization of Tasso, *Il Pastor Fido* 4.9, although for Fowler, Milton "seems to go beyond Guarini, and to entertain the conception of an honour like that of a Noble Savage—'primitive honour,' in Conrad's phrase" (630).

291–95. While this passage begins by firmly and clearly responding to Gen. 1.27, "So God created man in his own image," with the repetition of "severe" (293, 294) it turns, as it were, from the theological toward the political implications of the divine image. The earliest editors, almost to a person, discuss 291–95 as a unit, quickly moving to associate its initial theological import to the subsequent political overtones. Hume begins by noting that Adam and Eve were in "strict Conformity to their Makers Commands, exact and conformable to the Rectitude by him implanted in their Nature, and left subordinate to the Government and Guidance of their innate Free-Will." Filial freedom, Hume continues, therefore consists "in that Frank and ready Obedience that Sons pay to their Fathers, in which is founded all the Authority of Mankind, as being the result of Obedience from Children due to Parents, grounded on Paternal Authority, in respect of Prudence, Truth and Sanctitude" (144). The Richardsons bring even more emphasis to the political implications here, writing that "when they ['Truth, wisdome, Sanctitude'] are possess'd by Men, 'tis Their Best Title to Govern. Power may Usurp Dominion, and Extort Submission; but Filial Obedience is paid to None but Those who exercise a Legal Authority with Truth, Wisdom, and Purity of Life. And such are Secure of it." Quoting 2 Sam. 23.3–4, the

Richardsons conclude, "This was undoubtedly *Milton's* Notion, as appears by all his Political Writings; and seems to be his Meaning Here" (152–53). Newton encloses 294 in parentheses more tightly to identify the "qualities [listed in 293] that give to magistrates *true authority,* that proper authority which they may want who yet have legal authority" (250). David Masson, obviously referring to Newton, returns the reading to Hume's point of view, noting, "By some this passage is pointed so as to make the '*whence*' refer to '*sanctitude severe and pure,*' *i.e.* to imply that such sanctitude is the source of true authority in men. I conceive, however, that to make the '*whence*' refer to '*filial freedom*'—*i.e.* make such freedom the source of true authority in men—is more in accordance with Milton's mode of thought; and the original pointing seems to warrant this" (*Poetical Works* 3:173–47). Understanding "Truth, wisdome, Sanctitude" as "holiness," Verity (461) continues the emphasis of the early editors when he writes that it is "these qualities, not birth and position, conferring true authority." Verity then cites Edmund Burke's *Reflections on the Revolution in France* (*Works* 1:477): "There is no qualification for government, but virtue and wisdom, actual or presumptive."

Focusing more on the opening lines of this sequence, a number of the late twentieth century critics develop Milton's understanding of the image of God in man by uncovering its theological history. Asserting that Milton here describes Adam and Eve with the "conventional attributes of the divine image," John M. Steadman ("Heroic Virtue and the Divine Image" 98), for example, reports that for Gregory of Nyssa (*Contemplation sur la Vie* 36), these attributes were "purity, liberty, beatitude, dominion, justice, virtue, moral perfection, and the like. For Calvin [*Institutes* 1.164], similarly, it involved perfection, purity, righteousness, and holiness." C. A. Patrides refers his discussion of the image of God in man to Andrew Willet's survey in *Hexapla in Genesin* 14–15, and pointing to some of the many readings of the concept, he also notes differences between Milton's own remarks about the divine image in *Tetr* (Patterson, *Works* 4:74) and in *DocCh* (Patterson, *Works* 15:53). Rather like Masson, Patrides emphatically concludes, "Milton throughout *Paradise Lost* laid the greatest emphasis on free will" (*Milton* 51). Finally, Louis L. Martz discusses "the trinitarian way" in which the description of Adam and Eve is advanced by this line: "in words that seem to echo Augustine: through the human countenance shines the Truth of God the Father, the Wisdom of the Son, Word of the Father; and the Sanctity of the Holy Spirit" ("*Paradise Lost:* Princes" 240). While Balachandra Rajan emphasizes reason as part of the image of God in man, he also brings historical meaning to the theological concept when he elaborates the difference between servile and filial fear as he discusses the role of law in history (*Lofty Rhyme* 89–91, 68). With a somewhat similar approach, G. Wilson Knight and Ira Clark refer these lines to human history in conjunction with theological abstractions. Clark discusses the image of God as that "telescoping symbol" that expresses all of man's history: "The dogma of man's original perfection, fall, and regeneration are explained by the use of the image of God in *De Doctrina;* the emotive, sacramental pattern is embodied in *Paradise Lost* and *Paradise Regained*" (426). In the abstractions said to express the image of God in man, Knight finds the suggestion of a "nobly tragic destiny; the 'truth, wisdom, sanctitude, severe and pure' (IV.293) of Adam and Eve indicate rather a future perfection than an original innocency, the words denoting spiritual victory, not happy inexperience" (78).

Finally, C. S. Lewis and John Halkett note that Eve, as well as Adam, expresses the image of God. For Lewis, "the wisdom and sanctitude, not in Adam only but in both, were 'severe'—in the sense in which Cicero [*De Officiis* 1.69] speaks of a man as *severus et gravis;* that is, they were like a severe style in music or architecture, they were austere, magnanimous, and lofty" (118). Halkett, finding this initial presentation of Adam and Eve "an emblem of perfect matrimony" (103), asserts that Adam's "superior understanding and strength gave him a natural authority over woman," but "the possession of 'Truth, Wisdom, Sanctitude' by both Adam and Eve, in whom 'The image of thir glorious Maker shone,' made them 'Lords of all'" (103–04).

292. *glorious Maker:* acknowledging the ambiguity attending Milton's use of epic epithets and references for the Father and the Son, Kester Svendsen argues that one may nevertheless "recognize in Milton's epithets as narrator five major relationships or characteristics of the Son, and these varied to suit the stages of the story" ("Epic Address" 199–200). As the creator, the Son is named *glorious Maker,* as well as *Almighty Maker* (2.915) and *sovran Planter* (4.69); the remaining four relationships of the Son, Svendsen identifies as almighty power, Son of God, judge, and intercessor ("Epic Address" 200). Cf. Svendsen on Adam and Eve's references to the Son in **412–13**.

295–311. While in the preceding initial description of Adam and Eve (288–95) both are said to have "seemd Lords of all" (290), and both express "in their looks

Divine / The image of thir glorious Maker" (291–92), with this sequence, the two are separated on the basis of gender and declared "Not equal" (295). The early editors make some passing comments on the beginning of the sequence, praising either Eve's "Charms, from her pleasing and winning Behaviour" (Hume 144), or the "charming lines" themselves (Newton 251), but their fullest remarks gloss "Hee for God only, shee for God in him" (299), and at the core of all their commentaries lie the Pauline epistles. Hume quotes 1 Cor. 11.3, 7, and 9, and concludes with Adam's words in 8.540–46, although between the quotations, in his own voice, Hume explains, "Woman is the Glory of the Man; that is, for his Glory, Satisfaction and Delight, out of him made his Companion" (144–45). With the same quotations from St. Paul, the Richardsons cross-reference 440, 637, and 10.150, and finally note that "by Obeying her Husband she obey'd God, whose Substitute he was" (153). This note may indicate the Richardsons' rejection of Bentley's assertion two years earlier that 440–42 supports changing the line to "*He for God only, She for God AND Him*" (117), a change that Pearce (121), Hawkey ("Various Readings"), Stebbing (96), and even Newton (251) approve, although Newton does not print the change. Todd ([1801], 275–76; [1826], 2:298–99; [1842], 2:70) presents Newton's note in 1801, whereas in 1826 he adds both John Bowle's contribution of a reference to the fourteenth chapter of William Whately's *A Bride-bush* 189–216, which discusses the biblical authority for female inferiority, and Charles Dunster's contribution suggesting that for the "turn of the expression" in 299, Milton was indebted to Tasso's *Gerusalemme Liberata* 16.21. Dunster's note is supported by Giamatti in **297–99**.

The topic of gender inequality, as well as its Pauline underpinnings as established by early editors, provokes much more various and more vigorous commentary from twentieth century critics. True, at the beginning of the century, Walter Raleigh comments on the "Not equal" relationship between the sexes by stating that Milton simply "thought fit" to present Eve as "the embodiment of a doctrine" (143), and Verity finds "only a touch of exaggeration in Johnson's remark that Milton's works reveal 'something like a Turkish contempt of females, as subordinate and inferior beings'" (461; see Johnson, *Milton* 276), but later critics acknowledge a problem here. Focusing attention on 296–99, Helen Gardner indicates the extent of the problem when she admits, "No lines have, I suppose, been more quoted and quoted against Milton than these" (*Reading* 81), and Joseph H. Summers explains that the passage is "difficult for us" because of "modern ideas of the equality of the sexes" (95). A number of twentieth century critics respond to this topic of gender inequality in Milton's garden, seeking to distance it from personal attachment to Milton, by arguing that it is a seventeenth century commonplace. Douglas Bush, for example, claims that line 299 "has evoked both mirth and annoyance; but it simply embodies the hierarchical view of order and degree which . . . was a universal heritage, and which Shakespeare appealed to at the end of *The Taming of the Shrew*" (*"Paradise Lost" in Our Time* 74). Rajan, Daiches, Nicolson, and Gardner similarly comment: "the deepest and most impersonal feeling of the time" (Rajan, *"Paradise Lost" and the Seventeenth Century Reader* 66), "a commonplace of contemporary and earlier thought" (Daiches 187), "almost universally accepted in Milton's time" (Nicolson, *John Milton* 240), and "the orthodox view of his age" (Gardner, *Reading* 81). Rather than pointing to differences between the seventeenth and the twentieth century, Northrop Frye points to differences between the pre- and the postlapsarian worlds, explaining that line 299 "illustrates a central problem in reading the poem. This is the problem of the language of analogy. The statement is made of the unfallen Adam and Eve, and so is not literally true of men and women as we know them" ("Revelation" 20). Edward S. Le Comte goes a bit further with this approach, arguing that although Milton held the commonplace view "that women had their 'not equal' (iv.296) place and should keep it," he did so "more moderately than many" (*Yet Once More* 134–35). In *Milton and the Idea of Matrimony,* John Halkett gives this approach to the "Not equal" relationship between Adam and Eve its fullest development, as he distinguishes the traditional elements in 295–311 from those elements that he determines to be uniquely Miltonic. Halkett acknowledges, for example, that arguing "the inequality of the sexes from the differences in their appearance" (104), a common rhetorical tradition, is one Milton adopts: "Eve's longer hair is a sign of her femininity; its veillike quality suggests her modesty and submission; it is unadorned because she exists in the state of natural innocence; its golden color suggests her greater physical beauty; its 'wanton' curls suggest profusion, charming disorder, and the need for masculine government and authority" (104). Halkett also insists, however, that the specific oppositions established in Milton's text, the oppositions, that is, between *contemplation* (297) and *Grace* (298), and *valour* (297) and *softness* (298) are "particularly Miltonic" (103).

While some critics therefore recover the seventeenth century context for Milton's declaring Adam and Eve "Not equal, as thir sex not equal seemd" (296), others situate the topic within the dramatic context of *PL.* Jon S. Lawry, for example, contends, "This hierarchical order of the sexes, repugnant to many of Milton's readers, is not really tyrannical, for it can be broken all too easily—in the upshot, we see how easily. Nor is it 'unfair' to Eve, for if Adam is a reflection of God and shares God's 'contemplation,' Eve is a second reflection, sharing both God's grace and man's love. She was the first, as Christ is a second, gracious offering to man" (171–72). Elaborating on the "direct and unifying intercourse" between the unfallen world and unfallen humanity, Michael Lieb asserts, "The inequality of male and female adds to their glorification, for, since the implication of the 'two great Sexes' is that the female play the passive role and the male play the active role, the second must be superior to the first. And, ideally, such is the situation between the unfallen Adam and Eve: the male dominates and the female obeys with 'sweet attractive Grace'" (71). J. M. Evans references Calvin's *Commentary* 2.18 as he establishes Eve's traditional dependence on Adam, but Evans then proceeds to stress that "this inequality is one of the major themes of Book IV, in which our attention and, for the most part, our sympathy are focused on Eve. Indeed, if Raleigh's adjective 'sententious' is to be applied to Adam at all, then it is in this part of the poem, in which Adam's speeches are all admonitory" (252). See Raleigh on Adam as "sententious" in **288–1015**.

Yet another twentieth century critical approach to gender inequality in *PL* has been the recovery of the allegorical reading of sexual difference. The ancient allegorical tradition associating Adam with reason and Eve with passion has influenced or shaped a number of important responses. Denis Saurat, for one, argues, "Because of her passionate role, woman cannot participate fully in intelligence. She can only participate in it through submission to it, even as desire is legitimate when it submits to reason. And man is the representative of reason" (163). Maud Bodkin supports Saurat: "I think that Saurat is right in gathering from Milton's total representation of woman in *Paradise Lost* that she is to be thought of as in some sense representing desire and passion, while man is the representation of reason" (169). Marjorie H. Nicolson ("Milton" 15) extends this focus into the cabalistic treatises, quoting Henry More's *Conjectura Cabbalistica* 35: "The wisdome of God . . . saw that it was not good for the soul of man, that the masculine powers thereof should operate alone," because of his conviction that "the second principle, whether it be instinct as distinct from reason, matter as distinct from spirit, feminine as distinct from masculine, is inferior only in the sense that without the first principle it is not capable of true existence, whereas the first principle, though capable of existence without the second, is not capable of completion."

Still other twentieth century critics bring analogical thought to bear upon their reading of the "Not equal" relationship between Adam and Eve. For example, William B. Hunter ("Milton" 361) compares the union of Adam and Eve with the "union of 'predominance'" between the Father and the Son. Roy Daniells also parallels Adam and Eve with the Father and the Son, but in terms of a baroque reading of hierarchy: "Milton's innovation lies in the avoidance or minimizing of gradations on the vertical shaft. The Persons of the Trinity, though not viewed by Milton as co-eternal, are not conceived as in a sequence, either. Milton's angels are not arranged in the customary hierarchies.... Though Eve is in a sense beneath Adam, she receives direct warning, direct judgment, and direct revelation, from God" (*Milton* 82). In "Milton and the *Argumentum Paris*" 359, John Steadman associates Lucifer's relationship with God and Eve's with Adam. Steadman notes, "In Eve's case, as in Satan's, there is a significant distinction between likeness and equality. She is Adam's 'likeness' (VIII, 450), but not his equal (IV, 295–96), and her inferiority provides one of the topics for Adam's indictment after the fall," as God questions him in 10.145–56.

297–311. Southey and Landor wax rhapsodic about this sequence, which Southey declares is "the triumph of our language." Landor reports that the poetry is "so harmonious that my ear is impatient of any other poetry for several days after I have read them," and, describing 310–11 as "the richest jewel that poetry ever wore," he admits, "I would rather have written those two lines than all the poetry that has been written since Milton's time in all the regions of the earth" (20–21).

297–99. A. Bartlett Giamatti (314) examines the "Satanic style" of implication, obliquity, and echo in Milton's presentation of Adam and Eve, as well as paradise, identifying in this passage, as did Charles Dunster, a structure syntactically similar to one in Tasso's *Gerusalemme Liberata* 16.21: "L'uno di servitu, l'altra d'impero / si gloria, ella in se stessa ed egli in lei," which Giamatti translates, "One glories in slavery, the other in command, / She in herself and he in her." Giamatti concludes, "Rinaldo and Armida are as different from Adam and Eve as Armida's enchanted garden is different from the true earthly paradise. But the echo from the epic of Milton's favorite Italian poet implicates Adam and Eve in the theme of the Italian passage. The figure to suffer most by this allusion is Eve, for the narcissism and sensuality of Armida fleetingly touch Eve even as the differences between the two become apparent" (314–15). Todd ([1826], 2:298–99; [1842], 2:70) acknowledges Dunster's point in **295–311**.

contemplation: Merritt Y. Hughes identifies Adam's attribute of contemplation as a key patristic tradition and explains that "before the Fall Adam's purity permitted his constant contemplation of the image of God in his Word, in the image of which Adam himself was made. His Fall consisted in the diversion of his contemplation from God to himself and the cravings of his body" ("Variorum").

softness: Allan H. Gilbert identifies Eve's *softness* as "something good, not something bad," signifying "gentleness, tenderness, mildness, refinement, and delicacy" ("Milton on the Position" 246).

sweet attractive Grace: Edward S. Le Comte drops the adjective *sweet* as he cross-references Eve's *attractive Grace* with Sin's "attractive graces" (2.762) to conclude that "Eve is associated with evil" (*Yet Once More* 41), but Anne Davidson Ferry and Dorothy Durkee Miller reject Le Comte's reading. Ferry finds difference, not similarity, underscored by the cross-reference: "Sin's 'attractive graces' are not, like Eve's 'sweet attractive Grace'…a divine gift of inner beauty expressed in outward form, but the empty seductions of an abstraction" (*Milton's Epic Voice* 133). Miller points out, "Grace is also a divine attribute and…it was through Eve that Adam was saved from despair; and…even more significantly, through woman came the means of man's salvation" (544). Also see Lawry in **295–311**.

299. Harris Francis Fletcher (178) refers this line to *Tetr* (Patterson, *Works* 4:76): "He not for her, but she for him." To the *Tetr* reference, Edward S. Le Comte (*Yet Once More* 87) adds "Who can be ignorant that woman was created for man, and not man for woman" from *DDD* (Patterson, *Works* 3:475). Le Comte then acknowledges, "Whatever we may think of it, it is straight out of Saint Paul, 'Neither was the man created for the woman, but the woman for the man' (1 Cor. xi.9)." Glossing this line with Eve's later statement that Adam is her "Author and Disposer" (635), B. A. Wright repeats the explanation that such statements of male authority were commonplaces in the seventeenth century. Wright adds that "most love poetry from the twelfth to the seventeenth century, in one way or another, shows an awareness of this conflict between human and divine love. Milton too believes that human love can be noble and ennobling, but not by the adoration of woman or by submission of the mind to the passion of love" (*Milton's "Paradise Lost"* 158).

Hee...shee: in the introduction to her 1952 edition of *PL,* Helen Darbishire presents her theory on Milton's pronoun spellings: "the pronouns have their emphatic, stressed forms, and their unemphatic, unstressed forms marked out by spelling: *hee, mee, wee, yee, you, their* emphatic; *he, me we, ye, thir* unemphatic" (*Poetical Works* 1:xxxiii). While he concedes that the emphatic-versus-unemphatic distinction is the usual explanation for the spelling difference, Robert Martin Adams tracks down many examples for which that explanation does not hold, to conclude that "the principle on which Milton, or his amanuensis, or his printers, distinguished 'he' from 'hee' is not an obvious one" (63–64).

300–51. This is the only entry under "Adam and Eve in Paradise" in section 3 of Edward Bysshe's *The Art of English Poetry.* Milton similarly dominates the entry "Paradise." Despite the authority Bysshe thereby yields to Milton's presentation of the Edenic experience, he makes some striking deletions throughout this sequence. Omitting 308–24, for example, Bysshe omits references to Eve's submission, Adam and Eve's nakedness, and the "honor dishonorable" of the narrator's world. Omitting 328–30, Bysshe deletes the reference to Edenic labor, and omitting 337–40, he avoids referring to Adam and Eve's "youthful dalliance" (300).

300–11. This 12-line unit focuses attention on Adam and Eve's hair, first literally describing Adam's hair, and then—as that objectivity ebbs—figuratively describing Eve's hair. Source studies dominate early criticism as editors trace connections with the Bible, with ancient and early modern literature, as well as with the visual arts, and while twentieth century scholars continue to pursue the relevance of the sources for this passage, they bring considerably more attention to the symbolic significance of the descriptions. As Davis P. Harding expresses it, "Milton, cheated by the hard facts of Genesis of any opportunity to exploit clothes symbolism in Adam and Eve, makes up for the deficiency by ascribing symbolic or quasi-symbolic values to their hair" (*Club* 71).

300–03. Although this series culminates with the description of Adam's hair, it opens by drawing attention to his forehead and his eyes (300–01). Eighteenth century editors offer no commentary whatsoever on Adam's eyes and forehead, unlike several twentieth century editors. John T. Shawcross, for example, glosses *sublime* as "upraised" (*Complete Poetry* 325), and Alastair Fowler glosses it as "uplifted" (631), while *OED* 3 cites Milton's line to illustrate *sublime* as "Of lofty bearing or aspect; in a bad sense, haughty, proud." Allan H. Gilbert contends that "the 'absolute rule' apparent in Adam's 'fair large front and eye sublime' is, so far as Eve is concerned, wholly a matter of influence, depends on her free will, and endures only while her mind agrees with that of Adam" ("Milton on the Position" 249). Wayne Shumaker somewhat similarly contends that, as Milton points to Adam's forehead and eyes, he is not so much describing those physical features as he is directing his reader how to see both Adam and Eve. Arguing that *PL* is "suffused with affective overtones" (*Unpremeditated Verse* 47) that limit or shape the reader's reaction to sensory images, Shumaker explains, "What is properly descriptive here is merely the declaration that Adam's forehead was large (or perhaps broad) and his eyes raised from the ground. The first detail points forward to the rather limited visual sharpness which is soon to come, the second backward to the framework of meaning, partly rational and partly affective, within which we must limit the activity of our imagination" (50). Shumaker then labels as "purely descriptive" the subsequent lines dedicated to Adam's hair (301–03): "Only the adjective 'manly' is interpretative here." Beginning with the passage on Eve's hair, however, Shumaker notes that "sensory details are given together with the meaning they imply" (51).

Hyacinthin: pointing out that *Hyacinthin* describes Adam's hair as well as Ulysses's hair in *Odyssey* 6.230–31, Hume (145) provides additional supporting quotations from various classical authors, especially Virgil (*Eclogues* 2.18, 3.63, *Georgics* 4.183), to suggest that *Hyacinthin* means Adam's hair was "Black, Red, and a Colour of these mixt, that of rusty Iron." Supplying a handful of quotations from the *Aeneid*, Hume cautions, however, "It is very observable, that such Epithets as this are not to be taken in too strict a sense; for Gold being the most excellent among Metals, Purple among Colours, the Rose, and anciently the Hyacinth, among Flowers." Newton and Todd present the Ulysses comparison that Hume had mentioned earlier, Newton adding the probability that "the hyacinth among the Ancients might be of a darker color than it is among us" (251–52), and Todd, quoting William Cowper's translation of Homer's *Odyssey* 6.286, suggesting that *Hyacinthin* might also mean that Adam's hair "curled like the blossoms of the hyacinth, without any allusion to the colour." In later editions, Todd presents Charles Dunster's unpublished observation that Queen Helen is said to have had "*iacinth hair curled* by nature, but intercurled by art" ([1826], 2:299–300; [1842], 2:70). Paterson (309), like the Richardsons (153), darkens the color reference, describing it as "Raven-black." Masson finds in *Hyacinthin* authority for both the dark color and the curl of Adam's hair (*Poetical Works* 3:174), and Verity reports that some think Adam's shoulder-length hair indicates Milton's condemnation of longer hair as "effeminate" and to be associated with the Cavaliers (462). To the early editors' reference to Ulysses as the source for Adam's "Hyacinthin Locks," Harding adds Virgil's first description of Aeneas (*Aeneid* 1.590–91), given "the grace of clustered locks" by Venus (*Club* 70), one of the passages from the *Aeneid* first cited by Hume (145).

Clustring: developing Milton's etymology, Hume writes, "curl'd round in Clusters like the Vines swelling bunch. *Cluster,* of the Sax. *Clurster,* a Bunch of Grapes" (145), and the Richardsons, without attribution, repeat Hume's point, but then also move to 1 Cor. 11, where Paul asserts that "the Sexes are thus Distinguish'd, Long Hair is a Glory to the Woman, but to the Man a Shame" (154). Newton draws a pastoral association between the description of Adam's hair and the subsequent description of Eve's hair: "His hair hung *clustring,* or like bunches of grapes, as her's was like the young shoots or *tendrils* of the *vine*" (252). Todd ([1842], 2:70) glosses *Clustring* by reference to *Mask* 54, as does the *OED*.

Some commentators see Adam's hair as a link not so much between Milton's Adam and the classical gods, but between Milton's Adam and Milton himself. Certainly, the Richardsons note that both have shoulder-length hair, and they claim that Milton thought that "a Beauty" (158). Newton seems to be the first to assert that Milton "drew the portrait of Adam not without regard to his own person, of which he had no mean opinion" (253). In his *Milton,* Johnson similarly reports that Milton's "hair, which was of a light brown, parted at the foretop, and hung down upon his shoulders, according to the picture which he has given of Adam" (273). Verity (461) seems to contrast the dark color of Adam's hair and the auburn of Milton's hair and quotes Newton's remarks in addition to referencing Milton's own description of his appearance in *Def 2* (Patterson, *Works* 8:58–63). Alastair Fowler (631) suggests, "The elaborateness of the present passage lends some support to the theory that M[ilton] had a special sexual interest in hair," and in support, Fowler sends readers to the later description of Eve's hair at 495–97, as well as the descriptions of "the tangles of *Neaera's* hair" and the shepherd's "oozy Lock's" in *Lyc* 69, 175.

Dismissing Verity's remark about Milton's self-portrait in Adam, Sister Mary Irma Corcoran insists instead that in portraits and descriptions of Christ, one glimpses not only Milton's Adam but also his Eve. Corcoran glances at the art of

Raphael, Titian, and others, but explains that the closest resemblance to Milton's Adam is a verbal description of Christ in an apocryphal, but widely circulated, thirteenth century letter said to have been written by Publius Lentulus during the reign of Tiberius, and published in London in 1650. Corcoran argues that Milton's description of the length of Adam's hair, for example, "reads like a contradiction of a positive statement such as that of 'Lentulus' that it [Christ's hair] was *ab humeris deorsum pendentes.*" She also points to "frequent verbal parallels which are sometimes literal and sometimes merely visual: *severitate,* severe; *vinei,* vine; *erecti,* erect; *frons,* front; *purs,* pure; *ingenuus,* gentle; gratia, grace. Both descriptions mention the parted, wavy hair, *vinei coloris* or hyacinthine, and each concludes with the Biblical statement that its object was the most beautiful of the sons of men" (47).

Adam's lack of a beard puzzles several early critics, beginning with Bentley. Bentley's (117) concern develops because the heroes of Homer and Virgil have beards, as do Spenser's youthful Verdant and Timias (*The Faerie Queene* 2.12.79 and 4.7.40). The Richardsons ponder some possible explanations for the absent beard: "perhaps because the Statues of the Gods or Men I have spoken of as Helps to Conceive properly on This Occasion have none; Perhaps because *Rafael* and others have painted him Without one; Perhaps because Hair hanging down to the Shoulders, and which he [Milton] thought was a Beauty (he wore his Own so) would not Look well with more on his Upper Lip and Chin,…perhaps because the Scripture, which he for the most part Scrupulously follows, mentions None" (158). The Richardsons then also suggest that if the reader wishes a bearded Adam, the reader may "Suppose" such "Downy Hyacinthin Blackness on the Lower part of his Face" (158–59). Newton reports that the major painters "always" present a beardless Adam, and Milton, according to Newton, "frequently fetches his ideas from the works of the greatest masters in painting" (252). Agreeing that Milton's Adam lacks a beard because of the influence of the visual arts, Alastair Fowler (631) references background studies by Erwin Panofsky, *Meaning in the Visual Arts* 249–65, and Vincenzo Cartari, *Le Vere e Nove Imagini de gli Dei delli Antichi.*

304–11. Milton's initial description of the color and the length of Eve's hair in 304–05 is seen straightforwardly by the critics, as is also the veil metaphor, which they inevitably read according to the Pauline tradition, but the more provocative language describing and interpreting the curl of Eve's hair evokes considerable commentary from modern critics, commentary about the vexed relationship between Adam and Eve, about the relationship between them and the garden, and about the relationship between Eve and evil.

vail: early editors quickly associate the veil metaphor describing Eve's hair with Paul's directives on hair in 1 Cor. 11. For Hume and the Richardsons (154–55) Eve's veil of hair symbolizes her subordination to Adam, and they explain that even among the ancients the bride's veil indicated that she was being put "in the Power of her Husband," but bringing Milton's "requir'd with gentle sway" (308) to bear on Paul's arguments, Hume writes, "our Poet sweetens it, to be *required with gentle sway,* on soft and easie terms, to be grounded on Reason, on just and fit, and supported and maintained by all imaginable Tenderness, and soft Endearments" (145–46). Todd, of course, also cites Corinthians ([1842], 2:71). Among the moderns, Sister Mary Irma Corcoran similarly refers the veil to the relationship between Adam and Eve: "Of the utmost importance in Milton's paradise were chastity and its exterior corollary, modesty. Eve's hair was like a veil (IV, 304f.) although 'No vaile / Shee needed, vertue-proof, no thought infirme / Alterd her cheek' (V, 383ff.). Milton treated of chastity in *Paradise Lost* chiefly with regard to the marriage of the first couple, in which relationship it is one of the domestic virtues" (115).

golden tresses: as in their annotations on Adam's hair, early critics associate Eve's hair with classical beauty, especially because of its color. The Richardsons note that Eve's hair is "Fair, Bright, Yellowish Locks, the Colour of the Hair of *Venus, Helena* &c. Much esteem'd by the Ancients, and in Later times" (154). Newton also refers to Helen and "golden Venus," and then wonders whether Milton had here intended "a compliment to his wife in the drawing of Eve; as it is certain, that he drew the portrait of Adam not without regard to his own person" (252–53). Todd repeats Newton's note, but in the later editions, adds references to Spenser's description of Britomart's hair in *The Faerie Queene* 4.1.13, as well as St. Paul's remarks in 1 Cor. 11.15 ([1842], 2:71). Hume's note (145) on Eve's *golden tresses* stands apart from these other early annotations, however, for, acknowledging that "Golden Yellow Locks, in ancient times [were] of great esteem," Hume mentions neither Helen nor Venus, but most unexpectedly and rather abruptly refers Eve's hair to the golden hair of soldiers in the *Aeneid* 8.659, 11.642–43. Commenting on Eve's hair, Todd quotes—at considerable length—an unpublished note by Robert Thyer that probably sheds some light on Hume's not referring Eve's hair to Helen or Venus. Acknowledging the standard association between Eve's hair and Venus's hair by quoting Marino, who in *L'Adone* 8.46 describes Venus's hair as golden ("aurei capelli"), Thyer moves to consider the challenge facing Milton of celebrating Eve's physical beauty without compromising her spiritual and intellectual beauty. "The poet has, I think, showed great judgment and delicacy in avoiding in this place the entering into a circumstantial description of Eve's beauty.... But, as a picture of this kind would have been too light and gay for the graver turn of Milton's plan, he has very artfully mentioned the charms of her person in general terms only, and directed the reader's attention more particularly to the beauty of her mind" ([1842], 2:71). Most recently, Stella Revard (182–84) also resists the long-standing association between Eve and Homer's Aphrodite when, questioning Merritt Y. Hughes's repetition of the association (*Complete Poems* 285), she points to one of Milton's contemporaries, Sir William Alexander, in whose *Dooms-Day* (*Poetical Works* 2:23) Eve is presented as beautiful, but also temperate and stately. While early editors and critics list parallels between Milton's Eve and beautiful females in other epics, William Hazlitt, in his appendix "On the Character of Milton's Eve," brings sustained attention to the differences between Milton's Eve and Shakespeare's female characters. Hazlitt explains that Eve is described "as devoted to her husband, as twining round him for support, 'as the vine curls her tendrils,' but her own grace and beauty are never lost sight of in the picture of conjugal felicity" (333–34). Shakespeare's female characters, Hazlitt argues, "seem to exist only in their attachment to others" (334). Also see Hazlitt in **440–91**.

A number of the modern critics continue to develop the metaphors comparing Eve's hair to a veil and a vine as symbols of her subordination to Adam. John Diekhoff, for example, brings "Absolute rule" (301) into conjunction with the description of Eve's hair to conclude, "Adam...should rule—should be granted obedience, that is to say, not exacting it by force" (*Milton's "Paradise Lost"* 53). While explaining how carefully Milton controls the reader's affective reactions to this detailed description of Eve, Wayne Shumaker moves to a similar understanding of the simile's meaning: " 'Slender,' although sufficiently denotative to be visually rather precise, carries connotations of gracefulness as distinct from strength; 'unadorned' may suggest innocent simplicity. Otherwise the specifications are mainly sensory. At once, however, the meaning of the [vine] image is made explicit: 'which impli'd / Subjection' (307–08). Because Eve's hair is wavy, we are to understand that she is Adam's hierarchical inferior—an implication, we now realize, which had already been insinuated in the simile of the vine" (*Unpremeditated Verse* 51). Michael Lieb associates Eve's submission to Adam, as symbolized by her hair, with Adam's later remarks on gardening (625–29, 5.211–19): "The mode of that submission would be characterized by the submission of the hair, which would resist order with a 'sweet reluctance.' Such an implication reveals a good deal about the love relationship itself: sexual union in the unfallen world is not mere dalliance but has the higher and more creative purpose of the submission of disorder or wantonness to the temperance of a higher or superior order. And, remarkably, we shall find that the act of ordering, of subduing wantonness characteristic of the sexual union, is exactly what defines the creative occupation of the unfallen gardeners" (72).

Besides discussing Eve's hair as a symbol of her relationship with Adam, and their relationship with the garden, a number of twentieth century critics ponder its significance as a symbol of evil. While A. Bartlett Giamatti, for example, looks to 5.383–85 when he considers Eve's hair as a veil, he also looks to 9.1054–58, as well as Italian epics: "The motif of the partially veiled woman has already been noted in the gardens of Alcina and Armida. Indeed, like Marino, Milton calls the hair a 'veil,' and the notion of a veil is to play an important role in the garden, for like the 'mazy' brook, the word for a physical fact becomes a metaphor for a mental or spiritual state" (321). In 9.1054–58, Giamatti explains, "The potentiality of the 'veil' and Venus allusions in Books IV and V are fulfilled" (322). Also see Giamatti in **492–97**. Davis P. Harding argues that as Milton sought to present prelapsarian sinlessness, he also "sought to implant in the minds of his readers a secret, furtive tentative uneasiness" (*Club* 69), and Harding finds some of that uneasiness in Milton's description of Eve's hair, arguing that because they imply subjection, the curled tendrils also imply "the kind of encroachment which may ensnare and destroy as well." Harding then "somewhat tentatively" suggests that "in this strangely troubling description of Eve" Milton may be indebted to Horace, who in *Odes* 1.5.5 describes Pyrrha's coiffure as "simplex munditiis," "simple elegance" (72). Stanley Fish similarly argues, "the fallen reader betrays himself when he feels obliged to pass moral judgment on every action or utterance. 'Wanton' and 'loose' and 'error' trouble us because we cannot help but read into them moral implications that are not relevant until the Fall has occurred" (*Surprised* 100). In addition to 1 Cor. 11.10, James H. Sims brings Ps. 128.3 and *PL* 9.214–19 to carry through with his understanding of the uneasiness in Milton's description of Eve's hair: "the allusion here [9.214–19] is to the psalmist's simile: 'Thy wife shalbe as a fruitfull Vine by the sides of thine house' (Ps. 128:3). The dramatic irony lies in Eve's suggesting that Adam go lead the woodbine and ivy where and how to climb when she, the main vine Adam has the duty and responsibility of directing, most needs him with her" (*Bible* 212). Indeed, by referencing the Bible, especially 1 Cor., Sims concludes that Milton "foreshadows the means by which Satan will manage to separate them" (25). Quoting Harding and acknowledging Hughes's note (*Complete Poems* 307) that associates the "vine-propp elme" of *The Faerie Queene* 1.1.8 with Adam and Eve's responsibility to lead the vine to *wed* the elm (5.215–19), Giamatti also more closely examines that vine metaphor, which links Adam and Eve as gardeners to the garden, and presents its more troubling implications. Giamatti looks at the context of the Spenserian precedent: "the Redcross Knight and Una are riding through a most ambiguous 'mixed forest' (8–9) which finally becomes 'the wandering wood…Errours den' (13); there is no need to comment further on the significance of 'wandering' and 'error' in *Paradise Lost;* could this landscape of *The Faerie Queene* have been somewhere in the poet's mind?" (323–24n27). William Empson most vigorously develops the dangerous implications of the provocative language describing Eve's hair. Empson associates Eve's curls and the tendrils to which they are compared with the image of the serpentine demons in Book 10 climbing the trees with the apples of ash (558–60). Empson argues that Eve's hair, while "modest," is "requiring" and "clutches at Adam like the tendrils of a vine. Eve now then is herself the forbidden tree; the whole face of Hell has become identical with her face; it is filled, as by the mockery of the temptress, with her hair that entangled him; all the beauty of nature, through her, is a covering, like hers, for moral deformity" (*Some Versions* 168–69).

306. *Disheveld:* "*Dischevele,* Fr. loose, hanging down at length" (Hume 145). In the second edition of his essay "On Picturesque Beauty," William Gilpin endeavors to support his notion of the picturesque as that which pleases "from some quality capable of being illustrated by painting" (9) by quoting Milton's description of Eve's disheveled hair. Gilpin adds the Milton citation to earlier references to Joshua Reynolds, who, will make your portrait "picturesque by throwing the hair dishevelled about your shoulders," and to Virgil, who achieves a picturesque effect when he describes Venus's windblown hair in *Aeneid* 1.350. To his essay, Gilpin appends a brief letter to him from Reynolds who suggests that "*picturesque* is somewhat synonymous to the word *taste,* which we should think improperly applied to Homer or Milton, but very well to Pope or Prior. I suspect that the application of these words are to excellences of an inferior order, and which are incompatible with the grand style" (35).

Allan H. Gilbert ("Milton and the *Aminta*" 97) finds a parallel between this description of Eve's hair and the hairstyle "a l'aura sparte" ("loosened by the breeze") described by the chorus celebrating the "bella eta de l'oro" ("beautiful golden age") at the end of the first act of Tasso's *Aminta* (trans. C. Fresch).

307–11. Listing the 52 examples in *PL* of rhyming lines separated by two unrhymed lines, John S. Diekhoff points to this sequence as he notes that in several of the examples, "the enclosed lines themselves contribute to other rhymes" ("Rhyme" 541).

308–11. In this description of Eve's obedience, Walter Raleigh finds an example of what he designates the "packed line": "The packed line introduced by Milton is of a greater density and conciseness than anything to be found in English literature before it. It is our nearest native counterpart to the force and reserve of the high Virgilian diction" (202).

Wayne Shumaker argues that in these lines "we have the description not of sensory qualities but of attitudinal. If we allow images to form in our minds as we read, they are our images, not Milton's" (*Unpremeditated Verse* 51). For Shumaker, the reader's experience is therefore "kept from being passive, so that the experience is not that merely of 'entertainment'" (52).

308. John T. Shawcross looks closely at this line; he glosses *Subjection* with "both 'being under control' (ironically) and their 'lying beneath,'" and he explains that "requir'd with gentle sway" means "both 'necessary for gentle undulation' and 'demanding of gentle governing.' The hair image implies Eve's vacillation and her need to be controlled" (*Complete Poetry* 325). Louis L. Martz finds that the "gentle sway" Adam is to exercise over Eve is most remarkably seen as Adam attempts to argue against her suggestion that they work apart in Book 9 ("*Paradise Lost*: The Power" 43).

310–11. As Newton first acknowledges, Roman love poetry reverberates in 311 and thereby foreshadows the narrator's remarks about sex—prelapsarian and postlapsarian—in the subsequent sentence. Admiring Milton's insistence that Eve's subjection is "requir'd with gentle sway" (308), Newton declares these two lines more elegant than a passage from Horace's *Odes* 2.12.26 ("aut facili saevitia negat"; "or in teasing playfulness refuses"), which Newton assumes to have been in Milton's thoughts (253). Subsequent editors, such as Todd and A. W. Verity, return to Newton's focus on 311, as both establish that later poets also obviously admire the passage. Todd ([1842], 2:72) claims that Pope (*Poems* 9:303) copied it when translating Homer's *Odyssey* 9.32, while Verity (462) asserts that Milton's line is the "obvious original" for William Collins's "Reluctant pride, and amorous faint consent," line 19 of "Written on a paper, which contained a piece of Bride Cake given to the author by a Lady" (*Works* 24). More recently, B. A. Wright adds an Ovidian source to the Horatian one established by Newton, tracing Milton's 311 to Ovid's *Art of Love* 2.718: "Sed sensim tarda prolicienda mora"; "but gradually lured on by slow delay." Wright presents the connection between the two as "proof that Milton's attitude to love in *Paradise Lost* was as sensual in the old pagan way as that expressed in his early love poems" (*Milton's "Paradise Lost"* 57). Wright also insists upon the importance of this recognition: "The distinction of love and lust is at the centre of his treatment of the Fall; but this quotation from Ovid is meant to show unmistakably his view that physical love is an essential and inseparable element in human love at its best" (58). Also see Wright's "Note on *Paradise Lost.*" Hume's response to 310–11, however, suggests a discomfort here similar to that felt by those translators who, Wright reports, usually leave Ovid's line "in the decent obscurity of a learned tongue" (*Milton's "Paradise Lost"* 57). Hume considers only the Latin etymology of *reluctant* in his annotation on 311, but he goes on at length to assert the meaning of 310. After defining *coy* as "shy," Hume explains that "modest pride" "seems to imply, that just Value and modest Self-esteem, that the Fair sex ought to regard; that *Conscience of their Worth* [cf. *PL* 8.502], which if well managed, sets off the soft Submission of a kind Companion" (146). If Hume bypasses the sexually charged nature of 311, C. S. Lewis focuses on it as he expresses concern that prelapsarian sex in Milton's epic is tainted with postlapsarian sex: "The defence of Milton's treatment must consist in distinguishing bodily shame as we now know it from some kind of bashfulness or modesty which can be conceived as existing before the Fall." Lewis then tries to make that distinction, but he sounds rather unconvinced by his own explanation when he concludes, "If this is what we mean by shame we may, perhaps, conclude that there was shame in Paradise" (123). John Halkett draws out the meaning in 310–11 in terms of their paradoxes, which "help to characterize the mixture of retirement, love, modesty, sense of equality, and sense of shame which the matrimonial writers attributed to the ideal wife. The final line is particularly rich in possibilities of interpretation; not only is 'amorous delay' paradoxical, implying desire and refusal, but 'reluctant' can apply to either of the terms which follow it, or both together: *reluctant-amorous* (implying the conflict between modest unwillingness and passionate assent); *reluctant-delay* (implying the unwillingness to withhold submission, along with its necessity); *reluctant-amorous-delay* (implying the unwillingness to show either indecent haste or misinterpreted indifference). 'Sweet' has a similar complexity, since both the person and the quality to which it refers are ambiguous" (104).

312–18. Although the description and explication of Adam's and Eve's hair end at 311, the *Nor* with which this next sentence begins implies a coordination of sorts between the two units of thought. If prelapsarian gender roles are symbolized by the descriptions of hair in 300–11, the topic of prelapsarian sexuality, grimly overshadowed by the narrator's personal remarks on postlapsarian sexual hypocrisy, is asserted in this second sentence. Any syntactical separation is further obscured by the suggestion of a blazon of beauties as Milton's description of Adam and Eve moves downward from their hair to "those mysterious parts" (312). J. B. Broadbent extends this sense of ongoing development back even further, drawing attention to the quality of the verse from 295 forward as "mysterious parts" is approached: "At first entirely abstract, and with no active verbs, the language slowly proceeds to conventional physical details. The rhythm undulates sleepily, then rises in pitch until it is quivering at Eve's 'sweet reluctant amorous delay' but at once her artfulness of love is checked by Milton's own bass voice declaring 'Nor those mysterious parts were then conceald'" (*Some Graver Subject* 186).

The earliest of Milton's early annotators, Patrick Hume, who hears no echoes of Roman love poetry in 311, directly focuses on the phrase that Broadbent sees as the end point of this extended sequence, but noting only its religious connotations, Hume, unlike later critics, has very little to say about human sexuality: "All the Secrets of Heathen Religion and Philosophy were carefully concealed from the Vulgar, and therefore called…Mysteries, not exposed to common and profane Eyes" (146). Highly critical of Milton's entire presentation of prelapsarian sexual life, Lewis has no tolerance for such concealment. Lewis writes that Milton "seems to think that by twice using the word *mysterious* in this connection (IV, 743, and VIII, 599) he excuses his very un-mysterious pictures" (124). Recalling Hume, Helen Gardner later chides Lewis for assigning *mysterious* "its modern sense of 'vague'" and for not admitting, "Milton is using it here in its older sense of 'religious,' pertaining to what is divinely received and beyond the reach of natural reason" (*Reading* 85). It is Broadbent, though, who finally confronts the complications of the sexual and the spiritual involved in *mysterious*. Returning to Lewis's cross-referencing of 743, Broadbent insists that "in both cases the word refers at once to the dark animal fact and the human significance. The materials are here waiting to be realised in either lust or love, by Adam and Eve, and the reader" (*Some Graver Subject* 186).

"Unfallen Sexuality" may be the shortest chapter in *A Preface to "Paradise Lost,"* but Lewis's reading of 311, which argues that prelapsarian sex in Milton's epic is inextricably entangled with postlapsarian sex, triggers the modern debate about the topic of human sexuality in *PL*. Among the first to speak to Lewis's reading is A. J. A. Waldock, who sees the critical effort to distinguish prelapsarian sex from postlapsarian sex as a non-topic. Waldock, in fact, flatly denies the possibility of sex without sensuality (about which Augustine had theorized), claims that even Milton himself could not imagine it, and believes that Lewis is therefore making "an unnecessary to-do about the provocativeness of Eve's sexual modesty" (62). Few other critics writing through the 1950s or 1960s appear quite that dismissive, and most continue to follow the lead of Lewis and to ponder the relationship between prelapsarian and postlapsarian sexuality. Sharing Lewis's concern with the theological issues involved in prelapsarian sex, and also looking at these lines, Dennis Burden, for example, admits that there are "difficulties" in Milton's description of Edenic sex: "Eve's tresses are 'wanton' but nevertheless imply 'subjection'; her 'sway' is 'gentle'; her coyness is…submissive; her 'pride' is 'modest.'" Burden finds, "All this manner of description exploits the puzzles in the matter" (47). Jackson I. Cope and Helen Gardner rather more confidently tackle the "difficulties" of discussing Edenic sex. Unlike Waldock, Cope does not suggest that Milton could not imagine prelapsarian sexuality, but rather that, for Milton, it serves as "an unrealizable symbol of innocence" and is therefore "perhaps the most important single stroke of unifying genius in the epic" (80). Cope's reading develops the association between the prelapsarian lushness of the garden and prelapsarian sexuality: "The breeding and multiplying of nature and of man are at one level God's reaction to Satan's active seduction of and by Sin; and, like nature's seasonal cycles, like the matter of the world itself, the sexual act is patterned into the inevitable but not yet unfolded imperfection of the fallen world created in consequence of the first fall" (82–83). While Helen Gardner shares Waldock's impatience with Lewis's "disquiet" about prelapsarian sexuality, she does not share Waldock's opinion about the nature of sex in Milton's garden. Instead, Gardner argues that Milton rejects Augustinian theories of "cold copulation" before the Fall, and contending that Milton does indeed present prelapsarian sex as pleasurable, yet not sensually tainted, she concludes, "Other feelings than shame make the heart beat faster and bring the blood to the cheeks" (*Reading* 85).

Two years before Lewis published *A Preface to "Paradise Lost,"* Grant McColley had launched the modern critical effort to establish the theological background for Milton's presentation of sex in the prelapsarian marriage. McColley writes, "Among Protestants it was, as with Calvin [*Commentaries* 2.25], not uncommon to defend somewhat vehemently the 'chaste use of the lawful and pure ordinance of God,' or with Willet, to speak emphatically against the 'popish inhibition of marriage' [*Hexapla* 21]. Satan was held up as a foe of matrimony, in part because he desired both to increase license and to diminish population" (*"Paradise Lost": An Account* 150–51). Explaining that Christian marriage was seen "as serving three desirable ends, 'domestic sweets,' procreation, and the taming of lust," McColley argues, "This interpretation of marriage, together with the remaining themes clustered about it, Milton set forth as effectively and much more attractively than his predecessors and contemporaries" (150–51). McColley's effort to establish the theological traditions against which Milton's presentation of Edenic sexuality might more accurately be understood is pursued by others during the 1940s. Sister Mary Irma Corcoran, for example, uncovers a number of traditional hexameral explanations for Adam and Eve's lack of shame, concluding that Milton "preferred the opinion that it was because of their innocence that the first couple were not ashamed" (77). Like McColley, surveying both Protestant and Catholic opinion on prelapsarian marriage and sexuality to clarify Milton's presentation, Arnold Williams points to the importance of Gen. 4.1 ("And Adam knew Eve his wife") and reports, "The most striking evidence of the pristine state of man in this happy garden was his lack of shame.... In Paradise there was no law of the members repugnant to the law of reason. The inferior parts had not revolted against the superior, and hence there was nothing in the body to be fought or to be ashamed of" (*Common Expositor* 109). Williams adds that while Benedictus Pererius (*Commentariorum* 215–16), representing "enlightened Catholic opinion," believes that "lust and immoderate passion" characterize postlapsarian intercourse, Andraeus Rivetus (*Operum Theologicorum* 106–07), the Protestant commentator, "maintains that the act is of divine origin, and though it is now frequently accompanied by passion, it is not necessarily so" (89).

Complementing this effort to establish the theological background, several other twentieth century critics consider the literary background for prelapsarian sexuality, and both Allan H. Gilbert and Frank Kermode focus on the golden-age topos presented in Tasso's *Aminta*. Gilbert admits that Tasso is hardly Milton's only source, but Gilbert also finds that the parallel between Milton's description of the "innocent nakedness of Adam and Eve" in this sequence stands as a "most striking resemblance" ("Milton and the *Aminta*" 97) to the chorus concluding the first act of Tasso's pastoral. Frank Kermode (111) similarly considers the literary background for Milton's presentation of Adam and Eve's naked innocence, quoting several lines from Henry Reynolds's 1628 English translation of Tasso's *Aminta,* which celebrates the ease, natural fecundity, and sexual freedom of the golden age before "Honour . . . lewdly did instruct faire eyes / They should be nyce, and scrupulous [sig. D2]."

Several critics during the 1960s bring the reader's reaction to bear on Milton's presentation of prelapsarian sexuality. Not sharing Addison's view that the passage is a beautiful digression (3:61), John Peter, for example, involves the reader's response with the narrator's response to Adam and Eve's nudity, and he finds the passage cathartic for both. Peter believes the narrator's personal reaction is "no more intrusive than the autobiographical exordium to Book Three, and . . . might almost be called cathartic, an emotional release" (92). So, too, when we, as readers, "encounter a representation of desire and fulfillment from which these doubts have been purged off, our reaction is accordingly not so much envy as pure relief" (93). Somewhat similarly, Wayne Shumaker considers the reader's response to this passage: "if there is imagery of a kind in the denial that sexual organs were hidden, the pictures must be supplied by the reader. All Milton has done is to jerk away a veil; what lies behind it he does not tell us. But the lack of concealment is not accompanied by shyness" (*Unpremeditated Verse* 52). Also recalling Addison, Shumaker characterizes 312–17 as a "digression on shame," after which "our attention is recalled to the ostensible objects of description by the phrase 'Simplicitie and spotless innocence' (318): and this again carries vague implications about bearing" (52). Stanley Fish, of course, most fully develops this reader-response approach, writing, "Adam and Eve are not troubled by their nakedness, but we are. Shame is described by Adam in his first awareness of sin, as 'the last of evils' (IX.1079) especially difficult to bear because it sits there to '*reproach* us as unclean' (1098, emphasis mine). Shame is 'guilty' because it wells up in us involuntarily to testify to an inner corruption. 'Shame to Milton,' writes Northrop Frye [*Return* 37], 'is something deeper and more sinister in human emotion than simply the instinctive desire to cover the genital organs. It is rather a state of mind which is the state of the Fall itself: it might be described as the emotional response to the state of pride.' This is the emotional response the reader gives to the description of Eve, and subsequently to the unfallen embrace.... If he does not immediately recognize his uneasiness at 'wanton' and 'dishevell'd' for what it is, he will certainly do so when Milton reminds him that 'nature's works' remain spotless and innocent unless they are perverted by the sin-bred mind of a guilty mankind" (*Surprised* 129). Also see Davis P. Harding on "guiltie shame" in **313**.

312–13. In his analysis of the "then-now" pattern as a feature of Milton's apocalyptic vision, Leland Ryken draws attention to these lines: "Prelapsarian sexuality, for example, was wholly innocent, but from the vantage point of the fallen narrator and reader such innocence is a past vision, contrasting with present reality" (46–47).

313. Rejecting Bentley's full stop after "guiltie shame" (117), Helen Darbishire explains that the punctuation she retains "expresses the indignant rush of Milton's thought here" (*Poetical Works* 1:296). Alastair Fowler similarly comments (632).

guiltie shame: Harding cross-references 9.1057–58, "naked left / To guilty shame," and explains that this technique of deliberately borrowing from himself is one Milton "probably learned from Virgil, who employs it constantly." Harding believes that the purpose of the continued passage (313–20) is to make us "almost ashamed of any suspicions we may have momentarily entertained" (*Club* 73).

dishonest shame: "Unseemly Shame, the Off-spring of Guilt and Sin: *Dishonest,* ugly, disgraceful" (Hume 146). John Shawcross (*Complete Poetry* 325) glosses *dishonest* as "unchaste," a definition the *OED* 2 illustrates with Shakespeare's *Henry V* 1.2.50.

314. *honor dishonorable:* the Richardsons comment that "the Distinction shewn to Those Parts is in Reallity a Dishonour; a Token of our Fall from a State of Happy Innocence when no such Regard was paid to them" (155). Newton believes that the phrase alludes to 1 Cor. 12.23, "And those *members* of the body which we think to be less honourable, upon these we bestow more abundant honour"

(253), a reference to which Todd adds the following passage from Milton's *Colas* (Patterson, *Works* 4:239): "Belike then the wrongful suffering of all those sad breaches and abuses in marriage to a remediless thraldom, is the strength and honour of marriage; a boisterous and bestial strength, a dishonourable honour" ([1842], 2:72). Also referring the phrase to 1 Cor., A. W. Verity (462) notes that Milton "often uses this classical figure of speech called *oxymoron*," and he records Tennyson's echo of Milton in *Lancelot and Elaine* 871 (*Poems* 3:447): "His honour rooted in dishonour stood."

320. Stanley Fish explains the revealing nature of the reader's response to the second half of this line: "The implication of the concluding half line, 'for they thought no ill,' is inescapable: they thought no ill but we do, and therein lies our shame and our guilt" (*Surprised* 130). Ryken develops the opposition between the reader's fallen world and Adam and Eve's paradisal world, an opposition that lies at the heart of Milton's device of the apocalypse through negation: "The perfection of Adam and Eve, like that of the garden, is frequently described in terms denying imperfection" (100). Ryken (101) points to the recurrence of this device at 313, 320, 495, 761, and 765–70.

321. *hand in hand:* turning to Philipp Camerarius's survey of the image's ancient origins in *The Living Librarie* 121–22, Kester Svendsen identifies "hand in hand" as a "hallowed image of unity" and "consecration of faith" (*Milton and Science* 111), a reading several other critics echo and develop. John Halkett, for example, explains that the image "suggests the unity and fidelity of the marriage bond" (105). Edward S. Le Comte (*Yet Once More* 41) follows Milton's emphasis on Adam and Eve's clasped hands at 4.689, 5.17, 9.385, and 12.648, and B. A. Wright focuses attention on Adam and Eve's joined hands to underscore the central importance of the love story in *PL:* "Their mutual love, in relation to their loving obedience to God, on which it depends, is the key to the harmony of their world. This is the central theme of their story, symbolized by the recurrent phrase 'hand in hand.' Through Adam and Eve in paradise Milton depicts his ideal of wedded love. It is the same ideal as Spenser had portrayed in Book III of *The Faerie Queene,* a natural sexual love that is also chaste" (*Milton's "Paradise Lost"* 156). Mario A. DiCesare considers this phrase in a somewhat broader focus on "the image of the hand reaching" (" 'Advent'rous' " 20). DiCesare explains that the image appears in three different, but at times combined, areas: "the hand as creative, the hand as symbolizing power, and the hand as symbolizing relationship" (20–21). Extending Le Comte's list of cross-references, DiCesare concludes, "From context to context, this simple gesture contains and expands our apprehension of their love, their individuality, their mutuality" (22).

323–24. Praising the "close couched" expressive power of these lines and, unlike several of his successors, never suggesting that they present a grammatical or logical challenge of any sort, Hume explains the theological basis of Adam and Eve's superiority: "That the Protoplast, the first Man, came most compleat out of the Hand of his Creator, perfect in all the Powers and Faculties both of Body and Soul: That his Comfort and Derivative *Eve* was also accomplish'd in like manner, in the full Bloom of Beauty, and all the Charming Ornaments of which her Sex was capable, is beyond all question." Hume concludes that "therefore doubtless they did not only excel all their Descendents, as the first Originals of Mankind, but as the most exact Image of their Maker, while they continued in glorious Innocence, which in their sinful Posterity is so defaced, that the most accomplish'd of either Sex, is but a dull Copy of those Master-Pieces of the Almighty" (146). Setting these lines against 2.678–79 ("God and his Son except, / Created thing naught valu'd he"), Addison in *Spectator* 285 faults but then forgives what he considers Milton's "little Blemishes," explaining, "It is plain, that in the former of these Passages, according to the natural Syntax, the Divine Persons mentioned in the first Line are represented as created Beings; and that in the other, *Adam* and *Eve* are confounded with their Sons and Daughters. Such little Blemishes are these, when the Thought is great and natural, we should, with *Horace,* impute to a pardonable Inadvertency" (3:10). Richard Bentley, however, is not forgiving, and with him begins a rather lengthy discussion of syntax and meaning in these two lines. First, Bentley paraphrases: Adam is "one of his Sons, and Her one of her Daughters. Besides, *His* Sons, *Her* Daughters; as if *His* Sons were not Her's too, and *Her* Daughters His." Then, so entangled with grammatical and logical concerns, Bentley declares, "But the whole is silly, superfluous, and spurious" (118). Pearce seeks to deflect Bentley's attack by offering classical precedents, such as the description of Diana as the loveliest of her attendant nymphs ("comitum pulcherimma"), and a number of later critics follow Pearce's example (122). The Richardsons (155) point to Horace's *Satires* 1.100 and Homer's *Iliad* 2.673. Newton supplies additional references to the *Iliad* and opines, "I believe a man would not be corrected for writing false

English, who should say *the most learned of all others* instead of *more learned than all others*" (254). Todd ([1842], 2:72–73) sustains the discussion by quoting Newton and adding to the list of precedents Sir David Lyndsay's *Ane Dialogue betuix Experience and ane Courteour, off the Miserabyll Estait of the Warld* 1:222, while he also ridicules Sir John Carr, who identified these two lines by Milton as "the prize bull" in his collection of bulls in *The Stranger in Ireland* 277. To this lengthening list of precedents authorizing Milton's syntax, Thomas Keightley (*Poems* 1:350) adds Tacitus's *Histories* 1.50, as well as Thucydides's *History of the Peloponnesian War* 1.1, in addition to references to *Orlando Furioso*. Asserting that Milton's lines exemplify "an idiom often used by Elizabethan, as it had been by Greek, writers," Verity (18) locates the idiom in the works of numerous Elizabethan writers such as Sir Thomas Browne, who in *Pseudodoxia Epidemica* 1.1 (*Works* 2:18) reports that "some affirm" Adam was "the wisest of all men since." Verity also explains: "Its independent existence in Greek and English proves that the idiom, though illogical, is natural—due perhaps to over-emphasis. It is just the sort of combined construction into which people slip in conversation" (462). Even before Verity offers his list of precedents, however, De Quincey decides that "the authority of Milton, backed by that of insolent Greece, would prove an overmatch for the logic of centuries. And I withdraw, therefore, from the rash attempt to quarrel with this sort of bull" (415). Tillyard shares De Quincey's impatience with the debate, but, unlike De Quincey, he enthusiastically praises the passage: "what simplicity, what daring, and what freedom!" (*Miltonic Setting* 127). Tillyard adds, "Milton was probably aware of the classical precedent, when he wrote the passage, and wished his readers to give it a glance if they felt inclined. He wrote his lines to stand on their own feet as English, yet through a hint of Homer he was able to ensure the epic decorum demanded by his contemporaries" (125). The accommodations—rather than the divisions—between syntax and thought draw the attention of the most recent critics attending to this crux. Frank Kermode explains that the seemingly illogical Greek syntax is actually a device by which we are included in the experience of Adam and Eve, and he associates these lines with other reminders throughout the epic to conclude "that the whole of history 'since created man' is somehow being enacted here and now in the garden" (113). J. B. Broadbent reasons that the purpose of Milton's here naming Adam and Eve by reference to their sons and daughters is to establish that they "share the artifice of eternity with paradise. Their love is not urgent because they are perpetually in love. They process through the garden with a dignity immune to the pressure of lapsarian time." Adam and Eve's children, Broadbent declares, "spring eternally from a syntactical union" (*Some Graver Subject* 190). Recalling Kermode's reading, Christopher Grose adds, "The anachronism involves the reader as well as Satan and what Satan is seeing: Milton's drama, in fact, seems to involve his reader *in* what the devil sees" (219). While these recent critics look at the sense of time established in these lines as all-embracing, Jon S. Lawry finds "a tremulous insistence on the past tense for Eden," which deepens the elegiac feeling that Satan's presence creates (172).

323. *Adam:* pointing out that the Hebrew word for *man* transliterates as "Adam," and that while the poem's first line refers to man, *Adam* does not appear until 3.734, when Uriel identifies paradise as "*Adams* abode" (*Bible* 66), James H. Sims focuses on this line: "Once inside the Garden of Eden, Satan views for himself the object of his evil purpose, '*Adam* the goodliest man of men since borne' (IV, 323), a phrase in which the poet very effectively brings together the transliterated name and its meaning. It is Satan, however, who brings together all the possible meanings of Adam's name and [in 9.175–78] adds to them his own resentful interpretation" (70).

John T. Shawcross explains that *Adam* is "derived from a word meaning 'dust,' 'soil,' and thence 'man'" (*Complete Poetry* 325).

324. *Eve:* John T. Shawcross explains that the name is "derived from a word meaning 'live,' 'be,' and thence 'Mother of Mankind' (V, 388)" (*Complete Poetry* 325).

325–40. As Adam and Eve move to enjoy "thir Supper Fruits" (331), the narrator mentions "thir sweet Gardning labour" (328) to introduce the topic of prelapsarian work, but while twentieth century critics maintain a vigorous discussion about Adam and Eve's work, early editors do not mention it. Adam himself refers to that prelapsarian gardening in his first speech (437–39), but it becomes the main subject of his second speech (610–33), and at that point, the topic is fully developed. Among the early editors, Todd alone comments on this sequence, but, considering a similarity between Milton's description of the evening meal and one in 1:93–94 of Jacob Masenius's *Sarcotis,* he gives no notice to the narrator's reference to Adam and Eve's working through the earlier part of the day ([1842], 2:73–74). Also observing the evening meal in Eden, Walter Raleigh memorably describes Adam and Eve as "nut-eaters" who " have not the art of cooking, and do not ferment the juice of the grape" (122), but he no more understands the evening meal as marking the end of a working day than does Tillyard, although Tillyard more emphatically engages with the topic of prelapsarian labor in his commentary on **610–33** (*Milton* 282–83).

While several modern critics note the easy informality of Adam and Eve's evening meal, they often also find ominous elements in the description of the scene. Roy Daniells points out that the setting for this informal evening meal differs from the one for the next day's midday meal with its "formal square table...set for a heavenly guest" ("Happy Rural Seat" 8), and John R. Knott identifies here the motif of "bucolic repose" ("Symbolic Landscape" 45), which may be traced to Virgil's first *Eclogue,* but as he continues, Knott allows that such "bucolic repose" is more often recalled in the "enervating repose shown in the false paradises of Ariosto, Tasso, and Spenser" (46) than in the presentations of the biblical paradise. "If one needs an emblem to represent the Arcadian world," Knott explains, "it should be a reclining or seated figure, suggesting by his relaxation and his harmony with nature a profound calm of mind. Milton's tableau is perhaps the richest statement of this motif in English poetry. Yet the frisking of all the animals about Adam and Eve in itself sufficiently indicates that their 'ease' goes beyond the *otium* of pastoral poetry. As Adam is reminded in his discourse with Raphael on astronomy, their contentment depends upon obedience" (46). Elsewhere, Knott advances this point by drawing attention to the ominousness of Satan's entering the garden at evening, "a time of security" in the pastoral tradition, "the most tranquil hour of the day, a time of relaxation and special intimacy for Adam and Eve" ("Pastoral Day" 175). John F. Huntley describes the meal as "*au natural,*" and explains, "Its simple privacy and unabashed sexiness are apt to shock us unless we view the scene with minds raised up from the darkness of Book 1 to the light invoked in Book 3." Huntley notes that, in describing this evening meal and the next day's lunch, Milton inverts traditional descriptions of grotesque scenes of gluttony, as well as scenes of gluttony associated with evil in *PL* (48). Just such provocative associations strike yet other critics as disconcerting. Although Broadbent, for one, appreciates that the sensuousness of Adam and Eve's eating "unqualified by art or reason" is most appropriately stressed here, he also admits that "even here there is danger." Broadbent writes, "The compliance of the boughs becomes sinister, the sidelong relaxation of Adam and Eve is a perilous declination from erectitude, and in a moment Satan's curses break in on us." As a result, Broadbent concludes,

"The overall feeling we have about Adam and Eve in Book IV is of stability on the brink of change: it can, will fall, but it could be no more blessed than it is" (*Some Graver Subject* 186). Finally, in "to thir Supper Fruits they fell," Jackson I. Cope hears "a pun that resounds with the infernal snicker" (112).

325–26. The very reason why "on a green" (325) here offends Bentley is the same reason it meets with Helen Darbishire's approval. Bentley describes the phrase as "poor stuff indeed" and complains that the writer "seems to have fansied himself in some Country Village, and to have forgot that the Scene was Paradise." Referring to "Where winds with reeds and osiers whispering play" in *PR* 2.26, Bentley contends that the line should read "*Under a tuft of shade, that* TO THE BREEZ / *Stood whispering soft*" (118–19). Darbishire considers Bentley's complaint, but she argues that neither the printer nor the poet is to be faulted, for "Milton had a true taste in country words." While she disagrees with Bentley, she does concede that his "strictures on Milton's language open our eyes, if they need opening, to the surprising variety, the changes and contrasts of mood and style which enliven it." To support and elaborate her understanding of Milton's language, Darbishire refers to Pope's remarks on the same (*Milton's "Paradise Lost"* 12). Also see Darbishire on "charm of earliest Birds" in **642**). Defending Milton's style, Pope explains that "it should have been observed of *Milton,* that he is not lavish of his exotick words and phrases every where alike, but employs them much more where the subject is marvellous vast and strange, as in the scenes of Heaven, Hell, Chaos &c. than where it is turn'd to the natural and agreeable, as in the pictures of Paradise, the loves of our first parents, the entertainments of Angels, and the like" (*Poems* 10:390).

In his 1795 edition of *PR,* Charles Dunster, like Bentley, juxtaposes 4.325–26 and *PR* 2.26. Dunster does so, however, as he argues that the whispering of the wind is one of Milton's favorite images. Considering 5.15–17 as well, Dunster explains that Milton "also applies whispering to the flowing of a stream; to the air that plays upon the water, or by the side of it; and to the combined sounds of the breeze and the current" (66).

325. *shade:* B. A. Wright and Anne Davidson Ferry have been most attentive to Milton's use of the word *shade.* Understanding *shade* as "tree," Wright adds that "'tuft' means 'clump (of trees)'; Shakespeare has 'tuft of Olives,' 'tuft of Pines,' 'tuft of trees.' A shade, in the ordinary sense, it may be noticed, does not whisper" (*Milton's "Paradise Lost"* 71). Also see Wright in 138n for *shade* as "tree." Ferry finds *shade* a very significant and subtly meaningful word recurring throughout the epic. She points out that it is especially important to the descriptions of Eden and "grows in meanings with the effect of a sacred metaphor" (*Milton's Epic Voice* 169). Milton's repetition of the word, Ferry contends, "identifies Eden with the qualities associated with 'shades'; it is a region holy, refreshing, benevolent, protected. The same associations accumulate around unfallen man, appropriately, since Eden is a 'state' of innocence, both a place and a condition" (171).

329. *To recommend coole Zephyr:* the list of both classical and Miltonic references to the west wind has been growing ever since Hume's initial annotation. "To make the soft West-Wind more pleasing," notes Hume, who then cites Pliny's *Natural History* 4:448; Virgil's *Eclogues* 5.5; and Homer's *Odyssey* 4.567, where the west wind is described as cooling men's souls in Elysium, and *Odyssey* 7.118, where the west wind ripens the fruits of Alcinous's garden (147). Reinforcing Hume's understanding of *Zephyr* as a soft and pleasing wind with a few more classical citations, Charles Grosvenor Osgood also points out, however, that in *Iliad* 23.200, 208, 214–15, Zephyrus is described as stormy (86). Merritt Y. Hughes (*Complete Poetry* 286) adds a reference to Milton's *El* 5.69. "The frolic wind that breathes the spring" in *L'All* 18 is the west wind cross-referenced by Alastair Fowler (633), who, invoking the authority of Edgar Wind (*Pagan Mysteries in the Renaissance* 103, 113) explains, "In Neoplatonic mythology, the enlivening touch of Zephyr begins the initial phase in the generative progression." Fowler adds, "From the time of Ovid (in his account of the Golden Age, *Met*[*amorphoses*] i 107[–8]), Zephyr had figured in most poetic visions of eternal spring," but in Ben Jonson's *The Vision of Delight* (*Ben Jonson* 7:461–71), Zephyr "received particularly elaborate treatment."

330–31. *appetite / More grateful:* Hume's annotation combines his dogged attention to etymology with a bit of late seventeenth century social commentary: "Hunger more pleasant in being satisfied: Hunger the best Sawce, tho' seldom served to the best furnish'd Tables" (147).

330. *easie:* "luxurious, comfortable" (Fowler 633).

332. *Nectarine:* Hume notes, "sweet like Nectar" (147), while Alastair Fowler (633) reports that "the variety of peach called nectarine was known at least as early as 1616."

    compliant: Todd ([1842], 2:74) suggests a reference to Theocritus (*Poems* 7:144–46), Verity (462) discusses etymology: "probably in the rare sense 'pliant, easily bent,' due to the false derivation from Fr. *plier,* Lat. *plicare;* the true etymological connection being with Ital. *complire,* Lat. *complere,*" and Alastair Fowler (633) adds that the *OED* 2 cites Milton's use here as the "earliest instance" in the sense of "pliant." One might also note, as the *OED* 5 does, that Eve is herself described in terms of *compliance* as Adam tells Raphael, "All her words and actions mixed with love / And sweet compliance" (8.603–04). Perhaps suggesting Patrick Hume's recognition of the association between Eve, whose "Subjection" is to be "yielded" to Adam (308–09), and the garden that yields to her is the collation of Hume's gloss on *Nectarine,* "sweet," and his annotation on those "compliant boughes [which] / Yielded" (332–33) such fruits: "willing, yielding, of the Verb to comply, that is, to yield, to agree to" (147).

    Allan H. Gilbert ("Milton and the *Aminta*" 96) draws a parallel between the compliant boughs in Milton's garden and the similar presentation of nature's yielding the fruits of the earth without cultivation in the chorus's celebration of the golden age at the end of the first act of Tasso's *Aminta.*

333. *recline:* Fowler notes: "recumbent, reclining (Lat. *reclinis*); the only instance of this Latinising coinage listed in *OED*" (633).

334. *damaskt:* with an eye to this word, Todd suggests similarity between Milton and his poetic predecessors, although several centuries later, J. B. Broadbent considers difference. Todd ([1842], 2:74) notes, "To damask the ground with flowers, was a favourite phrase among our old poets," and cites Phineas Fletcher, *The Purple Island* 12.1; Giles Fletcher, *Christs Victorie* 2.41; and Michael Drayton, *The Muses Elysium* 1.21 (*Works* 3:248). Against Milton's "Bank damaskt with flours" Broadbent sets Michael Drayton's *Endimion and Phoebe* 37 (*Works* 1:130), describing trees along a walk serving "for hangings and rich Tapestry," in which Broadbent claims, "Drayton is being carried towards the economic extravagance that Milton avoids. Milton chooses static phrases—'vegetable Gold,' 'fruit burnisht with Golden Rinde,' which simply equate nature with art, or balance them against each other. The 'soft downie Bank damaske with flours' (IV.334) is not elaborated into the appearance of an ottoman" (*Some Graver Subject* 179–80).

Leland Ryken (82–83) develops Milton's various apocalyptic techniques by reference to 334: "In such a description associations both of color and texture combine to form a composite enameled image. The streams of Paradise, in reflecting the vegetation growing on their banks, act as a 'chrystal mirror' (IV, 263), and the permanence which we associate with human artifice becomes linked with the vegetation of the garden when we read of 'the soft downie Bank damaskt with flours' (IV, 334)."

Merritt Y. Hughes reports that the *OED* 3 quotes the line to illustrate *damaskt* meaning "to ornament with or as with a variegated pattern or design." Of *damaskt*, Hughes adds, "The accent is on the last syllable" ("Variorum").

335–36. Gilbert (*Geographical Dictionary* 153–54) associates this passage with the more detailed description of the food that Eve prepares during Raphael's visit in Book 5, and suggesting that Milton "seems to have been especially attracted by descriptions of Indian fruits," Gilbert wonders whether some of Milton's language may have been inspired by Linschoten's report on the coconut as found in Purchas's *Hakluytus Posthumus, or, Purchas His Pilgrimes* 2:1778: "The huske being taken off, the shell serveth for many uses."

335. *savourie:* Fowler glosses this as "appetizing, fragrant. Note that the word often meant 'spiritually edifying'" (633).

337–40. Hume provides a note on "nor youthful dalliance," which stresses the "*Sportiveness and Youthful Pleasure, such as becomes Young Persons joyn'd in matrimonial State, when by themselves alone*" (147), and John Peter most recently develops the importance of such shared playfulness: "an absence of false delicacy, of poetic self-consciousness—the positive side of that tactlessness which is displayed in the matter of angelic substance and diet—and it does much to validate the remoter beauties of Paradise. It does still more to validate the relationship between Adam and Eve, for it persuades us that we are in contact less with paragons, unreal idealizations, than with a man and woman as human as ourselves. The inclusiveness extends particularly to that side of love most often glossed over in elevated modes of writing, and to the flesh through which it operates" (92).

Diametrically opposed to Patrick Hume and John Peter on this topic are Joseph Addison and C. S. Lewis, for whom Adam and Eve are paragons and idealizations. Neither Addison nor Lewis comments on Adam and Eve's "youthful dalliance," and their remarks elsewhere reveal the reason for their silence. For Addison, "*Milton's* Characters, most of them, lie out of Nature, and were to be formed purely by his own Invention" (*Spectator* 2:586). Prelapsarian Adam and Eve, for Addison, "are a different Species from that of Mankind, who are descended from them" (2:587). Insisting that Adam and Eve "were never young, never immature or underdeveloped" (115), Lewis argues, "The task of a Christian poet presenting the unfallen first of men is not that of recovering the freshness and simplicity of mere nature, but of drawing someone who, in his solitude and nakedness, shall *really be* what Solomon and Charlemagne and Haroun-al-Raschid and Louis XIV lamely and unsuccessfully strove to imitate.... And from the very first sight we have of the human pair Milton begins doing so" (118).

337. *gentle purpose:* all the editorial glosses define *purpose* as "conversation" and quite often refer to Spenser's similar use of the word. Robert Thyer, according to Todd, refers Milton's use to Spenser's in *The Faerie Queene* 3.8.14, where Braggadocchio turns to the false Florimell and "'gan make *gentle purpose* to his dame" ([1842], 2:74), and Merritt Y. Hughes cites *The Faerie Queene* 1.12.13 where Redcross and Una "fitting purpose frame" (*Complete Poems* 286). Alastair Fowler (633), qualifying the conversation as "polite," looks to *Much Ado about Nothing* 3.1.11–12. Pursuing the implications of the Spenserian associations in Milton's description of Adam and Eve enjoying "gentle purpose" along with their "Supper Fruits," A. Bartlett Giamatti does not note the conversation between Redcross and Una but, in addition to the Braggadocchio and false-Florimell passage, considers *The Faerie Queene* 1.2.30, where Redcross and the disguised Duessa share "goodly purposes, there as they sit." According to Giamatti, "What is immediately striking in this juxtaposition of passages is the vast difference between the kind of love implied in Milton's poem and that found in Spenser's, though one could see again how by allusion Milton might be preparing for the role of lust after the fall. But there is something deeper and more interesting here: the fact that the women of *The Faerie Queene* whom Milton evokes are the two (and the only two in Spenser's poem) who are simply not what they appear to be. And the result...is that we wonder about Eve" (318).

338. *dalliance:* Fowler (633) rejects the meaning "conversation," the first meaning listed in the *OED*, to argue that it "would be pleonastic after *purpose*," and defines *dalliance* instead as "caressing," which is the second meaning listed in the *OED*.

340–52. As Adam and Eve's lack of shame sharpens the topic of prelapsarian versus postlapsarian sexuality, so the behavior of the animals in the garden draws attention to the divide between the unfallen and the fallen world. Immediately remarkable is the peacefulness of the animals, which Hume refers to the Messianic vision in Isa. 11.6–7, 65.25, but, citing Theocritus (*Poems* 31) and Virgil's *Eclogues* 5.60–61, Hume explains that "general Opinion" also has it that before the Fall "there was an Universal Peace, even among the fiercest Beasts, throughout the whole Creation" (147). Supplying the mythological introduction and notes for the Loeb translation of Nonnos, H. J. Rose (3:211) suggests that Milton's description of the peaceful animals may also be a "possible imitation" of a passage in Nonnos's *Dionysiaca* 41.185–203. Also see Mabbott. Several modern critics bring detailed development to Hume's suggestion that the tradition of the peaceful prelapsarian animals was a popular one. In *Complete Poems* 286, Hughes cross-references 8.345–54 and quotes from Samuel Pordage's *Mundorum Explicatio* 58: "ADAM is Lord, and King: each animal / Comes at his beck, and doth obey his call." In "Variorum," Hughes adds a reference to the lengthy catalog of animals in Sylvester's translation of Du Bartas's *The Divine Weeks and Works* 1.6.25–418, while he also quotes from the seventh stanza of the sixth day in Thomas Traherne's *Meditations on the Six Days of the Creation* (*Centuries* 2:198). Sister Mary Irma Corcoran notes that while some authors believed that the animals entered paradise only to be named, other authors, like Milton, "regarded them as sources of delight to man" (28), as "part of the charm of Paradise" (29). Milton's most charming elephant, Corcoran points out, "like that of Blaeu's atlas [*Le Theatre du Monde* title page], wreathed his trunk ... and the serpent ... followed that of St. John of Damascene [*De Fide Orthodox,* col. 910] in conversing with man with pleasing motion." Corcoran also indicates that, as here in *PL,* so, too, in Sylvester's translation of Du Bartas's *The Divine Weeks and Works* 1.6.22, 1.6.297, and 1.6.299, bears, tigers, ounces, and pards are identified among the animals in the garden (29). Fowler (633) refers the popular presentation of the animals surrounding Adam and Eve to the visual arts: "Among fine examples are Cranach's painting *The Garden of Eden* (Vienna,

Kunsthistorisches Museum), Durer's engraving *The Fall of Man* (Bartsch I) and Goltzius's Windsor Castle ink drawing (No. 4758); among popular examples, the frontispiece to 'Eden' in Sylvester's 1613 Du Bartas. Contrast the scene of enmity at x 710–14." In his 1795 edition of *PR*, Charles Dunster associates the playful animals here with the animals that at the sight of Jesus in *PR* 1.310 "grew mild," Dunster noting, "upon the appearance of perfect innocence in a human form amongst them, they begin to resume a certain proportion of their Paradisiacal disposition" (35).

th' unwieldy Elephant... Proboscis: the playfulness of the animals, as Corcoran notes, is memorably expressed by the elephant, and modern critics have been attentive to that creature's efforts to entertain Adam and Eve, although Patrick Hume is impressed, more than amused, by the creature, reporting that its trunk is "so pliant and useful to him that Cicero calls it 'elephantorum *manum*,' the elephant's *hand* [*De Natura Deorum* 2.47]." Hume adds that the trunk is "common to this Creature with others much his Inferiours, Flies and Fleas" (148). Subsequent editors occasionally repeat this note; see, e.g., Todd ([1842], 2:75). Geoffrey Bullough indicates the elephant's humorous presentation in the Dutch edition of Jacob Cats's *Trou-Ringh* 3, as well as the 1643 Latin version of the poem, both of which included an engraving of an elephant "wreathing 'his Lithe Proboscis'... among the animals round the rustic throne of Adam and Eve" (122). Recalling Milton's much earlier prose reference to Adam and the animals in *Tetr*, where they were said "to make him sport" (Patterson, *Works* 4:83), Edward S. Le Comte goes on, "This is carried through in the elephant's 'lithe proboscis' passage, which some critics persist in being solemn about, though it contains the words 'Sporting' (iv.43) and 'To make them mirth' (346)" (*Yet Once More* 101). Elsewhere, Le Comte concedes, however, that "it may be that we are too sadly far from unfallen man to share Adam's innocent 'mirth' (IV, 346) on the occasion of the elephant's wreathing 'His Lithe Proboscis'" ("Milton as Satirist" 47). Dennis Burden and Roy Daniells do not qualify their appreciation for the elephant's maneuvers with his trunk, Daniells identifying the humor as baroque (*Milton, Mannerism* 128), and Burden describing it as "a circus act designed providentially to please the human pair, 'to make them mirth'" (51). J. B. Broadbent associates Milton's description of the elephant with contemporary travel literature, explaining that the elephant was a great favorite with readers, "appearing on almost all maps of the East" ("Milton's Paradise" 163). Broadbent faults Milton's presentation, however, because "the zoological facts had…not been properly subdued. The interest aroused in this elephant is amusement and curiosity of the 'Believe It or Not' kind, whereas Milton's fiction ought to be stranger than fact" (164).

unwieldy: Bentley admires Milton's "great Art and Judgment" here as "following his Principals *Homer* and *Virgil,* he made the Verse it self *unwieldy.*" Bentley also cautions the reader that the accent here is on the first syllable, unlike *unwieldy* describing the leviathan in 7.412, where the accent falls on the second syllable (119). Bentley's praise for the unwieldy nature of the verse in this passage is echoed in both Le Comte's approval of *Proboscis,* a "deliberately ponderous noun" ("Milton as Satirist" 47), and Arnold Stein's remarks on the entertainment all the animals provide: "Nowhere else, I think, does Milton so indulgently imitate physical movements by the sound of his verse as in his amused description of the prelapsarian zoo" (71).

Theodicy, rather than prosody, gains the attention of several other twentieth century critics as they ponder the elephant's ungainliness. Edward Chauncey Baldwin (368) reports that the unwieldiness of both the elephant or behemoth (7.470–72) and the leviathan (7.411) was intended for the Lord's entertainment, according to rabbinical authority, such as the *Midrash Konen* 26: "He created Behemoth of the thousand mountains, as well as the ox who uproots a thousand mountains daily; and both appear daily in Paradise to make merry in the presence of the Lord." Burden concedes that the unwieldiness of both the leviathan and elephant might appear to compromise divine providence, but the leviathans "demonstrate the overwhelming might of God. And they do not harm Adam in any way because their life is entirely separate from his. But with this distinction between the land and sea animals in mind, it is easy to see why Milton made his elephant in Paradise a comic turn" (51).

Tygers, Ounces, Pards: Hume provides etymological and descriptive comments on all three cats in this line and points to Virgilian references for tigers and ounces, and for the most part, subsequent editors have added nothing to Hume's annotations. By reference to Virgil's *Eclogues* 5.29, Hume explains, "A Tyger is a swift and very fierce Beast; *Tigris* is an *Armenian* word for swift, signifying this *Beast,* an *Arrow,* and the *Famous River* of that Name, all from their swiftness and impetuosity." Citing Virgil's *Georgics* 3.264, Hume identifies an ounce as "a Beast engendred between a Wolf and a Stag, therefore *e luporum cervariorum genere,* exceeding quick of sight, his Skin speckled and spotted with various Colours. *Ounce,* of the Span. *Lonza,* the Corruption of the Ablat. *Lynce,* of *Lynx.*" Pards, Hume reports, are "Male *Panthers,* or *Leopards*"

(147–48). Of the *Ounces,* Alastair Fowler writes, "properly 'lynxes'; but in the seventeenth century applied loosely to various feline beasts" (634). The *OED* 1 quotes Milton's line here to exemplify the definition Fowler summarizes.

the Serpent sly: the actions of the serpent, described in more detail than any of the other animals entertaining Adam and Eve, has long evoked critical discussions of the distinction between prelapsarian and postlapsarian behavior. The Richardsons identify the "intricate form, into which he [the serpent] put himself" as "a sort of symbol or type of his fraud, though not then regarded" (159–60). Newton argues that Milton "judiciously" devotes most of his attention to describing the serpent that will become "the instrument of so much mischief." The poet's intention, Newton reasons, is "to prepare the reader for what follows" (256). A number of twentieth century critics wrestle rather more vigorously with the problem of the prelapsarian serpent's slyness and guile. Arguing that there is no division between appearance and reality in *PL* until after the Fall of man, Raymond B. Waddington believes, "Milton explicitly represents the serpent as sufficiently evil in his own right for Eve to be able to detect his nature if she is alert" (393). Disagreeing, Burden does not find the prelapsarian serpent evil, although he admits that it was in other accounts. Burden explains that while the subtlety assigned the serpent in Genesis suggests that God is "improvident," Milton writes to prohibit that understanding "by making that slyness quite visible and apparent (even if, through Man's fault, it went unheeded)" (53). Fowler responds to Burden's reading of "proof unheeded" by suggesting that the phrase "may only be meant to point the irony that no one is paying any attention to the creature who will have the most momentous importance; 'proof' need only have been chosen for the sake of the context it suggests: the serpent's very movements are dialectical" (634). Arnold Williams investigates the theological uncertainty suggested by the serpent's slyness by looking at the Renaissance commentators on Genesis. Williams reports that "common opinion" was that the serpent was to be understood as neither a metaphor for Satan nor an image feigned by Satan, but rather as "a real, natural serpent, into which the devil had insinuated himself. The serpent was but the tool of Satan." Commentators also pondered why Satan chose the serpent, and while some followed St. Augustine (*The Literal Meaning of Genesis* 11.27), who, echoing the Jewish exegetes, contends that God permitted Satan to use only the serpent, others, according to Williams, "thought that the serpent's winding and sinuous way of locomotion fitted Satan's designs and gave outward evidence of a crafty and tortuous nature" (*Common Expositor* 115). Leland Ryken's emphasis on the apocalyptic nature of our vision of paradise brings yet another understanding to the prelapsarian-postlapsarian complications of Milton's "Serpent sly." Ryken explains: "Slyness and subtlety in our thinking denote achieving an end by devious means, but surely delicate artfulness can be a good quality when achieving a good end; we should, therefore, divest these descriptive words of pejorative associations in order to make the description accord with the innocence which we knew existed before the Fall. If the terms linked with the serpent seem difficult to interpret with positive meanings only, it is perhaps a measure of the distance between the fallen reader and the apocalyptic vision" (68). Allan H. Gilbert ("Milton and the *Aminta*" 96–97) points out that the serpents mentioned as the chorus celebrates the golden age at the end of act 1 of Tasso's *Aminta* are similarly innocent.

The notion of man's superiority to the earthly creatures, a theme usually involved with foreshadowing the postlapsarian world, is also established as Milton describes the animals of Eden. Kester Svendsen, considering the apparently deliberate actions of both the elephant and the serpent, cross-references 8.369–75 and 9.553–61, and also refers to *Prol 7* (Patterson, *Works* 12:246–85), which opposes reason and instinct. "The usual view, echoed many times in Milton, was that animals possessed highly developed instincts but not reason; and Milton's whole concept of Adam's superiority was that his moral responsibility rested upon his unique power of right reason" (*Milton and Science* 163). Noting that the animals "keep exactly the proper distance from Adam and Eve," Roy Daniells refers to God's earlier directive to Adam to "Find pastime" but also "beare rule" (8.375) over the animals. That directive, Daniells reasons, points to the postlapsarian world: "Clearly this adumbrates the domestication of animals, but, like the adumbration of Eve's maternal role, it is fulfilled only after the expulsion. In the meantime, there are token performances" ("Happy Rural Seat" 13). Dennis Burden and Leland Ryken also develop the association between pre- and postlapsarian animal life. Burden explains, "God in Genesis gave Adam dominion over all the creatures but Milton did not take this to imply that the animals needed to be tamed. In the Garden they are naturally well-behaved . . . and this friendliness of their manner enables Milton to make a nice point about the difference between the unfallen and the fallen satanic world" (49–50). Ryken's study of Milton's apocalyptic vision discusses both sameness and difference as the playful animals of the garden are juxtaposed to the postlapsarian animals known to Milton's readers from their maps, travel literature, or engravings. First, Ryken explains that the apocalyptic experience, being "other" than our ordinary experience, can most simply be established through the technique of contrasts, and, pinpointing "since wilde" in 341, he identifies "a whole pattern of 'then-now' temporal contrasts underlying the portrayal of prelapsarian perfection" (44). Second, reminding readers that the animals, like the plant life, in the garden "are essentially those of our own experience" (126), Ryken explains, "The poet who is portraying apocalyptic reality can qualify, negate, and distance the empirical images which he uses, but unless there is first a foundation of analogy established between the known and unknown worlds the apocalyptic vision ceases to be intelligible" (128).

342. Seeking to establish the elements of Milton's syllabic prosody, S. Ernest Sprott points to this line, as well as 219, as he explains one of the principles of the inversion of feet within the epic: "The rule, generally, is that in order that inversion may take place there must be a diaeresis [the end of the foot coincides with the end of the word] between the inverting and the preceding foot ['Wilderness, Forrest'], and the stress syllable of the preceding foot must be strongly accented or followed by a definite compensatory break" (100). Also see Sprott in **219**.

343. *rampd:* A. W. Verity glosses this as "sprang" (462) but more fully considers the meaning in his "Glossary," where he notes that it can mean "to rage" as in the Prayer Book text of Ps. 22.13 ("a ramping and a roaring lion"); "to tear, snatch"; and "to rear up on the hind legs" (715). To illustrate the figurative application of the meaning "To climb, scramble," the *OED* 2 cites Milton's *Animad*: "Surely the Prelates would have Saint Pauls words rampe one over another, as they use to clime into their Livings and Bishopricks" (Patterson, *Works* 3:150).

345–52. Arnold Stein settles this sequence into his overall view of Milton's presentation of the garden. "This is program music that expresses one of the human attitudes evoked by the pastoral theme—in which the artist's awareness of exaggeration is functional in the art, for this art is the grown man's conscious love for the childhood of nature in which he once unself-consciously participated with a child's love" (71).

345. *Gambold:* S. Ernest Sprott, insisting that Milton's prosody is syllabic, rather than accentual, considers this word as he looks at the entire line. Examining

elision due to the "y-glide" in Gambold, also Sprott explains that in the case
of the adjacent vowels ending one word and beginning the next ("unwieldy
Elephant"), the second vowel is stressed, not suppressed (78–80).

348. *Insinuating:* Hume's definition, derived from the word's Latin roots, is
"wrapping, or rolling up, and so it were embosoming himself," which Hume
then associates with Virgil, and which later commentators continue to develop.
Noting, "*Sinuosus* and *sinuare,* are words often used by Virgil, to express the
winding Motions of this wily Animal," Hume quotes from the *Aeneid* 2.208
and 11.753 (148). Todd condenses Hume's note ([1842], 2:75). Mario A.
DiCesare develops the connection between Virgil's and Milton's language of
insinuation. Acknowledging that until possessed by Satan, the serpent, according
to the narrator, remains "Nor nocent yet" (9.186), DiCesare (" 'Advent'rous' "
8–9) argues that the serpent has nonetheless an "aptly Satanic texture," expressed
here in Book 4 in "the sinuosity of the verse," which the Virgilian text (*Aeneid*
2.228–29) demonstrates with equal clarity: "Tum vero tremefacta novus per
pectora cunctis / insinuat pavor"; "Then indeed a strange terror steals through
the shuddering hearts of all." John T. Shawcross recalls the obsolete meaning of
train (349) "wile" to point out that the "coiling" (*Insinuating*) of that *breaded*
or "braided" *train* entangles it even more. "The spelling," Shawcross adds,
"implies the method used for his guile" (*Complete Poetry* 326).

    Gordian twine: Hume rehearses the ancient fable of the Gordian knot "hung
up in *Apollo's* Temple, by *Gordius* King of *Phrygia,* but formerly a Husbandman
who coming first on a fatal Day into the Temple, was by the Oracle declared
King of that Country, and in memory of his Preferment, hung up the Ropes that
formerly fasten'd his Team to the Plough, pleated in so strange a manner, that
the Sovereignty of those Countries (some say of the World) was predicted to
any one that could untie the intricate and perplext Knot, whence the Proverb,
Nodus Gordianus, for an inextricable Difficulty; and *Horace, Dignus vindice
Nodus* [*The Art of Poetry* 191]. *Alexander the Great* cut it in pieces with his
Sword, resolving to frustrate, if he could not fulfil the Prophesie" (148). The
Richardsons repeat this version of the fable (159–60) but are then charged with
misrepresentation by James Paterson, who reports that the knot was hung in
the temple of Jupiter (311–12). R. C. Browne (1:352) cross-references Milton's
earlier reference to the "Gordian knot" in *Vac* 90.

    twine: to the story of the Gordian knot, Alastair Fowler (634) adds that *twine*
"could also mean 'division, separation, disunion,' " as he cites the *OED* sb. 2,

which quotes Josuah Sylvester's translation of Du Bartas's *The Divine Weeks and Works* 2.4.2.1328. In this meaning, Fowler suggests, is "an allusion, perhaps, to the division made by Satan between Adam and Eve." Referencing *The City of God* 14.11, Fowler notes, "St. Augustine says that Satan chose the serpent for his instrument because it was a creature slippery, pliable, wreathed in knots, and fit for his work." Cf. *Nat* 226: "Not *Typhon* huge ending in snaky twine."

349. *breaded:* exemplifying the substantive *brede,* meaning "Anything plaited, entwined, or interwoven; a plait," the *OED*'s first entry is from Milton's *DDD:* "His silk'n breades untwine, and slip their knots" (Patterson, *Works* 3:401).

351–52. *Coucht…/…ruminating:* F. T. Prince identifies the structure of this pairing as an example of the Italian element in Milton's epic verse. Evident here, he explains, is the device of adding "a second adjective as an interjection or afterthought, to an already qualified substantive" (*Italian Element* 112).

Coucht, and now fild: studying Milton's prosody, S. Ernest Sprott points out that, of the three ways that the final *–ed* of the past tense and past participle may be spelled in Milton's poetry, this is the third: "Both *e* and the apostrophe are omitted to indicate there is no metrical syllable and the preceding vowel is short" (9).

Coucht: inserting an apostrophe, Newton (256) much admires "how artfully the word *couch'd* is placed, so as to make the sound expressive of the sense." Adding, "Such a rest upon the first syllable of the verse is not very common, but is very beautiful when it is so accommodated to the sense," Newton then lists similar occurrences in Homer's *Iliad* 1.51, 5.146, 5.156, as well as in Pope's translation.

sat: the *OED* cites Milton's line under definition 11, "Of animals: To rest the body in a manner analogous to that of a seated person." It also cites 5.24–25.

ruminating: simply and directly, Hume writes, "Chewing the cud before they go to rest" (148). Repeating Hume's gloss, Todd in 1801 reports a note from John Bowle suggesting that *Orlando Furioso* 6.22 may here have been in Milton's thoughts: "Senza temer, ch' alcun gli uccida, o pigli, / Pascono, o stansi ruminando l'erba"; "[the deer] not fearing that anybody would kill them or take them, are feeding or chewing their cuds" (trans. Allan Gilbert, *Orlando*) (282). In 1826, Todd (2:306–07; [1842], 2:75) adds that in *Summer. A Poem* 35, James Thomson "paints his herds from Milton: 'on the grassy bank / Some *ruminating* lie.'" David Masson returns to the simplicity of Hume's note (*Poetical Works* 3:174), while Merritt Y. Hughes suggests a pun, "to chew the cud and to meditate or contemplate" ("Variorum").

352–55. Early editors pay considerable attention to the astronomical details in this sequence. Hume first establishes the ancient belief that "the Sun set in, and arose out of the Sea"; then he precisely comments on Libra, "th' ascending Scale," to establish the seasonal time as the equinox (148). Newton reports Hume's note, and bringing additional emphasis to "ascending scale," quotes from Virgil's *Georgics* 1.208 as he explains, "The *balance* of Heaven or Libra is one of the 12 signs, and when the sun is in that sign, as he is at the autumnal equinox, the days and nights are equal, as if weigh'd in a balance" (257). Todd acknowledges Newton's note but drops the Virgilian reference ([1842], 2:75). Fowler develops the astronomical precision marking the earliest commentaries, although he sees a "serious pun" in the "ascending Scale": "Since the sun is in Aries (iii 555–61*n*, x 329*n*), the *stars that usher evening* rise in Libra, the Scales, the portion of the sky exactly opposite. But *scale of heaven* implies also the balancing of light and darkness that originally determined the visual representation of the equinoctial sign.... For the culmination of the constellation Libra at midnight, six hours after the time of the present passage, see ll. 1014f; and for the equinoctial theme elsewhere in *PL*, see ll. 280–5*n*, ix 50f, x 651–706*n*" (634). Fowler's detailed discussion of the "golden Scales" (997) sequence at the end of Book 4 returns considerable attention to his understanding of this earlier sequence.

Less taken up with the astronomical specifics of this setting, the majority of twentieth century critics bring broader attention to evening as a dramatic setting for this first scene in Eden. J. B. Broadbent explains that this description of evening, like that in 590–609, is a chronographia, the descriptive capture of a moment of time, which in this case gives "assurance of the smooth working of the divine laws of nature," and thereby distinguishes the garden from hell and the fallen world, where "endlessness and vicissitudes are modulated by no chronographias" (*Some Graver Subject* 199). Similarly, David Daiches explains that such scenes in the fallen world "are pettier and less involved in a whole cosmic pattern" (188). Developing the metaphoric and structural significance of scene throughout the epic is Jackson I. Cope: "With his [Satan's] coming there is another change in scenic texture, a definite turn and foreshadowing which thrusts us into the declining obscurity of Paradise lost" (112). Laurence

Stapleton suggests that evening permits a prompt emphasis on both the love-making and the troublesome dream when Adam and Eve retire, and adds that "no doubt Milton also wished to follow the Hebrew custom of taking sundown as the beginning of the day" (741). John R. Knott considers it ironic that Satan should invade the garden as the peace of evening descends, but he points to how life in Eden is patterned on the rising and falling of the sun: "This pattern—rising at dawn, taking refuge from the heat of the sun at noon, and retiring in the evening—owes little to the epic antecedents of *Paradise Lost*, . . . but descriptions of the three primary times of the day are commonplace in classical and Renaissance pastoral poetry" ("Pastoral Day" 168).

Edward Bysshe registers his approval of this description by including it under "Evening" in the "Collection" section of *The Art of English Poetry* (127). Also see Bysshe in **606–09** and **776–77**.

354. *th' Ocean Isles:* several later editors narrow down Hume's "the Islands sprinkled o'er the Western Ocean" (148). Verity, cross-referencing 8.631–32, as well as *Mask* 95–97, suggests that Milton understands these islands as the Cape Verde Islands (463). On the basis of 592, however, Hughes identifies the islands as the Azores (*Complete Poems* 286).

355. *usher:* Verity indicates a parallel in Shakespeare's Sonnet 132: "Nor that full star that ushers in the even" (463).

356–57. Newton finds "very beautiful" the dramatic delaying of Satan's second soliloquy: "Tho' Satan came in quest of Adam and Eve, yet he is struck with such astonishment at the sight of them, that it is a long time before he can recover his speech, and break forth into this soliloquy: and at the same time this dumb admiration of Satan gives the poet the better opportunity of inlarging his description of them" (257). Todd ([1842], 2:75) and Verity (463) repeat Newton's note. The *OED* 3.b definition of *gaze* supports Newton's reading: "attitude of gazing in wonder, expectancy, bewilderment."

358–92. Tone is the principal concern of most of the critical commentary prompted by this, Satan's second, soliloquy, but while editors and critics, both early and late, acknowledge the sincerity of Satan's immediate emotional reaction to Adam and Eve, as well as its effect on the reader's reaction to Satan, a debate develops in the early twentieth century about the sincerity of Satan's plans for Adam and Eve, about his stated intent, that is, to *entertain* (382) them in hell.

The Richardsons first remark on Satan's sensitive awareness of the blessedness of Adam and Eve: "without being capable of Joy Himself, [he] saw it plentifully possest by Others" (161). Most certainly, Shelley has this second soliloquy in mind when he describes Satan as "for ever tortured with compassion and affection for those whom he betrays and ruins; he is racked by a vain abhorrence for the desolation of which he is the instrument; he is like a man compelled by a tyrant to set fire to his own possessions, and to appear as the witness against, and the accuser of his dearest friends and most intimate connexions; and then to be their executioner, and to inflict the most subtle and protracted torments upon them" ("On the Devil" 7:96). So, too, early in the twentieth century, P. T. Forsyth comments that Satan's "resolution falters as he sees and feels the beauty and innocence of the first pair" (459). Seeing Adam and Eve "momentarily suspended in stylized innocence and archetypal bliss," as Satan soliloquizes, makes Satan appear even "more human...than they are," claims William McQueen ("'Hateful Siege'" 62). Jon S. Lawry writes that Adam and Eve's beauty moves Satan "to the edge of worship for both creature and Creator" (173), and G. Rostrevor Hamilton finds "something approaching tenderness in his [Satan's] character" (25). In his 1795 edition of *PR*, Charles Dunster associates Satan's claim that he "could love" Adam and Eve, with his words to Jesus in *PR* 1.379–82. With these two passages, Dunster also cross-references *PL* 4.844–49 (*Paradise Regained* 43).

While there is an enduring critical consensus on the sincerity of Satan's initial response to Adam and Eve, so beautiful that he "could love" them, that unanimity splinters as critics consider his subsequent remarks about seeking "mutual amitie" (376) with them. In *Milton* (1900), Walter Raleigh's understanding of Satan's plans for Adam and Eve initiates the twentieth century debate about the tone of Satan's vow, "Hell shall unfold, / To entertain you two, her widest Gates" (381–82). Arguing that Satan's response to Adam and Eve reveals that Milton "was not fully conscious, it seems, of what he was doing" (133), because "here surely was a chance for attributing to him the foul passions of envy and hate unalloyed" (137), Raleigh recognizes that Satan is instead "struck with admiration for their grace and infused divinity" (137). Raleigh then maintains that Satan's subsequent attitude regarding Adam and Eve does not change, but rather his plans for them continue to develop his initial claim that he "could love" them: "He seeks alliance with them, and is prepared to give them a share in all he has—which, it must be allowed, is the spirit of true hospitality. He finds it beneath him to attack innocence and helplessness, but public reasons compel him to do what otherwise he would abhor" (137–38). Raleigh finds that "no imputation is cast on the sincerity of the plea," and, recalling Shelley's reference to Satan's being "compelled" to destroy, Raleigh says, "we are left to conceive of Satan as of a lover of beauty reluctantly compelled to shatter it in the pursuit of his high political aims" (138). While he suggests that Raleigh makes his point "with evasive humour," William Empson also believes that Satan's offer of "mutual amity" and entertainment is sincere and that "the irony is that of Milton's appalling God" (*Some Versions* 160). The key biblical text supporting Empson's indictment is Isa. 14.9–15, a biblical text first applied to Satan's second soliloquy by Todd ([1842], 2:76), who credits John Gillies, as does Masson (*Poetical Works* 3:174). In *Milton's God*, Empson develops his understanding of the significant resonance between Satan's words and the Isaiah passage: "I would still deny... that this is meant only as the leering irony of the stage villain. It may seem absurd to suppose that he could have any good intentions towards them, but the text seems designed to leave the point open. They are pawns in his game, but he may prefer to have them do comfortably once they are on his side" (67). Also see Empson on *all* in **383**. Moving to settle his view of the characterization of Satan in the context of the larger debate about Milton's handling of Satan from Books 1–2 into Book 4, Empson explains that "what the critic has to deal with is not a 'complex personality' but one plain character superimposed on another quite separate from it. The most striking single example of this dissolving-view method of characterisation occurs when Satan is struck 'stupidly good' on his first view of Adam and Eve" (*Some Versions* 159). Of course, Satan is struck "stupidly good" not when he sees Adam and Eve in Book 4, but when he sees Eve alone in Book 9, as Robert Martin Adams points out (114n4). G. Wilson Knight and A. J. A. Waldock support the views of Raleigh and Empson. Knight admits that "as his story develops, Satan certainly becomes more distant, our subjective sympathies transferring to Adam and Eve," but he also contends that this second soliloquy, recalling those of Shakespeare's Claudius (*Hamlet* 3.3.36–72) and Angelo (*Measure for Measure* 2.2.161–87), is marked by "generous and noble emotions" (77). Like Raleigh, Waldock believes that Milton's Satan is escaping his creator's control (88). Cf. Werblowsky 15.

Among the first to reject these understandings of Satan's plans to entertain Adam and Eve are S. Musgrove and Balachandra Rajan. Musgrove describes Satan's expressions of pity for Adam and Eve as about "as sound as a rotten nut," and he insists that in Satan's voice is a "bitter irony hiding (or revealing) bottomless cruelty" (308). Maintaining his emphasis on Satan's degeneration, Rajan finds that degeneration most impressively revealed in the second soliloquy: "The lamentations mingled with the macabre gloating, the horrific irony seasoned with complaint are all confessions of his inner emptiness" (*"Paradise Lost" and the Seventeenth Century Reader* 100). John Peter and James Holly Hanford continue to counter the views of Raleigh and Empson. Identifying the second soliloquy's effects as "equivocal," Peter (53) admits, "Here we are at first won over by the unwonted generosity of his reaction to their beauty (360–5), and in what follows there is an undertone of pity, touched with gentleness." Peter nevertheless senses the developing complications in Satan's words: "Yet at the same time we feel the incongruity of Satan's pity when it is extended to his victims (366–73), and can detect the self-pity that goes with it (373–5), a self-pity that becomes insincerity with his almost jocular offer to 'entertain' the human pair in Hell (375–87)." Proposing an association that Empson will reject in *Milton's God*, Hanford argues that Satan is "of the lineage" of Elizabethan stage villains ("Dramatic Element" 189). Hanford associates Satan's "ironical" references to *League* and *mutual amity* with Richard of Gloucester's "grimmer but less tragic words of Clarence [*Richard III* 1.1.118–19]" (190). Also rejecting Raleigh's remarks about Satan's hospitality, yet insisting that Satan "is not the tyrant," G. Rostrevor Hamilton's reading pulls away from the critical argument about the ambiguity of Satan's intent to entertain Adam and Eve to emphasize Satan's final—and terribly clear—intent to revenge himself. Hamilton follows the dynamic development of the entire speech: "It is no special pleading to say that his gentler feelings might prevail over his envy, were he seriously not driven by a thirst to avenge himself on God, for behind the mean form of his action is that sole and terrible purpose. It is there, in the proud spirit of vengeance, that the weight of the charge against him lies, and it is precisely there that he has already succeeded in stilling the voice of conscience" (26). The more recent responses of J. B. Broadbent, Mario A. DiCesare, Alastair Fowler, John M. Steadman, and J. M. Evans bring the same emphasis to Satan's resolve at the end of the second soliloquy. Broadbent believes this second is the "most successful" of Satan's three soliloquies. Emphasizing the reader's relationship with Satan, Broadbent explains, "We are identified with him in fascination with the scene so that his cry of destruction and grief comes as a genuine dramatic shock. He goes on to admire the man and woman, then to fondle them horribly—'Ah gentle pair....' His voice lisps as a snake: 'League with you I seek, and mutual amitie so straight, so close,' perverting the 'happie nuptial League' of Adam and Eve in the previous paragraph. In the third act of *Adamus Exul* Satan actually offers alliance with Adam, who spurns it. Grotius's instinct was right, for it is as a politician that Satan appears at his most irrelevant and uncomprehending in relation to the calm pastoralism of Paradise" (*Some Graver Subject* 170). DiCesare tightens the focus on the relationship between Satan and Adam and Eve as he reacts to them in this second soliloquy: "Satan begins to feel their wholeness, a feeling that reaches its climax in their sexual union. The cold-blooded deliberateness of his second speech...argues his solitude. The overbearing irony and the pose of reluctant conqueror, even the sardonic pity, do not obscure the metaphor of relationship." Like Broadbent, DiCesare considers the connections with the third act of *Adamus Exul,* but he sees in 32–113 only "a thin reflection" of the earlier drama and finds that Broadbent's remark about Satan as a politician "misses the glacial malevolence underlying the metaphor of relationship" ("'Advent'rous'" 7). DiCesare continues to develop "the metaphor of relationship" in **375–85.** To Empson's argument, Fowler (636) responds, "One may agree that Satan does not sustain the irony of 375f or of the understatement *may not please* (l. 378), and that 385f is in a certain narrow sense 'sincere.' If high honour is accompanied with woe and opposed to joy (ll. 367–9), however, it is hard to see how it could be offered other than maliciously, to harm God's image in Adam and Eve—out of *revenge,* in fact, as Satan himself admits at 386f. Besides, the offer of room (l. 383) is belied in advance by the sinister *so strait, so close* (l. 376)." Referring the second to the first soliloquy, Steadman points out that in both Satan responds to the divine image, as represented first by the sun, and now by Adam and Eve: "Satan, who had once known the Beatific Vision, can still behold the image of God with wonder, and indeed almost with love. He can still contemplate the Creator in the creature." Steadman explains, however, that despite his ability to see the image of God, Satan "neither can nor will direct this recognition to its true end. Against God's image in created man he turns the same destructive intent he had earlier directed against God himself. Even the limited understanding that remains in him in his fallen state he distorts to serve his purpose of revenge" (*Milton* 56). Finally, referencing several features of the earlier debate about the tone of Satan's offer of "mutual amitie," Evans almost formally marks that debate's conclusion as he, like Steadman and Hamilton, stresses Satan's final determination to revenge himself. While Evans agrees with Hanford's earlier argument that Satan is related to the Elizabethan stage villains, he also tends to agree with Raleigh and Empson: "Satan's malevolent desire to make Man a partner in his ruin can be presented as 'amitie' without any melodramatic irony, for he does not yet regard him as an upstart creature destined to enjoy the glories he has lost." Evans moves beyond this point, however, as he argues that Satan's "speech reveals something infinitely more terrible than the hostility of a disinherited son towards the new heir; like a typical Elizabethan revenger, Satan proposes to kill the son simply to spite the father, recognizing his victim's beauty even at the moment he takes the decision to destroy it" (229).

To rather different ends, Grant McColley, Anne Davidson Ferry, and William McQueen also consider the dramatic associations of Satan's second soliloquy. McColley looks at the soliloquy as he studies the stages of the composition of *PL*. In pointing out that in the fourth of Milton's early drafts of a drama on the Fall, Gabriel—not Lucifer—describes Adam and Eve, as well as paradise, McColley reasons that Lucifer's "declaration that he could love Adam and Eve because they so closely resembled God" is what one would expect of Gabriel rather than Lucifer. McColley then suggests, "It well may be that the nontraditional admiration and sympathy which at times crept into Satan's discourse resulted in part from a transfer of Gabriel's role to the Apostate" (*"Paradise Lost": An Account* 289). Ferry and McQueen ponder the oddly dramatic nature of Satan's directly addressing Adam and Eve as he admits, "League with you I seek" (375). Describing the tone of the entire speech as "unctuous geniality," Ferry writes, "Satan speaks to himself as if he were talking to them [Adam and Eve]; even his solitary utterances are framed as if to persuade, since language for him has no other use or value" (*Milton* 54). McQueen declares that the direct address is "curiously out of place within a soliloquy" and "wonders whether it was at one time intended to be spoken to them" ("'Hateful Siege'" 63).

358. *O Hell!:* Frank Allen Patterson enters the critical discussion about Satan's tone in this second soliloquy by emphasizing its opening exclamation: "this is not simply an oath, but an integral part of the text; it reveals the deep anguish of Satan's envy, his wrath and despair—proper words to express his emotion as revealed by his soliloquy" (83n358).

359. *room:* glossing this word as "place," Fowler (635) cross-references 7.189–90. Illustrating *Room,* "In one's room, in one's place, denoting substitution of one person or thing for another," the *OED* 13.b quotes 3.285–86, where the Father addresses the Son: "Be thou in *Adams* room / The Head of all mankind."

360. *mould:* Verity claims that this is Milton's "constant word for 'material, substance'" (463).

earth-born perhaps: focusing on this phrase, Hume (149) considers Satan's first thoughts on the contingency of Adam and Eve's creation, and quickly and clearly presents several of the major authorities in the long-enduring theological debate about why and when mankind was created. "That Mankind was created to repair the Ruine of the Rebellious Angels, and to repeople the Heavenly Palaces, depopulated by many Millions of the Coelestial Tribes (the ancient Inhabitants of those blest Abodes), was the Opinion of *Rupertus* [Rupert of Deutz, *Commentariorum in Genesim* 2.9]. But *Pererius* [*Commentariorum* 154] and others conceive, that this World, and Man the height of the Terrestrial Creation, had in the Almighties appointed time, been made, although the whole Angelick Nature had stood firm and obedient in their holy state; which our Poet has intimated in Book I [650–54]." Cf. 7.189–90 and 4.359.

As he concludes his analysis of the epic texture created by Milton's references to the "Earth-born" (1.198) monsters Typhon and Briareos, and their Virgilian and Dantean antecedents, Mario A. DiCesare considers Satan's painful uncertainty about Adam and Eve's origins: "They are ['earth-born'], of course, but not of that giant race with which he is sinuously connected" ("'Advent'rous'" 11).

362. *Little inferior:* Newton (257) references Ps. 8.5 and Heb. 2.7.

363–65. Anne Davidson Ferry and Leland Ryken comment on the abstract nature of Satan's descriptive terms for Adam and Eve in these lines. Ferry explains, "Even Satan recognizes the outer and inner harmony of innocence, when he first sees Adam and Eve, and the fact that he does recognize it suggests both that he is still at moments capable of something like angelic vision and that their absolute unity of being is unmistakable" (*Milton's Epic Voice* 127). Even Satan, who so deviously corrupts language, is here, in Ferry's words, "forced to use language which has at once physical and moral meanings" (128). Discussing Milton's apocalyptic vision, Ryken makes a similar point as he notes that Satan sees Adam and Eve conceptually in this sequence; Satan sees those "qualities which differentiate unfallen human experience from fallen experience" (196). Cf. the bard's description of Adam and Eve at **288–95**.

366–73. Frank Kermode refers to this sequence as he discusses rhyme, pseudo-rhyme, and conjunctions of opposites, which he identifies as the epic's "counterlogical elements" (97). Kermode explains that the structure of the entire epic "is based on a series of massive antitheses, or if you like huge structural pseudo-rhymes, and the central pseudo-rhyme is *delight/woe*" (99).

366. *gentle pair:* Edward S. Le Comte directs readers to Milton's *Mask* 236, where the Lady applies the same phrase to her lost brothers (*Yet Once More* 59).

367. Supplying a lengthy list of cross-references, John Halkett points out how often Satan uses such words as *delicious, bliss, joy,* and *delight* to describe Adam and Eve's love. Halkett adds that Adam and Eve also invoke such language and similarly understand that their relationship, "the enjoyment of human love, is the epitome of all the delights of the garden itself" (102).

368. *ye:* Helen Darbishire contends, "As accusative of the first and second person plural Milton uses *ye* for the unemphatic form, *you* for the emphatic" (*Poetical Works* 1:296).

370–74. Alastair Fowler (635) claims, "Satan's pity is by no means to his credit. He is unable to act as firmly as Michael, because he knows himself to be in the wrong." Fowler rules that "the implied accusation of God for making man too frail is false. Man is 'sufficient to have stood'—as indeed Satan's fear of approaching Adam shows (ix 483ff.)."

370. Fowler clarifies the meaning here: "not so well secured as one would expect in the case of such happy creatures" (635). See Fowler on *secure* in **186**.

372. *for Heav'n:* "considering it is your heaven" (Fowler 635).

373–92. While J. M. Evans considers the absence of envy and hate in Satan as he here first views Adam and Eve, Irene Samuel explains how Satan's envy shapes his determination to destroy them. Researching the traditional reasons assigned to Satan's rebellion, Evans (227–28) reveals that "from Avitus [*De Originali Peccato* 77–88] onwards the Devil was usually presented as seducing Adam and

Eve in order to prevent them from enjoying the benefits which he himself had lost. Milton, however, made little or no use of this traditional motive until Book IX. Instead he laid all the emphasis on Satan's desire to be revenged on God, the motive favoured by Calvin [*Commentaries* 3.1]." This departure from tradition, Evans argues, then influences Satan's first reaction to the sight of Adam and Eve as registered in this second soliloquy: "Whereas in every previous treatment of this dramatic moment the Devil had expressed hate and jealousy, Milton's Satan is deeply moved by the beauty and innocence of the newly created pair" (229). Looking at this second soliloquy with no particular theological crux in mind, Samuel argues, "That grudging of other people's pleasure Milton shows as allied to the determination to cause pain; so too he allies the contempt, rooted in envy, that calls other people inferior to the determination to use them for one's own purpose" ("*Paradise Lost* as Mimesis" 21).

375–85. In his close reading of this sequence Mario A. DiCesare develops the metaphor of relationship extending throughout the texture of *PL*: "The first words of the passage—'League with you I seek'—harshly contrast with Adam and Eve's 'happy nuptial League' (IV, 339). Satan plans 'mutual amity so strait, so close,' but he can define this relationship only by prepositions of accompaniment (*with* in IV, 375, twice in 377). He proposes a domesticity (*dwell, dwelling*) that is really an absorption, a devouring. The heavy irony he directs at the Creator's work expands the implications of *give* (IV, 380–81), the grotesque exchange he anticipates. The language then returns to *amity;* the unfolding of Hell's widest gates produces a sense of straitness and closeness that clashes with what he calls 'these narrow limits'—actually their Paradise 'Imparadis't.' We recall, too, that Hell's gates, however wide, belong to monstrous Sin and Death and their horrid offspring, in whose circuit we see the referent for the close *amity* Satan offers to *give*." The clustering of these "images of relatedness," DiCesare argues, develops as "a metaphor for the straitened concentricity of Satan's nature, for the selfward impulse, the obscene gesture of self-embrace" ("'Advent'rous'" 7–8). Also see DiCesare on "the metaphor of relationship" in **358–92**.

375. *Though I unpittied:* With nearly 8 percent of the lines in *PL* containing ellipses, Janette Richardson argues that Milton is "deliberating writing Virgilian English" (331), and, like Virgil, Milton frequently omits various forms of *to be,* as he does here (326).

376. *streight:* printing it as *strait,* Alastair Fowler glosses this as "intimate" on the authority of the *OED* definition 14, but he notes that it also carries "the sinister overtone 'involving privation'" on the authority of the *OED* definition 6.b. Fowler adds, "The *Ed I* and *Ed II* spelling 'streight' allows a play with *straight* = honest; but this must be considered very secondary in view of the continuation *so close*" (635). Cf. *strait* in 405.

377. For Balachandra Rajan this line, "symptomatically lacking any sense of direction," reveals Satan's "tiredness" (*"Paradise Lost" and the Seventeenth Century Reader* 100). Alastair Fowler, however, reasons that Satan may not sound so tired "to readers who appreciate the villainous implication of the sequence *I with you* (i.e., temptation and sin, the inner hell): *you with me* (damnation, the external hell)" (635).

378–81. Several recent critics have identified biblical passages echoing through this sequence. James H. Sims reminds readers that in Matt. 10.8, Christ, speaking to his disciples, declares "freely ye have received, freely give." Finding the sarcasm therefore "intensified by the ironic reversal of purpose which Satan gives to the words of Christ," Sims also points out that God, of course, "did not really consign him to Hell 'freely,' as though for no cause, as Satan implies. Recognition of Satan's reversal of Biblical language increases the bitterness of his heavy sarcasm, making his plan to ruin man appear even more fiendish" (*Bible* 164). Fowler (636) adds a reference to Rom. 8.32: "He that spared not his own Son, but delivered him up for us all, how shall he not with him also freely give us all things?" DiCesare ("'Advent'rous'" 26n15) also considers the irony of *freely,* adding that associations with 9.732, 988, 996 enhance the force and implications of Satan's word choice here.

379. *fair:* noting Satan's frequent use of "fair" (521; 9.489, 538, 602–09), William G. Madsen wonders whether it "might almost be called Satan's favorite word" (*From Shadowy Types* 151), assigned him by a poet who, "in spite of his own sensitivity to the beauties of sight and sound, was deeply suspicious of man's response to physical beauty" (149).

381–85. Discussing directions in *PL,* H. F. Robins explains, "The three gateways in *Paradise Lost,* to Heaven, to Hell and to the Garden of Eden, are designed with reference to the fate of man" (96), and then Robins clarifies that, like the Edenic and the celestial gate, "the infernal gate is in the wall, rather than in the roof of Hell." Walter Clyde Curry believes the infernal gate is in the roof (97). See Curry 144–57.

381. R. C. Browne (1:352) cites Isa. 14.9: "Hell from beneath is moved for thee to meet thee at thy coming."

383. *all:* William Empson argues for the sincerity of Satan's offer to share empire with Adam and Eve and for the exclusive attribution of irony to "Milton's appalling God" by bringing a great deal of attention to *all,* which Empson identifies as Milton's "key word," a word that the poet uses only for "a wholesale and unquestioned emotion; what we are to feel here is the ruined generosity of Satan and the greatness of the fate of man" (*Some Versions* 161). In 1948, Empson retracts much of this argument, but insisting that "heroic generosity" still remains in the phrase "all her Kings," he contends that Milton's "feelings were crying out against his appalling theology in favour of freedom, happiness, and the pursuit of truth was I think not obvious to him, and it is this part of the dramatic complex which is thrust upon us by the repeated *all*" ("Emotions" 600 and *Structure* 104). Also see Empson in **705–08**. Robert Martin Adams believes that "more than a grain of salt" is needed to accept Empson's argument: "Disregarding compounds like 'almighty,' Milton uses 'all' no less than eight times during the speeches of Belial and Mammon. Presumably their feeling is very wholesale indeed, and one would be hard put to find a retail passage in Milton" (116). Of Empson's follow-up publication on *all,* Adams says that, although it "withdraws the original generalization ... [, it] ... puts forward so many new ones that a volume would be required to cope with them" (116n).

386. In his notes for an edition of Milton's works, which were passed on to Todd ([1842], 2:7), Benjamin Stillingfleet glosses Satan's claim to be "loath to this revenge" as an echo of Euripides's *The Madness of Hercules* 858: "Witness, Sun, that I am doing that which I would fain refuse."

388–94. Newton and Todd illuminate Satan's "Tyrants plea" (394) with seventeenth century politics, and several twentieth century editors continue to recover pertinent historical texts. Newton (257), for example, suggests that Milton may be recalling King Charles's plea for ship money. Todd ([1842], 2:7) repeats Newton's note but adds, "The same plea is said to have been Cromwell's apology for the murder of the king. For it is related that, on the evening of the execution of Charles, the arch-hypocrite walked round the corpse, as it lay in one of the rooms at Whitehall, muffled up in a long black cloak, and repeating to himself, 'Dreadful *necessity!*'" To illuminate Satan's appeal to "public reason," Frank Allen Patterson (*Student's Milton* 83) turns to the *The Life and Death of Sir Henry Vane* 122: "One main ground of the unjust proceeding of worldly powers against righteous and conscientious men, is Reason of State." Patterson concludes, following Newton's reasoning, by suggesting that Milton "may even have been thinking of the reason given for the execution of his friend, Vane." Against a rich background of classical and modern, religious and historical, writings on tyrants, Merritt Y. Hughes ("Satan" 171–72) also studies Milton's presentation of Satan as a tyrant, insisting, for example, that Milton "would never have disagreed with the opinion of St. Thomas Aquinas in the *De Regimine Principum* (I.6.52) that…'Sin therefore must be done away with in order that the scourge of tyrants may cease.'" In his edition of Milton's *Complete Poems* 287, Hughes settles the Ciceronian declaration "salus populi suprema lex esto" (*De Legibus* 3.3.8), which Hughes translates as "the good of the people is the supreme law," at the core of his consideration of Satan's perverse invocation of "public reason." Situating Satan's phrase in the context of early modern political history, Hughes reports, "In *The Contra-Replicant* (1643, p. 19) Henry Parker approved its use by Parliament and condemned the Royalists for too frequent appeals to it. In the *Advancement* [*of Learning* (*Works* 6:101)]…, Bacon recalled that its abuse in Italy under the name *ragione di stato* had been condemned by Pius V as an invention 'against religion and the moral virtues.' In *Adamo caduto* V, ii, Salandra has Satan tell the devils that they are going to corrupt mankind by inventing *ragione di stato*." Cross-referencing Dalila's excuse in *SA* 865–70 in which she claims, "to the public good / Private respects must yield," and recalling that in *Educ* (Patterson, *Works* 4:279), Milton "sneers at those to whom 'tyrannous aphorisms appear…the highest points of wisdom,'" A. W. Verity (463) repeats the comments of Todd and Newton, while he also points out that Dryden ironically puts the plea in the mouth of the Panther in *The Hind and the Panther* 3.835–38 (*Works* 3:185–86).

The sincerity or insincerity of Satan's sentiments, rather than their historical or philosophical vintage, concerns other critics. Walter Raleigh, like Shelley, as noted earlier, describes Satan as "reluctantly compelled to shatter it [Eden] in the pursuit of his high political arms" (138), but R. J. Zwi Werblowsky finds that Satan's lines "bear the stamp of dishonesty and hollowness" (15), and David Daiches describes them as "high-sounding nonsense" (154). Marjorie H. Nicolson similarly describes Satan: "Casuistical as he had become, he justifies his action by 'public reason,' political expedience, leading Milton to brief 'double talk' of a Puritan about 'necessity,' the tyrant's plea" (*John Milton* 241). Finally, Edward S. Le Comte points out that while in *Eikon* (Patterson, *Works* 5:83) Milton defines *law* as "public reason," in Satan's mouth, *public reason* becomes "the tyrant's plea" (*Yet Once More* 95–96).

393–95. John S. Diekhoff notes the rhyme in this passage ("Rhyme" 540).

395–408. The expressive appropriateness and the theological significance of Satan's animal disguises have been the topics of critical attention. Hume (149) emphasizes the cat disguises and the ferocity of the cats' eyes, as does Milton's text. Hume also associates Satan's disguise as "a furious ravenous Tyger" with Seneca's comparison between Atreus preparing to sacrifice his nephews and a tigress wavering between two bulls and doubtful as to where first to set her fangs in *Thyestes* 707–11. While Todd ([1842], 2:77) adds the transformation of Bacchus to a lion in Euripides's *The Bacchanals* 1017–19, Verity strengthens the sinister emphasis of Hume's annotation with biblical authority, 1 Pet. 5.8: "Be sober, be vigilant; because your adversary the devil, as a roaring lion, walketh about, seeking whom he may devour" (463). Verity also cross-references his note on 1.428, "in what shape they choose," which supports the popular understanding that evil spirits were often thought to appear in the shapes of wild animals (386). A series of twentieth century critics has continued to elaborate the theological significance of Satan's animal disguises. Raymond B. Waddington explains that each disguise "is representative of a particular quality of his nature, revealing his dominant mood at that moment" (391). Discussing idols and idolatry, and quoting Pss. 115.8 and 135.18, Northrop Frye explains, "The devils cannot inspire idolatry without becoming idols themselves: once again we have the biblical judgment on idols: 'They that make them are like unto them.' This identification with the evil that one creates is also symbolized by the variety of disguises that Satan assumes" (*Return* 76). Jon S. Lawry (172) tends to seal the evil expressed by Satan spying as lion and tiger when he identifies the "two gentle Fawns" in this sequence (404) with "the brace seen fleeing

Eden at the end of *Paradise Lost* [11.187–89]." Marjorie H. Nicolson ("Spirit World" 438) groups together all of Satan's animal identities as she argues for the similarities between Henry More's views on the spirit world and Milton's views. Nicolson notes that both More and Milton understood that "the baser spirits frequently descend to animal shapes in order to carry out their purposes" and that the animals associated with Milton's Satan appear appropriate according to More's explanation in *The Immortality of the Soul* 193–94 that base spirits "turn themselves into one brutish shape rather than another; as envying, or admiring, or in some sort approving and liking the condition and properties of such and such beasts." Finally, A. Bartlett Giamatti turns to classical, rather than biblical, demonology when he notes that Satan is now comparable to Circe as one who "can infect and affect Nature" (333), as one, that is, who has "the power to seduce and to control beasts" (334).

How literally to understand Satan's animal disguises is an issue raised by Northrop Frye, who cautions, "He [Milton] is not saying that Satan [moving through the garden] actually took these forms; he merely wants the reader to visualize them in connection with Satan" (*Return* 76). Douglas Bush and Dennis H. Burden disagree with Frye. Bush writes that once Satan assumes the disguises, the animals "become beasts of prey, unlike the actual animals of Eden" (*Complete Poetical Works* 284), and Burden contends that Satan "becomes the animals as they are in their savage post-lapsarian state" (50). Thomas Greene also puzzles over the nature of the disguises: "Satan as tiger seems to stray into a simile while still remaining outside it" (386n38).

The associations between Milton's Satan as spying animal and Du Bartas's similarly disguised Satan, first noted by David Masson (*Poetical Works* 3:174), have elicited a bit of controversy. Developing Masson's point, George Coffin Taylor looks to Sylvester's translation of Du Bartas's *The Divine Weeks and Works* 2.1.2.106–12, where Satan "tries the different animals before deciding on the serpent." With both Du Bartas and Milton, Taylor claims, "we find the same attempt to give the impression of a hidden danger ready at any moment to pounce upon its prey" (74). Robert Martin Adams rejects Taylor's argument that Du Bartas influenced *PL,* insisting that Du Bartas hardly could have impressed the mature Milton, and finding that most of the links between *Divine Weeks* and Milton's epic are coincidental and conventional (154–57). Merritt Y. Hughes quotes from Sylvester's Du Bartas (*Complete Poems* 288), but thereby also reveals that the predatory cats dominating Milton's passage are missing from Du Bartas's list (*Complete Poetry* 288). Kester Svendsen's note that Milton's Satan chooses "ominous" animal disguises also sharpens the point blurred by the attention to Du Bartas as a precedent for Milton's presentation (*Milton and Science* 165).

Unique in the criticism gathering about this sequence is John M. Steadman's reading, which examines Satan's animal disguises against the heroic convention of the ignoble disguise. Glancing at Odysseus disguised as a beggar in *Odyssey* 4.240–51 and Alfred as a fiddler, which Milton himself reports in his *HistBr* (Patterson, *Works* 10:214), Steadman argues that Satan's disguises "possess a recognizable affinity with heroic tradition—an affinity which critics have largely ignored" ("Satan's Metamorphoses" 81).

404. *Purlieu:* while he glosses this as "the outskirt of a forest" (463), A. W. Verity presents the more intriguing history of the word in his edition's "Glossary": "Sometimes land which had been taken from its owner and made part of a forest was restored to him or his successor" (714). Similarly glossing *Purlieu* as "land on the fringe of a forest," Alastair Fowler adds, "The more specific sense—land disafforested, but still subject to the provisions of the forest laws—does not seem to apply" (637).

405. *Strait:* Fowler has the word spelled *Straight*. He defines it as "at once; but punning with 'Strait,' 'tightly' (*OED* s.v. *Strait* adv. I). *Ed I* and *Ed II* 'Strait' could indicate either word, and made the play more obvious" (637n). Cf. *streight* in 376.

408–10. One critical crux here is the identity of the character who is "Turnd…all eare" (410). Bentley first comments on the phrase, describing it as "A pretty Expression, borrow'd from the Latin, *Totum te cupias, Fabulle, nasum,*" but he does not suggest to whom Milton's phrase refers (121). The referent problem becomes clear when Pearce admits that he "should have lik'd it better if the Poet had said *Turn'd* HER *all ear* &c.," for "*Eve* was the person to hear." Pearce (125) then cross-references *Mask* 559, "I was all ear." Two years later, the Richardsons' reading (163) counters Pearce's: "*Adam* turn'd the Devil, made him *All Ear,* Eager to hear what he had never heard yet, Human Speech, and to Learn from Thence what might be for his Purpose, as v. 401." Newton (260) presents Bentley's note without comment and attributes to the Richardsons the reference to *Mask.* Describing the crux as "no inconsiderable obscurity," Todd prints the response Charles Dunster had passed on to him: "it is in fact Satan, who, upon this occasion, turn'd him, all ear. &c. A comma, should be placed after *when,* to indicate *Adam's moving speech* to be in the ablative case absolute" ([1842], 2:77–78). Later votes for Satan as the one "Turnd...all eare" are registered by David Masson (*Poetical Works* 3:174) andVerity (463), and therefore, with the exceptions of Pearce and Bentley, the early editorial consensus appears to be that Satan is the one "Turnd...all eare."

Although the majority of modern editors agree with this reading, several twentieth century responses become rather creative. In 1940–41, G. G. L. and E. H. V. revive the discussion through several issues of *Notes and Queries,* with E. H. V. setting forth a Romantic reading, arguing that Adam is the referent for *him* because Adam himself "speaks...for the sake of making Eve speak" (95). In her edition of *PL* Helen Darbishire moves the comma after *speech* to follow *Eve,* and inserts a comma after *him,* explaining, "The commas are necessary to make the sense clear: it is Eve who is all ear" (*Poetical Works* 1:296). Douglas Bush adopts Darbishire's punctuation, also noting, "Eve is 'all ear'" (*Complete Poetical Works* 284). Merritt Hughes and Alastair Fowler maintain the punctuation of the seventeenth century editions of *PL.* Hughes concedes that either Adam or Satan could be the one turned "all ear" (*Complete Poems* 288), and Fowler argues, "The momentary uncertainty [about the referent of *him*]...is enough to give the impression that Satan has insinuated himself into Adam's grammatical place." Fowler also suggests that "all ear," the English version of a Latin idiom Bentley first identified, "is perhaps the earliest instance in English" (637). Supporting Fowler's suggestion is the *OED,* which lists the earliest occurrence of "all ear" (*ear* 3.d) as "He was all ear to her charming voice" in the 1868 translation of William Beckford's *Vathek* 88.

Satan's position as an eavesdropper in this episode has prompted a sustained search for Milton's source. The eavesdropping device, while first noted by the Richardsons (163) in 1734, was not tracked to a source until Todd's final edition more than 100 years later. Commenting on what Satan says to himself in his following, third soliloquy, "Yet let me not forget what I have gain'd" (512), Todd writes, "This is the ancient opinion of the devil's excitement to the temptation of Eve" ([1842], 2:83). The theological authority Todd then quotes is Moses Bar-Cepha, *De Paradiso Commentarius,* chap. 28. Without such detail, David Masson echoes Todd, referring the eavesdropping to the "fancy" of the "Jewish commentators" of Gen. 3, who, according to Masson, claimed "that Satan first learnt the prohibition imposed on Adam as to the Tree of Knowledge by overhearing him conversing on the subject with Eve; and Milton has adopted this fancy" (*Poetical Works* 3:175). In his 1921 edition of *PL,* Verity reports that "the device is said to come from the Talmud" (463). Grant McColley moves to the same conclusion, adding, "In hexameral and related literatures, we rarely meet the idea which Milton stressed here. Lancetta described Satan as having overheard in concealment a conversation between Adam and Eve [*La Scena Tragica d'Adamo et Eva* 2.4]. His work, if Milton knew it, may have suggested the Apostate as an eavesdropper. The basic idea—that Satan heard Adam convey the precept to Eve—probably reached Milton through the *Paradise* of Moses Bar Cepha" (*"Paradise Lost": An Account* 155). Watson Kirkconnell (306) reveals that the eavesdropping device also occurs in Salandra's *Adamo Caduto* 2.6.408–10, where Lucifer and his henchmen exult as they witness Eve succumb to the serpent's temptation. Hughes ("Variorum") notes that in the medieval English *Creation* plays, however, Satan learns the command by eavesdropping when God delivers the prohibition to Adam, or else he is simply aware of it. Howard Schultz traces what he understands as a commonplace to the *Displaying of Witchcraft* 219–20, where John Webster asserts that the fallen angels have but "spurious, erroneous, fallacious knowledge," and therefore, Schultz explains, "Satan and his brood could not know, for instance, the mind of a man who kept his mouth shut. This common bit of demonology, consonant with Augustine and the Talmud, obliged Milton's Satan to eavesdrop" (*Milton* 86).

Rather than the source of the eavesdropping device, its narrative function in the epic concerns John S. Diekhoff, who endeavors to deflect any suggestion that Adam's rehearsal of the command might suggest incipient rebellion: "Adam's gratitude and his remembrance of the prohibition are indeed in close juxtaposition here, but not necessarily to indicate a lurking discontent. There is the narrative function of the speech to consider. Satan, listening, must be told of the prohibition so that he may engineer the fall" (*Milton's "Paradise Lost"* 52).

408. *first of men / To first of women:* Leland Ryken explains temporal distancing as one of the techniques by which Milton establishes his apocalyptic vision. Referencing similar expressions, such as "our first-Parents" (6) and "Nations yet unborn" (663), Ryken explains, "The temporal distance which removes Adam and Eve from the reader of *Paradise Lost* is established largely through a group of epithets which are based on the principle that Adam and Eve are the first parents of the long succeeding line of the human race" (182).

411–91. This first spoken exchange between Adam and Eve, like the majority of their prelapsarian conversations, has been variously appreciated and deprecated. On the one hand, Addison's praise has no match. Contending that "there is scarce a Speech of *Adam* or *Eve* in the whole Poem, wherein the Sentiments and Allusions are not taken from this their delightful Habitation," Addison describes their thoughts as "always *Paradisical*" (*Spectator* 3:171), and their speeches to each other as "full of Warmth; but at the same time founded on Truth. In a word, they are the Gallantries of *Paradise*" (3:175). On the other hand, Walter Raleigh, describing Adam and Eve as "harmless tame creatures," whom he finds uninteresting before the Fall, is especially critical of Adam's speechifying: "And Adam, from the wealth of his inexperience, is lavishly sententious; when anything is to do, even if it is only to go to sleep, he does it in a high style, and makes a speech" (143). Stopford Augustus Brooke is disappointed by the beginning of this conversation but admires Eve's subsequent autobiographical reflections: "when Eve glides from describing her relation to Adam into a remembrance of her own coming into life and meeting with him, the poem becomes beautiful again in a series of soft and vivid pictures" (103). Also see Brooke on the later bedtime conversation in **610–88.** Both Grant McColley and C. S. Lewis attempt to counter adverse criticism of Adam's conversational skills by reminding readers that Adam is prelapsarian. Evoking theological tradition, McColley (*"Paradise Lost": An Account* 153) explains, "The extended discourse to Eve on the subject of angels, stars, and celestial influences, suggests definitely the learned and contemplative Adam envisioned by Calvin [*Commentaries* 125, 58, 162], [Tommaso] Campanella [*A Defense of Galileo* 157], [John] Mercer [*Commentarius in Genesin* 55], [Benedict] Pererius [*Commentariorum* 5.35ff., 44ff.], and [Alonso] Tostatus [*Commentaria in Genesim* 2.23]." C. S. Lewis attempts to discomfort modern readers who smile at Adam's "lectures" to Eve with similar logic: "He is not merely her husband, he is the sum of all human knowledge and wisdom who answers her as Solomon answered the Queen of Sheba." Lewis describes the prelapsarian life of Adam and Eve as "ceremonial— a minuet, where the modern reader looked for a romp" (119). For the Queen of Sheba's visit to Solomon, see 1 Kings 10. A number of later critics develop Lewis's point, explaining that the formality of Adam and Eve's discourse expresses and establishes their nobility. Sister Mary Irma Corcoran, for example, examines the terms by which prelapsarian Adam and Eve address each other: "Courtesy, gravity, and respect were particular marks of the salutation with which each speech opened . . . and all of the dialog is resonant with veracity and candor" (118). Echoing Corcoran, J. B. Broadbent insists, "The courtliness of Adam and Eve does not vaunt. It is a habit of behaviour directed always at the honour of another, not of the self." Broadbent explains, "Adam and Eve realise the highest purpose of politeness, to recognise and celebrate the precise nature of the being addressed" (*Some Graver Subject* 191). To Cecil Maurice Bowra, Adam's expressions of loyalty to God and Eve "constitute his *pietas*, and show a nobility of character worthy of so noble an appearance" (201). Northrop Frye and Harold E. Toliver attempt to move beyond the formality of Adam and Eve's language to focus on its energy. Frye describes their language as "stylized hierarchic language which indicates their exuberance in the possession of language as a new and fresh form of intellectual energy" (*Return* 68). Toliver labels the prelapsarian speech modes in Eden as "priestly-poetic" and specifies "Adam's chief modes" as "celebrational modes of love, both human and divine—hymns, orison, and song—which have the task of naming and worshipping aspects of the creation" (162). The critical rejection of Walter Raleigh's remarks about Milton's "lavishly sententious" Adam is not without exception, however. Arguing that Milton's portrayal of both Adam and Eve is most unsteady in their first speeches, John Peter claims, "Adam sounds like a Victorian governess, turning the children's blessings sour with every attempt to count them," and Peter finds "there is even a suggestion of disingenuousness when, having spoken pointedly of death, he has to pretend that the point is a vagary." Eve does not fare much better: "For her part Eve seems rather a ninny when she accepts what he has been saying as 'just and right' (iv.443), though fortunately she soon escapes from sententiousness into narrative" (93).

411–39. Like the God of Gen. 2, Milton's God first gives Adam the command not to eat of the forbidden tree and then gives him Eve, and in this, Adam's first speech in *PL,* Milton begins most directly to set forth the challenges Adam assumes as he seeks to love both the God whom "to love is to obey" (8.634) and the woman who declares him her "Guide / And Head" (442–43).

Frequently involved in critical discussions of Adam's understanding of God's injunction "not to taste that onely Tree" (423) are the critics' own uncertainties about the prohibition, the sanguine assent marking Newton's annotation seldom reappearing in later commentary. Describing it as "very natural" for Adam to talk about the command with Eve, Newton traces Adam's words back to the words in Genesis and contentedly leaves it at that: "this was what Satan wanted more particularly to learn: And it is expressed from God's command, *Gen*. ii.

16, 17" (260). Be it the biblical text or Adam's paraphrase of it, the command itself provokes questions and inquiry, however, as Satan well knows when he later tempts Eve, and from the mid-1930s through the 1940s the prohibition regarding the Tree of Knowledge in *PL* is more rigorously examined than ever before. In *The Seventeenth Century Background* (1934), Basil Willey puzzles the meaning of the command in conjunction with Adam's twice describing it as *easie* in this speech (421, 433). Quoting from Milton's *DocCh* 1.12 (Patterson, *Works* 15:207), Willey reasons that the command may be designated *easie* only if it is understood as a test of obedience, involving "an act 'indifferent in itself,'" but, Willey continues, "It would *not* have been 'easy' to abstain from knowledge freely to be grasped, and in fact it was by insisting upon the magic virtue of the fruit that Satan successfully tempted Eve" (258). A few years later, in *Milton and Wordsworth,* Herbert J. C. Grierson brings the notion of the taboo to bear upon Milton's presentation of the command: "It is a little strange to hear Milton speaking of the tree as a holy thing, in view of his general refusal to recognise holiness in things at all. Is he not here confounding the holiness of principles, of justice, etc. and the sacredness of tabus, the breach of which entails mischief on good and bad alike?" (96–97). Toward the end of the 1940s, A. J. A. Waldock also ponders the problem of the command, echoing Grierson's notion of the taboo, and, like Willey, quoting from Milton's own *DocCh,* but Waldock sees that Milton was "trapped, in a sense, by his theme," which required him to "deplore the coming of thought into the world (for that is what it really amounts to) and represent man's best state as that original featureless blessedness" (23). John S. Diekhoff (*Milton's "Paradise Lost"* 105) firmly rejects the notion of the command as a taboo and, like Willey, emphasizes the theology of obedience: "Grierson says the prohibition is arbitrary, is a tabu. Satan also calls it 'suspicious, reasonless.' But it is not that, and it is not merely a tabu. Lest the reader also think it reasonless, Milton lets us hear Adam accept the prohibition at the very moment when he first speaks of it in our hearing as 'the only sign of our obedience left.' God has spoken of it in the same terms in Book III [94–95], foreseeing the fall of man and predicting that he will 'easily transgress the sole Command, / Sole pledge of his obedience.'"

The foundation for the conviction of critics such as Diekhoff is the historical-theological research of such scholars as Grant McColley, C. S. Lewis, Sister Mary Irma Corcoran, and Arnold Williams, who unpack the traditional—yet diverse—theological understandings of the command. Focusing on Adam's rehearsal of the command in his first speech, McColley discusses the theology of obedience, arguing that Milton supported "a broad and popular tradition, one which held it not only necessary, but also proper, that Adam should obey his Creator. To do this man was particularly obligated, for he had received but a single and easy commandment, which was chiefly a pledge or just lesson in obedience. To reject the one simple precept was obviously to be ungrateful, haughty, and indifferent toward God" (*"Paradise Lost": An Account* 154). McColley locates this same orthodox defense of the ways of God in Augustine's *City of God* 14.13; Giovanni Diodati's *Pious Annotations upon the Holy Bible* 1; Josuah Sylvester's translation of Du Bartas's *The Divine Weeks and Works* 2.1.1.147–55; Joseph Beaumont's *Psyche* 6.162; Hugo Grotius's *Adamus Exul* 2.1; Andrew Willet's *Hexapla in Genesin* 33–34; and others ("Paradise Lost" 203). Lewis emphasizes Augustinian authority to assert, "The Fall consisted in Disobedience. All idea of a magic apple has fallen out of sight. The apple was 'not bad nor harmful except in so far as it was forbidden' and the only point of forbidding it was to instill obedience, 'which virtue in a rational creature (the emphasis is on *creature;* that which though rational, is merely a creature, not self-existent being) is, as it were, the mother and guardian of *all* virtues' (*De Civ[itate] Dei* [*The City of God*], xiv, 12). This is exactly the Miltonic view" (68–69). Corcoran reports, "Commentators generally construed the prohibition of the tree of knowledge of good and evil not as a deprivation of a positive good but as a mark of man's dignity and superiority over beasts in that, by virtue of his freedom, he was worthy to receive the law of God, and as a test of his obedience by abstention from an indifferent act, from something which contained some admixture of evil, or from something which good in itself, would have harmed Adam because of his immaturity" (52). Corcoran concludes, "To Milton the command was above all else a simple, literal injunction not to eat . . . by observation of which Adam was to prove his fealty to God" (53). Corcoran strengthens her views by citing *DocCh* 2.3 (Patterson, *Works* 17:51). Williams discusses the prohibition as a "special law," according to Pererius's understanding of the types of laws in his *Commentariorum* 143–44. A special law was necessary in the garden, Williams explains, because natural law "does not show simply and directly the power of God. Furthermore, a special positive law was needed, as one preacher observed, because Adam and Eve had such excellent endowments, 'Without any disorder in their affections, or defect in their intellectuals, that they were naturally carried to observe all moral laws of themselves.' Hence the test had to be 'a law of another nature, prohibiting a thing in itself neither good nor evil'" (*Common Expositor* 106). The annotations in Alastair Fowler's 1968 edition of *PL* reflect the outcome of the earlier debate about the nature of the command not to eat from the Tree of the Knowledge. Like Diekhoff, Fowler (638) cross-references 3.95, where God refers to the command as the "Sole pledge of his [man's] obedience." Fowler adds cross-references to 5.551 and 8.329, and *DocCh* 1.10, which he quotes: "The tree of knowledge of good and evil was not a sacrament, as it is generally called; for a sacrament is a thing to be used, not abstained from: but a pledge, as it were, and memorial of obedience" (Patterson, *Works* 15:115). Acknowledging Lewis, Fowler quotes the passage from Augustine that Lewis quotes in 1942, and McColley cites in 1939. See additional remarks on both the Tree of Knowledge and the Tree of Life in **194–204**, **218–22**, and **513–27**.

Rather than stressing obedience, Millicent Bell understands the command as a test of faith: "As a Puritan Milton believed that it was necessary finally to reach God by an accession of confidence which Reason knoweth not. The prohibition, to be a test of faith, *had* to be incomprehensible" (880).

As the command itself seems not to puzzle Newton, so he declares it "very natural" (260) that Adam here talks to Eve about the command, but again, Newton's reaction to this episode is not much in evidence in twentieth century criticism on this topic. Max Bertschinger, for example, finds it provocative rather than "natural" that Adam here talks to Eve about the command. Furthermore, arguing that his remarks reveal Adam's preoccupation with the prohibition, Bertschinger goes so far as to trace the beginning of the Fall to this first speech: "The strange inflection of 'needs must the power / That made us... / Be infinitly good' as well as the juxtaposition of God's goodness and what to Adam and Eve might have looked like God's wilfulness suggest Adam's peculiar interest in the subject" (55). Bertschinger proceeds to considers Eve's situation here: "If we take into account her strong susceptibility to Adam's reasoning—from her belief that it is superior to hers and therefore 'right'—we may say that, in a way, Adam tempts Eve by probing her with his mention of the Tree" (61). Also see Bertschinger on *easie* in **433**. While Bertschinger believes that Adam seems preoccupied with the command, Cecil Maurice Bowra maintains that Adam is "entirely contented. Therefore he does not question God's command not to eat of the Tree and cannot conceive that he should ever wish to do so" (202). Grant McColley and Dennis H. Burden also draw attention to the transmission of the command from God to Adam, and then from Adam to Eve. McColley explains, "By taking the position that the Creator delivered the precept to Adam and Adam, as master, transmitted the commandment to Eve, Milton made use of the opinion most common among theologians" (*"Paradise Lost": An Account* 154). Burden (97), concerned about the difficulty raised by Eve's modifications of God's commandment when she talks with the serpent, draws attention to Adam's preliminary restatement of it here, as well as to Eve's restatement of it immediately before she later chooses to break it: "she (unlike the Eve of Genesis) makes no mistake when she is talking with Satan: 'In the day we eate / Of this fair Fruit, our doom is, we shall die' (IX, 762–763)."

Less focused on Adam's remarks about man's relationship with God, as reflected in this first speech, Anne Davidson Ferry and Jon S. Lawry more directly consider Adam's relationship with Eve, the immediate audience for the speech, and both critics detect troubling undercurrents. Ferry explains, "When Adam in the first line of his first speech calls Eve 'Sole partner and sole part of all these joyes' (IV, 411), the echo of the word 'soul' reminds us that they are one soul and also that she is part of his soul, a principle within him" (*Milton's Epic Voice* 100). Also reverberating in Adam's first line are *partner* and *part,* and that echo, Ferry (100–01) explains, "recalls the creation of Eve from a part of Adam, an association confirmed by Eve's memory of Adam's first speech to her: 'Part of my Soul I seek thee, and thee claim / My other half' (IV, 487–88). The reiteration of these words with their combined double meanings seems to foretell the real separation of Adam and Eve 'The Morn when first they parted' (IX, 848)." The note of concern in Ferry's closing remark is heard more strongly in Lawry's reading, for in Adam's first words, Lawry hears a Satanic echo: "If we have forgotten paradigmatic Satan, Adam's first words recall him; Adam elevates Eve as dangerously as Satan had 'raised' Sin" (173).

411. *Sole partner and sole part:* cross-referencing 8.383–84 and 4.487, the Richardsons (163) comment that Adam "had none but Her to partake with him in what he Enjoy'd," paying no heed to the difficulties that distressed Bentley two years earlier and that would continue to demand editorial and critical consideration. Bentley (121) flatly declares that the line "could not come from the Author. How can a *Part* be *sole? sole part* is a self contradiction. If *Part* is admitted; it must have been, BEST *part.* If *Sole* be prefer'd, several Words may be substituted for *Part:* This may serve for one, *Sole Partner and sole* JOY *of all these Joys.* Or thus, *Sole Partner and sole* CAUSE." Bentley offers support from *SA* 377, "Sole Author I, sole cause." Pearce responds to Bentley by inserting a comma after *part,* explaining, "The sense is, among all these joys Thou alone art my partner, and (what is more) Thou alone art part of me, as in ver. 487."

Surveying Milton's writings, Pearce reports, "*Of* in Milton frequently signifies *among*. The want of observing this made Dr. Bentley read *best part* for *sole part*, thinking that *sole part* is a contradiction, and so it is as he understands *of* here, to be the mark of the genitive case govern'd of *part*" (125–26). Newton (260–61) and Todd ([1842], 2:78) follow Pearce, inserting a comma after *part* and reporting much of Pearce's comment.

The wordplay here, more than what Bentley considered frayed logic, elicits twentieth century commentary, and for A. W. Verity and Robert Martin Adams, that wordplay is not very appealing. Verity (463) finds in the line "an almost quibbling use of *sole* = (1) 'only,' (2) 'unique' (implying 'chief')," while Adams hears jangling. Adams does acknowledge the problem with meaning but concludes, "In the end there is a sort of plain grammatical sense at the foot of the passage; but if anything is clear at all, it is that Milton wanted the jangle on 'partner' and 'part' even at the cost of possible, indeed probable, misunderstanding of the literal sense" (107). Also see Adams in **530**. For F. T. Prince, however, puns, conceits, and other forms of verbal wit in *PL* evidence Milton's "extreme intellectual energy" from which the success of the entire poem derives (*Italian Element* 123).

412–17. Merritt Y. Hughes ("Variorum") sets Adam's reasoning about the goodness of the creator in this sequence against Milton's discussion of creation in *DocCh* 1.7, where, Hughes explains, "Milton inverts Adam's argument . . . and affirms that because man was made in the image of God he was necessarily endowed with 'natural wisdom, holiness, and righteousness' [Patterson, *Works* 15:52–53]. But the reasoning implies Plato's argument that the supreme originating principle of the Universe was its Maker's freedom from any trace of envy and his desire to make the cosmos good like himself (*Timaeus* 30E). Milton could assume acceptance of such reasoning in the form that St. Basil fixed upon it for the hexameral tradition when he wrote in his commentary on Genesis that the beginning of all existing things, the fountain of life, the spiritual light and immense wisdom which made Heaven and earth, was the infinite goodness which is most dear to all rational beings (*Homily*, col. 10)."

Leland Ryken looks to this sequence as he identifies two of Milton's strategies to establish his apocalyptic vision: distance, that is, adapting "the theological idea that God can be known through his Creation, which is a kind of extension of many of his qualities" (155), and the "renunciation of empirical qualities" (96).

412–13. Examining epic address and reference as functions of decorum in *PL*, Kester Svendsen notes, "Adam and Eve speak of the Son variously as the creator, the redeemer, the lord of creation, and their judge. Such epithets of Adam as *the Power that made us, high Creator, author of this Universe,* and *creator bounteous and benigne* illustrate the first of these types of reference" ("Epic Address" 201).

414. Edward S. Le Comte notes that Adam again describes God as "infinitely good" in 7.76 (*Yet Once More* 35).

416–18. Sister Mary Irma Corcoran sets these lines against the traditional explanations for Adam's being created outside the garden and placed in the garden only subsequently. The traditional explanations focused on God's knowledge that Adam would eventually have to live outside the garden, that Adam had to know that he was only the caretaker of the garden, that Adam needed to understand that he had received the garden not through merit but through grace, that his home was not the terrestrial but the celestial garden, and that his first journey into the terrestrial garden foreshadowed his final journey into the celestial garden (49). Furthermore, Corcoran reports the traditional allegorical reading: "the translation of Adam to Paradise signified the bringing of man from the world into the Church" (50). Corcoran (50) also refers the commentators' concerns with this topic to 8.338–39 and 11.339. Also see the *OED* on *possess* in **431**.

417. *happiness…hand:* Leland Ryken discusses *happiness* as well as Adam's reference to God's *hand* as exemplifying two techniques by which Milton establishes his apocalyptic vision: the techniques of conceptual imagery and anthropomorphism. Happiness, Ryken explains, is a conceptual image by which Milton "transcends the world of sense impressions by entering a conceptual realm of qualities and essences" (201). The anthropomorphism that references God's hand is "designed to describe concretely and symbolically specific functions of God; a reference to his hand depicts vividly his bestowal of bounty or his creative craftsmanship" (131–32).

happiness: insisting that from beginning to end *PL* "is concerned with the nature, conditions, and loss of original happiness," John Steadman ("Felicity and End" 126) examines the concept of happiness in Milton's paradise with an emphasis on ethical, political, and theological traditions. Steadman argues that in both *PL* and *PR*, Milton achieves "a conscious reorientation of the epic towards the end and final cause of ethics, politics, and theology — the *summum bonum* and true felicity of man" (132).

418–20. Todd attributes to John Gillies a reference to Acts 17.25: "Neither is [God] worshipped with men's hands, as though he needed any thing, seeing he giveth to all life, and breath, and all things" ([1842], 2:78).

425–27. As Adam here first ponders the meaning of death, Sister Mary Irma Corcoran (110) considers the concept of fear as a prelapsarian virtue: "At this point in his career, Adam had little fear, his obedience appearing as an act of obedient absolute love of God rather than of fear of offending the beloved. There is a suggestion of vague natural fear, however, in Adam's speculation that death is 'Some dreadful thing no doubt' (IV 426), since God has warned them against the act which would cause it. The virtue of fear of God occurs more definitely in God's commission to Raphael to warn Adam (V, 237[–45]). It appeared tentatively in the soul of Adam upon Raphael's account of the fall of the angels (V, 553[–57]), temporarily subsided (VII, 59[–60]), and appeared reintensified in his warning to Eve (IX, 353[–56])."

429. *many signes:* Werblowsky considers that the *many signes* that Adam lists (430–32) "are rather meagre and tame, consisting, as they do, mainly of the privilege to praise the Lord" (23).

430–32. See Gen. 1.26: "Let us make man in our image, . . . and let them have dominion over the fish of the sea, and over the fowl of the air, and over the cattle, and over all the earth." Merritt Y. Hughes cross-references 341–51, 8.338–47 ("Variorum").

Dorothy Durkee Miller points out that Adam here "reminds her [Eve] of her equal share" in dominion over the other creatures (543).

431. *possess:* "occupy" (Verity 464). The *OED* 1 cites this line to illustrate the obsolete meaning applicable to "a person or body of persons: To hold, occupy (a place or territory); to reside or be stationed in; to inhabit (with or without ownership)." Cf. Corcoran in **416–18**.

433. *easie:* as so often in Milton's poetry, this simple little word is anything but simple, as Adam's repetition of it in 421 suggests, and as various glosses and commentaries acknowledge. Patrick Hume reasons that the command struck Adam as "easie, because but one" (150). C. S. Lewis, supplying a reference to St. Augustine's *City of God* 14.12, describes the disobedience of Adam and Eve as "heinous precisely because obedience was so easy" (69), Sister Mary Irma Corcoran suggests that the "simple" nature of the command made it easy (53), and Alastair Fowler glosses *easie* as "Easy to keep; involving no effort; not constraining or oppressive" (638). Several decades before Basil Willey settles his attention on *easie,* A. W. Verity explains that he finds "an unconscious irony" in the word because it as appropriately describes keeping as breaking the command (464). In *The Seventeenth Century Background* (1934), Willey puzzles the meaning of the command in conjunction with Adam's twice describing it as *easie* in this speech. Quoting from Milton's *DocCh* (Patterson, *Works* 15:112), Willey reasons that the command may be designated *easie* only if it is understood as a test of obedience, involving "an act 'indifferent in itself,'" but, Willey continues, "It would *not* have been 'easy' to abstain from knowledge freely to be grasped, and in fact it was by insisting upon the magic virtue of the fruit that Satan successfully tempted Eve" (258). In a 1950 article, Max Bertschinger brings additional significance to Adam's adjective, concluding "there can be no doubt about his preoccupation with a vital part of his immediate condition of life, which he fails to understand and about which he seems constantly to have to check himself." To Bertschinger, Adam's statement "sounds a little like saying, 'Never mind about that tree,' when, in point of fact, he minds very much" (55). See Bertschinger in **411–39**.

436. Leland Ryken, explaining how analogy functions to establish Milton's apocalyptic vision of paradise, sees that prelapsarian, like postlapsarian, worship is in "an essentially ecclesiastical and devotional idiom," and "centers in the act of praise to God" (148). Ryken cross-references 444–45, 734–38.

437–39. See the full review of the critical discussion of prelapsarian work in **610–33**.

Merritt Y. Hughes notes "an ironic link" between Adam's closing remarks here about their "delightful task" and Eve's suggestion in 9.207 that they separate to work at their "pleasant task enjoyn'd" ("Variorum").

440–91. The entirety of Eve's first speech, but especially her narrative about her experience at the "Smooth Lake" (459), has revealed her innocence to some, but her sinfulness to others, and—for the most part—those others are twentieth century critics. While no one more passionately praises Eve's first speech than does Addison, none of the major early editors and commentators denies the image of Eve that he describes. Declaring Eve's autobiography "as beautiful a Passage as any in *Milton,* or perhaps in any other Poet whatsoever," Addison in *Spectator* 321 contends, "A Poet of less Judgment and Invention than this great Author, would have found it very difficult to have filled these tender parts of the Poem with Sentiments proper for a State of Innocence; to have described the warmth of Love, and the Professions of it, without Artifice or Hyperbole; to have made the Man speak the most endearing things, without descending from his natural Dignity, and the Woman receiving them without departing from the Modesty of her Character; in a word, to adjust the Prerogatives of Wisdom and Beauty, and make each appear to the other in its proper Force and Loveliness. This mutual Subordination of the two Sexes is wonderfully kept up in the whole Poem, as particularly in the Speech of *Eve*...and upon the Conclusion of it in the following lines. '*So spake our general mother*...'" (3:176). Addison's well-known remarks on Eve were preceded by a briefer, yet equally forceful, appreciation from the writer of a letter "*To Mr.* T. S. *in Vindication of* Mr. Milton's *Paradise* lost" in 1694. The author, "I. I.," celebrates Milton as the singer "of *Matchless Beings, Matchless Things,* before *unknown* to, and even *unthought* of, by the *whole* Race of Men" (200), and among those "*Matchless Beings,*" the writer points to Milton's Eve: "behold *Woman* appearing *Inferiour* to both these [angels and man], and yet more *Ambitious* than either, but then *softer* much in her *Make* and *Manners* than her *rougher Spouse,* whom down right *Sincerity* and unaffected plainness seem mostly to Delight. Nor can I now forget with what *vast complacency* we have oft together read the most *Natural, Lively,* yet (as their Sexes) different Descriptions our first *Parents* separately make of their own Apprehensions of themselves at their *first finding* themselves *Living Creatures*" (199). William Hazlitt develops this writer's sense of Eve's ambition as he later compares Milton's heroine with Shakespeare's females: "*Eve* is not only represented as beautiful, but with conscious beauty. Shakspeare's [*sic*] heroines are almost insensible of their charms, and wound without knowing it. They are not coquets. If the salvation of mankind had depended upon one of them, we don't know—but the devil might have been baulked. This is but a conjecture! *Eve* has a great idea of herself, and there is some difficulty in prevailing on her to quit her own image, the first time she discovers its reflection in the water" (336).

One of the sources of the twentieth century controversy about Eve can be identified as Walter Raleigh's influential *Milton* (1900). Without specifying Eve's first speech, Raleigh claims, "It would be a wearisome and fruitless quest to journey through the *Paradise Lost* in search of those profound touches of humanity, and those sudden felicities of insight, which abound in the Elizabethans. Subtleties of thought, fine observation of truths that almost evade the attempt to express them, sentences and figures illuminative of the mysteries of human destiny and the intricacies of human character—of all these there is none" (115–16). Raleigh continues, "In Milton's poetry we find ourselves in a remote atmosphere; far indeed from the shrewd observation of daily life, farther even from that wonderful analysis of emotion which is the pastime of Shakespeare and of Meredith. Beautiful figured writing and keen psychological observation of this kind are beside the purpose of Milton, and beyond his power" (117–18). Questioning Raleigh's assumptions about Milton's "purpose" in *PL,* James Holly Hanford insists, "It is only the Satan-blinded critic who will say that their [Adam and Eve's] story does not claim us. Involving as it does the elements of human strength and human weakness…it is the type of all subsequent tragic experience" ("Dramatic Element" 183). As Hanford therefore praises Milton's characterization of Adam and Eve, he does perhaps begin to blur the distinction between their prelapsarian and their postlapsarian identities, and to compromise their free will. Hanford claims that Milton "marks with a distinctness unknown in epic the precise weaknesses in both Adam and Eve which lead them to destruction" (183), and the "weaknesses" Hanford finds revealed in Eve's first speech are her "intellectual inferiority" and her "Instinctive desire for admiration" (184). While Hanford sees "weaknesses" in prelapsarian Eve, Howard Schultz sees "velleities toward sin which, long before the fact, make her fall credible" ("Satan's Serenade" 18). On Eve's recollection of yielding to Adam, for example, Schultz writes, "her reconciliation to manly grace and wisdom (she does not appreciate them by simple and immediate intuition) seems importantly bound up with her delight in Adam's society and the 'kisses pure'" (19). Schultz sees similar motives in Eve when she later chooses Adam, rather than Raphael, as her astronomy teacher (19). In A. J. A. Waldock's analysis the line separating prelapsarian and postlapsarian life, over which Hanford and Schultz perceive Eve hovering, is crossed, or rather erased, for Waldock considers Adam and Eve to be fallen from their very first appearance: "There was no way for Milton of making the transition from sinlessness to sin perfectly intelligible. It is obvious that Adam and Eve must already have contracted human weakness before they can start on the course of conduct that leads to their fall: to put it another way, they must already be fallen (technically) before they can begin to fall" (61).

Critical voices denying this claim are soon heard, however, the voices of Cleanth Brooks, Charles Monroe Coffin, and Arthur E. Barker being among the most forceful. Brooks stresses Eve's intellectual capacities upon her awakening to life: "She has been created mature, and moreover she represents unfallen humanity with its keen preceptions [*sic*] and its vigorous and powerful intellect. These she proceeds to apply at once to the situation in which she finds herself. Rene Descartes could do no better: she says not *Cogito, ergo sum*, but *Admiror, ergo sum*—I wonder, therefore I am" ("Eve's Awakening" 282–83). Coffin insists that Eve "has an identity as unique as Adam's, and in fact, a superior independence. *Separateness* would be a better word than independence, for the latter suggests self-sufficiency, and no creature in Milton's world has that" (14). Barker rejects all arguments about prelapsarian incidents foreshadowing the Fall. Pointing to Eve's response to the voice that calls her from the lake, Barker explains that such prelapsarian incidents "illustrate the kind of active response that is according to the norm of right. Milton's Creator does not punish his creatures for the limitations and even degrees of impercipience he has given them, even *un*fallen, to use instrumentally in the development of the potentialities they have as his image, only for wilfully not so using them" ("Structural and Doctrinal Pattern" 189). J. M. Evans and Barbara Kiefer Lewalski continue to develop Barker's understanding that Eve's autobiography reveals her growth toward fulfillment as a creature made in the image of God. Elaborating the emphasis he brings to the associations between the garden and the couple in the garden, Evans explains, "The point of this episode [Eve's experience at the smooth lake], one of Milton's most beautiful and perceptive inventions, is that 'Kind nature' does not on this occasion make the vine embrace the elm . . . that Eve's untutored feelings, like the natural growth of the plants around her, do not grow in the right direction spontaneously. They have to be 'reformed,' and it is necessary for God to check the 'fruitless embraces' she seeks in her reflection and lead her to 'wed her Elm'" (253). Lewalski reasons "that in his treatment of the prelapsarian state, Milton is not only, and not primarily, foreshadowing the Fall, but that he is undertaking to create, in quite unusual terms, the Life in Innocence" (116), and she locates in Eve's autobiographical speech evidence for that thesis: "Eve's creation story . . . displays an impressive advance in knowledge after some false starts: indeed she tells it to illustrate how she came to understand her right relationship to Adam and the true scale of human values" (101). J. B. Broadbent's admiration for Milton's characterization of Eve develops his argument that she is without any literary antecedent: "Epics had presented figures like Circe and the sportive damsels in Tasso's Fortunate Isle [*Gerusalemme Liberata* 15.58–65] and Spenser's Bower of Bliss [*The Faerie Queene* 2.12.42–82], or patient Penelopes, green maidens on whom knights could hang their honour; they had not offered anything like 'the Virgin Majestie of *Eve*' [9.270]. Heroines were deteriorating in 17th century narrative verse" (*Some Graver Subject* 187).

As Rosalie L. Colie argues that Milton's emphasis on creation shapes the organization of *PL,* she glances at this episode: "The actual narrative of the creation, broken at so many points, begins with the making of the last creature, Eve, who in Book IV tells Adam of her own sensations at the beginning of her conscious life" (136).

440–48. While Addison hears Eve announce a theory of the "mutual Subordination of the two Sexes" at the conclusion of her first speech (*Spectator* 3:176), subsequent critics instead hear her announce a theory of sexual hierarchy at the beginning of the same speech, and that theory, not the one Addison notes, stirs heated critical discussion. C. S. Lewis (79) glances at the dialog between Adam and Eve as he discusses "the Hierarchical principle" and Milton's love of it. Lewis writes that Milton "pictures the life of beatitude as one of order — an intricate dance, so intricate that it seems irregular precisely when its regularity is most elaborate (V, 620)." Epithets such as those by which Eve here addresses Adam are for Lewis "the ceremonious interchange of unequal courtesies," and he explains, "This is not the writing of a man who embraces the Hierarchical principle with reluctance, but rather of a man enchanted by it" (80). About 20 years earlier, however, Allan H. Gilbert had cautioned that the opinions Eve announces are those of a woman in love and must not be assigned to Milton: "Though these speeches of Eve's [throughout Book 4] are founded on the facts as Milton represents them, they are nevertheless the strong language of the greatest affection, and quite in accord with human nature. In her love for Adam, Eve is eager to acknowledge the superiority of her devoted husband." Recalling Johnson's opinion of Milton's contempt for women, Gilbert explains, "It should be unnecessary to say that this language of Eve's affection is not Milton's statement of the attitude he believed the wives of his day should take, yet some who have been blinded by the tradition of Milton's Turkish opinions, and are forgetful of the dramatic character of the poem, have gone to the length of supposing that it is" ("Milton on the Position" 247; for Milton's "Turkish opinions," see Johnson, "Milton" 276). Yet other critics continue to consider the impact of Eve's human nature as she asserts the theory of the sexual hierarchy when first addressing Adam. Denis Saurat, for one, claims, "Eve accepts her inferiority, not as a degradation, but as a privilege the more, since thus she has more to receive, more to admire, more to possess—a typically feminine solution to the whole problem" (161). Noting that in her first speech answering Adam's emphasis on the command, Eve "waves the idea of the Tree aside and utters what in its touching obliqueness is her naive expression of love for Adam" (56), Max Bertschinger believes that she "reacts in a truly womanly way" (61), for she simply tries to "distract him from his worried absorption in the Forbidden Tree" (57). Douglas Day describes Eve's behavior here as "typically feminine" (378), for, Day suggests, Adam's opening remarks are not what Eve had hoped to hear, and her reply, "though full of indisputable humility and piety, [is] a very short prayer of thanksgiving indeed" (369). Also emphasizing that Eve is a woman in love, John Steadman's focus is less on Milton the man than on Milton the poet confronting the challenge of presenting marital love within a Christian epic: "In building up his idyllic picture of the first and archetypal marriage, the poet consciously represents the ideal of wedded happiness as contingent on masculine dominance" (*Milton* 116). Steadman explains that Milton's development of *amor* as one of the major epic formulae complicates that archetypal marriage as it expresses both the valid image and the false idol of *amor:* "Wedlock serves as a matrix for a wide variety of related ideas. Within this single motif Milton introduces an extensive range of romantic conventions as well as Biblical concepts. Some of these are paradoxical or mutually exclusive. Like Chaucer before him, he has perceived the essential contradiction between the theological doctrine of marriage and the poetic tradition of courtly love" (115). In Adam and Eve's relationship, Steadman sees both concepts, but argues, "Milton accentuates their inherent contradiction by seizing on the essential point of difference—the issue of sovereignty and obedience" (115).

440–43. Eve's statement of the theory of male dominance, which constitutes her first extended epic epithet for Adam, rests upon the history of her creation and resonates with the Pauline scriptures responding to the creation narrative in Genesis, as critics have pointed out. Alastair Fowler (638–39) identifies three biblical echoes in Eve's words here: Gen. 2.23, "Adam said, This is now bone of my bones, and flesh of my flesh: she shall be called Woman, because she was taken out of Man"; 1 Cor. 11.3, "The head of every man is Christ; and the head of the woman is the man; and the head of Christ is God"; and 1 Cor. 11.9, "Neither was the man created for the woman; but the woman for the man." Fowler also cross-references 299. Sister Mary Irma Corcoran presents commentators' understandings of the creation of Eve from Adam's rib and then proceeds to Eve's response to her origin: "Commentators taught that God fashioned Eve from the rib of her husband so that he might love her as his own flesh, or for the sake of mutual harmony, that she might submit willingly to him, or that Adam might be the principle of the whole race" (64). Turning to Eve as she first speaks to Adam in *PL,* Corcoran observes, "Eve's origin from Adam motivated her humility and her reverence for him...and their mutual love." Corcoran (64–65) cross-references 482–88 and 635–37.

Other modern critics attend less to the echoes between the Bible and Eve's epic epithets for Adam and more to the echoes between passages in Milton's texts. C. S. Lewis admires and believes Milton "delights in" the "interchange of unequal courtesies" between Adam and Eve (79), but Jon S. Lawry finds a disturbing similarity in the terms of that interchange: "We uneasily notice that for our generating parents human self-definition begins in peril of Satanic pride. As Adam has perhaps unduly elevated Eve, so Eve places Adam in a position not only of superiority to herself but to any divine creativeness" (174). While situational irony colors this first dialog between Adam and Eve, for Satan is eavesdropping, John Halkett (105) argues that "the subtler irony is that Eve's words to Adam echo Sin's declaration of kinship to Satan [2.864–66]."

Examining epic address as a feature of decorum in *PL,* Kester Svendsen ("Epic Address" 193–94) agrees with Lewis that Eve's epithets are marked by "ceremonious formality," but Svendsen also notes that those epithets change to reflect the poem's action: "the epithets she uses up to Book IX are subjective.... In the persuasion scene of Book IX, however, the point of view and the tone change; there he is objectively described as *Offspring of Heav'n and Earth and all Earths Lord.* After she has sinned, her epithet reasserts the dependence stated in those earlier; she implores him as *my onely strength and stay.*"

445–47. In a letter to his wife, Mary, dated May 9–13, 1812, William Wordsworth assumes Eve's voice and grants to Mary the preeminence Eve yields to Adam: "I am the blessedest of Men, the happiest of husbands — How often does that passage of Milton come to my mind; 'I chiefly who enjoy so far the happier lot, enjoying thee, preeminent, etc.'" (8:66).

447–48. Patrick Hume annotates "Praeeminent by so much odds" with "More excellent by divers degrees; raised above me by so many degrees," but then moving to the Latin etymology of *Praeeminent* and *consort,* also suggests some ambiguity in Eve's words: "*Praeeminens,* Lat. raised, high, excellent, of *praeeminere,* Lat. to excel. *Consort,* Companion, of the Lat. *Consors,* of the same Size and Condition; hence a Wife, and especially that of a King, called *Queen Consort,* attaining that Title by her Marriage with a Soveraign Prince" (150). While two modern editors, A. W. Verity and Alastair Fowler, focus their attention on *odds* (447), C. S. Lewis considers the complications Hume's annotation suggests. Verity (464) glosses *odds* as "superiority" and finds it frequently so used by Shakespeare, as in *Richard II* 3.4.89 and *Titus Andronicus* 5.2.19, and Fowler's gloss maintains the same basic meaning: "difference, superiority, advantage; usually construed as singular, in the seventeenth century" (639). Lewis explains, however, that the "royalty" assigned to both Adam and Eve "is less apparent in Eve, partly because she is in fact Adam's inferior, in her double capacity of wife and subject, but partly, I think, because her humility is often misunderstood. She thinks herself more fortunate than he, because she has *him* for her companion while he 'like consort to himself can nowhere find' (IV, 448) and obeys his commands 'unargued' (IV, 635). This is humility, and, in Milton's view, becoming humility" (120). Also see Lewis in **288–1015.** Lewis also acknowledges, however, that grandeur is another significant feature of Eve's character: "There is no question, you see, of a boy and a girl tumbling on a bank; even for him there is that in Eve which compels deference, the possibility of *Daungier.*" For Lewis, Eve's "grandeur, and a certain aloofness in her, live in some of Milton's most memorable phrases: 'with sweet austere composure thus reply'd,' or 'to whom the virgin majestie of Eve.' Virgin, that is, in majesty: not, at the time to which the words refer, in body, and never virginal in the sense of being immature. Maidenly ignorance had never existed in Eve" (121).

449–52. While Milton's Eve awakening to life silently wonders about her situation, Dryden's Eve immediately talks. In *The State of Innocence, and Fall of Man* 2.3.8–10, Dryden (*Works* 12:110) assigns Eve the words that Milton attributes to the newly born Adam in 8.273–77. Also see Dryden and Anne Davidson Ferry in **460–91**.

449–50. Hume acknowledges that Eve's sleep metaphor is commonplace, but he realizes it is uniquely appropriate to both Adam's and Eve's autobiographies; indeed, writes Hume, the metaphor "cannot square with any Persons but those of our two first Progenitors, so it is exactly suitable to them, created certainly at full growth, perfect in Body, Mind and Memory" (150). Like Hume, Newton compares Eve's remarks upon awakening to life to Adam's at 8.253 and comments on the effect of the comparison: "the beauty and propriety of each will appear to greater advantage" (262–63). Todd quotes Newton ([1842], 2:79).

449. Critical opinions on how much time Adam and Eve have spent in the garden before Satan enters it have varied from the eighteenth through the twentieth century. Richard Bentley concludes that Eve's reference to *day* should have been *hour:* "A whole *Day* is too long to reckon by, when perhaps in the Poet's Plan they had not yet liv'd above Three or Two" (122). Cross-referencing 639–56, 680–88, and 712–13, Pearce rejects Bentley's assumption about the number of days Adam and Eve have been in the garden (126). To Pearce's cross-references, the Richardsons add 5.31, 5.253, 8.25, 8.253, and 9.1022 (164). Newton, quoted by Todd, believes that Adam and Eve "have lived many days in Paradise before the Fall" (Newton 262; Todd [1842], 2:79). Cf. Masson, *Poetical Works* 3:175. Twentieth century critics agree with Newton about Adam and Eve's tenure in the garden. Cross-listing a variety of time references, as do Pearce and the Richardsons, Allan H. Gilbert concludes, "The general impression is that the two in Paradise did not feel anything of novelty about their situation. When the effect of a long stay is clearly descried, we need only accept it" (*On the Composition* 150). Alastair Fowler observes, "The impression that they have been in Paradise for some days is confirmed by many other passages...; though it is of course possible that M[ilton] meant us to assume that man was created with a ready made understanding of seasonal change" (639). Change and development figuring so significantly in her discussion of the life of innocence, Barbara Kiefer Lewalski argues that Eve's earliest memory makes the point that Milton's Adam and Eve have enjoyed many prelapsarian days, although Lewalski reports that "most exegetes allowed Adam and Eve only one day in the Garden" (89).

450. *repos'd:* Hume (150) acknowledges the unusual transitive form here with his gloss "*Laid under a Flow'ry Shade,*" and he notes that it is "used by the wary Virgil in the same sense" in the *Aeneid* 4.391–92.

451. *of:* Newton points out that *on* occurs in the first edition, *of* in the second. He prints *on* (263). Todd also has *on,* explaining, "The second edition reads, 'Under a shade *of* flowers,' which has been followed in Tonson's earlier editions; but Tickell, Fenton, Bentley, and Newton, rightly follow the first edition, 'Under a shade *on* flowers.' To repose *on flowers under a shade,* is so elegant an expression; and to repose *merely under a shade of flowers,* so insignificant; that I am persuaded the reading of the second edition must be an errour of the press" ([1842], 2:79). Surveying the responses of ten of Milton's modern editors to this textual difference, Robert Martin Adams points out that only the Columbia edition's editors print *of* rather than *on.* Adams feels that, because either reading is "more or less acceptable" (80), it is "curious that nine editors of ten are sure that Milton did not intend a reading which is inferior neither in sense, sound, coherence, nor propriety to that of the first edition. The trees of paradise have flowers on them, and the very fact that Eve lies *on* flowers elsewhere may be a reason that Milton would have wanted her to lie *under* them here" (102).

    shade: see B. A. Wright's and Anne Davidson Ferry's earlier notes on *shade* in **138**. Merritt Y. Hughes finds that *on* "seems justified if *shade* means a shady grove of trees, as it does in 4.138 and 141" ("Variorum").

453–56. Christopher Ricks focuses considerable attention on this passage, stressing "Milton's recurring insistence that sound is a movement of the air, that an air is the air" (101). Establishing *sound* as "air," Ricks pursues the subsequent involvement of water and air: "Upon this mirroring of the airy sky in the lake depends the whole important episode. But perhaps 'mirroring' judges the situation more knowledgeably than Eve could—say rather, indistinguishability: 'Uncertain which, in Ocean or in Air' (III.76). Milton insists on the indistinguishable commingling not only by the explicit comparisons, but also by the syntactical mingling in a 'sound . . . spread into a liquid Plain.' It is not entirely accidental that we might talk of the *fluidity* of such syntax" (101). Ricks acknowledges that the mingling of the air and water, expressed by a phrase such as "the liquid air" is a "commonplace," but he also insists that "it is one of great use and importance when Eve as it were regards herself as Narcissus—one of the most poignantly significant of her appearances before the Fall. Milton brings this commonplace to life by blurring the distinction between air and water in his syntax" (102). Quoting from Ricks, Alastair Fowler (639) continues to develop the significance of this description. Fowler directs readers, "Notice, though, that *issued, spread* and *stood* could just possibly all be transitive past participles describing *waters*. (For the trans. use of *issue*, see *OED* 11[.]7.) The landscape is probably meant to be philosophically significant; for the water and the cave recall a Homeric image interpreted by Porphyry as a symbol of the descent of the soul (*De antro nympharum*, discussed in Henry More, *Conjectura Cabbalistica*, Defence i 6). See Homer, *Il.* v 872, 'low Hyle's [Matter's] watery plain.'"

In discussing Milton's apocalyptic vision, Leland Ryken examines the sustained attention to aural imagery in paradise: "Sound is thus one of the dominant sense impressions which we gain from descriptions of the garden, and the intangible nature of aural imagery accords well with the apocalyptic nature of the subject" (226).

453. *murmuring:* Robert Bridges finds that this word exemplifies the "Rule of R": "If two unstressed vowels are separated by *r* there may be 'elision'" (29).

457–58. Edward S. Le Comte (*Yet Once More* 50) cross-references *PR* 4.586–87: the angels "set him down / On a green bank."

460–91. Critics have always examined Eve's experience at the "Smooth lake" (459) by reference to the classical myth of Narcissus, but while the early editors describe Eve's behavior with terms like *natural, probable,* and *beautiful,* as do many twentieth century critics, several influential modern critics disagree, finding Eve's behavior "fallen" or "partly-fallen." Hume's (150) evaluation of the association between Eve and Narcissus sets the tone that is sustained and elaborated by all early editors. Sealing his comment by quoting *Metamorphoses* 3.425–26, Hume explains, "*Milton* has improved the Fable of *Ovid*, by representing *Eve* like a She *Narcissus* admiring her self; and has made it much more probable, that a Person who had never seen any thing like her self, should be in love with her own faint reflected Resemblance, than that a Man acquainted with the World and himself, should be undone by so dull a Dotage." Within a week of his declaration that Eve's autobiography is "as beautiful a passage as any in *Milton*, or perhaps in any other Poet whatsoever" (*Spectator* 3:176),

Addison publishes a letter from "RT" who writes that he had read "with great Satisfaction" Addison's essay, but wonders "whether there may not also be some Moral couched under that Place in the same Book where the Poet lets us know, that the first Woman immediately after her Creation, ran to a Looking-glass, and became so enamoured of her own Face, that she had never removed to view any of the other Works of Nature, had not she been led off to a Man. If you think fit to set down the whole Passage from *Milton,* your Readers will be able to judge for themselves." Addison fulfills that reader's request, printing the entire autobiographical passage (449–92), but once more declaring it "one of the most Beautiful Passages in the whole Poem" (*Spectator* 3:191–92). Addison also speaks to Eve's experience at the lake in his notes on the *Metamorphoses,* where, describing Eve as "a raw unexperienced Being," he, much like Hume, finds Eve's "surprize at the sight of her own face in the water, far more just and natural" than Narcissus's behavior (3:176n2). Newton's and Todd's commentaries are in line with Hume's as they too find that Eve's Narcissus experience is to her credit, as well as Milton's. In his notes, Newton reports RT's question, describing it as sarcastic, and proceeding to insist that Eve's experience "is much more probable and natural, as well as more delicate and beautiful, than the famous story of Narcissus in Ovid, from whom our author manifestly took the hint, and has expressly imitated some passages, but has avoided all his puerilities without losing any of his beauties" (264). Dropping the reference to RT, Todd repeats Newton's note, and quotes a note contributed by Benjamin Stillingfleet, who, after insisting that Milton has "improved" the Narcissus myth, asserts, "The same might be said of almost every passage Milton has borrowed from the ancients." Stillingfleet proceeds to conclude his praise for Milton's achievement by suggesting, "We may apply to Milton on this occasion what Aristotle says of Homer, that he taught poets how to lie properly" ([1842], 2:80). When he attributes speech to Eve at the Fountain in *The State of Innocence, and Fall of Man,* Dryden blurs the distinction that lies at the heart of the future debate about Milton's presentation of Eve's behavior: the distinction between prelapsarian and postlapsarian life. In 2.3.26–27, Dryden's Eve, for example, is angry when she exclaims to the image in the Fountain, "Ah fair, yet false! ah, Being, form'd to cheat, / By seeming kindness, mixt with deep deceit!" (*Works* 12:111). In addition, Dryden's Eve—unlike Milton's—also speaks later in 2.3.53–55 as she rejects Adam at first sight, her words echoing Adam's explanation of that rejection in his conversation with Raphael in *PL* 8.500–10 (*Works* 12:112). Also see Dryden in **449–52**. On such features of Dryden's dramatic adaptation of *PL,* Anne Davidson Ferry explains that the "vanity, suspicion, jealousy, fear, lust, [and] disappointment" Dryden attributes to his Adam and Eve are "appropriate to romance, satire, and farce rather than to the pastoral mode that Milton, fusing Biblical and classical traditions, designed for his early scenes in Eden" (*Milton* 89).

While Douglas Bush glimpses a hint of vanity in Eve's Narcissus experience (*"Paradise Lost" in Our Time* 76; also see Bush, "Ironic and Ambiguous Allusion" 638), and Howard Schultz spots velleities to sin ("Satan's Serenade" 18), A. J. A. Waldock's declaration in 1947 that both Adam and Eve "must already be fallen (technically) before they can begin to fall" (61) triggers the animated debate about the Narcissus scene that stretches over the following several decades. Among the most influential critics agreeing with Waldock are E. M. W. Tillyard and Millicent Bell. The term Tillyard introduces as he reconsiders prelapsarian scenes like Eve's "Smooth Lake" scene is *faking.* Milton, Tillyard explains, "resorts to some faking: perfectly legitimate in a poem, yet faking nevertheless. He anticipates the Fall by attributing to Eve and Adam feelings which though nominally felt in the state of innocence are actually not compatible with it" (*Studies* 10–11). Tillyard therefore declares, "The Fall…must be extended back in time; it has no plain and sensational beginning" (13). Bell writes that in Eve's Narcissus experience, "we have glimpsed a dainty vanity in 'our general Mother' which the Serpent will put to use" (871). Bell argues that Milton, not as concerned with identifying the prime cause of the Fall as are his modern critics, "subtly obscured any sharp division in the drama, any 'before' and 'after'" (864). Without directly acknowledging these earlier views, Don Cameron Allen looks at Eve's experience at the lake as a foreshadowing of Raphael's narrative of the angels' fall: "When the angels were created they looked first at themselves, surprised at their own existence. Then some looked upward and found the source of creation in the Word. Others fell in love with themselves and sank in their own darkness" ("Milton's Eve" 108). Milton's Eve, Allen explains, "was more fortunate than the angels, because the Word conveyed her to the thing that she was created to love" (109). In that same year, 1960, John Peter and J. B. Broadbent engage with Bell's reading of Eve's Narcissus experience. Bell's glimpse of "a dainty vanity" in Eve is "fallacious" in Peter's opinion, as he explains, "fallacious, at any rate if we are to give to 'vanity' a tone of incipient reproof, as her context suggests we should. The incident [at the smooth lake] is actually one of the most engaging glimpses we have of Eve's artless simplicity" (102). Broadbent's rejection of Bell's reading rests in part on theological tradition: "The identification of Adam and Eve with fallen man is not a peculiarity of Milton's but a characteristic of Protestant theology forced on it by taking the myth seriously." More significant, however, Broadbent's refusal to see Adam and Eve as partly fallen is involved with his view of the dynamic, challenging nature of Milton's presentation of prelapsarian human nature: "our first impression is of a balanced perfection, not the less perfect for being balanced. But it is true that this condition becomes less stable: the knife-edge between man's 'disposition to do good' and his 'liability to fall,' as Milton puts it in *De Doctrina* [1.11 (Patterson, *Works* 15:181)], is sharpened through Books V, VII and VIII, especially where Adam's relations with Eve are concerned, and by reflection from the liability of even angels to fall away from God" (*Some Graver Subject* 197). Joseph H. Summers and Davis P. Harding offer similar under-standings of Eve's situation, and this important and influential new view of the dynamic and challenging nature of Adam and Eve's prelapsarian life continues to develop throughout the 1960s. Juxtaposing Eve's response to her image in the lake with Satan's response to his image, Sin, and with the Father's pleasure in his image, the Son, Summers points out, "Eve's situation differs from both. Her fascination with her own image is a natural and inevitable potentiality for any free creature of perfect beauty, unaware of its relationships to the freedom and beauty of other creatures and ignorant of love; unchecked (or undirected) it would result in sterility, frustration, and inaction which we can only imagine in terms of death" (97–98). Harding recalls what eighteenth century editors stress, that Eve does not repeat Narcissus's mistake, and to Harding, the scene at the lake is therefore a "trifling display of natural vanity," but he also points to the lesson Eve learns from her experience. Harding argues that Milton "compels" the reader "to underplay the vanity motif by permitting it to become swallowed up and almost lost in the professed moral of the episode," as Eve states it in 490–91 (*Club* 74). Michael Lieb continues to elaborate the difference between Eve's experience with the reflection of herself and Satan's experience with Sin. Lieb draws immediate attention to the water casting the reflection, for example: "The water that reflects Eve's image is both the holy water of birth and, because it is 'Pure as th' expanse of Heav'n' (IV, 456), that substance which mirrors the world of Eve's spiritual origin. The water is also a vehicle of birth in the sense that it helps to generate a new awareness in Eve, an awareness that concerns true knowledge of the self" (148). Lieb contrasts Satan's response to his image and Eve's to hers: "Eve's relation with Adam, whose image she is, will result in healthy and glorious offspring; on the other hand, Sin's relation with Satan, whose image she is, will result in monstrous offspring. The reason for this is that Adam's image in Eve is ultimately God's image, whereas Satan's image in Sin is nothing more than Satan himself" (149). Therefore, Lieb concludes, through Adam "Eve unites with God," while "Sin's image in no way leads to God but leads inwardly and back again to the self" (150).

It is true that in the 1960s C. A. Patrides, echoing Waldock, continues to find that Eve is "partly fallen before she actually ate the forbidden fruit" (*Milton* 105), and Roy Daniells sees in Eve "the tragic flaw which will lead to her fall" (*Milton* 115), but there is clearly a stepping back from such terminology. John Halkett's engagement with Marjorie H. Nicolson's reading of the smooth lake scene most firmly indicates the rising critical discomfort with terms like "flaw" and "partly fallen." Unable to accept the notion of Eve's being flawed, Nicolson stresses the infantile quality of her innocence: "It is merely difficult for me to understand how Milton could have believed that Eve, as created by God, had an 'original flaw.' It seems entirely possible to explain Eve's supposed 'narcissism' by saying that Eve was still an infant—just now created—and her experience was that of any child for the first time noticing its reflection in mirror or water" (*John Milton* 242). In *Milton and the Idea of Matrimony*, Halkett directly responds to Nicolson's reading. While finding her reading "not entirely sound," Halkett does similarly reject the idea of a "flaw" in Eve: "Eve's inclination to vanity is not a weakness of her nature; it is a consequence of the fact that she is the more immediately attractive of the two. Vanity simply presents a greater temptation to woman than to man." Halkett agrees with Nicolson: "Eve's vanity is not the focal issue in Eve's account. Milton seems to be emphasizing, rather, certain differences between Adam and Eve, man and woman" (106). A few years before Halkett speaks to the issue of Eve's experience at the lake, Northrop Frye and David Daiches suggest that the episode had been overread, Frye seeing in it the revelation of "not pride but the kind of vanity that we find amusing and disarming, and so innocent" (*Return* 77), and Daiches "a winning innocence which is differentiated from Adam's more self-conscious dignity" (190). The resolution to the debate might be seen in remarks by A. Bartlett Giamatti and Alastair Fowler. Giamatti recalls the views of Frye and Daiches when he, too, advises that one ought not to read too much into Eve's experience at the smooth lake, but he also contends that "it would be a stubborn reader who would refuse to see the narcissism here, as some have done, or who would insist on completely underplaying its implications. The poet has made this overt suggestion of narcissism, not to lessen our immediate estimate of Eve so much as to provide a repository of doubt for later exploitation" (316). Similarly, Fowler (640) discusses the scene in terms of dramatic foreshadowing, "for we know that Eve is to fall into precisely this error of seeking an end in herself or desiring an ideal self, until like Narcissus she 'loves an unsubstantial hope and thinks that substance which is only shadow' (*Met*[*amorphoses*] iii 417)."

During the 1960s, then, the critical tide turns from the issue Waldock, Tillyard, and Bell present as they consider Eve's Narcissus experience to move in the direction set by such critics as Summers, Harding, Broadbent, and Peter. Terms like *unchecked, undirected,* and *sterility* point to a recognition of the similarity between the nature of Milton's garden and its gardeners, and that similarity becomes a focus of critical attention, as does the understanding that Adam and Eve are educated by prelapsarian experiences such as Eve's at the "Smooth Lake." Admitting that while Eve's experience "may prefigure a vanity and self-love which will prove destructive, it is…innocent," Charles Monroe Coffin, for example, contrasts Eve's initial—illusory—encounter with "what is other than herself" with Adam's, but also makes it clear that Eve, like Adam, does grow, does achieve that higher stage of understanding: "Adam, it will be recalled, experiences what is external, as the prior phase of the apprehension of self-existence; but Eve presumably would not have reached this stage…had not the 'warning' voice told her what she was staring at in the pool" (14–15). Mistakenly attributing Eve's understanding that "beauty is excelld by manly grace / And wisdom" to Adam, William G. Madsen nevertheless points to the intellectual development of both characters. Madsen acknowledges that Adam, however, fails to apply the lesson derived from Eve's experience to his own situation, for when he accepts the forbidden fruit from Eve, "he is choosing the physical shadow over the moral substance" (*From Shadowy Types* 104). Albert W. Fields finds Eve's experience at the lake parallel to Adam's admission to Raphael: "All higher knowledge…falls" (8.551) when he is in Eve's presence: "Eve and Adam were enamored of false images of self, such images as 'came and go.' Each has experienced 'evil concupiscence,' but neither has recognized it as a latency, as a feature of self unlike their Creator, in whom they see themselves mirrored" (397). Dennis H. Burden argues that, at the smooth lake, "What Eve is experiencing is a need of her nature but one which needs to be directed to its proper end. God, creating the need, has providentially arranged for its satisfaction" (83–84). J. M. Evans perhaps most emphatically establishes the pedagogical nature of Eve's Narcissus experience, which he describes as "one of Milton's most beautiful and perceptive inventions" (253). Evans argues that the point of that invention is "Eve's untutored feelings, like the natural growth of the plants around her, do not grow in the right direction spontaneously. They have to be 'reformed,' and it is necessary for God to check the 'fruitless embraces' she seeks in her reflection and lead her to 'wed her Elm' " (253). The notion of a line of separation between fallen and unfallen experience Evans finds misleading, and instead suggests, "The difference between unfallen and fallen Man is simply the difference between a well and a badly tended garden. It is a difference of degree, not of kind" (271).

Stanley Fish and Jon S. Lawry involve the reader in Eve's learning experience at the lake. Fish understands it as one of "a series of scenes [in the middle books] which provide a continuing test of the reader's steadfastness and honesty. The technique is again the technique of the 'good temptation' whereby the reader is left to choose, in a controlled situation, which of two roads he will take" (*Surprised* 216). Fish rejects Tillyard's explanation that in the Narcissus scene Milton is "faking" (*Studies* 10) and argues that it is the "abruptness" of Adam and Eve's fall in Book 9 "in relation to the movement of the narrative before that time" that "Milton wishes to emphasize; and he leaves us to work out the implications of these domestic adventures in the hope that we will use them to counterpoint, not circumscribe, the fatal act" (*Surprised* 227). Adapting terms like Patrides's *partly fallen* (*Milton* 105) to serve his different critical purpose, Lawry associates Eve's earliest experiences with the audience's earliest reading experience: "Guiding the search of the audience, Eve's first quest for identity is not promising. Opposing Adam's preceding stand, it is a form of fall, the first of three such separations from Adam and God. Narcissistically she half falls in love with her own image in a pool. As self-love had undone Satan and given birth to Sin, so it openly threatens mankind through our great mother." Lawry then parallels Eve's initial response to Adam, her "resistance to godlike virtues," with the audience's response to God in Book 3 (175).

Finally, Leland Ryken identifies the apocalyptic technique of distance (165) and "the conceptual background of apocalyptic innocence" (74) at work in Eve's narrative, and in a footnote contribution to the discussion about the meaning of the Narcissus episode, Ryken suggests that those assured of Eve's vanity might consider that what attracts Eve to her image is not physical beauty but the qualities of "sympathie and love" (195n34).

467–75. Cleanth Brooks identifies the *voice* (467) that speaks to Eve at the lake as God, but Allan H. Gilbert pauses to reconsider that designation. Assuming that "Eve is called away by the voice of God," Brooks explains, "He is invisible but by addressing her as 'Fair creature,' He takes cognizance of her love of beauty, and by telling her that what she sees is an image of herself, he takes account of her bewilderment and her need for companionship" ("Eve's Awakening" 283). Gilbert, however, notes that Eve identifies the guide as "a voice," not the voice of God, the narrator identifies Eve's guide as "the genial Angel" (712), and Adam "her Heav'nly Maker" (8.485). Gilbert traces these shifting designations to Milton's early plans for a drama on the Fall (*On the Composition* 45).

469–71. John S. Diekhoff notes the rhyme in this sequence ("Rhyme" 540). See Diekhoff in **222–24.**

471–72. In his review of Bentley's edition, Zachary Pearce responds to Bentley's manipulations and alterations of these two lines, as does Samuel Say ten years thereafter, but it is the much later commentary by Robert Martin Adams which perhaps most fully develops the expressiveness of Milton's grammar and syntax, the expressiveness that Bentley would sacrifice. Bentley finds that the "Accent is so absonous; that our Author, well skill'd in Music, could not be guilty of it. He must give it thus; *Thy coming and thy soft embrace: he whose / Image* thou art; HE WHOM *thou shalt enjoy*" (123). Pearce answers: "the Accent should be on *Thou,* because part of the force of the Sentence is in that word, and therefore the common reading is better than that which throws the Accent upon the less significant word *art*" (127). With considerable zeal, Say declares that "as the editor [Bentley] very often does not so much as understand his author, nor is sensible in the least of beauties which the numbers unavoidably offer to a proper reader, he attempts by his rash corrections to render it forever impossible to be perceived by others"—and, for Say, the "glaring instance" of this is Bentley's emendation of these lines (482). Also see Say's response to Bentley's emendation of **474.** Acknowledging, "In this passage the Deity muddles inextricably two simultaneous assertions while describing the mutual delights of Adam and Eve," Adams explains: "The peculiar virtue of 'shall' is that both 'hee' (with the object of 'thy soft imbraces') and 'thou' (with the object of 'him') can govern it; and though some editors, sensitive to subject-and-verb agreements have corrected it to 'shalt,' they have obviously narrowed Milton's meaning in the process" (90).

472. *image:* Sister Mary Irma Corcoran and C. A. Patrides establish the theological context for the voice's describing Eve as the *image* of Adam, Corcoran by reference to hexameral commentators, Patrides by reference to Milton's own writings. Corcoran explains that some commentators argued that as Adam was made in the image of God, Eve was made in the image of Adam, but, "the greater number of exegetes held that Eve was made directly in the image of her Creator" (66). Corcoran then notes, "Milton, as he had done with regard to the derivation of the soul of the woman from that of the man, again went counter to the strongest tradition by stating that Eve was the image and glory of Adam" (67). See Corcoran in **487**. Patrides draws 472 into association with 5.95 and 8.450, 543, as well as with selections from the prose, most importantly *Tetr* (Patterson, *Works* 4:76), to establish Milton's understanding that Eve was created in the image or likeness of Adam, not in the image of God (*Milton* 179).

473. *Inseparablie:* Dennis Burden (169) considers the significance of this word in the context of the argument for divorce in *Tetr*, where Milton stresses the difference between prelapsarian and postlapsarian marriage: "the institution it selfe from the first beginning was never but conditional, as all cov'nants are: because thus and thus, therefore so and so; if not thus, then not so" (Patterson, *Works* 4:171). Burden also notes that this word "has of course an additional force when it is said to Eve since it enables Milton to look forward at the same time to the fact that it was her separation from Adam that brought about her downfall. God's words to Adam about marriage however . . . say nothing about inseparability and indicate what reservations are made about the union of man and woman [8.444–51]." Alastair Fowler makes the same point about *Inseparablie:* "Literally true before the Fall, when Sin and Death had not yet entered the world" (640).

474. *Multitudes like thy self:* Bentley, who finds this phrasing illogical, emends it to provide what he is sure Milton intended: "What! all her Progeny to be Female? no doubt he gave it, '*Multitudes like* YOUR SELVS'" (123). Designating Bentley "the grammarian," Samuel Say asks, "Are *multitudes all*, then? Or were *all* mankind to be such pretty images of Eve as this which she saw in the water that separated her and the other Eve, which came and went with her?" Say's exasperation with Bentley swells: "But the editor was so far from apprehending the thought of the poet here that he has not so much as a suspicion of it" (482), and at this point, Say proceeds to deal with Bentley's handling of 471–72, cited earlier.

Multitudes: Purvis E. Boyette's reading of this word recalls Patrick Hume's reading of *wisdom* at **489–92**, Boyette writing, "The themes of love and fertility are thus linked through Milton's allusions to the Graces and to the Zephyr-Flora configuration, which together function as an expositor of a Neoplatonic metaphysic of love. When raised to its highest symbolic level, the promise of 'multitudes' is the assurance of grace. Adam follows Eve into disobedience because he is reluctant to turn away from what God has given him as a vehicle of revelation" (344). Also see Boyette in **481–91**.

475. *Mother of human Race:* like Merritt Y. Hughes (*Complete Poems* 289), Alastair Fowler (640) refers Adam's naming Eve to Gen. 3.20 and notes that the Authorized Version of the Bible provides a marginal gloss on *Eve,* "Chavah, or, living." Fowler observes, "The commentators made much of the fact that this name was given only after the Fall (before, she was called simply 'woman': see Gen. ii 23, and Willet [*Hexapla*] 54), so that M[ilton] may be deliberately correcting the conventional chronology, to enhance the status of sexuality and motherhood. See ll. 741[–47] for a similar piece of ideology, and on Eve's name see also xi 168[–69]."

Kester Svendsen points to the irony of the contrast between God's address to Eve here and his ironic reference to her as Adam's *God* or *guide* when he later judges Adam (10.145, 146). Svendsen finds that most of the narrator's epithets for Eve are of three types: "those indicating her relation to Adam . . . , those used during the temptation scene . . . , and those indicating her relation to posterity" ("Epic Address" 189).

476. Arguing that "all the quotations and echoes from liturgy, all the religious rites and ceremonies suggested or presented" (46) in the epic anticipate the future, Thomas B. Stroup finds here the inauguration of the "original . . . marriage ceremony" in which "the Son, the Creator-God Himself, invisible, leads Eve on to Adam. By so doing He institutes this honorable state, as the marriage rite of the Book of Common Prayer tells us He did" (26–27). Furthermore, Stroup observes, "as Eve remembers, Adam had pronounced unpremeditated the ceremony" (27).

strait: this is the spelling in the first and second editions, but Alastair Fowler, like A. W. Verity, spells it *straight.* Fowler defines *straight* as "immediately," and acknowledges that the spelling *strait* "could also indicate 'closely'" (640).

478–80. Critical opinion on Eve's turning from Adam is as divided as are the readings of her entire autobiography. See **440–91** and **460–91.** Jon S. Lawry, for example, refers to Eve's turning here as one of her preliminary separations from Adam anticipating the Fall (175). Douglas Day also faults Eve, explaining that she is rejecting God's earlier words in 467–75 and "succumbing instead to a mistaken impulse" (371). Cleanth Brooks contends that Eve turns because "she finds it easier to love the image of herself as mirrored in the forest pool than the image of herself as mirrored less obviously in Adam" ("Eve's Awakening" 284). Arguing that while this "strange episode" (84) of Eve's turning from Adam was invented by Milton to establish the importance of free and mutual consent in marriage, Dennis H. Burden concedes, however, that it is also for Adam "a warning episode" (85).

478. *Platan:* early editors clarify that this is the plane tree, not the plantan, and provide several literary cross-references, and Alastair Fowler reveals the tree's theological significance. Supporting his gloss with a passage from Virgil's *Georgics* 4.146, Hume observes that the plane tree is named for "the breadth of its Leaves" and is "useful and delightful for its extraordinary Shade" (151). Hawkey ("Various Readings") notes that "all the later editions" had "corruptly" printed *plantan* for *platan,* and that the error had thereby even appeared in number 326 of Addison's *Spectator.* Reprinting Hume's note and Hawkey's, Todd ([1842], 2:81) associates Milton's tree and "the platane round" in the tree catalog in Spenser's *The Faerie Queene* 1.1.9. Mitford (130) adds a reference to the third act of Hugo Grotius's *Adamus Exul.* Alastair Fowler explains, however, that the platan, the plane tree, "was a symbol of Christ, his head' (see Raban Maur, Migne cix 931; and cp. **299, 443**). The basis of this well-known allegory was *Ecclus.* xxiv 14–16: 'I . . . grew up as a plane tree [Vulg. and Tremellius *platanus*] by the water . . . [;] my branches are the branches of honour and grace.' This association seems more probable than those which made the platan tree a symbol of erotic love" (641).

481–91. While early editors are silent about Adam's pursuit of Eve, several modern critics have suggested a variety of sources for the episode. Sister Mary Irma Corcoran refers it to Marin Mersenne's *Questiones Celeberrimae in Genesim* col. 1228, Douglas Bush contends that it recalls the Apollo-Daphne episode in Ovid's *Metamorphoses* 1.452–567, and Purvis E. Boyette sees the continuing influence of the pursuit of Chloris by Zephyrus. After she locates in Mersenne "[a] happier concept of the woman than appears in any of the other commentaries," Corcoran quotes the "terms of endearment and hope for a long and happy companionship" that Adam there expresses (71–72). Corcoran also cross-references Adam's memory of his wooing in 8.491–99. Presenting Apollo's words as he pursues Daphne in *Metamorphoses* 1.504 and 514–15; "nympha, precor, Penci, mane! non insequor hostis.../...nescis, temeraria, nescis, / quem fugias, ideoque fugis"; "O nymph, O Peneus' daughter, stay! I who pursue thee am no enemy.../...Thou knowest not, rash one, thou knowest not whom thou fleest, and for that reason dost thou flee," Bush ("Ironic and Ambiguous Allusion" 638) points out that Sandys had translated Ovid's last phrase as "From whom thou fly'st, thou know'st not" (*Ovid's "Metamorphosis"* 1.513). In Milton's lines with their "brief but clear echo of Ovid," Bush (639) locates "the germ, no more, of the extravagant avowal of idolatry in VIII, 521–29." Boyette also places this scene within the context of classical mythology, as indicated in **474**. Boyette draws attention to Eve's identity as Flora and Adam's as Zephyrus at 5.16 and suggests, "Zephyrus' pursuit of Chloris which resulted in her transformation to Flora, as most memorably presented in Botticelli's *Primavera*, may also be influencing Milton's description of Adam's pursuit of Eve" (344).

Denis Saurat, Cleanth Brooks, and John Halkett consider the issue of power as Adam woos Eve. Saurat discusses Adam's pursuit of Eve in terms of woman's power over man: "woman has power over man, who needs her. First through passion, which through woman alone takes complete hold of him" (162). Second, Saurat observes, "woman has power also through the greater delicacy of her feelings." While Corcoran cross-references 8.491–99, Saurat (163) cross-references 8.596–603. Brooks brings attention not to Eve's power over Adam in this wooing episode but rather to Adam's power as expressed in his speech to Eve, which Brooks describes as "one of the most moving passages in the poem... and it moves Eve." Brooks then proceeds to examine the parallels between Eve's relation to Adam and Sin's to Lucifer, as well as the similarities and differences between Adam's and Eve's experiences as they seek to find their images ("Eve's Awakening" 283). Halkett similarly considers the power of Adam's words to Eve, observing the traditional nature of Adam's wooing, but adding that as he pursues Eve, Adam "emphasizes their union" and from that emphasis proceeds that affection which is the basis of Eve's obedience (107).

481. *faire Eve:* cross-referencing "fair Eve" at 8.172, "fair spouse" at 4.742 and 5.129, and "fair creature" at 4.468, which also identify Eve, Edward S. Le Comte (*Yet Once More* 35) notices that *fair* is applied to the forbidden fruit nine times, "and in the crucial book of the fall reference is significantly made to 'dalliance' on the part of the uxorious Solomon 'with his fair Egyptian spouse' (ix.443)."

482–83. Bentley complains about pronouns here: "By a needless changing of the Pronoun from the First to the Third Person; the Speech is made less passionate and endearing" (123), but Pearce authorizes the pronoun shift by reference to Virgil (127–28).

483–86. Arnold Williams surveys the views of Renaissance commentators on Genesis who ponder the choice of the rib for the origin of Eve. Williams concludes that Milton, like Du Bartas in Sylvester's translation of *Divine Weekes* 1.6.1017–18, found poetically appealing Pererius's explanation, *Commentariorum* 208, that God chose a rib from Adam's left side, where the heart lies, "because of the great love that should be between a man and his wife and the union of souls and concord of wills." Williams also points out that after the Fall, as indicated in 10.884–88, the "same ideas could be used for opposite effect" (*Common Expositor* 91).

483–85. Elmer Edgar Stoll draws attention to the poignancy in the voices of Adam and Eve even before the Fall: "in the more heart-felt emotions of the human pair, though still sinless, there is something of the seriousness or sadness of tone that to Milton, as to most artists, is inseparable from happiness." Even in Milton's paradise, Stoll observes, "there is no happiness unalloyed" ("From the Superhuman" 10).

483. *His flesh, his bone:* Newton (265) refers this line to Gen. 2.23.
    Anne Davidson Ferry argues that the narrator's "literal language of metaphor," by which literal and abstract meanings are unified, is used to realize even "the most fantastic, the most magical details of the legend from Genesis" (*Milton's Epic Voice* 108), and she suggests that the story of the creation of Eve may be the clearest illustration of this. Descriptions of Eve as "bone of my

bones, and flesh of my flesh" (Gen. 2.23) associate 4.440–43, 481–88, 8.495, 8.499, 9.911–16, and 10.884–88, and Ferry begins to explicate that association: "Because we know the story and because it is treated as sacred history, we accept these passages in one sense as literal statements." Ferry adds, however, that "in another sense we read these passages as metaphorical expressions of the inner, psychological unity of Adam and Eve, as a figurative way of describing their sexual and spiritual oneness" (110). The appropriateness of reading such passages both literally and figuratively, Ferry concludes that "even the characters in the poem recognize, for sacred events do express meanings, like terms in a metaphor" (110–11).

485. *Substantial Life:* situating *PL* in the context of the seventeenth century debate about the existence of spirits, William B. Hunter Jr. glances at this phrase as an expression of Milton's belief in "incorporeal substance" and adds, "Indeed, one of the probable reasons for the composition of *Paradise Lost* is opposition to 17th century materialism" ("Eve's Demonic Dream" 257).

486. *an individual solace:* Hume establishes the etymological richness of this phrase, which David Masson continues to probe and Mario A. DiCesare most recently reconsiders. Hume writes, "An Inseparable Companion and Comfort, made of a part taken out of *Adam's* Side, as intended for his *Associate,* not his *Servant. Individual, Individuus,* Lat. inseparable. *Solace, Solatium,* Lat. Comfort" (151). With cross-listing, Masson (*Poetical Works* 3:175) advances Hume's reading: "not to be divided, inseparable (La. *individuus*)." Masson cites *individual* in 5.610 and *Time* 12, and *dividual,* carrying "exactly the opposite sense—*i.e.* 'separable' or 'parted'" in 7.382 and 12.85. DiCesare explains, "Eve may be considered an 'individual' because she is distinct from Adam; she is the other whom, we discover later, he was impelled to seek, impelled even to the point of a quarrel with the Almighty. But it has another meaning, one perhaps best indicated by reference to the only other occurrence of the word in *Paradise Lost* [5.610]." Recalling Hume's and Masson's notes, DiCesare continues, "The Latinate meaning of 'undivided'—'unseparable'—is not only dominant here; the emphasis on union and wholeness, and the prominence of *Soul* with the obvious play on *sole* links this passage [609–12] with the earlier one [481–91]. The divine fullness and individuality are model for the source of the individual unity of Adam and Eve" ("'Advent'rous'" 4).

487. *Part of my Soul:* Newton and R. C. Browne identify Horatian parallels for Adam's phrasing here, while Sister Mary Irma Corcoran, Arnold Williams, and Merritt Y. Hughes ponder the theologically charged issue of the creation of soul. Newton (265) traces Adam's phrasing to Horace's description of Maecenas as "meae partem animae" ("the half of my own life") in *Odes* 2.17.5, and to that R. C. Browne (1:352) adds Horace's description of Virgil as "animae dimidium meae" ("the half of my own soul") in *Odes* 1.3.8. Identifying the phrase as a theological crux, Sister Mary Irma Corcoran sketches its history: "At the beginning of the fifth century, Eucherius [*Commentarii in Genesim* col. 909] wrote that it was questioned whether woman, formed from the side of man, derived her soul from his, and whether as the flesh is produced from flesh, so the soul is procreated through the soul, or whether new souls are always created by God out of nothing. Medieval and Renaissance authorities decided that the soul of Eve was not 'traduced' from that of Adam." The theological tradition thus sketched, Corcoran contends, "Milton's Adam implied the opposite view" (66). Arnold Williams also studies this issue, reporting the opinion of the Protestant commentator David Pareus (*In Genesin Mosis Commentarius* col. 433), whose opposition to the traduction theory rested on the text of Genesis. Williams wonders, "Perhaps it is Milton's belief in the traduction theory that leads him to add the phrase 'part of my Soul' in his paraphrase of Adam's greeting to Eve" (*Common Expositor* 87). Hughes ("Variorum") sets Adam's words in the context of Milton's remarks on the same topic in *DocCh:* "Milton may have thought of Eve's soul as traduced or drawn out of the soul of Adam, as in *DocCh* 1.7 he thought of the souls of all Adam's descendants as 'not created daily by the immediate act of God, but propagated from father to son in a natural order, as was considered as the more probable by Tertullian and Apollinarius, as well as by Augustine and the whole western church in the time of Jerome'" (Patterson, *Works* 15:43)."

489–502. As he ridicules Milton's presentation of Adam and Eve, H. A. Taine also mocks their creator. On the concluding lines of Eve's autobiography, for example, Taine writes, "Dear learned poet, you would have been better pleased if one of your three wives, as an apt pupil, had uttered to you by way of conclusion the above solid theoretical maxims" (2.2.297).

489–91. Eve's words, the "professed moral" of the episode, according to Davis P. Harding (*Club* 74), have drawn as much critical attention to Eve as to the lesson she announces. Cleanth Brooks, Charles Monroe Coffin, and Merritt Y. Hughes here see a process of socialization and/or education. In light of Eve's assertion, Brooks writes, "Milton has made Eve recapitulate the whole process of the child's growing up and transferring the affections to the other" ("Eve's Awakening" 284). Coffin considers Eve's yielding to Adam "less a mark of weakness than a sign of her detached condition. She feels no such large connections with the creatures of the world, or with 'some great Maker,' and, consequently, at loose ends so to speak, she wavers between herself and the outside attractions until she receives her proper location within the human situation. Looked at another way, she is nearly a center unto herself in a world whose geometry is being revised to accommodate just such terms of self-existence. She is, in short, the supreme human particular emerging from creation's individuating process" (15). Hughes ("Variorum") shares James Holly Hanford's suggestion to him in a letter that these closing lines match the climax of Diotima's revelation of love's development as Plato presents it in the *Symposium* 210. Perhaps not inappropriately associated with Hanford's suggestion, then, is Hume's annotation on *wisdom* (491): "The Character of our Saviour himself: *And the Child grew, and waxed strong in Spirit, filled with Wisdom. And JESUS increased in Wisdom and Stature, and in Favour with God and Man,* Luk. 2. Vers. 40, and 52" (151). While Douglas Day suspects Eve's sincerity as she states the "professed moral" of her autobiographical narrative, Stanley Fish questions her forgetting it later during her conversation with the serpent. Day finds that Eve's "reconciliation to reason and order comes suspiciously fast, and we are likely to feel that Eve's sudden humility is caused, partially at least, by the fact that she has just been flattered most fulsomely and effectively by a handsome young man" (371). Fish assumes that Eve is sincere as she speaks to Adam, but he observes that she is apparently forgetful when talking with the serpent: "There is at least one assertion of Satan's that Eve should challenge, since it contradicts something she herself has said earlier. The proper response to Satan's salutatory 'Fairest resemblance of thy Maker fair' ([9.]538) has been given, in effect, by Eve when she recognizes Adam's superior 'fairness' at IV.490.... Her failure to give that response again is hardly fatal, but it does involve a deviation (innocent but dangerous) from the strictness of her watch" (*Surprised* 13). Finally, J. B. Broadbent argues that Milton—more than Eve—is revealed in this sequence: "It was probably fear of his own voluptuousness, and perhaps of a homosexual tendency caused by his too-devoted father, with mixed pride and shame in his own physical beauty and his role as man of letters rather than action, that impelled him [Milton] to fondle every manifestation of Belialism, and then crush it with masculine hard rationality" (*Some Graver Subject* 93).

492–97. With the most notable exception of C. S. Lewis, commentators—early and modern—have admired Milton's description of Adam and Eve's first embrace. Their kiss serves as preamble to their later sharing "the Rites / Mysterious of connubial Love" (742–43), and both episodes define and describe Milton's presentation of prelapsarian sexuality. See **736–75**. Patrick Hume paraphrases the lines, offering only a few etymological notes, but his paraphrase celebrates Milton's presentation (151). Robert Thyer, contributing notes to Todd, is exuberant in his praise: "What a charming picture of love and innocence has the poet given us in this paragraph! There is the greatest warmth of affection, and yet the most exact delicacy and decorum. One would have thought that a scene of this nature could not, with any consistency, have been introduced into a divine poem; and yet our author has so nicely and judiciously covered the soft description with the veil of modesty, that the purest and chastest mind can find no room for offence" ([1842], 2:81). While impressed by the presentation of God in *PL,* Voltaire declares that Milton "hath especially an undisputable Claim to the unanimous Admiration of Mankind when he descends from those high Flights to the natural Description of human Things. It is observable that in all other Poems Love is represented as a Vice; in *Milton* only 'tis a Virtue.... There is Softness, Tenderness and Warmth without Lasciviousness; the Poet transports himself and us into that State of innocent Happiness in which *Adam* and *Eve* continued for a short Time; He soars not above human, but above a corrupt Nature, and as there is no Instance of such Love, there is none of such Poetry" (107). Voltaire's praise is not blanket praise, however, for he vigorously condemns the Jupiter-Juno simile at 497–502 (113; see Voltaire in **497–502**). Incorporated into Voltaire's deeply felt praise for Milton's presentation of prelapsarian love is also a passing reference to Giambattista Andreini's *L'Adamo,* a reference that Joseph Warton, Thomas Keightley, and William Vaughn Moody reconsider. Voltaire claims that Milton saw Andreini's play in Florence, but "pierc'd through the Absurdity of that Performance to the hidden Majesty of the Subject" (103). In *An Essay on the Writings and Genius of Pope,* Warton charges Voltaire with presenting "so false and so imperfect an account" (2:184) of Milton's debt to Andreini that in an appendix he provides a Latin summary of *L'Adamo,* after which he declares that "the copious, comprehensive, and creative mind of Milton, so rich in the stores of *nature,*" could never have been "a meer *borrower,* as Voltaire would insinuate" (2:419). Thomas Keightley also, albeit less passionately, contends that Voltaire charged Milton with plagiarizing *L'Adamo* (*Account* 401). After he condemns Voltaire for his dismissive remarks about *L'Adamo,* William Vaughn Moody considers Milton's "indebtedness" to Andreini: "Two circumstances lend weight to the theory of Milton's indebtedness to Andreini: the first is that after his return from Italy, when Andreini's play would have been still fresh in his mind, he proposed to treat the subject of Adam's fall in dramatic form...; the second is that in the early drafts of the proposed drama various allegorical personages appear, corresponding in some cases precisely to those profusely employed by Andreini, and so long before abandoned by serious dramatists in England" (94).

C. S. Lewis is perhaps the most outspoken critic condemning Milton's presentation of prelapsarian sexuality. He believes that Milton "should not have touched the theme at all" (124). R. J. Zwi Werblowsky also considers Milton's presentation here a failure, finding no sense of fecundity but only sensuality: "compared with the teeming life of hell it cannot but strike us as another Bower of Acrasia [*FQ* 2.12.69–80]" (23). The overwhelming majority of twentieth century critics, however, share the views of earlier critics. Joseph H. Summers, for example, praises Milton's bold achievement with prelapsarian sexuality: "Milton 'realized' his divine and all-embracing subject more often by sexual than merely sensuous metaphor and allusion." Summers favorably compares Milton's views on sex with those of William Blake and D. H. Lawrence, concluding that all three "are united in their rejection of the assumption that sexuality in man is a relatively unimportant part of normal animal behaviour" (88). J. B. Broadbent, somewhat reminiscent of Thyer, praises the "balance" of Milton's description: "we can see that Milton has avoided pornography on one hand and idealism on the other; that he has still not descended to witty brutalism, not sensationalised the contact; but that he has struck a balance which is also part of the larger, theological balance of Paradise" (*Some Graver Subject* 190). Mario A. DiCesare also sees this description in terms of epic balance: "The short simile [Jupiter-Juno] does not 'enlarge' the action except for the reader who has not yet perceived what the poetry is doing. The suggested identification with the order of nature is part of the superb balance which is also the 'larger, theological balance of Paradise'" ("'Advent'rous'" 5). Quoting Thyer, Davis P. Harding (*Club* 76) joins these critics to celebrate Milton's achievement in this description of Adam and Eve's kissing. Harding discusses the larger sequence (492–501) as a link between "Hee for God only, shee for God in him" (299) and Adam's later admission to Raphael that "when I approach / Her loveliness…All higher knowledge in her presence falls / Degraded" (8.546–52). In his reading, John M. Steadman emphasizes one of Voltaire's points, discussing how Milton develops the epic *amor* formula so as to reconcile marriage with romantic love: "In stressing the husband's '*maistrye,*' he not only represents it as the condition of marital bliss, but also invests it with many of the conventions of romantic epic and lyric. He consciously fits the ideal of romantic love into the context of masculine dominion. Adam's very embraces are attended with consciousness of 'superior Love,' and the sensuous details of Eve's beauty are linked with the idea of submission" (*Milton* 118). Developing the association that Thyer presents in commenting on 304–11, A. Bartlett Giamatti also sets 494–97 against Marino's *L'Adone* 8.46–47, in which Venus's hair is compared to a "thick, gilded veil" hiding her breast: "Within the obvious image of submission and meekness on the part of Eve toward her superior, there is implied a powerful, if innocent, sensuality. And the color of her hair picks up the fruits of 'vegetable Gold' and those 'burnisht with Golden Rind' as well as the 'sands of Gold' in that mazy brook; picks up, in fact, the other golden places in paradise which had such latent implications for evil" (321). Like Lewis, Stanley Fish and Jon S. Lawry are attentive to the gap between the experience of the fallen reader and the prelapsarian embrace the reader observes, but both of the later critics look at that separation as it functions to educate the reader. Fish writes, "The reader must admit that his perceptions do not extend to the object the poet would present, and, in addition, he is forced to come to terms with his tendency to remake everything in his own sinful image" (*Surprised* 104). Lawry describes the reader as the "unwilling but participatively implicated audience" (175).

Leland Ryken (196) stresses the conceptual imagery, in conjunction with the physical imagery, in this passage as he explains Milton's apocalyptic vision: "the erotic account of Adam and Eve's embraces…moves from the physical to the conceptual; Eve's 'swelling Breast' (IV, 495) leans on Adam's, but Adam, instead of viewing erotic physical details, is said to see such intangibles as 'Beauty,' and 'submissive Charms' (IV, 498)."

493. *unreprov'd:* editors have assembled a list of cross-references for this word. Todd applies Thomas Warton's gloss on *unreproved,* "blameless, innocent, not subject to reproof," in *L'All* 40 (*Poems* 47). Warton's note on *L'All* also cites "unreproved kisses" in George Sandys's *A Paraphrase upon the Song of Solomon* 8.1 and "I may safely play and unreproved" in Michael Drayton's "Eclogue" 3.23–24 (*Works* 2:527). Besides acknowledging Warton's gloss on *L'All*, Todd ([1842], 2:81; see 3:390 for the note on *L'All*) also supplies Robert Thyer's reference to Spenser's *The Faerie Queene* 2.7.16, "*unreprov'd* truth," and Robert Greene's *Greenes Groats-worth of Witte, Bought with a Million of Repentance* 50, "*unreproved* virtues." Masson (*Poetical Works* 3:175) contributes a reference to *unremoved* in 987. Explaining *unreprov'd* as "A Latin use of the past participle (e.g. *invictus,* unconquered, unconquerable) that M[ilton] was fond of imitating," Alastair Fowler (641–42) adds yet another cross-reference, "unenchanted eye" from *Mask* 395.

497–502. Early editors establish Virgil's *Georgics* 2.325–27 and Homer's *Iliad* 14.153–351 as the principal classical sources for Milton's that comparison, and present two different allegorical readings of Jupiter and Juno. Citing Virgil's *Georgics* 2, Hume writes, "*As the Air smiles upon the Earth, when it makes the Clouds fruitful in seasonable Showres and pretious Dews, which produce May's perfumed Flowery Offspring. By Jupiter and Juno* the Poets represent the Air and Earth, and though of Kin before, as *Et Soror & Conjux,* yet Marry 'em together" (151). Both the Richardsons (164) and James Paterson repeat this reading, Paterson adding that both the Air and the Earth "came both out of one Womb, the *Chaos*" (314). Newton proposes a second understanding of Jupiter and Juno: "As the Heaven smiles upon the air, when it makes the clouds and every thing fruitful in the spring. This seems to be the meaning of the allegory; for Jupiter is commonly taken for the Heaven or aether, and Juno for the air, tho' some understand by them the air and earth." To the Virgilian parallel, Newton joins a reference to *Iliad* 14 to enlarge the history of Juno and Jupiter's loves, and he adds, "That expression of *the clouds shedding flow'rs* is very poetical, and not unlike that fine one in the Psalms of *the clouds dropping fatness,* Psal. LXXV. 12. and it is said *May flow'rs* to signify that this is done in the spring, as Virgil describes it" (266–67). Todd excerpts Newton's response and notes that Pope apparently shared Newton's conviction about the Homeric influence upon Milton, for "in his translation [of the *Iliad*], he adopts Milton's phraseology, describing Jupiter 'smiling with superiour *love,*' v.387" ([1842], 2:82). Unlike Newton and Todd, Davis P. Harding most thoroughly pursues the ominous significance of the Homeric allusion. Harding emphasizes that Juno's deception of Jupiter on Mt. Ida in *Iliad* 14 establishes that marriage as "scarcely ideal even by Olympian standards" (*Club* 78). Articulating connections between his reading of this sequence and Pope's reading of 697–703, Harding agrees with Pope that Milton invokes the Mt. Ida episode to link prelapsarian and postlapsarian sexuality: "Milton has employed Virgil's figure of speech, but he has changed its terms, substituting for them a new set of terms—the moisture-dripping cloud and the spring flowers—derived from Homer's account of the amorous dalliance of Jupiter and Juno on Mount Ida. The clandestine discrediting of Adam and Eve, we are forced to conclude, begins almost with the first lines which describe them to us" (80). Unlike Harding, Charles Grosvenor Osgood is not disturbed by the Mt. Ida associations. Developing his thesis that Milton's descriptions of nature are usually involved with mythological allusions, Osgood argues that, "whatever the occasion of introducing the myth, if its persons or incidents connote even in the slightest degree the beauty or the power of nature, Milton makes us feel it." Looking at this sequence, Osgood then insists, "The luxuriance of spring is felt in a reference to the love of Zeus and Hera" (xxiii–xxiv). Among the moderns, Osgood (49), along with Merritt Y. Hughes and Alastair Fowler, espouses the allegorical reading of Jupiter and Juno as the upper air and the lower air that Newton first advanced. Hughes adds to the authority of this understanding by noting that Jupiter's name itself reflects his identity as "Lord of the sky," and Juno's identity as "ruler of the ayre" (*The Faerie Queene* 7.7.26) was similarly a matter of tradition (*Complete Poems* 290). Fowler explains, "The mingling of the two produces the spring with its flowers. The golden cloud represents those clouds which in the spring flash back the golden rays of the sun" (642). Jackson I. Cope, like Davis P. Harding, believes that the classical simile in this sequence discredits the prelapsarian love of Adam and Eve, but rather than referring the simile to Homer's Mt. Ida episode, Cope refers it to the description of Adam and Eve's lustful union after the Fall in 9.1039–42: "the fall of the lascivious first parents is upon a couch of flowers, just as the simile makes the sexual act of unfallen Adam and Eve in the heart of their bower an analogue to spring fertility" (83).

Not unexpectedly, Richard Bentley vigorously attacks the mythological context settled around Adam and Eve's kiss. The kiss itself Bentley finds "express'd with complete Dignity, and needed no filling up." But the introduction of Jupiter and Juno, he complains, is "mixing confess'd Fable with what is at least deliver'd as Truth. But to pardon him this; yet who can pardon what follows: *Juppiter* [*sic*] from a Person chang'd into the Element, *Pater Aether impregning the Clouds?* So *Adam* smil'd upon *Eve*, no otherwise than as the *Aether* smiles upon a Cloud. Is not this *Ixion*'s Deception, a *Cloud* instead of *Juno?* And then the Clouds, that shed *May-flours?* Why *May* here, proper only to the *Northern* Climates? No word should have been used here, but what is applicable to all the Earth" (124). Voltaire, too, is unhappy with the problematic associations of the Jupiter-Juno simile, condemning it as a "Fault" not to be excused in a poet who, in the epic's opening book (374–75), had declared that the classical "Divinities were but Devils worshipp'd under different Names" (113).

Several modern critics have pursued yet different readings of the mythological simile in this sequence. John T. Shawcross (*Complete Poetry* 329) and Michael Lieb, for example, understand Jupiter as the sun whose smile impregnates the clouds, as Lieb explains: "The mere act of smiling in Eden results metaphorically in impregnation: as the sun impregnates the womb world of earth, Adam's smiling with love upon Eve is compared with Jupiter's (sun) smiling upon Juno (air) thereby impregnating the clouds" (70–71). With Eve's identity as Flora (5.16) as a point of departure, Purvis E. Boyette proceeds to this passage: "Love, therefore, manifests itself in some pattern of fecundity that conforms roughly with the Zephyr-Chloris-Flora progression" (344; also see Boyette in **481–91**).

500. *impregns:* Patrick Hume supplies the Latin root, *impregnare,* which he defines as "to get with young" (151), and Todd ([1842], 2:82) points out that the word had occurred in Henry More's *Psychozoia, or The First Part of the Song of the Soul* 1.58.1–2: "This all-spread Semele doth Bacchus bear, / Impregn'd of Jove." The *OED* cites Milton's use in 9.737, where Satan's temptation of Eve is described as "impregned / With reason."

501. *Flowers:* Helen Darbishire notes, "This word is, in *Paradise Lost,* generally a monosyllable spelt *flours,* but once in mid-line clearly a disyllable spelt *Flowers* (iv. 709); possibly a disyllable where it is spelt *flowers* at the end of a line (e.g. i. 771), and here at the caesura where an extra syllable may be allowed" (*Poetical Works* 1:296). Also see Darbishire on *showers* in **646**.

Matron lip: Hume firmly establishes the purity of Adam and Eve's kiss by unpacking the Latin roots of *Matron,* which Bentley and Pearce also consider. Hume notes, "Her Married Lips. *Matron,* of the Lat. *Matrona* a *Matre,* or *Quasi Mater nati;* for Women as soon as Married were esteemed Matrons, as being obliged to a way of living more reserv'd and modest" (151). While Bentley objects to the adjective, he points out that Ovid, in *Fasti* 2.828, had established a precedent by describing the married Lucretia's cheeks as matron cheeks (124–25). Pearce approves the adjective, arguing that it makes the kisses "lawful, pure and innocent" (128). Todd ([1842], 2:82) and Newton (267) follow Pearce and Hume.

Stanley Fish develops the eavesdropping situation which brings dramatic, rather than etymological, meaning to Adam and Eve's kisses. Fish explains, "Raised to the level almost of ritual, the kisses become the visible signs of their [Adam and Eve's] inner (spiritual) unity, and the reader is left to ponder the discrepancy between his response and the purity of the action. If the distinction seems difficult or abstruse, it is made easier (and inescapable) by the sudden introduction of a third perspective." The effect of that sudden reminder that Satan has been observing the kiss, Fish considers, is "not unlike the effect of 'Then was not guilty shame' (313). The reader is alerted to the contrast between the 'kisses pure' and the impurity of the voyeur's response and is forced to acknowledge whatever part of that response he shares" (*Surprised* 106).

502–05. On Satan's hatred and envy of man, see Grant McColley in **9**.

502–04. Satan's eyeing the lovers' embrace with "envie" elicits thoughtful analysis from the Richardsons onward, but when that "envie" is conjoined with lust, especially for some twentieth century critics, Milton's description of Satan becomes much more controversial. Dryden's Lucifer announces both his envy and his lust as the Edenic lovers exit the first scene of act 3 in *The State of Innocence, and Fall of Man:* "Why have not I like these, a body too, / Form'd for the same delights which they pursue? / I could (so variously my passions move) / Enjoy and blast here, in the act of love" (*Works* 12:116). The Richardsons (164) quickly uncover Milton's earlier reference to the glance of the envious eye in *Patrem* 106, to which R. C. Browne (1:352) later adds *Mask* 413: "And gladly banish squint suspicion." Citing *The Faerie Queene* 3.12.15, Browne (1:291) claims, "Spenser makes Suspicion always look 'ascaunce.'" Paterson clarifies that *askance* means "side-ways, asquint, to look awry or enviously at one" (315), while Newton introduces what becomes one of the most controversial elements in the modern discussion of Satan's behavior at this point in the epic: "It was the innocence of their loves that made the devil turn aside" (267). In his last edition of *PL* ([1842], 2:82), Todd points out the notion that the Jews attributed envy to Satan, and he specifically names Jarchi, that is, Rashi, who in his commentary on Gen. 3 claims that the serpent coveted Eve. At the beginning of the twentieth century, Edward Chauncey Baldwin traces that commonplace to such late Jewish writings as Josephus's *Antiquities* 1.4, *Apocalypse of Moses* 19.3 (*Vita Adae et Evae* 137), Maimonides's *Guide* 30, and *Bereshith Rabba* 20 (*Midrash* 1:163), and focuses on the sexual aspect of the envy: "Satan's motive in seducing Eve was lust aroused in him by envy of Adam's marital relationship" (374). That firm coupling of envy and lust figures most influentially in C. S. Lewis's reading of this scene. Identifying Satan here as "a mere peeping Tom leering and writhing in prurience as he overlooks the privacy of two lovers," Lewis provokes the modern debate about Satan's response to Adam and Eve's embrace. Plotting Satan's degeneration, Lewis declares, "From hero to general, from general to politician, from politician to secret service agent, and thence to a thing that peers in at bedroom or bathroom windows, and thence to a toad, and finally to a snake—such is the progress of Satan" (99). Douglas Bush and, considerably later, Frank Kermode continue to see Satan as a voyeur. Bush asserts that Satan "feels the sensual sting of Iago or Leontes" (*"Paradise Lost" in Our Time* 74). Kermode explains that as Satan observes Adam and Eve's embrace, he "acquires some of the pathos of an old *voyeur*." Kermode claims, "Milton boldly hints that the fallen angel is sexually deprived. He has forfeited the unfallen delights of sense. There is, we are to learn, lovemaking in heaven, but not in hell; the price of warring against omnipotence is impotence" (114). In the early 1960s, several critics express reservations about the notion of Satan as voyeur, however. In 1962, Joseph H. Summers points out that Satan's reaction to the lovers' embrace is more painful than pleasurable: " 'Fierce desire' without any hope of fulfilment is more precisely the psychological state of his Hell. In that state all the energies which should be devoted to love are transformed into a lust which wishes only to destroy" (99). William Empson soon makes the same point, emphatically rejecting Lewis's reading: "C. S. Lewis need not have called Satan 'a thing which peers in through bathroom windows' because he feels jealous here of the sexual pleasure of Adam and Eve; God has recently cut him off from his own corresponding pleasures, and he is straightforward enough about it. But I agree that his temper has begun to spoil, so that he eyes them 'with leer malign' " (*Milton's God* 68). Pointing out that with Satan's "jealous leer" pure envy makes its first appearance in the poem, J. M. Evans concedes that, while "it is possible that both here and in Book IX, when the Devil admires Eve among the flowers, Milton had in mind the Jewish belief that the Tempter lusted after Adam's wife, it hardly seems necessary to invoke a source to explain why the sight of a man and woman making love should excite a being deprived of those pleasures to envy" (230). Robert C. Fox (272) observes that Satan's "method of viewing—half avoiding the hateful sight but unable to resist a sideways glance—is in the Ovidian tradition. In the *Metamorphoses* Invidia is first described as having eyes that are awry (*nusquam recta acies*); later, when Minerva departs with anticipations of joy at the thought of avenging Aglauros, Invidia eyes the goddess askance (*obliquo lumine*) [*Metamorphoses* 2.787]." Fox explains, "Like Ovid's Aglauros, grief-stricken because Herse enjoys the love of Mercury, Satan is tormented at the sight of Adam and Eve enjoying sexual and romantic love" (273). Also see Fox in **800–09**.

Several modern critics suggest meaningful cross-references for this passage. James H. Sims considers the contrast between Satan's leering reaction to the sight of Adam and Eve and Raphael's reaction to the naked Eve in Book 5: Raphael, although "possessed of as free a will as Satan, knows neither libidinous love nor jealousy, for he has chosen to follow God and good" (*Bible* 119). A. W. Verity cross-references 9.263–64, explaining, "From what Raphael tells him, Adam later imagines that conjugal love is likely to excite Satan's envy more than any other human bliss" (642). Harris Francis Fletcher explains the change in Satan's sentiments between the second and third soliloquies on the basis of his having observed the embrace of Adam and Eve: "Satan is now so envious of their bliss that, fully purged of his regret that he must cause their ruin, he leaves them; and the outcome of his venture is never again in doubt" (184).

Edward Bysshe offers this passage under "Envy" in the third section ("A Collection of...Allusions, Similes, Descriptions...found in the best *English Poets*") of his 1705 publication *The Art of English Poetry* (127).

502. *the Devil:* Balachandra Rajan plots Satan's decline by reference to the epithets identifying him: "Satan's dimensions are reduced so effectively that we hardly notice how, in the process, his titles lose their lustre, how the 'Archfiend' of the first book becomes 'the Fiend' or the 'arch-fellon' and how for the first time he begins to be 'the Devil'" (*"Paradise Lost" and the Seventeenth Century Reader* 99). Also see Rajan in **32–113**.

504–11. Michael Wilding (28–29) notes that Satan's "endless suffering is caught with the word-play of pain and pines picking up 'plaind,' and the dragging movement of the last two lines [502–03], broken by no caesura. And the happiness of

Adam and Eve—'thir fill / Of bliss on bliss'—contrasts not only with Satan's desire 'still unfulfilld,' rhyme and alliteration enforcing the contrast, but also with his earlier description of his own endless suffering [76–77]."

504. *askance:* explaining that the idea expressed by *To look, eye, view askance* "has varied considerably, different writers using them to indicate disdain, envy, jealousy, and suspicion," "suspicion" being the current one, the *OED* 2 cites Milton's line.

505–35. A number of twentieth century critics commenting on Satan's third soliloquy usually but briefly note that Satan is increasingly unattractive. Cecil Maurice Bowra, for example, argues that Satan is decaying: "Just as his appearance decays, so does his character, until he becomes wholly loathsome and even contemptible" (226). With very similar language, William Empson insists that Satan's "character rots away so fast now that his speech on first view of them [Adam and Eve in 357–92] is his only really puzzling one" (*Milton's God* 68). Also acknowledging the change in Satan between his first two soliloquies and this his third, J. B. Broadbent proffers a different explanation, finding that Satan's declaration "to corrupt man through the Tree of Knowledge, is merely a plot contrivance and probably derives from a dramatic version. When Satan says 'But first with narrow search I must walk round This Garden, and no corner leave unspi'd' (528–[29]) he is a melodrama villain sharing his stage secrets with the audience" (*Some Graver Subject* 170). John M. Steadman's reading of Satan takes issue with the notion that he is increasingly unattractive. Understanding him as falsely heroic, as an idol, that is, rather than as an image of heroism, Steadman sees little change in Satan: "From start to finish the poet consistently represents the Adversary in terms of the false-heroic, and this heroic *eidolon* is finally shattered only by the sudden intrusion of divine judgement in Book X" (*Milton* 49). Also see the review of commentaries on Satan's first two soliloquies in **32–113** and **358–92**.

505–11. Robert C. Fox (273) points to the smooth transition from the visual to the verbal expression of Satan's envy: "by turning aside and viewing Adam and Eve askance, then, Satan gives a silent manifestation of his envy. He gives a vocal manifestation immediately afterwards."

505. *Sight hateful:* John M. Steadman notes that all five of Satan's soliloquies (4.32–113, 358–92, 505–35, 9.99–178, and 9.473–93) are "prompted by an act of sight" ("Milton's Rhetoric" 80).

506. Hilaire Belloc (247) identifies this line, in addition to 773–75 and 602–04, as one of those "brief flashes of that pure lyric inspiration which had been the glory of his [Milton's] youth." Of this line, Belloc adds, "It has been repeated so often that men forget what a discovery it was, that impetuous embrace, the first four syllables, that grasping word 'imparadised'" (248). Roland Mushat Frye (159) sees in this line an expression of "The Puritan's experience of conjugal love [which] led him [Milton] to place it on the highest plane of human felicity," and supports this view with a passage from William Whately's *A Bride-bush* 16, which advises the married couple to "'request the Lords good will and blessing, and to give him due praises' for this greatest of temporal gifts."

Imparadis't: while early editors pursue this word's pedigree, several twentieth century critics reflect more on the irony of Satan's using it. Patrick Hume supplies this definition, "plac'd in a state of extraordinary Happiness," and he then claims that Milton coined *Imparadis't* (151). Bentley (125) corrects Hume, pointing to Sir Philip Sidney's use of the term in *The New Arcadia* 141, and adding, "And the *Italians* had prior Possession, *Imparadisato*." Addison notes that *Imparadis't* is one of the metaphors Milton uses throughout the epic to achieve the sublime style (*Spectator* 3:12). Todd ([1842], 2:82), declaring that the word was "common" in Milton's time, traces its "original" use to "'mparadisa la mia mente" in Dante's *Paradiso* 28.3. Among the moderns, Frank Kermode (114–15) establishes the significance of Satan's invoking this descriptive term: "Satan is so sure of their sexual joy that he anticipates later love poetry in making the body of the beloved a paradise in itself—his 'happier Eden' is not the same as that promised later to Adam (xii. 587)—and he uses a word, 'imparadis't' which was to have its place in the vocabulary of fallen love." Similarly, Alastair Fowler describes this as "A very romantic and poetic word," but one, "here used bitterly" (642). Mario A. DiCesare, declaring *Imparadis't* "striking in its uniqueness" ("'Advent'rous'" 5), underscores the intensity of Satan's reaction to Adam and Eve's embrace: "This is surely the bitterest moment Satan has yet experienced" (6). DiCesare highlights the word's thematic importance by associating it with two other words that develop the theme of union throughout the epic: "*imbrute* in Satan's bitter words referring to the serpent, 'This essence to incarnate and imbrute / That to the highth of Deity aspir'd' (IX, 166–67); and *imbosom'd* in 'the Father infinite / By whom in bliss imbosom'd sat the Son' (V, 596[–97]" (5).

513–27. Despite the vivid exclamation of envy erupting from him as he watches Adam and Eve kiss, Satan abruptly turns to what he has just heard, rather than what he now sees, and in this passage carefully weighs the meaning of the command. While Dryden's Lucifer in *The State of Innocence, and Fall of Man* 3.1.76 understands the command as evidence that God "sees they would rebel, and keeps them low" (*Works* 12:115), early editors and later critics have diverging opinions about Satan's understanding of the command. Early editors contend that Satan, knowing full well that the command is a test of faith, here deliberately misrepresents it, while twentieth century critics are far from certain that Satan understands God's law. Focusing on "By Ignorance" (519), Hume penetrates Satan's mind: "Satan would here insinuate, such a want of Knowledge, as was necessary to secure their happy and harmless Condition: Under so gross a want of understanding our first most perfect Patterns were not created; all the happy Ignorance they were in, was only want of knowing Ill, by the Commission of it, at once innocent and secure" (151). When they refer Satan's words about the command to Adam's remarks at 428 ("The only sign of our obedience left"), the Richardsons imply that in his reference to *faith* (520), Satan full well understands the nature of the command. Defining *faith* as "a Firm Perswasion of God's Sovereignty, Truth, Goodness, &c.," the Richardsons conclude, "This is what Satan meant by Faith. Himself had it not" (165). Newton is equally quick to expose Satan's motives: "This is artfully perverted by Satan, as if some useful and necessary knowledge was forbidden: whereas our first parents were created with perfect understanding, and the only knowledge that was forbidden was the knowledge of evil by the commissions of it" (269). Bentley enters this discussion from a unique—but relevant—angle. He wants to replace *more* (523) with "keen" because *more,* he reasons, "supposes they had already some desire [to know]: but it does not appear that yet they had any" (125). Pearce (129) counters Bentley's charge with the narrator's acknowledgment of Adam's thirst for knowledge in 7.59–69. While early editors characterize Satan's reflections on God's prohibition as insinuating or artfully perverting, such agreement is not to be found among twentieth century critics. S. Musgrove, for example, puzzles over Satan's reflections on "Knowledge forbidd'n" (515): "Now Satan knows (or knew) well enough that envy and a positive desire for suppression are not and cannot be parts of God's nature, which is wholly good, but these are arguments which could well be used to play on the credulous ignorance of Adam and Eve. But, as Milton's syntactical arrangement shows, these thoughts pass through Satan's mind not merely as possible arguments he might use, but as partly this, and partly Satan's own genuine reflections on the matter." Musgrove concludes, "Satan is beginning to believe his own propaganda" (309). Describing Satan's rhetoric in 514–20 as "forensic, flickering through ploce and traductio and erotema with suspicious speed; pragmatic, lacking the ceremoniousness that in places gives to what the Father (and especially Adam) says an aesthetic value," J. B. Broadbent shares Musgrove's belief that, when Satan quizzes himself "can it be sin to know" (517), he is expressing "a real spoken doubt, not a rhetorical question" (*Some Graver Subject* 151). William Empson insists that Satan's doubts about the command are sincere, not artfully perverse, and he firmly rejects Musgrove's claims about Satan's knowledge of God: "Satan always did say, from the start of his revolt, that God had such motives; and I do not see how a candid reader of the poem could disagree with him. Like most such characters, he could not have won his followers if he had not believed his own propaganda; probably he is beginning to doubt it here, but he can still feel genuinely indignant at the behaviour of God" (*Milton's God* 32). Jon S. Lawry focuses on 519, as does Hume, but unlike Hume, he contends that Satan "is sure that Edenic innocence is ignorance" (176). Basil Willey and John Peter repeat these several views on Satan's understanding of the command, but both argue that Milton's intent is not so much to lay bare Satan's mind as it is to educate the reader of *PL*. Willey explains that Milton, rejecting the belief that the forbidden fruit was a "magic sciential apple" (249), and attributing to Satan "almost every possible objection to the myth in its literal acceptation" (256), thereby indicated that "it was Satanic to suppose that the myth meant what it said; therefore it must mean something else" (257). For Milton the prohibition against eating the forbidden fruit, according to Willey, was a "taboo ... imposed simply as a test of man's obedience" (249). Peter reasons that Satan's remarks on the command deflect the reader's tendency to fault Milton's rather unattractive God: "by attributing to Satan unfair inferences about God's prohibition of the fruit of the fatal tree he [Milton] very effectively discourages us from making them for ourselves" (14). Finally, Alastair Fowler's commentary (643) neatly brings all these readings together. Describing Satan here as "exhilarated, because he has just thought of the basis of a scheme for the destruction of mankind," Fowler follows Satan's thoughts as "Enthusiastically he begins to rough out the speech with which he *will excite* (l. 522) Eve's mind. Thus *Equal with gods* (l. 526) corresponds to—though it is improved upon in—ix 547 'goddess among gods.' True, as Empson [*Milton's God*] 32 rightly remarks, Satan could only invent these arguments if he half believed them. But for M[ilton] what mattered would be what was just, not what Satan contrived to half-believe. And the injustice of Satan's argument is heavily underlined: as, e.g., in the irony that God not only intended Adam and Eve to be *equal with gods,* if they were obedient (v 499–501), but even to exalt manhood to the throne of God himself, when they were disobedient, fallen and redeemed (iii 303–17)." See other references to the Tree of Knowledge and the Tree of Life in **194–204** and **218–22**.

521–22. As he discusses the "rhetorical devices common and uncommon, of getting the effect of surprising rhyme without recourse to barbarous jingle" (97), Frank Kermode looks at the wordplay involving *foundation* and *ruine:* "This is, in the first place, a cruel paradox; one doesn't, or at this date didn't, build ruins. But there is also a pun-like effect using two senses of *ruin,* not only what is left after the destructive act, but also the fall itself—a sense which was still primary at the date of *Paradise Lost*" (98).

523. Fowler here supplies the text of Gen. 3.4–5: "The serpent said unto the woman…God doth know that in the day ye eat thereof, then your eyes shall be opened, and ye shall be as gods, knowing good and evil" (643).

525–26. In "Milton and the *Argumentum Paris,*" John M. Steadman notes that Satan's stated intent here is "on the whole, the same *argumentum paris* that he had utilized to justify his own revolt and persuade his companions," the argument to equal, not just to be like, God (358).

527. Merritt Y. Hughes ("Variorum") sets this line against Satan's contempt for the danger of death attached to violation of the forbidden tree in 9.692–97.

528–33. Researching *PL*'s stages of composition, Allan H. Gilbert compares this sequence with the Argument to Book 4, which states that Satan "then leaves them a while, to know further of thir state by some other means." In both cases there is created the expectation that Satan will search for and then interrogate another angel, as he did Uriel, but such an episode never occurs. All this leads Gilbert to conclude that, at some point, "there must have been in Milton's plan an incident that made Argument and verses necessary. Is it possible that the warning later given to Gabriel by Uriel may once have been given instead by an angel earlier encountered by Satan in the Garden itself?" (*On the Composition* 90).

529–31. John S. Diekhoff notes the rhyme in this sequence ("Rhyme" 540). Also see Diekhoff in **222–24**.

530. *A chance but chance:* the wordplay here disappoints several early editors, but the moderns express admiration, or at least appreciation, rather than disapproval. Considering that some readers might be offended by "this Jingle; as unbecoming *Satan* in this serious Juncture," Bentley suggests that "they may easily alter it thus, or several other ways; Some LUCKY *chance may lead*" (125). Reporting Bentley's censure and Pearce's effort (129–30) to remove the pun, "A chance (but chance) may lead," Newton announces, "But this sort of jingle is but too common with Milton. This here is not much unlike the *forte fortuna* of the Latins" (268). Todd ([1842], 2:83–84) presents Newton's reading and adds that he and Charles Dunster find Milton's "jingle" resembles Spenser's in *The Faerie Queene* 3.7.3: "Her [His in *Poetical Works* 177] *force,* at last, *perforce* adown did lie." A. W. Verity is impressed by the play on *chance,* describing the construction as "the grim sort of quibble in which bitterness (here jealousy) finds vent" (464). Discussing such wordplay in *PL* not as a regrettable lapse but as "a result of extreme intellectual energy" (*Italian Element* 123), F. T. Prince points to this line as one of those "instances in which a verbal flourish, sometimes empty enough in itself, is made to give interest or significance" (124–25). As he reviews the eighteenth century efforts to rectify the phrasing, Robert Martin Adams writes, "no set of grammatical connectives that one could import, would be esthetically worth the distraction of discovering or importing them. In reading Milton's poem, evidently one must have the restraint to subordinate effects of detail to those of structure, to pursue some curious inquiries and to refrain from pursuing others equally curious" (108).

Several modern critics point out that Satan's reflections on *chance* bring forward matters of theology. Dennis H. Burden observes that words such as *chance* and *hap* "indicate his [Satan's] belief in a universe of no pattern, a random world," and entering the garden in both Book 4 and Book 9, Satan is "taking a chance, running his luck." Later discovered at Eve's ear, Satan meets with bad luck, however, and "That capture of Satan itself provided a useful illustration of God's providence" (93). Describing Satan's language here as a "jaunty jingle" (643), Alastair Fowler (551) repeats Newton's note about the Latin phrase *forte fortuna* but also cross references "ill chance" in 2.935, where he considers the role of luck in the Fall: "Note that the temptation and Fall of man is made to depend not only on evil will, but on contingency. The threat to integrity comes *via* the realm of the chaotic and fortuitous. Although Rajan ridicules this idea, it seems to have been taken seriously by M[ilton], who frequently returns to it" (551). Besides 530, Fowler cross-references 9.85, 421, and 423.

533–35. Isabel Gamble MacCaffrey and J. B. Broadbent similarly comment on the significance of Satan's reference to time in these lines. MacCaffrey explains, "Satan brings the poison of time with him into Paradise, and the first breath of impermanence touches it" as Satan concludes this speech (80). Referencing *Godfrey of Bulloigne,* Fairfax's 1600 translation of Tasso's *Gerusalemme Liberata* 16.15.5, "O gather then the rose while time thou has," Broadbent (*Some Graver Subject* 190–91) points out that Milton takes the seduction theme "but makes it spiritual by channelling the conventional refrain into Satan's envy." Looking forward, Broadbent continues, "Satire on the coy mistress theme is explicit when Adam and Eve consummate their love, as consummation not to be found 'in the bought smile / Of Harlots' [765–66]."

538. Merritt Y. Hughes compares this line with 2.948 and notes in both cases the monosyllabic mimicry of the fiend's slow motion ("Variorum").
   roam: defining this as "the act of roaming," Alastair Fowler reports this as the earliest instance cited in the *OED* (644).

539. *Mean while in utmost Longitude:* Hume establishes that *Longitude,* from Latin, means "length, distance" (151). Newton (269) elaborates: "At the utmost length, at the farthest distance. *Longitude* is *length* in B[ook]. v.754; and it is particularly applied to *the distance from east to west* in B[ook]. iii. 576."

540–75. Developing the significance of direction, including the association of evil with the west and goodness with the east, H. F. Robins highlights Uriel's approach and entry to the garden: "Uriel, who descends to warn Eden's angelic guard of Satan's arrival, comes from the westering sun, but he alights near the eastern gate" (100). The angel's western approach, according to Robins, signifies the gravity of the news he brings (101).

540–43. Thomas Keightley is puzzled about "how the sun who was sinking in the west could level his rays directly against the eastern gate of Paradise," and while the earlier editors and critics seem not to notice the problem, several later critics share Keightley's concern. The first to ask the question, Keightley also attempts an answer: "It might be said, that it was against the inner side of the gate, and that the rays came over Paradise; but this is contrary to all analogy; for no one but Satan entered the garden except at the gate, and Uriel came on one of these beams" (*Account* 431). Some 19 years later, David Masson, too, expresses uncertainty: "Milton *may* have meant this; but it is hardly likely, since in what follows he seems to be describing the gate from the *outside*" (*Poetical Works* 3:175). While he accepts the explanation that Keightley proposes, Verity (464) points to yet another puzzle, the structure of the gate, which is discussed in more detail in 542–48: "The rays of the setting sun fell on the *inner* side of the towering rock which formed the gate of Paradise on the east (XII.638)." Fowler (644) posits a very high gate: "Since the gate is so high, even the setting sun's horizontal rays illuminate it, after passing over the 'insuperable height' of the western 'verdurous wall' (l. 143)."

541. *Slowly descended:* Bentley, Pearce, and then Newton are concerned about the apparent alteration in the speed of the sun's descent during this evening scene. Bentley (126) would have the line read "Had low descended" to establish that the speed of the sun's descent is even, while Pearce (130) argues that poetic license authorizes "Slowly descended." Newton glances back at 352–53, "The sun...was hasting now with prone career," and explains, "to reconcile them I think we must read 'Had low descended,' or perhaps 'Lowly descended,' or understand it as Dr. Pearce explains it, that the sun descended slowly at this time, because Uriel, its Angel, came on a sun-beam to Paradise, and was to return on the same beam; which he could not well have done, if the sun had moved on with its usual rapidity of course" (270). Reviewing the eighteenth century discussion, Fowler presents a reading based on Milton's being "further advanced in the study of astronomy" than were his early editors. Citing Giovanni Riccioli's discussion, "Tempus Apparens Ortus et Occasus Limborum Solis Definire" in his *Almagestum* 2.581.33, Fowler argues that Milton "allowed for the refractive effect of the earth's atmosphere during the ultimate phase of the sunset. This effect produces an apparent deceleration of the sun's descent" (644).

right aspect: Fowler notes, "direct view. Assuming that the gate is more or less vertical (547[–48]), the rays of the setting sun will be at *right* angles with it" (644).

542–50. The structure of the gate of paradise (542) is a perplexing topic, involved as it is with earlier descriptions of the mountain itself, as well as with the subsequent reference to the "Ivorie Port" at 778. While Hume ignores these challenges both at 778 and here, where he provides only a paraphrase (152), the Richardsons (165) directly confront the problem. Trying to relate this sequence to 778, they assert that the "Rock / Of Alabaster" (443–44) is "the Sides of the Gateway, call'd the Pillars, *v.* 549. the Gate it Self was of Ivory, *v.* 778." In their note on 547, they offer additional clarification (167): "Thus the Rock form'd a Gate of Alabaster, the Bottom, Sides, and Overhead; and This had a Door, or Gate to open and Shut on Occasion, which was of Ivory. the Rock was hung with Arms, Shields, and Armour, *v.* 553." Also see the Richardsons in **778**. The problem of the two mountains of paradise, presented at **131–48**, additionally complicates this description of the gate. Largely concerned with the literary source for Milton's presentation of the rocky, as opposed to the wooded mountain, Evert Mordecai Clark and Grant McColley point to Samuel Purchas's description of Mt. Amara in *Purchas His Pilgrimage* 566. Clark (146) quotes Purchas, who explains that, to someone looking up at it, Mt. Amara appears "like a high wall, whereon the heaven is as it were propped." As Purchas describes it, the top of Mt. Amara is "over-hanged with rocks, jutting forth of the sides the space of a mile, bearing out like mushromes, so that it is impossible to ascend it" except at "the ascending place, a faire gate." Noting that although Milton in 281 dissociates the mountain of paradise from Mt. Amara, McColley (*"Paradise Lost": An Account* 314) also accepts the probability of Milton's debt to Purchas, but in addition, he endeavors to determine the chronology of the composition of *PL* by reference to the two different descriptions of the mountain.

More recently, Alastair Fowler and Roy Daniells have directed critical attention away from the literary sources and architectural details of Milton's description of the gate to its meaning. Finding this a "complex and highly condensed" passage, Fowler (644–45) recites the essence of the source studies but claims that "earlier readers would also be quick to recognize the iconographical features of the description." Fowler identifies five such features: (1) "The rock ascending *to the clouds* is a supraterrestrial Paradise"; (2) "The way to its *entrance high* is an arduous Path of Virtue"; (3) "Its *pillars* are Pillars of Virtue"; (4) "The *craggy cliff* that overhangs symbolizes impending divine punishment"; and (5) "The mention of *alablaster* directs attention to the receptacle in which the ointment of faith was kept uncorrupted." Fowler draws all these features into an allegorical reading. While Roy Daniells sees the baroque artist at work in Milton's description of the gate, he locates one of the artist's "occasional lapses" in this sequence: "Eden's gate must, like the gates of heaven and hell, receive a proper Baroque emphasis. Set in a structure of alabaster, it is formed with armorial bearings (in the literal sense of a stand of arms) and with pillars between which sits the captain of the guard. Yet it performs no function" (*Milton* 91).

542. *eastern:* the Richardsons, cross-referencing 178, which establishes that the garden had only one gate, explain, "*Eastern* Here is an Epithet, not a Distinction" (165).

544. *Alablaster:* Hume (152) spells this *Alabaster,* as do Richard Bentley (126) and A. W. Verity (115), but the *OED* sheds light on the matter, noting that *alablaster,* the usual spelling in the sixteenth and seventeenth centuries, is apparently "due to a confusion with *arblaster,* a cross-bowman, also written *alablaster.*" While Merritt Y. Hughes finds *alablaster* or *alabaster* defined in Henry Cockeram's *English Dictionarie* as "a very cold Marble, white and clear" (*Complete Poems* 291), Alastair Fowler describes it as "a specially white variety of marble, variegated with other colours; carbonate of lime, used by the ancients for holding and preserving unguents" (645). The *OED* supports Hughes's definition, contrasting alabaster with the variegated marble that Fowler describes. R. C. Browne (1:353) cross-references *Mask* 660, which he annotates (1:294) with a nod to Spenser's "old (but incorrect) form" *alablaster* in *The Faerie Queene* 2.9.44.

549–50. Establishing Gabriel's role as ambassador and guardian, Patrick Hume presents the fundamentals developed by later editors and critics. Hume provides biblical authority for Gabriel as divine ambassador: "One of the Arch-angels sent to shew *Daniel* the Vision of the Four Monarchies and the Seventy Weeks, *Dan.* Chap. 4. and 9. and to the Virgin *Mary* to reveal the *Incarnation of our Saviour,* Luke. 1. Vers. 26." The basis of understanding Gabriel as a guardian is not biblical, however, but etymological, as Hume reports that Gabriel's name means "the *Man of God, or the Strength and Power of God,* well by our Author posted as chief of the Angelic Guards placed about *Paradise*" (152). Supporting Hume's first point is Verity's reference to a passage in *Jerusalem Delivered* 1.11, Fairfax's 1600 translation of Tasso's *Gerusalemme Liberata,* which also establishes Gabriel's role as ambassador from God to man. In *PR* 1.129, 4.504, Verity finds a similar notion of Gabriel's role (464–65). In the twentieth century, Hume's understanding of Gabriel, *"the Strength and Power of God,"* as guardian as well as ambassador continues to be developed. In her 1936 dissertation, Clara Starrett Gage refers Milton's presentation of Gabriel to Enoch 20.7, where Gabriel is included among the seven supreme angels and is set "over Paradise and the serpents and the Cherubim" (109). Acknowledging the absence of biblical authority for Gabriel's role as the "Chief of th' Angelic Guards," and, indeed, for angels guarding prelapsarian Eden, Grant McColley suggests the relevance of Ps. 91.11: "For he shall give his angels charge over thee, to keep thee in all thy ways." McColley traces the idea's development from Aquinas's *Summa Theologica* 1.113.4 through *The Glasse of Time* 29, where Thomas Peyton declares to the unfallen Adam, "God hath...charged the angels for thy fence and guard." As he notes that *Gabriel* means "the strength of God," McColley then refers to St. Gregory the Great (*In Evangelium Homily XXXIV* 34, col. 1251) and Bonaventure. In addition, McColley writes, "The *Cornish Creation* [*The Creacion of the World* 321–26] pictured Gabriel as the outstanding angelic warrior, and [Joost van den] Vondel's *Adam* [*in Ballingschap*] made him leader of the angels guarding the wedding feast of Adam and Eve" (*"Paradise Lost": An Account* 164; also see McColley, "Paradise Lost" 203). Finally, McColley suggests that the guards assigned to Mt. Amara also probably influenced Milton to assign guards at this point (*"Paradise Lost": An Account* 165). Robert H. West and Dennis H. Burden provide similar readings. West reports that, for the Catholic Church, Gabriel, Michael, and Raphael were protectors to whom worshipers "sanctioned prayer by name" (62). Burden balances the angels guarding Milton's prelapsarian garden not with the guards on Mt. Amara but with the guards assigned "to secure the Garden after the Fall" (19). More than 30 years after Clara Starrett Gage referred Gabriel's role as guardian to Enoch 20.7, Fowler reconsiders the association. He notes, however, that that particular verse "does not seem to have occurred...in the parts of Enoch accessible to M[ilton]." Furthermore, pointing out that Milton's Gabriel is not just a guardian of paradise, but also a warrior, Fowler claims, "M[ilton] followed a Jewish and cabbalistic tradition that identified Gabriel with Mars." Cross-referencing his note on 3.648, which associates Milton's presentation of the angels with Jewish and cabalistic tradition, Fowler explains that Gabriel is "one of the four archangels ruling the corners of the world, and one of the angels of the cosmic chariot" (645). Hughes reminds readers that Milton had selected Gabriel to deliver the prologue for "Adam Unparadiz'd" ("Variorum").

Discussing Milton's distinctive diction, which "brings a situation before us in two lines, every word contributing its share" (201), Walter Raleigh quotes these lines: "The packed line introduced by Milton is of a greater density and conciseness than anything to be found in English literature before it. It is our nearest native counterpart to the force and reserve of the high Virgilian diction" (202).

550. As he notes that "angelic guards" recurs in 10.18, while the identifying tag "heavenly spirits" recurs three times (361, 6.788, 8.615), Edward S. Le Comte argues that the repetitions of these "fixed epithets for angels" make us "very much aware of the unique privileges of Adam and Eve." Le Comte notes that the epithets stress the angels' brightness, rank, function, and place of origin (*Yet Once More* 39).

551–54. Considering angelic, as well as human nudity in the epic, Roy Daniells brings considerable attention to the viewer's perspective when glimpsing the unarmed angels: "When we first view them ... by the great gate, we get the same effect as when we reach the Arc de Triomphe and find a stand of arms looming above our heads." The visual experience changes however, as the reader or viewer nears the gate: "As we approach, we see that this unarmed 'youth of Heaven' is engaged in heroic games; they are now antique Grecian athletes, like undraped youths upon a frieze" ("Happy Rural Seat" 8).

551–52. Hume establishes the basic classical associations here, glossing the angels' "Heroic Games" as "Noble Sports and Pastimes" and identifying them as "an Allusion to the four celebrated Games of *Greece, th' Olympick, Pythian, Isthmian and Nemaean*" (152). The Richardsons (166) associate the angels' games with those of Achilles' followers during his dispute with Agamemnon, and they observe that Satan's followers similarly entertained themselves following Satan's departure in Book 2, a cross-reference that Stanley Fish and Alastair Fowler also consider. Fish agrees with the Richardsons that the angelic and the demonic games are comparable, but Fowler does not. Asking "what distinguishes these games," Fish replies, "The answer is, nothing" (*Surprised* 171). In his gloss on *unarmed,* Fowler rules the demonic games described in 2.532–38 as "more aggressive" (645).

552–54. Identifying those structural patterns contributing to the Italian element in Milton's verse, F. T. Prince points to this sequence as he discusses how associated adjectives "may be balanced against adverbial phrases or participles" (*Italian Element* 117–18).

554. Hume and Todd establish the conventionality of the flaming weaponry carried by the angelic guards. Hume (152) writes, "Flaming Helms, the Lustre and Brightness of Polish'd Shields and Helms, is by most of the Poets liken'd to Fire." Hume proceeds to Homer's descriptions of Diomedes's armor (*Iliad* 5.4–8) and Achilles's shield (*Iliad* 19.373–80), and concludes by quoting several of Virgil's descriptions of flaming armor. To the same purpose, Todd ([1842], 2:85) contributes Dunster's reference to Tasso's *Gerusalemme Liberata* 7.82. Several more recent editors point out that weaponry "with Diamond flaming" also functions metaphorically in Milton's theological writing. From *Apol* (Patterson, *Works* 3:313–14), Mitford (133) quotes Milton's description of the Reformers' spirit, "Zeale whose substance is etherial, arming in compleat diamond," and Merritt Y. Hughes ("Variorum") refers to *RCG* (Patterson, *Works* 3:230), where Milton claims that "no Diamond can equall" the outward glory of the truth.

555–56. Addison is disappointed with the manner of Uriel's transportation to and from the sun, and a few later critics share his objections, but by and large, the early editors appear quite content with the angel's use of the sunbeam and supply the description with supportive authority. In *Spectator* 321, devoted to *PL* 4, Addison considers Milton's epic machinery: "*Uriel*'s gliding down to the Earth upon a Sun-beam, with the Poet's Device to make him *descend,* as well in his return to the Sun, as in his coming from it, is a Prettiness that might have been admired in a little fanciful Poet, but seems below the Genius of *Milton*" (3:174). For Bentley's response to Addison's reading, see **589–92.** Unlike

Addison, the Richardsons (166–67) are apparently impressed by the practicality of Uriel's mode of transport: "*Uriel* coming from the Sun to the Earth, his Direct way was to keep with That of it's Beam which pointed on the Spot of Ground on which he intended to Alight, the Gate, there where *Gabriel* sate; 'twas a Level flight, 543, 549." Equally impressed by Uriel's common sense as he makes this trip, Newton glances at a pictorial precedent: "As Uriel was coming from the sun to the earth, his coming upon a sun-beam was the most direct and level course that he could take; for the sun's rays were now pointed right against the eastern gate of Paradise, where Gabriel was sitting, and to whom Uriel was going. And the thought of making him glide *on a sun beam,* I have been inform'd is taken from some capital picture of some great Italian master, where an Angel is made to descend in like manner" (271). Todd ([1842], 2:85–86) reports a note from Farmer, which glances at Addison's response, identifies Annibal Caracci as the Italian master to whom Newton refers, but concludes that Milton's description is indebted to James Shirley's *The Brothers, a Comedie* 9. Todd also presents Thomas Warton's commentary linking Uriel's ride on the sunbeam to Michael Drayton's earlier *The Tragicall Legend of Robert, Duke of Normandy* 46.4–5 (*Works* 2:391), "As on the *sun-beams* gloriously I ride, / By them I *mount,* and down by them I *slide,*" and Edward Young's later "Night Thoughts" 9, "Perhaps a thousand demigods *descend* / On every *beam* we see, to walk with men." Finally, Todd wonders, "perhaps Milton had in mind what Sandys relates of the traditions of the Jews respecting our Saviour, in his *Travels,* ed. 1615, p. 147. 'They say that he got into the Sanctum Sanctorum, and, taking from thence the powerful names of God, did sew them in his thigh: By vertue whereof he went invisible, *rid on the Sunne beames,* raised the dead to life, and effected like wonders.'" Todd concludes with cross-references to *Arc* 15–16 and *Mask* 80.

One of the best-known responses to Uriel's ride is Samuel Johnson's, of course. Pointing out that Uriel's riding on a sunbeam evidences his materiality, Johnson argues that one of the defects of Milton's poem is that his "infernal and celestial powers are sometimes pure spirit, and sometimes animated body" ("Milton" 290). While Johnson's criticism of Uriel's mode of transport is well known, however, it appears not to register very compellingly with such twentieth century critics as Robert H. West, J. B. Broadbent, and Roy Daniells. In *Milton and the Angels,* West subtly refutes Johnson as he explains, "Uriel's ride down the sunbeam is not angelology" but is "predominantly literary and so outside angelological 'science'" (104), and Broadbent contrasts the "heaving, shifting flying" of the demons with "the effortless gliding of unfallen angels, the deliberate movements and stances of Adam and Eve, and the immobility of God" (*Some Graver Subject* 87). Similarly concerned with the literary, rather than the angelological, significance of the episode, Daniells discusses Uriel's "switchback" as baroque: "Uriel's switchback is one of several machines which Milton produces in the space between heaven and hell where he can, as it were, spread himself. They are devices of which Inigo Jones might well have been proud" (*Milton* 126).

The modern reaction to Uriel's ride is not unanimous approbation, however; John Peter, for example, seems to be developing Joseph Addison's description of the episode as an inappropriate "Prettiness." Peter condemns not only Milton but also his lazy angel. Contending that Milton's "inappropriate and refractory" (22) presentation of the angels in *PL* encourages readers to be "alert to all their more ridiculous attributes" (23), Peter notes that Uriel "seems to disapprove of laziness in angels (iii. 700–01), yet he himself slides down the sunbeams like a lazy child instead of flying" (23–24).

555. *Eeven:* the critical discussion about Uriel's gliding through time, rather than place, begins with Bentley's changing *Eeven* to *Heav'n* and extends into the mid-twentieth century, when both William Empson and Isabel Gamble Mac-Caffrey present two different arguments for the correctness of *Eeven*. As he edits Milton's text, Bentley explains, "I never heard but here, that the *Evening* was a Place or Space to *glide* through. *Evening* implies Time, and he might with equal propriety say, *Came gliding though* [*sic*] *Six a clock*" (126). Unlike Bentley, Pearce (130–31) finds precedent to support Milton's expression, as do the Richardsons, who write, "*Uriel* is said to be Arriv'd from the Sun's Decline, no more a Place than the Evening, but Beautifully Poetical; and Justify'd by *Virgil, Georg.* IV. 59 where a Swarm of Bees Sails through the Glowing Summer" (166). Empson believes that Milton is punning here: "the angel is sliding, choosing a safe gradient, down a nearly *even* sunbeam; like the White Knight on the poker. But as so often when Milton is on the face of it indefensible the line seems to absorb the harshness of its absurdity; the pun gives both Uriel and the sunset a vast and impermanent equilibrium; it is because of the inevitable Fall of our night that he falls to earth, in the hush and openness of evening, himself in a heroic calm" (*Some Versions* 150). Alastair Fowler (645) applauds Empson's insight and goes on to cross-reference not only Uriel's return on a sunbeam (590–91) but also the scale image at the close of Book 4. Elucidating

Milton's handling of time in conjunction with space as a structural pattern in *PL*, MacCaffrey also speaks to Bentley's rejection of *Eeven:* "Whether or not it was always conscious, Milton experiences the world of his epic architecturally, in terms of mass and space" (76–77).

556–60. This extended metaphor of a "shooting Starr" (556) is very fully examined by Patrick Hume, who summarizes classical scientific discourse on the phenomenon of shooting stars and presents the metaphor's classical literary pedigree, leaving later scholars to deal with the relationship between Uriel and the ominous metaphor here applied to him. Hume's paraphrase introduces his emphasis on the science of the "shooting Starr": "*Swift like a darting Star, that in the Autumn crosses the Night, when Fat and Oily Vapours taking Fire, with their Activity, hurry the Air into Violence, and by their shining Path direct the Seaman, from what Quarter of the Heavens to beware of stormy, boisterous Winds*" (152). To debunk the "vulgar Opinion" about shooting stars, Hume paraphrases the views of Pliny, *Natural History* 2:22, and Servius Grammaticus, *Qui Feruntur in Vergilii Carmina Commentarii* 2:204–05, and summarizes Aristotle's explanation in *Meteorologica* 1.4 that shooting stars are "Fat and Oyly Exhalations, drawn up from the Earth into the middle Region of the Air, and there by the extraordinary Cold so compress'd and condens'd, that they took Fire by his unintelligible *Antiperistasis;* or by their own violent Circumgyration." Also see Hume's note on *Impress* in **558**. Establishing the metaphor's literary tradition, Hume cites Virgil's *Georgics* 1.365–67, Ovid's metaphor comparing the fall of Phaeton to a star (*Metamorphoses* 2.322), and Homer's metaphors comparing both the armed Achilles (*Iliad* 22.25–29) and the armed Diomedes (*Iliad* 5.4–8) to shooting stars. Hume insists, however, that *Iliad* 4.73–78, describing Minerva's descent into the Trojan camp, is "the most Parallel place at which our Authors imitation seems to have aim'd, and to have outdone" (152–53). Newton underscores Hume's comment on the shooting star as a warning by adding that such stars "usually portend tempestuous weather" (271–72), but Newton leaves it for several twentieth century critics to dissociate the ominous quality of the metaphor from the angel to whom it is applied. Merritt Y. Hughes ("Variorum") acknowledges the tonal complications of the metaphor, clarifying its "note of the sinister or dangerous" by cross-referencing 1.745, where the image of a "falling Star" is applied to Mulciber, but Kester Svendsen and Fowler separate Uriel from that sinister note. Establishing that "No one in Milton's generation could fail to know this superstition," Svendsen adds, "nor would he find anything strange in the comparison to Uriel, for that angel is here a sign of tempest between Gabriel and Satan and an omen of disaster for the latter as well as for Adam and Eve" (*Milton and Science* 89). Fowler writes, "Uriel's arrival is like the *shooting star* not only in visual respects, but also because he brings a warning to the *mariner* (Gabriel) and so temporarily *thwarts* the powers of darkness" (646). Also see MacCaffrey in **555**. In his edition of *PR* in 1795, Charles Dunster (264) associates this description of Uriel as a "swift shooting Starr / In Autumn" with the metaphor the angels in *PR* 4.619–20 invoke as they forecast Satan's end "like an Autumnal Star / Or Lightning thou shalt fall."

556. David Masson (*Poetical Works* 3:175) admires the music of this line, describing it as "One of the many lines in which Milton, by a beautiful fitness of metre and of component letters, makes the sound suggest the sense. Compare *Comus* 80." See Todd ([1842], 2:85–86) in **555–56**.

   swift: Alastair Fowler is somewhat puzzled by this adverb considering "Uriel has taken some considerable time over a journey that Satan accomplished almost instantaneously (see ll. 30 and 564). Perhaps the inference to be drawn is that Uriel had to wait until sunset, when a sun god's mythological task is completed for the day, before leaving his post" (646).

557. *thwarts:* again sounding the ominous note carried by the entire shooting star metaphor, Patrick Hume glosses this word, "Comes across the Night, thwarts and affronts the dismal darkness of the Night" (153), and while "crosses," the first element in Fowler's note, accords with Hume's much earlier annotation, Fowler adds that because *thwarts* appears "often in a nautical context" it is "appropriate diction here" (645). The *OED* supplies several nautical definitions of *thwart,* such as *thwart of,* "Transversely to, across the direction of," which is exemplified with 10.703; it also exemplifies the third meaning of the preposition *thwart,* "Across the course of, so as to obstruct," with a passage from Milton's *Ref:* "Cross-jingling periods which come thwart a setl'd devotion worse then the din of bells and rattles" (Patterson, *Works* 3:34). Also see MacCaffrey in **555**.

558. *Impress:* this word has military associations that Patrick Hume and John Upton highlight. Hume writes, "Here we have the Philosophy of these shooting Stars, that they are Unctuous Exhalations, which being fired, assault the Air, and move it violently. *Impress,* of *imprimere,* Lat. to use force upon, to make impression on, and in this sense *Impressio,* signifies an Assault, an Onset given by engaging Armies" (153). Also see Hume in **556–60**. John Upton (411) refers the word to Shakespeare's use in *Macbeth* 5.8.9–10: "As easy mayst thou the intrenchant air / With thy keen sword impress."

Hughes cross-references 150, where the sun "more glad impress'd his beams" on the colors of Eden's fruit ("Variorum").

559. *Compass:* Hume clarifies the nature of this instrument: "From what part of the Sky, from what Quarter of the Heav'n: The Compass here meant is a Circle set round with the 32 different Points from which the Winds have their Denominations" (153).

561. *by Lot:* Hume (153) establishes the first items in a growing list of biblical references where lots are cast to settle a variety of affairs. Hume begins with Num. 26.55, followed by Num. 33.55 and finally Acts 1.26, "And they gave forth their Lots, and the Lot fell upon Matthias." Referring to Luke 1.8–9 and 1 Chron. 3.6, the Richardsons (167) explain the assignment of duty by lot. Both Todd ([1842], 2:86) and Masson (*Poetical Works* 3:176) credit an unpublished note from Callander with the reference to Luke 1, as well as a cross-reference to 5.655. To this list of biblical references, Hughes adds Prov. 16.33 and 1 Chron. 25–26, as well as Euripides's *Rhesus* 544 and 564, where the practice of assigning watches by lot is treated as usual among the troops of Troy ("Variorum").

564. *at highth of Noon:* in a rich discussion of the noonday timing of the Fall, Jackson I. Cope, cross-referencing 9.219, 397–403, and 739–44, identifies Satan's first act of betrayal in this universe, his noon betrayal of Uriel, as one element in "the series of 'high Noon' preparations for the fall of Man" (136), but Alastair Fowler (646) interjects a note of caution. Because "M[ilton]'s universe is throughout on 'Paradise Time,'" Fowler argues that "the term *noon* can have no meaning unless a particular horizon is specified." Fowler parallels this *Noon* to *noon* in the argument to Book 4, and Hughes ("Variorum") refers it to the description of the sun on which Uriel stands in 3.616–17, "all Sun-shine, as when his Beams at Noon / Culminate from th' *Aequator.*"

565–66. Verity (465) compares Gabriel's description of Satan with Satan's words to Uriel at 3.667–76.

566–67. Uriel's declaration here that *Man* is "Gods latest Image" has stirred editors from Patrick Hume on to clarify the nature of God's other images. Hume reasons that "it is not to be doubted, that if Man in [*sic*] part of a Corporeal Substance, yet bears his Maker's Image; the Angels, those much more Pure and Spiritual Beings, are more exact Resemblances of that Eternal Purity and Perfection that Created them, as being more perfect Approximations to their Maker" (153). The Richardsons (167) consider Christ as God's "Earliest" image by reference to Heb. 1.3 and Col. 1.15, whereas Newton's note (273) gives all three of the usual understandings of God's image: "For the first was Christ; and before Man were the Angels." Newton also cross-references 3.151, where man is identified as God's "youngest Son." Alastair Fowler brings a more expansive reading to the concept of the image of God: "God's first *image* being Christ, and the intervening images the angels, heaven and the products of the first five days of mundane creation" (646).

566. *chiefly Man:* Edward S. Le Comte (*Yet Once More* 35) points to the repetition "chiefly Man, / His chief delight" (3.663–64) in Satan's dialog with Uriel, and "chief delight" in the Father's reply to the Son in 3.168.

567. *describ'd:* looking to 9.60 and 10.325 for support, Bentley (127) would replace *describ'd* with *descri'd,* but for the most part, editors do not accept his emendation. Both Pearce (133) and Newton (273) reject the change, whereas the Richardsons very precisely distinguish between *describ'd* and *descri'd:* "*Uriel* is said to have *Descry'd* his Entrance into *Eden;* Here he Describes his Way Thither. This *Entrance Descry'd,* and the Description of the *Way* mention'd in the first Line of the present Passage are plainly two Distinct things" (167–68). Helen Darbishire and Merritt Y. Hughes, however, establish the interchangeability of *describ'd* and *descri'd.* Rejecting Bentley's emendation, Darbishire claims that "*describe* was used in the meaning of *descry* in the 17th century" (*Poetical Works* 1:296n567), while Hughes ("Variorum") points out that the *OED* cites Milton's line under "'describe' (¶7) to illustrate its occasional, two-way confusion with 'descry' (To catch sight of [*OED* III.7])." Robert Martin Adams notes that all ten of the modern editions that he surveys accept *describ'd* (83).

568. *Aerie Gate:* Hume glosses *Gait* as "speedy March, or his passage through the Air, or his giddy and indecent Carriage; not well suiting a Spirit seemingly so zealous" (153), and the Richardsons pick up that notion: "He [Uriel] Directed him [disguised Satan] in his Way (he appearing to be in Violent Haste) Observ'd a Particularity in his Motion" (167–68). *Aerie* differently catches the attention of Marjorie H. Nicolson; arguing the similarities between the spiritual worlds of Milton and Henry More, she notes that Milton's *aerie* and *aerial* convey "something of the neo-Platonic significance they had for More" ("Spirit World" 436n7).

569.   *the Mount:* Hume (153) cross references 3.742 and paraphrases Uriel, who identifies Mt. Niphates as the place "where his Hellish Conscience and Devilish Despair disfigured him, and discovered his seeming Saintship."

571.   Hughes cross-references 18–19 and 23, where are displayed "the passions of horror, doubt, and despair which are now shown to have identified Satan (to Uriel) as having impaired his angelic nature" ("Variorum").

572.   *shade:* when they explain that Satan's "Looks were Suspicious, and he Hid himself in Darkness, by which Means he [Uriel] knows not what became of him" (167–68), the Richardsons' understanding of *shade* as "Darkness" prepares the background for several twentieth century considerations of Uriel's report that he lost sight of the "Spirit, zealous" (565). John Peter does not consider the nature of the *shade* concealing Satan, but he complains because Uriel "unaccountably loses sight of Satan's movements on the earth" (25), although earlier the angel had been described as "the sharpest sighted Spirit of all in Heav'n" (3.691), but both Anne Davidson Ferry and B. A. Wright understand the concealing *shade* as the trees of Eden. Ferry establishes the difference between Edenic and Satanic shade, as she explains, "In Eden Satan is associated with night and darkness, when he can best accomplish his 'dark' purposes. He seeks the protection of the 'shades' to hide him or to disguise him, again sundering a sacred metaphor by dividing the moral meaning of protection from the physical fact of cool dimness. When he is discovered lurking in Eden, he escapes from the sight of Gabriel [*sic*—should read Uriel] by fleeing 'under shade' " (*Milton's Epic Voice* 174). Directly responding to the Richardsons, Wright assumes that when they claimed Satan "Hid himself in Darkness," they meant that Satan "assumed a magic cloak of invisibility," and Wright rejects that understanding: "there is no suggestion here or elsewhere that Satan so hid himself. What he does . . . is to enter the thicket on the lowest slopes of the mount of Paradise" (*Milton's "Paradise Lost"* 71). Wright insists that *shade* makes no sense unless read as trees, which, he points out, has Virgilian authority, and he finds it "strange that this sense should not have been noted in commentaries or in the O.E.D." (72). See both Ferry and Wright on *shade* in **137–42**, and see Wright's expanded study of *shade* in " 'Shade.' " See also the *OED*'s definition 3.8 of *shade:* "Cover afforded by the interposition of some opaque or semi-opaque body between an object and light, heat, etc.; esp. the shelter from the sun afforded by trees; quasi-*concr.* (*sing.* and *pl.*) overshadowing foliage." The *OED* cites 1.303–04: "In *Vallombrosa,* where th' *Etrurian* shades / High overarch't imbowr."

576. *winged Warriour:* Edward S. Le Comte (*Yet Once More* 108) cross-references "Volatiles…milites"; "winged soldiers" in *Eli* 47 and "winged Warriours" in the opening line of *Circum.*

579–81. See H. F. Robins in **178–83**.

580. Hume (154) acknowledges Milton's use of metonymy: "The Watch here kept. *Vigilance, Vigilantia,* Lat. Watchfulness; *Vigilia* Lat. the Watch." A. W. Verity (465) cross-references "Armed watch" in 2.130, and Merritt Y. Hughes ("Variorum") cross-references similar metonymies in 1.435, 6.250, and 6.371–72. Robert Bridges finds this line the only exception to Milton's elision rule of L, and he therefore considers the line's prosody "an error of the text" (32).

589–92. Richard Bentley understands that Uriel's sunbeam is not "a flowing Punctum of Light, but…a continued Rod extending from Sun to Earth," and considers Uriel's exit in conjunction with Addison's understanding of the angel's entrance at 555–56. Looking back at 540–43, Bentley proceeds to correct Addison by arguing that Milton "makes *Uriel* come from the Sun, not on a *descending,* but on a *level* Ray, *v.* 540.… Here's no trick then or device: but perhaps a too great Affection to shew his Philosophy" (128). Also see Bentley in **592–97**.

590–92. Noting the presentation of vistas in *PL,* Roy Daniells associates these lines with the earlier reference to the vista seen from the wall of Eden (210–12): "when the sun sets in utmost longitude 'beneath th' Azores,' it is we who watch while Uriel glides back to his station. Interestingly enough, Gabriel, though posted in the gateway on top of the eastern cliff, sees nothing. As a guard, he never lets his gaze wander" ("Happy Rural Seat" 5).

592–97. As Uriel rides the sunbeam back to the sun, Milton's narrator ponders a matter of astronomy, anticipating Adam and Raphael's discussion in Book 8 and also provoking a steady stream of critical commentary. The narrator is uncertain "whither" (592) the rolling of the "less volubil Earth" (594) or the rolling of "the prime Orb" (592) has brought forth the evening. Much of Hume's note is paraphrase, but he does declare that "the prime Orb" (592) is "the first, the chief Circle, the *Primum Mobile*" (154). Newton and Bentley prefer *whether* to *whither* in 592, but astronomy, more than spelling, concerns them as both establish that the narrator's two options describe the Copernican and the Ptolemaic systems. Newton explains that it is "a less motion for the earth to move from west to east upon its own axis according to the system of Copernicus, than for the Heavens and heavenly bodies to move from east to west according to the system of Ptolemy. Our author in like manner, III. 575. questions whether the sun was in the center of the world or not, so scrupulous was he in declaring for any system of philosophy" (274–75; see **593** for Fowler's comment on Newton's phrase "less motion"). Bentley (128) similarly notes that Milton "starts a Doubt" as to whether the sunset "is produc'd in the *Ptolemaic* or *Copernican* way," but he adds that this doubt, as well as the business of Uriel's transport on the sunbeam, is a "little Foible he makes ample amends for." Also see Bentley in **589–92**. Throughout the nineteenth century, commentators such as Thomas Keightley, Robert Vaughan, and David Masson echo Newton's response to this sequence. Keightley (*Account* 434) finds that, "when a theory or an interpretation was not, as appeared to him, certain, he [Milton] would give the different views at different times. Thus, though he generally follows the Ptolemaic astronomy, as most accordant with the literal sense of Scripture, he yet occasionally hints that the Copernican might be the truth." Vaughan briefly comments, "It is observable that Milton will not here say whether the Ptolemaic or the Copernican system is the true one" (101), and Masson expresses his belief that Milton "was probably more of a convert to it [the Copernican system] than most of his contemporaries; and hence, though he retains for his general purposes the Ptolemaic system, he takes the precaution in this passage of suggesting, as perhaps more plausible scientifically, the Copernican alternative" (*Poetical Works* 3:176). Well into the twentieth century, Grant

McColley develops this opinion ("Astronomy" 220). Reconsidering this issue a few years later, as he studies the dating of the composition of *PL*, McColley assigns this sequence to 1655–58, when the poet's "associations [especially with Henry Oldenburg] would have influenced him to take a sympathetic attitude" toward the new astronomy, unlike the attitude expressed by Raphael during the dialog on astronomy in Book 8 (*"Paradise Lost": An Account* 322). During the 1960s, Balachandra Rajan and Fowler bring new information to bear upon the Copernican-versus-Ptolemaic debate. Arguing that to assume Milton's preference for the Copernican is misleading, Rajan explains, "It was the geo-heliocentric Tychonic System which was contending with the Copernican for supremacy; both in learned treatises and in popular almanacs opinion was divided fairly evenly." Because the Tychonic is not even mentioned in *PL*, however, Rajan concludes, "it seems probable that Milton's knowledge of astronomy has been overestimated," but, as Raphael later advises Adam, Rajan suggests that some matters are better left hidden (*"Paradise Lost" and the Seventeenth Century Reader* 153). See Fowler in **592** and **593**. Anne Davidson Ferry and Roy Daniells express more interest in the shape of the universe that Milton describes than in the uncertainty about whether the earth or the "prime Orb" moves. Ferry establishes Milton's use of circling imagery to reflect the shape of the unified prelapsarian universe, and she then argues, "The shape of the universe in *Paradise Lost* is clarified by still another repeated device. Distance in the poem is measured by lines within circles, 'As from the Center thrice to th' utmost Pole' (I, 74), and angelic characters travel within these circles so that we feel even the space in Milton's universe to be curved as it is in Einstein's. Standing apart with the narrator so that we can view through his eyes the whole world of the poem, we see figures circling the heavenly spheres or flying [as does Uriel in this sequence] from circumference to center of the universe" (*Milton's Epic Voice* 159). As he discusses the baroque nature of *PL*, and the shape Milton attributes to his physical universe, Daniells sets the Renaissance preference for the circle in church architecture against the baroque preference for the oval: "It may be objected that Eden being the centre of the universe the use of the word oval is unwarranted. But even if we take the word literally there is the curious supporting fact that Milton not only elongates the space of the universe by directional activity but also repeatedly (e.g., in IV, 592ff.) suggests the sun as an alternative centre, and two foci are, in a geometrical sense, the essentials for realizing an oval" (*Milton* 92).

592–94. Arguing that Du Bartas was a major influence on Milton, George Coffin Taylor points out that both writers invoke the "whither…or" construction "as the formula of scientific doubt" (77). Robert Martin Adams dismisses Taylor's argument (154–57).

592. *Azores:* Hume (154) identifies the Azores as "Islands of the *Western Atlantick Ocean,* Nine in Number, commonly called the *Tercera's,* of *Tercera,* the largest of 'em," and faults Edmund Bohun, whose *Geographical Dictionary* sig. D4 confuses the Azores with the Canaries. Allan H. Gilbert (*Geographical Dictionary* 42) locates the Azores 800 miles west of Portugal; cross-references 354 ("th' Ocean Iles") and 8.631 ("Beyond the Earth's green Cape and verdant Isles"); and adds another modern travel reference, *Purchas's Hakluytus Posthumus, or, Purchas His Pilgrimes* 4:1935, which explains that the islands became famous because of the Earl of Essex's 1597 voyage. Gilbert declares that Milton used the Azores "as a figure for the extreme west, where the sun sets," and he references *Mask* 97, which describes the sun setting "In the steep Atlantic stream," according to Gilbert, "an obvious imitation of the classics, not modified by a knowledge of modern geography, as are the passages in *Paradise Lost.*"

    whither: while both Bentley (128) and Newton (274) prefer *whether,* Robert Martin Adams points out that *whether* and *whither* were "interchangeable" for the seventeenth century reader (100–01).

    the prime Orb: the identity of this astronomical phenomenon is very unsettled, slipping from Hume's "Primum Mobile" (154) to Newton's "the Heavens and heavenly bodies" (274–75) and A. W. Verity's (466) "surely the sun," which he supports with cross-references to 3.576, 589, and 10.1069. Alastair Fowler (647) understands Milton's "dizzying series of verbal and syntactical ambiguities" as an effort to avoid choosing between the Ptolemaic and post-Copernican models, and Fowler glosses *the prime Orb* accordingly: " 'whether the *primum mobile* (*prime orb* = first sphere) had rolled there carrying the sun with it, or the turning earth had left him'; and 'whether the sun (*prime orb* = principal planet) had rolled there, or etc.' "

593. *Incredible how swift:* Fowler (648) clarifies Newton's reference in his commentary on 592–97 about the "less motion" involved in the Copernican system: "According to Copernicus's, Kepler's and later estimates, the velocity of the earth's diurnal motion had only to be about 0.06 German miles per second, as against 70 Ger. m.p.s. for the velocity of solar diurnal motion. And even the velocity of terrestrial annual motion was estimated at only 12.3 Ger. m.p.s." Fowler cross-references Adam's remarks to Raphael on this matter at 8.25–38.

594. *volubil:* Hume presents the Latin root, *volubilis,* defining it as "that may be turn'd round; *a volvendo,* turning or running round" (154). Noting that the *OED* I.2 (*voluble*) quotes Milton's line to illustrate this now-rare meaning, "Capable of ready rotation on a centre or axis; apt to revolve or roll in this manner," Merritt Y. Hughes cross-references 661–64 and 8.25–38 ("Variorum"; *Complete Poems* 292).

The Richardsons, Newton, and Verity comment on the word's pronunciation. The Richardsons explain, "*Volubil,* with the Second Syllable Long is Latin, and the Measure of the Verse requires it to be So pronounc'd" (168). Newton makes the same point, noting, however, that Milton "writes it *voluble,* when he makes the second syllable short, as in B[ook]. ix. 436" (275). Verity adds, "The Latin accentuation of words derived from Latin was very marked in Elizabethan E[nglish]; it has steadily declined, the Teutonic tendency in E[nglish] being to throw the accent forward" (466).

596. *Purple:* Robert Bridges (31–32), establishing the rules of Milton's prosody, points to this word as exemplifying the third rule of pure *L,* by which "unstressed vowels before pure *l* may be elided" (11). Bridges continues to discuss the third rule of pure *L* with commentary on *amiable* in **250,** *miserable* in **73,** and *Insuperable* in **138.**

598–609. With Richard Hurd the only exception, editors and critics from 1695 through the mid-twentieth century have admired, often fervently, this chronographia describing the coming of evening into the garden. Patrick Hume is particularly attentive to the scene's visual effects: "Now the quiet Evening came on, and dusky Twilight with her grave Livery cover'd every thing: The Sun was described according to his high Quality, arraying the Clouds with reflected Gold and Royal Purple. Here the Evening is as exactly delineated suitable to her obscure Condition, habited in Gray, and bestowing her sad-colour'd Livery on her Attendants" (154). Noting, "This is the first evening in the poem," Newton's praise is effusive: "surely there never was a finer evening; words cannot furnish out a more lovely description. The greatest poets in all ages have as it were vy'd one with another in their descriptions of evening and night; but for the variety of numbers and pleasing images I know of nothing parallel or comparable to this to be found among all the treasures of ancient or modern poetry." Newton (275) claims that the only description to approach the beauty of Milton's is the description of "a fine moon-shiny night by way of similitude in Homer, *Iliad* VIII.551." Quoting much of Newton's note, Todd ([1842], 2:87–88) balances it against Richard Hurd's disappointment with 598–600, which Hurd considers an inadequate imitation of Tasso's "Usci la Notte, e sotto l'ali / Meno il silentio" in *Gerusalemme Liberta* 5.79: "The striking part of Tasso's picture is, '*Night's bringing in Silence under her wings.*' So new and singular an idea as this had detected an imitation. Milton contents himself then, with saying simply, '*Silence accompanied.*' However, to make amends, as he thought, for this defect, *Night itself,* which the Italian had merely personified, the English poet not only personifies, but employs in a very becoming office: 'Now came still Evening on, and Twilight gray / Had in her sober livery all things clad:' Every body will observe a little blemish, in this fine couplet. He should not have used the epithet '*still,*' when he intended to add, '*Silence* accompanied'; But there is a worse fault in this *imitation.* To hide it, he speaks of '*Night's livery.*' When he had done that, to speak of her *wings* had been ungraceful. Therefore he is forced to say obscurely, as well as *simply,* '*Silence accompanied*': And so loses a more noble image for a less noble one. The truth is, they would not stand together. *Livery* belongs to *human grandeur; wings* to *divine* or *celestial.* So that in Milton's very attempt to surpass his original, he put it out of his power to employ the *circumstance* that most recommended it" (279–80). Todd also quotes a note from Robert Thyer who, like Newton, claims that Milton's lines are without parallel, adding, "I have often thought that the weakness of our poet's eyes, to which this kind of light must be vastly pleasant, might be the reason that he so often introduces the mention of it" ([1842], 2:88). Without naming Thyer, Stebbing (103) finds absurd the remark about Milton's weak eyes, though Verity (466) approves it. Hurd's fault-finding, which Todd attenuates with Newton's and Thyer's praise, never finds a second in later critical responses. Even H. A. Taine, who so derisively condemns Milton's presentation of Adam and Eve, lavishes praise on this sequence. In it he finds that "the sublime is born in the poet.... The changes of the light become here a religious procession of vague beings who fill the soul with veneration" (314–15). Like Taine, several early twentieth century critics who similarly condemn Milton's presentation of prelapsarian life also respond to this chronographia with enthusiastic praise. As he lists the details of Milton's "wonderful passage," Walter Raleigh, for example, closes with a question, "Yet did ever such beauty fall with night upon such peace, save in Paradise alone?" (106). So, too, G. Wilson Knight, who condemns the "stony, carven immobility" that he finds in so much of Milton's description of Eden, greatly admires this description of the approach of night: "There is an exact wedding of Milton's mind and manner with the mysterious nature of a *living* universe: one does not ask that his manner be changed, only that it shall be fitted, subdued, to his matter; and here it is so fitted. Though the stars are 'sapphires' note that they are 'living' ones: and this blend of the pulsing *with the solid* is all but the supreme excellence, as Keats knew, in any poetry. Life breathes from the description" (101). Knight then discusses the subsequent conversation between Adam and Eve as a development of the quality of this evening (see Knight in **635–88**). Elmer Edgar Stoll finds: "It is a felicitous arrangement that this account of the first day on earth should include its close. Sunlight is not easily distinguishable from the light of Heaven; but twilight and the nightingale, the moon and the stars, are neither of Heaven above them nor of Hell under the earth; and they are indissolubly associated with the mingled emotions of our common humanity" ("From the Superhuman" 10). Milton's admirers maintain this note of praise well beyond the midcentury mark. In 604–09, Anne Davidson Ferry, for example, finds what "is perhaps the speaker's most beautiful description of nature's wheel" (153). Applying Johnson's understanding of the sublimity of *PL,* F. T. Prince similarly admires these lines: "Milton's swan, Milton's moon, are not stage properties; but they are playing their part in a great dramatic exhibition of the fitness of things, as God first ordered them. Milton's Creation is like a cosmic pageant, every creature or element 'conscious of doing what it ought'" ("Milton" 60). J. B. Broadbent associates this chronographia with the one in 352–55: "Again there is a suggestion of balance, but the device functions mainly as an assurance of the smooth working of the divine laws of nature; a reminder of the physical position of Paradise in the world; and a contrast with Hell and the fallen world, whose endlessness and vicissitudes are modulated by no chronographias" (*Some Graver Subject* 199). Sharing and developing Broadbent's attention to this passage's "balance" is Alastair Fowler (647), who explains that the balance between "the hemispheres of light and dark at sunset . . . prepares for the important scales image of ll. 997ff (Note the pun in *beam*—sunbeam, balance beam—and cp. the 'scale of heaven' at 354ff, a passage linked to the present one by its mention of the 'Ocean Isles.')." Fowler concludes, "Moreover, the numerological pattern demands that prominence be given to the precise moment of sunset," and he cross-references his commentary at 777.

598–99. Todd ([1842], 2:88) refers the metaphor of Twilight cladding all things in her "sober Liverie" to Phineas Fletcher's *The Purple Island* 6.54, "The world late *cloth'd* in *Night's* black *livery*" and 8.5, "*Night's* sad *livery.*" Todd also traces the description to "*Night's livery*," a phrase in Sir Richard Tempest's *An Entertainment of Solitarinesse* 15, and, crediting Edmund Malone (20:341), to Shakespeare's Sonnet 132. A. W. Verity and Merritt Y. Hughes recall Milton's own phrasing "the grey-hooded Even" in *Mask* 188, Verity (466) repeating Todd's note on Robert Thyer's theory about the weak-eyed Milton's sensitivity to twilight (see Todd in **589–609**), and Hughes ("Variorum") observing, "The personification of *Eevning* gains by the suggestion that all things don her *livery* in the sense of a 'distinctive dress worn only by a person's servants' (*OED* 1)."

Mary Steward Leather (401) notes echo of Milton's lines in Pope's translations of Homer's *Odyssey* 3.422.

still Eevning: Mary Steward Leather associates Pope's *Iliad* 22.648 (*Poems* 8:483) and *Pastorals: Winter* 79 (*Poems* 1:99) with Milton's phrase.

600–02. In his 1795 edition of *PR*, Charles Dunster (54) associates these lines with *PR* 1.501 ("Fowls in thir clay nests were couch't") and with *PR* 2.282–83 ("As lightly from his grassy Couch up rose / Our Saviour").

600. *accompanied:* see Fowler on *descant* in **603**.

602–04. See Hilaire Belloc in **506**.

602. *the wakeful Nightingale:* cross-referencing Milton's own poetry as well as similar descriptions of the singing of the nightingale in other literary works has concentrated most of the commentary here. John Bowle reports to Todd ([1842], 2:88) that the wakefulness of the nightingale is a feature of the description of evening in Thomas Lodge's contribution to Robert Allot's compilation, *Englands Parnassus* 251, and to Bowle's note Todd adds a reference to Petrarch's Canzoniere 10. Verity (466) glances ahead to 5.40–41, where "the night-warbling Bird... / Tunes sweetest his love-labor'd song," and also offers a final reference to Virgil's *Georgics* 4.511–15. Milton's own Sonnet 1, of course, is addressed to the "nightingale, that on yon bloomy spray / Warblest at eve." Also see *Mask* 234–35 and *PL* 7.436.

603. Edward Bysshe quotes this line, as well as 5.40–41, under "Nightingale" in the "Collection" section of *The Art of English Poetry* (283).

descant: Hume (154) notes that *descant* derives from "*Discantare,* Lat. to sing over again, to vary, in repeating a strain in Musick," and Todd ([1842], 2:89) provides a number of citations from other literary works associating *descant* with birds, especially, as Todd notes, the nightingale. To John Bowle's example from George Gascoigne's *Philomene* 5–6, "Late in an even I walked out alone, / To heare the *descant* of the nightingale" (*Works* 2:175), Todd adds references to Sylvester's translation of Du Bartas's *The Divine Weeks and Works* 1.5.685, "The first replyes, and *descants* thereupon"; Izaak Walton's *The Compleat Angler* 21, and Euripides' *Rhesus* 548. Verity (466) observes that Thomas Gray "borrowed" from Milton when he wrote "The Birds in vain their amorous Descant join," in "On the Death of Mr. Richard West" 3.

Alastair Fowler later focuses even more attention on *descant* by drawing it into association with "Silence accompanied" (600). Fowler refers to the *OED*'s definition of *to accompany:* "To associate in a company" (II.5), as well as "To join a singer or player by singing or playing on any instrument an additional part or parts" (II.10). Fowler explains, "The second sense is supported by *descant,* but not demanded by it; when used of a bird it could mean simply a melodious warbled song, without necessarily implying polyphony" (648). The *OED*'s first definition of *descant* reads, "A melodious accompaniment to a simple musical theme (the plainsong), sung or played, and often merely extemporized above it."

604. *Silence was pleas'd:* this second mention of Silence's behavior as the nightingale sings (cf. 600) prompts praise from the Richardsons and additional cross-referencing from subsequent editors. "Beautifully Poetical!" exclaim the Richardsons. "Silence is Personiz'd, and made to Listen Delighted" (169). Todd ([1842], 2:89) presents Joseph Warton's reference to the *Hero and Leander* of Grammaticus Musaeus 280, and Mitford (135) points to Joseph Beaumont's *Psyche* 6.174 and 19.160. Verity (466) notes the association with *Mask* 556: "when 'The Lady' sang, 'even Silence' was enchanted" and Fowler (648) glances at *IlPen* 51–56: "with thee bring…mute Silence…'Less *Philomel* will deign a Song."

605–09. Concerned with the various spatial features of the garden, Roy Daniells elaborates on Adam's place beneath the circling skies: "Adam suffers neither the terror of looking out into Chaos nor the claustrophobia of living within a shell." Secure, "Adam always finds himself directly under Heaven, the dwelling place of his Creator and Sustainer" ("Happy Rural Seat" 9).

605. *living Saphirs:* Hume (154) explains that the stars are *living* "because shining, as if they burnt, as we use the same word, *a live Coal*," a reading that the Richardsons develop: "the *Saphir* is a Blew Stone; 'till the Absence of the Sun all the Stars were Invisible in the Azure Sky, and as of the Same Colour with it, Now they seem to be Li't up, to be Alive, in Effect Dead Before, So we say a Live Coal when the Fire is in it" (169). A. W. Verity (466) and Alastair Fowler (648) cross-reference heaven's "Battlements adorn'd / Of living Sappire" (2.1049–50) and the garden's "Saphire Fount" (237). Thomas Keightley (*Poems* 1:605) argues that stars are no more comparable to *"Saphirs"* than to emeralds or rubies, and that an editor had pluralized the similar *Saphir* with which Milton intended to describe "the rich blue of the antediluvian sky."

Hesperus: earlier, especially classical, references have been brought to bear on *Hesperus* ever since Patrick Hume (154) first identified it as "the Evening Star, *Venus* so called when she follows the Sun" and "the Forerunner of Light when preceding him." To this Hume subtends "Accendit Lumina Vesper"; "Vesper is kindling his evening rays" from Virgil's *Georgics* 1.251. As with "living Saphirs," the Richardsons (169) repeat Hume's identification of Hesperus but also exclaim, "Surely Here is the most Inchanting Description of the Ev'ning that ever was made!" Todd ([1842], 2:89) offers John Bowle's contribution of a quotation from Spenser's *Epithalamion* 288–89, where the evening star is addressed as "Faire child of beauty, glorious lamp of love, / That all the *host of heaven* in ranks dost *lead*" (*Poetical Works* 583). In his 1900 survey of Milton's classical mythology, Charles Grosvenor Osgood draws together the several references to Hesperus throughout *PL* (3.568, 4.250, 9.49, 11.589) and more closely examines the star's classical underpinnings. Like Hume, Osgood (42–43) turns to the classics, but Osgood quotes *Iliad* 22.317–18, where Homer compares the light gleaming from the spear of Achilles to "Hesperus, fairest of all stars set in heaven." Osgood's remarks on the Hesperus reference at 9.49–50 ("Hesperus, whose Office is to bring / Twilight upon the Earth") are also apropos here since Adam and Eve are about to retire. Tracking the Hesperus reference in Book 9 to Catullus's *Poems* 62.85–91, Claudian's *Rape of Proserpine* 2.361, and Seneca's *Hippolytus* 749–51, Osgood notes, "In the citations from Catullus and Claudian Hesperus is hailed more than once as the bringer of Hymen and the wedding-night, and is thus 'Love's harbinger.'" Finally, glancing at 3.568 and 4.250, as well as *Mask* 982, Osgood also considers the relationship between Hesperus and the Hesperides: "While the ancients generally speak of the gardens of the Hesperides, he [Milton] prefers the adjective Hesperian." Osgood cites *Mask* 982 as he points out that Milton "makes the Hesperides daughters of Hesperus," adding that the genealogy of the Hesperides "varies from Hesiod down..., but Milton follows Servius [1.552–53] who adds that there were but three."

Grant McColley looks at this reference to *Hesperus* as he studies the epic's development from its dramatic inception. Asserting that "the characters and incidents found in the two first acts of these drafts [drafts 1–3] foreshadowed sections from Books III and IV of *Paradise Lost*" (*"Paradise Lost": An Account* 282), McColley especially notes the description of the evening star Hesperus and the references to the angels singing the marriage hymn. In "Adam Unparadiz'd," draft four, the description of the evening star is omitted, and the angelic marriage hymn is rendered as Gabriel's speech to the chorus (286–87). Cf. McColley in **1–12**.

606–09. In this description of the rising of the moon, Patrick Hume concentrates on the phrase "Apparent Queen" (608), as other early editors and critics do not, but it is "Apparent Queen" that gains the critical attention of several twentieth century critics. On "Apparent Queen," Hume comments, "Undoubted Sovereign of the Night display'd her matchless Light. She is said to rise in Clouded Majesty, in respect of the gross Mists and Vapours that hang about the Horizon, hiding and veiling her fair Face, till she get higher and emerge from among them. *Apparent, apparens,* Lat. Visible, clear, manifest: An exact and curious Description of a Moon-Light Night" (154). Somewhat later, John Dennis and Edward Bysshe simply register their admiration for the extended description. Dennis points to it in his discussion of "the Enthusiasm of Admiration," a "Passion" produced by "the great Phaenomena of the Material World" (1:348), and Bysshe includes it under "Moon" in the "Collection" section of *The Art of English Poetry* (263). Also see Dennis in **32–113**, and Bysshe in **352–55**, and **776–77**. As the twentieth century begins, Charles Grosvenor Osgood (29) picks up on that element in Milton's description to which Hume may be referring when he admits to finding the description "curious." Looking not only at this sequence but also at 5.41 and 7.381, Osgood reports, "The regal character of the moon is not common in the classics. The brightness of her golden crown is mentioned in *Hom[eric] Hy[mn]* 32.5 [*Homeric Hymns* 460–61], and Horace calls her 'siderum regina bicornis' ['the constellations' crescent queen'] (*C[armen] Saec[lare]* 35). The queenly nature of Diana is easily transferable to the moon." Osgood refers Milton's description of the moon throwing "o're the dark her Silver Mantle" (609) to *Homeric Hymn* 32.8 (*Homeric Hymns* 460–61). Frank L. Huntley and Alastair Fowler continue to pursue the subtleties of meaning in the description of the moon's rising. In conjunction with the second mode of systasis in *PL,* that involving "the conflict and reconciliation in plot of the *union-with* and the *separation-from* good" (3), Huntley points out, "almost from the beginning their [Adam and Eve's] morning and evening prayers and repasts of both food and love are threatened" (7). In all the prelapsarian night scenes, Huntley contends, the moon's "unforgettable presence…anticipates change. The moon rising in 'clouded Majesty' is 'apparent queen' in two senses, manifest and in appearance only. And all night long the nightingale, that 'solemn bird,' sings a song that to Milton and to us, though not to Adam and Eve, is a song of passion, pain, separation, change, and eventual triumph." Huntley adds that Wallace Stevens's "Let *be* be the finale of *seem,*" line 7 of "The Emperor of Ice-Cream" (*Collected Poems* 64), is evoked by this and similar "urgings of the plot" in Milton's epic (7). Intriguingly slipping from Hume's understanding of "Apparent Queen" as "Undoubted Sovereign," Fowler (648) glosses the phrase as "manifest queen," adding that Milton's phrase is "also playing on 'heir-apparent' (often shortened to 'apparent'). While the moon was clouded (l. 607) her majesty was only presumptive; now, like her light, she is peerless, her succession unchallenged. The effect of the queen's sudden disrobing is heightened by the elaborate images of clothing at ll. 596–9."

608. *peerless:* "Matchless, incomparable, for the *Moon* is the greatest Light then, and darkens *Venus,* by a *Fig.* of *Rhet.*" (Paterson 318). The *OED* cites Milton's line to illustrate the meaning "Without peer; unequalled, matchless."

609. *Silver Mantle:* Hume (154) refers the moon's mantle to the *Aeneid* 7.8–9. Edward S. Le Comte (*Yet Once More* 64) recalls "Over the Pole thy thickest mantle throw" in Milton's *Passion* 30.

610–88. As he notes in his discussion of the first conversation between Adam and Eve (411–91), Stopford Augustus Brooke again sees a movement from "cold philosophy" to "joy" in their second conversation: "Adam calls Eve to sleep; she answers, praising him, in verses, soft as her breath and as the tropic night; and Adam's answer, dull at first in its cold philosophy, passes into poetic beauty when he speaks of the unseen spirits of the Heaven; and his joy at their songs, heard as they haunt the garden, adds a new touch to the interest of Heaven in Man, and to the beauty of Paradise." Brooke also points out, "From noon to midnight we have heard the tale of their hours, as in the next book we hear it from morn to noon—a whole day" (104).

610–33. The main subject of this, Adam's second, speech is prelapsarian labor, as Adam now fully develops the brief remarks about work that he and the narrator make earlier in Book 4 (327–30, 437–39), and the even briefer remark about Adam and Eve's work when the Father in Book 3 looks down "His own works and their works at once to view" (58–59). In *The State of Innocence, and Fall of Man* 3.1.82–91, Dryden's Adam beckons Eve to their "mornings task," claiming that "Some labor ev'n the easiest life would choose: / Our is not great; the dangling boughs to crop, / Whose too luxuriant growth our Alleys stop, / And choak the paths: this our delight requires, / And Heav'n no more of daily work desires." And Dryden's Eve, ominously recalling one of the arguments for separation presented by Milton's Eve at 9.220–25, light-heartedly replies, "I fear small progress will be made this day; / So much our kisses will our task delay" (*Works* 12:115–16). Prelapsarian gardening is seldom discussed, or even noticed, by the early editors and critics, however, with the exception of the Richardsons, who glance at the topic in their impassioned praise of Milton's powers of imagination at 236 ("if Art could tell"). At one point the Richardsons praise the "Picture" of "Paradise and it's Inhabitants, and How they are Employ'd!" (148), and later they contrast the sight of the animals to the "far more Noble Picture...of our First Parents, the Outward and the Inward Man; and How they were Employ'd" (149). After 1734, however, the topic of prelapsarian labor appears to lie dormant until twentieth century critics take it in hand, acknowledging, as does John Halkett, that "Book IV of *Paradise Lost* refers to two external signs of human reason and dignity: labor and love. Both of these are proper only to man" (108).

To be sure, those twentieth century critics do not always agree on how to understand either of those "two external signs of human reason and dignity." In 1900, Walter Raleigh expresses one side of the modern debate about prelapsarian labor, as suggested in **325–40**. He claims that Adam and Eve "have little to do but 'to lop and prune and prop and bind,' to adore their Maker, and to avoid the prohibited tree" (141). While he lists a variety of challenging gardening chores, Raleigh reduces that list to "little," and—unlike the critics writing about prelapsarian labor several decades later—Raleigh separates the gardening chores from Adam and Eve's adoration of God, their love of each other, and the prohibition of the tree. Without addressing Raleigh's dismissal of prelapsarian labor, Allan H. Gilbert ("Milton and the Mysteries" 149) points to a parallel emphasis on Adam and Eve's work in the fourth York play, "God puts Adam and Eve in the Garden of Eden," where God tells both of them, "Looke that ye bothe save and sett, / Erbes and treys for nothyng lette, / So that ye may endower / To susteyn beast and man" (24–27), but it is E. M. W. Tillyard who brings the topic to full-fledged controversy in 1930. His understanding of prelapsarian life is involved in his understanding of Satan as the hero of the poem. Tillyard claims that Milton "fails to convince us that Adam and Eve are happy, because he can find no adequate scope for their active natures." The garden's fecundity renders the gardeners' work "ridiculous," according to Tillyard, and puts Adam and Eve "in the hopeless position of Old Age Pensioners enjoying perpetual youth" (*Milton* 282). At "the climax" of *PL,* then, their virtues, pitted against Satan's "heroic energy," are "inactive virtues" (290). By 1951, though, Tillyard changed his understanding of Satan and the poem's dramatic structure, explaining, "the chief point of the crisis is the delusion of Satan and the ironic defeat of his apparently gigantic efforts by the small decencies of the human pair" (*Studies* 51), but while acknowledging the significance of Adam and Eve's "small decencies," Tillyard does not reconsider the topic of prelapsarian gardening. Opposed to Tillyard's opinion of Milton's pastoral vision, John Crowe Ransom believes that Milton "complicated the simplicity of Eden so that it could not be mistaken for emptiness. He did not leave Adam and Eve stranded without a natural career. Nor had Genesis: for it tells how 'the Lord God took the man and put him into the garden of Eden to dress it and to keep it.' Milton greatly developed this provision, and gave to the man, and the woman too, a fairly realistic occupation. He goes even so far as to risk the critical suggestion that their labor came to seem to them a little burdensome" (*God without Thunder* 128). Through the 1940s, Grant McColley, Sister Mary Irma Corcoran, and Arnold Williams authorize and explicate Milton's presentation of prelapsarian labor by reference to theological tradition. McColley explains that life in paradise is not to be understood as merely contemplative: "In full harmony with Calvin [*Commentaries* 125, 58, 162], [Sylvester's translation of] Du Bartas

[*Divine Weeks and Works* 2.1.1.299–304], Mercer [*Commentarius in Genesin* 55], Pererius [*Commentariorum* 5.35, 44], Willet [*Hexapla in Genesin* 25], and other writers, Milton declared that man should labor, and not live idly, even in Paradise" (*"Paradise Lost": An Account* 153; also see "Paradise Lost" 210n135). Corcoran develops this focus, reporting that, along with Milton, most of the hexameral commentators "held that Adam's days were filled with unarduous and delightful labor which provided salutary discipline and employment with enough pleasant exercises to give him an appetite" (55). In Milton's paradise, however, the work was also "urgent enough to require perseverance if the inhabitants of the garden were to 'tread with ease' (IV, 632)." Corcoran further notes that in the pseudepigrapha, "Eve was thought to have shared equally with Adam in the manual labor required to keep the garden" (77). Finally, Corcoran points to a difference between Milton's views on prelapsarian work in *DocCh* and in *PL*. In the treatise, Milton asserts, "No works whatever were required of Adam" (Patterson, *Works* 15:113), while in the poem, "labor and responsibility were marks of the superiority of man to beast" (56). As he examines the commentaries on Genesis written between 1527 and 1633, Arnold Williams more exclusively focuses on the tension between the figurative and the literal reading of God's command to Adam "to dress . . . and to keep" the garden (Gen. 2.15). Williams (*Common Expositor* 110) reports that, "Though some, following Augustine [*The Literal Meaning of Genesis* 8.10], allegorized this phrase to mean that man should care for his soul and keep it from all evil, the general opinion was that it was to be taken literally. God put man into Paradise to work." Finally, Williams adds, "Donne even construes the dressing and keeping of Paradise into a reason for the active against the contemplative life. Man, he preaches, 'is not sent into this world to live out of it, but to live in it'; Adam was not put into Paradise, only in that Paradise to contemplate the future Paradise, but to dress and keep the present' [*Sermons* 7.04]." This literal-figurative or active-contemplative split figures more and more importantly in the critical discourse about prelapsarian labor through the middle decades of the twentieth century. As one might expect, R. J. Zwi Werblowsky, discussing Satan as hero, echoes Tillyard's view of prelapsarian labor, finding energy and power in Satan but only "quietistic adoration" (69) and "sham activity" (70) in Adam and Eve. Contending that Milton himself could not really believe in the prelapsarian life he assigns to Adam and Eve, David Daiches continues to maintain that Milton "is unable to make their [Adam and Eve's] daily life convincing" (191), but critical opinion appears to swell in such firm opposition to Tillyard's understanding of Edenic gardening that few critics after 1950 even recall it in order to reject it. Instead, the critical intent through the middle decades of the century is to establish the important significance of prelapsarian labor. Taking that work literally, some critics, for example, discuss Adam and Eve's gardening as an expression of the natural human need and desire to work and to establish society. When Adam tells Eve that at dawn, "we must be ris'n, / And at our pleasant labour" (624–25), John Peter reasons, "it is a gardener's 'must,' marking the incentive they both feel to keep their home attractive, neat and trim.... Being the persons they are they naturally take their employment seriously, and it is quite right that they should" (97). Describing Adam and Eve as "suburbanites in the nude," who "are preoccupied with gardening, with their own sexual relations, and with the details of their rudimentary housekeeping," Northrop Frye denies anything humorous in Milton's presentation, and argues instead, "it is Milton's belief that the original state of man was civilized, and that it was far closer to the average life of a seventeenth century Englishman than it was to that of a noble savage" (*Return* 66). Dennis H. Burden similarly understands that Milton "provides labour of a uniquely light kind" as he brings an unusual "marital and domestic" quality to the traditions of pastoral (42). Although he describes the popularity of gardening in Milton's time as "a fashionable high-brow activity," Alastair Fowler nevertheless firmly acknowledges the very literal nature of Adam and Eve's gardening (632). Leland Ryken associates gardening with "a principle of order and civilized regularity"; although set against the garden's abundance, it functions as a mystic oxymoron in Milton's apocalyptic vision (93). In Michael Wilding's analysis, prelapsarian gardening satisfies Adam and Eve's "stimulation drive, involving a need to explore, to manipulate things, a need for stimulation," and as basic to the human condition as the drives of hunger, thirst, and sex (86). Included in the development of figurative readings of prelapsarian work is the concept of worship. Wilding, for example, sees that while the gardening satisfies Adam and Eve's "stimulation drive," it is simultaneously "a manifestation of their worship and love of God" (86), and J. B. Broadbent describes Edenic gardening as "a sacramental expression of Christian love" (*Some Graver Subject* 177), while John Peter (97) finds "it is seemly that Adam and Eve's gratitude should express itself in the desire 'To prune these growing Plants and tend these Flours' (438)." Also quoting Adam's own words (618–19), Leland Ryken similarly describes gardening as "a means of praising the God" (146). As Adam himself states, prelapsarian work simultaneously figures forth, "declares," man's "Dignitie, / And the regard of Heav'n on all his waies" (619–20). Dennis H.

Burden's analysis is typical of this critical understanding: "Indeed Milton makes the command to work itself a mark of God's providence. None of the other creatures are so exhorted, so that the command can be read as a mark of Man's uniquenesst" (44).

Writing in 1960, John Peter and J. B. Broadbent introduce yet another understanding of prelapsarian gardening, however, an understanding that over the following ten years most richly illuminates the roles of Milton's gardeners. Lines 618–19 anchor Peter's remarks: "When Adam says 'Man hath his daily work of body or mind Appointed' (618–19) he reminds us that exertion need not be exclusively physical, and this in turn should remind us that much of their time, like that of children, is spent in discovery, in learning what to think and how to behave" (98). Gardening as education figures as well in Broadbent's reading when he explains that working in their garden, "Adam and Eve do not exploit nature but literally educate her." Broadbent (*Some Graver Subject* 177) elaborates this point when he refers to prelapsarian labor as "a model of order in the commonwealth like the gardening in *Richard II* (III.iv; there are explicit references to Adam and Eve at 73ff.)." The recognition developing here, of course, is that the garden is a metaphor for the gardeners, that the nature of the garden and nature of the gardeners are involved, implicated with each other. The description of the tendrils of Eve's hair (305–9) connects her and Adam to the garden in which they work. In 1945, Corcoran describes prelapsarian gardening as a matter of "control and direction," and that understanding assumes central importance with critics at the close of the 1960s as they explain that in controlling and directing the growth of the garden, Adam and Eve are learning to control and direct their own growth. While Tillyard believed that the garden's lush fecundity had rendered prelapsarian gardening "ridiculous," later critics understand the garden's "excessive luxuriance" (Knight 83) as challenging Adam and Eve to learn about controlling and ordering nature—the garden's, as well as their own. Considering God's command to Adam to "Be fruitful, and multiply, and replenish the earth, and subdue it," Dennis H. Burden probes the association between the lush abundance of nature in the garden and human sexuality: "Since the word [*subdue* in Gen. 1.28] might seem to suggest some wildness on the Garden's part, some possible misrule, Milton has to make it clear that this represents no threat to Man. His first tactic is to read the Garden's wildness as an aspect of its enormous fertility, and hence as an exemplification of the profusion of God's goodness. The common enough distinction between art and nature, between control and abundance, helped to carry him across this problem of the Garden that, though innocent, needed to be subdued.... His second tactic is to link the wildness of the Garden with God's command to the human pair to multiply . . . so that God's promise of children is remedial, providing assistance for their work" (44–45). J. M. Evans and Barbara Kiefer Lewalski present the most thorough analyses of prelapsarian gardening as a propaedeutic activity. Both scholars establish the uniqueness of the garden's lush fecundity and therefore the demanding nature of prelapsarian gardening. The garden's "surprising tendency to excess and disorder," Lewalski explains, "makes Adam and Eve's labor not merely the expected ritual gesture, but a necessary and immense task" (93). Seeing Milton's nature as an anticipation of the Romantic view of nature, Evans notes, "In no previous Eden had there been anything 'overgrown' or 'wanton,' 'unsightly' or 'unsmooth,' to demand Adam's urgent attention" (248). If Adam and Eve failed to tend the garden, Evans argues, "the wilderness outside would soon engulf it," and this situation, he contends, makes for "the most strikingly original feature of Milton's treatment" (249). Evans and Lewalski also most rigorously examine the condition of prelapsarian perfection characterizing both the gardeners and the garden they tend. As Evans implies in the preceding quotation, "The perfection of Adam and Eve no less than the perfection of the garden they inhabit is nothing if not conditional, for it requires their constant vigilance to preserve the balance of forces on which it depends. These forces, being natural, are always trying to grow, so they must be controlled" (268–69). Lewalski describes prelapsarian perfection as "a mode of life steadily increasing in complexity and challenge and difficulty but at the same time and by that very fact, in perfection." Very much aligned with Evans, Lewalski also explains, "Much of the work Adam and Eve perform in Eden is an image of the work they should accomplish in the paradise within" (93). Evans takes his understanding of prelapsarian life back to Philo, who reads the Fall story allegorically in *Allegorical Interpretation of Genesis* 2.3. In Philo's reading, Evans writes, "the tree of knowledge had little or no part to play, and the main emphasis was placed on the command to keep the garden, which meant that Reason was to control the Passions, protect the Virtues, and generally keep the Soul in good order" (249). Suggesting that this moral interpretation "may well have furnished him [Milton] with the theme of his description of the state of innocence" (250), Evans concludes, "Adam and Eve's physical relationship to the garden is in fact an image of their psychological relationship to their own passions and to each other" (250). Frank L. Huntley also brings considerable attention to the significance of prelapsarian gardening, including the difference between the gardening tasks performed by Adam and those performed by Eve. Huntley explains, "Adam's job seems mostly to bind up and cut away the excess branches of the fruit-trees for their growth, while Eve's is to prop up the flowers and to pluck the fruit" (4). While he acknowledges that "Milton avoids a systematic division of labour," Huntley claims, "the simply male and female tasks of Adam and Eve become a metaphor for the whole poem. Paradoxically, Satan lops away their innocence that God's grace may burgeon. And the punishment for disobedience is that mothers create fruit within their wombs and fathers support the children with the sweat of their brows while it is Death who holds the pruning shears" (5). Huntley follows the metaphor's development into the divine scheme of salvation by means of engrafting and transplanting.

610–22. Mockingly critical of Milton's presentation of Adam and Eve, H. A. Taine here compares Adam's remarks to the "pithless sentences" of a "bachelor of arts, in his inaugural address," adding, "This is English virtue and morality; and at evening, in every family it can be read to the children like the Bible" (2.2.298).

610–14. With several cross-references (1.65–67, 183–85, and 2.802), Isabel Gamble MacCaffrey focuses her discussion of *rest* in *PL* on these lines. Identifying the Satanic element in *PL* with restlessness, "the eternal restlessness that is the result of imperfection striving to regain, or attain, perfection" (185), MacCaffrey finds its "antithesis" in Adam and Eve's retirement into the bower (186). When he enters the nuptial bower, Satan violates the order that marks the Edenic experience: "The unquiet of evil is manifest in its disregard for the orderly cycles of rest and waking that are the basis of health in living things" (187).

610. Establishing the principles of Milton's syllabic prosody, S. Ernest Sprott points to the end of this line: "With a classical precedent Milton permits elision of a vowel before an initial *h* which is followed by another vowel, as if in pronunciation the *h* were completely absent" (86–87).

614. *the timely dew of sleep:* editors have always associated this metaphor with a number of literary parallels. Hume (154–55) presents a passage from the *Aeneid* 3.511 as he explains, "Seasonable Sleep is compared to a gentle refreshing

Dew, from its stealing on us, as that descends upon the Earth, at the same time, and as imperceivably." The Richardsons are not specific about the other poets comparing sleep to dew but are much more zealous in their admiration: "What a Description of Drowsiness! the Dew of Sleep; falling on the Eye-lids Soft as Dew, yet giving a Grateful kind of Heaviness, Inclining, bearing down, from the Latin *Inclino*. Did not the Beauty of the Poetry keep the Mind Awake, the Words would Lull the Reader Insensibly" (170). Verity (466) specifies two Shakespearean references to the dew of sleep: *Richard III* 4.1.84 and *Julius Caesar* 2.1.230, to which Merritt Y. Hughes ("Variorum") adds *The Faerie Queene* 1.1.36.

624–26. As he argues that English Renaissance tragedy transformed Milton's concept of epic, James Holly Hanford ("Dramatic Element" 181) points to this sequence and 646–49: "The utterances in *Paradise Lost* are, on the whole, less static than is common in earlier epics, and more responsive to the situation. The setting is more often brought before us, not in the narration, but through description put into the mouths of the characters in the scene." The specific dramatic parallel Hanford cites here is *Romeo and Juliet* 3.1.1–8.

625–29. Isabel Gamble MacCaffrey, asserting the importance of the concept of rule in *PL*, contends that the main effect of the "submerged suggestion of unruly nature" in this sequence is "to enhance the power and wisdom of Adam, ruling the wilderness. The notion of order as something positive and created, to be maintained by effort of will, is consonant, however, with Milton's general view of the contending forces in the universe, and with one strenuous strain in Puritanism" (154–55).

626. *Arbors…Allies:* Hume endeavors to establish the practical difference between these two features of the garden: "*Arbors*, Coverts, made shady by the Boughs of Trees, of *Arbor*, Lat. a Tree. *Allies*, Close Walks, of *Aller*, Fr. to go" (155). B. A. Wright ("Note on Milton's Diction" 147) concedes that Hume's understanding of *Arbors* might be accurate, but he also offers the obsolete meaning of "A flower garden or bed [*OED* 2]." The *OED*, however, also indicates the interinvolvement of *Arbors* and *Allies*. *OED* definition 5.b, for example, cites Milton's use here to illustrate another obsolete meaning for *Arbor*, "A shaded or covered alley or walk." Defining *Alley* (II.2) as "A walk in a garden, park, shrubbery, maze, or wood, generally bordered with trees, or bushes; an avenue; also the spaces between beds of flowers or plants, or between the rows of hops in a hop-garden," the *OED* cites Milton's *Mask* 311–12: "Each lane, and every alley green Dingle or bushy dell of this wild wood." Also see the Richardsons in **627**.

John R. Knott associates the alley of trees with the reference to God as a "sovran Planter" (691): "Wherever Milton got the idea for his alley of trees, he presents them as part of the order in the mind of God, one more example, of the way in which God has combined order with delight in the Garden" ("Symbolic Landscape" 45).

627. The Richardsons point out that the plural *walks* appears in the first but in no subsequent edition, and they suggest that the change was made "because it might be Understood as if the Arbours were for Walking in as well as the Alleys, whereas Those were for Repose after Weariness by Walking in the Long Alleys, Dressing the Garden. *&c.*" Sensitive to the practical details shaping life within the garden throughout the course of a day, the Richardsons then turn to "branches overgrown," understanding them as "too Luxuriant, So as to be Troublesome, and therefore wanted to be *Reform'd:* not that they grew Over the Alleys, so as to make what they call *Berceau* Walks; Such indeed These were, they were their Noon Walks, and the more Overgrown in That Sense the Better" (170). Also see **626**.

628. *manuring:* Hume and the Richardsons establish the meaning through the French *manoeuvre,* Hume defining it as "Labouring, Tilling, Cultivating the Earth" (155), and the Richardsons defining it as "Working with Hands... 'tis, as immediately after, to Lop, to Rid away what is scattered" (170–71).

R. C. Browne (1:353) points out that Iago similarly uses this term in *Othello* 1.3.324, while Robert Vaughan (102) cross-references Milton's *RCG:* "The manuring hand of the tiller shall root out all that burdens the soil" (Patterson, *Works* 3:214).

629. *wanton:* this word is one of several recurring not only in Book 4 but also between Books 4 and 9, and, as is explained in the commentary on Eve's "wanton ringlets" (see **304–11**), *wanton* is one of the most provocative words in Book 4. While *wanton* describes Eve ringlets, for example, it will shortly come to describe the mask (768) so vigorously condemned in the narrator's hymn to wedded love. The very phrase "wanton growth" appears in Book 9 as Eve initiates the separation debate with Adam (9.211), and when the serpent later approaches her, he does so curling "many a wanton wreath" (9.517). *Wanton* recurs in *PL* 1.414, 1.454, and 11.583, as well as frequently throughout the shorter poems. In the "Glossary" to his edition, A. W. Verity defines *wanton* as literally meaning "'unrestrained'; hence 'luxuriant,' as used of growth, IX. 211," and he refers this understanding to *A Midsummer Night's Dream* 2.1.99–100. When *wanton* describes motion, such as the serpent's at 9.517, Verity explains that "it implies 'tossing about'" (723).

630. Merritt Y. Hughes ("Variorum") cross-references 248: "rich Trees wept odorous Gummes and Balme."

632. *Ask:* A. W. Verity (466) glosses the word with *require* and explains it as a common Elizabethan usage.

634. Richard Bentley (129–30) here makes the intriguing suggestion that Milton is courting the favor of female readers: "Our Author, through his whole Poem, had certainly that in his View, to make the Female Sex favour it. But here he seems to incline needlesly [*sic*] too much to *Eve's* outside, even with straining of his Verse. I would have made it, to comprehend both her outward and inward Endowments, *To whom thus Eve with perfect* GIFTS *adorn'd.*"

635–88. The intensity of Addison's praise for the earlier exchange between Adam and Eve (411–91) carries into his commentary on their second conversation, and especially Eve's reply to Adam, which, Addison writes, "is dress'd up in such a soft and natural Turn of Words and Sentiments, as cannot be sufficiently admired" (*Spectator* 3:177). See Addison in **411–91**.

G. Wilson Knight and, considerably later, Philip Brockbank admire the interconnections between the evening conversation of Adam and Eve and the actual celestial order that brings on night as they talk. According to Knight, Milton creates "the very mystery of darkness, of otherness, of nothingness charged with a presence," and this mystery "is the concern of Eve's question…concerning the stars, so beautiful while men sleep." When Adam, answering Eve's question, refers to the "spiritual creatures" who "walk the earth / Unseen" (677–78),

Knight argues that those creatures "are continuous with the nightingale itself, their 'celestial voices' [682] sounding from 'hill' [681] and 'thicket' [681]. They grow from a soil, an atmosphere, already realized" (191). Knight also notices how the setting contributes to the Edenic love theme: "Finally, this new and atmospheric recognition, itself a kind of love, blends delicately into the human love of Adam and Eve: the two are interdependent" (103). Brockbank explains that both Eve's love song and Adam's reply express aesthetic and moral values by reference to the astronomical order of Eden: "Eve's love for Adam is expressed through hyperboles that seem both to transcend and to intensify the ceremonious daily round" (203). So, too, Brockbank continues, "Adam's love responds with a grave and marvelling account of the celestial order, and of the voices that sing to the midnight air (IV, 659–88). Milton in this passage may well be remembering Lorenzo's nocturnal courtship of Jessica in Shakespeare's Belmont [*The Merchant of Venice* 5.1.1–22]; but, together with a comparable eagerness to find cosmic sanction for the tenderness of lovers, there is an austerer purpose; Milton is out to offer a humanly satisfying astronomical teleology" (204).

635–58. Eve's love poem (639–56), the heart of this, her second, speech, has probably received more unreserved critical admiration than any other set piece in Book 4, the spirit of B. A. Wright's question, "Where is there a lovelier love poem?" coloring much of the criticism of the passage (*Milton's "Paradise Lost"* 57). In Eve's brief remarks framing that love poem, however, in her opening formal address to Adam (635–38), that is, and in her final abrupt inquiry about the stars (657–58), several critics have heard disturbing suggestions about the character of the woman who sings, "Sweet is the breath of morn" (641).

635–38. Apparently first to suspect the sincerity of Eve's address to Adam is James Paterson, who snappishly attacks Milton's Eve, as well as all her daughters, when he exclaims, "Here, is Eve's supposed Answer, full of Duty and Obedience to her H[u]sband.... A most excellent and useful *Lesson* to all *Wives*. Happy they, if they would take it!" (319). Two centuries later, Denis Saurat and Howard Schultz also question Eve's integrity as she opens this speech, and their readings, unlike Paterson's, elicit critical replies. While he acknowledges that Eve asserts Adam's superiority, Saurat claims that she does so "with a modesty which is mostly coquetry, and certainty of her own power" (161). Childishness, the "pleasant pout," is what Schultz sees in Eve at this point, and what he hears is "the reluctance of a girl too fond of the night to wish to leave it." Schultz contends that a sigh marks Eve's concession of "Adam's right to command. Like a child when thus told to go to bed, she does indeed go, but not before she has had another word. In the rest of the same speech she does not quite leave Adam's bidding 'unargued'" ("Satan's Serenade" 20). Firmly opposed to these readings are those of Balachandra Rajan, Sacvan Bercovitch, and J. M. Evans. In *"Paradise Lost" and the Seventeenth Century Reader,* published a year before Schultz's essay, Rajan hears Eve's epithets for Adam as notes contributing to the "gentler, more nostalgic music" that he understands as the verbal style associated with paradise. Rajan contends, "The resultant lyricism, which could be cloying more often than it is, is saved usually by an insistent sense of proportion and by the severe yet joyous formality of its ritual. The elaborate, studied, courtesy of Adam and Eve's addresses to each other helps to stabilize this structure of ceremony which is buttressed also by the recurrent hymns. One thinks first in this connection of the stately, reiterated cadences of Eve's second address to Adam and the fervid solemnity of the hymn on wedded love" (130). In Eve's words here, as in Adam's successful argument for a mate in Book 8, Bercovitch finds evidence that "Adam and Eve before their fall embody respectively the concepts of justice and love" (250), the values that Bercovitch argues are first expressed in the union of the Father and the Son, and the values that "combine to show man the way to obedience" (243). J. M. Evans (254) believes that, in these lines, Eve "affirms her duty, her submission to and love for her husband," and he argues that such is "the criterion by which we are to judge her response to Adam's arguments during the crucial discussion that prefaces the Fall in Book IX."

The association that Evans makes between Eve's assertion of submission to Adam as her "Author and Disposer" and their separation debate in Book 9 is one several other modern critics mention. Louis L. Martz, for example, contrasts these "grand titles" that descibe Adam and Eve in Book 4 with the terminology used for the separation debate, where they are introduced as "the human pair" (397) and where they address each other as "Adam" and "Eve." Martz's point is, "The more we see of them and the more we hear them talk, the more they seem like us" (*"Paradise Lost:* The Power" 39). Marjorie Barstow (120) identifies the epithets exchanged by Adam and Eve as "poetic conventionalities" that immediately disappear from postlapsarian conversations, while Merritt Y. Hughes specifically traces those epithets to Homer's heroes (*Complete Poems* 293). Alastair Fowler (650) identifies as "prelapsarian" such titles as these with which Eve addresses Adam, but Fowler believes that they "are as much Biblical, however, as epic," and he specifically links Eve's "My Author" (635) to the Authorized Version's marginal note on Acts 3.15, which describes the second Adam as the "author of life," and to Heb. 12.2, which describes him as the "author and finisher of faith."

635–37. Patrick Hume (155) cross-references earlier passages in Book 4: "Hee for God only, shee for God in him" (299), and "O thou for whom / And from whom…" (440–41).

635. *My Author:* "*Fr. Lat.* The first Cause of a Thing, a Beginner and Head of a Society or Party. Here *Adam* is so called by *Eve*" (Paterson 319).
   Disposer: "*Fr.* from the *Lat.* i.e. A Placer; a Commander, Manager, Ruler. Here, *Adam*, by a *Fig.* of *Rhet.*" (Paterson 319). The *OED 2*, "One who regulates or governs; a controller, manager, director, ruler," cites Milton's use here.

639–56. While Patrick Hume's earliest annotations, much like Todd's, trace a number of the pastoral elements in Eve's love poem to classical parallels, it is Addison who clearly acknowledges how those elements function as a vital context for Eve's declaration of love for Adam. Quoting from Virgil's *Eclogues* 3.87–88 and *Georgics* 4.169, 511, Hume declares the sequence "An Imitation of Virgil's Pastoral Plainness and Sweetness" (155; also see Todd [1842], 2:90–91). Addison, however, considers the more dynamic nature of the pastoral element in Eve's love poem: "*Eve,* tho' in Paradise it self, [is] no further pleased with the beautiful Objects around her, than as she sees them in Company with *Adam*" (*Tatler* 2:184). In addition, Addison observes, "though the sweetness of these Verses has something in it of a Pastoral, yet it excels the ordinary kind, as much as the Scene of it is above an ordinary Field or Meadow" (2:246). Later critics and commentators continue to develop the pastoral element of Eve's love poem. David Daiches notes that the theme of Eve's love lyric "has long been a stock one in love poetry from the mediaeval lyric to the love songs of Hollywood—nature is beautiful, but without the loved one its beauty is meaningless" (192).
   More like Addison, a number of other modern critics, however, emphasize how Eve's expression of love within this pastoral setting "excels the ordinary kind." Douglas Bush, for example, believes, "It would not be easy to find the equal of that [Eve's love poem] in English pastoral verse, but it is clearly not

human dialogue. It is a carefully composed poem on the beauty of human love and its harmony with nature" (*"Paradise Lost" in Our Time* 114). Roy Daniells and Peter Berek also emphasize the extraordinary quality of Eve's words. Daniells sees here, as in Adam's later cry that Eden without Eve would be "wild Woods forlorn" (9.910), the "psychological counterpart" to the "magnificent world in which they live" ("Happy Rural Seat" 15). Berek writes, "In their state of innocence, they [Adam and Eve] are capable of using language not to manipulate the facts of the real world [as do the fallen speakers of the epic] but simply to reveal it." Eve's love poem to Adam beautifully demonstrates this quality of innocent human speech: "Eve fixes upon the loveliness of nature. But she singles out the *process* of nature.... And nothing could be more orderly than its [the poem's] structure" (244).

It is Joseph Addison who first anticipates such tributes to the "orderly...structure" of Eve's love poem. Describing the lyric as "inexpressibly charming" (*Tatler* 2:184), he quotes it in its entirety in the *Tatler* (2:181–85), and then praises the poem's remarkable structure as evidence refuting Dryden's charge, presented in the *Discourse Concerning the Original and Progress of Satire* that he could find "no Elegant turns, either on the word, or on the thought" in Milton (*Works* 4:84–85). Addison not only points to Eve's poem as a example of epanadiplosis, "turn of words or thoughts," but he recognizes the inextricable involvement of that rhetorical device with the nature of her love for Adam. "The Variety of Images in this Passage is infinitely pleasing, and the Recapitulation of each particular Image, with a little varying of the Expression, makes one of the finest Turns of Words that I have ever seen" (2:185). Concluding his essay, Addison quotes 2.557–61 as another example of Milton's success with the rhetorical figure of the epanadiplosis (2:185). The "Turns of Words" that Addison first praises continue to gain the attention of twentieth century critics. Steadily acknowledged as an impressive rhetorical flourish, the epanadiplosis is increasingly appreciated as a device descriptive of the complexity of the paradisal love encircling Adam and Eve. As the century opens, Walter Raleigh recalls Addison's reproach of Dryden, and while he admits that there are rhetorical turns in Milton's longer poems, Raleigh specifies none, concluding, "Yet in the main Dryden is right, for even instances like these are not many" (208). Less grudging is A. W. Verity (466), who, declaring Eve's love poem "A striking example of the poetic artifice called *epanadiplosis* or 'repetition,'" cross-references Milton's use of the same rhetorical device at 7.25–26. Edward S. Le Comte identifies Eve's love poem as "Milton's masterpiece of repetitive art, which is to say that English poetry can produce no equal to it" (*Yet Once More* 26), and in the following year, 1954, W. K. Wimsatt, pointing to 3.294–98, similarly writes, "These are the figures which Dryden in 1693 calls 'turns, both on the words and on the thought,' and which, despite a report by Dryden to the contrary, are nowhere better illustrated than in Milton's *Paradise Lost*" (179). Helen Darbishire ("Milton's Poetic Language" 50–51), also recalling Dryden's words, notes the turns in *PL* 1.66, 2.623–24, and 9.648, while Warren Chernaik sets the turn in Eve's love poem against Satan's turn on "know" in his retort to Ithuriel and Zephon: "In Milton, the turn is a central element in the structure and progression of the blank verse line and is capable of wide variations in tone. The lyric simplicity of the first example [641–56] and the power and subtlety of the second [828–30] are appropriate to the two speakers, Eve and Satan" (215–16). As she considers this topic, Isabel Gamble MacCaffrey adds greatly to the modern critical appreciation of the relationship between Adam and Eve's love and the circling processes of the natural pastoral world containing it. Discussing Milton's ability to modulate time into spatial effects in *PL,* MacCaffrey declares, "The finest of all the transformations of time in Eden takes place when its changing sameness is re-enacted in Eve's beautiful iterative speech to Adam." For Eve, "Adam *is* Eden," MacCaffrey argues: "In her communion with him, the constancy of Paradise, the sweetness and benevolence underlying all its superficial changes, reach their culmination." Of the element of repetition in Eve's lyric, MacCaffrey writes, "The repetition, almost word for word, of her speech, enacts a timeless recurrence that is confirmed both in the sense of the words and in Milton's picture of Paradise as a whole" (77). Anne Davidson Ferry's analysis of the structure of Eve's love poem also continues more closely to scrutinize the link between the lovers and the temporal world of recurrent change in which they love. Establishing the embracing Adam and Eve as the center of all the poem's circling, Ferry details how even the language of Eve's "loveliest speech, her archetypal love poem…revolves in circles around him" (*Milton's Epic Voice* 161). Ferry sees the poem's structure as "an unbroken circle of repetition upon repetition," and she points out how individual words and word patterns are repeated, while the poem's first section is repeated, yet reversed and negated, in the poem's second section. "Patterns of sound are repeated," Ferry also explains, "especially soft *f, s,* and *r* sounds which elsewhere throughout *Paradise Lost* are associated with 'fair' Eve's 'sweetness' and 'grace.' By this association Milton suggests that the qualities of pastoral nature are the qualities of Eve. She is as 'sweet' as the morn (to which Adam, who rarely uses similes, twice compares her), as 'soft' as showers, as 'fair' as the moon. Throughout the poem her inner and outer natures are described by these adjectives (which characteristically have both concrete and abstract meanings), and she is repeatedly associated with the image of the moon as she personifies it here" (162–63). Rehearsing MacCaffrey's reading, Alastair Fowler more emphatically heightens the level of praise for the structure of Eve's "Sweet" poem and brings even more detail to Addison's appreciation of its "Turns" by naming yet other rhetorical figures at work in 639–56: epanalepsis, epanodos, merismus, and irmus. While Ferry discusses Eve's poem as an eighteen-line unit consisting of eleven (639–49) plus seven (650–56) lines, Fowler looks at it as a sixteen-line unit (641–56), which he sees divided into sections of nine and seven: "Numerologically, 16 divided in this way, into portions of 9 and 7, symbolizes virtue harmoniously adjusting the mutable to the heavenly, *anima* to *mens,* soul to mind." Fowler continues, "Note that the 9-line spiritual portion refers to Paradise with Adam, the mutable 7-line portion to Paradise without Adam. In the latter portion each item in the former suffers alteration; though this alteration is as yet hypothetical and held in check by negation" (650; also see Fowler in **652–53**).

A few years earlier, Louis L. Martz, similarly recalling MacCaffrey's provocative phrase "transformations of time," presents a reading of Eve's love poem that acknowledges its elegiac undercurrent. Explaining that Eve's love song expresses the qualities marking paradise as a whole, "all organic, all alive, all a harmony," Martz acknowledges that "an effect of ritual celebration certainly emerges here, as it does elsewhere, on specific, local occasions" (*Paradise Within* 120), but referencing MacCaffrey's reading, Martz (121) glances ahead to hear a threatening note in Eve's sudden question about the stars, reminding readers that such timeless moments "cannot be maintained for long."

Finally, John Halkett (102) contends that the "sophisticated repetition" of Eve's love poem "resembles the chiming speeches of characters in Shakespeare's comedies — for instance Orlando and the Duke Senior in *As You Like It,* II.7.113–126."

639. Todd suggests, "This beautiful and affectionate avowal may remind the reader of a similar picture of patriarchal simplicity, *Gen.* xxix.20. 'And Jacob served seven years for Rachel; and they seemed unto him but a few days, for the love he had to her'" ([1842], 2:90).

640. *seasons:* the Richardsons establish meaning and cross-reference 5.170, 9.200: "All Times, Morning, Noon, *&c.* as it is explain'd Immediately Afterwards. 'tis not Spring, Summer, *&c.* Those were not Yet Changing, 'twas Now an Eternal Spring, *v.* 268. He uses Seasons for Hours, as the *Greeks* do Hours for Seasons" (171). Agreeing with the Richardsons, Alastair Fowler (650) cross-references 8.69, where Raphael directs Adam to pursue knowledge of God's "Seasons, Hours, or Dayes, or Months, or Years."

641. *Sweet:* Edward Bysshe offers this line as one of the entries under "Sweet" in *The Art of English Poetry* (391; Bysshe prints *is* in "Sweet is" as *as*).

the breath of morn: Todd ([1842], 2:90) first refers this phrase to "the original passage in *Solomon's Song,* ii.17. 'Till the day *breathe*'; which in our translation of the Bible is rendered, less poetically, 'Till the day *break*,' " and James H. Sims returns to that association in *The Bible in Milton's Epics.* Sims's reading of Eve's love poem focuses on the similarity between Eve and the bride in the Song of Solomon who desires to rise "By night … and go about the city," and especially significant to Sims is that like the bride, Eve speaks of the rising of the morning as "the breath of morn." Sims explains that the Hebrew word translated as "breath" in this verse elsewhere in the Authorized Version is translated as " 'blow,' 'puff,' 'utter,' and 'speak.' The Biblical Bride is thinking of the day, or morning, as breathing soft airs as it rises; Eve speaks of the breath of morn in its rising, accompanied by 'charm of earliest Birds' wafted on gentle breezes. This brief Hebraic phrase … is followed, after Eve's Satanically induced dream, by Adam's awaking Eve in Book V (ll. 17–25) in language strongly reminiscent of the Bridegroom's words to the bride in the Song of Solomon 2:10–13" (93). Also see Sims in **657–58.**

642. *charm:* tracing this word through the Latin *carmen* to the Italian *ciarma,* Patrick Hume glosses it as "Song" (155), as do such modern editors as Alastair Fowler (650) and Merritt Y. Hughes (*Complete Poems* 293), who supplies a cross-reference to *PR* 4.257, while A. W. Verity unpacks the word's more complicated etymology, first suggested apparently in R. C. Browne's annotation. Browne (1:353) points out that in Old English "*charm* was a low, murmuring noise, whence a *charm* (or flock) of goldfinches." In his notes, Verity (466) glosses *charm* as "song," notes that it is "used sometimes in the wider sense of harmonious notes, music," and quotes the following passage from John Bunyan's *The*

Holy War 219: "The men of Mansoul also were greatly concerned at this melodious charm of the trumpets." In the "Glossary," Verity elaborates: "M[ilton] may have supposed it to be derived from Lat. *carmen*, 'song,' but really *charm* as used of the song of birds is of Anglo-Saxon origin. It is a variant form of Middle E[nglish] *cherme* or *chirm* = A[nglo] S[axon] *cirm*." Verity goes on to report several dialect expressions with *charm*, and then praises Tennyson's accurate use in the fourth stanza of *The Progress of Spring:* "I hear a charm of song thro' all the land" (*Poems* 1:519). Finally, Verity returns to *carmen:* "Probably *cherme* or *chirm* would never have got this variant form *charm* but for the influence of Lat. *carmen*" (700–1). Verity's remarks accord with the *OED* 1: "The blended singing or noise of many birds; the blended voices of school-children, and the like." The *OED* cites Milton's line. Helen Darbishire and B. A. Wright present the same argument about the etymology, Wright identifying *charm* as one of the "homely" words (*Milton's "Paradise Lost"* 74) and Darbishire as one of the poet's "country words" (*Milton's "Paradise Lost"* 12). James H. Sims (*Bible* 135n18) cross-references *charm* in 9.999.

Allan H. Gilbert (*Geographical Dictionary* 20) and Evert Mordecai Clark (140) point out that, in *Purchas His Pilgrimage* 7.5, Purchas similarly describes the sound of the birds in his description of Amara.

644. *orient:* Anne Davidson Ferry discusses this word as one of those ritualistically repeated words with multiple meanings most characteristic of the narrator's metaphorical style because they "express divine unity of vision" (*Milton's Epic Voice* 98). Pointing out that *orient* means "resplendent," "rising," and "eastern," and is often associated with the sun, Ferry writes, "The most familiar because the most effective use of 'orient' occurs in Eve's beautiful love lyric" (99). Verity finds that the meaning "rising" from the Latin *oriens* "is possible" (713).

645. *Glistring . . . fragrant:* Hume, ending with a quotation from Virgil's *Georgics* 4.169, notes, "Shining with Pearly Dew-drops. *Glist'ring. . . . Fragrant,* Lat *Fragrans,* smelling sweet" (155). Todd ([1842], 2:91) glosses Milton's line with a quotation from "A Remedie for Love," a poem attributed to Sidney that was printed at the end of the thirteenth edition of the *Arcadia* published in 1674: "And sweet, as after gentle showers / The breath is of some thousand flowers."

646. *showers:* referencing her preceding note on *Flowers* (501), Helen Darbishire explains that *showers* "is always a monosyllable in *Paradise Lost* spelt *showr* or *showre* (*v.* xi. 883); except sometimes at the end of the line, *v.* l. 653 *infra,* and here at the caesura where it is spelt *showers*" (*Poetical Works* 1:296).

646–49. See James Holly Hanford in **624–26.**

647. *silent Night:* Edward S. Le Comte acknowledges that Milton's phrase may be found in both Virgil and Homer, as well as in Milton's *El* 4.114 and *Idea* 27, but, Le Comte adds, "it does not matter," for in this sequence, "Milton is the magician (song is indeed 'charm' with him), holding us fascinated by his incantation and his rhythmical movement" (*Yet Once More* 28).

648. *her solemn Bird:* Hume's rather detailed annotation on *solemn* suggests something of the feeling in Louis L. Martz's reference to "ritual celebration" in his commentary in **639–56.** As he so often does, Hume considers the meaning of the word's Latin root, *solemnis:* "perform'd at certain times of the Year, thence the word is used for *accustomed, usual.*" To establish that definition, Hume cites line 101 of Horace's first epistle, to Maecenas, "insanire putas sollemnia me"; "you think my madness is the usual thing." Quoting from Virgil (*Aeneid* 6.380), Hume adds, however, "*Solemn* does also signifie serious, grave, stately, as the Shews, Pomps and Assemblies, at Funerals and other Ceremonious Meetings," as he concludes, again citing Virgil (*Georgics* 4.511), as well as Tasso's *Gerusalemme Liberata* 18.18: "So that in this sense the Nightingal may be esteem'd a solemn mournful Bird" (155).

Quoting *IlPen,* which establishes the nightingale as "most musical, most melancholy," Newton (279) cross-references 7.435, where the bird is described as "the solemn nightingale."

649. Todd ([1842], 2:91) lines up a series of similar metaphors from Spenser's *Hymn to Heavenly Love,* where the heaven is "adorned with ten thousand *gems* of shining gold" (*Poetical Works* 593), to Sylvester's translation of Du Bartas's *The Divine Weeks and Works* 1.4.540, to Pope's *Odyssey* 15.123 (*Poems* 10:74), to Ben Jonson's "On the Lady Jane Pawleet, Marchion: of Winton" 87 in *Underwood* (*Ben Jonson* 8:271).

652–53. Alastair Fowler (651) continues his close analysis of the rhetorical devices in Eve's love poem as he focuses on these lines: "Note how *herb…dew,* merismus at ll. 644f, is now varied to an independent *enumeratio.* The passage is full of such theme-and-variation effects, which enact Eve's responsiveness to Adam, and perhaps (proleptically) the effect of her independence." See Fowler in **639–56**.

653. *showers:* Dennis H. Burden identifies the watering of the garden as one of the problems facing Milton: "Genesis 2:5–6 says that the earth is without rain though there is a mysterious dewfall, but it appears later in the same chapter (V.10) that there is a river which waters the Garden. Genesis does not say how this river is replenished, nor whether there is thereafter rain. Milton's Garden however is typically unmagical and is watered by mists and showers" (42). Also see earlier discussion of the garden's river and irrigation system in **223–40**.

654–56. Acknowledging that "the preposition 'without' has always, I believe, taken the accent on the second syllable in English speech," B. A. Wright observes, "Milton not infrequently in *Paradise Lost* accents the first syllable and his treatment of this word illustrates some points of his technique" ("Stressing" 202). Wright then comments on these concluding lines of Eve's love poem, insisting that "to accent otherwise is to deny the full stress, the proper dwelling of the voice on 'thee,' and to spoil the conclusion of one of the most beautiful lyrical movements in English verse" (203). Also see Wright on "without Thorn the Rose" in **256**.

654. *Eevning:* Helen Darbishire (*Poetical Works* 1:296) points out that the spelling in the first edition is *Evening,* and she supports the spelling of the second edition by reference to the same explanation that she provides for *Eevning* in **151**.

657–58. Eve's questioning Adam about the shining of the stars has provoked a wide range of twentieth century commentary; initially criticized—even condemned—Eve has more lately come to be commended, however, for her inquiry. Those condemning Eve have found her approaching, if not revealing, sins such as pride, curiosity, selfishness, and greed. A. W. Verity (466), for example, associates Eve's question with Pope's *Essay on Man* 1.131–32 (*Poems*

3.1.31): "Ask for what end the heav'nly bodies shine, / Earth for whose use? Pride answers, ''Tis for mine.'" Writing in 1948, Howard Schultz contrasts Eve's concern with the pleasures of the night and Adam's concern with their daily work: "She has now to add, this time clearly on the intellectual side, the gravest of her faults—an imprudent question which, though innocent in itself, in the light of what Adam has just told her, constitutes an approach to the grievous sin of curiosity" ("Satan's Serenade" 21). Also contrasting Eve's question and Adam's focus on their work, Jon S. Lawry (177) similarly brings charges against Eve: "Against Adam's reasonable image of man's duty to 'lop [the] wanton growth' (IV, 629) of otherwise too luxuriant nature, Eve opposes a selfish question indicting God of waste or of abundance in the nature of things, almost as if to anticipate not only her prelapsarian greed but also her postlapsarian suggestion that all procreation cease [10.979–89]." Although he does not so forthrightly indict Eve for her question, Merritt Y. Hughes ("Variorum") associates her admiration of "This glorious sight" with Comus's joy in "the Strarry Quire" in Milton's earlier *Mask* 112. While in his 1948 essay he contends that Eve's question "constitutes an approach to the grievous sin of curiosity," in *Milton and Forbidden Knowledge* (1955), Howard Schultz takes another look at this episode, as he juxtaposes Eve's question to Adam's later remarks about nature's "disproportions" (8.27) and "superfluous hand" (8.27) during his dialog with Raphael: "Adam erred more seriously than his mate in that he impugned not only the wisdom of God, but also the dignity of man by his criticism of man's dwelling" (182). As the 1960s draw to a close, censuring Eve because of her inquiry about the "glittering Starr-light" ceases, and critics, especially Barbara Kiefer Lewalski and J. M. Evans, move instead to argue that Eve's question, as well as Adam's answer, is to be commended. Although he believes that in Eve's concern with the stars is found "a tincture of questioning God's creative purpose," Michael Lieb rules that her question is "innocent" (188), and Leland Ryken describes the question-and-answer session as "an exhibition of Adam's superior knowledge" (166). More precisely situating Eve's question and Adam's answer within the challenging nature of prelapsarian life, Lewalski and Evans emphatically reject any charge against Eve and instead look at her dialog with Adam as evidence of their intellectual and moral growth. Lewalski explains, "Eve's query about astronomy is a response to the challenge of Nature, an effort to extend knowledge of Nature's ways by speculation." Nevertheless, Lewalski continues, "the question involves certain faulty assumptions—that not only the earth but the entire cosmos was made for man, and that it was made somewhat inexpertly...—assumptions that, if uncorrected, could lead to overweening human pride" (101). As he corrects those "dangerous assumptions," Adam, Lewalski argues, "reestablishes the right moral context for speculations about nature" (101–02). Similarly underscoring how the episode presents the intellectual and moral growth of Adam and Eve, Evans believes this is their "first experience of night," and he builds his reading upon the significance of Milton's response to the rabbinic tradition of the first night: "The Rabbis...had portrayed Adam's fear of the approaching darkness as a symptom of his fallen ignorance and guilt, and Dracontius [*Carmen de Deo*, col. 732] had readapted the incident to illustrate unfallen Man's gradual realization of the natural cycle of day and night. Milton follows Dracontius in placing the episode before the Fall, but uses it to reveal not Adam's original innocence but his wisdom" (254). Geoffrey Bullough and James H. Sims trace Eve's interest in the night to a similar interest shared by several other women. Bullough points out that not only does Eve in Jacob Cats's *Trou-Ringh* 7 initially resist Adam's advances, as does Milton's Eve, but Cats's Eve, like Milton's, also asks Adam why the stars shine at night. Bullough concludes that the "comparison between the poems illustrates the two poets' participation in the Protestant culture of their century and their individual approaches to theological and moral topics of importance at the time" (120). As in his earlier note on "the breath of morn," Sims (93) compares Milton's Eve with the bride in Song of Sol. 3.1–2, "who desires to rise 'by night...and go about the citie.'" See Sims in **641**.

660–88. Adam's reply to Eve's query consists of two distinct, yet interrelated, sentences, the first (660–73) a brief astronomy lecture, and the second (674–88) a description of the praise offered God by those "Millions of spiritual Creatures" who "keep watch" throughout the night.

660–73. The Richardsons set Adam's brief remarks to Eve about astronomy against Raphael's astronomy lecture in 8.66–178, while Patrick Hume, like several twentieth century critics, attempts to clarify Adam's knowledge of science. As Adam "talks very Naturally, as not being yet Better instructed," so, the Richardsons claim, "Eve is as Naturally Fully Satisfy'd with Her Husband's Superiour Understanding," but when Raphael delivers his astronomy lecture, "Neither Then was he [Adam] Taught Much more Philosophy of This Kind, but far Better" (171). Also see Schultz in **657–58**; Hughes, *Complete Poems*

293; Fowler 651. Unlike the Richardsons, Patrick Hume engages with the "Philosophy" in Adam's comments to Eve, specifically the topic of "stellar vertue" (671). All plants, vegetable, and "superiour living Creatures," Hume reports, are said to "have one at least of these celestial eyes, that with its Astral influence particularly regards and cherisheth all of its kind; hence that Astrological division of 'em into *Saturnine, Jovial, Martial, Mercurial, Venereal,* and *Lunar* Plants, according to the respective qualities *shed down* and *infused* into them by their presiding Planets" (156). Among the moderns, George Wesley Whiting, Merritt Y. Hughes, and Alastair Fowler add to and clarify the discussion of "stellar vertue" that Hume initiates, while they, like others, also often touch on the literary or scientific sources of Milton's knowledge. Whiting sets Adam's words against Sir Walter Ralegh's remarks on astral influence in *The History of the World* 1.1.11. Quoting Ralegh's claim that stars were created as "instruments and Organs of his [God's] divine Providence, so far as it hath pleased his just will to determine," Whiting believes that "Raleigh is fully convinced that the stars have decided effects." Cautious about source studies, however, Whiting merely concludes that Ralegh and Milton may have "shared the belief in a mild form of astrology" (*Milton's Literary Milieu* 44). Like Whiting, Hughes ("Variorum") refers Adam's views on "stellar vertue" to Ralegh's *History* but adds, "The biblical authority is the 'sweet influences of Pleiades' (Job 38.31), to which Milton expressly alludes in 7.374–75." Even more emphatically, however, Hughes develops the similarity between Adam's reply to Eve and George Hakewill's *An Apologie or Declaration of the Power and Providence of God* 98, in which Hakewill explains that "the *Sunne* and the *Starres* infuse a warmth into these *Sub-celestial* Bodies." Hakewill argues that it is "very reasonable...that light, the most *Divine* affection of the *Celestiall* Bodies, should be the cause of *warmth,* the most *noble, active,* and excellent quality of the subcelestiall." Strengthening the Hakewill-Milton association, Hughes ("Variorum") recalls, is the fact that Hakewill's treatise stirred the debate at Cambridge that is reflected in Milton's youthful *Naturam* (Patterson, *Works* 1:260–66). Hume's reference to "Astrological division" is clarified by Alastair Fowler, who, referencing Marsilio Ficino's *In Timaeum* (*Opere* 2:1468), explains, "in Neoplatonic astrology, Sol was said to accomplish the generation of new *life* by acting through each of the other planets in turn; their function was only to modulate his influence, or to select from his complete spectrum of virtues" (652). In the mid-1940s, William B. Hunter comments on this passage as he discusses Milton's "optimistic materialism" ("Milton's Materialistic Life Principle" 69), and in Adam's remarks to Eve, Hunter finds support for his argument that "light...becomes for Milton the agent or force back of life, the true *élan vital;* since its source is the Sun, that body takes on a tremendously enhanced position, comparable to that which it enjoys among Sun worshippers" (71). Associating this sequence with 3.606–12, Walter Clyde Curry concludes that the "physics involved is generally hazy, and except by implication indeterminate" (137), but, Curry points out, "Milton is not more vague in these matters than most of his contemporaries" (138). Focusing particular emphasis on *Temper* (4.670) and *Humor* (3.610), Curry also considers the possibility of Milton's alluding to Aristotle's theory of two types of exhalations from earthly bodies, vaporous and dry exhalations (140–42). Milton's sources, rather than his science, gain more ascendency in other commentary on this sequence. Kester Svendsen, who publishes a series of articles through the 1940s and early 1950s, culminating in *Milton and Science* in 1956, finds that the verbal parallels between Adam's explanation to Eve and the relevant passages in such popular encyclopedias as Bartholomaeus's *De Proprietatibus Rerum* Book 8, chapter 17, titled "De luna et eius proprietatibus," and Caxton's *Mirrour of the World* 144–48 "indicate how thoroughly the language of the encyclopedias had permeated poetic vocabulary" (*Milton* 77). From Caxton's *Mirrour* 147–48, Svendsen (*Milton* 77) quotes the following explanation of the relationship between the sun and the less powerful stars: "yet somtyme they restrayne his heetes and after they enlarge them, after that they be set [fer] or nygh, as he otherwhile hath nede." George Coffin Taylor (78–79) juxtaposes Adam's response to Eve to Sylvester's translation of Du Bartas's *The Divine Weeks and Works* 1.4.431–42, while Grant McColley (*"Paradise Lost"* 210n135) finds that Adam's words echo Andrew Willet's *Hexapla in Genesin* 33, in which Adam is described as "occupied in continual beholding of the goodly plants in Paradise, [that] he might thereby be stirred up to acknowledge the goodness and bounty of the Creator." Questioning the arguments of Taylor and McColley, Robert Martin Adams insists that both critics make too much out of random similarities of phrasing and thought (154–55).

Merritt Y. Hughes has gathered a number of additional cross-references to those included in the preceding commentary on Milton's science and sources. Like Curry, Hughes cross-references 3.598–612, but he also relates this sequence to 5.171–84 and 8.85–97, in addition to 9.107, where Satan assumes that the stars have a "sacred influence"; 8.511–13, where Adam claims, "all Heav'n, / And happy Constellations" shed their "selectest influence" on his wedding night; and 10.662, where the bard suggests that an "influence malignant" from the planets is possible after man's fall ("Variorum"). In his edition of Milton's *Complete Poems* 293, Hughes contrasts this sequence with 7.171 and 8.150.

Anne Davidson Ferry's reading of Adam's answer to Eve's question proceeds out of her earlier reading of Eve's love lyric, reinforcing the integrated presentation of the themes of love and knowledge here, as well as elsewhere in Milton's description of prelapsarian life: "As her world turns upon Adam, the heavens and the seasons rotate around the earth. Their benevolent purpose Adam explains to Eve in the speech which follows her love lyric. By attributing to the heavenly spheres a 'kindly' intention of 'Ministring' to nations (IV, 660–674), Adam reveals his understanding that their physical power to enlighten is an expression of the moral design of the creation" (*Milton's Epic Voice* 163–64).

660. *accomplisht:* while Hume defines this word in terms that remain acceptable to twentieth century critics, Landor's Robert Southey, highly critical of the entire line, almost explosively condemns Adam's adjective. Hume's note begins, "Most perfect, most excellent and compleat Consort *Eve;* the first, best-finished Original of the Fair Sex her charming Descendants." Tracing *accomplisht* to its Latin roots, *ad* and *complere,* Hume elaborates, "to fulfill, furnished and stored with all the beauties of Body and perfections of Mind" (156). Newton's note, presenting Pope's explanation that "Appellations of Praise and Honour" (*Poems* 7:91n97) are appropriate to the style of classical literature, registers no discomfort with Milton's word choice: "Milton has not been wanting to give his poem this cast of antiquity throughout which our first parents almost always accost each other with some title, that expresses a respect to the dignity of human nature" (1:279). Landor's Southey, however, exclaims, "Surely she was not daughter of *man;* and, of all the words that Milton has used in poetry or prose, this *accomplisht* is the worst. In his time it had already begun to be understood in the sense it bears at present" (21). Illuminating Southey's concern, the *OED* presents two senses of the past participle, the first emphasizing process, "Fulfilled, completed, finished, perfected," and the second emphasizing the achievement itself, "Complete, perfect; *esp.* in acquirements, or as the result of training." A. W. Verity (467), like the majority of his successors, understands the word as a compliment to Eve, comparing Milton's use to Shakespeare's in *Twelfth Night* 3.1.95: "Most excellent accomplished lady." Merritt Y. Hughes (*Complete Poems* 293) defines *accomplisht* as "full of accomplishments" and cross-references *SA* 230 where Samson describes Dalila as "most accomplisht snare." Kester Svendsen notes the responses of Landor and Newton as he argues, "Adam's epithets for

Eve deepen the reader's impression of Adam's fascination, his delight, and his disappointment, according to the changing state of their relationship" ("Epic Address" 190–91). John T. Shawcross understands that the term *accomplisht* is "ironically indicating her lack of need of further accouterments such as those to which she later succumbs" (*Complete Poetry* 333). In "The Balanced Structure of *Paradise Lost*," Shawcross elaborates on the notion of ironic humor appropriate to the epic genre: "The sum total of Milton's humor is a ridiculing of sinners, sin itself, and sin-begetters. Milton's object lesson is the foolishness of men" (716).

661. *Those:* Newton (279) and Todd ([1842], 2:92) first change *Those,* the reading in both of the first editions, to *These,* and while Masson reports that he finds "no good ground for the change" (*Poetical Works* 3:177), A. W. Verity, glancing at *these* in 657 and 674, thinks the change may be right (467). In her 1952 edition, Helen Darbishire prints *These* (1:296), and Robert Martin Adams approves (67–68). Alastair Fowler prints *Those* in his edition but notes, "Perhaps 'These' was intended" (651).

664. Alastair Fowler (651) cross-references 724–25, "Thou also madst the night, / Maker omnipotent, and thou the day," and associates both passages with Ps. 74.16, "The day is thine, the night also is thine: thou hast prepared the light and the sun."

665. Alastair Fowler (651) cross-references 3.725–32, "where Uriel explains that Night has invaded the nocturnal hemisphere, but that the moon's 'pale dominion checks the night' and prevents a return to the 'original darkness' (ii 984) of chaos."

667. The Latinate construction of the first half of this line prompts the Richardsons (171) to invoke Virgilian authority, explaining that Virgil writes "Munera Laetitiamque Dei" for "Munera Laeta" in the *Aeneid* 1.636 and "Squamis Auroque" for "Aureis squamis" in the *Aeneid* 8.436. The Richardsons (172) paraphrase Milton's text: "in all Natural things, in all Nature, the New Creation. *Milton* has a like Phrase (X.345) with Joy and Tydings for Joyful Tydings."

674–88. The nature of the "Millions of spiritual Creatures [who] walk the Earth /
Unseen" (677–78) has been pursued into various pneumatological writings,
but critics and editors—early and late—usually present these references more
as influences than as the sources for Adam's remarks. Although rather impatient
with Milton's "little affectation of showing his learning of all kinds" and his
making "Adam discourse here somewhat like an adept in astrology," Newton, for
example, suggests that what Milton's Adam says "seems to be an imitation and
improvement of old Hesiod's notion of good geniuses, the guardians of mortal
men, clothed with air, wand'ring every where through the earth" (280). Todd
([1842], 2:92–93) quotes Newton but also suggests a link to Richard Crashaw's
"Charitas Nimia. Or the Dear Bargain" 9–28 (*Poems* 280–81). Irene Samuel,
Merritt Y. Hughes, and Marjorie H. Nicolson develop the pneumatology topic,
Samuel looking at Platonic philosophy, Hughes and Nicolson more narrowly
at the Cambridge Platonists of Milton's own age, although Hughes continues
to consider an influence from Hesiod. While Samuel associates the "Millions of
spiritual creatures" to the Hermetic daemons of *IlPen* 93–96, "those *Daemons*
that are found / In fire, air, flood, or underground, / Whose power hath a
true consent / With Planet, or with Element," Samuel believes that the spirits
Adam references are part of the Platonic tradition of daemons, or divine spirits,
"between immortal and mortal who convey men's prayers to the gods and the
blessings of the gods to men" (*Plato* 35). In his edition of Milton's *Complete
Poems,* Hughes, like Newton, claims that Hesiod influences Milton here, but
Hughes compares Milton's "spiritual Creatures" not with Hesiod's geniuses but
with the muses in the *Theogony* 3–21, 35–52, who, according to Hughes, sing
"the greatness of their father Zeus, the earth and heaven, in ceaseless concert as
they mount the cloudy slope of Olympus in the darkness" (294). In "Variorum,"
Hughes suggests, "Milton may have been influenced by the mixed Neoplatonic
and Cabalistic theories of Robert Fludd's conception in *Mosaical Philosophy* 147
of the air as filled with 'heavenly spirits, by which it is informed and vivified.' "
In addition, Hughes glimpses a resemblance between these "spiritual Creatures"
who "keep watch" and the Attendant Spirit in Milton's *Mask,* whom Sears Jayne
(536) identifies as one of the host of daemons that Marsilio Ficino found in the
Neoplatonic tradition. Asserting that "rapturous and ecstatic praise" of God
defines the continual music of the angels in the garden, Marjorie H. Nicolson
("Spirit World" 448) more assuredly claims a link between the spiritual creatures
in this passage and the spirit world of Henry More, who, in *The Immortality
of the Soul* 199, writes, "Sacred hymns and songs, sung with voices perfectly

imitating the sweet passionate relishes of the sense of their devout minds, must even melt their souls into divine love, and make them swim with joy in God." Finally, Alastair Fowler returns the pneumatology topic to the classical tradition with a reference to *De Rerum Natura* 4.586–90, where Lucretius establishes that the music is Pan's pipes "often interpreted allegorically as the music of the spheres." Fowler brings unique attention to Adam's description of the voices singing "Sole, or responsive each to other's note." Fowler (652) cross-references the description of angelic polyphony at 3.370–71, adding, "Socrates Scholasticus (258v) tells how Ignatius 'saw a vision of angels praising the Holy Trinity in responsive hymns,' and how this vision was the source of antiphonal music in the Church…; a tradition referred to by M[ilton] in his *Commonplace Book* [Patterson, *Works* 18:140]."

674. *deep of night:* Verity (467) references *Julius Caesar* 4.3.226 ("The deep of night is crept upon our talk"), as well as *The Merry Wives of Windsor* 4.4.40 ("In deep of night to walk by this Herne's Oak").

675–88. In letter 963, dated January 10, 1836, William Wordsworth argues that with a bit of rewriting ("Think not beloved Eve though Men were none"), one would have here, "in blank verse, all the essentials of a Sonnet" (*Letters* 6.3.150).

675. Helen Darbishire (*Poetical Works* 1:90) replaces the comma after *vain* with a colon, while Alastair Fowler, who keeps the comma, admits that it "may be in error for a heavier point" (652).

none: A. W. Verity (467) acknowledges the emphasis created by placing *none* at the end of this line, as also at the end of 704 and 11.612.

677–78. The closeness of the relationship between Adam and Eve and the "spiritual Creatures" whose song they hear has been quite differently understood by Evert Mordecai Clark and Roy Daniells. Pursuing Milton's debt to descriptions of Abyssinian paradises, Clark notes that while both Edenic and Abyssinian paradises are guarded and "closed to all unwarranted access from below, these Gardens are ever open to celestial visitants. 'The gods if ye beleeve Homer, (that they feasted in Ethiopa) could not there, nor in all the world,' says Purchas [Samuel Purchas, *Purchas His Pilgrimage* 565], 'find a fitter place for entertainment'" (148). Daniells, however, does not see much entertaining in Milton's paradise. Other than Raphael, the angels seem to avoid Adam and Eve, for the reasons Daniells presents: "In a sense, the *donnée* of the story would suffer, the rigour of the great moral experiment would be compromised, and our focus on archetypal man and woman would be blurred if the presence of an angelic guard led to toing and froing, chatting, picnicking, and asking advice. Yet angels are, *ipso facto*, messengers. Some real rapport must be established. We get it in the deep concern of Gabriel and his subordinates for the safety of Adam and Eve" ("Happy Rural Seat" 12).

678–80. John S. Diekhoff notes the *sleep-steep* rhyme in this passage ("Rhyme" 540). See Diekhoff in **222–24**.

681. Setting forth the principles of Milton's syllabic prosody, S. Ernest Sprott finds in this line an example of elision due to a "w-glide" in the first of two consecutive vowels in a word ("echoing") whereby neither vowel is stressed (85).

682. Newton (281) associates this line with Virgil's *Eclogues* 1.57, "canet frondator ad auras"; "the woodman's song shall fill the air." He also references Lucretius's *De Rerum Natura* 4.586, while Charles Dunster, contributing notes to Todd's edition, finds in it "something of Shakespeare's spiritual musick," as described in *The Tempest* 3.2.144–52. Todd quotes Newton as well as Dunster ([1842], 2:93).

684–87. As he persistently questions verbal repetitions throughout *PL*, so Bentley (131) objects here: "*Singing* would otherwise do well enough; but within the third Line he repeats again *Their Songs*. So I believe he gave it, HYMNING *their great Creator;* As IV.944. *With Songs to* hymn *his Throne.*" Also see Bentley on "Mysterious" in **743**. Pearce, however, recognizes the rhetorical device as a feature of Milton's style: "M[ilton] So often joyns Verbs and Substantives of the same root in the same verse" (137).

686. *touch:* exemplifying the definition "a note or brief strain of instrumental music," the *OED* 5.b quotes 686, as Merritt Y. Hughes notes ("Variorum"). The *OED* also quotes Milton's youthful *Vac* 37–38: "Listening to what unshorn *Apollo* sings / To th' touch of golden wires."

688. *Divide the night:* Hume refers this phrase to the classical military tradition of the *gallicinia,* by which the night was divided into watches, a reference most later editors accept and develop (156). Supplying a quotation from Silius Italicus's *Punica* 7.154–55, "cum Buccina Noctem / Divideret"; "when the bugle sounded the midnight hour," the Richardsons reinforce Hume's note, explaining that the night was divided "into Watches, as the Trumpet did among the ancients, sounding as the Watch was reliev'd." They add, "This was in full Chorus, and with Instruments…but besides these Regular Watches, other Spiritual creatures were often heard among the Distant Hills, or in the Woods, Singing Single or in Duette, at any time of the Night Indifferently. v.680, &c." (172). To the precedent in Silius Italicus, A. W. Verity (467) adds "dividere horas; "to divide the hours" in Lucan's *The Civil War* 2.689, and notices that Tennyson "gives a fresh turn to the phrase" with *A Dream of Fair Women* 225: "Saw God divide the night with flying flame" (*Poems* 1:490). Verity also argues that in this sequence Thomas Campbell found the inspiration for lines 25–38 in *The Pleasures of Hope* 2. While he, too, acknowledges the military annotation that Hume first supplies, Alastair Fowler wonders whether "perhaps there is also a play on the musical sense of *divide* (*OED* 11[.]a, perform with 'divisions'—florid melodic passages or descants)" (652).

lift our thoughts: Todd ([1842], 2:94) associates this expression with the sonnet "To a Nightingale" 12 in William Drummond of Hawthornden's *Flowres of Sion or Spirituall Poems,* where the nightingale's song can "lift a reverent eye and thought to heaven." Todd also points to Shakespeare's *Henry VIII,* where Buckingham asks his friends to "Make of your prayers one sweet sacrifice, / And lift my soul to heaven" (2.1.78–79), which, Todd adds, Pope combines with Milton's development of the expression to conclude his *Ode for Musick on St. Cecilia's Day* 133–34 (*Poems* 6:34): "His [Orpheus's] Numbers rais'd a shade from Hell, / Hers lift the Soul to Heav'n."

Heaven: studying Milton's prosody, S. Ernest Sprott (144) notes that on the five occasions where *heaven* ends a line in *PL,* the word is dissyllabic, "being allowed to constitute final extrametrical syllables." Besides 688, Sprott lists 3.60, 7.43, 10.467, and 10.598.

689. *alone:* Bentley sounds petulant, but his objection draws attention to this word's importance: "'Tis no great Discovery to tell us, they were *alone;* unless we could suppose, that the Beasts accompanied them, who were already gone to roost. But the POET gave it, *Thus talking, hand in hand* ALONG *they pass'd"* (132). See Le Comte, *Yet Once More* 321.

690–705. With but a few provocative exceptions, Milton's description of the "blissful Bower" has prompted sustained critical praise. Hume begins by providing detailed notes on the classical associations of nearly every plant figuring in the bower while constantly noting their scents. Of the bower's walls, for example, Hume admiringly explains, "Within each lovely Flower, fair to the sight, or fragrant to the smell, all-colour'd *Iris,* and the blushing Rose, and snowy Jessemin advanc'd their flowry Heads, mix'd and inwoven, chequer'd the beauteous Bower with the most charming variety of view. *Iris,* the *Flower-de-luce,* called so of its imitating the divers Colours and their confusion in the Rainbow, thence interpreted *All-hues. Jasmin,* Fr. an Arbor-Plant, bearing a white fragrant Flower" (157). Echoing Hume's joyful reaction to Milton's description, the Richardsons describe the "blissful Bower" as "Inchanting" (173), and in the twentieth century, Douglas Bush maintains that it is "the perfection of natural beauty" (*"Paradise Lost" in Our Time* 105).

One of the most significant elements in the critical grist that lifts the commentary on the bower from adulation to analysis, however, is the ancient literary topos of art versus nature, which the narrator himself first formally announces in the earlier panoramic view of the entire garden, when he refers to the *Flours* as those "which not nice Art / In Beds and curious Knots, but Nature boon / Powrd forth" (241–43). Commenting on the bower, Hume echoes a key phrase, "curious Knots," from that earlier lengthy description, as he draws attention to such words as *Mosaic* and *Emblem,* which will remain important in future discussions of this sequence and the art-versus-nature topos. As he does almost routinely, Hume begins with a note on etymology, deriving *Mosaic* from the Latin "*Musivum*" or "*Musaicum*...whence the Fr. *Mosaique,*" and then defining *Mosaic* as "a curious Chequer-work of Stones of divers colours, and several sorts of Metals, wrought into shapes of Birds, or pretty Knots, with such exactness, that it seems one entire Stone, or piece of Metal, the production of Nature, rather than the performance of Art, abundance whereof are to be seen in St. *Mark's* Church in Venice." Glossing *Emblem,* Hume writes, "More curious in its natural Colours, than if inlay'd with Parian Marble, or precious Stones more costly Ornaments. An *Emblem* is a Representation, in Painting, or Carving, or Inlaying" (157). The Richardsons also carefully attend to the art-versus-nature topos, emphasizing the element of imitation and precisely setting this description of the bower against the earlier description of the garden, as does Hume. Finding the entire description "Inchanting," the Richardsons conclude, "Here was *Nice Art in Beds and Curious Knots,* &c. not as in the rest of Paradise, where Nature was left to Work in her Own way" (173). Perhaps the first important critic to disapprove of Milton's description of the bower on the basis of its unnaturalness is Southey, in his imaginary conversation with Landor in the early eighteenth century. Looking at the description of the walls that Hume so admires, Southey objects that Milton "had before told us that there was every tree of *fragrant* leaf: we wanted not 'each *odorous* shrub.' Nor can we imagine how it fenced up a verdant wall: it constituted one itself; one very unlike any thing else in Paradise, and more resembling the topiary artifices which had begun to flourish in France. Here is indeed an exuberance, and 'a wanton growth that mocks our scant manuring.'" Southey also complains, "The *broidery* and *mosaic* should not be set quite so closely and distinctly before our eyes" (22). As the discussion about the naturalness or the unnaturalness of his garden flares into a prominent controversy in the 1930s, as surveyed in the commentary in **205–87**, Milton's description of the "blissful Bower" is often referenced. G. Wilson Knight's view of the bower, like his view of the garden, is one of the most influential, but when Knight sets the bower in the garden, his evaluation is strikingly different from Southey's, for while he disapproves of the elaborate description of the garden, declaring it "deliberating aestheticism," Knight praises Milton's "exquisite" description of the bower (83). Don Cameron Allen looks at the bower in the context of the earlier description of the entire garden, his attention directed to the quality of the visualization, which, of course, also figures significantly in the discussion of Milton's description of the garden as a whole. Allen contends that the "generalized and allusive" view of the garden that we see "through the darkened eyes of cormorant Satan" ("Description" 104) contrasts with the view of the nuptial bower: "It is evident that when we view the bower through the still sinless eyes of Adam and Eve, we see each plant in particular, but the shades that the sinful demon sees are wanting. Satan sees color—'vegetable Gold,' 'gay enameld colours mixt,' 'Golden Rinde,' 'Purple grapes'—but this squinting vision fails to make specific distinctions because white radiance is no longer his" (105). Contributing to this discourse about the "blissful Bower" and the art-versus-nature topos during the middle decades of the twentieth century is a number of other critics. Douglas Bush, for example, insists that the "artificial words 'inlay' and 'Broider'd' are employed precisely for their artificial value; the terms of sophisticated art emphasize the natural simplicity of Eden" (*"Paradise Lost" in Our Time* 105). Roy Daniells makes a similar point as he observes that we cannot be sure where the bower is located within the garden: "The scene, unmapped, combines effects of ornamental planting with pastoral landscape" ("Happy Rural Seat" 4). William G. Madsen's opinion is that "Adam and Eve's bower is a work of art as much as it is a work of nature," as he explains: "The 'natural' is superior to the 'artificial,' but nature in the Garden would be unsightly were it not for the 'art' of cultivation. It is not 'nature' as the primitive or instinctive or irrational that we are dealing with—those terms better describe Chaos; it is 'nature' as the divinely ordained hierarchy of essences. And it is not 'art' as such that is condemned but art as the symbol of existence, human and angelic, without God" ("Idea" 263). Also see Madsen in **205–87**. The concept of the theatrical sublime dominates F. T. Prince's view of Milton's description: "The poet's intention reaches into every detail of the style, and transforms the Latinate neo-classical formulas by giving them a new purpose. Thus the use of terms from human art to heighten descriptions of nature helps to sustain the impression of conscious display" ("Milton and the Theatrical Subline" 59). Leland Ryken's study of Milton's apocalyptic vision also comments on the art-versus-nature topos and Adam and Eve's nuptial bower, the bower's enameled imagery, writes Ryken, giving "a quality of static permanence to it despite its vital greenery" (83). J. B. Broadbent contributes significantly to this discussion of the Edenic bower by sketching the development of the art-versus-nature topos from classical into Renaissance thought, bringing special emphasis to *The Faerie Queene,* which, as noted subsequently, figures importantly in the commentary on the bower's poetic antecedents and analogs. Developing his emphasis on the value of balance or reciprocity in Milton's presentation of prelapsarian life—both natural and human—Broadbent also reveals his concern, shared with Don Cameron Allen, about the identity of the eye viewing the garden and the bower. In paradise, Broadbent reasons, the "equation" between art and nature "represents the omniprovidence of nature as she appears to the innocent contented soul. Greek and Renaissance philosophers and artists were sharply aware of a dichotomy between nature and art, and of the need to resolve it. The dichotomy became a symbol of human imperfection, hence of evil: in Spenser's Bower [of Bliss in *The Faerie Queene* 2.12.42–82] nature and art are rivals" (*Some Graver Subject* 178–79). If nature should "behave artistically," Broadbent (179) explains, it "symbolised innocence. So the bower in Spenser's Garden of Adonis [*The Faerie Queene* 3.6.29–45] is 'nor by art but of the Trees own inclination made' (*F.Q.* III. vi. 44)." Also see Broadbent in **691, 694,** and **700–03**.

The Spenserian antecedents to which Broadbent draws attention are the very ones Patrick Hume sets against Milton's "blissful Bower," although Hume also considers the Virgilian and Homeric allusions here, as do a number of other commentators. As he reviews the bower's flowers, Hume first looks to Homer's *Iliad* 14.346–49: "*Homer* makes the top of Mount *Ida* fertil in some of the same Flowers, where he describes the amorous *Jupiter* caressing his jilting *Juno*." Second, Hume looks to Spenser. After quoting *The Faerie Queene* 2.5.29, which describes Acrasia's Bower of Bliss, Hume asserts that Spenser's bower is "as far short of ours, as his Garden of Adonis, Bo[ok] 3. C[anto] 6. Stan[za] 30. is of inimitable *Eden*" (157). Hume similarly responds to Spenser in a much earlier note on the topography of paradise. After he quotes from Homer's descriptions of Alcinous's garden and Calypso's "shady Grotta," Hume quotes the description of the Bower of Bliss in *The Faerie Queene* 2.12.42, having introduced Spenser as "a Poet of our own Nation, and famous in his time; but 'tis *impar congressus!* and Rhyme fetter'd his Fancy" (134). See Hume on "Laurel and Mirtle" (694) for the Virgilian allusions. Like Hume, Newton (282) sees Homer's presence in the references to the "Violet, / Crocus, and Hyacinth" of the bower's floor, and recalls that Pope also makes the association in *The "Iliad" of Homer* 14.395–400 (*Poems* 8:181–82). Footnoting the episode on Mt. Ida in his translation of *The Iliad*, Pope had actually commented at length on Milton's having "imitated the several beautiful Parts of this Episode, introducing them upon different Occasions as the Subjects of his Poem would admit." In Milton's description of the "blissful Bower," Pope claims that "the very Turn of *Homer's* verses is observed, and the Cadence, and almost the Words, finely translated." Pope finally notes that Milton again refers to the Mt. Ida episode in 9.1029–45, thereby setting the "lascivious Rage of the Passions" of that sexual encounter against prelapsarian love (*Poems* 8:181–82n395). Twentieth century critics continue to note, and sometimes pursue anew, the Homeric and Spenserian associations with Milton's "blissful Bower." Like Hume, for example, Douglas Bush recalls Milton's allusion to Homer's Mt. Ida episode, and like Pope, Bush sees that Milton makes this allusion both here and in Book 9 (*"Paradise Lost" in Our Time* 105). In the 1960s, A. Bartlett Giamatti returns to the Spenserian echo (*The Faerie Queene* 2.12.42) in Milton's "it was a place / Chos'n by the sovran Planter" (690–91), and describes it as "strikingly" evocative: "Of course, the crucial and important difference between Spenser's and Milton's Bowers is that the latter is the work of God, or at least innocent man, while Spenser's was a trap set by Acrasia. However, we cannot ignore the implied similarity even while we underscore the basic differences; in the echoes of the verse, and the fact both Bowers are artifacts, something has happened to the Bower in Eden. Some damage has been done" (312). To the well-established Homeric and Spenserian associations with the flowers of Milton's "blissful Bower," Alastair Fowler (653–54) adds associations with the flowers of the Atlantic Isles as described in Natale Conti's *Mythologiae* 143. As both the Homeric and the Spenserian pastoral retreats are most famously and firmly associated with love—ideal or corrupt—so, too, of course, is Milton's "blissful Bower," which Adam later calls "the nuptial bower" (8.510) and in which "Espoused Eve decked first her nuptial bed" (4.710). At the end of his lengthy footnote on *Emblem* (703), for example, Fowler concludes: "More generally, the bower as a whole is an emblem of true married love. Thus its seclusion and concealment (ll. 693, 704) reflect the privacy and particular belonging of the marital relation" (654). Dennis H. Burden, Michael Lieb, and John Halkett present similar readings. It is "Milton's sense of the necessary privacy of unfallen love," Burden explains, "that leads to his invention of the nuptial bower for Adam and Eve." Quoting from Milton's witty description of More's sexual misconduct in a garden in *Def 2* (Patterson, *Works* 8:31–33), Burden continues: "If bowers and gardens offer convenient privacy for illicit love, it would have been unjust of God not to provide a private bower for Adam and Eve's wedded love" (48). Developing the dialectics of creation in *PL,* Lieb considers the associations between Adam and Eve's creative withdrawal into the "blissful Bower" and the creative withdrawals of God and the poet: "This retreat within the retreat of Eden has overtones of God's holy Hill, where the Father dwells alone and unapproached from all eternity. In their own sacred 'inmost' place of seclusion, the unfallen couple perform the mysteries of love. They withdraw into the privacy of the enclosed area to create as the poet withdraws into himself to meditate. However, Adam and Eve's withdrawal does not have the same implications as the poet's: their enactment of the introverting pattern does not represent a return to the chaotic state but a return to a womb from which birth issues effortlessly and naturally" (74). In the nuptial bower, Halkett sees the "perfect symbol of the holy uniqueness of their [Adam and Eve's] love. The place is never entered by the lower creatures (IV.703–05); its natural beauty, as opposed to the artificial pomp of a building like Pandemonium, is suggested by the use of architectural terms to describe vegetable forms (e.g. 'roof,' 'fenc'd up,' 'wall,' 'Mosaic,' 'inlay,' IV.692–703); and it surpasses in shade, holiness, and secrecy the bowers in which mythological creatures of uncontrolled sexual appetite—Pan, Silvanus, and Faunus—diverted themselves (IV.705–08). Matrimonial love, like the hut which houses it, is proper to man alone" (109).

690. *Bower:* the only entry under "Bower" in the "Collection" section of Edward Bysshe's *The Art of English Poetry* 37 is Milton's description of the nuptial bower at 692–708, to which Bysshe fuses a version of 5.377–79.

691. *sovran Planter:* with Gen. 2.8, "And the Lord God planted a garden eastward in Eden," Patrick Hume supports his gloss, "By God, the Sovereign Creator of the World, as well as the Planter of this particular place, and pleasant Garden" (156). Several modern critics commenting on this epithet for God continue to limn the relationship between art and nature in Milton's garden. J. B. Broadbent explains, "Nature's artistry is also a symbol of perfection because it reveals the designs of God. The plateau paradise in Drayton's *Endimion and Phoebe* [1–81 (*Works* 1:129–30)] is the scene of innocent but physical love between mythical but solid characters. There is a coniferous umbrella, occurring naturally but 'thus divinely made' as in Paradise the natural canopy of the bower has been framed by 'the sovran Planter' (IV.691). Indeed, the more artificial nature's works appear, the more they illustrate the immanence of God" (*Some Graver Subject* 179). Michael Lieb describes the relationship between the creative work of God, Milton's "sovran Planter," and the creative work of Adam and Eve: "Following the lead of the 'sovran Planter'...who is also the Creator, the unfallen gardeners in their own way perform the creative act of effecting union and tempering what is otherwise 'wanton' like Eve's ringlets or like Eve herself without the sexual superiority of Adam" (73). Also see John R. Knott in **626.**

694–99. In a letter dated May 21, 1807, Wordsworth explains to Lady Beaumont "that the mind can have no rest among a multitude of objects, of which it either cannot make one whole, or from which it cannot single out one individual, whereupon may be concentrated the attention divided among or distracted by a multitude." Asserting that eventually "we must either select one image or object, which must put out of view the rest wholly, or must subordinate them to itself while it stands forth as Head," Wordsworth then quotes Milton's lines (*Letters* 2:148)

694. *Laurel and Mirtle:* Patrick Hume (256–57) initially establishes some of the mythological associations for these plants, which, given more detailed development by Alastair Fowler and J. B. Broadbent, also contribute to the bower's association with love. Hume notes that both trees are "remarkable for their lasting greenness," and he identifies the laurel as "*Apollo's* favourite Tree, and from his honouring it, used to encircle the Victors brows; *Myrtle, Myrtus*...an everlasting Green, of pleasant smell, dedicated for its delicacy to *Venus.*" Hume concludes by quoting Virgil's *Eclogues* 2.54–55. After first referencing "the arbour of generation within the 'grove of myrtle' in the Garden of Adonis in Spenser, *F.Q.* III vi 43–4, which is certainly sexually, and probably even anatomically, symbolic," Fowler translates lines 54–55 from Virgil's second eclogue ("You too will I pluck, laurels, and you their neighbour myrtle, for so placed you blend sweet fragrance"). Also carefully cross-referencing 9.430–31, where Eve supports the flowers "Gently with myrtle band" immediately before Satan begins his temptation, Fowler believes that in this context in Book 4, "the trees seem...to symbolize the complementary roles of Apollo and Venus, male and female, *mens* and *anima,* reason and virtue. The force of the passage lies in the suggestion of a comprehensive polarity" (653). Broadbent looks at the *Laurel and Mirtle,* along with the trees listed at 139, but he rejects the attention to symbolism marking Fowler's and Hume's remarks. Broadbent contends that Milton's "re-creative and serious treatment of convention" is evident here as "he did not allow all the realities to steam away into idealism, allegory or wish-fulfilment" (*Some Graver Subject* 182). Instead, Broadbent observes, Milton "simply names the trees," while earlier poets, guilty of "mishandling Paradise," set about to "expound...their emblemism," and that tradition "had become part of that dreary world of title-pages and emblems that makes the 17th Century look, from outside, so musty and dull" (182–83).

696. *Acanthus:* very similarly structuring their commentaries, Patrick Hume (157) and Alastair Fowler (653) continue to reveal their attentiveness to the art-versus-nature topos throughout the extended sequence (690–719) describing Adam and Eve's bower. Both editors consider the "Acanthus" as a plant in nature. Hume, uncertain if *Acanthus* is a tree, as Theophrastus claims in *De Historia Plantarum* 1.4.112, a "spicy shrub," or "a Thorn, because beset with multitudes of 'em," describes the leaves as "long, large, and winding," while Fowler, on the basis of Virgil's *Georgics* 2.119, suggests that Milton may not be referring to the acanthus flower, but "the Egyptian acacia, the evergreen tree that Virgil describes as *semper frondens*"; "ever-blooming." Both Hume and Fowler also consider the acanthus as an architectural decoration, Hume referencing Virgil's *Eclogues* 3.45. Fowler adds that metamorphosis stories are common to both the hyacinth (701) and the acanthus and notes that Spenser has a list of such metamorphosed lovers in the Garden of Adonis in *The Faerie Queene* 3.6.45.

699. *Rear'd high:* Edward S. Le Comte (*Yet Once More* 58) cross-references 1.463–64, Dagon's "Temple high / Rear'd," and *Mask* 798, "magic structures, rear'd so high."

  flourisht: Hume's definition is "flourishing," as he traces the term to the Latin *florere*, which he defines as "to spring" (157), while Merritt Y. Hughes's definition (*Complete Poems* 294), like John T. Shawcross's (*Complete Poetry* 334) and Alastair Fowler's (654), is "flower-laden, or adorned with flowers."

700–03. When "terms of art predominate," J. B. Broadbent (*Some Graver Subject* 180) maintains, "the reference is usually to the bower of Adam and Eve which had been deliberately made for them by God." Broadbent adds that contributing to the description here is "Ezekiel's vison of Adam's kingly splendour [28.13]...as well as the amorously emblematic jewellery of the Song of Solomon [5.11]."

700. *Mosaic:* Todd ([1842], 2:95) identifies a similar description in Sir Philip Sidney's *New Arcadia* 14: "Of each side the green, a thicket, and, behind the thickets, again new beds of *flowers*, which being under the trees, the trees were to them a pavillion, and they to the trees a *mosaical floor*." In the *OED* (a.1 Obs.), Sidney's is the earliest citation.

  Patrick Hume's gloss (157) anticipates the *OED*'s primary definition of the noun *mosaic*, and Merritt Y. Hughes notes that the *OED* quotes Milton's line to illustrate the transferred and figurative application of that meaning: "The process of producing pictures or decorative patterns by cementing together small pieces of stone, glass, or other material of various colours; pictures or patterns produced in this manner; the construction of decorative material composed of small pieces of coloured material cemented together" ("Variorum").

702–04. John S. Diekhoff notes the *stone-none* rhyme in this passage ("Rhyme" 540). See Diekhoff in **222–24.**

702. In this line, as well as in 711 and 3.359, 361, Samuel Johnson locates examples of "harmony arising principally from the collocation of vowels and consonants" (*Rambler* 4:100).

 Broiderd: Hume glosses, "inlay'd the fragrant Floor, with soft and sweet Embroidery" (157). The *OED* 2 quotes Milton's line as it defines the term: "To adorn as with embroidery, to inlay *with* (pearl, ivory, gold, etc.)."

 Todd ([1842], 2:94–95) recalls that Tonson's 1711 edition reads "*Border'd* the ground," perhaps in response to 9.438 ("flowers *imborder'd* on each bank"), but Todd himself retains *Broiderd* as "the reading of Milton's own editions." Todd also refers readers to *violet-embroider'd* in *Mask* 233.

703–05. John Upton identifies two literary parallels in which animals are excluded from a sacred site. One is Callimachus's *Hymn* 1.10–13 and the site where Rhea brings forth Jove, to which Todd also points ([1842], 2:95). The second is *A Midsummer Night's Dream* 2.2.9–12 and the site where Titania will sleep after the fairies' protective song, which commands a variety of creatures "Come not near our fairy queen." Upton believes "Milton doubtless had both Callimachus and Shakespeare in mind" (413).

 Sister Mary Irma Corcoran notes that explanation for the animals' exclusion from the nuptial bower appears later, in the narrator's celebration of wedded love (750–75), which "in its emphasis upon reason as the foundation of the nuptial relationship and the distinguishing mark of human love, bears some resemblance to St. Thomas' [*Summa Theologica* 4.369] broader explanation of the reservation of the garden to rational beings" (30).

703. *Emblem:* some uncertainty about level of meaning immediately develops with the eighteenth century notes on this word, and while the Richardsons take on that ambiguity, Alastair Fowler's commentary reconsiders the limited meaning that they impose. Hume's 1695 definition bears repeating, however: "An *Emblem* is a Representation, in Painting, or Carving, or Inlaying" (157). Discarding Hume's reference to "Painting, or Carving," Bentley rules that "*Emblem* is here in the *Greek* and *Latin* Sense for inlaid Floors of Stone or Wood, to make Figures Mathematical or Pictural" (132). Explaining that the "*Mosaic* Pavements of the *Romans*…consisted of Small Square Stones call'd *Emblemata,* from their being In-laid," the Richardsons insist that this "is the Import of the *Greek* Word, to Distinguish These from what was done with *the*

Pencil; for they were Generally form'd into Pictures. and as the Subjects were Commonly Moral and Allegorical, We have Transferr'd the Signification of the Word to the Subject." They then conclude, "*Milton* has restor'd it to the Original Sense" (173). While Merritt Y. Hughes glosses "stone / Of costliest Emblem" with "stone inlaid with precious metal" (*Complete Poems* 294), and in "Variorum" reports that the *OED* 1 quotes 703 to exemplify *Emblem* in its obsolete meaning of "an ornament of inlaid work," Alastair Fowler (654) reflects on the possibility that Milton's *Emblem* carries a more complicated meaning. Quoting Rosemary Freeman (37), who supplies Geoffrey Whitney's definition, "such figures, or works, as are wrought in plate, or in stones in the pavements, or on the walls, or such like, for the adorning of the place" ("To the Reader" 2), Fowler announces, "it is difficult to think that the other sense of *emblem* (pictorial symbol) is not also meant to operate here, and to draw attention to the emblematic properties of the flowers (the humility of the *violet,* prudence of the *hyacinth,* amiability of the *jessamin,* etc.)."

705–08. While the deities mentioned in this passage obviously charm Patrick Hume, they drive Richard Bentley to a burst of rewriting that removes them entirely from Milton's text; not to be dismissed, however, several twentieth century critics, perhaps most notably William Empson, share Bentley's distress with this list of classical deities. Hume devotes more than a page to this four-line sentence, providing detailed information on each deity and fondly supplying abundant quotations from a variety of classical poets. While Hume groups Pan, Silvanus, Faunus, and the nymphs as "the Rural Deities" at one point, he later identifies them as "these false Gods" but nevertheless continues comfortably to sketch their histories, and he never suggests that they are anything but beneficent (158). Opposite is Bentley's reaction. After describing Pan, Silvanus, and Faunus as "salvage and beastly Deities, and acknowledg'd feign'd," Bentley rules the entire sentence an editorial interpolation. He moves 705 into 708 and declares that the line should read, "Such was their INSTINCT. Here in close recess" (132). As the twentieth century opens, Charles Grosvenor Osgood asks the question that Bentley's editing prohibits. Setting 250–51, "*Hesperian* Fables true, / If true, here only," against this sequence, Osgood asks, "how are we to reconcile this view with his [Milton's] frequent and loving and reverent treatment of the myths?" Osgood concludes that Milton understood the classical myths as "the gift of divine inspiration," which he shaped according to his Christian moral purpose (xlviii). Decades later, in "Milton and Bentley," a chapter in

Some Versions of Pastoral, William Empson ponders the nature of Milton's engagement with "paganism." Empson argues, "the fall from paganism is like the fall from paradise" (177), and as he concludes his essay, Empson considers this four-line sentence in which Adam and Eve's earlier "blissful Bower" (690) becomes their "shadie Bower" (705). Empson shares Bentley's immediate reaction: "Surely Bentley was right to be surprised at finding Faunus haunting the bower, a ghost crying in the cold of Paradise, and the lusts of Pan sacred even in comparison to Eden. There is a Vergilian quality in the lines, haunting indeed, a pathos not mentioned because it is the whole of the story. I suppose that in Satan determining to destroy the innocent happiness of Eden, for the highest political motives, without hatred, not without tears, we may find some echo of the Elizabethan fulness of life that Milton as a poet abandoned, and as a Puritan helped to destroy" (182–83). In *The Structure of Complex Words,* Empson continues to hear a haunting sadness in these lines, describing them as "one of the most echoing bits of pathos about the nuptial bed of Eden" (102).

Pan or Silvanus…nor Nymph, / Nor Faunus: Charles Osgood adds more cross-references and classical sources to those Hume cites, and some of this additional material conflicts with or complicates Hume's notes, but as Alastair Fowler reminds us, ambiguity often attends the representations of the classical gods.

Pan: acknowledging the authority of both Homer and Virgil to identify Pan as "the Protector of Sheep and Shepherds," Hume (158) then adds that it is "most probable" that Pan "had many celebrated Groves and Bowers in his beloved *Arcadia,*" and he supports that understanding by citing Virgil's *Eclogues* 10.26 and *Georgics* 1.16–18. Hume sends readers back to Milton's earlier reference to Pan at 266. Osgood (68) adds a cross-reference, *EpDam* 52, where Pan is described as sleeping beneath the shade of an oak, a description that Osgood relates to Theocritus's "Poems" 1.16, where a goatherd claims that "high noon's his [Pan's] time for taking rest after the swink o' the chase." Fowler finds that in the context of the "blissful Bower" description, Pan is "more specifically a symbol of fecundity and a god of *sequestered* places" (654).

Silvanus: Hume, quoting Virgil's *Eclogues* 10.24–25, and more specifically the *Aeneid* 8.597–601, identifies *Silvanus* as "The God of Woods and Groves" (158). Osgood (87) invokes the authority of the *Aeneid* 8 to identify Silvanus as "the god of the fields and flocks" but immediately adds, "Servius in his comment [*Servii Grammatici Qui Feruntur in Vergilii Carmina Commentarii* 2:282] says that this was the popular belief, but that more strictly Silvanus was a god of the woods." Osgood also cross-references *IlPen* 134. Heightening the uncertainty about several of these figures by noting that Silvanus, Pan, and Faunus—all half man and half goat—were often confused, Alastair Fowler adds, "Silvanus, said by some to be the son of Faunus, was a god of woods, gardens and limits" (654).

Nymph: Hume identifies nymphs as "Daughters of *Thetis* and the *Ocean*" according to Orpheus, "To the Nereids" 1 (*Orphic Hymns* 705–08), and reports that according to Homer, some of the nymphs "belong'd to Rivers, others to the Woods, the rest to Mountains and Fields." Hume (158) pursues etymology to add that the nymphs always looked young, and that Pausanias (*Description of Greece* 10.31.10) considered them "Feminine Deities, not absolutely Immortal, but of an unaccountable Longaevitie." In *Complete Commentary,* James Paterson initially repeats Hume's understanding of the etymology, but adds a derivation from Hebrew: "*Nephesh,* i.e. *A Soul:* They were supposed to be the *Souls* of the *Dead.* Any *Goddess* of the *Waters, Rivers, Springs, Mountains, Fields:* for the *Heathens* imagined that some inferior *Deities* presided over these: And hence the *Papists* dedicated these to their *Saints,* as St. Patrick's, St. Bridget's, St. Winifred's Wells, &c" (321). The *OED* presents only the Latin and Greek roots. Osgood brings more detail to the divisions among the various nymphs and provides abundant cross-referencing, from Milton's invocation of the nymphs in *Lyc* 50–57 to his use of *nymph* as a synonym for *maiden.* Furthermore, Osgood points out that "Milton dwells often upon the beauty of places haunted by the nymphs," and in addition to 705–08, he lists *PR* 2.184–92, 289–97, 354; *IlPen* 133–46; *Arc;* and *Mask* 119–21, 230–43, 423, 964; as well as numerous classical analogs for such descriptions (64–65).

Faunus: this may be the most intriguingly ambiguous figure in this list of classical deities. Hume names only one source for his annotation, the *Aeneid* 7.48–49. Faunus, according to Hume, was "the Son of Picus King of the Latins, who reigned in Italy about the time of Pandion's ruling at Athens." Hume explains that because Faunus "was a pious Prince, and a great Improver of Agriculture," he was "therefore admitted amongst the Italian deities, as the Tutelary God of Husbandmen, of whom descended all the *Fauni,* to part of this fabulous Story *Virgil* subscribes." Finally, citing Virgil's *Georgics* 1.10, Hume explains that the Fauni were so called because of "their prophetic foretelling of future Events" (158–59). Osgood does not cite the *Aeneid,* but rather Ovid (*Fasti* 3.84, 299–316), when he identifies Faunus as "a Latin divinity of the woods, sometimes confounded with the Greek Pan" (87). Osgood also notes,

"The fauns seem to have been the Latin form of the Greek *Satyrs*" (87). Fowler adds to this richly provocative complexity, noting that, like Pan, Faunus was "a benignly priapic wood god…who haunted the forest as an oracle," according to Horace and Virgil (*Aeneid* 7.81–84), but as "the father of satyrs, an emblem of Concupiscence," according to the Renaissance emblem books such as Andrea Alciati's *Emblemata cum Commentariis* 321–24 and Cesare Ripa's *Iconologia* 315, "or even of Satan, tempter of Eve" (654).

705. *shadie:* the Richardsons point out that in the first edition the adjective is *shadier,* but "Alter'd in the Second." While they declare that both words are "Well," the Richardsons prefer *shadie,* finding it "preferable because Thus the Circumstance of the Shadiness is most Strongly mark'd, as 'tis a very Material and Beautiful One; and is accordingly much insisted on Afterwards" (174). Hawkey returns to *shadier,* understanding it as "more strongly painting the shade, which is a material part of the picture in the description of the bower" ("Various Readings" n.p.). With a similar explanation, Newton also prints *shadier* (283). Surveying the decisions of ten of Milton's modern editors, Robert Martin Adams feels that either reading is "more or less acceptable" (80).

See Anne Davidson Ferry's earlier comment on *shade* in **138.**

706. *sacred and sequesterd:* these adjectives draw some remarkably diverse responses. Patrick Hume emphasizes the Latin root of sacred, *sacer,* "Holy, set apart for Divine Service." Hume then associates the "blissful Bower" with the sacred laurel that stood in the midst of Latinus's palace in the *Aeneid* 7.59–60: "Virgil makes Latinum his Laurel as sacred as this awful Bower" (157). Deriving *sequesterd* from the Latin *sequestrare* and *sequestratio,* Hume explains them as "Law-terms, signifying the separating and setting aside any thing in Controversie from the possession of those that contend for it" (158). Outrage colors Richard Bentley's response because, he insists, an intrusive editor has described as *sacred* the "wild Grottos" of the "beastly Deities" (132). For John Peter, these adjectives qualify Adam and Eve's sexual intimacy, rather than their "blissful Bower." Explaining Adam and Eve's strong appeal to the reader, Peter stresses their "quite untainted, pure and immaculate" sexuality: furthermore, he argues, as secrecy marks the sexual relationship between Satan and Sin, which is "the only type of sexuality we encounter before Adam and Eve's[,] theirs naturally tends to seem all the more wholesome, 'sequesterd' and private no doubt (iv. 706) but in no sense surreptitious" (91).

feignd: like his notes on the "Rural Gods" themselves, Hume's definition of *feignd* suggests the tender warmth of his appreciation for this entire passage (705–08): "contrived as the Poets do the imaginary Groves and Grottoes, where they sent their Rural Gods to Nurse, or under cool refreshing Shades lay'd 'em to sleep" (158). Merritt Y. Hughes refers this word to *As You Like It* 3.3.21–22, "the truest poetry is the most feigning," adding that feigning implies such myths "were pagan fabrications" (*Complete Poems* 294), but in "Variorum," Hughes sounds rather less sanguine, glossing *feignd* as "the falsity of a classical myth," and identifying Silvanus and Faunus as "questionable characters" in *PR* 2.191 and *El* 5.137.

707–08. Examining Milton's strategies for presenting similes against the strategies of his epic predecessors, James Whaler notes the remarkably "simple and rapid" compounding of the four similes in these two lines, while in the *Aeneid*, for example, he finds that "no more than two similes ever occur together" ("Compounding" 315).

708–10. This charming recollection of Eve's marriage preparations has won admiring comments from several modern critics, Marjorie H. Nicolson describing it as "one of the most idyllic scenes in the earlier books of *Paradise Lost*" (*John Milton* 242) and Roy Daniells noting that Milton does not specify the flowers and herbs with which Eve "deckt first her nuptial Bed," but "leaves this to Eve, as her private affair" ("Happy Rural Seat" 6).

709. *Flowers:* describing Milton's syllabic, rather than accentual, prosody, S. Ernest Sprott explains that, though Milton intended a ten-syllable blank verse line, supernumerary syllables and elisions are frequent. "Within the line, certain words retain certain values. Thus *power,* and other hypermonosyllables such as *bower, flower* (except only *flowers* at *P.L.,* IV, 709), *shower, tower, prayer, eev'n* (adv. and subs.) and *sev'n* are always monosyllabic" (55–56). Also see Darbishire in **501** and **646**.

711. In this line, as well as in 702, 3.359, and 361, Samuel Johnson finds examples of "harmony arising principally from the collocation of vowels and consonants" (*Rambler* 4:100).

heav'nly: Leland Ryken explains that *heav'nly* is one of the many stock epithets that Milton uses to "modify a noun naming an empirical phenomenon" to achieve his apocalyptic vision. Listing many other such adjectives, Ryken identifies *celestial* as the most frequently used (54).

Hymenaean: Hume sketches the classical background, noting that derived from Greek, this is "a Song usually sung in Praise, and to the Prosperity of the married Mates," which takes its name from Hymen, who was either "a jolly Deity, the first Institutor of, and Instigator to Matrimony" or "the Name of an *Athenian,* who restored certain Virgins, seized upon by Thieves, entire and inviolated to their Parents, who was ever after honoured with Memorials and Invocations at all succeeding Marriage Festivals" (159). The *OED* B.1 cites Milton's line to illustrate the obsolete noun meaning "wedding-song." James Paterson and Alastair Fowler contribute a few cross-references, Paterson (321) to Catullus's marriage songs and Fowler (654) to the echo from those marriage songs in Milton's *El* 5.106, "io Hymen."

Philip Brockbank, pursuing the moral and aesthetic values conveyed in Milton's astronomical references, writes, "The heavenly choirs that celebrate the diurnal motion of the celestial spheres sing Eve's Hymenaean too (IV, 711), and the relationship between human love and the astronomical order is, in this movement of the poem, perfected with the prayer that preludes the 'Rites Mysterious of connubial Love'" (204).

712. *genial Angel:* while the early editors Patrick Hume and the Richardsons are apparently untroubled as they explain who this figure is, several twentieth century critics more cautiously consider the angel's identity. Like Hume, the Richardsons (174) assert that this is "the Friendly Angel, that took Care of the Propagation of Mankind" (174), but Hume's annotation on the etymology of *genial* also highlights the joy attending the Edenic marriage: "*Genius,* the God of Pleasure. Hence *genio indulgere,* to make good Cheer; they derive it *a generando*" (159). Cross-referencing other descriptions of Eve's marriage procession in *PL* creates uncertainty for both Allan H. Gilbert and then John Peter, however, as they consider the identity of the one leading Eve to Adam. Gilbert points out that Eve's earlier mention of the *voice* (467) that led her to Adam and Adam's later description of Eve being led to him by "her Heav'nly Maker" (8.485) contrast with the narrator's present reference, "the genial Angel." Gilbert attributes the differences to the shifting plans involved in the composition of *PL* (*On the*

Composition 45). Also see Gilbert in **467–75**. Considering the contrast between the "genial Angel" and Adam's report in 8.485 naming God as Eve's guide, Peter suggests that Milton is using both understandings of the Hebrew phrase *mal'ak Jahweh:* "angel of Jahweh" or "special visitation of Jahweh" (25). In his footnote on this phrase, Alastair Fowler acknowledges Gilbert's response and concedes that perhaps there is a "discrepancy" between the several passages, but, without mentioning Hume, Fowler first heads back to reject the understanding of *genius* that the early annotator presents: "The role that in poetry of a different mode would be taken by Genius, the deity presiding over generation and marriage (cp. 'Old Genius' the porter of Spenser's Garden of Adonis, *F.Q.* III vi 31f.), is here instead taken by the mysterious invisible *genial* angel" (655). Also see Giamatti in **713–19**.

713–19. Hesiod's *Works and Days* is the seminal text for the story of Pandora, and from it, Patrick Hume first begins to draw the key elements in his synopsis of the ancient myth, but the history of the critical response to this sequence in *PL* is a history of intervening readings of that myth, including Milton's own earlier reading in *DDD*. When they rehearse the classical myth, the early editors more certainly state the foolishness of Hesiod's Epimetheus, as they also more certainly acknowledge the charm of Hesiod's Pandora than do twentieth century critics. Hume cites Virgil's *Eclogues* 6.42, Ovid's *Metamorphoses* 1.82–83, Horace's *Odes* 1.3.28–31, and Cicero's *Tuscan Disputations* 5.3.8, but he immediately and most fully quotes from and paraphrases Hesiod's *Works and Days* 54–105. Initially, Hume describes Pandora as "a most beautiful Virgin, sent by *Jupiter* to ensnare Mankind," but then he identifies her as a "lovely Sorceress [who] brought in her hand a Box close shut, which being opened by the unwary *Epimetheus,* filled the World with all manner of Mischiefs, that flew out of it, leaving only flattering and deceitful Hope at the bottom." Hume concludes that sentence by almost matter-of-factly presenting the traditional Christian "Parallel" that sees the consequences of Pandora's behavior as "like that *Patrimony* the charming and audacious *Eve* transmitted to her sinful and sad Posterity." Hume then explains Epimetheus's motivation, as Hesiod does not, when he asserts that the "unwary" Epimetheus opened the box in order "to satisfie his heedless Curiosity" (159). The Richardsons and Paterson continue to acknowledge the element of male responsibility in the Greek myth. The Richardsons write that Pandora "Enticed" Epimetheus, but what she enticed, according to them, was "his Foolish Curiosity" (175). In his summary, Paterson says that while Pallas gave wisdom to Pandora, Aphrodite gave her beauty and Mercury gave her eloquence; although Hesiod's account (77–79) is rather more detailed, as he writes that Mercury contributed "lies and crafty words and a deceitful nature at the will of loud thundering Zeus, and the Herald of the gods put speech in her." Like Hume and the Richardsons, Paterson (322) notes the quality in Epimetheus that Hesiod describes as "scatter-brained" in *Theogony* 513: "*Jupiter* sent her to *Epimetheus* with a Box, which he rashly opened." William Hazlitt makes Milton's Pandora reference somewhat more dynamic by placing it in a wider context, one that includes the description of Eve "in naked beauty" (713) being led to Adam: "That which distinguishes Milton from the other poets, who have pampered the eye and fed the imagination with exuberant descriptions of female beauty, is the moral severity with which he has tempered them. There is not a line in his works which tends to licentiousness, or the impression of which, if it has such a tendency, is not effectually checked by thought and sentiment" (339). As the twentieth century opens, Charles Grosvenor Osgood (68) maintains a reportorial focus on Hesiod's *Works and Days* and *Theogony*, but A. W. Verity brings another very significant text to bear on 4.713–19. While Verity (468) glances at other classical versions of the story of Pandora, noting that in some versions Pandora's box contains "all human ills," while in others it contains "blessings," he also points out that in *DDD* Milton first presents the comparison between Pandora and Eve, describing Eve as "a consummate and most adorned Pandora," as well as the comparison between Epimetheus and Adam, "our true Epimetheus" (Patterson, *Works* 3:441). With this redirection of critical attention from Milton's primary source toward Milton himself, the consensus among the early editors' readings begins to splinter. William Empson proceeds out of Bentley's troubled effort to see why "to be aveng'd" (718) is applied to Pandora, who "had no hand nor thought in it: it was all Juppiter's [*sic*] studied design" (132–33). Bentley faults Milton's editor, of course, but Empson faults Milton, labeling the passage a "queer smack at Eve" and "a more serious piece of comparative mythology." Empson reasons, "Not only was Eve not trying to avenge Satan but Pandora was not trying to avenge Prometheus" (*Some Versions* 171). Pearce, in his much earlier response to Bentley's edition, claims that Pandora was but an "Instrument" of revenge (138). Also see Bentley and Pearce in **715–17**. Answering what he understands as Empson's "queer smack at M[ilton]," which he finds "beside the point," Alastair Fowler explains, "it is not Satan who steals the authentic fire of forbidden knowledge. Man is both Prometheus and Epimetheus: so long as he has foresight and wisdom, he enjoys (as here) divine gifts; but when in the *sad event* (result) he is *unwiser,* he comes to resemble Epimetheus, and to experience the consequences of sin" (655). In his extensive footnote on 714–19, Fowler then reflects the renewed critical attention to *DDD*. After he asserts, "M[ilton] had applied the [Pandora] myth in a similar manner" in the divorce pamphlet, he more fully quotes from the sentence in *DDD* that Verity cites decades earlier: "*Plato* and *Chrysippus* with their followers the *Academics* and the *Stoics* who knew not what a consummat and most adorned *Pandora* was bestow'd upon *Adam* to be the nurse and guide of his arbitrary happinesse and perseverance, I mean his native innocence and perfection, which might have kept him from being our true *Epimetheus*" (655). At about this same time, A. Bartlett Giamatti also draws these texts together: "The angel who brought her to Adam is compared to Hermes, Eve to Pandora, and Adam, implicitly, to Epimetheus, whose wife brought woe to all the world. And if this sinister analogy were not clear enough, elsewhere Milton is even more explicit." Giamatti then quotes the sentence on Eve-Pandora and Adam-Epimetheus from *DDD* (325). About ten years earlier, Don Cameron Allen illuminates the Pandora-Eve association in **713–19** by citing Tertullian, *Liber de Corona* 85. According to Allen, the parallel between Eve and Pandora is so "conventional" that the "foolish Pandora hardly needs the testimony of a Father as old as Tertullian to inform us that she is the pagan half-memory of silly Eve" ("Description" 126). Yet another of the intervening texts juxtaposed to this extended passage is the entry on Pandora in Carolus Stephanus's (Charles Estienne's) *Dictionarum Historicum, Geographicum, Poeticum* 334, brought to critical attention in 1955 by Starnes and Talbert in *Classical Myth and Legend in Renaissance Dictionaries*. They concede that "Hesiod could have been Milton's source," but they argue that the phrasing in Stephanus's version of the Pandora myth is much closer to Milton's than is the phrasing in either Hesiod or Comes (Conti). Starnes and Talbert bring considerable attention, for example, to *prima mulier,* which appears in the first line of Stephanus, and in Stephanus's *ornauerunt* they see the inspiration for Milton's *adorned* (l. 713); "'donata' or 'dotata' suggests 'Endow'd' (715); the 'singulis…donis suis' and 'omnium donum' emphasize 'with all their gifts'; and 'quam singuli dij donis suis ornauerunt' (cf. 'donata' and dotata') is parallel in structure and meaning to 'whom the God Endow'd with all their gifts'" (270). Alastair Fowler also finds that the verbal parallels suggest Milton "followed" the account in Stephanus (655).

While all of these editors and critics see a comparison between Eve and Pandora, Leland Ryken (49) sees a contrast, a contrast that permits Milton to create the apocalyptic vision of a prelapsarian Eve. Ryken also points to the comparative superiority of Eve established in 5.380–82.

715–17. More than the problem of Pandora's apparently seeking revenge concerns William Bentley as he proceeds through this sequence. Of the phrase, "O too like / In sad event," for example, Bentley asks, "Would Milton have anticipated this, which his Poem afterwards deducts in several Branches, as News to his Reader?" Also problematic for Bentley is "the unwiser Son / Of *Japhet*." Identifying this son as Epimetheus, Bentley reasons, "unwiser...supposes that his Brother too was *unwise:* and yet *Prometheus* in all Mythology is character'd as the *wisest* of Men" (132–33). Pearce responds, "Surely it may be reckon'd want of wisdom in *Prometheus* that he stole *Jove's* fire, and thereby provok'd him to revenge himself: however wise *Prometheus* might have been in Arts and Sciences, he was *unwise* in this action" (138). Also see Bentley and Pearce in **713–19.** Todd, citing John Jortin's *Tracts, Philological, Critical, and Miscellaneous* 1:309, offers a different understanding of *unwiser:* "The epithet *unwiser* does not imply that his brother Prometheus was unwise. Milton uses *unwiser*, as any Latin writer would *imprudentior*, for *not so wise as he should have been*" ([1842], 2:95–96).

715. *all:* see Empson in **705–08.**

717. *Japhet:* in Hesiod's myth, Japetus is the father of Epimetheus and Prometheus, but Milton here identifies him as Japhet, who is named as one of the sons of Noah in Gen. 10.2. Hume (159) first reports that Japetus was "supposed by some to have been the same with *Japhet* the son of *Noah*," but leaves it to others—twentieth century commentators—to track down the names of those authorities. Verity (468) begins that work when he supplies a list of cross-references: Gen. 10.2, Isa. 66.19, *SA* 715–16, as well as *PL* 1.508. What Verity's cross-references draw attention to, however, is the Japhetic line; they do not clarify Milton's substituting Japhet for Japetus. Charles Grosvenor Osgood (46) references both St. Jerome's *Liber Hebraicarum Quaestionum in Genesim* 10.2 and Sir Walter Ralegh's *The History of the World* 1.8.1 on the Japhetic line from which sprang, in Jerome's words, "Iones, qui et Graeci" (col. 999), but Jerome also names none of those who, like Milton, identified Japetus with Japhet. In his chapter "The Dispersal and the Chosen People," Arnold Williams pursues the Japhetic line topic most attentively, since Japheth "was the father of the Gentiles," but first Williams firmly takes up the Japetus-Japhet name shift and begins to identify a few of those authorities Hume clusters together as "some." Citing Pareus's *In Genesin Mosis Commentarius* cols. 908–10 and Pererius's *Commentariorum* 545–49, Williams reports, "Several of the commentaries mention the frequent identification [of Japheth] with the Iapetus of Greek myth, the Titan and father of Prometheus." Williams concludes, "None of the commentaries, however, accepted this identification" (*Common Expositor* 155). William Empson heads toward taking on the Japetus-Japhet issue, but veers off track and settles for an ad hominem attack on Ralegh's handling of Gen. 10.2 by locating him within "the wild gang of comparative anthropologists he collected round him in his great days" (*Some Versions* 171). About 20 years later, Starnes and Talbot contend, "the interesting identification of Iapetus and Iaphet" perhaps occurred to Milton because those two entries in Stephanus's *Dictionarium* are back-to-back (260). Responding to these last several critics, Robert Martin Adams and Alastair Fowler validate the tradition of identifying Japetus with Japhet. Adams dismisses Empson's finger-pointing but, turning back to the identity of Japetus and Japhet, discusses the association between Noah and his sons, and Iapetos and his sons. Moving beyond the Renaissance commentaries on Genesis that Arnold Williams cites, Adams (85) explains that such mythological parallels involving Noah and his descendants can be found as far back as Flavius Josephus, *Jewish Antiquities* 1.6. Fowler (655) simply characterizes as "rash" Starnes and Talbot's theory on Milton's identification of Japetus as Japhet, explaining, "In fact the identification was an established piece of syncretism," and in support, Fowler quotes from the chapter "Iapetus" in the anonymous *Observationum Libellus* appended to Natale Conti's *Mythologiae* 598.

719. *stole:* R. C. Browne (1:354) points out that in *Mask* 194, Milton had earlier changed the more grammatical *stol'n,* which appears in the manuscript version, to *stole.* Browne then explains, "If we read *stol'n, who had* will coalesce—a frequent use in Milton. In iii. 398–402, there are three instances." Verity (468) compares Milton's verb form to Shakespeare's in *Macbeth* 2.3.73 ("murder hath broke ope") and *Julius Caesar* 2.1.237–38 ("Y' have ungently, Brutus, / Stole from my bed"). Merritt Y. Hughes reports that the *OED* recognizes *stole* as a frequent participle from the fourteenth to the eighteenth centuries ("Variorum").

    authentic: following the gloss "Properly belonging to," Hume (159) cross-references 3.656. The *OED* 4 cites Milton's line to illustrate the obsolete definition "Original, first-hand, prototypical; as opposed to *copied*," whereas the *OED* 7 cites *Eikon* 28, "[For justice] to put her own authentic sword into the hands of an unjust and wicked man" (Patterson, *Works* 5:293), to illustrate the obsolete definition "Belonging to himself, own, proper."

720–75. Drawing attention to Satan's absence, which now makes Adam and Eve "the exclusive center of interest," John Halkett describes this scene as the culmination of Milton's presentation of the Edenic marriage, and also brings additional attention to the relationship between unfallen Adam and Eve and the unfallen world surrounding them. "At this point," Halkett writes, "their relationship, soon to change, is presented at its most ideal. The earlier scene had demonstrated not so much the ideal of human happiness as its frailty; the whole scene had been framed by Satan's presence and his self-absorbed commentary on it: all good is to become his prey, all potential weakness his weapon. But now the sense of danger is diminished, and the paradisal amity of Adam and Eve is shown in its perfection as a symbol of cosmic order" (107–08).

720–35. The great majority of the editorial and critical comments on Adam and Eve's evening prayer traces sources, influences, and analogs — both classical and biblical. Hume (160) and Newton (284) begin by hearing an echo of Virgil's *Aeneid* 6.725, "Lucentemque globum Lunae"; "and the shining orb of the moon" in Milton's phrase "the Moons resplendent Globe" (723), and Newton extends this into the next phrase, linking Milton's "And starrie Pole" with Virgil's subsequent "Titaniaque astra"; "and Titan's star." Addison enriches the inquiry into the classical influences by drawing attention to the transition from the bard's narrative voice in 720–24 to the voices of Adam and Eve in 724–35. Describing that transition as "Masterly," Addison explains, "Most of the Modern Heroic Poets have imitated the Ancients, in beginning a Speech without premising, that the Person said thus or thus; but as it is easie to imitate the Ancients in the Omission of two or three Words, it requires Judgment to do it in such a manner as they shall not be miss'd, and that the Speech may begin naturally without them. There is a fine Instance of this Kind out of *Homer,* in the Twenty Third Chapter of *Longinus*" (*Spectator* 3:177). Newton (285) quotes Addison's remarks, and clarifies his citation of Longinus on Homer (*On the Sublime* 51–52), but also enriches the critical discussion of the evening prayer's associations with classical literature by drawing attention to another transition, the transition from *The God* (722) to *Thou* (724): "I conceive Mr. Addison meant Sect. 27. And the instance there given is of Hector being first nam'd, and then of a sudden introduced as speaking, without any notice given that he does so. But the transition here in Milton is of another sort; it is first speaking of a person, and then suddenly turning the discourse, and speaking to him. And we may observe the like transition from the third to the second person in the hymn to Hercules [*Aeneid* 8.293–302]." A few years later, in his "Notes" for *The Works of Virgil,* Joseph Warton makes the same point, adding that Milton "has finely imitated" Virgil's achievement (3:400). The first editor to consider the influence of the Psalms on Adam and Eve's prayer is Todd, and who also finds in the Psalms the phenomenon Newton discusses by reference to classical precedent, the shifting from the third to the second person. Todd draws attention to Ps. 127, but especially to Ps. 74, because it shifts persons in its references to God: "the hymn of our first parents commences with the acknowledgement of God's power, made by David in the 16th verse, 'The day is thine; the night also is thine': And, in the 14th verse, God is thus addressed, 'For God is my king of old; the help that is done upon earth, *he* doeth it *himself*.' Then follows immediately a transition from the *third* person to the *second*, in the five succeeding verses: '*Thou* didst divide the sea,' &c" ([1842], 2:96). Verity later registers his approval of Todd's reading (468). Twentieth century critics continue to comment on sources, influences, and analogs as they discuss Adam and Eve's prayer. For the notion of the "gift of sleep" (735), for example, Verity (468) specifies one Homeric parallel in *Iliad* 9.713, and one Virgilian in *Aeneid* 2.269. Edward Chauncey Baldwin adds Ps. 92 to those listed by Todd, reporting that the rabbis, who called Ps. 92 the "Sabbath Psalm," identified the fallen Adam as its author: "He composed it, they said, out of gratitude because the Sabbath appeared before God as his advocate, pleading that he be not expelled from Paradise on the Sabbath" (368). Thomas B. Stroup contends that Adam and Eve's prayer is to be associated with the Evensong in the Book of Common Prayer, which calls for Pss. 74 and 127 to be read or chanted. Stroup adds that Pss. 98 and 67, which "were used as canticles for Evening Prayer in Elizabeth's Prayer Book," also "in word, doctrine, or imagery contribute either to the adoration or to the hymn itself." Stroup concludes by claiming that the last two lines of the couple's prayer "remind us of the Second Collect at Evening Prayer: that we 'may passe our time in rest and quietnes' " (29). Focusing on this evening prayer, in addition to the following morning's prayer, Sister Mary Irma Corcoran agrees that "the prayers are hymns compiled from various sources, chiefly the Psalms and the Canticle of the Three Children" (111), but she cautions, "many of the Psalms have ideas and phrases in common with each other and with other portions of Scripture, notably with the Canticle of the Three Children, Job, Wisdom, and the Epistles of St. Paul, so that the exact source of a passage can not be determined without further evidence than mere verbal parallels" (133). Corcoran concedes, however, that "the close correspondence of most of the lines of Adam's prayers not only to Psalms recited during Matins, Lauds, Prime, and Vespers of the Roman Breviary, but yet more strikingly to hymns peculiar to that office, together with the reference within the morning prayer (V, 170) to 'that sweet hour of prime,' suggests that Milton at least was familiar with the Breviary" (133–34). Finally Corcoran finds it very probable that Milton was also indebted to the doxology of Cornelius à Lapide (134).

Rather than associating Adam and Eve's prayer with the Psalms or classical literature, Kester Svendsen associates it with Satan's earlier address to the sun: "Milton repeatedly moves from circumference to center, retracing through stock images the arcs of focus upon earth and man. And it is a two-way passage. Satan and Adam are centers from which radiates the flow of imagination, as when Adam and Eve contemplate the heavens and pray or Satan apostrophizes the sun after he had flung himself from its sphere to the top of Mount Niphates" (*Milton and Science* 45).

In their readings of the evening prayer, Grant McColley and Jon S. Lawry find that Adam and Eve express their intellectual and spiritual growth, their developing awareness of and appreciation for the ways of God. Quoting Andrew Willet's *Hexapla in Genesin* 33, McColley explains that the evening prayer recalls the concept of the intellectual nature of work in the garden: "being thus occupied in continual beholding of the goodly plants in Paradise, he [Adam] might thereby be stirred up to acknowledge the goodness and bounty of the Creator" ("*Paradise Lost*" 210n135). Also see McColley in **610–33** and **660–73**. Similarly, Lawry writes, "in their vesper hymn our first parents again choose rightly within God's abundance, recognizing that, whereas Satan would prevent human love (IV, 749), God has promised them 'a Race / To fill the Earth' (IV, 732–733). Milton perhaps touched the words faintly with prophetic tragic irony, indicating the grave which Adam and Eve will 'fill' with their race, but the principal meaning is clear: they forego their own questioning of God's abundance, 'understanding' him joyfully rather than merely questioning without thought" (177).

Speaking against the conventional eighteenth century opinions on versification, most notably expressed by Samuel Johnson in a series of *Rambler* essays published in early 1751, Samuel Say praises the "variety" he hears in Milton's verse, especially pointing to Adam and Eve's hymns and the narrator's hymn to wedded love. In "An Essay on the Harmony, Variety, and Power of Numbers," Say explains the "variety" of numbers as that which "arises from the different length and form of the periods; the different structure and composition of the parts; the different quantity of time in which they move; the force of consonants or sweetness of vowels, chosen with art or suggested with felicity, the ready attendant on art and exercise. And a proper mixture, exchange, agreement, or opposition of such a variety of parts, sounds, and numbers—and sometimes a sudden and seasonable start from all rules, to awaken attention or imitate the passion—seems to be that 'hidden soul of harmony,' as Milton calls it, which secretly informs the whole composure and animates every word, and even every syllable" (466). While Johnson, a few years later, declares the "pure" measure in English verse as iambic, Say, focusing on the hymns in *PL,* explains that in the hymns "you will find the same strong iambics as industriously avoided; and all is slow and solemn, in airs that breathe or inspire devotion. And the grave and sacred spondees are the sounds that justly prevail" (476). Also see Say on Milton's "Haile wedded Love" in **736–75**. For Johnson, Milton's "starting[ing] from all rules" is "licentious," as he argues in *Rambler* 86 (4:91). Johnson describes the versification in Adam and Eve's evening hymn as "the mixed measure," which, "always injures the harmony of the line considered by itself," although he concedes that the "mixed measure" does "relieve…us from the continual tyranny of the same sound, and makes us more sensible of the harmony of the pure measure" (4:90). Finding only lines 724 and 728 "regular," Johnson rules that "the rest are more or less licentious with respect to the accent" (91). Quoting Johnson's use here, the *OED* 1 defines *licentious* as "Disregarding commonly accepted rules, deviating freely from correctness, esp. in matters of grammar or literary style; overstepping customary limits."

720–22. Several forms of repetition function through this series of lines describing Adam and Eve preparing to pray before "thir shadie Lodge." Newton first directs attention to the structural parallel between the last foot in 720 and the first foot in 721: "A great admirer of Milton observes, that he sometimes places two monosyllables at the end of the line stopping at the fourth foot, to adapt the measure of the verse to the sense; and then begins the next line in the same manner, which has a wonderful effect. This artful manner of writing makes the reader see them *stand* and *turn* to worship God before they went into their bower. If this manner was alter'd, much of the effect of the painting would be lost" (284). Christopher Ricks identifies the "great admirer of Milton" as William Benson in *Letters Concerning Poetical Translations* 48. Of the structural device, Ricks admits, "Plainly there will always be differences of opinion about such effects, but Benson does seem to be pointing to a genuine function of the line-ending: the verse wheels, just as Adam and Eve wheel" (79–80). The second form of repetition in this sequence is the three-time repetition of *both,* once in each line. Todd reports that while Dunster admires the structural repetition between 720 and 721, he regrets that *both* is repeated a third time: "What poetical effect is here produced by the repetition of *both,* is much frustrated by the unfortunate and unmeaning introduction of the word in the next line, where, from the words that follow ['Skie, Air, Earth and Heav'n'], it not only loses all the force, but has no propriety." In this same note contributed to Todd's edition of Milton's *Works,* Charles Dunster then cites a Virgilian precedent in *Eclogues* 7.4–5 ([1842], 2:96). Masson (*Poetical Works* 3:178) responds to Dunster's disappointment, considering but dismissing the possibility that Milton intended a comma after the third *both,* and finally pointing out that in his earlier poetry (Sonnet 11.2), Milton refers *both* to more than two items: "both matter, form, and stile." Verity, followed by Alastair Fowler, brings additional legitimacy to *both* being applied to more than two items. Verity explains that such a usage is "quite Elizabethan," and he offers an example from Shakespeare's *Venus and Adonis* 747: "Both favour, savour, hue and qualities" (468). Fowler brings forward the authority of the *OED both* B.I.b to legitimize Milton's usage (656).

724–29. Bentley (133) struggles with the syntax of these lines, assuming that "this delicious place" (729) must be the direct object of the far-removed "Thou also mad'st" at 724, and the Richardsons, as well as Newton and Todd, are drawn to comment. The Richardsons admit, "We should not have taken Notice of This Passage if it had not been Strangely Mistaken of Late. the Sense, as 'tis pointed in the Best Editions, is Sufficiently plain. Happy in our Mutual Help, in our Mutual Love, the Chief of All Our Bliss, thy Gift, and Happy in this Paradise" (175). Accepting both readings, Newton (285–86) adds a third, "Happy in our mutual help and mutual love, the crown of all our bliss, and *of* this delicious place," and while Todd presents all three, he believes that the Richardsons' reading best captures Milton's meaning ([1842], 2:96–97).

724–25. Conceding that this allusion to Ps. 74.16 ("The day is thine, the night also is thine") "makes it clear that God still controls things, even though a fateful night is falling," James H. Sims notes, "Although God has control of both night and day, in poetic consistency with the opposition of light and darkness in the setting, when Satan flees [as Book 4 ends], the shades of night flee with him" (*Bible* 112).

724. *Pole:* Merritt Y. Hughes (*Complete Poems* 295) glosses this as "the entire sky," and cross-references *Mask* 99.

732–33. In Adam and Eve's words about "a race / To fill the earth," Alastair Fowler (656) hears Gen. 1.28, "God said unto them, Be fruitful, and multiply, and replenish the earth," and describing that text as "very controversial," Fowler proceeds to present Willet's understanding in *Hexapla* that it not only established marriage as an "institution in mans innocencie" (21) but also established that marriage was open to all men. Fowler (657) points out, however, that for the Catholic Robert Bellarmine and his fellow Jesuits (*Disputationes* 327) as well as Benedictus Pererius (*Commentariorum* 184), Gen. 1.28 "contained no precept to marry, but only an 'institution of nature.'" Cf. **736–75**, and Hume's distinction between a benediction and a command. James H. Sims (*Bible* 26) hears Gen. 1.28 at 748–49: "Our Maker bids increase, who bids abstain / But our destroyer."

735. Again, Bentley stirs several other editors to pause when he decides that "the gift," not "thy gift," was what Milton, influenced by Homeric precedent (*Iliad* 5.742), had intended (133). Pearce (139–40) cross-references 612 as he argues for "thy gift," and he invokes Virgilian authority from the *Aeneid* 2.269, "Dono divum gratissima serpit"; "and by grace of the gods [their first rest] steals over them most sweet." Todd reports both references, but asserts the more compelling authority of Ps. 127.2, "so he giveth his beloved sleep" ([1842], 2:97). Most recently, Fowler adds another Homeric precedent (*Iliad* 9.713), yet admits that "the idea of sleep as a divine gift is almost universal" (656).

736–75. Having expressed their love for God in prayer "unanimous, and other Rites / Observing none" (736–37), Adam and Eve approach the nuptial bower, and the narrator's voice—no longer joined with theirs—becomes something like a voice-over as the prelapsarian couple proceeds to share "the Rites / Mysterious of connubial Love" (742–43). Strikingly memorable visual details anchor the paragraph at its beginning and its end, but when the opening image of Adam and Eve holding hands (738–39) fades to a glimpse of prelapsarian lovemaking that he cannot actually see but can only "weene" (741), the postlapsarian narrator assumes a much more rhetorical role, as he alternates between defending—or celebrating—marriage, and condemning all that threatens it. To be sure, the paragraph's first section (736–49) structurally stands apart from the subsequent formal hymn to "wedded Love" (750–75), but the two sequences merge thematically as they develop the narrator's views on marriage, as well as the views of those against whom he argues. Finally, while the narrator is speaking about marriage, he is also speaking about marital sex, and this theologically charged sequence therefore brings variation to the theme of prelapsarian sex introduced with the description of Adam and Eve's kiss at 292–97.

Providing more than two pages of annotations, Patrick Hume most energetically initiates the critical response to the theological issues, and while his successors seldom cite him, the soundness of his annotations remains unquestioned until the mid-twentieth century, when Milton scholars bring extraordinary attention to the very complicated and controversial topic of Adam and Eve's marriage. Hume declares that he has not a doubt "but all the sensitive Appetites were in absolute obedience to Reason before *Adam's* transgression, and the most brutal Passions easily governable; and that by sin entred that irregularity which brought forth shame, and the disguise of his leav'd Apron" (161). Against the opinions of such church fathers as John of Damascene (*De Fide Orthodoxus* 1.4.25, 1.2.30) and Chrysostom (*Homily* 18 on Gen. 4), Hume charges that they "fortify...their Reason with v. 12 of Psal. 49 ['Nevertheless man being in honour abideth not: he is like the beasts that perish']...as if that Text did imply that Mankind (if sinless) was to have been propagated some nobler way than by that of Generation, now common to the Beasts with them: A *Dogma* which some have pursued to such a height of presumption as to affirm, That *Eve* her self was the forbidden Fruit. *St. Augustine* [*The Literal Meaning of Genesis* 9.3–4] himself went so far, as to say, That Carnal Knowledge and Consanguinity proceeded from sin; that is, that *Adam*, during his Innocency and abode in Paradise, knew not his fair *Eve*. An assertion he could no way be certain of" (160). After thus presenting the opinions of these "ancient Fathers and great Doctors," Hume highlights the scriptural authority for condemning their views and for justifying the prelapsarian physical union. Juxtaposing Gen. 1.27–28 to Gen. 2.18, Hume concludes that "it will be hard to assign any thing in which Adam wanted a help meet for him more properly, than in that of the Production of his own Kind" (160). Hume also invokes the authority of St. Paul, whose opinions figure importantly to all who consider Milton and marriage, in whatever context. Hume cites Eph. 5.32 and Heb. 13.4, "Marriage is honourable in all, and the Bed undefiled," before he circles back to God's own words in Gen. 1.28, and to those who insist, "Be fruitful, and multiply" is not a command but "a Benediction." Those "Catholic Encouragers of the Celibat," Hume concludes, "are approving thereby and fulfilling the Prophecy of St. *Paul* amply verified in them. *Now the Spirit speaketh expresly, That in the latter times some shall depart from the Faith, giving heed to seducing Spirits, and Doctrines of Devils, speaking Lies in Hypocrisie, having their Consciences seared with a hot Iron, forbidding to marry.* 1 Tim. ch. 4. v. 1, 2, 3. to which our Author seems to have had regard, from V.744. to this place" (161). While eighteenth and nineteenth century editors gloss 736–75 with the same scriptural references, none sketches out a background for the narrator's debate with those "Hypocrites" who "austerely talk / Of puritie and place and innocence" (744–45), as Hume does. Masson (*Poetical Works* 3:178), for example, writes that Milton "had in view not merely the general discouragement of the married state by the Roman Catholic advocates of monasticism, but also the opinion of some theologians that in the state of innocence there was no exercise of marriage-rights. In combating either view, or both, Milton refers to Scriptural texts—Gen. i.28; I Cor. vii.28 and 36; I Tim. iv.1–3; Heb. xiv.4; &c." Also see Newton 286; Todd (1842), 2:97; Stebbing 107. In 1929, Edward Chauncey Baldwin aligns Milton with the rabbis who also "insisted... upon the blamelessness of sex relations before the Fall" (376), but the relationship between Milton's views and Catholic views on the Edenic marriage remains as Hume describes them until such critics as Grant McColley, C. S. Lewis, Sister Mary Irma Corcoran, and Arnold Williams return to the topic. In his study of the major origins of *PL*, McColley (*"Paradise Lost": An Account* 151–52) looks anew at the Catholic fathers and describes their view as follows: "*if* copulation had occurred in Paradise prior to man's fall, it would have been effected without lust." In support of his claim, McColley refers to Tostatus's remarks (13.770) on pre- and postlapsarian copulation in his commentary on Genesis, and to Augustine's *The City of God* 14.23.

See, however, Robert Martin Adams's objections to McColley's methodology (152). "Unfallen Sexuality," the shortest chapter in *A Preface to* Paradise Lost, becomes the most well known of these very important re-examinations of the theological background of Adam and Eve's marriage. With the chapter's opening sentence, C. S. Lewis, unlike McColley, gives nearly exclusive authority to Augustine's influence on Milton's presentation: "Milton and St. Augustine agree in contrasting the fallen sexuality which we now know, and which is conditioned by the disobedience of our members, with an unfallen sexuality." Lewis points out, however, that Augustine and Milton disagree about what actually happened in the garden, Augustine believing that unfallen sexual intercourse never occurred, and Milton insisting that it did. Furthermore, while Augustine thought that any effort to describe such unfallen sexual intercourse was bound to contaminate it, Milton dared to present just such a description, although Lewis concludes, "I cannot make up my mind whether he was wise" (122). Corcoran sets Milton's presentation of prelapsarian sexual intercourse against the hexameral background, considers the modulations in Catholic opinion over time, and acknowledges the personal element in the voice of Milton's narrator. While there was a strong "disapproval of conjugal union" (73) during the early Christian era, Corcoran reports that "the greater number of commentators...agreed that human life in the state of original justice would have been propagated in the manner natural to the species with the exception that, in this as in all human acts, all bodily and spiritual powers would have been in perfect harmony and due order, with reason and will supreme" (74). Corcoran finds that the narrator's adamant insistence on Edenic sex, however, tends to "arouse doubt" about its being unlibidinous, and "to make the couple's serene hope of parenthood (IV, 732) seem perfunctory" (75). Arnold Williams situates Milton's views on copulation in the state of innocence in the context of the commentaries on Genesis published between 1527 and 1633, and while he acknowledges that those commentaries clearly indicate the split between Catholics who support and Protestants who oppose celibacy, Williams cautions that it is "unfair...not to note that Catholic commentators like Pererius list among the ends of marriage the social, though they do insist on the higher merit of the celibate life for those who can receive it" (*Common Expositor* 86). Furthermore, Williams explains that, though in his *Commentariorum,* Pererius explains that "the natural method of procreation among animals, including man, ...would have obtained in the state of innocence just as it did after the fall," he, and others like him, did not believe that Adam and Eve had ever had sexual relations in the garden, and those commentators would have denied Milton's insistence upon it (*Common Expositor* 89). While they, like the critics just surveyed, never specifically refer to Hume, Merritt Y. Hughes and Geoffrey Bullough qualify any similarly sweeping condemnations of Catholic opinion on sex and marriage, both before and after the Fall. After he quotes John Salkeld, whose remarks on the early Catholic fathers in *A Treatise of Paradise* 178–79 accord with Hume's, Hughes turns to C. S. Lewis's presentation of medieval theological thought in *The Allegory of Love* 15, where Lewis writes that Albertus Magnus (*In Petri Lombardi Sententiarum* 4.26.7) had "swept away 'the idea that the [sexual] pleasure is evil or the result of the Fall: on the contrary, pleasure would have been greater if we had remained in Paradise'" (*Complete Poems* 295). As he considers the parallels between the Edenic marriage in *PL* and the one in Jacob Cats's *Trou-Ringh,* Bullough moves the consideration of Catholic opinion on the Edenic marriage from the early fathers to the Scholastic fathers. In *Trou-Ringh,* Philogamus expresses concern about the propriety of prelapsarian sex and is answered by Sophroniscus, who reports that "the Scholastic writers concluded that in the primal state fleshly union took place." Bullough cautions that the parallel is not evidence of Milton's debt to Cats because "the same problems faced writers everywhere who wished to describe the paradisal state" (119). In tandem with these scholarly efforts to clarify Catholic opinion are efforts to clarify the Protestant opinion on marriage, prelapsarian and postlapsarian. In "The Puritan Art of Love" William and Malleville Haller argue, "Up to a point Milton was merely presenting in the poetic idiom of *Paradise Lost* what most men and women in his day, certainly most Puritans, thought about marriage, had often heard from the pulpit, and could have read in a large number of edifying books" (235). Roland Mushat Frye works with Puritan sermons, marriage manuals, and conduct books in "The Teaching of Classical Puritanism on Conjugal Love." Frye (159) finds that Milton's entire presentation of Edenic love through this section of Book 4 accords with what Daniel Rogers tells newly married husbands in *Matrimoniall Honour* 19: "Thy wife shall be a blessing, no snare; thy liberties shall be pure unto thee, and thou shalt visit thine habitation without sinne." Early Puritanism, Frye explains (155–56), insisted upon "the purity, legality, and even obligation of physical love in marriage," and he glosses Milton's 4.762 with a passage from *The Office of Christian Parents* 140 asserting that the married couple "may ioyfully give due benevolence one to the other; as two musicall instruments rightly fitted, doe make a most pleasant and sweet harmonie in a well tuned consort." More widely focused, C. A. Patrides presents much the same conclusion a decade or so later, finding the "standard Protestant views on conjugal love" in Milton's presentation of Adam and Eve's marriage, but similarly acknowledging that Milton "insists" on the physical consummation of that marriage (*Milton* 167). As he considers seventeenth century opinion on the purposes of marriage ("society, procreation, remedy for lust"), Alastair Fowler (658) places Milton in the company of Anglicans, rather than Puritans, Anglicans such as John Hooper (*A Declaration of the Ten Commandments* 381), Thomas Becon (*The Booke of Matrimony* fol. DCxlviii recto), and Jeremy Taylor ("The Marriage Ring" 219); "the majority of Anglican divines," writes Fowler, "unlike Donne, who emphasised remedy [e.g., *Sermons* 2:335–47], placed society first." Quoting *DocCh* 1.10 on this point ("The *form* of marriage consists in the mutual exercise of benevolence, love, help, and solace between the espoused parties.... The end of marriage is nearly the same with the form" [Patterson, *Works* 15:155]). Fowler traces the same emphasis in the presentation of marriage in Book 4 of *PL*. Reviewing much of the critical discourse on the Edenic marriage, Fowler brings up yet another thorny theological concern: "If Adam and Eve share the fertility of Paradise, must they not conceive before the fall, and thus bear a child free from original sin?" (657). This very question had haunted many pondering the first marriage, and Patrick Hume is no exception. Hume follows his criticism of St. Augustine's view that Adam "knew not his fair Eve," as he explains that Eve "conceived not during his stay there" (160). Fowler cites not Hume, but rather Andrew Willet, who, according to Fowler, "was quite capable of believing both that marriage was instituted 'in man's innocencie' (*Hexapla* 21) and that 'Adam in the state of innocencie should [sc. would] not have gotten so ungratious a sonne, as Caine was'" (60). According to Fowler, "It was possible to hold that Adam and Eve made love in Paradise without conceiving. But in any case, traditional embryological theories allowed ample opportunity for the subsequent infection of children conceived in innocence" (657). Also see Kermode on this point (103). Such critical efforts to understand the prelapsarian marriage carry into John Halkett's *Milton and the Idea of Matrimony*, which re-engages with much of the material earlier critics examined, but also more emphatically brings Milton's divorce tracts to bear on the topic. Halkett insists that the marriage in Book 4 is "fully chaste because it is 'wedded Love,' human love informed by reason and by the law of God, and also fully sexual" (102). The marriage "is a sign of the full humanity of man, of his reason, will, emotions, and appetites operating in harmony; and it is the culmination and epitome of human happiness" (109).

What is sometimes forgotten, or only briefly, and perhaps uncomfortably, acknowledged in these more polemical efforts is the sensuous joy of "the Rites / Mysterious of connubial Love" (742–43). When Dennis H. Burden approaches this element in the marriage of Adam and Eve, for example, his focus remains on theodicy: "it was not simply Man's possession of sexual appetite that was responsible for his fall, since that would be to indict the providence of God who had created Man's particular nature" (159). The importance of sex in Milton's unfallen garden has not gone unappreciated, however. Unburdened by Christian theodicy, Denis Saurat in the early 1920s, for example, argues that if "the physical inclination, far from 'subduing the soul of man,' is only the realization on the material plane of the whole soul, the material union of two beings already united morally and intellectually, then sex is the mysterious consecration of the whole of man, and becomes sacred: it is the instrument of God for the transmission of life" (157). Through the middle decades of the twentieth century, as the so-called sexual revolution began to reshape Western society, a number of Milton critics focus attention on the joy of prelapsarian sex, not to advance Saurat's thesis, but to temper or counterbalance the criticism that authorizes the Edenic marriage by theological debate; for these critics, Milton's poetry, more than theological history, speaks most meaningfully. Against the polemics defending marriage, and insisting on harmony between reason and passion in the prelapsarian marriage, is a body of criticism that hears such harmony in Milton's musical celebration of marriage, the encomium "Haile wedded Love" (750–75). Douglas Bush chronologically heads up these moderns. He completely agrees that the role of reason in prelapsarian life "is nowhere more strikingly illustrated than in his [Milton's] account of love between man and woman. This has been regarded, with favor or otherwise, as the Puritan ideal of marriage set forth in a versified Puritan conduct book." Bush insists, however, that Milton is "decidedly more emphatic and outspoken than most Puritans in exalting the physical expression and enrichment of love." Recalling Saurat's argument, Bush contends, "The importance he [Milton] gives to 'Love's due Rites' has a metaphysical basis, namely, his belief in the essential oneness of matter and spirit, yet this emphasis is part of, and not at odds with, his larger emphasis on the rational nature of human love" (*"Paradise Lost" in Our Time* 75). Also see Bush on the prelapsarian marriage in *Mythology* 266–67.

Like Bush, Frank Kermode, Joseph Summers, and David Daiches, as well as William Haller, present their reservations about too strong an emphasis on "wedded Love" as something adequately presented within the bounds of a theological debate. A few years after "The Puritan Art of Love," William Haller returns to Milton's marriage encomium, giving more attention to its poetry, in addition to its theology, and underscoring the place of marriage within society: "Plato and the poets had taught him [Milton] that the office of love begins and ends in the soul. Spenser and the preachers in their several ways had taught him that the love whose office is in the soul must be sealed in marriage" (95). Such an understanding of marriage, Haller continues, makes it "the focus of all interest and meaning in *Paradise Lost*. It is the consummation of God's plan of creation on earth. It is the projection of the divine order, of the order of nature and of the soul, into human society. It is the whole of human society in germ, the living microcosm, truly, of family, church, and state" (97). With a nod to the earlier work of such scholars as Haller, Frank Kermode concedes that "the Puritan cult of married love" may have authorized the prelapsarian sexual consummation of Adam and Eve's marriage, but he insists that "it could not account for what has been called Milton's 'almost Dionysiac treatment' of sexuality before the Fall" (103; see Harris Francis Fletcher 185). Kermode declares that "nothing in the poem is more beautifully achieved" (104) than Milton's presentation of that sexual joy, and dismissing Corcoran's fear, he insists, "The loves of Paradise must be an unimaginable joy to the senses, yet remain 'unlibidinous'" (105). Summers emphasizes the importantly personal authority for Milton's celebration of sexual love in the garden: "Despite all the possible sources, the intensity of his conviction that there could be no original paradise for man without sexual love seems personal and original" (99). For Daiches, Milton's marriage encomium "is one of the strongest expressions of Milton's views on the place of sex, and makes clear once and for all that his views were far from those conventionally labelled Puritan" (192). Finally, Leland Ryken discusses prelapsarian sexuality as a feature of the apocalyptic vision of paradise. "The prelapsarian relationship of Adam and Eve...is essentially humanistic in its portrayal, both in its insistence on the presence of physical love and its portrayal in images taken from the institution of civilized marriage" (145).

With the eighteenth century editors and critics, the topic of sexual love is seldom, if ever, so directly encountered, but rather channeled through discussions of "Haile wedded Love" as it responds to a variety of poetic traditions. The vigor of Hume's debate with the "Hypocrites" indicted by Milton's narrator is missing from his rather fragmented commentary on "Haile wedded Love," but the editors who immediately succeed Hume greatly admire the hymn. Hume glosses 750–75 with passages from Ovid (*Metamorphoses* 1.468–71), Virgil (*Georgics* 2.458–59, 4.373; *Aeneid* 1.73), and Horace (*Odes* 3.10.1–8,

4.1), but when he describes "Cupid" inflicting wounds that bring on "Pains and Pangs," and the "shifting Inconstancies" of "that unruly Passion," Hume seems to let the Roman poets' views on love overshadow the views of Milton's narrator (162). Considering "Haile wedded Love" in its entirety, Newton (287) credits an "ingenious friend" for identifying Milton's praise of wedded love with one of Torquato Tasso's letters: " 'O dolce conguintione de' cuori, o soave unione de gli animi nostri, o legitimo nodo,' &c. [Lettura Sol Matrimonio 36]. The quotation would swell this note to too great a length; but the reader, who understands Italian, may, if he please, compare the original with our author, and he will easily perceive what an excellent copier Milton was, as judicious in omitting some circumstances, as in imitating others." In addition Newton refers "Haile wedded Love" to Cicero's *De Officiis* 1.17. Also see Newton on *Charities* in **756**. Todd most extensively develops the consideration of literary sources. Glancing at Cupid's "purple wings" (764) by reference to "March" 33 in Spenser's *The Shepheardes Calender* (*Poetical Works* 593) and, crediting a note from Charles Dunster, Ovid's *The Remedies of Love* 701, Todd proceeds to present Newton's note on Tasso but adds Robert Thyer's unpublished note on "Reigns here and revels" in 765 of Milton's hymn: "What our author here says of marriage, Marino applies in the same terms to Venus [*L'Adone* 2.114]." Thyer adds, "it is probable, that Milton alluded to this and other such extravagances of the poets, and meant to say, that what they had extravagantly and falsely applied to loose wanton love, was really true of that passion in its state of innocence." Todd also finds it "probable" that Milton was here influenced by two other eulogies on love: Lodovico Dolce's "Dialogo del modo di tor moglie [*Dialogo... nel Quale si Ragiona della Institution della Maritata* 2.36v–61]" and "an eulogy on matrimony in the fifteenth Canto of Murtola's 'Creatione del Mondo.' " Finally, Todd offers a note from Dunster identifying the "ground-work" of Milton's celebration of marriage as Sylvester's translation of Du Bartas's *The Divine Weeks and Works* 1.6.1055–78, "where the poet, having described the marriage of Adam and Eve, proceeds in terms of abundant but certainly not very poetical eulogy on wedded Love" ([1842], 2:97–99). In *Considerations on Milton's Early Reading and the Prima Stamina of His "Paradise Lost,"* Dunster compares Du Bartas with Ennius, and Milton with Virgil, concluding that the readers of both "will be pleased... to see how a Virgil has improved and decorated the primary thought of an Ennius" (149). Contemporary with Todd, Mitford (140–41) refers Milton's "Haile wedded Love" to Thomas Middleton's *The Phoenix* 2.2.161–70: "Reverend and honourable matrimony." Several other twentieth century critics reconsider Dunster's reference to Du Bartas and Milton's "Haile wedded Love." Contending that "no other work of the Renaissance had a more important and definite influence on *PL* than Sylvester's translation of Du Bartas," George Coffin Taylor brings special attention to the marriage songs: "Du Bartas follows his hymn in praise of marriage (which somewhat resembles Milton's after the creation of Adam and Eve) by saying—as Milton does here—that 'increase' is 'Rather commanded then allowed'" (44). In "Variorum," Merritt Y. Hughes considers the parallel between the human marriage and the divine marriage with which Du Bartas opens his epithalamium: "Source of all joyes! Sweet Hee-Shee-Coupled-One!... / O blessed Bond! O happy Marriage! / Which dost the match 'twixt Christ and us presage!" (1.1062, 1066–67). Robert Martin Adams rejects such arguments about Du Bartas's influence on the poet of *PL,* however, reasoning that Milton "is unlikely to have thought highly of an author whose literary tastes and talents were unashamedly pedestrian" (154–55). Finally, while parallels and sources connect Milton's "Haile wedded Love" with earlier literature, several critics have read the marriage song as an anticipation of future literature. The late nineteenth century French critic H. A. Taine may mock Milton's failure to humanize prelapsarian Adam and Eve, but he celebrates Milton's achievement in the hymn to "wedded Love," pointing out that Milton "justifies" prelapsarian sex "by the example of saints and patriarchs. He immolates before it 'the bought smile' and 'court-amours, mix'd dance or wanton mask, or midnight ball, or serenate.' We are a thousand miles from Shakespeare; and in the Protestant eulogy of the family tie, of lawful love, of 'domestic sweets,' of orderly piety and of home, we perceive a new literature and an altered time" (2.2.315–16). Four decades later, G. Wilson Knight also comments on this point, comparing Milton's views on "sexual energy" with D. H. Lawrence's, and arguing that both writers attack "primarily a lustful or unduly mentalized development of sexual energy, as well as many sophisticated and respectable pleasures, indeed the whole chivalrous and idealistic approach." For Milton, Knight proceeds to argue, "The Fall is therefore carefully shown as inducing a peculiarly mental lasciviousness" (71).

Among the early editors, none admires "Haile wedded Love" more deliberately than Joseph Addison, but his criticism moves away from the poem's literary sources to ponder its appropriateness within the epic and to provoke a debate that proceeds into twentieth century criticism. Addison discusses what he names Milton's "Panegyrick on Marriage" in *Spectator* 297, which considers the faults in *PL*. Digressions, Addison asserts, "are by no means to be allowed of in an Epic Poem" (*Spectator* 3:60), but identifying digressions in Milton's epic, he defends them with a precedent from the *Aeneid*, in which Virgil reflects on Turnus's donning the spoils of Pallas: "As the great Event of the *Æneid*, and the Death of *Turnus* whom *Æneas* slew because he saw him adorned with the Spoils of *Pallas*, turns upon this Incident, *Virgil* went out of his way to make this Reflection upon it, without which so small a Circumstance might possibly have slipped out of his Reader's Memory." Addison argues that although they too are digressive, "*Milton's* Complaint of his Blindness, his Panegyrick on Marriage, his Reflections on *Adam* and *Eve's* going naked, of the Angels eating, and several other Passages in his Poem are liable to the same Exception, tho' I must confess there is so great a Beauty in these very Digressions, that I would not wish them out of his Poem" (*Spectator* 3:61). Newton responds that "tho' this panegyric upon wedded love may be condemn'd as a digression, yet it can hardly be call'd a digression, when it grows so naturally out of the subject, and is introduced so properly, while the action of the poem is in a manner suspended, and while Adam and Eve are lying down to sleep; and if morality be one great end of poetry, that end cannot be better promoted than by such digressions as this" (288). Newton is quoted by Todd ([1842], 2:99). Voltaire considers the "digression on love" in Book 4 while responding to critics who condemn Milton for intruding himself into his epic. Voltaire distinguishes Milton's prologues from those interruptions in the narration "which he intersperses now and then upon some great incident, or some interesting circumstance. Of that kind is his digression on love in the fourth book." Very much recalling Newton's defense of Milton's panegyric on marriage, Voltaire continues, "I am so far from looking on that Liberty as a fault, that I think it to be a great Beauty" (112). In the twentieth century, Anne Davidson Ferry brings fresh attention to this critical issue. Designating the hymn to wedded love an "author-comment," rather than a digression, and keeping Waldock's condemnation of Milton's authorial intrusions in mind, Ferry develops her argument about the narrator's role throughout Milton's epic: "The direct addresses by this voice are not nervous attempts to correct the dramatic direction of the poem. They are reminders of the speaker's identity, that the reader may never lose his awareness of that distinctive voice in its unique situation. The explicit comments by the narrative voice are part of the total pattern, are essential to the expression of the speaker's vision, which directs the reader's interpretation by controlling the mood and meaning of every scene in the poem" (*Milton's Epic Voice* 51).

In his "An Essay on the Harmony, Variety, and Power of Numbers," Samuel Say focuses on Milton's "Haile wedded Love," as well as Adam and Eve's hymns, and, rejecting Richard Bentley's emendations in this passage, Say writes, "And why should not the mind and judgment of the reader have some pleasure in the power and variety of the numbers, where the ear is pleased to an excess and soothed with the sweetness of...a dozen such lines [764–75] as can scarce be met with in any other poet?" (481). See Bentley and Say in **765–69**. Also see Say in **720–35**.

736–38. Editors and critics have steadily echoed Milton's attention to the simplicity of prelapsarian *Rites* of worship, often emphasizing the difference between that worship and postlapsarian worship. Describing Adam and Eve's vesper prayer as "short," and "said by them with mutual consent," Hume paraphrases the bard: "No other Customs or Ceremonies observing, but standing and looking up to Heaven, they pray'd" (160). Vaughan, a mid-nineteenth-century editor, underscores Adam and Eve's praying *unanimous:* "By both—with one heart" (105). As he offers the support of *DocCh* 2.4, where Milton writes, "No particular posture of the body in prayer was enjoined, even under the law" (Patterson, *Works* 17:91), A. W. Verity (468) asserts that "M[ilton] often shows his dislike of ceremonies and forms in worship." Verity also notes that, after the Fall in *PL*, Adam and Eve pray standing at one point but kneeling shortly thereafter (11.1–2, 150), and later Michael explains that some of their sinful descendants "Will deem in outward Rites and specious forms / Religion satisfi'd" (12.534–35). Two later critics develop Michael's forecast about future worship. Walter Raleigh firmly sets Adam and Eve's worship against seventeenth century ceremonies: "In the Garden of Eden he [Milton] might present to an age which was overrun with a corrupt religion and governed by a decadent court the picture of a religion without a church, of life in its primitive simplicity, and of patriarchal worship without the noisome accretions of later ceremonial" (91). A. J. A. Waldock looks from the worshipers in the garden to the twentieth century readers observing them: "the ritual act for the moment sets the two apart from us and they take on a remoteness of majesty. At such moments the effect of nobility and loftiness that Milton perhaps was striving for was very nearly secured. At such moments the Adam of the poem is very close to the Adam that Milton had in mind" (28). Also see Cecil Maurice Bowra in **214**.

738. *inmost bowre:* the Richardsons explain that this phrase refers to "the Inmost, the Farthest part. the Word is us'd in the same Sense. V.302. ['Earths inmost womb'] in Both very Poetically" (175). The *OED* 1 quotes this line to illustrate the literal meaning of *inmost:* "In reference to spatial position: Situated farthest within, most inward, most remote from the outside." With 1.168, where Satan reveals to Beelzebub that he intends to "*disturb*" God's "inmost counsels from thir destind aim," the *OED* 2 illustrates the figurative meaning of *inmost:* "Of thoughts or feelings, the mind or soul, personal relations, etc.: Most inward or intimate; deepest; closest." Cf. Lieb in **690–705**.

739. *Handed:* in "Variorum," Merritt Y. Hughes reports that to illustrate *handed* meaning "hand in hand," the *OED* 3 quotes this line, as well as Milton's reference in *DDD* to the mutual obligations of "any two [who] be but once handed in the Church" (Patterson, *Works* 3:382). Hughes also cross-references 321–24.

740. *disguises:* "Cloaths, the covertures and concealments of our shame, the reproach of sin, and yet improved to the height of Pride and Vanity" (Hume 160).

742. *Rites:* glancing back at *Rites* in 736, Merritt Y. Hughes and Thomas B. Stroup comment on the association Milton thereby draws between religious worship and sexual communion. Hughes (*Complete Poems* 295) points out that Joseph Beaumont similarly associates religious worship and marital joy in *Psyche* 1.203–06: "Except the venerable Temples, what / Place is more reverend than the Nuptial Bed? / Nay, heav'n has made a Temple too of that / For Chastitie's most secret rites." To this repetition of *Rites,* Stroup draws in Eve's earlier recollection of her marriage ceremony (481–91): "If the form of the wedding ceremony is so casual and 'natural' as to seem pagan, the pagan consummation rites have been so transformed as to seem utterly Christian in both form and meaning" (28).

743. *Mysterious: Mysterious* strikingly resounds not only in Book 4 of *PL* but also, of course, with major Pauline statements about marriage, as critics have unfailingly noted, some, such as Richard Bentley and C. S. Lewis, finding those repetitions poetically ineffectual. Hume (161) associates Eph. 5.32

with *Mysterious* at its second appearance in this verse paragraph, at 750, which opens the hymn to "wedded Love." In Eph. 5.32, Paul writes, "For this cause [marriage] shall a man leave his father and mother, and shall be joined unto his wife, and they two shall be one flesh. This is a great mystery: but I speak concerning Christ and the church." After Hume explains that in this text "the Apostle makes Matrimony a representative of Christs Union with his Church by his Incarnation," he cross-references 312. The echo of the Pauline text is so clearly audible, however, that a simple "See *Ephes.* v.32" suffices for the Richardsons (176). James H. Sims (25) adds another Pauline reference, 1 Cor. 7.4–5, but maintains the emphasis on Ephesians. A dutiful nod to the Pauline texts is not what Milton's *Mysterious* elicits from Bentley and C. S. Lewis, however. Bentley claims that Milton "wears this Epithet threadbare. He had it once before, IV.312. *Mysterious Parts:* and what is worse, he repeats it within six Lines, *Hail wedded Love, mysterious Law.* I persuade my self, he gave it here, *Nor* Eve *the Rites /* SOLEMNIOUS *of connubial Love refus'd*" (134). Pearce (140) predictably offers Eph. 5.32 to justify *Mysterious,* but two centuries later, C. S. Lewis continues to share Bentley's dissatisfaction, adding that Milton again invokes *Mysterious* at 8.599, and complaining that Milton "seems to think that by twice using the word *mysterious* in this connection…he excuses his very un-mysterious pictures" (124). Merritt Y. Hughes explains that *Mysterious* also resonates with Milton's prose. Acknowledging Milton's attention to 1 Cor. 7.4–5 and Eph. 5.31–32, Hughes (*Complete Poems* 295, "Variorum") points to *Colas,* where Milton refutes an objection to his description of marriage as "a mystery of joy" (Patterson, *Works* 4:263) and *Apol,* where he asserts his mastery of "the doctrine of holy Scripture unfolding these chaste and high mysteries…that *the body is for the Lord, and the Lord for the body*" in marriage (Patterson, *Works* 3:306).

747. Alastair Fowler (657) here directs attention to *DocCh* 1.10, " Of the Special Government of Man before the Fall, Including the Institutions of the Sabbath and of Marriage," where Milton asserts that "marriage is honourable in itself, and prohibited to no order of men," and, drawing on the authority of 1 Cor. 7.1–2 ("It is good for a man not to touch a woman. Nevertheless, to avoid fornication, let every man have his own wife") concludes, "Hence marriage is not a command binding on all, but only on those who are unable to live with chastity out of this state" (Patterson, *Works* 15:155).

Pure: in his examination of the caesuras in Milton's poetry in *Rambler* 90, Samuel Johnson points to *Pure* to exemplify the following argument: "when a single syllable is cut off from the rest, it must either be united to the line with which the sense connects it, or be sounded alone. If it be united to the other line, it corrupts its harmony; if disjoined, it must stand alone and with regard to musick, be superfluous; for there is no harmony in a single sound, because it has no proportion to another" (4:111–12). Johnson concludes this essay, however, by asserting that, in regard to pauses in his poetry, Milton "has performed all that our language would admit" (115).

748–49. James H. Sims hears an allusion to Gen. 1.28, "Be fruitful and multiply," and reasons that Milton apparently considers "this command a more important argument for including wedded love in Paradise than the statement that Adam knew Eve after their expulsion (Gen. 4:1) is for excluding it" (26). See **736–75**.

750–75. See **736–75**.

750–70. This passage, along with Adam's later recollection of his wedding day, heads the list of 13 quotations under "Marriage" in Edward Bysshe's "Collection of…Descriptions and Characters, of Persons and Things…in the best *English* Poets" in *The Art of English Poetry* (250–51).

750–60. Michael Lieb (74–75) associates the invocation of "wedded Love" with the invocation of "holy Light" that opens Book 3: "Like the animating 'Fountain' (III, 8) of the poet's own inspirational source, the mysterious source of human animation and human offspring becomes the 'Perpetual Fountain of Domestic sweets' (IV, 760). The dialectic views both these sources, poetic and biological, with the highest reverence, for they are both of divine origin; they both inspire; and the miraculous operations of both are one of the mysteries of life." Lieb acknowledges the additional "associations of promised regeneration" in Gabriel's biblical Annunciation in Luke 1.26–38.

750–57. Identifying the *amor* formula, in addition to the *fortezza* formula, as one of the most persistent epic motifs, John M. Steadman explains: "Contrasting modes of *amor* (concupiscence and charity) motivate antithetical actions (disobedience and obedience) and achieve antithetical rewards (damnation and salvation). In Miltonic epic, as in the heroic poems of earlier Renaissance poets, love spurs the hero's principal act. The chief difference is that the warfare is spiritual rather than carnal, ethical rather than physical." Steadman continues, "Beauty supplements Valour as a heroic motif, and the heroine's charms complement the hero's prowess" (*Milton* 113). See Balachandra Rajan in **291–95**.

750. *mysterious Law:* Bentley (134) objects to *Law,* proposing "League" instead: "A *Law,* that's suppos'd *mysterious,* is no Law at all; which Word in its very Notion implies Publication and general Knowledge." Against this understanding, Bentley explains his preference for "League": "A *League* may be as mysterious, as the contracting Powers shall agree: and the matrimonial League always admits of secret Articles. IV.339. *Fair Couple, link'd in happy* Nuptial League." The Richardsons (176) and Todd ([1842], 2:98) follow Pearce (140) in simply glossing *mysterious* by reference to Eph. 5.32.

751–54. John S. Diekhoff notes the rhyme (*proprietie* and *thee*) in this sequence ("Rhyme" 541). See Diekhoff in **130–33**.

751. *sole propriety:* Hume (161) explains that "wedded Love" (750) is "the one only thing *Adam* could have called his own, had he continued in Paradise a sharer with his Sons," and he refers that understanding to Virgil's *Aeneid* 1.73: "Connubio jungam stabili, Propriamque dicabo"; "I will link to thee in sure wedlock." Alastair Fowler refers this feature of prelapsarian life to both Adam and Eve: "the exclusive relationship and mutual rights of Adam and Eve were the only propriety (proprietorship, ownership) in Paradise. The institution of marriage was prelapsarian, but not that of property rights" (658).

753–57. Sister Mary Irma Corcoran (30) points out that this passage explains the rationale for the announcement in 703–05 that the animals are excluded from the nuptial bower; the passage's emphasis on "reason as the foundation of the nuptial relationship and the distinguishing mark of human love, bears some resemblance to St. Thomas' broader explanation of the reservation of the garden to rational beings." See *Summa Theologica* 4.369.

756. *Charities:* Hume notes, "All the endearments of Fathers and Children," and he lists "Friendship, Benevolence, Beneficence, all the good Offices and reciprocal Kindnesses of *Relations. Relatio,* Lat. for relatives; of *referre,* Lat. to belong to; Relatives do *mutuo se* ponere, as Father and Child imply one the other" (161). Newton (287) adds classical and modern authority to Hume's note, supplying a reference to Cicero's *De Officiis* I.17 — "Cari sunt parentes, cari liberi, propinqui, familiares; sed omnes omnium caritates patria una complexa est"; "Parents are dear; dear are children, relatives, friends; but one native land embraces all our loves" — and adding that the word *Charities* "is used likewise in this manner in the Italian, and by Tasso in the place which our author is here imitating, *Ma la charita del sglivolo, e del padre*" (*Lettera* 40). Todd ([1842], 2:98) quotes Newton.

757. Jon S. Lawry believes that "the capitalized words in 'Father, Son, and Brother' half insist that the love between God, the Son, and the altogether human 'Brothers' of Christ is based on such a generative 'mysterious Law.'" Furthermore, Lawry contends that Milton "sees in the image of 'wedded love' the sense of oneness in love and will that can bind the Church to Christ, Christ to God, and men to one another and to God. It totally opposes the isolation and forgetfulness involved in the 'love' of Satan with Sin and Death" (178). See Hume on Eph. 5.32 in **743.**

758–60. A. W. Verity suggests that Milton "may have had in mind the charge brought against him of belittling marriage in his Divorce-tracts" (469).

761. The allusion to Heb. 13.4 has been established since Hume's *Annotations* (161). James H. Sims reasons that Milton's "projections of New Testament standards of Christian morality back to Paradise, though anachronistic, is deliberate" (*Bible* 26).

762. *Saints and Patriarchs:* Merritt Y. Hughes ("Variorum") clarifies the distinction here: "From Adam to David the *Patriarchs* were primarily the men whose faith is celebrated in Heb. 11.4–40. The *Saints* of the Old Testament were the whole congregation of the righteous whose way God 'preserveth' (Prov. 2.8)."

Patriarchs: Patrick Hume concentrates his attention on the concept of patriarchal power, tracing *Patriarch* to the Greek for "Father, and thence Governor of a Family," and then referencing Acts 7.8, "Jacob begat the twelve Patriarchs," on which Hume comments: "All Government took its Original Power and Authority from that of Fathers over their Children; and *Adam* was the first grand universal Patriarch and Monarch of Mankind" (161).

Masson admits to his uncertainty about Milton's intent here: "I am not sure but here Milton introduces a touch of his peculiar views of marriage. He seems to mean 'whether in our present form of the institution, or in that known to saints and patriarchs in the old dispensation'" (*Poetical Works* 3:178).

763–73. William G. Madsen points to the contrast between "the theoretical truths of his [man's] nature or essence" and "the facts of his fallen existence" ("Idea" 249) by highlighting "the contrast between the natural love of Adam and Eve in the Bower, lulled to sleep by the spontaneous song of the nightingale, and the artificialities of the Petrarchan love tradition" (262).

763–65. Early editors, especially Hume and Todd, identify and trace the traditions of Roman love poetry surfacing in this passage as they comment on the entire extended verse paragraph (see **736–75**), but a number of more recent critics and editors also continue to pursue Milton's debt to those Roman poets.

Love: describing the misery of the stereotypical victim of Love in the Roman poetic tradition, for example, Hume acknowledges the Ovidian (*Metamorphoses* 1.468–71), Virgilian (*Georgics* 1.373), Juvenalian (*Satires* 6.139), and Horatian (*Odes* 4.110) ancestry of Love as a mythological figure, but his annotation also intimates that the classical tradition is overshadowing his reading of Milton's text (162). Charles Grosvenor Osgood (26) looks more widely at Milton's references to Love, pointing out that Milton only infrequently refers to Love as a divinity, and when he does "he follows the later conception of Love as a sportive, winged boy, armed with the bow, arrows, and firebrands." Osgood clarifies that Milton here is reversing Ovid's description in *Amores* 3.9.7–9: "ecce, puer Veneris fert eversamque pharetram / et fractos arcus et sine luce facem; / adspice, demissis ut eat miserabilis alis"; "See, the child of Venus comes, with quiver reversed, with bows broken, and lightless torch; look, how pitiable he comes, with drooping wings."

golden shafts: A. W. Verity reports that in the legend, as it appears, for example, in *A Midsummer Night's Dream* 1.1.170, Cupid "had two sorts of arrows, one tipped with gold to inspire love, the other with lead to repel love," and Verity, like Hume, traces this legend to Ovid's *Metamorphoses* 1.468–71. Noting that Cupid's arrow here becomes a "rich golden shaft," as it also does in *Twelfth Night* 1.1.35, Verity concludes that Love's weaponry is an Elizabethan poetic commonplace (469). Also consulting the passage from *Metamorphoses* 1, Alastair Fowler (659) adds, "Cupid's *golden shafts* were sharp and gleaming, and kindled love; while those of lead were blunt, and put love to flight." Furthermore, Fowler points out that Erasmus, in his colloquy *Courtship* 1–5, anticipates Milton in associating Cupid's golden arrows with marital love.

constant Lamp: Verity (469) contrasts this with the lighting of the "Nuptial Torch" in 11.590, and he contrasts *constant* here with *casual* in 767. The contrast between prelapsarian and postlapsarian love is also Fowler's point when, referencing Valeriano's *Hieroglyphica* 46.19, "Mulieris Amor," he notes, "a lamp usually symbolized inconstancy of love, particularly woman's inconstancy." Fowler associates Love's "constant Lamp" with the lamps of the constant virgins awaiting the bridegroom in Matt. 25.1–13, insisting that the biblical parable "must surely constitute an allegorical overtone" (659).

purple wings: according to Patrick Hume (162), such wings are "no more than shining gawdy, glittering," as he quotes from Virgil's *Georgics* 4.373 and Horace's description of a swan's wings in *Odes* 4.1.10. Todd ([1842], 2:97) adds Spenser's *The Shepheardes Calender*, "March" 33 (Spenser 429), but concurs with Charles Dunster that both English poets are indebted to Ovid's *The Remedies of Love* 701, "Nec nos purpureas pueri resecabimus alas"; "I shall not clip the Boy's bright wings." Alastair Fowler acknowledges the meaning of the Latin *purpureas,* but adds that "Reigns" in the next line would have prompted Milton's seventeenth century readers to understand "that purple as an emblem of sovereignty was intended. Note also that purple was the distinctive colour of Hymen" (659).

Reigns here and revels: Todd presents Newton's note on Tasso (see **736–75**) but adds Robert Thyer's on 765: "What our author here says of marriage, Marino applies in the same terms to Venus in his description of her, *Adon.* [*L'Adone*] cant. ii. st. 114; and it is probable, that Milton alluded to this and other such extravagances of the poets, and meant to say, that what they had extravagantly and falsely applied to loose wanton love, was really true of that passion in its state of innocence" ([1842], 2:99).

765–69. Samuel Say, hearing "the very hiss of the serpent" (481) in this passage, has little patience with Richard Bentley's emendations: "the editor, with a great deal of compassion indeed for the lover and the harlot, but with no compassion to the author or regard to the pleasure of the reader, saith, 'Rather let it be "th' half-starv'd lover," and his case will be bad enough.' But the poet was of a differing opinion, and therefore has *starved* him *quite* to everyone that reads with a natural voice and gives to every sound its proper accent and quality of time" (480). See Bentley on Milton's "stumbling Verse" (134).

765–66. James Sims suggests that Heb. 13.4, "but whoremongers and adulterers God will judge," might have inspired Milton's "the bought smile / Of Harlots" (26). Sims explains that "such allusions placing Adam and Eve's relationship in alignment with New Testament (and seventeenth century Christian) concepts of the order of the sexes and the marriage relationship were doubtless intended to suggest to Milton's audience a convincing contemporary reality. At the same time, these allusions to the 'Rites / Mysterious' establish a vertical or figural connection between the pair in Paradise and Christ as the Bridegroom of his bride, the Church" (*Bible* 26–27).

766. *Harlots:* defining *Harlots* as "lewd Strumpets, empty of Love, Satisfaction, and all Endearments of the soft Sex," Hume, as he so often does, considers etymology: "*Harlot,* tho some will have it a derivation of *Arletta,* the Name of *William* the Conqueror's Mother, and others his Mistress, is doubtless from the Italian *Arletta,* a proud, insolent Mistress, or a contraction of *Horelet,* a Wench, a little wanton" (162). The *OED* quotes Milton's line to illustrate meaning 5c, "An unchaste woman; a prostitute; a strumpet," but one of the more intriguing features of the *OED* on *Harlot* is its tangled struggle with etymology. Admitting "Of this widely-diffused Romanic word, the ulterior history and origin are uncertain," the *OED* concludes the section on etymology with the following: "The random 'conjecture' of Lambarde, 1570–6, retailed by many later writers, that *harlot* in sense 5c was derived from the name of Arlette or Herleva, mother of William the Conqueror, could have been offered only after the earlier senses and uses of the word were forgotten."

767–70. David Masson admits, "The general Puritanism of this passage is obvious," but recalls "that Milton had seen masques acted and had himself written two of a peculiar kind, both acted—*Arcades* and *Comus*" (*Poetical Works* 3:178). Several later editors develop Masson's note. Assuming that Milton is probably "glancing particularly at the dissolute court of Charles II," A. W. Verity (460) cites the appearance of similar sarcasm in 1.497 describing the sons of Belial and in *PR* 2.183. Verity also explains that Puritans "greatly disliked the practice of men and women dancing together," and he quotes from *Ref,* where Milton combines in one condemnation "gaming, [jigging,] wassailing, and mixed dancing" (Patterson, *Works* 3:53). To Masson's acknowledgment that, while Milton here condemns masques, he had after all written two of them, Merritt Y. Hughes ("Variorum") similarly points out that in *L'All*, Milton invokes the spirit of "mask, and antique Pageantry" (Patterson, *Works* 1:39).

769. *Serenate…starv'd:* emending *Serenate,* which is the spelling in both the first and second editions, to *Serenade,* Hume brings attention to the coolness of the evening: "An evening Song, performed under the Window of some Lovely or Beloved Mistress; of the Fr. *Serenade,* of *serain,* Fr. the cool, or the cool Air of the evening." The lover is *starv'd,* suggests Hume, because of being "exposed to the accidental injuries of the Weather" (162), an understanding supported by the *OED* 4, which, quoting Milton's line, defines *starv'd* as "perished with cold." Again quoting Milton's line, the *OED* 1 defines *Serenade* as "A performance of vocal or instrumental music given at night in the open air, esp. such a performance given by a lover under the window of his lady." A. W. Verity (469) cross-references *starve* in 2.600 and refers the passage to "Horace's picture of a lover shivering by night outside the house of his 'proud fair' Lydia or Lyce (*Odes* I.25 and III.10)."

Dennis H. Burden compares this "contemptuously characterized" kind of poetry with Satan's voice in Eve's dream (5.38–47), which "has charm but no sense" (130), and he contrasts this Satanic poetry with Adam's words to Eve after that dream (5.122–28), which Burden describes as "a model of the right sort of love song" (131).

770. *quitted:* repaid, requited (Hughes, "Variorum").

771. Todd ([1842], 2:99–100) credits Callander with identifying an "affinity" between this description of Adam and Eve, asleep and embracing, with lines from Thomas Kyd's *The Spanish Tragedy* 2.2.45–51.

772–73. Three different parallels have been uncovered for this description of the roses showering down on Milton's sleeping Adam and Eve. Todd ([1842], 2:100) refers to John Harington's translation of Ariosto's *Orlando Furioso* 44.29: "And damsels from the windowes high and towres, / To gratulate their prosperous deeds and haps, / Cast showres of roses from their tender laps." Todd also finds the showering roses here comparable to the "Sweet showers of flowers" cast upon the head of Solomon's bride in Sylvester's translation of Du Bartas's *The Divine Weeks and Works* 2.4.2.812. Geoffrey Bullough (115–16), translating from the Dutch, notes a parallel scene in Jacob Cats's *Trou-Ringh* 659–61: "And [water] rises on all sides in fountain-spray / Filled with sweet scents the air plays round the pair [Adam and Eve] / While strewing over them a shower of roses."

773–75. Hume (162), seconded by Douglas Bush, refers the narrator's benediction over the "Blest pair" to Virgil's *Georgics* 2.456–57: "O fortunatos nimium sua si bona norint / Agricolas!"; "O happy husbandmen! Too happy, should they come to know their blessings!" According to Bush, Milton's recollection of Virgil's peasants "adds a note of human actuality to the pathos of idyllic innocence." Furthermore, Bush continues, "Although we think of Milton as an exponent of moral choice, of conscious virtue, the impending ruin of Adam and Eve evokes his nostalgic compassion for the simple innocence that is unaware of evil" ("Ironic and Ambiguous Allusion" 637; also see Bush on *repair'd* in 773). Bush's "note of human actuality" is more complicated to Christopher Grose, who in these lines sees evidence that Milton "keeps us keenly aware of the limits of poetry, as well as the fallibility of our own vision. There is no 'outside' to this poem, he [Milton] would seem to suggest; his Adam and Eve are real enough to address directly . . . or artificial enough to become pageantry" (222).

In his paraphrase, Hume acknowledges Milton's wordplay in "know to know no more," but most intriguingly complicates that wordplay by introducing—and by repetition, emphasizing—the concept of desire. Hume exclaims, "O happy Couple, at the height of happiness as yet, if you attempt and seek after no higher Happiness, and understand but to desire no more, and know your condition so well as to desire nothing above it" (162). Merritt Y. Hughes glosses 775 with "be wise enough to seek no more knowledge (i.e. of good and evil)," and, recalling Hume's paraphrase, Hughes cross-references 7.119–20, where Raphael reminds Adam that he had been sent "to answer thy desire / Of knowledge within bounds" (*Complete Poems* 296).

While Southey (23) disapproves of the "unfortunate recurrence of sound" throughout Milton's lines, several modern critics offer more subtle responses to the repetition. Cleanth Brooks ("Milton" 1052) sees here Milton's clearest statement of the paradox involved in the issue of prelapsarian, as opposed to postlapsarian, knowledge: "The good that Adam possesses, he does not 'know' he possesses. He will know that he had it only after he has lost it. Adam states this in so many words after the Fall [9.1071–73]." Discussing such wordplay in *PL* not as a regrettable lapse, but as "a result of extreme intellectual energy," F. T. Prince (*Italian Element* 123) sees here one of those "instances in which a verbal flourish, sometimes empty enough in itself, is made to give interest or significance" (124–25). Consulting the *OED*, Alastair Fowler somewhat differently distinguishes between the first and the second *know:* "Either 'know that it is best not to seek new knowledge (by eating the forbidden fruit)' or 'know (*OED* IV[.]12) *how to* limit your experience to the state of innocence'" (660).

Hilaire Belloc identifies these lines, in addition to 506 and 602–04, as evidence of those "brief flashes of that pure lyric inspiration which had been the glory of his [Milton's] youth" (247).

773. *repair'd:* A. W. Verity defines this as "made good the loss of, i.e. with fresh roses" (469), and Merritt Y. Hughes, supplying a similar definition, cross-references 7.153, where the "'detriment' of Heaven's loss of a third of its inhabitants is to be repaired" (*Complete Poems* 296; "Variorum"), while Douglas Bush and Anne Davidson Ferry settle the idea of repair into the context of the poem's action. Bush suggests another echo of Virgil's *Georgics* 2.200–02, "where Virgil says that what the herds crop in the long days the cool dew will restore in one short night: 'exigua tantum gelidus ros nocte reponet.' In Virgil the idea is merely nature's quiet, perpetual renewal; in Milton it becomes ironical because the morning's repairs will not go on much longer" ("Ironic and Ambiguous Allusion" 637). Also see Bush in 773–75. Irony is integral to Ferry's reading. The cyclical patterns of nature symbolize order for Adam and Eve, Ferry explains: "The endless rotation of day and night told them that nothing in nature was lost or wasted, just as we are told that before the Fall the bower of Adam and Eve 'Showrd Roses, which the Morn repair'd' (IV, 773). But to the fallen reader and the fallen narrator, the changing light of nature means what it means to Adam and Eve after the Fall—that nothing in nature is permanent, that everything vulnerable is threatened and everything beautiful will fade, like

the garland that Adam weaves for Eve which, after her sin 'Down drop'd, and all the faded Roses shed' (IX, 893)" (*Milton's Epic Voice* 31).

776–98. David Masson appears to be the first critic to give sustained and detailed attention to the military maneuvers of the angelic squadron guarding Eden, tracing Gabriel's orders here through to their fulfilment in the descriptions of the squadron's movements in 861–64 and 977–84. Masson first clarifies that at nine o'clock, the angels under Gabriel "issued *not* out at the eastern gate of Paradise, so as to be beyond the walls, but only from one of the inner ports of that gate into a space *within* the walls, ready for the duties of the night-watch." Masson then explains that Gabriel orders Uzziel to "lead half of the armed Angels round the walls of Paradise on the inside, taking the southern circuit from the eastern gate, while he himself, with the remaining half, would make the northern circuit inside from the same gate.... They would thus meet at the west, or at the point of the circumference of Paradise exactly opposite the gate from which they set out" (*Poetical Works* 3:79–80). Also see Masson in **861–64** and **977–80**. In his *Life of John Milton* 2:472–77, Masson returns to this extended sequence as he argues for Milton's more than literary acquaintance with such battlefield maneuvers. Also see James Holly Hanford's qualifications of Masson's claims about Milton's practical experience of war in "Milton."

Alastair Fowler (660–61) suggests a parallel between the movements of the guardian angels and the movements of the constellations: "Uzziel's detachment are (as it were) the stars of the southern hemisphere, Gabriel's those of the northern." Fowler concludes with a cross-reference to Andrew Marvell's *Upon Appleton House* 313–14, "the vigilant *Patroul* / Of Stars walks round about the *Pole*" (*Poems* 72).

776–77. The early commentators set the hour by clarifying the astronomical details in this description of nighttime. Hume (162) and the Richardsons (177–78) fix the time as 9 P.M., Bentley, "the Third Hour of the Night" (135). The Richardsons and Bentley report that this is the traditional hour for the watch to be set, Bentley specifying it as the first watch. In their commentary on 688, the Richardsons join other editors to supply details about the Hebrew and Roman traditions for assigning the night watches. Also see the Richardsons and others in **561**, where the watch is assigned "by Lot." Disagreeing with Bentley, Alastair Fowler claims that "the second watch is just beginning," and he then explains the numerological significance of Milton's precisely setting the time at line 777: "Numerologically, as the content demands, l. 777 exactly marks—'measures'—the *Half way* point between l. 539, when the sun *in utmost longitude* begins its descent beneath the horizon at six o'clock, and l. 1015, the last line of Bk iv, when 'the shades of night' first begin to flee at midnight" (660).

shaddowie Cone: the fundamentals of Hume's description are repeated by other early editors as they set the time: "*Conical,* because the Earth, an opaque spherical Body, being extremely less than the vast Luminary that enlightens it, casts on its adverse side a decreasing and sharp shadow, like in shape to a *Cone*" (Hume 62; also see Newton 289). Todd ([1842], 2:100) quotes Bentley, and much of the Richardsons, but also presents Dunster's disapproval, "I do not much admire the poetical imagery of this passage," and his reference to Henry More's *Psychozoia* 1.25.6–8, which describes Night's "Conique tire" by which "she doth assay / To whelm on th' earth." Although Charles Dunster does not "much admire" this description, Edward Bysshe indicates his approval by including it under "Midnight" in the "Collection" section of *The Art of English Poetry* (283). Also see Bysshe in **352–55** and **606–09**. Like the early editors, Alastair Fowler notes the astronomical precision of Milton's description, but he adds that, for Milton, the cone also carries symbolic meaning "as another form of a thematic shape common in *PL,* the pyramid of pride." Fowler (660) cross-references 5.758–59 and quotes from *RCG*, where Milton describes "hierarchies acuminating still higher and higher in a cone of Prelaty" (Patterson, *Works* 3:218). To Dunster's note on Henry More, Charles Grosvenor Osgood and Kester Svendsen bring additional literary sources for night's "shaddowie Cone." Osgood (xlvi) notes that Plutarch's "The Obsolence [Cessation] of Oracles," which is echoed in *Nat* as well as *PR*, describes the earth's shadow as "conical" (355). Explaining that Milton's description of the "shadowy Cone" recalls similar descriptions in the encyclopedias of the thirteenth through the seventeenth centuries, Kester Svendsen ("Milton" 325–26; *Milton and Science* 41–42) adds Pierre La Primaudaye's *French Academie* 722, Bartholomaeus's *De Proprietatibus Rerum* 8.31, and Caxton's *Mirrour of the World* 3.130–33.

777. *Sublunar Vault:* some uncertainty about Milton's "Sublunar" develops among early editors. The Richardsons (177–78) explain that it is "a Vault whose top reaches not so high as the Moon, (Sublunar, Under the moon): for as the Point of the Cone could not be suppos'd to extend to a more Distant

Sky, *Milton* has Imagin'd a certain portion of the Heavens, not reaching so far as the Moon, to be the Limit of *this Circling Canopy of Night's extended Shade,* III.556." If he does not flatly disagree with the Richardsons' understanding of "Sublunar Vault," Newton does extend it, explaining that "the shadow of the earth sweeps as it were the whole arch or vault of Heaven between the earth and moon, and extends beyond the orbit of the moon, as appears from the lunar eclipse" (289). Masson, too, understands "Sublunar" as under the moon, but he faults Milton for claiming that "the apex of the shadowy cone fell short of the Moon, or only just reached it" (*Poetical Works* 3:178). The *OED* A, referencing *sublunar* as *sublunary,* cites Milton's line, and defines *sublunary* as "Existing or situated beneath the moon; lying between the orbit of the moon and the earth; hence, subject to the moon's influence."

778–81. Critics have advanced Milton's views on the angelic orders in notes to passages throughout *PL,* but Robert H. West, identifying the angelic orders as one of the three principal angelological controversies between Protestants and Catholics, offers the following overview in *Milton and the Angels,* an overview that later critics support: "He [Milton] is not exact about them [the orders] nor combative and uses a terminology that is familiar and traditionally appealing to all, yet is offensive to no one, and is serviceable to the turns of his story" (132). Supporting this overview, West points to the terminology of order and hierarchy in 550, 778, and 864 to conclude that, while suggesting the Dionysian scheme, set forth in *Celestis Hierarchia,* Milton "uses the terms of rank so fluidly that no one has been able to organize his use into a consistent pattern" (134). West notes, for example, that "Gabriel as leader of the angelic guard is simply 'Chief' (IV.550, 864), though his detail is 'the Cherubim' (IV.778). Obviously Milton sometimes uses the hierarchical terms virtually without hierarchical meaning, since he can mix them easily with such variations as *Chief, Guard, Warriors, Armies, Sanctities, Ardors*" (134–35). West concludes, "Both Milton's flirting with the Dionysian orders and his evasions are entirely in the Protestant tradition" (135). C. A. Patrides and Roy Daniells present similar understandings. Patrides points out that "Milton refused to name all the angelic orders, still less commit himself to the widely accepted ninefold arrangement proposed by Dionysius the Areopagite," and he explains that by the mid-seventeenth century, "the tendency among Protestants was to reject the 'palpable follie' of the 'high soaring (though counterfeit) Dionysius,' but to maintain, just as categorically, that the angels are indeed 'Legioniz'd in Rankes' " (*Milton* 64). Also see Patrides's earlier essays on the orders of the angels, "Renaissance Thought" and "Renaissance Views." Approaching this topic from the point of view of baroque aesthetics, Daniells acknowledges, "Milton's angels are not arranged in the customary hierarchies" (*Milton* 82).

Pondering the question of why Milton assigns cherubim to guard duty, A. W. Verity explains, "Cherubim had a wondrous power of vision: hence their main duty in *Paradise Lost* is to keep watch" (681).

778. *Ivorie Port:* the Richardsons are the first to express concern about the description of the "Port," and the critical issues they raise continue to demand explanation. Juxtaposing "Ivorie Port" to the earlier reference to the "Gate of Paradise" (542) as "a Rock / Of Alablaster" (543–44), Hume reveals no uneasiness (162), but the Richardsons are deeply puzzled, as they are by the earlier description itself. The Richardsons admit that "this Ivory port, Gate, or Door was not mention'd when the Rocky Gate or Portal was describ'd, *v.* 543. but Such Must be Suppos'd, and is Here Expressly given. the Rocky Portal form'd a Streight, or a Narrow Passage; but 'twas So Wide, and Continu'd so far as to give room for the Angels Unarm'd to Divert Themselves, and *Gabriel* their Leader, with *Heroic Games;* forth of this Narrow way (where was the Ivory Gate, and in that Part of it as was next the Garden) the Cherubim issu'd into the Wide Space of Paradise Adjoyning." The Richardsons also ponder the material of the gate because it brings to mind Homer's description of the gates of sleep, one ivory, the other horn, in the *Odyssey* 19.562–65: "True Dreams passing through That of Horn, and False Ones through the Ivory Gate. *Virgil* is generally thought to have Alluded to This Passage of *Homer,* Aen[eid] VI.895. where he makes *Aeneas* go out of Hell through a Gate of Ivory to Suggest that All he had said of *Aeneas's* Descent into That Place, and what he saw There, was to be consider'd only as a Pure Fiction, and Poetical Invention. in like manner *Milton* might intend to Intimate Here that what he said of These Guards and Fortifications about Paradise was Fictitious, as indeed they did not Answer the End. This is only Offer'd as a Conjecture; but most Certain it is He could not Forget this Ivory Gate of *Homer;* whether he Alluded to it or No" (178–79). Newton (289–90) finds such a conjecture anything but compelling: "We cannot conceive that here is any allusion to the ivory gate of sleep, mention'd by Homer and Virgil, from whence false dreams proceeded; for the poet could never intend to insinuate that what he was saying about the angelic guards was all a fiction. As the rock was of alabaster, ver. 543. so he makes the gate of ivory, which was very proper for an eastern gate, as the finest ivory cometh from the east…and houses and palaces of ivory are mention'd as instances of magnificence in Scripture, as are likewise doors of ivory in Ovid, *Met*[*amorphoses*] IV.185." Todd ([1842], 2:100–01) presents Newton's reading, as well as a suggestion in a note from Benjamin Stillingfleet that the angelic guard is "designed only as a poetical embellishment." Alastair Fowler offers a fresh solution to the problem of the Homeric associations clinging to Milton's "Ivorie Port": "Since the cherubim are to interrupt a false dream, it is the ivory gate they use" (660).

In Milton's "Ivorie Port," Allan H. Gilbert finds suggested "a building intended for the guard, more suitable for Purchas' Amara than for Paradise," and it also figures in his arguments about the different times of composition for *PL* (*On the Composition* 40n5; cf. Gilbert in **131–48**).

780. *in warlike Parade:* Hume glosses this phrase as "In Martial Order and Array," and derives *Parade* from the French *Parade,* "the place where Soldiers in a Garison or Town draw up together, in order to a Sally, Shew, or to relieve the Guard" (162). Quoting this line, the *OED* 2 reads: "An assembling or mustering of troops for inspection or display; esp. a muster of troops which takes place regularly at set hours, or at extraordinary times to hear orders read, as a preparation for a march, or any other special purpose."

781–89. *Gabriel…Uzziel…Ithuriel…Zephon:* commentators have always been intrigued by the names of Milton's angels—both the upright and the fallen. Patrick Hume first traces the names to their Hebrew roots, pointing out that Uzziel's name means "*Strength of God*" and derives from the Hebrew word that means "*to be strong,* as all God's mighty Angels are." Ithuriel's and Zephon's names, Hume believes, serve "as indication of their Offices," *Ithuriel* in Hebrew meaning "*Discovery of God*," and *Zephon,* "*a Secret*." Hume then concludes that both angels are "the Searchers and Spies, as *Uriel* is stiled God's Eye" (163). Subsequent critics from Newton (290) to Hughes (*Complete Poems* 296) repeat these readings, although A. W. Verity (470) and R. C. Browne (1:355), following Thomas Keightley (470), report that *Zephon* means "a looking out" (470). Edward Chauncey Baldwin (369) traces the idea of two guardian angels assigned to Adam and Eve to the *Vita Adae et Evae* 33.1–3. Robert H. West attempts a broader examination of this topic. Pointing out that the Bible supplied Milton with names for only his principal angels, West considers the names of Milton's lesser angels and the expanded lists of angelic names available in angelological and occultist writings. Both Milton and the angelologists, for example, shared angel names that in the Bible were the names of men and places: "*Arioc, Abdiel, Uzziel* [Ex. 6.18, Num. 3.19], and *Zephon* [Num. 26.15] are all in the Bible as names of men or places, and in various religious or occult writings as of angels. *Abdiel* and *Uzziel* are both in the *Sepher Raziel* f. 34b and 40a, for instance, and *Uzziel* in several other mystical and Cabalistic works" (154). While *Zephon* occurs as a human name in Num. 26.15, John Selden in *De Diis Syriis* 1.3.43 had also identified it as the name of a heathen idol, worshiped at the city of Baal-Zephon, but West suggests that Milton may have agreed with Agrippa, *Three Books of Occult Philosophy* 3.27, that "as divers men have many times the same name, so also spirits of divers offices and natures may be noted or marked by one name" (155). Not to be found in the Bible or in the literature of angelology, the name *Ithuriel*, West suggests, might be found in *The Key of Solomon the King*, an even more unsavory association (155). All of this supports West's view that Milton "shows not a jot of interest in the names for their own sake or in the special powers supposed to go with them" (151).

782–87. The rhythm developed in this verse paragraph wins praise from James Whaler. In his study of the arithmetical patterns in the rhythmic groupings and progressions of Milton's epic verse, Whaler explains that the "circular rhythmic continuum" of this paragraph parallels the military maneuver being executed by the angelic guards (*Counterpoint* 76).

783. *wheel:* Thomas Keightley (437) points out that, like the Latin poets, Milton here uses the simple *wheel* for the compound "wheel to." Keightley identifies the same phenomenon in Milton's *drive* at 155. The *OED* 6.b cites Milton's line to illustrate the obscure and rare meaning "To encircle, surround, encompass."

784–85. Full of praise for this *flame* metaphor, all the early editors acknowledge the biblical authority for understanding the angels as creatures of fire (Ps. 104.4, Heb. 1.7), and all agree that the metaphor therefore more appropriately describes Milton's angels than the Trojans Homer similarly describes in the *Iliad* 2.780.

Hume explains that the guardian angels "move like flame, as quick as darting Lightning" (163), while the Richardsons suggest two possible readings of the metaphor: "Either 'tis meant they divided as Flame divides it self into Separate Wreaths, Or that they went with the Velocity and Vigour of Flame" (179–80). Newton adds another level of meaning: "This break in the verse is excellently adapted to the subject. They part as the flame divides into separate wreaths. A short simile, but expressive of their quickness and rapidity, and of their brightness and the splendor of their armour at the same time" (290). Todd ([1842], 2:101) quotes Newton.

The description of the parting angels *wheeling* to either the shield on their left or the spear on their right has been traced to a number of classical texts. The Richardsons (180) refer it to Aelian's *Tactics* 73. Without reference to classical authority, Bentley associates the shield with the left and the spear with the right, and finds in Milton's description "a dignity of expression, more than the common words have" (135). Quoting Hume and Bentley, Todd ([1842], 2:101) contributes the parallel in Giovanni Trissino's *Italia Liberata* 6.55–56. Masson mentions that "the Greeks had had a similar phrase" (*Poetical Works* 3:180). In this century, James Holly Hanford ("Milton" 254) indicates how common the expression was by providing the English version of the command as it appeared in Robert Ward's *Animadversions of Warre* 254: "Wheel your battle to the right; wheel your battle to the left."

785–86. Criticizing Pearce criticizing Bentley criticizing Milton, William Empson tangles up both himself and his reader at this point. Bentley (136) indicates no concern about rhythm with these lines in Book 4 but complains of "bad Measure" in 5.786, which reads "Our minds and teach us to cast off this Yoke," but that Bentley would have read "Our Minds, to quit the Yoke, hard and unjust." In his chapter on Milton and Bentley in *Some Versions of Pastoral*, Empson (151–52) changes Milton's 4.786 to "Our minds, and teach us to cast off this yoke." Then bringing Bentley's commentary, as well as Pearce's (141) commentary on 5.786 into the mix, Empson ends up creating what Robert Martin Adams calls "a specially odd muddle" (114n4).

786. *suttle:* Bentley's objection is probably the stimulus for the Richardsons' note. Explaining that subtlety is not what the angels need on this occasion, Bentley (136) changes the word to "nimble," and points to "I hear the tread of nimble feet" at 866 for support. The Richardsons explain that "Subtilty does not Always imply what is usually meant by Craft; 'tis us'd in a Good Sense, *Prov.* viii.12. *I Wisdom dwell with Subtilty,* for So the Margin says 'tis in the *Hebrew.* and Thus the Latins frequently use the Word. Cunning, Sagacity, Prudence was Necessary to Those Sent as well as Strength" (180).

788–91. In the difference between Gabriel's more general orders to the angelic guard in these lines and the description of those orders in the Argument to Book 4 (Gabriel "appoints two strong Angels to Adams Bower, least the evill spirit should be there doing some harm to Adam or Eve sleeping; there they find him at the ear of Eve, tempting her in a dream"), Allan H. Gilbert finds more evidence of the relationship between the epic and Milton's earlier plans for a drama on the Fall (*On the Composition* 30).

791. *secure of harm:* A. W. Verity interprets this phrase to mean that Adam and Eve were "unsuspicious of, not fearing" harm (470). Cf. *secure* at 186.

793. *Who:* A. W. Verity notes this as a Miltonic response to the Latin *qui,* meaning "one who," and refers, of course, to Uriel (470).

795. *errand bad:* Edward S. Le Comte cross-references "bad errand" (10.41), the Father's term for Satan's quest (*Yet Once More* 37).

796. *hither:* Harris Francis Fletcher takes this to mean that Gabriel remains at the eastern gate after he sends the guards out to scour the garden on the heels of Uriel's warning. Fletcher (248) bases his understanding on the *Midrash to Numbers* 2:10 (*Midrash* 3:39). Other critics, however, describe Gabriel accompanying the guards that "wheel the North" who will meet their colleagues at the opposite side of the garden. See Masson and Fowler in **776–98.** Robert Martin Adams, surveying studies of Milton's rabbinical learning that appeared in the 1920s and 1930s, responds to Fletcher's reading: "The arguments from 'angelology' which make up the last half of Mr. Fletcher's book are even more marginal than those which relate to rabbinical commentary. They center upon such points as the fact that by a complex deduction from IV, 782–85, Gabriel can be seen to face the East at this point, and a medieval Jewish tradition says his station is to the east of the heavenly throne" (145). Rejecting the body of claims advanced by studies such as Fletcher's, Adams concludes, "The price of

Milton the rabbinical scholar seems to be the conversion of England's greatest writer of epic into a seventeenth century amalgam of Madame Blavatsky and a Byzantine mosaicist" (147).

797–1015. Studying the purposes and effects of the contrast Milton establishes between exact and vague time in the epic, Laurence Stapleton explains how Milton's emphasis on the exact time of Satan's capture by Gabriel's angels creates immediacy and suspense: "this event, the threatened fight and its suspension last through the hours of darkness. On Satan's baffled departure, 'with him fled the shades of night.' The next event follows without interval: dawn, and the awakening of Adam to find the sleeping Eve discomposed by her dream" (741).

799–809. Satan's efforts to tempt the sleeping Eve, a "revolutionary addition" to the traditional literary treatment of the Fall, according to Grant McColley (*"Paradise Lost": An Account* 158), have prompted the inevitable search for literary sources or parallels, but the challenge of sorting out the uncertain strategies of Satan's demonic art has prompted even more provocative critical attention, for entangled in those uncertainties are elements of the debates about Milton's characterization of Eve, as well as his characterization of Satan, debates that sound throughout the critical response to Book 4.

What might be considered the first critical commentary on this episode, the so-called dream temptation, is Dryden's dramatic adaptation of it in 3.3 of *The State of Innocence, and Fall of Man* (*Works* 12:18–22). Dryden brings forward from Milton's Book 5 Adam's discourse on dreams, incorporating it into a soliloquy he assigns to Lucifer who explains, "Their Reason sleeps; but Mimic fancy wakes, / Supplies her parts, and wild Idea's takes / From words and things, ill sorted, and misjoyn'd" (5–7). As Dryden's undisguised Lucifer then whispers in Eve's ear, a vision appears on stage: "*a Tree rises loaden with Fruit; four Spirits rise with it, and draw a canopie out of the tree, other Spirits dance about the Tree in deform'd shapes; after the Dance an Angel enters, with a Woman, habited like Eve*" (12 s.d.). After the Spirits in that dream dramatization eat the fruit offered by the Angel, "*they immediately put off their deform'd shapes, and appear Angels*"; then "*The Angel gives to the Woman who eats*" (28 s.d.). Finally, after she admits, "Ah, now I believe; such a pleasure I find / As enlightens my eyes, and enlivens my mind" (36–37), the Woman flies with the Angels "out of sight" (45 s.d.).

As noted earlier, editors and critics have long sought to identify literary sources for the dream temptation, and to pursue the more modern studies of demonology that may have influenced Milton's presentation of it. Puzzling, therefore, especially to anyone at all acquainted with his 1695 *Annotations,* is Patrick Hume's not mentioning those Virgilian parallels so apparent to his immediate successors; instead Hume briefly quotes Hippocrates's *Dreams* 194 ("corpus dormit, Anima vigilat"; "the body sleeps, the soul is awake," trans. Cheryl Fresch), paraphrases Milton's narrator, and, like Dryden's Lucifer, anticipates Adam's discourse on dreams the next morning. Hume, however, supplies an intriguing note on "animal Spirits" (805), one that glances at the description of Eve's awakening the next morning with "startl'd eye" (5.26): "Others liken 'em ['animal Spirits'] to rays of Light issuing out of the Bloods vital and florid Flame, which the vivid and equal shining that shews it self in the eyes of those in health, as that dull deadness that appears in those drawing to their end, and the fierce, sparkling and wild disorders that manifestly discover themselves in the looks of Lunatics, does sufficiently evidence" (163). Finally, while Hume seals his summary remarks with a firm statement of faith in God's omnipotence, his understanding of the dream's effect on Eve remains provocatively unclear: "That the Devil, by his great sagacity, may be able so to distemper the humours of human Bodies, to heat and inflame the Blood and animal Spirits, and by them so to disorder the Fancy, that many evil thoughts, inductive of sinful desires, may assault us, is not to be doubted: but that *God, who is faithful, and will not suffer us to be tempted above that we are able,* (1 Cor. 10.13.) should let the Temptation surmount the regency of our Reason, and the freedom of our Will, is not without Blasphemy to be supposed *of that most Pure and Compassionate Being*" (164; also see Hume in **808**). The Richardsons (181) first associate Eve's dream temptation with the victimization of Amata in the *Aeneid* 7.349–51, when Alecto casts a snake into the already angry Amata's breast and it "creeps softly over her, *Viperearn Inspirans Animam*"; "[and] breathes into her its viperous breath." Both Newton (292) and Todd quote the Richardsons, and Todd ([1842], 2:102) supplies a later reference to another dream inspired by a Fury, the dream Erinnys sends Herod in Marino's *La Strage de Gl'Innocenti* 1.53–59. Among the early editors, Paterson claims a biblical parallel in the diabolically inspired dream of Pilate's wife, mentioned in Matt. 27.19 (324).

More recently Robert C. Fox and Davis P. Harding have identified classical literary parallels for Eve's dream. Fox associates Eve's dream temptation with Ovid's story of Aglauros, envious of Mercury's love for her sister Herse

(*Metamorphoses* 2.708–832). Common to both episodes, Fox writes, are "the night scene, the unwary victim asleep, the insomniac tempter, the infusion of venom" (274). Explaining that dreams in epics may warn, foreshadow, and motivate, Harding notes that "as a rule a dream performed only one of these possible functions, rarely two, never, I believe, all three at once" (*Club* 82). When he turns to sources for Eve's dream, Harding argues that Milton synthesizes various sources, the first being Alecto's dream visitation of Turnus in *Aeneid* 7.406–60, the second the parallel the Richardsons (181) had noted: "Eve's dream, like that of Turnus, bears directly on the crisis of the poem, and a verbal parallel [Virgil's 'viperam inspirans animam' and Milton's 'inspiring venom'] increases the likelihood that Milton had his dream in mind." Harding also suggests that Eve's dream is influenced by Medea's dream in the *Argonautica* of Apollonius Rhodius (3.451–70), which "reflects her subconscious desires," and Dido's dream in *Aeneid* 4.464–68, which foreshadows her abandonment (*Club* 82–83).

While Todd, acknowledging similar episodes in Virgil and Marino, affirms the value of identifying possible literary sources for Milton's dream temptation, he also introduces another critical approach by citing the discussion "De Phantasia" in Johann Wierus's (Weyer's) *De Lamiis* 3.8, where the "power of evil spirits over the fancy and animal spirits, is minutely discussed" ([1842], 2:102), and subsequent critics have moved in that direction, endeavoring, that is, to situate Satan's "Devilish art" (801) in the context of sixteenth and early seventeenth century demonology and angelology. For example, George Wesley Whiting (*Milton's Literary Milieu* 156) juxtaposes 801–09 and Robert Burton's explanation in *The Anatomy of Melancholy* 1.2.1.2 that the Devil "begins first with the phantasy, and moves that so strongly, that no reason is able to resist." Whiting then broadens the implications of this parallel: "Burton and Milton...deal with orthodox material in a fashion that reveals fundamentally sympathetic tastes and tendencies" (170–71). Merritt Y. Hughes (*Complete Poems* 297) also looks to Burton's *Anatomy* 1.1.2.2, clarifying the physiology of the various human spirits vulnerable to demonic powers. In "Variorum," Hughes cites Kathleen Ellen Hartwell's study *Lactantius and Milton* 52 for patristic opinion on the "mystery of diabolic psychosomatic power over men" and translates the following from Lactantius's *Divinarum Institutionum* 2.13.13–14: "Demons, which are rarefied spirits, slip unperceived into men's bodies and secretly destroy health, cause diseases, terrify their souls with nightmares, and plague their minds with passions." Grant McColley (*"Paradise Lost": An Account* 163) surveys not only Wierus's (Weyer's) text, to which Todd first refers, but also the following writings on demonology, spirits, and witchcraft: Michael Psellus's *De Operatione Daemonis* ch. 12, Reginald Scot's *The Discoverie of Witchcraft* 15.2, 31, and Thomas Heywood's *The Hierarchie of the Blessed Angells* 497. Much like George Coffin Taylor (75–76), however, McColley insists that the following passage from Sylvester's translation of Du Bartas's *The Divine Weeks and Works* 2.1.2.135–40 is "our most complete single analogue" for the dream temptation in *PL:* "Sometimes, me seems, troubling Eve's spirit, the / Fiend made her this speaking fancy apprehend... / The evil angels slide too easily, as subtle / Spirits, into our fantasy." Also see Adams *Ikon* 156–57. In "Eve's Demonic Dream" 261, William B. Hunter explains that much of the seventeenth century popular understanding of dreams and demons continued to express the theological views systematized by St. Thomas Aquinas, who concedes in the *Summa Theologica* 1.114.2.3 that a demon "can change the inferior powers of man, in a certain degree: by which powers, though the will cannot be forced, it can nevertheless be inclined."

Besides developing a more detailed historical context emphasizing demonology and theology, Hunter's article importantly shifts attention to another, and decidedly more controversial, feature of the dream temptation, the effects of Satan's "Devilish art" (801) on Eve, an aspect of the dream temptation that Grant McColley glosses over by simply describing Satan's efforts as "unsuccessful" (*"Paradise Lost": An Account* 160). Also see McColley "Paradise Lost" 210–12. By the mid-1940s, much of the critical attention on Eve is directed, of course, to her experience at the "Smooth Lake" (459), with critics detecting hints of vanity, or velleities to sin in her, until several—most notably Waldock, Bell, and Tillyard—conclude that Eve is fallen before she eats the apple. See **449–91**. Looking at Eve's demonic dream, William Hunter does not join that group, does not claim Eve is fallen before she eats the apple, but he does open his study with this statement: "To a great degree the dream exactly anticipates the actual events which followed, and it thus may be argued that the Fall, which occurs in Book IX, is a direct sequel of the dream" ("Eve's Demonic Dream" 255). A few years before Hunter's article, P. L. Carver discusses the dream temptation with equal care. Like Hunter, he distinguishes the dream from the "real deception" of Book 9, and like Hunter, he explains that in his efforts at Eve's ear, Satan "thus prepared the way for the real deception" (426). Carver looks for theological guidance as he discusses this sequence: "It is probable that the whole of this episode...was designed to dramatize a fact mentioned by St. Augustine and recalled by St. Thomas [*Summa Theologica* 94.4]: 'The woman could not have believed the words of the serpent, had she not already acquiesced in the love of her own power, and in a presumption of self-conceit.'" Carver contends that Eve's tears upon awakening the next morning "must be taken as a sign" that Satan had indeed "induced Eve to acquiesce" (427). John S. Diekhoff, publishing his study in 1946, as does Hunter, more directly states his point when he locates the "beginning of the fall" in Satan's efforts at Eve's ear: "the dream is the beginning of the temptation, the beginning of the fall." In the dream temptation, Diekhoff argues, "The desires that are to lead to her downfall have been aroused in her" (*Milton's "Paradise Lost"* 56). Surveying the debate about fallible perfection some 20 years later, however, Diekhoff reexamines the dream temptation, and his reading shifts: "Satan is not in the poem a metaphor for man's evil impulses. He is the source of them and a real agent in Milton's fable. The dream is not of Eve's devising; it springs not from her unconscious but from Satan's conscious. Squat like a toad at her ear, he dictated it. It reveals his ethos, not Eve's" ("Eve's Dream" 6). Diekhoff's debate with himself reflects the larger one within the community of Milton scholars through the middle decades of the twentieth century. Endeavoring to refute criticism that contends or intimates that the dream temptation compromises Eve's perfection are critics such as John Peter and Balachandra Rajan, both of whom broaden the debate to acknowledge the poetic or structural, as well as the philosophical or theological, challenges confronting Milton. Peter identifies Eve's dream as Milton's effort "to bridge a possible gap between Book Four and Book Nine," and, he argues, "Two processes can be distinguished here, and neither implies the slightest corruption in Eve herself. If Satan uses 'The Organs of her Fancie' to create the dream he uses them as a material, not a co-operative agency.... If on the other hand he succeeds in tainting her 'animal Spirits' that is not because they are already tainted. It is because his 'art' is powerful enough to force its way into her body, like an infection, disturbing the innate harmony that exists there." When Eve awakes, Peter points out, "she is herself again, though naturally troubled by the memory of what has been intruded into her mind" (100). Developing Milton's use of correspondences as a feature of the architecture of *PL*, Rajan, much like Harding and Hunter, asserts that "poetic reasons" prompted Milton to create the dream temptation: "Eve's dream is effective as an omen, it involves a deft use of supernatural machinery, and besides providing a pretext for a discussion on faculty psychology, it makes possible an encounter between Gabriel and Satan which no reader of Milton would like to see omitted. But what is most important for my purpose is that the actual temptation is anticipated in Eve's dream" (*"Paradise Lost" and the Seventeenth Century Reader* 49–50). Frank Kermode somewhat similarly focuses on Milton's poetic craft, and also sees "the theme of physiological perturbation" as a vital link between the dream temptation and the actual temptation (115). Also see Kermode in **114–23**. Keen to dismiss the notion that Milton must have believed in witchcraft, John M. Steadman situates Eve's dream within the conventions of witchcraft, but he, too, rules that Eve commits no sin while she dreams: "Unlike the deluded sorceresses among her posterity, Eve is still unfallen and is therefore able to recognize her aerial journey as a mere 'dream'" ("Eve's Dream" 569). While Steadman's investigation of witchcraft theories exonerates Eve after her encounter with Satan's "Devilish art," Northrop Frye's application of Freudian theory condemns her: "In its manifest content," Frye argues, the dream itself "was a Freudian wish-fulfillment dream" (*Return* 75). Stanley Fish, however, firmly rejects Frye's reading. "Notice that Frye assumes Satan's success, while the verse itself leaves the matter in doubt. Satan is *assaying* to reach her Fancy, in the *hope* that he could then 'forge / Illusions as he list'; or, barring that, he will see if he can infuse venom into her which *might* then taint her animal spirits. There is more than a hint that his calculations may prove incorrect" (*Surprised* 219–20).

When A. Bartlett Giamatti considers Satan at Eve's ear, he does not describe the dream as a "wish-fulfillment dream," but he suggests a similar inclination: "Satan knows what others in gardens have learned: that man's greatest snare is his own illusions about himself." Giamatti's commentary moves the critical discussion to ponder the effects of this episode on Milton's presentation of Satan. Directing attention to terms such as "Fancie," "Illusions," "Phantasm and Dreams," Giamatti points out, "This is the first time his [Satan's] power is specifically called his 'art,' although Satan as actor or artist has been implied before. Now the old theme of art and nature takes on its widest implications as this art is obviously opposed to all that is natural" (334; see Giamatti in **141**). To practice this "Devilish art," of course, Milton's Satan assumes a disguise, again not something that as an "actor or artist" he has not done before, but the toad disguise brings complications to his characterization that his earlier disguises — "stripling Cherube" (3.636), cormorant, lion, or tiger — did not. Reporting the general understanding that spirits might choose to assume any form, for example, Grant McColley (*"Paradise Lost": An Account* 163) quotes Reginald Scot's "Inventory of Devils and Spirits" in his *Discoverie of Witchcraft* as saying that the "first and principal king," when conjured, has three heads, "the first, like a toad" (15.2, 31). Robert C. Fox (274) presents the narrower, yet also damning association between the toad and envy, pointing to its occurrence in both Spenser (*The Faerie Queene* 1.4.30 and 3.10.59–60) and Du Bartas, who, in Sylvester's translation of *The Divine Weeks and Works* 1.120, describes Envie's anger as "Toad-like swelling anger." In his study of Eve's dream, John Steadman sweepingly reminds readers that Satan's toad disguise was "one of the most conventional forms which familiar devils assumed in their association with the sorceress" ("Eve's Dream" 568), though in another study, Steadman also discusses Satan's disguise as a heroic convention, "the ignoble disguise," associating Satan as a toad with Ulysses as a beggar. Steadman therefore reasons that the disguise does not degrade Satan ("Satan's Metamorphoses"). For those critics who track Satan's degeneration, and for those who track his degradation, the toad disguise marks a very low point. P. T. Forsyth, for example, asserts, "Disguise is inconsistent with majesty. And by the disguises which Satan does not hesitate to adopt the poet indicates the progress of that decay which leaves the great figure finally stripped of all his personal glory" (460). When he considers Satan "like a Toad," P. L. Carver, however, speaks of degradation rather than progressive decay: "It seems to be true, on a general view of the poem, that the Satan who extorts our admiration at the beginning is the Satan of orthodox theology, and that the degraded Satan is Satan as the school of Tertullian might have imagined him" (431). Michael Wilding presents yet another view. Wilding agrees that Satan experiences "an overall decline," but, pointing out that after he is discovered "Squat like a toad" (800) and leaves "murmuring," Satan appears in Book 5 "as one of the first of the angels," thus demonstrating that the process of decline "is neither one of steady descent...nor one originating from initial pure glory" (20). Also see 987, where Satan is compared to Teneriff, and for additional commentary on Satan's disguises, see the earlier presentation of the degeneration-versus-degradation debate in **32–113**.

Finally, it is probably Samuel Johnson who has drawn more enduring critical attention to this sequence than has any other critic. Identifying "the agency of spirits" as one of the major defects of *PL*, Johnson explains that Milton "saw that immateriality supplied no images, and that he could not show angels acting but by instruments of action; he therefore invested them with form and matter. This, being necessary, was therefore defensible; and he should have secured the consistency of his system, by keeping immateriality out of sight, and enticing his reader to drop it from his thoughts. But he has unhappily perplexed his poetry with his philosophy. His infernal and celestial powers are sometimes pure spirit, and sometimes animated body. When Satan walks with his lance upon the *burning marle,* he has a body; when, in his passage between hell and the new world, he is in danger of sinking in the vacuity, and is supported by a gust of rising vapours, he has a body; when he animates the toad, he seems to be mere spirit, that can penetrate matter at pleasure; when he *starts up in his own shape,* he has at least a determined form; and, when he is brought before Gabriel he has *a spear and a shield,* which he had the power of hiding in the toad, though the arms of the contending angels are evidently material" (*Milton* 290). At least two earlier critics anticipate Johnson's concerns. While John Dennis focuses his reading on the war in heaven in the third letter of his series of "Observations on the *Paradise Lost* of Milton" (*Critical Works* 2:228), he also announces that he intends to discuss "an Objection, which no one that I know of has made against those very Machines of *Milton,* from the Force and Power of which those sublime Beauties were drawn." Dennis states his objection: "the Poet seems to confound Body and Mind, Spirit and Matter." Unlike Johnson, however, Dennis placidly accepts Milton's explanation in 1.423–31 as an answer to the problem of angelic matter (2:228). A bit less clearly, the Richardsons also appear to recognize the philosophical complexity of the sequence presenting Satan as toad. After they insist that the "venom" Satan may be inspiring into Eve is "a real Poisonous Vapour," the Richardsons direct readers to Raphael's discourse with Adam on angelic digestion in Book 5, adding "*Milton's* System appears to be that the Souls of Men, as the Angels, are Spirits, but not in the Highest Sense; That he reserves to God Only. Whether This be Right or Not let Divine Judge, and *Milton* answer, but 'tis Fine Poetry" (181). Lord Macaulay is apparently the first to reply to Johnson's famous criticism. Macaulay argues, "It was impossible for the poet to adopt altogether the material or the immaterial system. He therefore took his stand on the debatable ground. He left the whole in ambiguity. He has, doubtless, by so doing, laid himself open to the charge of inconsistency. But, though philosophically in the wrong, we cannot but believe that he was poetically in the right" (1:226–27).

The principal twentieth century respondents to Johnson's remarks include C. S. Lewis, A. J. A. Waldock, and Robert H. West, and none of them is as sanguine about it as Lord Macaulay. Lewis's *Preface* features the entire chapter "The Mistake about Milton's Angels," and Lewis identifies that mistake as Johnson's belief "that the corporeality of Milton's angels was *a poetic fiction*" (108). Lewis proceeds to discuss "Platonic Theology" by quoting Henry More, among others, who, in his third letter to Descartes, explains, "I was always disposed to agree with the Platonists, the ancient Fathers, and almost all the magicians, in recognizing that all souls and genii, whether good or evil, are plainly corporeal" (110). Therefore, Lewis argues against Johnson, "When Satan animates the toad this does not prove that he is immaterial, but only that his subtle body can penetrate a grosser body and contract itself to very small dimensions. When he meets Gabriel he dilates" (112). Without addressing Samuel Johnson's remarks, P. L. Carver (418) reports that Tertullian wrote, "Spirit has a bodily substance of its own kind, in its own form [*Adversus Praxean* 346]." One of a number of later critics supporting Lewis on the Platonic underpinning for Milton's view of angelic corporeality is C. A. Patrides, who surveys the writings of a variety of medieval theologians speaking to the topic of angelic corporeity (*Milton* 48). When A. J. A. Waldock enters the debate, he takes on C. S. Lewis, as well as Milton, although like Lewis, Waldock realizes that Johnson's error was his failure to recognize "the queer substance of angels, so different from 'gross' matter as we know it" (109). Mockery strongly colors Waldock's criticism: "The fact that he [Milton] believed in his absurdities—or was willing to risk suggesting that he did—surely has the effect of rendering them rather *more* (not, as Mr. Lewis thinks, less) reprehensible" (108). Moving from Satan "Squat like a Toad" to the war in heaven, Waldock exclaims that in so presenting spiritual matter, Milton is "treating us very nearly as morons" (111). Like Waldock and Lewis, Robert H. West finds that Johnson simply misunderstood Milton's philosophy, but rejecting Johnson's contention that Milton perplexed his poetry with his philosophy, West explains that the two independently coexist: "The first thing to do in considering Milton's handling of his angels is to distinguish the wholly literary pictorialization that was unavoidable if Milton was to present angels directly, from a special pictorialization that follows upon his 'philosophy'—a 'philosophy' that is not what Dr. Johnson thought it. When Satan expands and contracts himself and changes his shape…it is according to the 'philosophy' which Milton has chosen to follow, a Platonistic-Protestant angelology that ascribed ethereal body to angels. But when Satan walks on the burning marle or lies on the burning lake extended many a rood or does any other ordinary action according to the rules of extension, time, and place, Milton has conveyed nothing about special angelic metaphysics, but has simply represented the angel to us in the only way that the limitations of language allow—in what Dr. Johnson notes as 'images of matter.'" West concludes, "Milton is simply telling his story in the only way a story can be told, and the reader still may suppose that so far as the 'philosophy' is concerned his angels are abstract intelligences. The well-understood convention of the stage on this matter shows that such anomalous adaptations in *Paradise Lost* do not prejudice any 'philosophy' Milton may join to them. The 'image' and the 'philosophy' may co-exist peacefully" (109–10).

West's glance at Milton's early plans for a dramatic version of the Fall story and the problems of presenting spirits on stage is developed by Allan H. Gilbert as he studies the composition of *PL*. While Satan's confrontation with the angels guarding Adam and Eve is a part of the early dramatic sketches, Gilbert reasons that "the description of Satan's attempt on Eve must be later. It can have been written only after Milton decided to give something on life in the Garden before the Fall. Even the tragedy mentioned by Phillips can hardly have contained it, because the action involving Satan in the form of a toad, suddenly restored to his normal form, is hardly possible on the stage. Unless assigned in drama to some narrator, it must have been written after the epic form was settled upon. Eve's dream itself, however, being necessarily a matter of narrative, could have been part of a drama" (*On the Composition* 91–92). As explained at the beginning of this note, Dryden, of course, dramatizes Eve's dream in the third act of *The State of Innocence, and Fall of Man* (*Works* 12:18–22), but Lucifer does not appear in disguise.

800. A. W. Verity (470) notes that in "An Epistle from Mr. Pope, to Dr. Arbuthnot" 319–22 (*Poems* 11:118–19), Alexander Pope alludes to this line: "Or at the Ear of *Eve*, familiar Toad, / Half Froth, half Venom, spits himself abroad, / In Puns, or Politicks, or Tales, or Lyes, / Or Spite, or Smut, or Rhymes, or Blasphemies." Verity also cross-references *SA* 857–58, "and the Priest / Was not behind, but ever at my ear" and *PR* 4.407–09, "for at his head / The Tempter watch'd, and soon with ugly dreams / Disturb'd his sleep."

Jon S. Lawry reasons why Satan positions himself at Eve's head, and Michael Lieb why Satan squats. Lawry explains that Satan "intends that his familiar horrors—isolation, sin, and death—will be generated from her 'head' (that is, from her reason and choice) as they once were from his" (179). Lieb (185) contrasts Satan's squatting with the Spirit of God, who "Dove-like satst brooding" (1.21) or with Beelzebub's claim that the demons in Pandemonium "sit in darkness... / Hatching vain empires" (2.377–78). Also see Lieb on the language of creation in **802**, **804**, and **810–19**.

like a Toad: in his response to Johnson's criticism of this entire episode, Robert West impatiently takes up Johnson's concern about how Satan managed his shield and sword during the dream temptation: "Dr. Johnson thought that Satan took his spear and shield with him into the toad; but Milton does not say that he did. In fact, Milton does not speak of Satan *in* a toad, but only of Satan squat *like* a toad. These vapid explanations are no more literal-minded than the objections they meet and only one step more conjectural; perhaps they are permissible if the objections are. But we have surely to be a little shamefaced about the whole paltry speculation" (111).

802. *The Organs of her Fancie:* in *Milton and the Angels,* Robert West concludes, "The general idea that angels touched the mind of a man by managing its bodily instruments was standard among pious angelologists," and glancing at the two "bodily instruments" ("Organs of her Fancie" and "animal Spirits") that Satan could have used to reach Eve's mind, West writes, "In these passages, which express no choice between alternatives, Milton seems to indicate both his acquaintance with angelological detail and his Puritan indifference to it" (126).

Michael Lieb, insisting that Satan's dream temptation of Eve is "clearly sexual in its implications" (184), explains that this phrase "combines both psychological and creational overtones. Once these particular 'Organs' are activated, for example, the potentially chaotic emotions, previously tempered by the rational faculties, gain sway. The impregnated 'Organs' then give birth to 'Illusions,' 'Phantasms and Dreams,' in which world the fallen Satan is himself forever confined" (185–86). Also see Lieb on the language of creation in **800, 804,** and **810–19**.

Todd ([1842], 2:102) refers this phrase to *The Merry Wives of Windsor* 5.5.55: "Raise up the organs of her fantasy."

Organs: Alastair Fowler (661) detects a pun "between 'instruments' and a sense nearer to the modern ('functionally adapted parts of the body')."

803. *list:* A. W. Verity (470) explains that this is the past tense, like "when they list" in *PL* 2.656.

Phantasms: Alastair Fowler glosses this as "illusions, deceptive appearances; mental images" (661), while John M. Steadman brings attention to the word's special philosophical meaning: "Eve's dream was likewise an *eidolon* or

phantasma. Plato had included the 'appearances in dreams' among *eidola*."
Steadman also notes, "Significantly, Eve had already displayed her vulnerability
to *eidola;* her reflection in the lake was an *eidolon*" ("Image and Idol" 653).
While the *OED* 2.3 does not cite 803, it does present the philosophical meaning that Steadman applies.

804. *inspiring:* arguing that "Satan wishes to initiate the process of impregnation
and consequently birth," Michael Lieb explains: "The presence of words such
as 'inspiring,' 'animal' (from *anima* or spirit), 'Spirits,' 'breaths,' 'raise,' 'blown
up,' and 'ingendring' merely serves to reinforce the idea previously mentioned.
Underlying the imagery is the concept of giving life through the breath as a
breathing into or inspiring. Ironically, Satan gives life in order to cause death."
Other words, such as *distemperd* and *inordinate,* Lieb describes as "implicitly
uncreative," reasoning that "healthful generation implies a tempering and
ordering of that which is chaotic and disordered" (186). Also see Lieb on the
language of creation in **800, 802,** and **810–19.**

    venom: Hume glosses this phrase as "a pois'nous Vapour" (163), and quot-
ing "Viperam inspirans Animam ... / ... pertentat Sensus" ("[a snake] breathes
into her its viperous breath ... / ... [and] thrills her senses") from the *Aeneid*
7.350–54, the Richardsons repeat Hume's "pois'nous Vapour" when they insist
that the venom Satan may be inspiring into Eve is "not a Meer Suggestion of
Discontent, Pride, &c. but a real Poisonous Vapour, Corrupting the Blood,
and by It the Mind, as appears by what immediately follows" (181). Also see
Newton 292.

808. *inordinate desires:* Hume's comment on this phrase suggests the twentieth
century debate about the dream's effect on Eve's spiritual state: "Unbounded
appetites, disorderly desires, exceeding the bounds of Reason. *Inordinate,* excessive, *extra ordinem.* The first steps and motions towards sin, are irregular desires,
and inordinate appetites" (163; also see Hume in **799–809**).

809. *ingendring pride:* Todd ([1842], 2:102) refers this phrase to Sir William
Alexander's *Tragedy of Julius Caesar* 245 (*Poetical Works* 1:354), "where the
poet is speaking also of those who deride the Omnipotent: 'Those that by follie
ingender pride.'"

810–19. The first of a series of scholars who have admired the explosive revelation of Satan at Eve's ear, Addison describes it as "wonderfully fine, both in the Literal Description, and in the Moral which is concealed under it" (*Spectator* 3:172 qtd. in Newton 293). Todd ([1842], 2:102) reports a note from Robert Thyer who associates this sequence with Ariosto, who "uses the same simile to describe a sudden start of passion" in *Orlando Furioso* 10.40: "Non cosi fin salnitro, e zolfo puro / Tocco dal foco, subito s' avvampa"; "Fine saltpeter and pure sulfur, when touched with fire, do not so suddenly blaze up" (trans. Allan Gilbert, *Orlando*). Tennyson's admiration is presented by A. W. Verity (471), quoting from one of Edward Fitzgerald's letters: "Tennyson [again] used to say that the two grandest of all Similes were those of the Ships hanging in the air [2.636–43], and 'the Gunpowder one,' which he used slowly and grimly to enact, in the Days that are no more" (Benson 156). Glimpsing evidence within the simile of the effects of Milton's blindness, Masson notes, "This is one instance, out of many in the poem, of an image drawn from the luminous effects of fire" (*Poetical Works* 3:180).

Michael Wilding, Alastair Fowler, and Michael Lieb develop readings that may clarify the "moral" Addison mentions but never elaborates. Wilding establishes a groundwork for his reading: "Most of the Devil's technology is military, and the imagery of gunpowder, cannon and explosions follows Satan as he travels. The technological achievements become converted into images of the state of being fallen." According to Wilding, Satan's explosive exposure is therefore "a vivid simile, suitable for the great energy of Satan, suitably destructive and aggressive. Appropriate to the whole imagery of Hell, moreover, it suggests he carries Hell with him" (35). Fowler (662) draws together the imagery of explosions, adding that "all these passages acquire new significance with Raphael's account of the invention of gunpowder, in vi 469–500. The present simile gains aptness from the fact that gunpowder was commonly called 'serpentine powder.'" Fowler also suggests that perhaps "smutty grain" (815) "sets up a resonance with the next simile, of corn and chaff (ll. 981–5)." Explaining the dialectics by which divine and demonic creation are associated in *PL*, Michael Lieb (187) describes this episode as "a kind of mock birth." "The idea of being fraudulently 'blown up with high conceits' is transferred to a more spectacular 'blow up.' Ithuriel's touching Satan lightly with his spear causes Satan to reveal himself explosively. The act recalls the igniting of the cannon fuses in the War in Heaven.... Here ... 'truth' explodes 'falsehood' with its store of debased associations, and the 'Smuttie grain...inflames the air' (IV, 810–818). The offspring of this explosive birth, Satan in his true shape, 'resembl'st now / [His] sin and place of doom obscure and foul' (IV, 839–840)." Like Lieb, Fowler, and Wilding, J. B. Broadbent identifies the "technological and mountainous imagery of Hell" (*Some Graver Subject* 200) that marks the descriptions of Satan even in paradise, but Broadbent (110) fits that imagery into "the process of alternating inflation and deflation of the devils begun in Book I, and continued for Satan all through the poem—his furious 'dilation' into the size of Teneriffe or Atlas (IV.986) followed by his slinking into the darkness; his explosion from toad to proper shape at the touch of Ithuriel's spear; and finally his expansion from plebeian disguise to 'shape Starr-bright' and then to 'Dragon grown, larger then whom the Sun Ingenderd in the *Pythian* Vale on slime, Huge Python' (X.450, 629)."

The issue of how the guards knew to test the toad's nature first troubles Bentley and remains a provocative critical concern through the mid-twentieth century. Between 810 and 811, Bentley inserts "*Knowing no real Toad durst there intrude,*" explaining, "For we know, the Bower was sacred and sequester'd to *Adam* and *Eve* only; IV.703. *Other Creatures there, / Beast, Bird, Insect or Worm, durst enter none.* This the Two Angels could not be ignorant of" (136). Implicitly acknowledging the problem Bentley's revision aims to remedy, Pearce nevertheless responds, "I can't find M[ilton] representing the Angels as acquainted with This or many other Circumstances of Paradise" (142). William Empson shares Bentley's sensitive awareness of the muddling of reason throughout *PL* and announces that he therefore views Bentley's "worst efforts with affection and pleasure, and...[is] properly charmed" by his efforts to make sense of Ithuriel's discovery of Satan in the toad (*Some Versions* 148). Later, Dennis H. Burden also takes on the problem that first perplexes Bentley: "If Uriel cannot penetrate Satan's disguise, then neither can the guard, and what is the use of a guard if it cannot distinguish friend from foe? Milton meets this awkwardness by providing the guard with a magic stick which has the power to restore any creature to its proper shape." Burden concedes that Milton's handling of this problem is "perhaps somewhat fanciful, but the point where it all started—Eve's failure to see through Satan's disguise—was too crucial to be ignored" (100). Alastair Fowler considers Burden's explanation but aligns himself with Bentley: "the fact that a toad has dared to enter the nuptial bower—an unnatural occurrence; see l. 704—is enough to alert the guard. The spear is rather an emblematic expression of their perceptiveness. It is necessary to the story in another way, however: Satan has to be got back into a presentable form for the confrontation that follows" (662).

While the notion of Milton's resorting to "a magic stick" discomforts Burden, it has literary authority, as a number of editors and scholars have acknowledged. Wayne Shumaker, for example, understands that Ithuriel's spear is magical, and sees it as the only exception to his thesis that Milton "had little use for magic," which figures so large in Italian Renaissance epics ("*Paradise Lost*" 96). Much earlier, in 1695, Patrick Hume (164) anticipates Shumaker's remarks about magic spears and Italian epics: "Well may the touch of *Ithuriel's* Spear, heavenly temper'd, return Satan to his own shape, when *Tasso* makes a whole Army of wild Beasts run away at the sight of *Ubaldos Sacred Switch* [*Gerusalemme Liberata* 15.52]." Edwin Greenlaw (352) argues that Ithuriel's unmasking of Satan is "exactly parallel" to the unmasking of the evil Titaness Mutability when Mercury "on her shoulder laid / His snaky-wreathed Mace," in *Cantos of Mutability* 6.18 (Spenser 396). Finally, Marjorie H. Nicolson ("Spirit World" 438) suggests that a remark by Henry More, in *The Immortality of the Soul* 204, "might almost have been the motivation" for the explosive revelation of Satan's identity in this sequence. A disguised demon, More contends, "upon command...will be forced to appear in his natural and usual form, not daring to deny upon examination to what particular subdivision he belongs." George Wesley Whiting takes issue with Nicolson's remarks on More and Milton. See Whiting in **838–40**.

F. T. Prince finds in Ithuriel's discovery of Satan an example of the theatrical sublime in *PL*, which he understands as "Milton's use of organized and enacted spectacle, his demonstration of the meaning of a dramatic moment: which leaves us with the impression of having witnessed a consciously complete *performance*, on the part of both the poet and his poem." Prince sees the theatrical sublime as the "detailed application" of Johnson's concept of Miltonic sublimity: "of displaying the vast, illuminating the splendid, enforcing the awful, darkening the gloomy, and aggravating the dreadful" ("Milton" 55).

812. *temper:* the Richardsons comment on the literal metallurgical meaning here, while later critics consider more figurative meanings. Tracing *temper* to "*Tempera*, and *Tempra*, (Ital.) Consolidation," the Richardsons (181) explain that it is "said of Iron put red hot into Cold Water to Harden, of This Celestial

Temper was the Head of *Ithuriel's* Spear, *v.* 553." A. W. Verity moves to a more figurative meaning: "a thing tempered, i.e. a weapon: abstract for concrete" (470). Merritt Y. Hughes ("Variorum") cross-references *distemperd* in 807, as well as Belial's prediction that in time the fallen angels will be "to the place conformd / In temper and in nature" (2.217–18). Alastair Fowler's note moves in a similar direction: "The primary reference is to the spear, which has been tempered in heaven; but the odd diction allows a secondary reference to Ithuriel's own spiritual constitution" (662). The play between *temper* and *distemperd* might also reverberate with *forge* at 802.

815. *nitrous Powder:* "Of Gunpowder made of Salt-Petre" (Hume 164). Milton's line is the first illustration of the *OED*'s definition 1.b: "Mixed or impregnated with nitre so as to form an explosive compound."

816. *Tun:* while the Richardsons (181) establish the French origin *Tonneau*, "any Cask or Vessel," Newton admits, "'Tis commonly call'd a *barrel*: but Milton for the sake of his verse, and perhaps for the sake of a less vulgar term, calls it a *tun*" (292).

   som Magazin: "A store-house of publick Provisions, of Arms, and other Utensils of all sorts for War" (Hume 164). The *OED* 2 cites Milton's line to illustrate this meaning.

817. *Against:* Verity (471) glosses the word as "in preparation for" and notes that "various battle-touches in *P.L.* (especially in bk. VI.) seem like a reminiscence of the Civil War."

818. *sudden blaze:* Edward S. Le Comte (*Yet Once More* 62–63) traces a progression from figurative to literal meaning in Milton's repetition of this phrase, moving from *Arc* 2 and *Lyc* 74 to *PL* 1.665, 4.818, and 10.453.

820. *amaz'd:* Merritt Y. Hughes cross-references *SA* 1286, where *amaz'd* is paired with *distracted* to describe alarm or terror caused by surprise ("Variorum").

821. *the grislie King:* the Richardsons (182) note: "Grisly, or Grieslie; Ugly, Dreadful; an *Anglo-Saxon* Word, and frequently used by *Chaucer* and *Spencer*.

the Verb is *Agrise*, to Fright, to Fear, to be Terrify'd. I.670. II.704." The *OED* cites Milton's *Nat* 208–09: "In vain with Cymbals' ring / They call the grisly King."

823–56. J. B. Broadbent, no admirer of Book 4's ending, nevertheless admits that the guards' initial confrontation with the revealed Satan "makes a dramatic impact after the somnolence of the Paradisal afternoon" (*Some Graver Subject* 199), and others have long shared his view. In addition to the spectacle of Satan's explosive exposure, other dramatic concerns, especially character and plot, but also thought (dianoia) have shaped the criticism of Ithuriel and Zephon's interrogation of Satan, but puncturing the drama of that confrontation is the sustained intrusion of the narrator's voice in 844–51, and that narrative commentary often provocatively enters the critical response to this dramatic scene. The Richardsons are perhaps the most effusive of all those who admire characterization in this episode, describing Satan as "a true Diabolic Character. he Pin'd, Griev'd at, the Loss of his Purity of Mind when he saw the Advantage it gave the Angel both in Strength and Beauty; but his Greatest Concern was that his Own Glory was Evidently Faded, and Observ'd to be So, yet put on a Pretence to a Courage he had not. Pride and Hypocrisy. What a Picture! the Angelic Grace, Heighten'd So as to be Invincible by his Grave Rebuke, Severe; Severity join'd with Youthful Beauty, Awfulness, Goodness; and These Contrasted with the Faded Lustre of the Apostate Spirit, and He Asham'd and Confounded! and What a Noble Moral does it Exhibit!" (182–83). Addison, too, admires the confrontation scene for its handling of character, noting, for example, that Satan's "Answer upon his being discovered, and demanded to give an Account of himself, is conformable to the Pride and Intrepidity of his Character." Addison praises Zephon's "Rebuke" of Satan, describing it as "exquisitely Graceful and Moral" (*Spectator* 3:172). Newton quotes Addison (293). In his 1795 edition of *PR*, Charles Dunster brings considerable attention to the contrast between the revealed Satan's angry response to Ithuriel and Zephon, who do not recognize him, and the disguised Satan's response when Jesus in *PR* rejects the first temptation and tells Satan, "I discern thee other then thou seem'st" (1.348). Dunster points out that following Jesus' rebuke, Satan "makes here no vaunt of his power or rank, as he had done in the other instance" (40). The contrast between Satan's behavior in these two situations, Dunster suggests, "may be considered as meant to elucidate and exalt the character of our Lord" (41).

With the fiery exchange between Satan and the angelic guards, Dryden ends the third act of *The State of Innocence, and Fall of Man* (*Works* 12:120–22). Merging this confrontation scene into the subsequent one in *PL* 4, Dryden has his Lucifer face Gabriel and Ithuriel together, and the scene ends not with Satan's flight after looking up and seeing the golden scales as in the epic but with Lucifer's disdainful refusal to fight with angels, and his demand to confront God: "let me with him contend / On whom your limitary pow'rs depend" (3.112–13). Twentieth century criticism has responded to the dramatic element in Satan's exposure by Zephon and Ithuriel. John M. Steadman discusses Satan's character by reference to sapience, one element of Renaissance heroism, and he identifies Satan as an idol of heroism whose guile "derives its full significance only from contrast with its opposite. As the false image of *prudentia*, it must be brought face to face with its contraries." Satan's discovery at Eve's ear creates such a confrontation: "In first tempting Eve, he finds his lies and excuses refuted by the angelic guard" (*Milton* 51). In an earlier article Steadman explains how the classical notion of the dramatic recognition, the Aristotelian anagnorisis, contributes to the scene's success: "The Recognition scene of Book II had stressed the moral deformity of Satan's daughter, Sin; the Recognition scene of Book IV emphasizes the spiritual foulness of Satan himself" ("Recognition" 165; cf. Steadman in **990–1004**). Allan H. Gilbert (*On the Composition* 15) studies the episode against Milton's early manuscript drafts for a drama. In the outline for act 2 in Milton's fourth draft, Lucifer encounters the chorus, which "prepare resistance at his first approach," and "after discourse of enmity on either side he departs" (Patterson, *Works* 18:231). In the scornful exchanges between Zephon and Satan in *PL* 4, Gilbert suggests, "It is possible, though not necessary, to find…something of the 'discourse of enmity' of Milton's fourth draft" (91). Gilbert notes that Zephon and Ithuriel's discovery of Satan at the ear of Eve is not in the Trinity Manuscript, and—of course—the confrontation between Satan and the angelic watch is necessarily as futile in the epic as in the dramatic draft 4 (41–42). Unlike Gilbert, J. B. Broadbent laments the dramatic remnants that appear to have made their way into the epic. The meeting of Gabriel and Satan, Broadbent argues, "insists on the involvement of Adam and Eve in cosmic politics—though the actual conduct of these politics, the need for sentries in Paradise, their failure to prevent Satan's approach to Eve, and God's release of Satan after his arrest, are absurd." Broadbent believes that when "these relics of Milton's early plans enter the poem they spoil it, not so much because they are ex-generic but because the genre they belong to is less serious than *Paradise Lost*" (*Some Graver Subject* 199–200).

Broadbent is not alone in his displeasure with the confrontation between Satan and the angelic guards. A number of those twentieth century critics who find that Milton degrades Satan give considerable attention to this scene, and perhaps even more attention to the narrator's commentary in 844–51. John Peter accuses Milton of sacrificing the characterization of Satan: "This is not the integration in a single form of majesty and evil; it is merely a description of pretence. A degree of expediency has appeared in Milton's presentation which was not there before" (55). A. J. A. Waldock contends that Satan is here "made to be 'abasht,'" as Milton continues "energetically pressing Satan down and down" (90). Waldock complains that the impairment of Satan's "lustre" (850) in this sequence is "merely another kind of 'interference,' taking us a step farther on the road to downright allegory: as is Satan's 'imbruting' of himself in animal forms" (90–91).

Opposed to those like Waldock and Peter, of course, are the critics who argue that Satan is not degraded or pressed down, but rather degenerates and declines on his own. On the heels of Waldock's and Peter's publications, Anne Davidson Ferry, for one, argues that Zephon's remarks about Satan's altered appearance simply point to evidence of demonic division, demonic disintegration: "Satan is the father of lies, the father of Sin, and, in a special sense, the father of allegory. The nature of his offspring which broke 'violent way' from him is a revelation of the division in his fallen experience, and his history in the poem is his disintegration under the pressure of the widening division within him. That disintegration is revealed in part by descriptions of Satan's changing appearance" (*Milton's Epic Voice* 133). John M. Steadman, recalling that the fall of Lucifer and his companions had traditionally "entailed a corresponding debasement in form" and "had been a recurrent theme in medieval and Renaissance art and literature" ("Archangel to Devil" 321), argues that Milton adapts the tradition to present Satan's "gradual degeneration in several stages" (335). See the fuller presentation of the critical debate about Milton's characterization of Satan in terms of degeneration versus degradation in **32–113**.

As modern critics debate the evidence of Satan's degeneration or his degradation in this scene, so within the scene itself an even more heated dispute grows out of the guard's opening question, "Which of those rebell Spirits adjudg'd to Hell / Com'st thou?" (823–24). Although Gabriel and Satan later call each other by name, Ithuriel and Zephon refer to Satan only as a rebel spirit or a "revolted Spirit" (835), and Satan never moves from "ye" in his replies to them. Do Satan and the angelic guard not know each other? The angels' question could simply be scornful, as Allan Gilbert reasons, but if not, "they do not recognize Satan because he is changed; moreover Satan, expecting to be recognized, does not realize that his lustre is visibly impaired" (*On the Composition* 95). This identity topic thus works into the discussion of character while it responds to the element of drama that Aristotle calls thought or dianoia: "The Thought of the personages is shown in everything to be effected by their language—in every effort to prove or disprove, to arouse emotion (pity, fear, anger, and the like), or to maximize or minimize things" (*Poetics* 1456b). Marjorie H. Nicolson comments on the development of the argument about identity that whips back and forth between Satan and the guard, but she also acknowledges the vigorous debate within Satan himself as he is forced to confront a new identity, as well as the "emotional effects" of both debates. She describes Satan as "disdainful of minor angels who fail to recognize one who was long their superior. The figures of speech, from grand to base, follow each other in rapid succession. The former good and the increasing evil in Satan are inextricably mingled here. For a moment he stands abashed before the severe purity of the youthful angels, feeling 'how awful goodness is' and 'virtue in her shape how lovely.' His indomitable Pride wins over momentary regret and remembrance of times lost" (*John Milton* 243). Raymond B. Waddington and Jacques Blondel similarly glance at Satan's reaction to this confrontation with self that Zephon forces on him. Waddington describes Satan rejecting the fact of his changed appearance, "despite being told...directly" (390), and Blondel suggests that this sequence might compel the reader, as well as Satan, to an altered sense of self, for when Ithuriel and Zephon here identify Satan, "his reality is laid bare and one discovers an overlapping of the post-lapsarian condition of man on the prelapsarian, which creates dramatic tension" (262). Stanley Fish's commentary on the syntax of Satan's reply to the question, "Which of those rebell Spirits adjudg'd to Hell / Com'st thou?" continues to reveal the intricate associations among character, plot, and thought: "By delaying the pronoun 'mee' [828], Milton emphasizes the 'selfness' of Satan's concern. It is for this that he has rebelled and in the context of his ego-centric vision 'nonrecognition' is more than a social slight" (*Surprised* 338). Recalling Satan's vaunt in 1.254–55, "The mind is its own place, and in it self / Can make a Heav'n of Hell, a Hell of Heav'n," Fish writes, "Satan's 'shape' like his mind, is now an extension of his place, which usurps the selfhood in whose name he had declared himself injured. The final proof of this of course is his involuntary metamorphosis (at X.511) into a shape that is not his own, or more properly into the shape that has overtaken and become him" (339).

Not always or completely overshadowed by Satan, the developing identities of his captors have also been critically considered. Thomas Newton points out, for example, that although the voice for the guard's first speech (823–26) is not indicated, the division of their roles in the scene individualizes them so "that each of them may appear as actors upon this occasion. Ithuriel with his spear restored the Fiend to his own shape, and Zephon rebukes him. It would not have been so well, if the same person had done both" (293–95). Todd ([1842], 2:103) quotes Newton. Reasoning that the guards as well as Satan have changed their identities, William Empson suggests why Zephon is the angel bold enough verbally to assault Satan. Empson notes that Satan treats Zephon "with wither-ing social contempt. Some critics have found an inconsistency here, because he accepts arrest by two angels and then threatens to fight the whole troop to which they lead him; but it is a point of honour to refuse to fight except with his equals. This is the reason he gives, and Milton does not contradict it, while adding that his feelings were more complex. He would be embarrassed at being caught as a toad, and he 'felt how awful goodness is' when confronted with the severe youthful beauty of the cherub. Milton of course is thinking of human youth, but there is no inconsistency in regarding Zephon as recently made a cherub; he has been fitted out with a new appearance, and is much keener than the old hands. The scene may be from an earlier play, as has been deduced from the words of Gabriel (870), and this might explain a confusion; but drama is needed here (Satan is relieved of his shame by the prospect of a fight), and no confusion need be found" (*Milton's God* 60–61). Alastair Fowler (664) does not find Empson's reading a compelling one: "But doesn't M[ilton] contradict Satan's reason? The point of honour is said to be part of his seeming daunt-lessness (ll. 850–2), whereas his true feeling is dismay at the visible difference between good and evil—a difference of which he has apparently repressed the full memory. We are explicitly told that Satan *to strive . . . held it vain* because he was awe-struck. Presumably this feeling has passed by the time he defies the whole squadron at l. 987." Finally, the identity topic that drives the debate between Satan and his captors is developed through "proof and refutation," as Aristotle puts it, and brings attention to two types of wordplay. First is Satan's play on *to know* in 827–31. Verity (471) cross-references *SA* 1081–82, "thou knowst me now, / If thou at all art known." W. K. Wimsatt considers the development of the rhetorical figure of the *traducio,* or the turn through the entire sequence: "The reiteration of the word *know*—dramatic and ironic emphasis—is the opposite of both Elegant Variation and slipshod verbal Repetition and is hence a logical virtue of style. But the modulation of the root—*know, knew, to know, unknown*—introduces another aspect of meaning which, though in this instance it is no doubt under logical restraint, is capable of greater liberty" (211). Also see Wimsatt in **639–56** and Le Comte, *Yet Once More* 29. Zephon refutes Satan's rhetorical gymnastics with his own play on *then-when* in 835–40, compelling Satan to confront his altered self as he confronts the angelic guard. Developing the *then-now* pattern as a feature of Milton's apocalyptic technique, where usually the present state in *PL* is the perfect state, Leland Ryken explains, "From a fallen viewpoint, however, the apocalyptic state is a past vision, with imperfection now the present reality," as Zephon here points out to Satan (45).

824. *transform'd:* Hume (164), pointing to Virgil's *Georgics* 4.383–419, sees here a link between Satan and Proteus: "Transformatus, Lat. disguis'd, of *transformare,* Lat. to shift shapes. *Omnia transformat sese in miracula rerum* ['changes himself into all wondrous shapes'] (*Georgics* 4.441). Of the various *Proteus.*"

829. *sitting:* quoting Greenwood, Todd ([1842], 2:103) establishes this word's significance to Satan's sense of self-identity: "As *sitting* is frequently used in the Scriptures, and in other ancient writers, for a posture that implies a high rank of dignity and power; Satan by this expression intimates his great superiority over them, that he had the privilege to *sit,* as an Angel of figure and authority, in an eminent part of Heaven, where they *durst not* soar, where they did not presume even to come." The same understanding prompts John Mitford's (144) reference to *The Tragedie of Claudius Tiberius Nero* 434: "Nor shall he hope to sit where *Nero* soares."

830. *argues:* in his edition of *PL,* R. C. Browne (1:355) supplies the definition "proves" while cross-referencing 931 and citing Shakespeare's *2 Henry VI* 3.3.30 and *Richard III* 3.7.40. Similarly defining the word in "Variorum," Merritt Y. Hughes adds, "As an example of this use of the word Milton quotes a Virgilian tag, 'Fear argues degenerate souls' (*Aen.* IV, 13) in *Art of Logic* I, ii" (Patterson,

Works 2:25). The *OED* 3 cites Milton's use here to illustrate the meaning "To prove or evince; to afford good ground for inferring, show weighty reasons for supposing; to betoken, indicate."

834–48. Leland Ryken, discussing Milton's apocalyptic technique of analogy, contends that Milton makes his angels even more anthropomorphic than God, attributing to them physical but also mental and emotional qualities, such as the laughter and scorn of Zephon and, later, Gabriel (903) as they confront Satan (134–37).

834. *scorn with scorn:* Stanley Fish explains, "The sneer in 'vaunting' is aimed equally at the performance and anyone who lingers to appreciate it (Satan himself delivers the final judgment on this and on all his speeches at IV.83)." Fish continues, "The danger is not so much that Satan's argument will persuade (one does not accord the father of lies an impartial hearing), but that its intricacy will engage the reader's attention and lead him into an error of omission" (*Surprised* 10).

835–36. Bentley and Pearce register difficulty with syntax here, and suggest changes, but subsequent editors and critics find Milton's meaning apparent. Bentley (138) thinks "undiminished brightness" should be "brightness undiminish'd," and Pearce (143) suggests "thy" should be "by." Newton, reporting the debate, concludes it: "But without any alteration may we not understand shape and brightness as in the accusative case after the verb think? Think not thy shape the same, or undiminish'd brightness to be known now, as it was formerly in Heaven" (294). Alastair Fowler contributes more imaginative support for Milton's construction: "*undiminished brightness* mimetically resists the grammatical pressure to alter" (663).

838–40. George Wesley Whiting asserts the conventionality of Zephon's retort by insisting that many of the early church fathers explained that when the rebel angels fell they "were changed into a more aerial and gross substance" (*Milton's Literary Milieu* 155). Bringing Robert Burton's *The Anatomy of Melancholy* to bear on the discussion, Whiting then counters Marjorie H. Nicolson's arguments about Milton's debt to Henry More's views on spirits in *The Immortality of the Soul:* "Relevant parts of the *Anatomy* [1.2.1.2] show that the spirit worlds of More and Milton include a number of conventional ideas" (156). For more commentary on More and Milton, see **20–26**, **127**, **223–40**, **295–311**, **395–408**, **674–88**, and **810–19**.

839. Examining Milton's prosody, and pointing to *thee* as a supernumerary in this line, Robert Bridges explains that such an extrametrical syllable in the middle of a line while "common" in Shakespeare is "disallowed" by Milton and that "the extra syllable is accounted for by Elision" (8).

843. As he establishes the principles of Milton's syllabic prosody, S. Ernest Sprott points to this line as well as 250 when explaining, "It seems generally better to elide *-able* words externally rather than internally" (92). Also see Sprott in **220** and **250**.

844–51. In this sequence, the narrator's interpretation of the effects on Satan of his confrontation with Zephon and Ithuriel, some moderns like A. J. A. Waldock charge Milton with pushing Satan "down and down," while other moderns like William Empson find Milton not imposing but exploring the demon's "more complex" feelings. See Waldock and Empson in **823–56**. An intriguingly prophetic reading is presented by P. T. Forsyth in "Milton's God and Milton's Satan" several decades before the degeneration-versus-degradation debate flared into prominence. "If he felt the awfulness of goodness," Satan, according to Forsyth, "was not utterly lost" (454). In this passage, Forsyth proceeds to locate evidence of Satan's "gradual process of moral decay and diminished dignity," and he finds that "degeneration" the "most absorbing feature in this character" (459).

The earlier editors give most of their attention to the literary sources for the idea of "Vertue" having a visible shape. Hume (164) attributes the idea to Juvenal's *Satires:* "A Virtutem videant, intabescantque relicta"; "Let them see moral excellence and let them pine at abandoning it" (the quotation is from Persius, *Satires* 3.38, not Juvenal, however). While Newton (295) repeats Hume's note, he also cites Cicero: "*Formam* quidem *ipsam* et quasi *faciem honesti* vides, quae *si oculis cerneretur,* mirabiles amores, ut ait Plato, excitaret sapientiae"; "You see here . . . the very form and as it were the face of Moral Goodness; 'and if,' as Plato says, 'it could be seen with the physical eye, it would awaken a marvelous love of wisdom'" (*De Officiis* 15; also see Plato *Phaedrus* 250D). Newton in addition refers the description of Zephon's "youthful beauty" and "grace / Invincible" to Virgil's description of Euryalus in *Aeneid* 5.344: "Gratior et pulchro veniens in corpore virtus"; "and worth, that shows more winsome in a fair form." Todd ([1842, 2:104] straightens out the Persius-Juvenal snag and adds Sir Philip Sidney's "if ever virtue took a body to show his else-inconceivable beauty, it was in Pamela" from *The New Arcadia* 421 to Hume's and Newton's classical references. In addition, Todd quotes the following three passages from Milton's *RCG:* "And certainly Discipline is not only the removal of Disorder; but, if any visible shape can be given to divine things, *the very visible shape and image of Virtue;* whereby she is not only *seen* in the regular gestures and motions of her heavenly paces as she walks, but also makes the harmony of her voice audible to mortal ears" (Patterson, *Works* 3:185); "*The lovely shapes of Virtues* and Graces" (3:191); and "The very *shape* and visage of *Truth*" (3:249). Several modern editors and critics, including Merritt Y. Hughes, Edward S. Le Comte, and Alastair Fowler, continue to pursue the classical philosophical expressions of the notion of virtue having a shape, and, underscoring the idea's appeal to Milton, they contribute cross-references to his other writings. In "Variorum," Hughes underscores the Persius parallel, first identified by Hume, by paraphrasing Isaac Casaubon's commentary (32–33): "all men are said to be capable of the vision of virtue, and those who refuse to see it are called almost no better than beasts." Hughes moves beyond both Persius and Milton to "Plato's faith in virtue as so beautiful that if its form could be visible it would be irresistibly lovely (*Phaedrus* 250D)." In *Mask* 214–16, where the Lady sees Hope as a "hov'ring Angel girt with golden wings," and Chastity an "unblemish't form," Hughes finds suggested this "Platonic conception of the virtues as capable of making their forms visible" (*Complete Poems* 298). Finally, in *PR* 3.10–11 Hughes notes the dramatization of Casaubon's point about the bestial nature of those who refuse the sight of virtue when Satan refuses the virtue he sees in Jesus, whose "heart / Contains of good, wise, just, the perfect shape" ("Variorum"). Le Comte (*Yet Once More* 95–96) cross-references 9.503–04, where Satan appears as serpent: "pleasing was his shape / And lovely." Fowler cross-references 9.457–65, where Satan is "overaw'd" by Eve's "Heav'nly form / Angelic," and, quoting Odes 3.7 and 2.4 from Dante's *Convivio,* Fowler goes on to argue, "The establishment of the idea as one of the principal doctrines of Renaissance love poetry was apparently due to Dante" (663–64). Finally, Irene Samuel's chapter "The Theory of Ideas" in *Plato and Milton* most thoroughly pursues the Platonic background of Satan's here seeing "Vertue in her shape how lovly" (848) as he beholds

Zephon. While Samuel does not specifically comment on Satan's experience with the angelic guard, she does look at a number of the passages other critics have cross-referenced in their responses to the episode, and she establishes that, "in general, the 'very visible shape and image of virtue' is the main contribution of the Platonic world of true being to Milton's thought—and not only where a phrase reveals his source, but throughout the moral substructure of his writings" (145).

Discussing the importance of grace, decency, and decorum to human behavior, Addison, in *Spectator* 292 (February 4, 1712), moves from the sources or parallels for the idea of virtue being visibly beautiful to its effect: "The Comeliness of Person and Decency of Behaviour, add infinite Weight to what is pronounc'd by any one. 'Tis the want of this that often makes the Rebukes and Advice of old rigid Persons of no Effect, and leave a Displeasure in the Minds of those they are directed to: But Youth and Beauty, if accompanied with a graceful and becoming Severity, is of mighty Force to raise, even in the most Profligate, a Sense of Shame. In *Milton* the Devil is never describ'd asham'd but once, and that at the Rebuke of a beauteous Angel" (3:41). John M. Steadman notes that as Milton "makes Satan contrast his own diminished luster with the beauty of the unfallen angels," he is "transforming the poetic fable into a rhetorical *exemplum*" in order to arouse his reader to pursue virtue and turn from vice ("Ethos and Dianoia" 202).

844–46. *rebuke…abasht:* pointing out that Spenser associates both terms very much as Milton does here, Hume (164) quotes *The Faerie Queene* 5.11.64: "Abash'd at his rebuke, that bit her near." The *OED* cites Milton's line to illustrate rebuke definition 2b, "A reproof, a reprimand."

845–47. A. W. Verity (471) claims that Dryden remembers these lines in *The Hind and the Panther* 3.1040–41: "For Vice, tho' frontless, and of harden'd Face / Is daunted at the sight of awfull Grace" (*Works* 3:192). Verity also sees a parallel between these lines and the scene in *PR* 3.145–49, "where Satan, not insensible to goodness, is abashed in the presence of the Saviour."

845–46. *grace / Invincible:* R. J. Zwi Werblowsky, referring to Tillyard's emphasis on the theme of "heroic energy" in *PL*, contends that "it is not the beauty of holiness, nor the holiness of beauty that appeals to Milton; it is the power of holiness, the power of beauty, the power of goodness, that carry him away" (68). In "Variorum," Merritt Y. Hughes cross-references *PR* 2.408, where Satan confesses that Jesus' temperance is "invincible."

846–50. Jackson I. Cope writes that "the wedding of his [Satan's] symbolic darkness and the scenic dark of the narrative setting is here consummated—a point underlined in the last words of Book Four—when Gabriel and his troops expel Satan from Paradise and 'with him fled the shades of night' (1015)" (113).

848. Establishing the rules of elision in Milton's verse, Robert Bridges finds the rule of open vowels exemplified by the juxtaposition of *e* and *i* in "Virtue in." "All open vowels," Bridges explains, "may be elided, whether long, short, double, or combined; and whether both the vowels be in the same word, or divided between two" (24).

849–50. John Peter notes that Satan's "dislike of ugliness," established when he earlier faced Sin and Death (2.745), "prepares us for his chagrin when told of his own" (47).

851–54. Walter Raleigh argues that in confronting both Michael in heaven and Gabriel on the earth, Satan "never falls below himself" (135). Describing Satan as an idol of heroic magnanimity, opposed to the true image of magnanimity—the Messiah—John M. Steadman explains that Satan's "desire to test himself against a worthy antagonist links him with various heroes in the *Iliad* and the *Avarchide*—Achilles, Hector, Ajax, Segurano, Galealto, Lancelot" (*Milton* 143).

854–56. Roy Daniells and John M. Steadman discuss the heroism of Zephon's reply. Daniells refers to these lines as he distinguishes between Catholic and Protestant concepts of martyrdom in baroque art. Milton, with an "emphatic dislike for the deliberately shocking presentation of the agonies of those done cruelly to death," possesses a "passion for 'heroic fortitude,'" here demonstrated by Zephon, according to Daniells (*Milton* 176). Steadman explains that Milton here counters mere strength (*mera fortezza*) with strength tempered by reason, as well as with the "better fortitude" of patience: "The paradox of strength in weakness is so closely interwoven with the formula of patient fortitude as to be virtually inseparable. Its obverse is the paradox of weakness in strength, whereby…Milton degrades the *fortezza* pattern. Satan's might is providentially exposed as 'light' and 'weak.' Zephon asserts the actual frailty of the strength dedicated to evil" (*Milton* 40).

856. Verity (471) refers this line to *SA* 834: "All wickedness is weakness."

858–61. Satan's state of mind here puzzles Allan H. Gilbert. While "awe from above had quelld / His heart" (860–61), when he faces Gabriel "he no longer holds resistance vain but collects his might for a conflict.… Evidently he is released from 'awe from above,' though only for the moment, for again, on seeing 'his mounted scale aloft,' he flees from the vain combat. Why did Milton thus rapidly alternate the Adversary's state of mind?" (*On the Composition* 43). Also pointing out that the chorus in the early dramatic drafts becomes the angelic guard in the epic, Gilbert proceeds to argue that while Satan's confrontation with the guard emphasizes his weakness, it also reveals "that God could have protected man, but preferred rather to leave him his independence and free will to choose good or evil as he would. An unrestrained Devil is the symbol of man's liberty" (44).

858–59. Todd ([1842], 2:105) presents a lengthy list of classical, as well as sixteenth and seventeenth century, parallels to this simile of the "proud steed." Crediting Robert Thyer, who finds the metaphor to be "literally from what Mercury says to Prometheus," Todd quotes Aeschylus's *Prometheus Bound* 1009–10, and crediting Benjamin Stillingfleet, he quotes from Apollonius Rhodius's *Argonautica* 4.1606–07. Todd then independently refers the simile to Spenser's *The Faerie Queene* 1.1.1, "His angry steede did chide his foming bitt, / As much disdayning to the curbe to yield"; Spenser's *Daphnaida* 194–95 (*Poetical Works* 530), "As stubborne steed, that is with curb restrained, / Becomes more fierce and fervent in his gate"; Sir John Harington's translation of Ariosto's *Orlando Furioso* 27.56; and Sylvester's translation of Du Bartas's *The Divine Weeks and Works* 2.1.4.449–53. In 1952, J. C. Maxwell reconsiders the link between Milton and Aeschylus that Thyer offers, and declares, as Todd's additions to Thyer make clear, that "the comparison is a very usual one." Maxwell suggests that although Milton knew Aeschylus, "it may be doubted whether he was very intimately familiar with him." While he therefore rejects Thyer's note on this point, Maxwell finds that of all the early commentators Thyer "comes off by far the best—his comparisons are never silly. Dunster is the worst. The others come in between" (370).

858. *hautie:* considering the challenge of editing Milton's text, Robert Martin Adams sets this spelling against *haughty* in 5.852 and *haughtie* in 6.109, and concluding that "there is no conceivable rationale, either of buried significance, of philological origins, or of euphony, for a very great number of his [Milton's] spelling variations" (74), Adams contends that "being a child of his age, he [Milton] had no interest in such matters; he left trivia of this sort to printers and pedantic syllable pickers" (75).

859–61. John S. Diekhoff notes the rhyme in this passage ("Rhyme" 540). See Diekhoff in **222–24**.

861–64. David Masson continues here to develop his close examination of the deployment of the subdivisions of the angelic guard, tracing their movements from Gabriel's initial orders in 782–84 and 788–90 through to their confrontation with Satan in 977–84. "Here again Milton keeps military exactness in his description," Masson explains; "The subdivisions have joined (by the military act known as *closing*), and are standing in line, as before, facing Paradise, Gabriel in front, when Ithuriel and Zephon arrive with their prisoner" (*Poetical Works* 3:181). Cf. Masson, *Life of John Milton* 2:476 and Hanford, "Milton" 252–53.

H. F. Robins, considering the significance of directions in Milton's universe, including the association between evil and the west, notes, "It is to the west wall, where the circling angels have again met, that Satan is escorted under guard." So, too, then, after the judgment scene with the golden scales, Robins goes on, "Satan flees westward—'and with him fled the shades of night' [4.1015]" (101).

862. *half-rounding:* Alastair Fowler reports that in the *OED* "no other instance of the use as a verb is given" (664). The *OED* (B.b.), identifying Milton's term not as a verb but as an adjective deriving from the noun *half-round*, defines *half-rounding* as "forming a semicircle."

863–64. As he develops an understanding of *PL* as a baroque poem in which the complex of unity, power, and will drives the epic argument, Roy Daniells (*Milton* 75) writes, "Not only is this great theme argued and demonstrated; there are in addition many symbols or symbolic instances of freely given obedience conducing to corporate power; for example, the angelic guard in Eden that 'closing stood in squadron join'd / Awaiting next command.'"

866–73. John Upton and, centuries later, Davis P. Harding comment on Milton's debt to Homer as Gabriel announces the approach of Satan and the angelic guards. Upton writes, "Milton, in this whole episode, keeps close to his master Homer who sends out Ulysses and Diomedes into the Trojan camp as spies" (237n3). The Homeric episode occurs in the *Iliad* 10.532–40 where Nestor no sooner reports to the uneasy Greeks that he hears the hooves of Ulysses's and Diomedes's horses than the two scouts actually enter the camp, so Ithuriel and Zephon's entrance follows immediately upon Gabriel's report to the angelic guard, "I hear the tread of nimble feet" (866). Davis P. Harding (*Club* 47) acknowledges Upton's reference to the *Iliad* and develops it, finding, for example, that Ithuriel and Zephon's earlier interrogation of Satan is a "reminiscence of the capture and scornful questioning of the spy Dolon by Odysseus and Diomedes [*Iliad* 10.371–453]."

Unlike Harding and Upton, who consider the scene's Homeric underpinnings, James Holly Hanford argues that Gabriel's announcement of the coming of the angelic guard is one of the many essentially dramatic devices in *PL* resulting from the enduring influence of Elizabethan drama on Milton's epic, and prompting Milton to "go...beyond all previous epics in his approximation to dramatic form" ("Dramatic Element" 181–82).

868. *shade:* in "'Shade' for 'Tree,'" B. A. Wright puts Gabriel's announcement of the guards' approach against the earlier description of their departure as "radiant Files, / Daz'ling the Moon" (797–98) and concludes that "the glimpses Gabriel now catches of Ithuriel and Zephon must be through the trees [*sic*] than just through the darkness" (207).

869. *port:* the Richardsons note that *port* derives from "*Porter* (Fr.) Kingly Carriage or Behaviour" (183). The *OED* does not support the Richardsons' attention to kingliness but cites Milton's line to illustrate definition I.1, "The manner in which one bears oneself; external deportment; carriage, bearing, mien." A. W. Verity (472) supplies a cross-reference to *Mask* 297, where Comus describes the Lady's brothers: "Their port was more then human."

870–71. Verity, referring to 830–31, explains that "Gabriel, belonging to one of the highest of the Heavenly Orders, has known Satan (an archangel) in the past, and so recognises him here; Zephon, an inferior angel, did not" (472). In accord with the spirit of Verity's note, Alastair Fowler adds that "Satan's gibe at l. 830 is evidently well-founded" (665). See **823–56**.

872. *contest:* Verity (472) points out that Milton "always accents the noun, as we do the verb," that is, on the second syllable, and Verity cross-references 11.800, "In sharp contest of battle found no aid."

873. Todd ([1842], 2:105–06) cross-references *SA* 1073, where the chorus describes Harapha, "His habit carries peace, *his brow defiance*," and Todd contends that Pope "copies" Milton's line in *The Temple of Fame* 343: "And proud *Defiance in their Looks* they bore" (*Poems* 2:280).

lours: Jon S. Lawry finds a pun with "lowers," as he considers the quality of Gabriel's triumph in his verbal sparring with Satan (180).

877. *stern regard:* Hume glosses the phrase as "angry looks," and, supplying quotations from the *Iliad* 3.342 and 4.349, writes that Milton is here "answering to the Homerick" (164). Todd quotes Hume ([1842], 2:106).

stern: Dennis H. Burden contrasts *stern* here, as well as in 924 and 9.15, which "is used of irreconcilable opposites," with the anger of Milton's God, which is based on justice and therefore "does not render God utterly implacable towards Man since God's intention is ultimately reconcilement and mercy" (11–12).

878–976. The dramatic excitement of the guard's interrogation is heightened and complicated as Satan verbally spars with Gabriel in this second confrontation scene, and that dramatic element has been greatly admired, especially among early editors. Addison, for one, is much impressed, and writes that Satan's "disdainful Behaviour on this occasion is so remarkable a Beauty, that the most ordinary Reader cannot but take notice of it" (*Spectator* 3:172). Addison then explains: "The Conference between *Gabriel* and *Satan* abounds with Sentiments proper for the Occasion, and suitable to the Persons of the two Speakers" (3:173). Newton (293) approvingly quotes Addison. With a note that is more celebratory paraphrase than critical comment, the Richardsons detail Gabriel's exposure of Satan's duplicity, arrogance, and foolishness. Satan, they relate, "had reproach'd the Angel (*v.* 887.) as having Ask'd a Silly Question; (878.) *Gabriel* replies, He was a Fit Person indeed to accuse Them of Folly who demanded of him How he Durst break Prison; and yet boasted his Own Wisdom, not as having fled from Pain, for That, Singly consider'd had been Right, but for daring to do so at all Adventures, at the Hazard of *Seven-fold* Vengeance for So doing" (183–84). Nineteenth century critics, early and late, continue to echo the earlier praise. Landor, looking specifically at Gabriel's second response to Satan (947–67), exclaims, "what a flagellation he inflicts on the traitor Monk!" Landor admits that when Gabriel "loses his temper he loses his poetry, in this place and most others. But such coarse hemp and wire were well adapted to the stripped shoulders they scourged" (24). Stopford Augustus Brooke rules the entire confrontation scene sublime, a term Addison applies to Satan at the end of the scene, and Brooke insists that "none but Milton could have conceived and expressed that meeting" (104). See Addison in **985–90**. As the twentieth century opens, one continues to find passionate appreciation for the battle of wits between the angel and the demon. Walter Raleigh, for example, argues that Milton's own mastery of taunts, insults, satire, and invective—flytings—in his prose controversies marks "the great close of the Fourth Book, especially, where the arch-fiend and the archangel retaliate defiance, and tower, in swift alternate flights, to higher and higher pitches of exultant scorn" (73).

There is a striking difference, however, between this early enthusiastic praise and the more restrained criticism of Gabriel's interrogation of Satan through the middle decades of the twentieth century. One might see certain remarks by Charles Williams in 1932 as announcing that change. "Having created Satan, Milton's poetry had to do something else," Williams explains: "It had also to deal with Adam who was the ostensible subject. By the end of the Fourth Book, Satan had been sufficiently achieved; indeed the episode of the 'back-chat' between him and Gabriel at the close of that book is, in a sense, a luxury. It recapitulates, condenses, and emphasizes all that has gone before—defiance, selfhood, and compulsion by superior power" (*English Poetic Mind* 127). Much of the subsequent criticism of the scene between Gabriel and Satan develops the staid overview of it that Williams presents. As he argues against C. S. Lewis's emphasis on Satan's absurdity, for example, G. Rostrevor Hamilton looks to the argument between Gabriel and Satan, and sets it against, as Williams puts it, "all that has gone before." Hamilton explains that in the first exchange between the angel and the demon, Gabriel, "taking a false point, the imputation of cowardice, . . . enables Satan to recover his dignity. But for a passing moment Satan certainly makes himself ridiculous" (18). And while admitting that in the confrontation with Gabriel, Satan initially seems to express "the old grand defiance and splendour" that he demonstrated in Books 1–2, S. Musgrove also proceeds to acknowledge that a change in Satan is here underscored, for in the early books, "Satan's desperate grandeur had been accompanied by an apparent wealth of intellectual activity, which, false though it was, sufficed to gloss over the surface. Now this veneer has gone; as we have just seen, Satan has reached the stage of fooling himself with his own lies, a state not conducive to intellectual integrity" (309). Later critics variously hone the notion that the debate with Gabriel reveals Satan "fooling himself." William Empson mockingly undermines Musgrove's reading, but also perhaps misrepresents it. Empson claims that Musgrove "rebukes him [Satan] for telling a lie; surely this implies a quaint innocence about what heroes on our own side might think proper when in enemy hands. And so forward; the steady flow of such arguments is enough to turn any fair-minded man into a Satanist" (*Milton's God* 32). Jon S. Lawry (180) avoids Musgrove's charge that Satan is "fooling himself with his own lies" and refers to Satan's "willful ignorance" instead: "In his supposed wit, Satan promptly demonstrates the Fall. Gabriel having asked why Satan has transgressed here, Satan taunts him for his angelic ignorance. The joke is on Satan, who of course has knowledge only of Hell. He also reveals his willful ignorance in yet another unwitting admission. To Gabriel, he says, flight from Hell is 'no reason' (IV, 895). There was no reason in the choice for Hell, and the flight is undone and without reason if, as Satan has already said, Hell is where he is. That realization, so easily forgotten, plagues his contemptuous statement that if God directs all, he should have bound Hell more tightly." With classical rhetorical theory in hand, John M. Steadman ("Ethos and Dianoia" 209) unpacks the significance of what he identifies as Satan's contradiction, bringing Satan's "falsehoods and fallacies" into association with his "false character." Establishing the debate as one of several debates between unjust and just discourse in *PL,* Steadman identifies the main features of Gabriel's victory. "Gabriel maneuvers him [Satan] into contradicting himself. His falsehoods and fallacies demand a rebuttal. . . . Thus Gabriel begins by countering Satan's opening jibe ('thou hadst . . . th' esteem of wise') and then challenges his second point ('Lives there who loves his pain?')." Steadman concludes, "Whereas Satan assumes a false character to acquire greater plausibility, the ethical proofs of Christ and Abdiel, Gabriel and Michael are based on their real character. In these cases, the disparity between rhetorical and poetic *ethos*...tends to disappear. Another result of the confrontation of these contrasting rhetorical modes is epistemological. It tends to reduce the dialogue to a clear-cut debate between truth and falsehood" (214). In *Milton and the Renaissance Hero,* Steadman advances much the same argument: "Exposing the apostate's pretensions to heroic leadership as false, the captain of the angelic guard argues that Satan is neither a true leader nor a faithful. He is only the spurious image—the idol" (94). Also see Steadman's discussion in "Milton's Rhetoric" 88–91. Closely reading the comparisons in Books 1–2 between Satan and the heroes of classical epics, comparisons that "serve to magnify our impression of Satan's heroic grandeur," but "also simultaneously provide the grounds for impugning him" (*Club* 44), Davis P. Harding contends that in Satan's encounter with Gabriel "our growing suspicions have been confirmed. Satan's conduct has opened our eyes to his real nature and also to the fact that even this nature is undergoing a slow but inexorable defilement" (47).

In praising Milton's achievement in this scene none of the early editors or critics suggests that Addison is off the mark when he finds the "sentiments...suitable to the Persons of the two Speakers," but several modern critics question Milton's characterization of the archangel Gabriel. John Peter, for example, condemns Milton's presentation of Gabriel in this scene almost as much as he condemns Milton's treatment of Satan throughout the epic. Peter finds troubling the contrast between the "military succinctness and decision" of Gabriel's earlier speeches (586–88, 789–91) and his manner with Satan: Gabriel's "brisk and soldierly manner disappears. Satan is described as speaking 'in scorn' (902), which seems from what he says to be a slight distortion, but the statement that Gabriel replies 'Disdainfully half smiling,' with its suggestion of supercilious vanity, agrees closely with the words of reply. As soon as he speaks it is obvious that Satan's questioning of his wisdom has stung him, and his response is to throw doubts on Satan's wisdom in return. His egotism, just here, seems very nearly as touchy as Satan's; and unlike Zephon's, which was grim (855), his irony is jeering. Indeed the tone of his speech is not very different from Satan's at iv. 375–87, where derisive irony also figures. Perhaps the pique and abusiveness of Milton's prose pamphlets has crept into both passages; in any case what is natural in Satan appears most unnatural in an angel as valiant and august as Gabriel" (26). Gabriel's second exchange with Satan (947–67) has elicited modern reactions strikingly different from earlier ones such as Landor's. Gabriel's accusation here that Satan "Once fawn'd, and cring'd" (958–60) is to A. J. A. Waldock, for example, the "most flagrant example" of Milton's "literary cheating" in his presentation of Satan throughout the epic: "Are we, then, on Gabriel's undocumented assertion, to make an effort to accommodate the Satan we know to a Satan who 'once fawn'd, and cring'd, and servilly ador'd'? Why should we accept this high-handed piece of unsupported calumny?" (81). Considering Waldock's reading of Gabriel's rebuke, R. J. Zwi Werblowsky muses, "I rather suspect that Milton, slightly off his track, gives away his real opinion (and, incidentally, that of many of his readers) as to what we should think about the revivalling crowd in heaven, who 'lowly reverent ... bow and to the ground with solemn adoration ... cast Their Crowns' (*P.L.* iii.349–52), as compared to the dashing self-reliance of Satan and his crew" (10). John Peter is similarly puzzled by Gabriel's assertion. If Gabriel's claim is true, Peter wonders if "the angels were fallen before their fall" (70). In *Milton's God*, William Empson boldly announces that Gabriel, like Raphael, has "a timid slavish mind," and when Gabriel charges that Satan "Once fawn'd, and cring'd," Empson hears "a quaint bit of spite," which leads him to conclude "that God had already produced a very unattractive Heaven before Satan fell" (111). Considering the implications of Empson's reading, Alastair Fowler believes "it seems more likely that Gabriel is simply falling in with Satan's choice of words (with *cringed*, cp. 'cringe' l. 945, with *servilely* cp. 'serve' l. 943), as people do in the heat of an argument. Thus he amplifies the effect of his counter-accusation of hypocrisy — 'If it's cringing you call it you've cringed too; and without even being sincere, either'" (668).

879. *transgressions:* Bentley's dissatisfaction with *bounds* (878) being prescribed to Satan's *transgressions* prompts his suggestion that the proper word is *transcursions* (140). Pearce (145–46) and the Richardsons (183) engage with Bentley, but Newton appears to bring the matter to a close: "the common reading is justifiable: for though (as Dr. Bentley says) no bounds could be set to Satan's *transgressions*, but he could transgress in his thought and mind every moment; yet it is good sense, if Milton meant (as I suppose he did) that the bounds of Hell were by God prescrib'd to Satan's transgressions, so as that it was intended he should transgress no where else, but *within* those bounds; whereas he was now attempting to transgress *without* them. And by this interpretation we shall not understand *transgressions* in the sense of the pure Latin, and *transgress*

in the very next line in the usual English acceptation, but shall affix the same notion both to the one and the other" (296–97). Todd excerpts Newton's note ([1842], 2:106).

charge: Alastair Fowler cites two possible meanings: "'task' (*OED* 12); perhaps also 'ward, person entrusted to the care of another' (*OED* 14)—i.e., Eve" (665). Merritt Y. Hughes sees both Adam and Eve as being entrusted to the protection of Gabriel's troop (*Complete Poems* 299).

883. *to violate sleep:* Hume (164) refers this phrase to the *Aeneid* 7.114: "Et violare manu, malisque audacibus Orbem"; "to profane with hand and daring jaw the [fateful] circles." Newton refers it to *Macbeth* 2.2.36 ("Macbeth does murder sleep") and considers "both equally proper in the places where they are employ'd" (297). Todd quotes Newton ([1842], 2:106).

John R. Knott finds in Gabriel's charge that Satan intends "to violate sleep" the angel's recognition that Satan intends "more clearly a disturbance of the order of nature" ("Pastoral Day" 174).

S. Ernest Sprott (79–80), analyzing Milton's syllabic prosody, points to this line and 995 as examples of elision by means of the so-called "y-glide," the *o* in *violate* being here elided, as is the *o* in *violence* in 995.

886. *esteem:* R. C. Browne (1:356) glosses this as "estimation, report," and notes Shakespeare's use in *Two Gentlemen of Verona* 1.3.40: "of good esteem."

888. Admiring Satan's heroic defiance and his magnificent verbal retorts as he encounters Ithuriel, Zephon, and then Gabriel, Michael Wilding is especially impressed by the question in this line, insisting that the phrasing "does not distress us as uncolloquial because it is so vividly terse. The staccato concision is so appropriate to Satan at this point, and Milton's verse is the superbly flexible medium that can create it, as well as create the rhetorical declamations of Satan addressing his followers in Hell. There he needed the rolling periods, the polysyllabism; here in a tough corner, he is the tight-lipped defiant soldier" (23).

893. *Torment with ease:* Bentley (140) would change this phrase to "Torment for ease," but Newton (298), quoting Virgil's *Georgics* 1.8, explains that Milton is following a Latin example. Todd ([1842], 2:106) repeats Newton's response to Bentley, and, crediting George Steevens, also notes that in *Cymbeline* 1.6.54–55,

Shakespeare's phrasing anticipates Milton's: "to shift his being / Is to exchange one misery with another."

894. *Dole with delight:* Todd ([1842], 2:107) points out that Shakespeare "uses the same antithesis" in *Hamlet* 1.2.13, "weighing delight and dole," and that a similar formulation occurs in the third act of *The Rare Triumphes of Love and Fortune,* sig. Diii: "Dole and despaire hencefoorth be thy delight." Alastair Fowler (665) suggests the possibility of irony here, for besides "grief, distress" (sb. 2.1) or "pain, suffering" (sb. 2.3), the *OED* defines *dole* as "guile, deceit, fraud" (sb. 3.1). The *OED* cites Milton's line to illustrate the first meaning, "Grief, sorrow, mental distress."

896. *object:* A. W. Verity explains, "urge as an objection to my breaking from Hell" (472), a definition that Alastair Fowler (666) refers to the *OED* vb. 3 and 4.

898–900. John S. Diekhoff notes the rhyme in this sequence ("Rhyme" 540). See Diekhoff in **222–24.**

899. *thus much:* Verity (472) paraphrases this as "thus much in reply to your question" and comments, "The style of the speech reflects Satan's 'contemptuous' bearing (885)."
   askt: B. A. Wright clarifies the archaic use of *askt:* "in reply to what was asked" ("Note on Milton's Diction" 144).

902. *in scorn:* David Masson finds "a strain of courtesy" in Satan's first speech to Gabriel (886–901), "as of a coequal to a coequal whom he has not seen for some time," but the narrator's reference here to Satan's concluding "in scorn," as well as the earlier description of Satan's speaking "with contemptuous brow" (885), leads Masson to conclude that "the courtesy must be supposed ironical" (*Poetical Works* 3:181). Also see Masson on *wise* in **904.**

903. *Disdainfully half smiling:* as Todd ([1842], 2:107) reports, the concision of Milton's expression wins praise from John Bowle, who points out that Tasso "uses two lines to express the same idea" in *Gerusalemme Liberata* 5.42 and 19.4: "Sorrise all' hor Rinaldo; e con un volto, / In cui tra 'l riso lampeggio lo sdegno"; "Rinaldo smiled at that, and in his smile / there flashed the slightest traces of disdain"; and "Sorrise il buon Tancredi un cotal riso / Di sdegno"; "a smile of disdain flashed on good Tancred's face" (trans. Anthony M. Esolen). To Bowle's note Todd adds Skelton's description of the moon in lines 5–6 of his prologue to *The Bowge of Courte: "smylynge halfe in scorne* / At our foly, and our unstedfastnesse" (*Complete English Poems* 46).

904. *wise:* David Masson, identifying Gabriel's tone as ironic, paraphrases this line, "O the loss that there has been in Heaven, since Satan fell, of one able to judge what wisdom is" (*Poetical Works* 3:181). Also see Masson on "in scorn" in **902.** Jon S. Lawry develops that ironic tone, claiming that Gabriel here recalls Satan's earlier use of *wise* (886): "Gabriel answers truly but most bitingly, playing Satan's chosen word 'wise' through as many ironies as Antony plays Brutus' 'honor' in *Julius Caesar* [3.1.78–112]." Lawry then traces Gabriel's use of *wise* forward into 947–53, insisting that the angel "sharply points out the unreason in everything said by the Father of Lies" (180–81).

906. *returns him:* stating that Satan is probably the subject of this verb, A. W. Verity (472) explains that the phrase illustrates "the reflexive use so common in Elizabethan E[nglish] with many verbs now intransitive," and he offers the example of *1 Henry VI* 3.3.56, "Return thee, therefore, with a flood of tears."

911. *However:* for the Richardsons (184), context tightens the meaning to "upon Any terms, at all Adventures. This is the Force of This Word, as appears by what follows Immediately, as well as by the Sense of the Place." See the rest of their comment in **878–976.**

916. *anger infinite:* Kester Svendsen ("Epic Address" 204), examining epic epithets for God as a function of decorum in *PL*, notes that, "except for Raphael's, the epithets of the angelic powers contribute little to dramatic characterization. Gabriel calls him *anger infinite,* Abdiel speaks of *th' incensed Father* [5.847] and *God ever blest* [6.184], and Michael refers to *the living God* [12.118] and *the holy One* [12.248]."

917–23. Referring to James Whaler's discussion of the play of cross-rhythmic currents in Milton's verse, which he demonstrates by contrasting this sequence with a restructured version of it (*Counterpoint* 20–21), Christopher Ricks notes how the contrast Whaler offers emphasizes the "surge of the verse" in the original, the "playing of the syntax against the metre," the "emphatic placing of 'Less pain' and 'Less hardie' at the opening of the lines, and above all the great weight which the last line of the speech received by being the only one where the sense-unit met and cinched the metre" (100).

918. Edward S. Le Comte hears an echo of this line in 3.87, "Through all restraint broke loose," adding, "The duplication points to an equation: all hell did break loose with Satan" (*Yet Once More* 38).

919. Identifying the elements of Milton's syllabic prosody, S. Ernest Sprott (100–01) examines the inversion of feet, and while he specifically points to this line as an example of Milton's inversion of the second foot, his chart on inversion is perhaps more revealing. In Book 4, 19.9 percent of the lines begin with inversion in the first foot; only Book 1, with 22.3 percent, ranks higher. Also according to Sprott's chart, Book 4 has the highest percentage of inversions in the third foot, 3.2 percent against 3.1 percent for Book 3. The percentage of lines of Book 4 that show inversions in the fourth foot is 2.9 percent, second only to Book 9, which has 3.3 percent.

925. A. W. Verity paraphrases this as "I do not come because I have less power to endure" (472).

926–27. *I stood / Thy fiercest:* Bentley triggers some discussion here by suggesting that "*the* fiercest" is the correct reading (141). Pearce (147) rejects Bentley's opinion, as do the Richardsons, who explain that "thy fiercest" is "very Concise, but very Intelligible and Strong; Enemy, Opponent is Understood" (184). Pearce and the Richardsons cross-reference other occasions in *PL* where Milton uses adjectives as nouns: 2.278, 4.852, 11.4, and 11.497. Newton (300) rehearses the discussion, and Todd quotes Newton ([1842], 2:108), while Verity (472) suggests yet another less preferable reading, "I proved myself," but all three agree with the logic of the Richardsons' explanation.

926. *Insulting:* Hume (165) understands this to mean "Jeering, Braving and insulting over us in misery," and he supports the attention to *misery* with the Latin root *Insultare,* which he translates as "to mock, properly at men in misery." Hume then supplies literary authority, quoting Virgil's *Aeneid* 2.329–30, "Victorque Sinon incendia miscet / Insultans"; "and Sinon, victorious, insolently scatters flames."

stood: Alastair Fowler (666) glosses this as "put up with, endured," and references the *OED* V.59.

928. *Thy:* the second edition replaces "The" with *Thy*, and there is some discussion of this change among early editors. Hume prints *Thy* in his text but shifts to *the* in his note: "When thou wert forced to call to thy speedy Aid the dreadful Thunder, born on Blasting Wings" (165). The Richardsons (184), Newton (301), and Todd ([1842], 2:108) print *The* from the first edition, the Richardsons commenting that *Thy* "is wrong no doubt. The word occurs very often thereabout, and probably occasioned the mistake. The sense requires it to be *The.*" Frank Allen Patterson's Columbia edition follows the 1674 text, but Robert Martin Adams argues that "to read '*Thy* blasting volied Thunder made all speed' would be to make Satan attribute mastery of the Thunder to Gabriel when the precise point is that Gabriel had to be helped in battle by God's thunder" (79). Alastair Fowler (667) supports and refines this point by glancing at Raphael's narrative of the war in heaven, where he recalls that "Messiah did not put forth all his strength, 'but checked / His thunder in mid volley, for he meant / Not to destroy' (vi 853–5)."

volied: the *OED* 2 quotes Milton's use here as the first illustration of the meaning "Of thunder or lightning: Discharged with the noise or continuous effect of a volley." The *OED* reports that such usage was "very common in poetry of the 18th century."

929. Todd ([1842], 2:108) takes this line back to the *Aeneid* 12.894–95, where Turnus scoffs at Aeneas's fiercely insulting words: "Non me tua servida terrent / Dicta, ferox: dii me terrent et Jupiter hostis"; "Thy fiery words, proud one, daunt me not; 'tis the gods daunt me, and the enmity of Jove."

930–34. Hume presents a careful paraphrase: "But still thy unwary words, as what thou saidst before, witness thy want of knowledge, how a trusty General ought to behave himself in hazardous Attempts, and under ill Success and Disappointments, ought not to venture all in dangerous ways untry'd and unessay'd by himself" (165).

930. *at random:* Hume (165) traces the meaning "heedlessly, carelessly, precipitately" to the French *Randon,* which he translates as "the violent course of a Torrent" or the French *Rendon,* "rashness, uncertainty." The *OED* 3.b, quoting Milton's line here, reports that *at random* used with substantives is somewhat rare.

931. *Argue:* Verity (472) cross-references *argues* at 949, and Merritt Y. Hughes (*Complete Poems* 300) cross-references *argues* at 830.

932. *assaies:* B. A. Wright explains that in this context *assaies* means "An attempt, endeavour," whereas at 9.747 it means "The trial of something by tasting." Wright also points out that since the end of the sixteenth century "*essay* has replaced *assay* exc. for the testing of metals" ("Note on Milton's Diction" 148).

938. *Fame:* A. W. Verity traces this word to the Latin *fama,* which, in the literal sense, translates as "report" (472).

939. *afflicted:* A. W. Verity (472) turns to the Latin root, *afflictus,* as he supplies the definition "struck down," and cross-references 1.186. The *OED* 1 also cites 1.186, where Satan describes the demons on the fiery lake as "our afflicted Powers," to illustrate the obsolete meaning of the transitive verb, *to afflict,* "To dash down, overthrow, cast down, deject, humble in mind, body, or estate."

940. A. W. Verity explains that "on Earth, or in mid Aire" alludes "to the Rabbinical view, commonly adopted by mediaeval writers, that the angels who fell with Satan were the same as the spirits or 'daemons' who inhabited the 'elements' of earth and air" (472). Verity references his appendix on "the middle air" mentioned in 1.516. In that appendix, he points to the term's currency in works such as Hugo Grotius's *Adamus Exul* 5 and Ben Jonson's *Masque of Hymen* (*Ben Jonson* 7:217), and he cross-references Milton's use of such terminology in *PR* 1.39–41, 2.117; *FInf* 16; *QNov* 12; *Vac* 41, 42; and *Prol* 2.14. Asserting that the term *middle air* "would be perfectly intelligible to all scholars of the 17th century," Verity (674) concludes, "The *media regio* is the place of clouds and heavy vapours," and is "peculiarly cold.... It extends to the top of high mountains; and Mount Olympus is the dwelling-place of the deities who 'rule the middle air,'" which "is capped by another, perhaps broader, belt of air" (676).

Merritt Y. Hughes (*Complete Poems* 300) points to Eph. 2.2, which refers to "the prince of the power of the air."

941. *put to try:* defining the phrase as "made, forced, to try," A. W. Verity (472) cross-references *Cymbeline* 2.3.110: "You put me to forget a lady's manners."

942. *gay:* A. W. Verity (473) suggests that *gay* as "fine" may be "a retort to 'obscure and foul' in 840."

943–44. Cf. Svendsen in **86**.

944–45. Bentley (142), as Pearce puts it, "is much disturb'd at the suppos'd Phrase of *hymning practis'd distances,* especially where *fighting* is concern'd: for (he says) that *to practise distances* there, is in order to retreat, not to fight." Pearce suggests following the punctuation of the 1667, rather than the 1674, edition; that is, putting a comma, rather than a semicolon, after *Throne,* to make the sense read, "To hymn his Throne with Songs, and not to fight, but to cringe with practis'd distances" (147–48). Newton (301) follows Pearce's advice, as have most subsequent editors (Todd, [1842], 2:109; Verity 127; Darbishire, *Poetical Works* 1:97; Hughes, *Complete Poems* 300; Patterson, *Works* 2:140). Fowler offers a sensitive response to Bentley's concern when he contends that there is a zeugma at work here: "*practised distances* goes with *fight* as well as with *cringe.* Footwork was no less important in combat than in court etiquette" (667).

Todd ([1842], 2:109) identifies Satan's mockery of the angels worshiping about God's throne with Prometheus's "untamed insolence" toward the chorus in *Prometheus Bound* 937–43. Masson (*Poetical Works* 3:182) and Verity (473) present Todd's note, as does Merritt Y. Hughes (*Complete Poems* 300). Todd's notes on 962, as well as 858–59, point to additional echoes of Aeschylus's *Prometheus Bound.*

945. *to cringe:* Hume (165) associates this action, "to bow very low to," with the Russians, who "lay their faces on the ground in approaching to their Monarchs, of the Teut. *Kriechen,* to creep to." Masson more broadly refers the action to "Oriental courtiers" (*Poetical Works* 3:182).

947–67. While Landor (23) admires the "flagellation" that Gabriel "inflicts on the traitor Monk," he claims that when the angel "loses his temper he loses his poetry," exemplified by the terminal rhyme of *supream* and *seem* at 956–57. Landor advises, "Great heed should be taken against this grievous fault, not only in the final syllables of blank verse, but also in the cesuras" (24). Also see Landor in **878–976** and Diekhoff in **956–57.**

949. David Masson (*Poetical Works* 3:182) notes that "Gabriel here retorts sarcastically on Satan's phrase in line 933," where Satan describes himself as "A faithful Leader."

Argues: A. W. Verity cross-references *Argue* in 931.

trac't: although Patrick Hume (165) prints *trac't* in the text of the poem, in his annotations he prints *Track'd* as he opens his note: "Caught, overtaken, follow'd close. *Track'd,* of the Verb to *trace,* to follow by the footsteps. See Bo[ok] 2. V. 1025." Alastair Fowler (667) moves from Hume's note on physically tracking to the *OED*'s definition of the verb *to trace,* which emphasizes intellectual activity (1.2.8), "discovered, searched out." Fowler questions whether there might be "a secondary implication" of "twisted, interwoven" deriving from the *OED*'s definition 3.1.

952. Arnold Stein points out, "The faith that goes only downward, never upward, exacts its penalties; and Satan is tied to his followers more than he realizes" (5).

953–57. A. W. Verity draws attention to the significance of Gabriel's pronouns: "In these lines Gabriel speaks to the host of Satan's followers, as though they were present; *your* refers to them—not, of course, to Satan, whom Gabriel addresses as *thou.* In Shakespeare *thou* is often a contemptuous form of address" (473). Masson presents the same understanding (*Poetical Works* 3:182). Alastair Fowler similarly reasons that Gabriel is addressing Satan's followers "through their *head* and representative Satan" (668).

956–57. John S. Diekhoff identifies this as one of the four couplets in Book 4 ("Rhyme" 539–40). See Diekhoff in **24–27**, and Diekhoff and Landor in **947–67**.

958. *Patron:* A. W. Verity cross-references 3.219 as he glosses this word *champion* (473). The *OED* 2.c quotes 3.219 to exemplify the meaning "A defender before a court of justice; an advocate, a pleader."

962. *arreede:* Hume's initial gloss, "appoint," "enjoyn," which he derives from the French *arrester* ("to determine, to decree"), is maintained but made somewhat more muscular in subsequent annotations (165). Paterson writes, "Fr. O[ld] E[nglish] Poet. To appoint, determine, judge, decree, order or pronounce a Sentence upon one; by a *Fig.* of *Rhet.*" (327). Todd develops this emphasis by pointing to a similarity between Gabriel's manner of threatening Satan and Mercury's denouncing punishment to Prometheus in Aeschylus's *Prometheus Bound* 1079. Todd ([1842], 2:109) also notes that it is with the sense of "to *appoint,* to *decree*" that *arede* appears in Chaucer's poems and Bishop Hall's satires. To the basic meanings of "advise" and "decree for," David Masson adds, "Originally the word meant to divine, to guess, to interpret, to read a riddle" (*Poetical Works* 3:182), an understanding with which A. W. Verity agrees (697). R. C. Browne (1:356) cross-references Milton's *DDD*, where he addresses any would-be reformer: "let me arreed him" (Patterson, *Works* 3:369).

Avant: establishing its French origins, Hume glosses this as "be gone; of *Avant,* Fr. before, forward, on" (165). Paterson (327) brings more vigor to this reading: "Away, begone out of my Sight. A Word of Disdain"; and the Richardsons (185) add figurative energy to that understanding: "On, Forward. the Beauty of the Word Here is, that it gives the Idea of One Driven before Another as a Beast is driven; it implies Contempt; *Satan* had before Observ'd That in him, *v.* 926. and with Reason, *v.* 903."

963–67. William Empson recalls, "Some critic has accused Gabriel of weakness here, taking him to mean 'Don't you dare come again,'" but Empson suggests that Gabriel "might mean to grant Satan one hour for decision whether to go of his own accord or be dragged in chains; it is a statesmanlike proposal, though no use because Satan decides to fight at once" (*Milton's God* 112).

965–66. Quoting Rev. 20.3, Hume (165) immediately identifies the apocalyptic allusion in Gabriel's threat: "This seems to allude to *the chaining of the Dragon, that old Serpent, which is the Devil and Satan,* mentioned in the *Revelations: And he cast him into the bottomless Pit, and shut him up.*" Merritt Y. Hughes and Alastair Fowler have added some biblical texts and several cross-references within *PL*. Hughes cross-references 1.45–48 (*Complete Poems* 300) and his footnote there (212) to Isa. 14.12, as well as Jude 1.6: "And the angels which kept not their first estate . . . in everlasting chains, under darkness." Fowler (668) cross-references *PL* 3.82.

965–67. R. J. Zwi Werblowsky finds it inconsistent that "Gabriel's regiment mount guard in Paradise, whilst God foresees and permits Satan to erupt from hell" (22).

965. *I drag thee:* Hume notes of the present tense that it is "used for the future, to signify the immediate execution of the menace" (165). Newton quotes Hume (302), and the Richardsons (185), explaining the phrase as "A Latinism, and very emphatical," offer examples from Virgil's *Aeneid* 3.367 ("Quae prima pericula Vito"; "what perils am I first to shun") and Seneca's *Troades* 975 ("Cui famula trador? quem Dominum Voco?"; "To whom am I given as slave? Whom do I call master?").

967. *The facil gates of hell:* in his 1795 edition of *PR*, Charles Dunster associates this phrase with Satan's reference to Adam's "facil consort *Eve*" in *PR* 1.51.

971. *limitarie:* this adjective catches the careful attention of many early editors and critics, and while they engage in etymological study, they are also keen to comment on the sarcasm of Satan's word choice. Dryden retains the sharp-edged word for Satan's use as he leaves the garden in *The Age of Innocence and Fall of Man,* disdainful of fighting with mere angels: "let me with him contend, / On whom your limitary pow'rs depend" (*Works* 12:122). Following a paraphrase that catches Satan's sarcasm, "Thou proud prescribing Angel that presumest to *limit* me, and appoint my *Prison,*" Hume (165) tracks the Latin origins of the word, and quotes Virgil's use of it in the *Aeneid* 12.898, where Turnus and Aeneas are about to clash. The Richardsons (185) underscore the mockery in Satan's word choice: "Set to Guard the Bounds, as *v.* 878. a Taunt, Insulting the Good Angel as one Employ'd on a Little, Mean Office." To the comments of

Hume and the Richardsons, whom he quotes, Newton adds, "*Milites limitanei* are soldiers in garrison upon the frontiers. So *Dux limitaneus*" (302). Paterson's note continues to develop the witty, double-edged wordplay in Satan's diction: "*Bounded within Limits,* i.e. *Gabriel,* who was either appointed to be in the *Boundary* of *Paradise* himself; or was now *limiting Satan,* to his *Bounds* in *Hell.* A Word of Disdain" (327). Todd reprints Newton's note, and reports a note from Robert Thyer who, like the earlier editors, considers *limitary* "as a scornful sneer upon what Gabriel had just said, 'if from this hour / Within these hallow'd limits thou appear'" (963–64). In addition, Todd presents a note from Benjamin Stillingfleet, who refers *limitary* to *limitour,* which "in Chaucer means a friar restrained to the exercise of function *in certain limits*" ([1842], 2:110). Most recently, Stanley Fish explains that, "if Gabriel assumes that because he has been given an assignment (don't let anything in) he will be able to carry it out, Satan is correct. Good intentions and a willingness to serve do not assure success, which comes only if God wills it" (*Surprised* 175).

   Cherube: Verity (473) points out that Gabriel was an archangel, not a cherub, but Alastair Fowler (645) traces the angel's identity as a cherub to Enoch 20.7: "Gabriel, one of the holy angels, who is over Paradise and the serpents and the Cherubim."

973–76. Hume (165) establishes the influence of Ezekiel's vision of the chariot of God throughout this sequence by quoting extensively from Ezek. 10–11, including 11.22: "Then did the Cherubims lift up their Wings, and the Wheels besides them; and the Glory of the God of Israel was over them above." Also referring Milton's lines to Ezekiel's vision is Newton (302), whom Todd ([1842], 2:110) quotes, while suggesting an additional parallel with Ps. 18.10: "He rode upon a Cherub, and did fly." Verity (473) points to the description of the same visionary chariot at 6.771 in the war-in-heaven narrative. In addition to these points, Alastair Fowler (602–03) refers this sequence back to his note on 3.656, which presents Piero Valeriano's explanation in *Hieroglyphica* 549 of one association between the chariot and the angels; the presence of specific angels is indicated by the letters in the Hebrew word for chariot *argaman,* Gabriel's presence, for example, denoted by the third letter, Raphael's by the second, and so on.

973. *Heavens:* studying Milton's prosody, S. Ernest Sprott explains that "Milton regarded this word [*Heav'n*] as being essentially monosyllabic but capable of expansion to two syllables before a consonant." This is one of Sprott's 14 examples of the dissyllabic *Heaven* (144).

976. *progress:* Hume defines this as "A Royal March, the stately and leisurely Journey of a Court, of *Progredi,* Lat. to more forward by degrees" (166).

the rode of Heav'n Star-pav'd: Todd ([1842], 2:110) refers to the epigrams John Ashmore added to his *Certain Selected Odes of Horace* 33: "The casements large of *Heaven* have open set, / And from their *star-pav'd floors* have sent me down." A. W. Verity (473) notes comparisons in *PL* 7.576–78 ("To God's Eternal house direct the way, / A broad and ample road, whose dust is Gold / And pavement Stars"), as well as *The Merchant of Venice* 5.1.58–59 ("Look how the floor of heaven / Is thick inlaid with patens of bright gold"), whereas Alastair Fowler (669) understands *the rode of Heav'n* as the Milky Way.

Star-pav'd: S. Ernest Sprott identifies this as a departure from Milton's standard pattern of hyphenation as described in **190**. Sprott suggests that in such departures from the pattern, "Milton used hyphens primarily to link together words of interlocking meanings and met the same difficulty as his reader experiences in deciding when the logical emphases demand prosodic stresses" (14).

977–80. As the heightening tension of the verbal sparring match between Satan and Gabriel plunges into abrupt silence following Satan's ironic anticipation of the language of the apocalypse, the response of the "Angelic Squadron," witnesses to the confrontation, underscores the ominous silence. Three visual elements in the description of that mute response are the main critical concerns in this passage. First, without a word the squadron moves to re-form itself. Referring *Phalanx* (979) back to 550, Hume describes that movement: "Extending their square Body into a round one, and so sharpning it into Horns, like those of the increasing Moon, endeavoring to inclose him" (166). Verity (473) somewhat blurs Hume's attention to the fluid movement from one formation to another as he explains that "the close array of angels spread itself out in the shape of a crescent moon," but he provides a parallel description from Fairfax's translation of Tasso's *Gerusalemme Liberata* (titled *Godfrey of Bulloigne*) 20.22.3, "Like the new moon, his host two horns did spread." Among modern editors, Alastair Fowler gives the closest attention to the crescent formation being created by the moving angels, reporting that such formations "were classic in warfare, and still often used in M[ilton]'s time." Fowler refers to stanza 125 of Dryden's *Annus*

Mirabilis (*Works* 1:78) and quotes from George Gascoigne's "Gascoignes Devise of a Maske for the Right Honorable Viscount Mountacute" in *A Hundreth Sundrie Flowres* 307: "The Christian crew came on in forme of battayle pight, / And like a cressent cast themselves preparing for to fight." Finally, Fowler considers the symbolism of the crescent: "the description is appropriate not only because images of Ceres-Isis anciently had crescent horns to indicate her lunar godhead...but also because Satan is an eclipsing power of darkness, occupying as it were the shadowed part of the imaginary lunar orb" (669).

The second visual element in this description occurs when the moving formation of angels appears to change color: "th' Angelic Squadron bright / Turnd fierie red." Not all critics see a color change, however. E. M. W. Tillyard, for example, argues that "one should surely imagine a comma between *turnd* and *fierie*. The angel guard, already fiery red, turned their flanks inward. Many readers, I dare wager, picture them as going red with rage; I cannot think they are right, or even that we must accept a double meaning" (*Studies* 63). Alastair Fowler acknowledges Tillyard's point that cherubim are naturally "fiery red," but he also stands with those who see a color change as "here indicating angry ardour" (669). Robert H. West contends that a change in color is indeed pictured here, but reflects the nature of angelic matter rather than angelic rage. West understands the angelic squadron's color change, as well as Satan's subsequent dilation, as dramatic demonstrations of Milton's Psellian views on angelic corporeality and spirituality: "the notification in Book I that demons can condense and dilate themselves enables the reader to see the marvelous as probable when the contracted multitude makes itself at ease in Pandaemonium...and when Satan expands himself against the angelic guard in Paradise.... The [Psellian] phrase on demons' power to be bright or obscure similarly supplies a rationalization for the guard's turning fiery red as it bends its horns in toward Satan" (146).

The third visual detail that focuses critical attention in this passage is the position of the squadron's spears, described by the narrator as *ported* (980). While early editors agree about the meaning of this phrase, controversy has arisen among several twentieth century critics. Hume (166) first explains that "ported Spears" are "born pointed towards him [Satan]." Newton (303) quotes Hume, as do Todd ([1842], 2:111) and Stebbing (113), while the Richardsons appear to describe a similar stance: "held Sloping towards the Enemy, the Right hand Before, and the Other Behind. a Defensive Posture, ready also to Attack" (185). Emphasizing Milton's "correct use of military terms," David Masson disagrees with these editors: "a body of men 'with ported spears' meant therefore, not...a body of men with their spears thrust straight out against an enemy, but a body of men with their spears held in their hands across their breasts and slanting beyond the left shoulder, ready to be brought down to the 'charge' if necessary. The Angels have not the points of their spears turned to Satan; they have them only grasped in the position preparatory to turning them against him. This explains the subsequent image; for a series of spears so 'ported' over the left shoulders of a body of men, being parallel to each other and aslant, *would* resemble, to a spectator, cornstalks in a field blown all one way by the wind" (*Poetical Works* 3:182–83; cf. *Life* 2:476–77). Verity (473), Hughes (*Complete Poems* 301), and Fowler (670) follow Masson's interpretation. Quoting such seventeenth century texts as Robert Ward's *Animadversions of Warre* 224, James Holly Hanford, however, moves to correct Masson: "The phrase 'with ported spears' Masson and subsequent commentators describe as if it were the equivalent of the modern 'port arms,' which would be inappropriate. The military books which Milton read give it correctly as the position intermediate between 'carry' and 'charge,' the point of the lance or pike being held directly forward, with the shaft at an angle of 45 degrees" ("Milton" 253). The *OED* quotes Milton's line as it refers the past participle *ported* to definition 2 of the verb *to port*. Quoting from Gervase Markham's *The Souldier's Accidence* 23 and Roger Boyle's *A Treatise of the Art of War* 190–91, the *OED* V.1, definition 2 *Mil*, supports Masson's definition: "To carry or hold (a pike or the like) with both hands; *spec.* to carry (a rifle or other weapon) diagonally across and close to the body, so that the barrel or blade is opposite the middle of the left shoulder."

977. *Angelic Squadron:* Todd, with quotations from Fulvio Testi's *Poesie* 473 and Andreini's *L'Adamo* 3, establishes that *angeliche squadre* "is a frequent phrase in Italian poetry" ([1842], 2:110–11).

980–85. More openly—and stridently—than any other critic, Richard Bentley (143) admits to considerable difficulty with this passage, an epic simile, but an epic simile that seems to fuse two separate similes, and while later editors never accept his proposal to delete the second half of the passage (983–85) as the "Manufacture" of a "pragmatical Editor," Bentley's problem with this two-part epic simile is one other critics, those discussing the waving-grain image of 980–83 or those discussing "the careful Plowman" of 983–85, have sometimes avoided rather than taken up.

980–83. The waving-grain simile in 980–83 has sent editors and critics in search of classical precedents and influences. Opening his lengthy annotation on 980–85, Alastair Fowler briefly notes, "The comparison of an excited army to wind-stirred corn is Homeric" (669), and the rest of the annotation, which covers nearly half a page, focuses on "the careful Plowman." While Fowler's cursory reading of the waving-grain image is correct, it is also significantly incomplete, for as both Patrick Hume and Davis P. Harding show, Virgil works several complications of meaning into Homer's image, and the Virgilian precedents as surely influence Milton's verse, as does the Homeric one. Hume (166) acknowledges that the "Field of Corn...is sufficiently significative of a vast number of armed Men ranged close together" and that the comparison is of "familiar use and occurrence amongst the best Poets." The first such poet Hume identifies is Homer, in the *Iliad* 2.147–50, where, according to Hume, "*Homer*...expresseth the power *Agamemnon*'s Oration to the *Grecian* Army had on the affected Multitude." Then Hume turns to the *Aeneid*, quoting the image's recurrence in Book 3, twice in Book 7, and finally in Book 12. In Book 3 and Book 7.525–26, the image describes a great number of weapons. In Book 3.45–46, for example, Polydorus recalls his own death: "Hic confixum ferrea texit / Telorum seges, & jaculis increvit acutis"; "Here an iron harvest of spears covered my pierced body, and grew up into sharp javelins." At 7.720, however, the image occurs in a catalog of the numbers of Ausonian soldiers flocking to Turnus: "Vel cum sole novo densae torrentur aristae"; "Or thick as the corn-ears that are scorched by the early sun." Finally, Hume records that in the *Aeneid* 12.662–64, Virgil again invokes the image to describe the weapons as an "iron harvest of swords." In a way, the proportions of Richard Bentley's note mirror those of Fowler's, for after he sweepingly rules the "*Phalanx with ported Spears*...justly compar'd" to the "Crop of ripe Wheat, which wav'd with a gentle Wind bend all their Heads, the same way," Bentley (143) attacks the second half of the sequence. The other early editors give but a glance to the literary precedents for the waving-grain image. The reference to the *Iliad* 2 is presented by Newton (303), whom Todd quotes, but citations from the *Aeneid* are not to be found in their editions, although Todd does point out that in "Nec galeis denisque virum *seges* horruit hastis"; " human crop ever bristled with helms and serried lances" (*Georgics* 2.142), "Virgil has compressed the simile into a single metaphor, equally significative" ([1842], 2:111). As he sets out to show that Milton's "normal procedure...was to blend together material from two or more different poets," Davis P. Harding once again presents Virgil's variations in the *Aeneid* on the image Homer establishes in the *Iliad,* and, unlike Hume, restricted to sketchy annotations, Harding discusses the development of the epic simile. In the passage from Homer, for example, Harding explains, "Agamemnon's speech sways his audience irresistibly in one direction, as a violent west wind stirs a field of wheat. Since he is adapting Homer's simile to a new set of circumstances, Milton deliberately makes his wind a variable one to suggest the prevailing atmosphere of uncertainty. In Homer's simile, furthermore, the stirring of the warriors, and not their vast numbers, receives the major emphasis." Without mentioning Hume's earlier notes, Harding then points out that while the image at the end of the *Aeneid* 7 ("vel cum sole novo densae") emphasizes the numbers of the soldiers, the one in Book 12.662–64 ("Circum hos utrimque phalanges / stant densae strictisque seges mucronibus horret / ferrea"; "Around these on either side stand serried squadrons, and a harvest of steel bristles with drawn swords") compares the grain not to the soldiers, but to their "ported Spears," which Harding finds more appropriate, "at least from a visual standpoint" (*Club* 97).

981.   *Ceres:* Hume makes the initial identification, which basically all subsequent editors repeat: "The Daughter of Saturn and Ops, was the first Discoverer, and thence the tutelar Goddess of Corn" (166). Charles Grosvenor Osgood (19) traces Ceres's story to Hesiod's *Theogony* 453, 912, and cross-references 4.271 and 9.395. Merritt Y. Hughes (*Complete Poems* 301) adds a cross-reference to *QNov* 32.

982.   *bearded Grove of ears:* E. M. W. Tillyard argues that this phrase, while describing grain, also implies thickly leaved trees, and so as with the humble plowman reference in the confrontation between Satan and Gabriel, "we get another case of big and small things brought together" (*Studies* 64).

  Merritt Y. Hughes reports that the *OED* 2 quotes this line "to illustrate *bearded* as applied to plants with 'bristles or hairy tufts' about their seeds, and [*Grove* 1.b] to exemplify the transference of *Grove* from its primary application to trees. In a general way, *ears* means the seed-bearing spikes of any cereal grass" ("Variorum").

983–85. While Hume's notes on the waving-grain simile firmly lay down its classical foundation, he offers no comment on "the careful Plowman," and indeed among the early editors, only Bentley speaks about this second half of the extended pastoral image (980–85). Contending that the "pragmatical Editor" inserted the image into Milton's text, Bentley then enters into that insertion's specific flaws, one of which, he claims, is the editor's changing the gentle breeze that bends the grain in the preceding lines into "a Tempest" that "frightens the Husbandman with the loss of all his Grain." Frustrated, Bentley asks, "What an Injury is this to the prior Comparison? What are Sheaves bound up in a Barn to the Phalanx, that hem'd *Satan?* Where's the least Similitude? Besides, to suppose a *Storm* in the Field of Corn, implies that the Angels were in a ruffle and hurry about *Satan,* not in regular and military Order" (143). Bentley's demanding questions set an important critical challenge before his successors. In a manner of speaking, A. J. A. Waldock responds to Bentley when he denies that the reference to the plowman is associated—even by contrast—with the scene of the angelic confrontation: "The sentence, that is to say, neither helps nor hinders the general comparison, for it has no connection with it. We have slipped off that comparison." Waldock, however, sees no problem with that dissociation between the two parts of the epic simile: "We are not (or ought not to be) thinking about it—about God or Satan or the angels or the imminent flight; we have turned our minds from all those, and for the moment are thinking only of the ploughman, who looks at his wheat and wonders how it will look on the threshing floor. The simile, in other words, is quite normal" (142). After he surveys Bentley's remarks, and agrees that the plowman image "makes the angels look weak," William Empson tacks off somewhat to wonder if the plowman is God or Satan. If God, reasons Empson, "he is anxious; another hint that he is not omnipotent." If Satan, "he is only anxious for a moment, and he is the natural ruler or owner of the good angels. The main effect is less logical; the homely idea is put before the description of Satan to make him grander by contrast, an effect denied to the other angels." In conclusion, however, Empson does return to Bentley's demanding questions about the integrity of the two-part epic simile: "first the angels lean forward, calm and eager, in rows, seeming strong; then as the description approaches Satan, who is stronger, they are in a ruffle and hurry" (*Some Versions* 164). Provocative though Empson's concern with the plowman's identity is, and thoughtful as his closing comments are, it is his reference to the homeliness of the image that the majority of later critics pick up and develop. With Empson on this point, for example, is Balachandra Rajan. Considering Milton's sometimes-digressive similes, Rajan explains that "they usually serve to accentuate by contrast the superhuman grandeur of the events which they relieve." Rajan then specifies the plowman image, contending that it "isolates all the more forcibly the great figure unremoved like '*Teneriff* or *Atlas*'" (*"Paradise Lost" and the Seventeenth Century Reader* 121). E. M. W. Tillyard claims that, because of his position "between the description of the angelic guard and that of Satan," the plowman "is the focus of the powers of Heaven of Hell and thus resembles Adam and Eve.... He attaches the gigantic play of the other actors to the homeliness of earth, as at the end of the poem the mist rising at the heel of the labourer returning home" (*Studies* 63). While Christopher Ricks describes the simile as "beautiful but digressive" (172), Louis L. Martz moves the critical appreciation of the plowman from his homeliness to the possibility of his heroism. Arguing that the heroism of the individual human consciousness is one of the epic's organizing themes, Martz explains that the "'careful Plowman doubting' is a little richer in Milton's English than in ours, for 'careful' has not only its modern implications of one who is attentive to his work, who takes care of things, but it also implies a person who is anxious and troubled, full of care; and the word 'doubting' implies both a state of uncertainty and also a state of fear lest some disaster happen. It is a superb image of the human condition, again displayed as superior to that of Satan, who, for all his appearance of power, flees abjectly before the sign that God hangs in the heavens. These glimpses of the cheerful ways of the true princes of exile are more frequent than we might think, for sometimes they flash upon us in only a line, or two, or three" (*"Paradise Lost:* Princes" 244). Davis P. Harding brings to his commentary on the second half of the pastoral simile the focus on Virgil that he maintains in discussing the earlier waving-grain image and, in doing so, supports A. S. Ferguson's argument, presented in 1920, that the waving-grain image initiates a series of associations between this sequence in *PL* 4 and the last 300 verses of the *Aeneid,* culminating in the scales and the darkness common to the end of Milton's Book 4 and Virgil's entire epic (168–70). Harding notes that when Virgil compares Turnus and Aeneas to two bulls about to rush each other in the *Aeneid* 12.715–22, the herdsmen in the metaphor "retire in terror, all the cattle stand dumb in dismay, and the heifers murmur in doubt which shall be lord in the woodland." Harding concludes, "The 'careful' and 'doubting' plowman is a decorous substitution for the cattle which stand 'dumb in dismay' (*metu mutum*) [718] and the heifers who 'murmur in doubt'" (*Club* 49). J. B. Broadbent similarly shifts the figure of plowman forward into association with the golden scales episode at the end of Book 4, but the Bible, not the *Aeneid,* serves to support this reading. While he agrees that the homely plowman "provides the usual mundane interval," as does the "belated peasant" witnessing the metamorphosis of the demons into "smallest dwarfs" in Book 1, Broadbent believes that Milton uses the plowman "to direct our attitude to Satan" by alluding to Daniel's interpretation of Nebuchadnezzar's dream. Like the giant image in the king's dream, Satan will be destroyed, will be "like the chaff of the summer threshingfloors" (Dan. 2.35), and as Daniel prophesies to Nebuchadnezzar, "Thou art weighed in the balances, and art found wanting" (5.27), so Satan is about to be weighed and found wanting when the golden scales tip against him at the end of Milton's Book 4 (*Some Graver Subject* 200–01). James H. Sims also brings the Bible to bear on this passage, but he seems to be echoing Bentley's demanding questions about the unity of the entire sequence when he asks why Milton expands the harvest image to include "the careful Plowman." Sims reports that in the Bible, the plowman represents both the servant of God (1 Cor. 9.10, Luke 17.7) and the Son of God (Matt. 13.37, Luke 9.62), and contends that Milton shifts the identity of his plowman from the servant to the Son when "God, immediately following this simile and the description of Satan's tremendous might, intervenes and doubles the strength of Gabriel's forces to 'trample...as mire' (l. 1010) the Fiend." Sims then proceeds to associate with this sequence Christ's words to Peter: "Satan may sift you as wheat" (Luke 22.31). Finally, Sims identifies one of the most puzzling details in the sequence and asks why Milton set a plowman, and not a reaper, in the middle of this harvest simile. "Perhaps the allusion is to the prophetic promise of God that in the days of the millennial reign of the Messiah, 'the plowman shall overtake the reaper, and the treader of grapes him that soweth seed; and the mountaines shall drop sweet wine, and all the hills shall melt' (Amos 9:13); when the seasons so merge into one another, the 'Eternal Spring' of Paradise will be regained" (*Bible* 232–34). The *OED* defines *ploughman* as "A man who follows and guides the plough," but adds that the word is "often used generically for a farm-labourer or rustic." Finally, in his extensive commentary, Alastair Fowler not only directly deals with both Bentley and Empson on this simile, but, like Sims, also pursues the simile's biblical associations. Looking at Empson's concern with the identity of "the careful Plowman," Fowler dismisses the possibility that he is Satan and cautions that if he is God, he cannot be God in all respects, for God remains omnipotent. At Bentley's feet, Fowler lays modern critics' difficulties with the simile, faulting Bentley for introducing an "irrelevant notion, that the ploughman is afraid of a storm." Then, unlike Harding, Fowler does not refer the image to the *Aeneid*, but rather to Virgil's *Georgics* 1.192 and 226 ("exspectata seges vanis elusit artistis"; "the looked-for crop has mocked [them] with empty ears"), both of which "refer to the consequences, not of storm damage, but of sowing at the wrong time." Finally, citing Jer. 51.33 and Hab. 3.12, Fowler turns to the Bible, where "*threshing* was a very familiar metaphor for divine judgment," and he concludes that Milton's meaning in this plowman simile may therefore be that "God is *careful* that the final judgment, and the final reckoning with Satan, should not be premature. It might even be maintained that the simile, by opening the theme of divine judgment followed up in the Scales image or ll. 997ff., actually contributes to an impression of God's secret transcendence" (669–70).

984. *hopeful:* A. W. Verity (473) presents two possible readings: "from which he had hoped so much; or 'which had made him so hopeful' (the epithet being transferred)," and, like Fowler in **983–85**, Verity believes that Milton is recalling Virgil's *Georgics* 1.226.

985–90. Unlike the illumination reflected on the figure of Satan in the preceding five-line simile, this description, comparing him to a mountain, aims a spotlight directly on him, and yet it, too, casts shadows as well as light. The critical response to this description has long been involved with the critical response to the parallel confrontation scene in Book 2 that pits Satan against Death. Todd quotes a note from Charles Dunster, for example, who sees the episode in Book 2 as "a fine description of two desperadoes, equally matched, from the violence of altercation rushing to furious combat; the result of which seems doubtful. But how different is the situation of Satan in this place! Satan is here so far from being unterrified, that he is absolutely alarm'd; and he only collects his might, and dilates himself, that is, makes the most of his personal bulk and stature, to take the finest possible position, and best to oppose the foes that encircle him. His object here is self-defence. But it is a self-defence worthy of the great Adversary of God and Man, one of the interesting features of whose character, as drawn by the poet, is resolution in danger. It therefore well admits the poetical decorations that follow" ([1842], 2:111–12). Twentieth century critics who juxtapose this confrontation to the one in Book 2 see the contrast rather differently, however, quite often directing their remarks to the degeneration-degradation debate most fully presented in **32–113**. Balachandra Rajan believes that "Satan dilated 'like *Teneriff* or *Atlas*' is never quite as impressive as the

'Unterrifi'd' Satan who challenges Death at the outset of his journey through Chaos. He is too concerned with winning verbal victories, with shifty deceits and elaborate evasions. He accepts (as one cannot imagine the earlier Satan accepting) the symbolic verdict of the scales suspended in Heaven. The implication plainly is that the heroic Satan is yielding to the perverted, and that the passions which led him to war with his creator are beginning to recoil on the intelligence which released them" (*"Paradise Lost" and the Seventeenth Century Reader* 101). Drawing attention to phrases such as "On th' other side," and "now had" or "might have," which are common to both passages, Stanley Fish even suggests that there may be more farce than drama in Satan who here stands "dilated" like a mountain (*Surprised* 173). A number of additional critics have associated Satan's presentation as a mountain with several other scenes in *PL*. One such is the earlier scene in Book 4 in which he is found "Squat like a Toad" (800). The change from toad to mountain is a drastic one, especially because it occurs within 200 lines, and it prompts Frank S. Kastor and Robert Martin Adams to much the same understanding. Kastor concludes that the change "dramatically underscores the relation of Satan's stature to his roles as well as the differences in the stature and size of each" (268). Adams, insisting that Satan "does not develop consistently in any single particular direction," argues against those who consider Satan a hero: "He is, at any given juncture, whatever it suits the needs of man's story to have him" (43). J. B. Broadbent understands Satan's comparison to "*Teneriff* or *Atlas*" as one of his several "metamorphoses," and he sets it against the shrinking of the crowd of demons entering Pandemonium in Book 1 who are compared to "Faerie Elves" (781) seen at midnight, not by a "careful Plowman," but by "some belated Peasant" (783), and in both episodes, Broadbent insists that Milton mocks "the falsely epical" (*Some Graver Subject* 106). Finally, although she does not specifically set this scene against any earlier one, Marjorie H. Nicolson does speak about Satan's appearances throughout the epic, and along with a contingent of twentieth century critics, she insists that Satan degenerates, and, indeed, that the greatness of his characterization lies in that "slow and steady degeneration" (*John Milton* 186). Nicolson nevertheless finds grandeur in him at this moment: "One of the last occasions that Milton uses a grand comparison for Satan is the scene at the end of Book IV in which the angelic squadrons begin to hem Satan round and he turns upon them with all the courage he still possesses" (187).

That "grand comparison," of course, relates Satan to "*Teneriff* or *Atlas*" (987), and those specific mountains have drawn critical attention to two principal topics, geography and literary parallels, with Hume's preliminary annotations not much altered by subsequent critics. Hume (165) begins by establishing geographical facts. "*Teneriffa*, or, as the Natives name, *Thenerife*, is one of the *Canary* Islands in the *Atlantick* Ocean, anciently called *Nivaria*, because its Peak (supposed the highest in the World) is seldom without Snow. The Basis of this Mountain is about 48 *Spanish* Leagues in compass, and its Summit about 15 miles high, to be seen about 120 *English* Miles at Sea." On Atlas, Hume reports that it is now named "*Aiducal*," and is "the greatest Mountain in all *Africa*, hiding its head in continual Clouds: It begins in *Mauritania*, near the *Atlantick* Ocean, which bears its Name, by Cape *de Guer*, by various windings and turnings, stretching it self Eastward to the Deserts of *Barca*. Its prodigious height occasioned the Fable of *Atlas* bearing Heaven." Hume establishes Milton's principal literary parallel for this simile, Virgil's description of Aeneas about to attack Turnus in the *Aeneid* 12.701–03: "That *Lucifer*, the Chief Leader and Champion of the lapse'd Angelick Host, should, swoln with rage, be compared to Mountains of such vast Immensity, will seem modest enough, when paralell'd with the liking of *Aeneas* by *Virgil* to some others, not so much inferior to these, as his *Heroe* must be allowed to have been below any one of those *Spiritual Beings:* 'Quantus Athos, aut quantus Eryx, aut ipse coruscis / Cum fremit ilicibus quantus, gaudetque nivali / Vertice se attollens pater Apenninus ad auras'; 'Vast as Athos, vast as Eryx, or vast as Father Apennine himself, when he roars with his quivering oaks, and joyously lifts heavenward his snowy head.'" Hume's immediate successors follow his approach to this passage, commenting on geography and literary antecedents. The Richardsons, for example, report that Teneriff is 45 miles high (186). Noting the difference between Hume and the Richardsons, Newton suggests that the Richardsons' 45 may be "a false print 45 for 15," and, accepting the report of "a gentleman who measur'd it," Newton concludes that "the perpendicular highth" of Teneriff "is no more than one mile and three quarters" (304). Newton dismisses Hume's emphasis on the difference between Milton's metaphor and Virgil's metaphor when he describes them as "the same" (304), while Todd ([1842], 2:112) reports Robert Thyer's comparison of Milton's Satan here to Tasso's Satan in *Gerusalemme Liberata* 4.6: "Ne pur *Calpe* s'inalza, o 'l magno *Atlante*, / Ch' anzi lui non paresse un picciol colle"; "[compared to Pluto] not Atlas nor the towering / Rock of Gibraltar is more than a small slope" (trans. Anthony M. Esolen). In his notes for Christopher Pitt's *The Works of Virgil, in Latin and English*, Joseph Warton reestablishes the spirit of Hume's annotation: "Indeed our great countryman would convey an idea different from Virgil's; he insists upon the fixedness of Teneriff or Atlas; whereas Virgil would represent Aeneas enraged, and accordingly mentions the oaks on the top of the Apennines, as resounding with tempests" (4:400).

While such twentieth century critics as Charles Grosvenor Osgood and Allan H. Gilbert gather more references to Atlas scattered through classical literature, as well as Milton's own poetry, much more commentary is directed at presenting the early modern geographers' and travelers' reports on Atlas and Teneriff. To Hume's reference to the *Aeneid* 12 passage, Osgood (14) adds references to Atlas in Aeschylus's *Prometheus Bound* 348–51; Homer's *Odyssey* 1.52; Ovid's *Metamorphoses* 4.631–38; and Virgil's *Aeneid* 4.481–83. Gilbert (*Geographical Dictionary* 39–40) reports that Atlas is referenced in 2.306, 10.674, and 11.402, as well as in *PR* 4.115 and *Idea* 24 (Patterson, *Works* 1:268). Allan Gilbert, Robert Ralston Cawley, Merritt Y. Hughes, and Alastair Fowler—unlike Newton—do not speak of having personal acquaintance with men who have visited Teneriff or Atlas, but they do present the reports of those early modern travelers who made such visits. Gilbert (*Geographical Dictionary* 39), for example, quotes Leo Africanus, who describes Atlas in *The History and Description of Africa* 1:15–16 as "in most places rounde, hard to ascend, craggie, steepe, impassable, cold, barren, shadie, and every where full of woods and fountaines, with cloudes alwaies hovering about the tops thereof, being forlorn and desolate toward the Ocean, but over against Africa minor, most fertile." The remarks of Sir John Hawkins, as presented in Richard Hakluyt's *The Principall Navigations, Voiages, and Discoveries of the English Nation* 3:502, compose Gilbert's note on Teneriff: "In this Iland of Teneriffe, there is a hill called the Pike, because it is piked, which is in height by their reports twentie leagues, having both winter and summer abundance of snowe in the top of it. This Pike may be seene in a cleere day fiftie leagues off, but it sheweth as though it were a blacke cloude a great height in the element. I have heard of none to be compared with this in heigth." Gilbert (*Geographical Dictionary* 289–90) adds new references to Teneriff found in Fairfax's translation of Tasso, *Jerusalem Delivered* 15.33–34, 46, 52, 53; and in Donne's "The First Anniversary" 286–87 (*The Epithalamions* 30). Robert Ralston Cawley acknowledges that Atlas is one of the best known of classical myths, but, he continues, "there had been almost as many new associations with Tenerife, the sky-pointing peak of the Canaries which seamen delighted to tell tall tales about. Because the mountain rose directly out of the ocean, it gave approaching ships an impression of loftiness far in excess of the truth. In addition, there seems to have been something of a contest to see who could indulge in the most extravagant hyperbole." Cawley concludes that Milton "could not have chosen an analogy which would create upon his reader's mind an impression of greater loftiness and stability" (132–33). Merritt Y. Hughes notes that both Teneriff and the Atlas range in Morocco were "dramatically conspicuous on the maps of Milton's time" (*Complete Poems* 301). Finally, Alastair Fowler (670) adds yet one more voice from the early modern literature of travel, as he quotes Peter Heylyn's *Cosmographie* 4:88 on Teneriff: "With truth enough most of our *Travellers* and *Geographers* hold it to be the highest in the whole world." Like Hume, Cawley, and others, Fowler considers how the mythological traditions complicate the geographical. He observes, for example, that the comparison to Atlas "is double-edged; since Satan sustains the pressure of the angels as Atlas sustained the weight of the stars..., but is also, like Atlas, a rebel against the supreme deity."

This description of Satan "Collecting all his might" as he faces Gabriel has also been invoked to exemplify aesthetic notions such as the sublime. Addison is the first to speak of it as sublime: "*Satan*'s cloathing himself with Terror when he prepares for the Combat is truly sublime" (*Spectator* 3:173), and as the nineteenth century nears its end, Stopford Augustus Brooke insists that the description of "'Satan *alarmed*,' (nothing can be more noble than the use, and the placing at the end of the line, of the word) 'Dilated stood,' fills the whole scene with sublimity" (104). Also see the commentary on "horror Plum'd" and the sublime in **988–89**. In the preface to his *Poems*, Wordsworth turns to Milton's description of Satan "Like *Teneriff* or *Atlas*" when he defines the poetic imagination as that which "recoils from every thing but the plastic, the pliant, and the indefinite.... Having to speak of stature, she does not tell you that her gigantic Angel was as tall as Pompey's Pillar; much less that he was twelve cubits, or twelve hundred cubits high; or that his dimensions equalled those of Teneriffe or Atlas;—because these, & if they were a million times as high, it would be the same, are bounded: The expression is, 'His stature reached the sky!' the illimitable firmament" (xxxiii–xxxiv). Returning to the distinction between Milton's and Virgil's mountain metaphors that Hume first makes, Davis P. Harding (*Club* 48–50) focuses on the phrase Wordsworth celebrates, noting that in Virgil's comparison between Aeneas and the "lord of the Apennine," it is only the mountain's "crest" that is reared into the air, whereas Satan's "stature reacht the Sky."

This five-line description of Satan comes into play in Allan H. Gilbert's work on the stages of the composition of *PL*. Gilbert (*On the Composition* 53) points out that the idea of combat between Satan and the angelic guard figures in Milton's notes for the second act of "Adam unparadiz'd," when Satan "seeks revenge on man," and "the Chorus prepare resistance at his first approach" (Patterson, *Works* 18:231). The Satan who "dilated stood, / Like *Teneriff* or *Atlas*," however, Gilbert considers a much later conception.

985–86. *allarm'd / ... dilated:* Todd ([1842], 2:111–12) reports that these adjectives describing Satan as he confronts Gabriel create a bit of controversy between two of those men contributing notes to his edition of Milton's poetical works. Contending that Milton's use of *dilated* is unique in English, Robert Thyer argues that Milton is borrowing "this nervous expression" from *Gerusalemme Liberata* 19.12, where Tasso applies the adjective *disteso* to Argantes as he confronts Tancred: "*Disteso* in Italian, is exactly the same with *dilated* in English, and expresses very strongly the attitude of an eager and undaunted combatant, where fury not only seems to erect and enlarge his stature, but expands as it were his whole frame, and extends every limb." Charles Dunster, however, brings *allarm'd* to bear upon *dilated* as he argues that Satan "is absolutely alarm'd; and he only collects his might, and dilates himself, that is, makes the most of his personal bulk and stature to take the finest possible position, and best to oppose the foes that encircle him." The *OED* quotes 985–86 as it defines both *dilated* and *allarm'd*. Defining *dilated* as "widened, expanded, distended, diffused," the *OED* traces the meaning back to the year 1450, and before quoting Milton's usage, cites Shakespeare's *Troilus and Cressida* 2.3.259–61, where Ulysses addresses Ajax on the heels of Achilles's refusal to fight: "I will not praise thy wisdom, / Which like a bourn, a pale, a shore confines / Thy spacious and dilated parts." Defining *alarm'd* as "Called to arms, aroused, on the watch," *OED* 1 precedes its citation of Milton's lines with Shakespeare's *King Lear* 2.1.55–56, where Edmund lies to Gloucester about an encounter with Edgar: "He saw my best alarum'd spirits / Bold on the quarrel's right." Masson's note on *allarm'd* supports the meaning presented in the *OED*: "on his guard," "fear is not implied" (*Poetical Works* 3:183). Also see Verity 473; Tillyard, *Studies* 63.

986. *dilated:* John Peter and Alastair Fowler understand that this term diminishes Satan. Peter writes that *dilated* and *horror* (989) are "pejorative touches" that "tend to flatten, reducing Satan to a cardboard silhouette" (55), whereas Fowler (670) notes, "The impressive stance is as usual bathetically punctured—here by the grumbling retreat of ll. 1014f."

987. *unremov'd:* Todd ([1842], 2:112) reports Robert Thyer's admiration and a Shakespearean parallel noted by Steevens: "*Unremoved* for *immovable,* Mr. Thyer adds, is very poetical, and justified by Milton's 'conjugal attraction *unreprov'd*' [493], and Spenser's '*unreproved* truth' [*The Faerie Queene* 2.7.16]. Mr. Steevens (*The Plays of William Shakespeare*) offers a parallel expression from the first part of Shakspeare's *K. Hen. VI.* [2.5.102–03] 'Strong-fixed is the house of Lancaster, / And, *like a mountain, not to be remov'd.*'" Todd closes his note suggesting a comparison with Ps. 135.1, and quoting Fairfax's translation of Tasso's *Gerusalemme Liberata* (titled *Godfrey of Bulloigne*) 9.31.1–4: "as a *mountain,* or a cape of land, / Assail'd with storms and seas on every side, / Doth *unremoved,* stedfast, still withstand / Storme, thunder." On Milton's earlier *conjugal attraction unreprov'd,* see **493.** Defining *unremoved* as "Fixed in place; firmly stationed," the *OED* 1.c quotes Milton's line after providing several sixteenth century examples.

988–89. *on his Crest / Sat horror Plum'd:* Patrick Hume here follows a rather predictable critical path as he identifies classical parallels, and explores the meanings of specialized diction such as *Crest* and *Plum'd,* but remarkable, rather than predictable, is his final annotation, which looks ahead to future critical discussions of Milton and the sublime. Describing Satan's helmet as "Dreadfully graven and delineated," Hume immediately associates it with the helmets of classical heroes that "were made terrible, by Horses Tails stuck in their Crests, and by representations of divers angry Animals." Hume then provides a long list of descriptions of such helmets, including the helmet Venus delivers to Aeneas in the *Aeneid* 8.620: "Terribilem cristis galeam flammasque vomentem"; "Terrific with plumes and spouting flames." *Crest,* Hume derives from *Crista,* "Lat. a Comb, or tuft of Feathers on a Bird's head, thence a Plume of Feathers, or any other Ornament on a Helmet." On *horror Plum'd* Hume notes, "Horror full-fledg'd, ready to fly upon the Enemy; Fury in perfection. *Plum'd,* of *Pluma,* Lat. Feathers; in imitation of which, any thing carved, graven or embroidered was called *Opus plumatile,* a kind of damasking Shields and Helms." Hume then cites a Virgilian approximation to this image in the *Aeneid* 11.770–71. Finally, however, the inclination to pedantry with which he has been charged disappears, as returning, yet again, to the phrase *Sat horror Plum'd,* Hume admits that it "has something in it, *quod nequeo monstrare, & sentio tantum*" (167).

Quoting only one classical parallel, Newton's admiration for Milton's description matches Hume's, although Newton (304) sharpens the picture of "horror Plum'd," clarifying that Horror personified is itself "made the plume of his [Satan's] helmet; and how much nobler an idea is this than the horses tails and sphinxes and dragons and other terrible animals on the helmets of the ancient heroes." Newton even rules that Milton's description surpasses Virgil's description of "the Chimaera vomiting flames on the crest of Turnus" in the *Aeneid* 7.785–86: "Cui triplici crinita juba galea alta Chimaeram / Sustinet, Aetnaeos efflantem faucibus ignes"; "His lofty helmet, crested with triple plume, upbears a Chimaera, breathing from her jaws Aetnean fires." The Richardsons, like Newton, establish that "Horror is Personiz'd," and similarly refer to Turnus's helmet, not Aeneas's, but they understand *Plum'd* literally, explaining that on the cone of the helmet, Horror "sits shaded with a Plume of Feathers, as the *Chimaera* on the Helmet of *Turnus,* Aen. VII.785. Feathers have always been a Military Ornament, and several together is call'd a Plume, Corruptly a Plum of Feathers" (186). The *OED* cites Milton's lines in the entries for both words, defining *Crest* 4 as "The apex or 'cone' of a helmet' hence a helmet or head-piece," and *Plum'd* 2.3.b as "To set or place as a plume." Todd's response to the description of Satan's helmet consists largely of a series of parallels from early modern literature, such as John Fletcher's *Bonduca* 3.1.7–8 (*The Dramatic Works* 4:191–92), Philip Massinger's *The Unnatural Combat* 2.1.171–72, and George Sandys's *A Paraphrase upon the Psalms of David*. Most intriguing, however, are Todd's prefatory remarks, which recall Hume's closing words on "horror Plum'd." Todd explains, "I will endeavour also to illustrate this passage, notwithstanding Mr. Warton discourages any explanation of it" ([1842], 2:112). Todd's reference is to Thomas Warton, editor of *Poems upon Several Occasions by John Milton,* who in his note on *exanguisque…Horror,* in *QNov* 148, announces that he refuses to analyze the construction because "we have no precise or determinate conception of what Milton means. And we detract from the sublimity of the passage in endeavouring to explain it, and to give it a distinct signification. Here is a nameless terrible grace, resulting from a mixture of ideas, and a confusion of imagery" (505). In his note on *horror Plum'd,* David Masson (*Poetical Works* 3:183) credits Hume, adding that the "personification" is "terrible in its very vagueness. The poet, imagining Satan, sees as it were the plumed crest of his helmet, but gives only this visionary metaphor of it." Masson establishes several additional parallels pointed out by Keightley (*The Faerie Queene* 2.7.23; Shakespeare's *Richard III* 5.3.35, "Victory sits on our helms"). Also see Joseph Addison and Stopford Augustus Brooke on the sublime in **985–90.** For the most part, the twentieth century response to *horror Plum'd* reinforces the work of the earlier editors. Charles Grosvenor Osgood (43–44) does push behind the Virgilian sources to the Homeric traditions associating Horror and war, and he specifically references the description of Agamemnon's preparation for battle in the *Iliad* 11.15–46. Davis P. Harding glances anew at Turnus's helmet, noting that Milton's description "distils the essence of Virgil's striking image of the horrible snake-like Chimaera, 'breathing from her throat Aetnean flames'" (*Club* 51), and to Harding's comment, Merritt Y. Hughes adds, "The implied association of Satan and the serpent here and elsewhere has also its latent threat of the doom of the serpent to be bruised by the 'seed of the woman' as the serpents Tityos and Typhon were slain by the arrows of Apollo or the thunderbolts of Zeus" ("Satan and the 'Myth'" 138). Standing apart from all these editors and critics, John Peter reports that he is as unimpressed by Milton's attribution of *horror* to Satan's appearance as he is by Satan's standing "dilated" (986), labeling both "pejorative touches" that "tend to flatten, reducing Satan to a cardboard silhouette" (55).

988. *His stature reacht the Skie:* the early editors and critics present several literary parallels. In *Observations on Shakespeare* 402, John Upton first associates this line with Wisd. of Sol. 18.16: "It [God's Word] touched the heaven, but stood upon the earth." Cf. Upton in **990–1004.** Addison (*Spectator* 3:173) points to Homer and Virgil, finding Milton's verse "at least equal to *Homer*'s Description of Discord [*Iliad* 4.441–45] celebrated by *Longinus* [15–16], or to that of Fame in *Virgil* [*Aeneid* 4.176–77], who are both represented with their Feet standing upon the Earth, and their Heads reaching above the Clouds." Like Upton, Newton (304) points to the Wisdom of Solomon while he also acknowledges Addison's reference to Homer's Discord and Virgil's Fame. Todd ([1842], 2:112) provides John Bowle's reference to Caxton's *Life of Saint Anthony* 333: "The *devil* appyered to hym in so grete a *stature* that he *touched the heven.*" Finally A. W. Verity (474) adds, "For now sits Expectation in the air" from the prologue to act 2 of Shakespeare's *Henry V.* Verity also cross-references 6.306–07, and lines 13–19 in Milton's *Prol* 7:13–19 (Patterson, *Works* 12:260). Also see Wordsworth and Harding in 985–90.

989–90. The critical problems deriving from Milton's insistent philosophy of spiritual materialism, problems most memorably attacked by Samuel Johnson in his remarks cited in **799–809**, are anticipated by earlier critics attempting to explain how Satan has managed to arm himself as he confronts Gabriel. Hume is silent on the topic, but Newton immediately asks where Satan's spear and shield came from when he had "just raised out of the form of a toad." Newton concludes that "we must suppose that his power, as an Angel, was such, that he could assume them upon occasion whenever he pleased" (304–05). The Richardsons tick off possible explanations as they reason their way through the problem: "*Milton* was Here under some Difficulty. *Satan* could not be Suppos'd to have brought Arms with him, nor was it proper to imagine he had Stollen any of those belonging to the Good Angels; to have Dis-arm'd Any of them had been Worse; he has therefore given him what only Seem'd to be Spear and Shield. nor yet is the Poet quite Extricated, the Reader must Assist him by Supposing *Satan*'s Power Exceeding Great, who even with Such could Defend himself So as to Endanger, not only Paradise, but the whole New Creation, as it follows; and This gives a Vast Idea of his Power, though Impair'd by Sin" (187). First quoting Newton, Todd reports that Charles Dunster—like the Richardsons—also contends that Satan's arms only "seemd both Spear and Shield," but Dunster does not follow the Richardsons in asserting that the reader's imagination enhances those arms. In his note contributed to Todd's edition, Dunster argues that unlike "the most sublime indistinctness" of Milton's description of Death in Book 2, "the intimation, that Satan's arms were a *mere semblance,* has a bad effect. Indeed it is absurd, and renders the description, which follows, of what might have happened had an encounter taken place, absolutely ridiculous" ([1842], 2:112–13).

Masson rejects Dunster's condemnation of the description, while bringing forward the philosophical issue at the core of the ongoing critical discussion: "Dunster and others after him object to the hesitancy here as spoiling the picture. 'The intimation that Satan's arms were a mere semblance,' says Dunster, 'has a bad effect;' and Mr. [R. C.] Browne [1:357] supposes that Milton here yielded to a sudden feeling that he was too *material* in his representations of spiritual beings. Nothing of the sort. Satan has just shot up to such vast stature that it is impossible to give precise visual descriptions of his helmet…or his arms. *That* is the true reason for the vague 'what seemed'" (*Poetical Works* 3:183). A. W. Verity follows Dunster to cross-reference the description of Death in Book 2, but not to fault the vagueness of "seem'd both Spear and Shield." Verity, rather, echoes the Richardsons in his praise: "The intentional vagueness of such descriptions is so effective because it stirs but does not satisfy the imagination, rousing a sense of the mysterious and indescribable" (474). Finally, one must recall that while Dunster finds "absurd" the semblance of arms in Satan's grasp, J. B. Broadbent finds "absurd" the entire confrontation between Satan and Gabriel. See Broadbent in **823–56**.

990–1004. Among all the episodes in Book 4, God's hanging forth "his golden Scales" (997) as Gabriel and Satan prepare for battle receives some of the most sustained criticism. Identifying the classical and biblical sources involved in the sequence forms the core of the early criticism, and, as so often, Hume lays a firm foundation. Hume (167–68) fixes the three key classical parallels: the episode in the *Iliad* 8.68–72 when Jupiter "weighs the Success of the engaging Armies of *Troy* and *Greece*," the episode in the *Iliad* 22.208–13 when Jupiter "ponders the Fate of *Achilles* and *Hector* in their single Combat," and the episode in the *Aeneid* 12.725–27 when Jupiter weighs the fates of Aeneas and Turnus. As do his eighteenth century successors, Hume notes Milton's adaptations: "It is observable, both in the Original and the Copy, that the heaviest Weight was unlucky and fatal; whereas our Author, keeping closer to the Simile, puts Satan, as the wicked and weakest, into the mounted Scale, as unable to preponderate and prevail against the Good and God-like *Gabriel*" (168). Hume also considers the astronomical ramifications of the "golden Scales, yet seen / Betwixt *Astrea* and the *Scorpion* signe" (997–98). With a supporting quotation from *Metamorphoses* 1.149–50, Hume identifies *Astrea* as "Justice…who during the Golden Age, with other Gods frequented the Earth, and was the last that left it, when defiled by all Abominations, and has her place among the Signs of the Zodiac" (167). On *Astrea,* also see Osgood in **998**. Moving out from its literary context, Hume notes that, as a constellation, Libra is located between the Scorpion and the Virgin, and he points out that when the sun enters Libra, "the Days and Nights are weighed equally" (167). Finally, Hume (167) moves to consider the biblical associations, explaining that Milton has "nobled this Sign…placing it among the Stars, in memory of the Almighty Creator, *Wherein all things created first he weigh'd; Who, as Job says, made a weight for the winds, and weigheth the waters by measure,* Chap. 28. v. 25. *Who knows the ballancing of the Clouds,* Chap. 37. v. 16. *Who weigheth the mountains in Scales, and the hills in a Ballance,* Isai. 40. v. 12." In the dedication to his translation of the *Aeneid,* Dryden also acknowledges Milton's adaptation of Virgil's scales episode, but, explains Dryden, "to a different end: for, first, he makes God Almighty set the scales for St. Michael [*sic;* should be Gabriel] and Satan, when he knew no combat was to follow." In addition Dryden suggests another biblical allusion, the passage in Dan. 5.27 "where Belshazzar was put into the balance and found too light" (*Works* 5:316–17). The Richardsons and Newton continue to pursue both these classical and the biblical associations. Like Hume, the Richardsons understand the weighing comments on "the Strength of each Contending Angel" (189), as well as "the Question…whether a Battle or Not" (188), and they underscore what Dryden recognizes, that the scales episode also clarifies the difference between Milton's God and Homer's Jupiter who learned "what was the Decree of Destiny, to which Himself was Subject; Whereas *Milton* says the Almighty us'd these Scales but as a Sign directing the Contending Parties to Act as Himself had Determin'd they should" (189). The Richardsons focus as well on the significance of *sequel* (1003): "*Milton* has Nobly extended the Thought, not only Parting and Fight, but all their Train of Consequences are Included, Each are the Sequel, One of This, the Other of That" (188–89). Like Hume, the Richardsons acknowledge Milton's nonclassical interpretation of the scales' dropping or rising, and like Hume, they celebrate the astronomical reality of the scales, which "does, as it were, Reallize the Fiction, and gives Consequently a Greater Force to it" (187). The biblical influences on Milton's scale image draw forth the Richardsons' highest praise, however, as they add New Testament references to God's providential wisdom to Hume's Old Testament references to God's creative power: "a Short and Noble Account of the Divine Wisdom in Creation and Providence! In the Beginning he Fitted All the Parts of the Great Work, All was Contriv'd with respect to Each as relating to the Rest, and to the Whole…and Thus Now, (for 'tis the Poet speaks) Now, and at all times, He, the same Eternal Wisdom, *Ponders all Events;* for Example, Battels, Which Side shall prevail, and What shall be the Consequences; So Realms, States, Monarchies, These also he Weighs; Which shall Subsist, which Decay, which Subdue, and Swallow up Which, *&c.* as *Job* xxviii.25. xxxvii.16. *Isa.* xl.12. *Matt.* x.30. *Ephes.* i.4. 2. *Thess.* i.9. &c." (187–88). While the Richardsons overlook the allusion to Daniel, which Dryden apparently first notes, John Upton, publishing his *Critical Observations on Shakespeare* a year before Newton brought out his annotated edition of *PL,* does not. In fact, Upton (401) dismisses the classical texts, insisting that Milton "is entirely governed by scripture; for Satan only is weighed, viz. his parting and his fight, Dan. V, 27. TEKEL, THOU *art weigh'd in the balances, and art found wanting.*" Commenting on the classical parallels for

Milton's scales, Newton paraphrases much of the Richardsons' commentary, stressing that in the heavenly sign Satan could "read his own destiny." To the earlier biblical references, Newton adds 1 Sam. 2.3 and Prov. 16.2 but stresses Dan. 5.26–27 (306–08).

Upton's and Newton's emphasis on the importance of the book of Daniel is sustained by Joseph Addison and continues to be developed into the mid-twentieth century. Stressing the biblical over the classical associations of the scales image, Addison points to Job 28.15, Isa. 40.12, and 1 Sam. 2.3, but it is Dan. 5.27 that he underscores, explaining that Milton is "more justified" than Homer and Virgil in his use of the "golden Scales" because "we find the same noble Allegory in Holy Writ" (*Spectator* 3:174; also see 134–35). Todd ([1842], 2:113) presents Addison on the classical parallels, and Newton on the biblical parallels, but then directs readers to Pope's notes on the *Iliad* 8 (*Poems* 7:399–401n88). Pointing to the Old Testament texts the early editors cite, Pope admits that the figure of the scales "was first made use of in holy Writ" (*Poems* 7:399n88), but he believes that Homer's presentation of the scale figure "appear'd so beautiful to succeeding Poets" that Aeschylus, according to Plutarch in "How the Young Man Should Study Poetry" 87, wrote *Psychostasia*, a tragedy based upon it. Considering why in Milton the ascending scale—not the descending, as in Homer—"denoted ill Success," Pope explains that Milton's "Reason was, because Satan was immortal, and therefore the sinking of his Scale could not signify Death, but the mounting of it did his *Lightness,* conformable to the Expression we just now cited from *Daniel*" (*Poems* 7:400n88). Pope concludes that Milton's image is superior "on account of the beautiful Allusion to the Sign of *Libra* in the Heavens, and that noble Imagination of the Maker's weighing the whole World at the Creation, and all the Events of it since; so correspondent at once to Philosophy, and to the Style of the Scriptures" (*Poems* 7:401n88). Several centuries later, as he refers the "golden Scales" of *PL* 4 to the "scales of the fates" (*fatorum lances*) in *Naturam* 35, A. W. Verity (474) praises Pope's achievement with the image in *The Rape of the Lock* 5.71–74 (*Poems* 2:206).

While early editors almost appear to be vying to outdo one another in praising Milton's image of the scales, several early critics nevertheless firmly condemn the episode. In the October 23, 1753, edition of the *Adventurer,* Palaeophilus (Joseph Warton) writes of the confrontation of Satan and Gabriel: "this horrid fray is prevented, expectation is cut off, and curiosity disappointed, by an expedient which, though applauded by ADDISON and POPE, and imitated from HOMER and VIRGIL, will be deemed frigid and inartificial, by all who judge from their own sensations, and are not content to echo the decisions of others." Furthermore, concludes Palaeophilus, "To make such a use, at so critical a time, of LIBRA, a mere imaginary sign of the Zodiac, is scarcely justifiable in a poem founded on religious truth" (Warton, *Adventurer* 185). Landor, some 75 years later, also speaks against this sequence, offended by its sounds, but even more offended by its meaning: "To pass over the slighter objection of *quick* and *kick* [1004] as displeasing to the ear, the vulgarity of kicking the beam is intolerable. He might as well…talk of *kicking the bucket*" (26–27).

A number of twentieth century critics also fault this episode, but for the most part, the moderns, both those admiring and those condemning Milton's image, respond to its role within Milton's epic more than to its relationship with literary and biblical parallels. For R. J. Zwi Werblowsky, John Peter, Marjorie H. Nicolson, and William Empson, the "golden Scales" sequence raises as many questions about Milton's God as about Milton's art. Werblowsky contends that God holds forth the scales "presumably with the sole purpose of enabling Satan to clear out in time to save his skin, and to be ready to attempt man's fall a second time with better success" (22). Peter writes, "We cannot believe that any real violence will follow when on one side there is merely a group of minstrels armed with toy spears—men, as it were, of straw—and when God intervenes to avert disaster it seems the act of a busybody or a poltroon. In view of Gabriel's assurance that Satan is 'Not likely to part hence without contest' (872), and the tremendous power previously attributed to the devil, it is even possible, just here, to feel that God knows Satan will prevail, and that his method of avoiding a defeat, even a minor defeat, is underhand and unfair" (24–25). Similarly, Nicolson finds the episode "basically unfair to the great Adversary of God and Man. Milton takes refuge in a device of old 'epic machinery,'" which, she contends, "has no artistic justification when used by Milton's Hebraic-Christian God to decide an issue in what might have proved a battle grander and more dangerous than that in Heaven." Up until this point, Nicolson explains, "the various steps in Satan's downfall have seemed just, right and inevitable, because he has taken each step of his own deliberate choice. This time his author has unfairly imposed the sudden ignominy upon him as a 'deus ex machina'" (*John Milton* 244). William Empson's reading is perhaps the most provocative, prompting a detailed reply from Alastair Fowler. Empson insists that when he stops the "horrid fray" (996) with the "golden Scales" (997), Milton's God reveals his true colors: "I do not see what the incident can mean except that God was determined to make man fall, and had supplied a guard only for show;

as soon as the guards look like succeeding he prevents them. No doubt the Latin pun on *ponder* helps to emphasize that the whole incident is meant to be allegorical, but no translation of it into more spiritual terms can alter the basic fact about it" (*Milton's God* 112–13). Defending Milton's God again Empson, and charging Empson himself with "anthropopathy," Fowler reasons that "God would have been reckless and partial if he had ignored the risk to other species inhabiting the starry cope. And besides, he is not interested in preventing the Fall by force; he has already explained in iii 90–133 about the degree of latitude to be allowed to Satan, in order that Adam's freedom may have real content." Fowler concedes, "It is in one sense true that the angelic guard—like every-thing else that is less than divine—is unnecessary and 'only for show,'" but he insists that they nevertheless "have ambassadorial dignity. And we are allowed to speculate that their interruption of Satan had critical significance, if he was to get in enough suggestion to be able later to tempt Eve, but not so much as to brainwash the freedom of choice out of her" (671). Even Empson's comment on *ponders* (1001) is corrected by Fowler, who accepts that it works as a pun with *weights* (1002) but contends that the wordplay is "not a Latinism, for the concrete sense of the English word was still current in M[ilton]'s time" (672). See Robert Martin Adams on *ponders* as a pun in **1001**.

Like Fowler, other twentieth century critics argue that the "golden Scales" episode reveals Milton's God as anything but a manipulative, if not malevolent, "busybody" or "poltroon." Anticipating the essence of Fowler's reading, and emphasizing that the God of *PL* is "the God of Order," C. A. Patrides, for example, finds that the episode is one of the "countless occasions" revealing "God's endless efforts to prevent the cosmic structure from collapsing into dis-cord" (*Milton* 58). James H. Sims concludes, "Milton has, within the framework of his epic, made the sign of Libra a heavenly symbol similar to the Scriptural rainbow (Gen. 9:12–16); as the rainbow signifies God's promise never again to destroy all terrestrial life by water, the constellation of the 'golden Scales' symbolizes God's power as Creator, His power of deciding the outcome of the actions of His creatures, and ... His power to defeat Satan whenever it is His will to do so" (*Bible* 146). For Dennis H. Burden, "Milton, making a rhetori-cal identification of God's scales with the Libra constellation which can still be seen, reminds his readers (quite without threat) that God's judgment does not cease." Burden also insightfully points out, "God's foreknowledge is here interestingly and deliberately made conditional: Satan will be defeated *if* he resists" (29–30).

As these modern critics emphasize that God's foreknowledge, as well as his omnipotence and goodness, is revealed in the "golden Scales" episode, other modern critics develop and detail another reading similarly glimpsed in some of the earlier commentary, a reading that views the episode as a learning situation for the two warriors preparing to enter the "horrid fray." John M. Steadman and Mario A. DiCesare, for example, discuss this episode in terms of the Aristotelian notion of recognition. As Satan's confrontation with the angelic guard begins with an "incomplete Recognition," when Ithuriel and Zephon do not recognize Satan, so, Steadman explains, "The scene concludes with a Discovery of a different sort—a Recognition not of persons, but of an 'inanimate thing,' the 'celestial Sign' whereby the Almighty prevents the outbreak of battle in Paradise" ("Recognition" 165; cf. Steadman in **823–56**). DiCesare understands the "golden Scales" as an epic device of recognition that removes the threat of the battle between Gabriel and Satan, reminding the epic characters, as well as the reader, that "the true contest is not between divinities or angelic powers, for those battles were over before they started" (*"Paradise Lost"* 43). Grant McColley suggests that Satan's own recognition may be incomplete, however, because, "without pausing to question the 'writing' in the heavens, Satan fled from Eden" (*"Paradise Lost": An Account* 162; also see Harding, *Club* 47–48). Esmond Marilla, Stanley Fish, and Alastair Fowler bring detailed attention to Gabriel's response to the "golden Scales." Marilla explains, "it is important to observe that even though Gabriel emphasizes his inability to conquer Satan, he nevertheless is resolute in his purpose to fight if Satan resists. It is Satan's own recognition of the meaning of the sign that averts the threatened onslaught, and in his flight we witness, in fact, the reward of Gabriel's sustaining faith in the celestial assurance of ultimate victory" (138). Asserting that God's judgment, as displayed by the scales, "extends to Gabriel in his capacity as a military functionary" (*Surprised* 174), Fish points out, "the scales are tipped against all battles ('all events, Battles, Realms'), and against all those who trust in their own strength," and "Gabriel knows it" (175). Fish explains that our reading of this incident in Book 4 will soon be influenced by Raphael's war-in-heaven narrative in Book 6, which will lead us to "realize that Gabriel is heroic here because he admits that, in the conventional sense, he cannot be" (176). Contending that "the weighing is quite differently understood by God, Gabriel and Satan," Alastair Fowler offers a very different reading of Gabriel's recognition experience. Fowler argues that "unless indeed he deliberately misapplies the omen in an exulting or gibing way, [Gabriel] clearly fails to grasp how much it signifies;

which is not surprising, in view of the strong probability that as yet he has had no news of the heavenly council on Predestination and the Fall." To Fowler's mind, what Gabriel sees in the movement of the scales is "simply a sign of judgment upon Satan, who is being weighed and found wanting." While God "is really pondering the consequences of Satan's 'parting' and of his remaining to 'fight'" as he hangs forth the scales, Fowler suggests that "Satan's interpretation may not be different from Gabriel's, if we take *scale* (1014) as 'balance.'" Because "the more usual sense of *scale,* except in a few set phrases, was 'pan of a balance,'" Fowler acknowledges, however, "that Satan may imagine that his destiny is being weighed against Gabriel's, in the Homeric (pagan) manner" (672–73).

The "golden Scales" episode figures significantly in a number of modern discussions of the overall structure of *PL.* Contending that Milton's purpose in moving from a ten-book to a twelve-book epic was "to reduce the structural emphasis on the Fall of man and to increase the emphasis on his restoration," Arthur E. Barker explains that "the prophetic note of *Paradise Lost* swells from the ambiguity of Satan's view from the steps that link Heaven and Earth, and of the scales seen aloft, through the victory of the Son in Heaven to Michael's final prophecy" ("Structural Pattern" 25). John T. Shawcross offers the traditional nod to the Homeric parallel for Milton's scales but brings more detailed attention to the epic's structure by considering Libra's place in the zodiac between "Virgo and Scorpio, that is, between innocence and evil." Developing this point, Shawcross explains, "At the same time Libra becomes Mercy set between Justice and the Truth of Man's failing (compare *Nativity Ode* 141–48), and the passage comments upon the beginning of Man's fall since the Sun enters Libra at the autumnal equinox, proceeding through evil (Scorpio), wounding (Sagittarius), and lust (Capricorn) before movement toward rebirth (Aries) is begun" (*Complete Poetry* 342). Also see Shawcross, "Balanced Structure" 708. Balachandra Rajan somewhat similarly points to the associations between the end of Book 4 and the epic's closing books. Discussing the style of *PL,* "the presence of the whole poem behind its details" (*Lofty Rhyme* 108), Rajan writes, "Nor must we forget the images that end Book IV and initiate Book XII, which whatever else they may be doing, also suspend process to make us aware of pattern" (109). Finally, drawing links with earlier passages such as 4.354–55 and 3.555–61, Alastair Fowler discusses the "golden Scales" episode as the "culmination in the development of the Balance image-complex." Fowler associates Milton's treatment of the image with Spenser's in *The Faerie Queene* and argues that in

Milton's presentation here in Book 4, "the emphasis is on the Balance as a sign of God's predestinating justice" (671).

Finally, returning to the allusion to Daniel that figures in this episode, J. B. Broadbent extends the standard eighteenth century reading by associating the gigantic figure of Satan with Milton's reference to an "unactive and lifeless Colossus" in *Animad* (Patterson, *Works* 3:140) which, like the idol of Nebuchadnezzar's dream, would be thrown down by Scripture "like the chaff of the summer threshing-floors." Broadbent concludes: "This quotation from *Daniel* (ii.35) relates both the colossus of the prose and Satan in the poem to Nebuchadnezzar's dream of the idol; so when a few lines later God hangs out the golden scales in Heaven the immediate reference is not so much to the *Iliad* ... as to Daniel's interpretation of the writing on the wall; 'God hath numbered thy kingdom, and finished it.... Thou art weighed in the balances, and art found wanting' (V.26). Thus the balanced frailty of Paradise is ultimately secure in the determination of God's will" (*Some Graver Subject* 200–01).

991. *nor onely Paradise:* Newton (305) comments, "This representation of what must have happen'd, if Gabriel and Satan had encounter'd, is imaged in these few lines with a nobleness suitable to the occasion, and is an improvement upon a thought in Homer, where he represents *the terrors which must have attended the conflict of two such powers as Jupiter and Neptune,* Iliad. XV.224."

992–93. Masson argues that "Milton distinguishes here between the distant sphere of the fixed stars and the elements of fire, air, earth, and water, employed in the composition of the terrestrial world itself" (*Poetical Works* 3:183).

992. *commotion:* citing this line, the *OED*'s definition 2 is "Physical disturbance, more or less violent; tumultuous agitation of the parts or particles of any thing."

Cope: Verity defines this as "canopy," by reference to 3.556 (cf. the *OED* 7.d) or as "roof." Verity (474) notes a parallel in Shakespeare's *Pericles* 4.6.132, "the cheapest country under the cope." Alastair Fowler adds that "the metaphor had long been a dead one" (671). As does the *OED*, Merritt Y. Hughes (*Complete Poems* 301) explains that etymology relates *Cope* and "cape," and he cross-references 6.215.

994. *had gon to rack:* Edward S. Le Comte (*Yet Once More* 39) points to the recurrence of this phrase in 6.670 and associates it with references to hell trembling in 2.676, 788.

    rack: The *OED* sb. 5.1 defines this as "Destruction" and cites 11.821.

995. *violence:* See S. Ernest Sprott's note on *violate* in **883**.

998. *Astrea:* Charles Grosvenor Osgood (51) points out that in Hesiod's *Works and Days* 197–201, "we find that Aidos and Nemesis, after the golden age, clothe their fair bodies in white robes, and ascend to the abode of immortals, leaving men to grievous affliction. In Latin writers it is Pudicita and Astraea (Justice) who are the last of the gods to leave earth (Juv[enal] *Sat[ires]* 6.19ff.; Ov[id] *Met[amorphoses]* 1.149). We find a slightly different grouping in Horace's lament for Quinctilius [*Odes* 1.24.6–7]: 'Pudor et Justitiae soror, Incorrupta Fides, nudaque Veritas'; 'Honour, and Justice's sister, Loyalty unshaken, and candid Truth.' Among later poets it is Dike (Justice) who leaves the earth and Aratus (*Phaen[omena]* 96ff) describes her in the form of the constellation Virgo (Astraea, P. L. 998), which she assumed in heaven." See Hume in **990–1004**.

1000–01. *with ballanc't Aire / In counterpoise:* Hume (167) explains, "Sustained and supported equally in the Air by its own counterpoise, according to the Opinion, That the Earth hangs by an Equilibration of its parts to the Centre of Gravity," and then adds the following passage from Ovid's *Metamorphoses* 1.13: "Ponderibus librata suis"; "Poised by her own weight."

1000. *The pendulous round Earth:* Hume (167) refers this phrasing to Job 26.7: "He stretcheth out the north over the empty place, and hangeth the earth upon nothing," to which Todd ([1842], 2:114) adds a reference to "pendulous air" in Shakespeare's *King Lear* 3.4.69, as well as "Qui *pendulum telluris orbem /* Iapeti colitis nepotes"; "Ye that dwell on the pendent orb of earth, ye children's children of Iapetus!" in Milton's own *Procan* 3–4. A. W. Verity (474–75) claims, "This is what Bacon means by 'the pensileness of the earth'" (*The Advancement of Learning* [*Works* 6:140]). Edward S. Le Comte (*Yet Once More* 105) cross-references 2.1052, "This pendent world," and adds "pendulus orbis" ("the pendent earth") from Milton's *El* 1.76 to Todd's earlier reference to *Procan*.

pendulous: A. W. Verity glosses this as "hanging," and "as the central body," and cross-references *hung* in 7.242 and in *Nat* 122. Citing this line from *PL* 4, the *OED* 1.c defines *pendulous* as "Hanging or floating in the air or in space."

1001. *counterpoise:* Hume defines this as "In equal weight" (167), while the *OED* 3.b, quoting Milton's line, defines it as "The state of being balanced; equilibrium." The first figurative use of this term as cited by the *OED* appears in Milton's *Tetr:* "Others coming without authority from God, shall change this counterpoise" (Patterson, *Works* 4:161).

ponders: while A. W. Verity simply notes "weighs" (475), and Merritt Y. Hughes (*Complete Poems* 301) supports that meaning by reference to the word's Latin roots, Robert Martin Adams identifies "a half pun" here where "either God or his heavenly scales may be the subject of the verb in the phrase 'now ponders all events,' since here the ideas of weight and reflection are almost equally balanced" (86). Cf. Hume's use of *ponder* and *preponderate,* as well as Fowler's response to Empson's claim about "the Latin pun on ponder" in **990–1004**.

1003. *sequel:* Bentley suggests that *signal,* not *sequel,* was Milton's intended word: "The Ascending Weight, *Satan*'s, was the Signal to Him of Defeat; the Descending, *Gabriel*'s, the Signal to Him of Victory" (144). In rejecting Bentley's proposed change, Pearce (150) anticipates the critical readings to follow: "They were both Signals (if Signals) to Satan only, for he only was *weigh'd, v.* 1012, and 1014." Pearce assumes that "Dr. B[entley] and probably many others have misunderstood M[ilton]'s Thought about the Scales, judging of it by what they read of *Jupiter*'s Scales in *Homer* and *Virgil;* the Account of which is very different from This of *Milton:* for in them the Fates of the two Combatants are weigh'd one against the other, and the descent of one of the Scales foreshew'd the Death of him whose Fate lay in that Scale, *quo vergat pondere lethum[;* 'and with whose weight death sinks down' (*Aeneid* 12.727)]: whereas in M[ilton] nothing is weigh'd but what relates to Satan only, and in the two Scales are weigh'd the two different Events of his Retreating and his Fighting" (151; see **990–1004** for the detailed critical discussion of Milton's debt to Homer and Virgil in the "golden Scales" episode). Newton (306–08) and Todd ([1842], 2:114–15) quote Bentley and Pearce, but their readings support Pearce's. Masson similarly concludes his rehearsal of the argument (*Poetical Works* 3:183–84). Merritt Y. Hughes simply glosses *sequel* as "consequence," without noting any of the debate about meaning (*Complete Poems* 301). Cf. *sequel* in 10.334.

1004. *and kickt the beam:* Hume explains, "The less Weighty Scale, signifying the Sequel or Issue of Satans encountring the Angelick Guard, was quickly mounted aloft, and smote the *Beam,* which is the Cross-piece to whose Extremities the Scales are fastened; the Balance equally pois'd upon its central Point" (168). Dryden, who deletes the scale device from the end of the third act of *The State of Innocence* and has Gabriel and Ithuriel simply walk Satan out of the garden, nevertheless reveals his approval of the image by adapting it, as Verity (475) notes, for use in *The Hind and the Panther* 2.622–24 (*Works* 3:157): "If such a one you find, let truth prevail; / Till when, your weights will in the balance fail; / A Church unprincipled kicks up the scale." Unlike Dryden, Landor disapproves of Milton's phrase, finding "the vulgarity of kicking the beam...intolerable" (26–27). Defining *beam,* the *OED* I.6.b considers the phrase *To kick* or *strike the beam:* "(of one scale of a balance) to be so lightly loaded that it flies up and strikes the beam; to be greatly outweighed." This entry is cross-referenced, and 1004 is cited, in the *OED*'s definition 4.d of *kick:* "To strike (anything) with a violent impact."

1005. Todd ([1842], 2:115) sees a verbal parallel between Milton's "Which *Gabriel* spying" and the beginning of a sequence in Giovanni Trissino's *Italia Liberata* 27.709–11, where with golden scales the Creator weighs the fates of the Romans and the Goths.

1006–13. E. M. W. Tillyard and John M. Steadman analyze the nature of Gabriel's heroism as he addresses Satan following the prophetic movement of God's scales. Tillyard writes, "The brevity and simplicity of his [Gabriel's] speech are the perfect mirror of what he and his guard stand for; absolute humility joined with absolute assurance. And yet in 'though doubld now / To trample thee as mire' Gabriel touches a height of passion not to be surpassed in poetry. Further, the speech is essentially (though not in any crude or offensive way) Protestant, in that it expresses that luminous sense of uninterrupted intercourse between creator and creature which though not in the least an exclusively Protestant doctrine was nevertheless the peculiar attribute of the highest Protestant vision" (*Studies* 65). In Gabriel's speech, Steadman hears Milton's critique of *fortezza* ("strength of mind or body"), which had "served as the normal standard for evaluating or comparing heroes of different ages, nations, or religions" (*Milton* 23), and, Steadman argues, "Since power is really the gift of God, bestowed on whom He wills, the creature has no just grounds for glorying in his own strength. He can only confess his own weakness and acknowledge his dependence on divine power. Trust in his own strength—or (in theological terms) 'carnal reliance'—thus stands in direct opposition to trust in God. The ideal of heroic fortitude yields inevitably to that of heroic faith" (29–30).

1008–09. Newton clarifies the meaning of the personal pronouns here: "*Thine* and *mine* refer to *strength,* v. 1006, not to arms, the substantive preceding" (308).

1010. *To trample thee as mire:* Todd ([1842], 2:115), crediting John Gillies, identifies the biblical parallel in Isa. 10.6, "To tread them down like the mire in the streets," and adds a reference to 2 Sam. 22.43.

    mire: the *OED* 2 cites this line as it defines *mire:* "wet or soft mud, slush, dirt."

1013–15. The critically contentious topic of Milton's characterization of Satan, which dominates so much modern criticism on *PL,* colors the reading of his exit, as it has colored the reading of his behavior in the garden throughout Book 4. Speaking for those who find that Milton degrades Satan is John Peter as he considers Satan's flight: "one of the most significant qualities that Satan has is suddenly abandoned, his habitual disregard for facts…[and] the poet's opportunism is even more blatant." Peter therefore once again concludes, "Waldock's interpretation is the simple truth: 'he is not a changed Satan, he is a *new* Satan.' Worst of all he is a Satan from whom all real interest has drained away" (55; in **32–113**, see Waldock, and see others contributing to the debate about Milton's presentation of Satan). A voice for those who find that Satan degenerates is James H. Sims: "He who proudly vaunts his undaunted courage while he is surrounded by his followers in Hell is full of doubt and inner turmoil when he is alone…; and when he is faced with clear evidence that God has determined the outcome of battle against him, he flies from danger" (*Bible* 179).

    Writing long before the debate about Milton's presentation of Satan erupted in the mid-twentieth century, Thomas De Quincey explains that he admires the "fine machinery" involved in Milton's presentation of Satan, including the unfolding of the association between Satan and darkness, an association that elicits commentary from a number of critics. Noting that as Satan flees the garden, he is now identified as "The Fiend…under the fine machinery used by Milton for exalting or depressing the ideas of his nature," De Quincey observes, "The darkness flying with him, naturally we have the feeling that he is the darkness, and that all darkness has some essential relation to Satan" ("Question" 418). Among the many who share De Quincey's understanding of the association between Satan and the darkness is Patrick Hume: "Darkness, and the Prince of it, took their flight together" (168). As additional editors and critics look to the final line in Book 4, the association between Satan and the darkness expands to enfold the murmuring that also marks his flight. Todd ([1842], 2:116), for example, offers Charles Dunster's glance at Tasso's *Gerusalemme Liberata* 9.65: "Essi *gemendo abbandonar'* le belle / Region' de la luce"; "Forsaking / the golden stars and the lovely realm of light, / they moaned" (trans. Anthony Esolen). Anne Davidson Ferry develops this image cluster as a device by which Satan's exit from the garden recalls his initial appearance in hell among its "doleful shades" (1.65), a phrase that Ferry argues "suggests not only shadows but ghosts, departed spirits mourning the loss of the world of light. This double meaning is again associated with Satan when he flees from Eden 'Murmuring, and with him fled the shades of night' (IV, 1015)" (*Milton's Epic Voice* 172–73; also see Ferry in **138** and **572**). For James H. Sims (*Bible* 112), the end of Book 4 recalls the allusion to Ps. 74 at 724–25, whereas for Merritt Y. Hughes it recalls the end of Book 2: "Like Book II, Book IV ends with a transition from darkness to day" (*Complete Poems* 302).

In Milton's description of Satan fleeing with "the shades of night" (1015), J. B. Broadbent sees "an ominously brief chronographia" (*Some Graver Subject* 201), and this attention to time is variously developed by critics commenting on the last line of Book 4. Jon S. Lawry, for example, explains that the "shades of night" indicate "both Satan's present identity and his eschatological fate," as the murmuring "suggests the inarticulate hissing of the serpent he is to become in his final degradation" (*Shadow* 181). Irene Samuel's appreciation for Milton's struggle to delay the losing of paradise touches not only her commentary on the opening 12 lines of Book 4 but also her commentary on its close: "His [Satan's] confrontation by Ithuriel and Zephon, and again by Gabriel, in which he has to hear some home truths, simply ends with his removal. And with that thrusting out of Satan, and the thrusting off of the fall until Book IX, Eden can become increasingly Edenic, not merely the place that is going to be lost, but positively the state of joyous growth, for which innocence, not hurt-fulness, is only the negative name" ("*Paradise Lost* as Mimesis" 22). Considering the relationship between the end of *PL* 4 and the end of Virgil's *Aeneid,* Davis P. Harding and Stanley Fish develop the chronographia topic. Harding explains that the death of Turnus that marks the end of Virgil's epic "did not have its complete meaning in itself. With him perished a whole creed, a whole outlook on life. Satan does not perish, but it is not only he who has been weighed in the balance and been found wanting. It is his code, the heroic values he incorporates, the principle of 'what arms can doe.' Henceforth he will forgo the methods of Achilles and Turnus and resort to guile, the method of Odysseus" (*Club* 50). Fish argues that Turnus's "defiance of the fates and his inevitable defeat" are "comprehensible only in the light of what Satan did in a past that our time signatures cannot name and is about to do in a present (poem time) that is increasingly difficult to identify. Whatever the allusion adds to the richness of the poem's texture or to Milton's case for superiority in the epic genre, it is also one more assault on the confidence of a reader who is met at every turn with demands his intellect cannot even consider" (*Surprised* 37). David Daiches anticipates Fish's reading of the atmosphere of darkness at the end of Book 4. To Daiches, the "sullen darkness, full of foreboding" is removed from Satan to the reader: "having seen a demonstration of God's intervention we are inevitably reminded again of the whole question of why God should stand idly by and allow Satan to corrupt and destroy His creatures, a question which Milton should not have allowed to emerge at this point" (*Milton* 194).

Bibliography

Editions

Bentley, Richard, ed. *Dr. Bentley's Emendations on the Twelve Books of Milton's "Paradise Lost."* London, 1732.

Browne, R. C., ed. *English Poems by John Milton.* 2 vols. 1866. New ed. edited by Henry Bradley. Oxford: Clarendon, 1906.

Bush, Douglas, ed. *The Complete Poetical Works of John Milton.* Boston: Houghton Mifflin, 1965.

Darbishire, Helen. *The Poetical Works of John Milton.* 2 vols. Oxford: Clarendon, 1952.

Dodd, William. *A Familiar Explanation of the Poetical Works of Milton.* London: J. and R. Tonson, 1762.

Fowler, Alastair, ed. *Paradise Lost.* In *The Poems of John Milton,* 417–1060. Ed. John Carey and Alastair Fowler. London: Longmans, Green, 1968.

Hawkey, John. *Paradise Lost. A Poem in Twelve Books.* Dublin, 1747.

Hughes, Merritt Y, ed. *Complete Poems and Selected Prose.* Indianapolis, IN: Odyssey Press, 1959.

Hume, Patrick. *The Poetical Works of Mr. John Milton.* London, 1695.

Keightley, Thomas, ed. *The Poems of John Milton, with Notes.* 2 vols. London: Chapman and Hall, 1859.

Masson, David, ed. *Poetical Works of John Milton.* London: Macmillan, 1874.

Mitford, John, ed. *The Poetical Works of John Milton.* Boston: Hilliard, Gray, 1836.

Moody, William Vaughan, ed. *The Complete Poetical Works of John Milton.* Boston and New York: Houghton Mifflin, 1899.

Newton, Thomas, ed. *Paradise Lost.* London, 1749.

Patterson, Frank Allen, ed. *The Student's Milton.* Rev. ed. New York: Appleton-Century-Crofts, 1933.

———. *The Works of John Milton.* 18 vols. in 21. New York: Columbia University Press, 1931.

Shawcross, John T., ed. *The Complete Poetry of John Milton.* Garden City, NY: Doubleday, 1963.

Stebbing, H., ed. *The Complete Poetical Works of John Milton.* New York: D. Appleton, 1856.

Todd, Henry John, ed. *The Poetical Works of John Milton.* 6 vols. London, 1801.

———. *The Poetical Works of John Milton.* 2nd ed. 7 vols. London, 1809.

———. *The Poetical Works of John Milton.* 6 vols. London, 1826.

———. *The Poetical Works of John Milton.* 4th ed. 4 vols. London: 1842.

Vaughan, Robert, ed., *Milton's "Paradise Lost." Illustrated by Gustave Dore.* London: Cassell, Petter, and Galpin, 1866.

Verity, A. W., ed. *Paradise Lost.* 1910. Reprint, Cambridge: Cambridge University Press, 1921.

Wright, B. A., ed. *Milton's "Paradise Lost."* New York: Barnes and Noble, 1962.

Commentaries and Reference Works

Abercrombie, Lascelles. *The Epic.* London: Secker, 1914. Reprint, Freeport, NY: Books for Libraries Press, 1969.

Adams, Robert Martin. *Ikon: John Milton and the Modern Critics.* Ithaca, NY: Cornell University Press, 1955.

Addison, Joseph. *The Spectator.* 5 vols. Ed. Donald F. Bond. Oxford: Clarendon, 1965.

———. *The Tatler.* 3 vols. Ed. Donald F. Bond. Oxford: Clarendon, 1987.

Aelian [Tacticus Aelianus]. *The Tactics of Aelian.* London: Cox and Baylis, 1814.

Aeschylus. *Prometheus Bound.* In *Aeschylus,* vol. 1, 209–315. Trans. Herbert Weir Smyth. London: William Heinemann; New York: G. P. Putnam's Sons, 1922.

Agrippa, Henry Cornelius. *Three Books of Occult Philosophy.* Trans. J. F. London, 1651.

Alciati, Andrea. *Emblemata cum Commentariis.* Padua, 1621. Reprint, New York: Garland, 1976.

Alexander, Sir William. *The Poetical Works of Sir William Alexander, Earl of Stirling.* 2 vols. Ed. L. E. Kastner and H. B. Charlton. Edinburgh and London: William Blackwood, 1921–29.

Allen, Don Cameron. "Description as Cosmos: The Visual Image in *Paradise Lost.*" In *The Harmonious Vision: Studies in Milton's Poetry,* 95–109. Baltimore: Johns Hopkins University Press, 1954. Enlarged ed., 1970.

———. "Milton's Eve and the Evening Angels." *Modern Language Notes* 75 (1960): 108–09.

Alley, William. *Ptochomuseion. The Poore Mans Librarie.* London, 1571.

Ambrose. *De Paradiso.* In *Patrologiae Cursus Completus. Series Latina,* vol. 14, cols. 275–314. Ed. Jacques-Paul Migne. Paris, 1845.

————. *Hexameron.* In *Patrologiae Cursus Completus. Series Latina,* vol. 14, cols. 123–274. Ed. Jacques-Paul Migne. Paris, 1845.

————. *In Psalmum CXVIII.* In *Patrologiae Cursus Completus. Series Latina,* vol. 15, cols. 1197–1526. Ed. Jacques-Paul Migne. Paris, 1845.

Andreini, Giambattista. *L'Adamo.* Milan, 1613.

Apollonius Rhodius. *The Argonautica.* Trans. R. C. Seaton. Cambridge, MA: Harvard University Press, 1912.

Appianus of Alexandria. *Appian's "Roman History."* Vols. 1–2. Trans. Horace White. New York: Macmillan, 1912.

Aquinas, Thomas. *De Regimine Principum.* Rev. ed. Taurini: Marietti, 1948.

————. *The "Summa Theologica" of St. Thomas Aquinas.* 22 vols. Trans. Fathers of the English Dominican Province. London: Burns, Oates and Washbourne, 1922–37.

Aratus. *Phaenomena.* In *Callimachus: "Hymns" and "Epigrams"; Lycophron; Aratus,* 206–99. Rev. ed. Trans. A. W. Mair and G. R. Mair. London: Heinemann; Cambridge, MA: Harvard University Press, 1955.

Ariosto, Lodovico. *Orlando Furioso.* Venice, 1584.

Aristotle. *De Partibus Animalium.* Trans. A. L. Peck. In *Parts of Animals. Movement of Animals. Progression of Animals,* 4–434. Rev. ed. Trans. A. L. Peck and E. S. Forster. Cambridge, MA: Harvard University Press, 1961.

————. *Meteorologica.* Trans. H. D. P. Lee. Cambridge, MA: Harvard University Press, 1952.

————. *Poetics.* In *Aristotle: The Poetics. "Longinus": On the Sublime. Demetrius: On Style.* Trans. W. Hamilton Frye, 1–118. Cambridge, MA: Harvard University Press; London: Heinemann. Rev. ed. 1932. Reprint 1960.

Arnold, Matthew. "The Study of Poetry." In *The Works of Matthew Arnold,* vol. 4, 1–41. London: Macmillan, 1903–04.

Ashmore, John. *Certain Selected Odes of Horace.* London, 1621.

Augustine. *The City of God.* Trans. Marcus Dods. New York: Random House, 1950.

————. *Confessions.* Trans. R. S. Pine-Coffin. Baltimore: Penguin, 1961.

————. *Contra Secundam Juliani Responsionem Imperfectum Opus.* In *Patrologiae Cursus Completus,* vol. 44, cols. 1049–1608. Ed. Jacques-Paul Migne. Paris, 1865.

————. *The Literal Meaning of Genesis.* 2 vols. Trans. John Hammond Taylor. New York: Newman Press, 1982.

Ausonius. "Epigram 72." In *Ausonius,* vol. 2, 196–97. Trans. Hugh G. Evelyn White. Cambridge, MA: Harvard University Press, 1919.

Avitus. *De Originali Peccato.* In *Patrologiae Cursus Completus. Series Latina,* vol. 59, cols. 329–38. Ed. Jaques-Paul Migne. Paris, 1847.

Bacon, Sir Francis. *The Works of Francis Bacon.* 14 vols. Ed. James Spedding, Robert Leslie Ellis, and Douglas Denon Heath. London: Longman, 1858–74.

Bailey, John Cann. *Milton.* London: Oxford University Press, 1915.

Baldwin, Edward Chauncey. "Some Extra-Biblical Semitic Influences upon Milton's Story of the Fall of Man." *Journal of English and Germanic Philology* 28 (1929): 366–401.

Barker, Arthur E. "Structural and Doctrinal Pattern in Milton's Later Poems." In *Essays in English Literature from the Renaissance to the Victorian Age: Presented to A. S. P. Woodhouse*, 169–94. Ed. Millar MacLure and F. W. Watt. Toronto: University of Toronto Press, 1964.

———. "Structural Pattern in *Paradise Lost*." *Philological Quarterly* 28 (1949): 17–30.

Barstow, Marjorie. "Milton's Use of Forms of Epic Address." *Modern Language Notes* 31 (1916): 120–21.

Bartholomaeus, Anglicus. *De Proprietatibus Rerum*. Trans. John Trevisa. In *"On the Properties of Things": John Trevisa's Translation of Bartolomaeus Anglicus "De Proprietatibus Rerum."* 3 vols. Ed. M. C. Seymour. Oxford: Clarendon, 1975–88.

Basil. *Homily 1*. In *Patrologiae Cursus Completus. Series Graeca*, vol. 29, cols. 3–28. Ed. Jacques-Paul Migne. Paris, 1857.

———. *Homily 5*. In *Patrologiae Cursus Completus. Series Graeca*, vol. 29, cols. 93–118. Ed. Jacques-Paul Migne. Paris, 1857.

———. *Oration 3*. In *Patrologiae Cursus Completus. Series Graeca*, vol. 30, cols. 61–72. Ed. Jacques-Paul Migne. Paris, 1857.

———. *Quod Deus Non est Auctor Malorom*. In *Patrologiae Cursus Completus. Series Graeca*, vol. 31, cols. 329–54. Ed. Jacques-Paul Migne. Paris, 1857.

Beaumont, Francis. *The Fair Maid of the Inn*. Ed. Fredson Bowers. In *The Dramatic Works in the Beaumont and Fletcher Canon*, vol. 10, 553–657. Ed. Fredson Bowers. Cambridge: Cambridge University Press, 1966–96.

Beaumont, Joseph. *Psyche, or Love's Mystery, In XXIV Cantos: Displaying the Intercourse Betwixt Christ, and the Soul*. 2nd ed. In *The Complete Poems of Dr. Joseph Beaumont*, ed. Alexander B. Grosart, vols. 1–2: 1–231. Edinburgh: Constable, 1880. Reprint, New York: AMS, 1967.

Beckford, William. *Vathek*. London, 1868.

Becon, Thomas. *The Boke of Matrimony*. In *The Workes of Thomas Becon*, vol. 1, 558–678. London, 1564.

Bede, the Venerable. *Bede's "Ecclesiastical History of the English People."* Ed. Bertram Colgrave and R. A. B. Mynors. Oxford: Clarendon, 1969.

Bell, Millicent. "The Fallacy of the Fall in *Paradise Lost*." *PMLA* 68 (1953): 863–83.

Bellarmine, Robert [Roberto Bellarmino]. *Roberti Bellarmini e Societate Jesu, S. R. E. Cardinalis, Disputationes de Controversiis Christianae Fidei*. Editio ultima. Vol. 3. Coloniae Agrippinae: Apud Joannem Gymnicum, 1628.

Belloc, Hilaire. *Milton*. Philadelphia: J. B. Lippincott; London: Cassell, 1935.

Benlowe, Edward. *Theophila, or Loves Sacrifice*. London, 1652.

Benson, A. C. *Edward Fitzgerald*. London: Macmillan, 1905.

Benson, William. *Letters Concerning Poetical Translations, and Virgil's and Milton's Art of Verse, etc.* London, 1739.

Bercovitch, Sacvan. "Three Perspectives on Reality in *Paradise Lost*." *University of Windsor Review* 1 (1965): 239–56.

Berek, Peter. "'Plain' and 'Ornate' Styles and the Structure of *Paradise Lost*." *PMLA* 85 (1970): 237–46.

Bertschinger, Max. "Man's Part in the Fall of Woman." *English Studies* 31 (1950): 49–64.

Biblia Sacra. Lugduni, 1558.

Blackmore, Richard. *King Arthur*. London, 1697.

Blaeu, Willem. *Geographie Blaviane*. Amsterdam, 1667.

———. *Le Theatre du Monde*. Amsterdam, 1638.

Blake, William. *The Marriage of Heaven and Hell*. In *The Complete Poetry and Prose of William Blake*, 33–44. New rev. ed. Ed. David V. Erdman. Berkeley and Los Angeles: University of California Press, 1982.

Blondel, Jacques. "Milton's Eden." *English Studies Today*, 4th ser., 255–65 Rome: Edizioni di Storia e Letteratura, 1966.

Bochart, Samuel. *Geographiae Sacrae*. Francofurti ad Moenum, 1646.

Bodkin, Maud. *Archetypal Patterns in Poetry*. Oxford: Oxford University Press, 1934.

Boethius. *The Consolation of Philosophy*. Trans. S. J. Tester. In *The Theological Tractates*, 130–435. New ed. Trans. H. F. Stewart, E. K. Rand, and S. J. Tester. Cambridge, MA: Harvard University Press, 1973.

Bohun, Edmund. *A Geographical Dictionary*. London, 1688.

Bonaventure. *Opera Theologica Selecta*. Florence: Typographia Collegii S. Bonaventurae, 1934–49.

Bowra, Cecil Maurice. *From Virgil to Milton*. London: Macmillan, 1948.

Boyette, Purvis E. "Milton's Eve and the Neoplatonic Graces." *Renaissance Quarterly* 20 (1967): 341–44.

Boyle, Roger. *A Treatise of the Art of War*. London, 1677.

Bridges, Robert. *Milton's Prosody*. Oxford: Clarendon, 1893. Reprint, 1965.

Bright, Timothie. *A Treatise of Melancholie*. London, 1586.

Broadbent, J. B. "Milton's Paradise." *Modern Philology* 51 (1953–54): 160–76.

———. *Some Graver Subject: An Essay on "Paradise Lost."* London: Chatto and Windus; New York: Barnes and Noble, 1960.

Brockbank, Philip. "'Within the Visible Diurnal Spheare': The Moving World of *Paradise Lost*." In *Approaches to "Paradise Lost": The York Tercentenary Lectures*, 199–221. Ed. C. A. Patrides. London: Edward Arnold, 1968.

Brooke, Stopford Augustus. *Milton*. London: Macmillan, 1879. Reprint, New York: AMS, 1973.

Brooks, Cleanth. "Eve's Awakening." In *Essays in Honor of Walter Clyde Curry*, 281–98. Ed. Alan Rudrum. Nashville, TN: Vanderbilt University Press, 1954.

———. "Milton and Critical Re-estimates." *PMLA* 66 (1951): 1045–54.

Brooks, Cleanth, and John Edward Hardy. *Poems of Mr. John Milton: The 1645 Edition with Essays in Analysis.* New York: Harcourt, 1951.

Browne, Sir Thomas. *The Works of Sir Thomas Browne.* 4 vols. 2nd ed. Ed. Geoffrey Keynes. Chicago: University of Chicago Press, 1964.

Bucanus, Guillaume. *Institutions of Christian Religion.* Trans. Robert Hill. London, 1606.

Bullough, Geoffrey. "Milton and Cats." In *Essays in English Literature from the Renaissance to the Victorian Age: Presented to A. S. P. Woodhouse,* 103–24. Ed. Millar MacLure and F. W. Watt. Toronto: University of Toronto Press, 1964.

Bunyan, John. *The Holy War, Made by Shaddai upon Diabolus.* Ed. Roger Sharrock and James F. Forrest. Oxford: Clarendon, 1980.

Burden, Dennis H. *The Logical Epic.* Cambridge, MA: Harvard University Press, 1967.

Burke, Edmund. *The Works of Edmund Burke, with a Memoir.* 3 vols. New York: Harper and Brothers, 1859.

Burton, Robert. *The Anatomy of Melancholy.* 3 vols. Ed. Thomas C. Faulkner, Nicolas K. Kiessling, and Rhonda L. Blair. Oxford: Clarendon, 1989–94.

Bush, Douglas. *English Literature in the Earlier Seventeenth Century, 1600–1660.* 2nd rev. ed. Oxford: Clarendon, 1962.

———. "Ironic and Ambiguous Allusion in *Paradise Lost.*" *Journal of English and Germanic Philology* 60 (1961): 631–40.

———. *Mythology and the Renaissance Tradition in English Poetry.* Minneapolis: University of Minnesota Press, 1932.

———. *"Paradise Lost" in Our Time.* Ithaca, NY: Cornell University Press, 1945.

———. *The Renaissance and English Humanism.* Toronto: University of Toronto Press, 1939.

Byron, Lord George Gordon. *The Complete Poetical Works.* 7 vols. Ed. Jerome J. McGann. Oxford: Clarendon, 1980–93.

Bysshe, Edward. *The Art of English Poetry.* 2nd ed. London, 1705.

Callimachus. "Hymn 1." In *Callimachus: "Hymns" and "Epigrams"; Lycophron; Aratus,* 36–47. Rev. ed. Trans A. W. Mair and G. R. Mair. Cambridge, MA: Harvard University Press, 1955.

Calvin, John. *Commentaries on the First Book of Moses Called Genesis.* 2 vols. Trans. John King. Edinburgh: Calvin Translation Society, 1847–50.

———. *Institutes of the Christian Religion.* Trans. Henry Beveridge. Edinburgh: Calvin Translation Society, 1845–46. Reprint, Grand Rapids, MI: Eerdmans, 1989.

Camerarius, Philipp. *The Living Librarie.* Trans. John Molle. London, 1621.

Camoens, Luis De. *The Lusiad, or Portugals Historicall Poem.* Trans. Richard Fanshaw. London, 1655.

Campanella, Tommaso. *A Defense of Galileo.* Trans. Richard J. Blackwell. Notre Dame, IN: University of Notre Dame Press, 1994.

Campbell, Thomas. *The Pleasures of Hope.* In *The Pleasures of Hope and Other Poems,* 8–51. New York: J. Gray, 1820.

Carew, Thomas. *The Poems of Thomas Carew with His Masque* Coelum Britannicum. Ed. Rhodes Dunlap. Oxford: Clarendon, 1949.

Carr, John. *The Stranger in Ireland.* London, 1806.

Cartari, Vicenzo. *Le Vere e Nove Imagini de gli Dei delli Antichi.* Padua, 1615. Reprint, New York: Garland, 1979.

Carver, P. L. "The Angels in *Paradise Lost.*" *Review of English Studies* 16 (1940): 415–31.

Casaubon, Isaac. *Auli Persi Flacci Satirarum Liber.* 3rd ed. London, 1647.

Cats, Jacob. '*S Weerelts Begin, Midden, Eynde, Bestoten in den Trou-Ringh, Met den Proef-Steen van den Selven.* In *Allede Wercken van den Herre Jacob Cats,* 2:1–48. Amsterdam, 1726.

Catullus. *The Poems of Gaius Valerius Catullus.* Trans. F. W. Cornish. In *Catulllus, Tibullus, and "Pervigilium Veneris,"* 1–183. Trans. F. W. Cornish, J. P. Postgate, and J. W. Mackail. Cambridge, MA: Harvard University Press, 1962.

Caussini, Niccolai. *De Eloquentia Sacra et Humana.* 3rd ed. Paris, 1630.

Cawley, Robert Ralston. *Milton and the Literature of Travel.* Princeton, NJ: Princeton University Press, 1951.

Caxton, William. *Life of Saint Anthony.* In *The Golden Legend,* vol. 1, 331–36. Ed. Frederick S. Ellis. Hammersmith: Kelmscott, 1892.

———. *Mirrour of the World.* Reprint, *Caxton's Mirrour of the World.* Ed. Oliver H. Prioe. London: Kegan Paul, Trench, Trubner and Oxford University Press, 1913 (for 1912).

Cervantes de Saavedra, Miguel de. *Don Quixote.* Trans. Edith Grossman. New York: Harper-Collins, 2003.

Chapman, George. *Ovid's Banquet of Sense.* In *The Works of George Chapman,* vol. 2, 19–37. Ed. Richard Horne Shepherd. London: Chatto and Windus, 1904–24.

Chaucer, Geoffrey. *Troilus and Criseyde.* In *Chaucer's Major Poetry,* ed. Albert C. Baugh, 74–211. New York: Appleton-Century-Crofts, 1963.

Chernaik, Warren L. *The Poetry of Limitation: A Study of Edmund Waller.* New Haven, CT: Yale University Press, 1968.

Chrysostom. *Homily 18 on Genesis 4.* In *Homilies on Genesis: 18–45,* trans. Robert C. Hill, 3–20. Washington, DC: Catholic University Press, 1990.

Ciardi, John, trans. *The Divine Comedy,* by Dante Alighieri. New York: W. W. Norton, 1961.

Cicero. *De Legibus.* In *De Re Publica, De Legibus,* trans. Clinton Walker Keyes, 296–519. Cambridge, MA: Harvard University Press; London: Heinemann, 1928; reprint, 1966.

———. *De Natura Deorum.* In *De Natura Deorum: Academica,* 1–396. Trans. H. Rackham. Cambridge, MA: Harvard University Press, 1933.

———. *De Officiis.* Trans. Walter Miller. Cambridge, MA: Harvard University Press, 1913. Reprint, Cambridge, MA: Harvard University Press; London: Heinemann, 1968.

———. "The Second Speech against Gaius Verres: Book IV." In *The Verrine Orations,* vol. 2, 282–467. Trans. L. H. G. Greenwood. London: Heinemann; New York: Putnam, 1928–35. Reprint, Cambridge, MA: Harvard University Press, 1960.

———. *Tusculan Disputations.* Rev. ed. Trans. J. E. King. Cambridge, MA: Harvard University Press; London: Heinemann, 1945.

Clark, Evert Mordecai. "Milton's Abyssinian Paradise." *University of Texas Studies in English* 29 (1950): 129–50.

Clark, Ira. "Milton and the Image of God." *Journal of English and Germanic Philology* 68 (1969): 422–31.

Claudian. *Rape of Proserpine.* In *Claudian,* vol. 2, 292–377. Trans. Maurice Platnauer. Cambridge, MA: Harvard University Press, 1922.

Cockeram, Henry. *The English Dictionarie of 1623.* London, 1623. Reprint, New York: Huntington, 1930.

Coffin, Charles Monroe. "Creation and the Self in *Paradise Lost.*" *ELH* 29 (1962): 1–18.

Coleridge, Samuel Taylor. "Kubla Khan," in *The Collected Works of Samuel Taylor Coleridge,* vol. 16, 512–14. Ed. Kathleen Coburn. Princeton, NJ: Princeton University Press, 1969–2001.

Colie, Rosalie L. "Time and Eternity: Paradox and Structure in *Paradise Lost.*" *Journal of the Warburg and Courtauld Institutes* 23 (1960): 127–38.

Collins, William. *The Works of William Collins.* Ed. Richard Wendorf and Charles Ryskamp. Oxford: Clarendon, 1979.

Conti, Natale. *Mythologiae.* Padua, 1616. Reprint, *Mythologiae. Natale Conti. Mythologia, M. Antonio.* New York: Garland, 1979.

Cope, Jackson I. *The Metaphoric Structure of "Paradise Lost."* Baltimore: Johns Hopkins University Press, 1962.

Corcoran, Sister Mary Irma. *Milton's Paradise with Reference to the Hexameral Background.* Washington, DC: Catholic University Press, 1945.

Cowper, William. *The Iliad and Odyssey of Homer, Translated into English Blank Verse.* 2 vols. London: 1791.

Crashaw, Richard. *The Poems English Latin and Greek of Richard Crashaw.* 2nd ed. Ed. L. C. Martin. Oxford: Clarendon, 1957.

The Creacion of the World: A Critical Edition and Translation. Ed. and trans. Paula Neuss. New York: Garland, 1983.

Curry, Walter Clyde. *Milton's Ontology Cosmogony and Physics.* Lexington: University Press of Kentucky, 1957.

Daiches, David. *Milton.* 2nd rev. ed. London: Hutchinson, 1959.

Damascene, John. *De Fide Orthodoxus.* In *Patrologiae Cursus Completus. Series Graeca,* vol. 94, cols. 789–1228. Ed. Jacques-Paul Migne. Paris, 1860.

Daniello, Bernardino. *L'Espositione di Bernardino Daniello da Lucca Sopra "La Comedia" di Dante*. Ed. Robert Hollander and Jeffrey Schnapp, with Kevin Brownlee and Nancy Vickers. Hanover, NH: University Press of New England, 1989.

Daniells, Roy. "A Happy Rural Seat of Various View." In *Paradise Lost: A Tercentenary Tribute*, 3–17. Ed. Balachandra Rajan. Toronto: University of Toronto Press, 1967.

———. *Milton, Mannerism and Baroque*. Toronto: University of Toronto Press, 1963.

Daniélou, Jean. *Origen*. Trans. Walter Mitchell. London: Sheed and Ward, 1955.

Dante. *Convivio*. In *Opere di Dante Alighieri*, 127–291. Ed. Fredi Chiappelli. Milan: Ugo Mursia, 1965.

———. *Inferno*. In *Opere di Dante Alighieri*, ed. Fredi Chiappelli, 449–568. Milan: Ugo Mursia, 1965.

———. *Paradiso*. In *Opere di Dante Alighieri*, ed. Fredi Chiappelli, 689–808. Milan: Ugo Mursia, 1965.

———. *Purgatorio*. In *Opere di Dante Alighieri*, ed. Fredi Chiappelli, 569–688. Milan: Ugo Mursia, 1965.

Darbishire, Helen. *The Early Lives of Milton*. London: Constable, 1932.

———. *Milton's "Paradise Lost."* London: Oxford University Press, 1951.

———. "Milton's Poetic Language." In *Essays and Studies, Being Volume Ten of This New Series of Essays and Studies Collected for the English Association by Margaret Willy*, 31–52. London: John Murray, 1957.

Davies, John. *Wittes Pilgrimage, through a World of Amorous Sonnets*. London, 1605 (?).

Day, Douglas. "Adam and Eve in *Paradise Lost*, IV." *Texas Studies in Literature and Language* 3 (1961): 369–81.

Denham, John. "Cooper's Hill." In *The Poetical Works of Sir John Denham*, 63–89. 2nd ed. Ed. Theodore Howard Banks. Hamden, CT: Archon, 1969.

De Quincey, Thomas. "On Milton." In *The Collected Writings of Thomas De Quincey*, vol. 10, 395–406. Ed. David Masson. Edinburgh: Adam and Charles Black, 1890. Reprint, New York: AMS, 1968.

———. "Question as to Actual Slips in Milton." In *Collected Writings*, vol. 10, 414–24. Ed. David Masson. Edinburgh: Adam and Charles Black, 1890. Reprint, New York: AMS, 1968.

Dennis, John. *The Critical Works of John Dennis*. 2 vols. Ed. Edward Niles Hooker. Baltimore: Johns Hopkins University Press, 1939–43.

DiCesare, Mario A. "'Advent'rous Song'; The Texture of Milton's Epic." In *Language and Style in Milton: A Symposium in Honor of the Tercentenary of "Paradise Lost,"* 1–29. Ed. Ronald David Emma and John T. Shawcross. New York: Frederick Ungar, 1967.

———. "*Paradise Lost* and Epic Tradition." In *Milton Studies*, vol. 1, 31–50. Ed. James L. Simmonds. Pittsburgh: University of Pittsburgh Press, 1969.

Diekhoff, John S. "Eve's Dream and the Paradox of Fallible Perfection." *Milton Quarterly* 4 (1970): 5–7.

————. *Milton's "Paradise Lost": A Commentary on the Argument*. Oxford: Oxford University Press, 1946.

————. "Rhyme in *Paradise Lost*." *PMLA* 49 (1934): 539–43.

Diodati, Giovanni. *Pious Annotations upon the Holy Bible*. London, 1643.

Diodorus Siculus. *The Library of History*. 12 vols. Trans. C. H. Oldfather. London: Heinemann; Cambridge, MA: Harvard University Press, 1933–67.

Dionysius Periegetes. *Dionysii Orbis Descriptio*. Oxford, 1697.

Dolce, Lodovico. *Dialogo di M. Lodovico Dolce, nel Quale si Ragiona della Institution della Maritata*. In *Dialogo della Institution delle Donne*, 36v–61. Vinegia, 1547.

Donne, John. *Devotions upon Emergent Occasions*. Ed. John Sparrow. Cambridge: Cambridge University Press, 1923.

————. *The Elegies and The Songs and Sonnets*. Ed. Helen Gardner. Oxford: Clarendon, 1965.

————. *The Epithalamions, Anniversaries, and Epicedes*. Ed. W. Milgate. Oxford: Clarendon, 1978.

————. *The Sermons of John Donne*. 10 vols. Ed. Evelyn M. Simpson and George R. Potter. Berkeley and Los Angeles: University of California Press, 1953–59.

Dracontius. *Carmen de Deo*. In *Patrologiae Cursus Completus. Series Latina*, vol. 60, cols. 679–902. Ed. Jacques-Paul Migne. Paris, 1862.

Drayton, Michael. *The Works of Michael Drayton*. 5 vols. Ed. J. William Hebel. Oxford: Published for the Shakespeare Head Press by Blackwell, 1961.

Drummond, William. "Song 1." In *William Drummond of Hawthornden: Poems and Prose*, 13–20. Ed. Robert H. Macdonald. Edinburgh: Scottish Academic Press, 1976.

————. "To a Nightingale." In *William Drummond of Hawthornden: Poems and Prose*, 111–12. Ed. Robert H. Macdonald. Edinburgh: Scottish Academic Press, 1976.

Dryden, John. *The Works of John Dryden*. 20 vols. Ed. Edward Niles Hooker and H. T. Swedenberg Jr. Berkeley and Los Angeles: University of California Press, 1956–96.

Dunster, Charles. *Considerations on Milton's Early Reading, and the Prima Stamina of His "Paradise Lost."* London, 1800

————. *Paradise Regained*. London, 1795. Reprinted in *Milton's "Paradise Regained": Two Eighteenth-Century Critiques by Richard Meadowcourt and Charles Dunster*. Intro. Joseph Anthony Wittreich Jr. Gainesville, FL: Scholars' Facsimiles and Reprints, 1971.

"E." "Milton's 'Par. L.' B. 4. V. 256." *The European Magazine, and London Review; for November 1795*, 296.

Eisenstein, Sergie. *The Film Sense*. Trans. Jay Leyda. New York: Harcourt, Brace and World, 1947.

Eliot, T. S. "Emotions in Words Again." *Kenyon Review* 10 (1948): 579–601.

————. "Milton." In *Proceedings of the British Academy*, 61–79. London: Oxford University Press, 1947.

———. "A Note on the Verse of John Milton." In *Essays and Studies by Member of the English Association,* vol. 21, 32–40. Collected by Herbert Read. Oxford: Clarendon, 1935.

Empson, William. *Milton's God.* Rev. ed. London: Chatto and Windus, 1965.

———. *Some Versions of Pastoral.* London: Chatto and Windus, 1935. Reprint, Norfolk, CT: New Directions, 1960.

———. *The Structure of Complex Words.* London: Chatto and Windus, 1951.

Erasmus. "Courtship." Trans. Craig R. Thompson. In *The Collected Works of Erasmus,* vol. 39, ed. R. J. Schoeck and B. M. Corrigan, 256–78. Toronto: University of Toronto Press, 1977.

Esolen, Anthony M., trans. and ed. *Jerusalem Delivered,* by Torquato Tasso. Baltimore: The Johns Hopkins University Press, 2000.

Eucherius (?). *Commentarii in Genesim.* In *Patrologiae Cursus Completus. Series Latina,* vol. 50, cols. 893–1048. Ed. Jacques-Paul Migne. Paris, 1846.

Euripides. *The Bacchanals.* In *Euripides,* vol. 3, 1–123. Trans. Arthur S. Way. Cambridge, MA: Harvard University Press, 1912.

———. *Hippolytus.* In *Euripides,* vol. 4, 157–277. Trans. Arthur S. Way. Cambridge, MA: Harvard University Press, 1912.

———. *Ion.* In *Euripides,* vol. 4, 1–155. Trans. Arthur S. Way. Cambridge, MA: Harvard University Press, 1912.

———. *The Madness of Hercules.* In *Euripides,* vol. 3, 124–247. Trans. Arthur S. Way. Cambridge, MA: Harvard University Press, 1912.

———. *The Phoenician Maidens.* In *Euripides,* vol. 3, 339–491. Trans. Arthur S. Way. Cambridge, MA: Harvard University Press, 1912.

———. *Rhesus.* In *Euripides,* vol. 1, 153–241. Trans. Arthur S. Way. Cambridge, MA: Harvard University Press, 1912.

Evans, J. M. *"Paradise Lost" and the Genesis Tradition.* Oxford: Clarendon, 1968.

Fairfax, Edward. *Godfrey of Bulloigne, or The Recoverie of Jerusalem. Done into English Heroicall Verse.* London, 1600.

Ferguson, A. S. "*Paradise Lost,* IV, 977–1015." *Modern Language Review* 15 (1920): 168–70.

Ferry, Anne Davidson. *Milton and the Miltonic Dryden.* Cambridge, MA: Harvard University Press, 1968.

———. *Milton's Epic Voice.* Cambridge, MA: Harvard University Press, 1963.

Ficino, Marsilio. *Opera Omnia.* 2 vols. Turin: Bottega D'Erasmo, 1962.

Fields, Albert W. "Milton and Self-Knowledge." *PMLA* 83 (1968): 392–99.

Fish, Stanley. "Discovery as Form in *Paradise Lost.*" In *New Essays on "Paradise Lost,"* 1–14. Ed. Thomas Kranidas. Berkeley and Los Angeles: University of California Press, 1969.

———. *Surprised by Sin: The Reader in "Paradise Lost."* Berkeley and Los Angeles: University of California Press, 1967.

Fletcher, Giles. *Christs Victorie, and Triumph in Heaven, and Earth, over, and after Death.* In *The Poetical Works of Giles Fletcher and Phineas Fletcher,* vol. 1, ed. Frederick S. Boas, 5–56. Cambridge: Cambridge University Press, 1905.

Fletcher, Harris Francis. *Milton's Rabbinical Readings.* Urbana: University of Illinois Press, 1930.

Fletcher, John. *The Dramatic Works in the Beaumont and Fletcher Canon,* 10 vols. Ed. Fredson Bowers. Cambridge: Cambridge University Press, 1966–96.

Fletcher, Phineas. *The Purple Island, or the Isle of Man.* Cambridge, 1633.

Fludd, Robert. *Mosaical Philosophy.* London, 1659.

Forsyth, P. T. "Milton's God and Milton's Satan." *Contemporary Review* 95 (1909): 450–65.

Fox, Robert C. "Satan's Triad of Vices." *Texas Studies in Literature and Language* 2 (1960): 261–80.

Fraunce, Abraham. *The Countesse of Pembroke's Ivychurch, Parts 1 and 2.* London, 1591.

Freeman, Rosemary. *English Emblem Books.* London: Chatto and Windus, 1948.

Frye, Northrop. *The Return of Eden.* Toronto: University of Toronto Press, 1965.

———. "The Revelation to Eve." In *"Paradise Lost": A Tercentenary Tribute,* 18–47. Ed. Balachandra Rajan. Toronto: University of Toronto Press, 1967.

Frye, Roland Mushat. "The Teachings of Classical Puritanism on Conjugal Love." *Studies in the Renaissance* 2 (1955): 148–59.

Gage, Clara Starrett. "Sources of Milton's Concepts of Angels and the Angelic World." Ph.D. diss., Cornell University, Ithaca, NY, 1936.

Gardner, Helen. "Milton's 'Satan' and the Theme of Damnation in Elizabethan Tragedy." *English Studies,* n.s., 1 (1948): 46–66.

———. *A Reading of "Paradise Lost."* Oxford: Clarendon, 1965.

Gascoigne, George. *The Complete Works of George Gascoigne.* 2 vols. Ed. John W. Cunliffe. Cambridge: Cambridge University Press, 1910.

———. "Gascoignes Devise of a Maske for the Right Honorable Viscount Mountacute." In *A Hundred Sundrie Flowres,* ed. G. W. Pigman III, 301–12. Oxford: Clarendon, 2000.

Genesis B. In *The Saxon Genesis: An Edition of the West Saxon Genesis B and the Old Saxon Vatican Genesis,* 207–31. Ed. A. N. Doone. Madison: University of Wisconsin Press, 1991.

Giamatti, A. Bartlett. *The Earthly Paradise and the Renaissance Epic.* Princeton, NJ: Princeton University Press, 1966.

Gilbert, Allan H. *A Geographical Dictionary of Milton.* New Haven, CT: Yale University Press, 1919.

———. "Milton and the *Aminta.*" *Modern Philology* 25 (1927): 95–99.

———. "Milton and the Mysteries." *Studies in Philology* 17 (1920): 147–69.

———. "Milton on the Position of Women." *Modern Language Review* 15 (1920): 240–64.

———. *On the Composition of "Paradise Lost": A Study of the Ordering and Insertion of Material.* Chapel Hill: University of North Carolina Press, 1947.

———. *"Orlando Furioso": An English Translation with Introduction, Notes and Index*. New York: S. F. Vanni, 1954.

Gilpin, William. "On Picturesque Beauty." In *Three Essays: On Picturesque Beauty; On Picturesque Travel; and On Sketching Landscape: to Which is Added a Poem, On Landscape Painting*, 3–33. 2nd ed. London, 1794.

Giovannini, Margaret. "Milton's *Paradise Lost*, IV, 131–193." *Explicator* 12 (1953): item 1.

Goldsmith, Oliver. *Collected Works of Oliver Goldsmith*. 5 vols. Ed. Arthur Friedman. Oxford: Clarendon, 1966.

Gray, Thomas. "On the Death of Mr. Richard West." In *The Complete Poems of Thomas Gray*, ed. H. W. Starr and J. R. Hendrickson, 92. Oxford: Clarendon, 1966.

Greene, Robert. *Greenes, Groats-worth of Witte, Bought with a Million of Repentance*. London, 1592. Reprint, London: John Lane, The Bodley Head; New York: E. P. Dutton, 1923.

———. *Menaphon: Camillas Alarum to Slumbering Euphues*. London, 1589.

Greene, Thomas. *The Descent from Heaven: A Study in Epic Continuity*. New Haven, CT: Yale University Press, 1963.

Greenlaw, Edwin. "Spenser's Influence on *Paradise Lost*." *Studies in Philology* 17 (1920): 320–59.

Gregory the Great. *In Evangelium Homily XXXIV*. In *XL Homiliarum in Evangelia. Patrologiae Cursus Completus. Series Latina*, vol. 76, cols. 1075–1314. Ed. Jacques-Paul Migne. Paris, 1849.

Gregory Nazianzen. *Christus Patiens*. In *Patrologiae Cursus Completus. Series Graeca*, vol. 38, cols. 137–338. Ed. Jacques-Paul Migne. Paris, 1862.

Gregory of Nyssa. *Contemplation sur la vie de Moïse ou traité de la perfection en matière de vertu*. Trans. Jean Daniélou. Paris: Editions du Cerf, 1941.

———. *De Hominis Opificio*. In *Patrologiae Cursus Completus. Series Graeca*, vol. 44, cols. 23–256. Ed. Jacques-Paul Migne. Paris, 1858.

Gossman, Ann. "The Use of the Tree of Life in *Paradise Lost*." *Journal of English and Germanic Philology* 65 (1966): 680–87.

Grierson, Herbert J. C. *Milton and Wordsworth*. New York: Macmillan, 1937.

Grose, Christopher. "Some Uses of Sensuous Immediacy in *Paradise Lost*." *Huntington Library Quarterly* 31 (1968): 211–22.

Grotius, Hugo. *Adamus Exul*. In *The Celestial Cycle*, 96–220. Trans. and ed. Watson Kirkconnell. Toronto: University of Toronto Press, 1952.

Guarini, Battista. *Il Pastor Fido: Tragi-commedia Pastorale*. Venice, 1602.

Hakewill, George. *An Apologie or Declaration of the Power and Providence of God in the Government of the World*. 2nd ed. London, 1630.

Hakluyt, Richard. *The Principall Navigations Voyages Traffiques and Discoveries of the English Nation*. 3rd ed. London, 1598–1600. Reprinted in 10 vols., Glasgow: MacLehose, 1903–05.

Halkett, John. *Milton and the Idea of Matrimony*. New Haven, CT: Yale University Press, 1970.

Hall, Joseph. *Heaven upon Earth*. In *Heaven upon Earth and Characters of Vertues and Vices*, 84–139. Ed. Rudolf Kirk. New Brunswick, NJ: Rutgers University Press, 1948.

Haller, William. "Hail Wedded Love." *ELH* 13 (1946): 79–97.

Haller, William, and Malleville Haller. "The Puritan Art of Love." *Huntington Library Quarterly* 5 (1942): 235–72.

Hamilton, G. Rostrevor. *Hero or Fool? A Study of Milton's Satan*. London: George Allen and Unwin, 1944.

Hanford, James Holly. "The Dramatic Element in *Paradise Lost*." *Studies in Philology* 14 (1917): 178–95.

———. "Milton and the Art of War." *Studies in Philology* 18 (1921): 232–66.

Harding, Davis P. *The Club of Hercules: Studies in the Classical Background of "Paradise Lost."* Urbana: University of Illinois Press, 1962.

———. *Milton and the Renaissance Ovid*. Urbana: University of Illinois Press, 1946.

Harington, Sir John. *The History of Polindor and Flostella*. In *The History of Polindor and Flostella: With Other Poems*, 1–160. 3rd ed. London, 1657.

———. *Orlando Furioso: In English Heroical Verse*. Ed. Robert McNulty. Oxford: Clarendon, 1972.

Hartwell, Kathleen Ellen. *Lactantius and Milton*. Cambridge, MA: Harvard University Press, 1929.

Hawkey, John. "Various Readings." Unpaginated. In *Paradise Lost. A Poem in Twelve Books*. Dublin, 1747.

Hazlitt, William. *Lectures on the English Poets*. 3rd ed. New York: Russell and Russell, 1841.

Herrick, Robert. *The Poems of Robert Herrick*. Ed. L. C. Martin. London: Oxford University Press, 1965.

Hesiod. *Theogony*. In *Hesiod: The Homeric Hymns, Epic Cycle and Homerica*, 78–155. Rev. ed. Trans. Hugh G. Evelyn-White. Cambridge, MA: Harvard University Press, 1936.

———. *Works and Days*. In *Hesiod: The Homeric Hymns, Epic Cycle and Homerica*, 2–65. Rev. ed. Trans. Hugh G. Evelyn-White. Cambridge, MA: Harvard University Press, 1936.

Heylyn, Peter. *Cosmographie in Four Bookes*. London, 1652. Reprint, *Cosmography in Four Books*. Ed. Robert Mayhew. Bristol, UK: Thoemmes, 2003.

———. *Microcosmos*. 5th ed. Oxford, 1631.

Heywood, Thomas. *The Hierarchie of the Blessed Angells*. London, 1635.

Hippocrates. "Dreams." In *The Medical Works: A New Translation*, 194–201. Trans. John Chadwick and W. N. Mann. Oxford: Blackwell Scientific Publications, 1950.

Homer. *Iliad*. 2 vols. Trans. A. T. Murray. 2nd rev. ed. Ed. William F. Wyatt. Cambridge, MA: Harvard University Press, 1999.

———. *Odyssey*. 2 vols. Trans. A. T. Murray. London: Heinemann; Cambridge, MA: Harvard University Press, 1919.

The Homeric Hymns. In *Hesiod: The Homeric Hymns and Homerica*, 285–463. Rev. ed. Trans. Hugh G. Evelyn-White. Cambridge, MA: Harvard University Press, 1936.

Hooper, John. "A Declaration of the Ten Holy Commandments of Almighty God." In *Early Writings of John Hooper,* 249–412. Ed. Samuel Carr. Cambridge: Cambridge University Press, 1843.

Horace. *The Art of Poetry.* In *Satires, Epistles and Ars Poetica,* 442–89. Rev. ed. Trans. H. Rushton Fairclough. London: Heinemann; Cambridge, MA: Harvard University Press, 1929.

———. *Carmen Saeculare.* In *The Odes and Epodes,* 349–57. Trans. C. E. Bennett. London: Heinemann; Cambridge, MA: Harvard University Press, 1952.

———. *Epodes.* In *The Odes and Epodes,* 359–417. Trans. C. E. Bennett. London: Heinemann; Cambridge, MA: Harvard University Press, 1952.

———. *Odes.* In *The Odes and Epodes,* 1–347. Trans. C. E. Bennett. London: Heinemann; Cambridge, MA: Harvard University Press, 1952.

———. *Satires.* In *Satires, Epistles and Ars Poetica,* 1–245. Rev. ed. Trans. H. Rushton Fairclough. London: Heinemann; Cambridge, MA: Harvard University Press, 1929.

Huet, Pierre Daniel. *Traitte de la Situation du Paradis.* Paris, 1691.

Hughes, Merritt Y. "'Myself Am Hell.'" *Modern Philology* 54 (1956–57): 80–94.

———. "Satan and the 'Myth' of the Tyrant." In *Ten Perspectives on Milton,* 165–95. Ed. Merritt Y. Hughes. New Haven, CT: Yale University Press, 1965.

———. "Variorum." Unpublished notes for a critical variorum on *Paradise Lost.*

Hume, Patrick. *Annotations on Milton's "Paradise Lost."* London, 1695.

Hunter, William B., Jr. "Eve's Demonic Dream." *ELH* 13 (1946): 255–65.

———. "Milton on the Incarnation: Some More Heresies." *Journal of the History of Ideas* 21 (1960): 349–69.

———. "Milton's Materialistic Life Principle." *Journal of English and Germanic Philology* 45 (1946): 68–76.

Huntley, Frank L. "Before and after the Fall: Some Miltonic Patterns of Systasis." In *Approaches to "Paradise Lost": The York Tercentenary Lectures,* 1–14. Ed. C. A. Patrides. London: Edward Arnold, 1968.

Huntley, John F. "Gourmet Cooking and the Vision of Paradise in *Paradise Lost.*" *Xavier University Studies* 8 (1969): 44–54.

Hurd, Richard. "A Dissertation on the Marks of Imitation." In *The Works of Richard Hurd,* vol. 2, 242–313. London, 1811.

I., I. "*To Mr. T. S. in Vindication of* Mr. Milton's *Paradise Lost.*" In *Miscellaneous Letters and Essays on Several Subjects.* Ed. Charles Gildon. London, 1694. Reprinted in *Critical Essays of the Seventeenth Century,* vol. 3, 198–200. Ed. J. E. Spingarn. Oxford: Clarendon, 1909.

James, William. *The Varieties of Religious Experience.* New York: Random House, 1936.

Jayne, Sears. "The Subject of Milton's Ludlow Mask." *PMLA* 74 (1959): 533–43.

Jerome. *Liber Hebraicarum Quaestionum in Genesim.* In *Patrologiae Cursus Completus. Series Latina,* vol. 23, cols. 986–1062. Ed. Jacques-Paul Migne. Paris, 1865.

Johnson, Samuel. *A Dictionary of the English Language.* 2 vols. London, 1755.

————. *The History of Rasselas, Prince of Abyssinia*. In *The Yale Edition of the Works of Samuel Johnson*, vol. 16, ed. Gwin J. Kolb, 1–176. New Haven, CT: Yale University Press, 1990.

————. "Milton." In *The Lives of the Most Eminent English Poets; with Critical Observations on Their Works*, vol. 1, 242–95. Ed. Roger H. Lonsdale. Oxford: Oxford University Press, 2006.

————. *The Rambler*. Ed. W. J. Bate and Albrecht B. Strauss. *The Yale Edition of the Works of Samuel Johnson*. Vols. 3–5. New Haven, CT: Yale University Press, 1969.

Jonson, Ben. *Ben Jonson*. 11 vols. Ed. C. H. Herford, Percy and Evelyn Simpson. Oxford: Clarendon, 1925–52. Reprint, 1963–67.

Jortin, John. *Tracts, Philological, Critical, and Miscellaneous*. 2 vols. London, 1790. Facsimile, New York: Garland, 1970.

Josephus, Flavius. *Jewish Antiquities*, in *Works*. Vols. 4–10. Trans. Henry St. John Thackeray et al. Cambridge, MA: Harvard University Press; London: Heinemann, 1926–81.

Justin Martyr. *Apologia Secunda pro Christianis*. In *Patrologiae Cursus Completus. Series Graeca*, vol. 6, cols. 441–70. Ed. Jacques-Paul Migne. Paris, 1857.

Juvenal. *The Satires of Juvenal*. In *Juvenal and Persius*, 1–307. Trans. G. G. Ramsay. London: Heinemann; Cambridge, MA: Harvard University Press, 1940.

Kastor, Frank S. "'In His Own Shape': The Stature of Satan in *Paradise Lost*." *English Language Notes* 5 (1968): 264–69.

————. "Milton's Tempter: A Genesis of a Subportrait in *Paradise Lost*." *Huntington Library Quarterly* 33 (1970): 373–85.

Keats, John. "Notes on Milton's *Paradise Lost*." In *The Complete Works of John Keats*, vol. 3, 256–65. Ed. H. Buxton Forman. Glasgow: Gowars and Gray, 1901.

Keightley, Thomas. *An Account of the Life, Opinions, and Writings of John Milton, with an Introduction to "Paradise Lost."* London: Chapman and Hall, 1855.

Kermode, Frank. "Adam Unparadised," In *The Living Milton*, 85–123. Ed. Frank Kermode. London: Routledge, 1960.

The Key of Solomon the King. Trans. and Ed. S. Liddell MacGregor Mathers. 1888. Reprint, New York: Samuel Weisor, 1978.

Kirkconnell, Watson. *The Celestial Cycle: The Theme of "Paradise Lost" in World Literature with Translations of the Major Analogues*. Toronto: University of Toronto Press, 1952.

Knight, G. Wilson. *The Burning Oracle: Studies in the Poetry of Action*. New York: Oxford University Press, 1939.

Knights, L. C. "Milton Again." *Scrutiny* 11 (1942): 146–48.

Knott, John R., Jr. "The Pastoral Day in *Paradise Lost*." *Modern Language Quarterly* 29 (1968): 168–82.

————. "Symbolic Landscape in *Paradise Lost*." In *Milton Studies*, vol. 2, ed. James D. Simmonds, 37–58. Pittsburgh: University of Pittsburgh Press, 1970.

Kranidas, Thomas. *The Fierce Equation: A Study of Milton's Decorum*. The Hague: Mouton, 1965.

Kuhns, Oscar. "Dante's Influence on Milton." *Modern Language Notes* 13 (1898): 1–6.

Kyd, Thomas. *The Spanish Tragedy*. Ed. Philip Edwards. London: Methuen, 1959.

L., G. G. "A Phrase in *Paradise Lost.*" *Notes and Queries* 180 (1941): 387.

Lactantius. *Divinarum Institutionum*. In *Patrologiae Cursus Completus. Series Latina,* vol. 6, cols. 111–822. Ed. Jacques-Paul Migne. Paris, 1844.

Lancetta, Troilo. *La Scena Tragica d'Adamo et Eva,* 1644. Synopsis in William Hayley's *The Life of Milton, in Three Parts,* 324–28. London, 1796.

Landino, Cristoforo. *La Commedia Divina*. Ed. Piero da Figino. Commentary by Cristoforo Landino. Venice, 1497.

Landor, Walter Savage. "Southey and Landor." In *Imaginary Conversations,* 4th ser., vol. 4, 1–53. Boston: Roberts Brothers, 1877.

La Primaudaye, Pierre. *The French Academie. Fully Discoursed and Finished in Foure Bookes*. Trans. Thomas Bowes, Richard Dolman, and William Phillip (?). London, 1618.

Lawry, Jon S. *The Shadow of Heaven: Matter and Stance in Milton's Poetry*. Ithaca, NY: Cornell University Press, 1968.

Leather, Mary Steward. "Pope as a Student of Milton." *Englische Studien* 25 (1898): 398–410.

Leavis, F. R. *Revaluation: Tradition and Development in English Poetry*. London: Chatto and Windus, 1936.

Le Comte, Edward S. "Milton as Satirist and Wit." In *Th' Upright Heart and Pure: Essays on John Milton Commemorating the Tercentenary of the Publication of "Paradise Lost,"* 45–59. Ed. Amadeus P. Fiore. Pittsburgh: Duquesne University Press, 1967.

———. *Yet Once More: Verbal and Psychological Pattern in Milton*. New York: Liberal Arts Press, 1953.

Leo, Africanus. *The History and Description of Africa*. 3 vols. Trans. John Pory. 1600. Reprint of 1896 edition by Hakluyt Society. Ed. Robert Brown. New York: Burt Franklin, 1963.

Lewalski, Barbara Kiefer. "Innocence and Experience in Milton's Eden." In *New Essays on "Paradise Lost,"* 86–117. Ed. Thomas Kranidas. Berkeley and Los Angeles: University of California Press, 1969.

Lewis, C. S. *A Preface to "Paradise Lost."* London: Oxford University Press, 1942.

Libanius. "Oration 11." In *Libanius Opera,* vol. 1, 412–535. Ed. R. Foerster. Lipsiae: Teubneri, 1903–22. Reprint, Hildescheim: Georg Olms, 1963.

Lieb, Michael. *The Dialectics of Creation: Patterns of Birth and Regeneration in* Paradise Lost. Amherst: University of Massachusetts Press, 1970.

Lockwood, Laura E. "A Note on Milton's Geography." *Modern Language Notes* 21 (1906): 86.

Lodge, Thomas. Selection in *Englands Parnassus; or, The Choysest Flowers of our Moderne Poets, with their Poeticall Comparisons,* 1600. Comp. Robert Allot. Ed. Charles Crawford. Oxford: Clarendon, 1913.

Longinus. *Longinus on the Sublime*. Trans. A. O. Prickard. Oxford: Clarendon, 1906. Reprinted with corrections, 1930.

Lucan. *The Civil War*. Trans. J. D. Duff. London: Heinemann; Cambridge, MA: Harvard University Press, 1928.

Lucretius. *De Rerum Natura*. Trans. W. H. D. Rouse. London: Heinemann, 1924. Reprint, Rev. ed. Ed. Martin Ferguson Smith. Cambridge, MA: Harvard University Press, 1975.

Lycophron. *Cassandra*. Trans. Joseph Scaliger. In *Lykophronos tou Chalkide os Alexandra*, 147–83. Oxford, 1697.

Lyndsay, Sir David. *Ane Dialogue betuix Experience and ane Courteour, off the Miserabyll Estait of the Warld*. Vol. 1. of *The Works of Sir David Lindsay of the Mount*. Ed. Douglas Hamer. Edinburgh: William Blackwood and Sons, 1931.

Mabbott, Thomas. "Milton and Nonnos." *Notes and Queries* 197 (1952): 117–18.

Macaulay, Lord. "Milton." In *Critical, Historical, and Miscellaneous Essays*, vol. 1, 202–66. New York: Sheldon, 1871.

Macaulay, Rose. *Milton*. New York: Harper and Brothers, 1935.

MacCaffrey, Isabel Gamble. *"Paradise Lost" as "Myth."* Cambridge, MA: Harvard University Press, 1959.

Mack, Maynard. *Milton*. Vol. 4 of *English Masterpieces*. New York: Prentice-Hall, 1950. Reprint, 2nd ed. Englewood Cliffs, NJ: Prentice-Hall, 1961.

Macrobius, Ambrosius. *Saturnalia*. Trans. Percival Vaughan Davies. New York: Columbia University Press, 1969.

Madsen, William G. *From Shadowy Types to Truth: Studies in Milton's Symbolism*. New Haven, CT: Yale University Press, 1968.

———. "The Idea of Nature in Milton's Poetry." In *Three Studies in the Renaissance: Sidney, Jonson, Milton*, 183–283. New Haven, CT: Yale University Press, 1958.

Maimonides. *Guide for the Perplexed*. 2nd rev. ed. Trans. M. Friedlander. London: Routledge; New York: Dutton, 1928.

Malone, Edmund, ed. *William Shakespeare: The Plays and Poems*. 21 vols. London, 1821.

Mandeville, John. *The Voiage and Travaile of Sir John Maundervile*. Introduction, notes, and glossary by J. O. Halliwell. London: F. S. Ellis, 1866.

Marilla, Esmond L. "A Reading of Two Episodes in *Paradise Lost*." *Études Anglaises* 12 (1959): 135–41.

Marino, Giovan Battista. *L'Adone*. 2 vols. Ed. Giovanni Pozzi. Milan: Arnoldo Mondadori, 1976.

———. *La Strage de Gl'Innocenti*. In *Dicerie Sacre e "La Strage de Gl'Innocenti,"* 443–600. Ed. Giovanni Pozzi. Turin: Guilio Einaudi, 1960.

Markham, Gervase. *The Souldiers Accidence*. London, 1635.

Marlowe, Christopher. *Doctor Faustus*. In *The Complete Works of Christopher Marlowe*, vol. 2, 121–271. Ed. Fredson Bowers. Cambridge: Cambridge University Press, 1973.

Martz, Louis L. "*Paradise Lost:* Princes of Exile." *ELH* 36 (1969): 232–49.

———. "*Paradise Lost:* The Power of Choice." *Ventures* 10 (1970): 37–47.

———. *The Paradise Within: Studies in Vaughan, Traherne, and Milton*. New Haven, CT: Yale University Press, 1964.

Marvell, Andrew. *The Poems and Letters of Andrew Marvell*. 2 vols. 3rd rev. ed. Ed. Pierre Legouis, with collaboration of E. E. Duncan-Jones. Oxford: Clarendon, 1971.

Masenius, Jacob. *Sarcotis, et Caroli V. Imp. Panegyris, Carmina*. London and Paris: Barbou, 1771.

Massinger, Philip. *The Unnatural Combat*. In *The Plays and Poems of Philip Massinger*, vol. 2, 181–272. Ed. Philip Edwards and Colin Gibson. Oxford: Clarendon, 1976.

Masson, David. *The Life of John Milton*. 7 vols. 1877–96. Reprint, New and rev. ed. Gloucester, MA: Peter Smith, 1965.

Maxwell, J. C. "Milton's Knowledge of Aeschylus: The Argument from Parallel Passages." *Review of English Studies*, n.s., 3 (1952): 366–71.

McColley, Grant. "Milton's Technique of Source Adaptation." *Studies in Philology* 35 (1938): 61–110.

———. *"Paradise Lost."* *Harvard Theological Review* 32 (1939): 181–235.

———. *"Paradise Lost": An Account of Its Growth and Major Origins, with a Discussion of Milton's Use of Sources and Literary Patterns*. Chicago: Packard, 1940.

———. "The Astronomy of *Paradise Lost*." *Studies in Philology* 34 (1937): 209–47.

———. "The Book of Enoch and *Paradise Lost*." *Harvard Theological Review* 32 (1939): 21– 39.

McQueen, William A. "'The Hateful Siege of Contraries': Satan's Interior Monologues in *Paradise Lost*." *Milton Quarterly* 4 (1970): 60–65.

Mercator, Gerhard. *Atlas*. Amsterdam, 1628.

Mercer, John. *Commentarius in Genesin*. Paris, 1598.

Mersenne, Marin. *Questiones Celeberrimae in Genesim*. Paris, 1623.

Middleton, Thomas. *The Phoenix*. In *The Phoenix by Thomas Middleton: A Critical Modernized Edition*. Ed. John Bradbury Brooks. New York: Garland, 1980.

Midrash Rabbah. 5 vols. Trans. and ed. H. Freedman and Maurice Simon. New York: Soncino, 1977.

The Mirror for Magistrates. London, 1610.

Miller, Dorothy Durkee. "Eve." *Journal of English and Germanic Philology* 61 (1962): 542–47.

Mohl, Ruth. *Studies in Spenser, Milton and the Theory of Monarchy*. New York: King's Crown, 1949.

More, Henry. *The Apology*. Appended to *A Modest Enquiry into the Mystery of Iniquity*. London, 1664.

———. *Conjectura Cabbalistica*. London, 1653.

———. *The Immortality of the Soul*. In *A Collection of Several Philosophical Writings of Dr. Henry More*. 4th ed. London, 1712.

———. *Psychozoia, or The First Part of the Song of the Soul, Containing a Christiano-Platonicall Display of* LIFE. In *The Complete Poems of Dr. Henry More.* Ed. Alexander B. Grosart, 9–39. Edinburgh: Constable, 1878. Reprint, New York: AMS Press, 1967.

———. "Third Letter to Descartes." In *A Collection of Several Philosophical Writings of Dr. Henry More,* 85–95. 4th ed. London, 1712.

More, Paul Elmer. "The True Theme of *Paradise Lost.*" *Independent* 54 (1902): 277–80.

Moses Bar-Cepha. *De Paradiso Commentarius.* In *Patrologia Cursus Completus, Series Graeca,* vol. 111, 481–609. Ed. Jacques-Paul Migne. Paris: 1864.

Musaeus, Grammaticus. *The Divine Poem of Musaeus.* Trans. George Chapman. London, 1616.

Musgrove, S. "Is the Devil an Ass?" *Review of English Studies* 21 (1945): 302–15.

Nashe, Thomas. *Anatomy of Absurditie.* In *The Works of Thomas Nashe,* vol. 1, 1–49. Ed. Ronald B. McKerrow. London: A. H. Bullen, 1904–10. Reprinted with corrections and supplemental notes. Ed. F. P. Wilson. Oxford: Blackwell, 1959.

Nicolson, Marjorie H. *John Milton: A Reader's Guide to His Poetry.* New York: Farrar, Straus, 1963.

———. "Milton and the *Conjectura Cabbalistica.*" *Philological Quarterly* 6 (1927): 1–18.

———. "The Spirit World of Milton and More." *Studies in Philology* 22 (1925): 433–52.

———. *The Breaking of the Circle.* Evanston, IL: Northwestern University Press, 1950. Reprint, Rev. ed. New York: Columbia University Press, 1960.

Nonnos of Panopolis. *Dionysiaca.* 3 vols. Trans. W. H. D. Rouse. Mythological introduction and notes by H. J. Rose. Notes on text criticism by L. R. Lind. Cambridge, MA: Harvard University Press; London: Heinemann, 1940.

The Office of Christian Parents. Cambridge, 1616.

Orpheus. *The Orphic Hymns: Text, Trans. and Notes.* Ed. Apostolos N. Athanassakis. Missoula, MT: Scholars, 1977.

Ortelius, Abraham. *Theatrum Orbis Terrarum. The Theatre of the Whole World.* Antwerp, 1592.

Osgood, Charles Grosvenor. *The Classical Mythology of Milton's English Poems.* New York: Henry Holt, 1900.

Ovid. *The Amores.* In *Heroides and Amores,* 313–508. Trans. Grant Showerman. Cambridge, MA: Harvard University Press; London: Heinemann, 1914. Reprint, 1963.

———. *Fasti.* Trans. Sir James George Frazer. London: Heinemann; New York: Putnam, 1931. 2nd ed. Reprinted with corrections and revised by G. P. Goold. Cambridge, MA: Harvard University Press, 1996.

———. *Metamorphoses.* 2 vols. Trans. Frank Justus Miller. Cambridge, MA: Harvard University Press; London: Heinemann, 1916. Reprint, 1968–71.

———. *The Art of Love.* In *"The Art of Love" and Other Poems,* 11–175. Trans. J. H. Mozley. Cambridge, MA: Harvard University Press; London: Heinemann, 1929. rev. ed. 1939. Reprint, 1969.

———. *The Remedies of Love*. In *"The Art of Love" and Other Poems*, 177–233. Trans. J. H. Mozley. Cambridge, MA: Harvard University Press; London: Heinemann, 1929. Rev. ed. 1939. Reprint, 1969.

———. *Tristia*. In *Tristia; Ex Ponto*, 1–262. Trans. Arthur Leslie Wheeler. Cambridge, MA: Harvard University Press; London: Heinemann, 1924. 2nd ed. reprinted with corrections and revised by G. P. Goold.

Panofsky, Erwin. *Meaning in the Visual Arts: Papers in and on Art History*. Garden City, NJ: Doubleday, 1955.

Pareus, David. *In Genesin Mosis Commentarius*. Frankfurt, 1609.

Parish, John E. "Milton's *Paradise Lost*, VI, 362–368." *Explicator* 24 (1965): item 15.

Parker, Henry. *The Contra-Replicant, His Complaint to His Maiestie*. London, 1643.

Paterson, James. *Complete Commentary, with Etymological, Explanatory, Critical and Classical Notes on Milton's "Paradise Lost."* London, 1744.

Patrides, C. A. *Milton and the Christian Tradition*. Oxford: Oxford University Press, 1966.

———. "Renaissance Ideas on Man's Upright Form." *Journal of the History of Ideas* 19 (1958): 256–58.

———. "Renaissance Thought on the Celestial Hierarchy: The Decline of a Tradition." *Journal of the History of Ideas* 20 (1959): 155–66.

———. "Renaissance Views on the 'Unconfused Orders Angelick.'" *Journal of the History of Ideas* 23 (1962): 265–67.

———. "The Tree of Knowledge in the Christian Tradition." *Studia Neophilologica* 34 (1962): 239–42.

Pausanias. *Description of Greece*. 4 vols., with a companion volume containing maps, plans and indices. Trans. W. H. S. Jones, with R. E. Wycherley editing vol. 5. Cambridge, MA: Harvard University Press; London: Heinemann; New York: Putnam, 1918–35.

Peacham, Henry. *The Complete Gentleman*. In *The Complete Gentleman, The Truth of Our Times, and The Art of Living in London*, 1–174. Ed. Virgil B. Heltzel. Ithaca, NY: Cornell University Press, 1962.

Pearce, Zachary. *A Review of the Text of "Paradise Lost": In Which the Chief of Dr. Bentley's Emendations Are Considered*. London, 1732.

Peck, Francis. *New Memoirs of the Life and Poetical Works of Mr. John Milton*. London, 1740.

Pererius, Benedictus. *Commentariorum et Disputationum in Genesin*. Venice, 1607.

Persius. *Satires*. In *Juvenal and Persius*, 41–125. Ed. and trans. Susanna Morton Braund. Cambridge, MA: Harvard University Press, 2004.

Peter, John. *A Critique of "Paradise Lost."* New York: Columbia University Press, 1960.

Petrarch [Petrarca], Francesco. *Sonnets and Songs*. Trans. Anna Maria Armi. New York: Grosset and Dunlap, 1968.

Peyton, Thomas. *The Glasse of Time, in the Two First Ages*. London, 1623.

Philo. *Allegorical Interpretation of Genesis II, III*. Trans. F. H. Colson and G. H. Whitaker. In *Philo*, vol. 1, 139–484. Cambridge, MA: Harvard University Press, 1929–62.

———. *Questions and Answers on Genesis.* Trans. Ralph Marcus. In *Philo,* vol. 11. Cambridge, MA: Harvard University Press, 1929–62.

Pindar. *The Odes of Pindar Including the Principal Fragments.* Trans. Sir John Sandys. London: Heinemann; New York: Macmillan; Cambridge, MA: Harvard University Press, 1915.

Pirke de Rabbi Eliezer. 2nd ed. Trans. Gerald Friedlander. New York: Herman, 1965.

Plato. *Cratylus.* In *Cratylus. Parmenides. Greater Hippias. Lesser Hippias,* 6–191. Rev. ed. Trans. H. N. Fowler. Cambridge MA: Harvard University Press, 1939.

———. *Phaedrus.* In *Euthyphro. Apology. Crito. Phaedo. Phaedrus.* Trans. Harold North Fowler, 405–579. Cambridge, MA: Harvard University Press, 1914.

———. *Symposium.* In *Lysis. Symposium. Gorgias,* 73–245. Trans. W. R. M. Lamb. Cambridge, MA: Harvard University Press, 1925.

———. *Timaeus.* In *Timaeus. Critias. Cleitophon. Menexenus. Epistles,* 1–254. Trans. R. G. Bury. Cambridge, MA: Harvard University Press, 1929.

Plautus. *Captivi.* Trans. Paul Nixon. In *Plautus,* vol. 1, 459–567. Cambridge, MA: Harvard University Press; London: Heinemann, 1916. Reprint 2006.

Pliny. *Natural History.* 10 vols. Trans. H. Rackham. Cambridge, MA: Harvard University Press, 1938–63.

———. *The Historie of the World: Commonly Called, The Naturall Historie of C. Plinius Secundus.* 2 vols. Trans. Philemon Holland. London, 1634.

Plutarch. "How the Young Man Should Study Poetry." In *Moralia,* vol. 1, trans. Frank Cole Babbitt, 71–197. London: Heinemann, Cambridge, MA: Harvard University Press, 1936. Reprint 2003.

———. "The Obsolence of Oracles." In *Moralia,* vol. 5, trans. Frank Cole Babbitt, 347–501. London: Heinemann; New York: G. P. Putnam, 1927. Reprint 2005.

Pope, Alexander. *The Poems of Alexander Pope.* 11 vols. Ed. John Butt. London: Methuen; New Haven, CT: Yale University Press, 1951–69.

Pordage, Samuel. *Mundorum Explicatio.* London, 1661.

Porphyry. *De Antro Nympharum.* In *Porphyriou Philosophou Pythagorikou,* 249–72. Cambridge, 1655.

Prince, F. T. "Milton and the Theatrical Sublime." In *Approaches to "Paradise Lost": The York Tercentenary Lectures,* 53–63. Ed. C. A. Patrides. London: Edward Arnold, 1968.

———. *The Italian Element in Milton's Verse.* Oxford: Clarendon, 1962.

Psellus, Michael. *De Operatione Daemonum.* Kiloni, 1688.

Pseudo-Dionysius, the Areopagite. *Celestis Hierarchia.* In *Opera Dionysii,* fol. I–CLXII. N.p., 1502.

Publius Lentulus. *Letter.* London, 1650.

Purchas, Samuel. *Hakluytus Posthumus; or, Purchas His Pilgrimes.* London, 1625. Reprinted in 20 vols., Glasgow: James MacLehose and Sons, 1905–07.

———. *Purchas His Pilgrimage*. London: 1613, 1617, 1626.

Rajan, Balachandra *"Paradise Lost" and the Seventeenth Century Reader*. London: Chatto and Windus, 1947.

———. *The Lofty Rhyme: A Study of Milton's Major Poetry*. Coral Gables, FL: University of Miami Press; London: Routledge and Kegan Paul, 1970.

Ralegh, Sir Walter. *The History of the World*. London, 1614. Reprinted in *The Works of Sir Walter Ralegh*, vols. 2–7. Ed. William Oldys and Thomas Birch. Oxford: Oxford University Press, 1829. Reprint, New York: Franklin, 1965 (?).

Raleigh, Walter. *Milton*. New York: Putnam, 1900.

Ramsey, Andrew. *Andreae Ramsaei, sacrocanctae theologiae in Academia olim Edinburgena Professoris, Poemata sacra*. 3rd ed. Edinburgh, 1752.

The Rare Triumphes of Love and Fortune. London, 1589.

Ransom, John Crowe. *God without Thunder*. New York: Harcourt, Brace, 1930.

———. "Mr. Empson's Muddles." *Southern Review* 4 (1938): 322–39.

Reclus, Elisee. *The Universal Geography: The Earth and Its Inhabitants*. 19 vols. Ed. E. G. Ravenstein. London: J. S. Virtue, 1876–94.

"A Remedy for Love." Appended to Sidney's *Arcadia,* 13th ed. London, 1674.

Revard, Stella. "Milton's Eve and the Evah of Sir William Alexander's *Doomes-day.*" *Papers on Language and Literature* 3 (1967): 181–86.

Reynolds, Henry. *Mythomystes*. London, 1632.

———. *Torquato Tasso "Aminta" Englisht*. London, 1628.

Riccioli, Giovanni. *Almagestum Novum*. Bononiae, 1651.

Richardson, Janette. "Virgil and Milton Once Again." *Comparative Literature* 14 (1962): 321–31.

Richardson, Jonathan, father and son. *Explanatory Notes and Remarks on Milton's "Paradise Lost."* London, 1734.

Ricks, Christopher. *Milton's Grand Style*. Oxford: Clarendon, 1963.

Riggs, William G. "The Poet and Satan in *Paradise Lost.*" In *Milton Studies*, vol. 2, 59–82. Ed. James D. Simmonds. Pittsburgh: University of Pittsburgh Press, 1970.

Ripa, Cesare. *Iconologia*. Padua, 1611. Reprint of 1779 ed., New York: Garland, 1976.

Rivetus, Andraeus. *Operum Theologicorum Quae Latine Edidit*. Rotterdam, 1651.

Robins, H. F. "Satan's Journey: Direction in *Paradise Lost.*" In *Milton Studies in Honor of Harris Francis Fletcher*, 91–103. Urbana: University of Illinois Press, 1961.

Rogers, Daniel. *Matrimoniall Honour: or, The Mutuall Crowne and Comfort of Godly, Loyall, and Chaste Marriage*. London, 1642.

Rogers, Nehemiah. *The Penitent Citizen; or, A Mirrour of Mercy*. London, 1640.

Ronsard, Pierre de. *La Franciade. Oeuvres Completes*. Vol. 16. Ed. Paul Laumonier. Paris: Librairie Marcel Didier, 1950.

Rupert Tuitiensis [Rupert of Deutz]. *Commentariorum in Genesim*. In *De Sancta Trinitate et Operibus Eius,* vol. 21, 129–578. Ed. Hrabanus Haacke. Corpus Christianorum, Continuatio Mediaevalis. Turnholti: Brepols, 1971–72.

Russell, John. *The Two Famous Pitcht Battels of Lypsich and Lutzen*. Cambridge, 1634.

Ryken, Leland. *The Apocalyptic Vision in "Paradise Lost."* Ithaca, NY: Cornell University Press, 1970.

Salandra (Serafino, della Salandra). *Adamo Caduto*. Cosenza, 1647. Facsimile, Cosenza: Effesette, 1987.

Salkeld, John. *A Treatise of Paradise*. London, 1617.

Samuel, Irene. *Dante and Milton: The "Commedia" and "Paradise Lost."* Ithaca, NY: Cornell University Press, 1966.

———. "*Paradise Lost* as Mimesis." In *Approaches to "Paradise Lost": The York Tercentenary Lectures,* 15–29. Ed. C. A. Patrides. London: Edward Arnold, 1968.

———. *Plato and Milton*. Ithaca, NY: Cornell University Press, 1947.

Sandys, George. *Ovid's "Metamorphosis". Englished, Mythologized, and Represented in Figures by George Sandys*. Oxford, 1632. Ed. Karl K. Hulley and Stanley T. Vandersall. Lincoln: University of Nebraska Press, 1970.

———. *A Paraphrase upon the Psalms of David*. In *A Paraphrase upon the Divine Poems,* 81–240. 4th ed. London, 1676.

———. *A Paraphrase upon the Song of Solomon*. In *A Paraphrase upon the Divine Poems,* 25–43. 4th ed. London, 1676.

———. *A Relation of a Journey*. London, 1615.

Saurat, Denis. *Milton: Man and Thinker*. London: J. Cape, 1924.

Say, Samuel. "An Essay on the Harmony, Variety, and Power of Numbers, Whether in Prose or Verse," 1745. All but section 7 reprinted in *Eighteenth-Century Critical Essays,* vol. 1, 456–83. Ed. Scott Elledge. Ithaca, NY: Cornell University Press, 1961.

Schanzer, Ernest. "Milton's Hell Revisited." *University of Toronto Quarterly* 24 (1955): 136–45.

Schultz, Howard. *Milton and Forbidden Knowledge*. London: Oxford University Press, 1955.

———. "Satan's Serenade." *Philological Quarterly* 27 (1948): 17–26.

Scortia, P. Joannes Baptista. *De Natura et Incremento Nili. Libri Duo*. Lugduni, 1617.

Scot, Reginald. *The Discoverie of Witchcraft*. Reprint, Ed. Brinsley Nicholson. London, 1886.

Scot, Thomas. *Philomythie*. 2nd ed. London, 1622.

Selden, John. *De Diis Syriis*. London, 1617.

Seneca. *Hippolytus*. In *Tragedies,* 2 vols., trans. Frank Justus Miller, 1:217–423. Cambridge, MA: Harvard University Press; London: Heinemann, 1917. Reprint, 1968.

———. *Thyestes*. In *Tragedies,* 2 vols., trans. Frank Justus Miller, 2:89–181. Cambridge, MA: Harvard University Press; London: Heinemann, 1917. Reprint, 1961.

————. *Troades.* In *Tragedies,* 2 vols., trans. Frank Justus Miller, 1:121–223. Cambridge, MA: Harvard University Press; London: Heinemann, 1917. Reprint, 1968.

Servius Grammaticus. *Servii Grammatici Qui Feruntur in Vergilii Carmina Commentarii.* 3 vols. Ed. Georgius Thilo et Hermannus Hagen. Reprint, Hildesheim: Georg Olms, 1961.

Shakespeare, William. *The Plays of William Shakespeare . . . to Which Are Added Notes by Samuel Johnson and George Steevens.* 10 vols. 3rd rev. ed. Ed. Isaac Reed. London, 1785.

————. *The Riverside Shakespeare.* Ed. G. Blakemore Evans. Boston: Houghton Mifflin, 1974.

Shawcross, John T. "The Balanced Structure of *Paradise Lost.*" *Studies in Philology* 62 (1965): 696–718.

————. "The Metaphor of Inspiration in *Paradise Lost.*" In *Th' Upright Heart and Pure: Essays on John Milton Commemorating the Tercentenary of the Publication of "Paradise Lost,"* 75–85. Ed. Amadeus P. Fiore. Pittsburgh: Duquesne University Press, 1967.

Shelley, Percy Bysshe. "A Defence of Poetry." In *The Complete Works of Percy Bysshe Shelley,* vol. 7, 109–40. Ed. Roger Ingpen and Walter E. Peck. New York: Charles Scribner's Sons, 1940.

————. "On the Devil and Devils." In *The Complete Works of Percy Bysshe Shelley,* vol. 7, 87–104. Ed. Roger Ingpen and Walter E. Peck. New York: Charles Scribner's Sons, 1940.

Shirley, James. *The Brothers, a Comedie.* London, 1652.

Shumaker, Wayne. "*Paradise Lost* and the Italian Epic Tradition." In *Th' Upright Heart and Pure: Essays on John Milton (Commemorating the Tercentenary of the Publication of "Paradise Lost"),* 87–100. Ed. Amadeus P. Fiore. Pittsburgh: Duquesne University Press, 1967.

————. *Unpremeditated Verse: Feeling and Perception in "Paradise Lost."* Princeton, NJ: Princeton University Press, 1967.

Sidney, Sir Philip. *The New Arcadia (The Countess of Pembrokes Arcadia).* London, 1590.

Sikes, George. *The Life and Death of Sir Henry Vane.* London, 1662.

Silius Italicus. *Punica.* 2 vols. Trans. J. D. Duff. Cambridge, MA: Harvard University Press, 1927–34. Reprint, 1950–61.

Sims, James H. "Camoens' *Lusiads* and Milton's *Paradise Lost:* Satan's Voyage to Eden." In *Papers on Milton,* 36–46. Ed. Philip Mahone Griffith and Lester F. Zimmerman. Tulsa, OK: University of Tulsa Press, 1969.

————. *The Bible in Milton's Epics.* Gainesville: University Press of Florida, 1962.

Skelton, John. *The Complete English Poems.* Ed. John Scattergood. New Haven, CT: Yale University Press, 1983.

Smith, Miles. *Sermon Preached at Worcester.* Oxford, 1602.

Socrates Scholasticus. *Ecclesiasticae Historiae Autores.* Paris: 1544.

Solinus. C. Julius. *Polyhistor.* Trans. Arthur Golding. London, 1587.

Sophocles. *Oedipus the King.* Trans. F. Storr. In *Sophocles,* 2 vols., 1:1–139. Cambridge, MA: Harvard University Press, 1912.

———. *Philoctetes.* Trans. Hugh Lloyd-Jones. In *Sophocles,* 2 vols., 2:253–407. Cambridge, MA: Harvard University Press, 1994. Reprinted with corrections, 1998.

Sozomen. *The Ecclesiastical History of Sozomen.* Trans. Edward Walford. In *The Ecclesiastical History of Sozomen, Comprising a History of the Church, from* A.D. *324 to* A.D. *440. Also the Ecclesiastical History of Philostorgus,* 1–424. London: Henry G. Bohn, 1855.

Spenser, Edmund. *The Poetical Works of Edmund Spenser.* Ed. J. C. Smith and E. De Selincourt. London: Oxford University Press, 1912. Reprint, 1959.

Sprott. S. Ernest. *Milton's Art of Prosody.* Oxford: Basil Blackwell, 1953.

Stapleton, Laurence. "Perspectives of Time in *Paradise Lost.*" *Philological Quarterly* 45 (1966): 734–48.

Starnes, DeWitt T., and Ernest William Talbert. *Classical Myth and Legend in Renaissance Dictionaries.* Chapel Hill: University of North Carolina Press, 1955.

Steadman, John M. "Archangel to Devil: The Background of Satan's Metamorphosis." *Modern Language Quarterly* 21 (1960): 321–35. Reprinted in *Milton's Epic Characters,* 281–97. Chapel Hill: University of North Carolina Press, 1968.

———. "Ethos and Dianoia: Character and Rhetoric in *Paradise Lost.*" In *Language and Style in Milton,* 193–232. Ed. Ronald David Emma and John T. Shawcross. New York: Frederick Ungar, 1967.

———. "Eve's Dream and the Conventions of Witchcraft." *Journal of the History of Ideas* 26 (1965): 567–74.

———. "Felicity and End in Renaissance Epic and Ethics." *Journal of the History of Ideas* 23 (1962): 117–32. Reprinted in Steadman, *Milton's Epic Characters,* 105–22.

———. "Heroic Virtue and the Divine Image in *Paradise Lost.*" *Journal of the Warburg and Courtauld Institutes* 22 (1959): 88–105. Reprinted in Steadman, *Milton's Epic Characters,* 23–43.

———. "Image and Idol: Satan and the Element of Illusion in *Paradise Lost.*" *Journal of English and Germanic Philology* 59 (1960): 640–54. Reprinted in Steadman, *Milton's Epic Characters,* 227–40.

———. "A Milton-Ariosto Parallel." *Zeitschrift für Romanische Philologie* 77 (1961): 514–16.

———. "Milton and the *Argumentum Paris:* Biblical Exegesis and Rhetoric." *Archiv für das Studium der Neueren Sprachen und Literaturen* 202 (1966): 347–60. Reprinted in Steadman, *Milton's Epic Characters,* 160–73.

———. *Milton and the Renaissance Hero.* Oxford: Oxford University Press, 1967.

———. *Milton's Epic Characters.* Chapel Hill: University of North Carolina Press, 1968.

———. "Milton's Rhetoric: Satan and the 'Unjust Discourse.'" In *Milton Studies,* vol. 1, 67–92. Ed. James D. Simmonds. Pittsburgh: University of Pittsburgh Press, 1969.

———. "Recognition in the Fable of *Paradise Lost.*" *Studia Neophilologica* 31 (1959): 159–73.

———. "Satan's Metamorphoses and the Heroic Convention of the Ignoble Disguise." *Modern Language Review* 52 (1957): 81–85. Reprinted in Steadman, *Milton's Epic Characters,* 194–208.

————. "The 'Tree of Life' Symbolism in *Paradise Regain'd*." *Review of English Studies*, n.s., 11 (1960): 384–91. Reprinted in Steadman, *Milton's Epic Characters*, 82–89.

Stein, Arnold. *Answerable Style: Essays on "Paradise Lost."* Minneapolis: University of Minnesota Press, 1953.

Stephanus, Carolus [Charles Estienne]. *Dictionarum Historicum, Geographicum, Poeticum.* Geneva, 1596. Reprint, New York: Garland, 1976.

Stevens, Wallace. *The Collected Poems of Wallace Stevens.* New York: Alfred A. Knopf, 1964.

Stoll, Elmer Edgar. "From the Superhuman to the Human in *Paradise Lost*." *University of Toronto Quarterly* 3 (1933): 3–16.

————. "Give the Devil His Due: A Reply to Mr. Lewis." *Review of English Studies* 20 (1944): 108–24.

Strabo. *The "Geography" of Strabo.* 8 vols. Trans. Horace Leonard Jones. London: Heinemann; Cambridge: Harvard University Press, 1917–32.

Stroup, Thomas B. *Religious Rite and Ceremony in Milton's Poetry.* Lexington: University Press of Kentucky, 1968.

Summers, Joseph H. *The Muse's Method: An Introduction to "Paradise Lost."* Cambridge, MA: Harvard University Press; London: Chatto and Windus, 1962. Reprint, New York: Norton, 1968. Reprint, Binghamton, NY: MRTS, 1981.

Svendsen, Kester. "Epic Address and Reference and the Principle of Decorum in *Paradise Lost*." *Philological Quarterly* 28 (1949): 185–206.

————. *Milton and Science.* Cambridge, MA: Harvard University Press, 1956. Reprint, New York: Greenwood Press, 1969.

————. "Milton and the Encyclopedias of Science." *Studies in Philology* 39 (1942): 303–27.

Sylvester, Josuah, trans. *"The Divine Weeks" and Works of Guillaume de Saluse Sieur Du Bartas.* 2 vols. Ed. Susan Snyder. Oxford: Clarendon Press, 1979.

Tacitus, Cornelius. *The Histories, Books I–III.* In *"The Histories" with an English Translation by Clifford H. Moore. The Annals with an English Translation by John Jackson*, vol. 1 (4 vols.). London: Heinemann; New York: Putnam, 1925–37.

Taine, H. A. "Milton." In *History of English Literature*, vol. 2.2, 239–318. New ed. Trans. H. Van Laun London: Chatto and Windus, 1897.

Tasso, Torquato. *Aminta.* Milan: Biblioteca Universale Rizzoli, 1976.

————. *Gerusalemme Liberata.* Ed. Luigi Bonfigli. Bari: Gius, Laterza and Figli, 1930.

————. *Il Mondo Creato.* Ed. Giorgio Petrocchi. Florence: Felice Le Monnier, 1951.

————. *Lettera sul matrimonio.* In *Lettera sul matrimonio, consolatoria all'albizi,* ed. Valentina Salmosa, 1–41. Rome, Padua: Editrice Antehore, 2007.

Taylor, George Coffin. *Milton's Use of Du Bartas.* Cambridge, MA: Harvard University Press, 1934.

Taylor, Jeremy. "The Marriage Ring; or, The Mysteriousnesse and Duties of Marriage." In *XXV Sermons Preached at Golden Grove*, 219–31. London, 1653.

Tempest, Sir Richard. *An Entertainment of Solitarinesse.* London, 1649.

Tennyson, Alfred. *The Poems of Tennyson.* 3 vols. 2nd ed. Ed. Christopher Ricks. Burnt Mill, UK: Longman, 1987.

Tertullian. *Liber Adversus Praxean.* Trans. Peter Holmes. Ante-Nicene Christian Library. Ed. Alexander Roberts and James Donaldson. Edinburgh: T. and T. Clark, 1870. Vol. 15, 333–406.

———. *Liber de Corona.* In *Patrologiae Cursus Completus. Series Latina,* vol. 2, cols. 74–102. Ed. Jacques-Paul Migne. Paris, 1844.

Testi, Fulvio. *Poesie.* Milan, 1658.

Theocritus. *The Poems of Theocritus.* In *The Greek Bucolic Poets,* 5–351. Rev. ed. Ed. J. M. Edmonds. Cambridge, MA: Harvard University Press; London: Heinemann, 1928.

Theophrastus. *De Historia Plantarum.* 2 vols. Trans. Arthur Hort. Cambridge, MA: Harvard University Press, 1916.

Thevenot, Jean de. *Travels of Monsieur de Thevenot into the Levant.* Trans. Archibald Lovell. London, 1686.

Thompson, Elbert N. S. *Essays on Milton.* New Haven, CT: Yale University Press, 1914.

———. "Milton's Knowledge of Geography." *Studies in Philology* 16 (1919): 148–71.

Thomson, James. *Summer. A Poem.* London, 1727.

Thucydides. *History of the Peloponnesian War.* 4 vols. Trans. Charles Forster Smith. London: Heinemann; Cambridge, MA: Harvard University Press, 1919–23.

Tillyard, E. M. W. *Milton.* Rev. ed. London: Chatto and Windus, 1966.

———. *Studies in Milton.* London: Chatto and Windus, 1951.

———. *The Miltonic Setting: Past and Present.* Cambridge: Cambridge University Press, 1938.

Toliver, Harold E. "Complicity of Voice in *Paradise Lost.*" *Modern Language Quarterly* 25 (1964): 153–70.

Tostatus, Alonso. *Commentaria in Genesim.* Venice, 1728.

The Tragedie of Claudius Tiberius Nero, Romes Greatest Tyrant, 1607. Reprint, Oxford: Oxford University Press, 1914.

Traherne, Thomas. *Centuries, Poems, and Thanksgivings.* 2 vols. Ed. H. M. Margoliouth. Oxford: Clarendon, 1958.

Trissino, Giovanni. *La Italia Liberata da Gotthi.* 3 pts. in 1 vol. Rome and Venice: 1547–48.

Upton, John. *Critical Observations on Shakespeare.* London, 1748.

V., E. H. "A Phrase in *Paradise Lost.*" *Notes and Queries* 182 (1941): 95–96.

Valeriano, Joannis Pierii. *Hieroglyphica.* Coloniae Agrippinae, 1632.

Valerius Flaccus. *Argonautica.* Trans. J. H. Mozley. Reprint, Rev. ed. Cambridge, MA: Harvard University Press, 1936.

Virgil. *The Aeneid.* In *Virgil,* vol. 1, 233–571; vol. 2, 1–367. Trans. H. Rushton Fairclough. Rev. by G. P. Goold. Cambridge, MA: Harvard University Press, 1999–2000.

———. "Culex." In *Virgil*, vol. 2, 370–403. Trans. H. Rushton Fairclough. Rev. by G. P. Goold. Cambridge, MA: Harvard University Press, 2000.

———. *Eclogues*. In *Virgil*, vol. 1, 1–77. Trans. H. Rushton Fairclough. Rev. by G. P. Goold. Cambridge, MA: Harvard University Press, 1999.

———. *Georgics*. In *Virgil*, vol. 1, 80–237. Trans. H. Rushton Fairclough. Rev. by G. P. Goold. Cambridge, MA: Harvard University Press, 1999.

Vita Adae et Evae. In *The Apocrypha and Pseudepigrapha of the Old Testament in English*, vol. 2, 34–54 (2 vols.). Ed. R. H. Charles. Oxford: Clarendon, 1913.

Voltaire. *An Essay upon the Civil Wars of France, Extracted from curious Manuscripts. And also upon the Epick Poetry of the European Nations from Homer Down to Milton*. London, 1745. Facs. ed. in *Le Bossu and Voltaire on the Epic*, 37–130. Intro. Stuart Curran. Gainesville, FL: Scholars' Facsimiles and Reprints, 1970.

Vondel, Joost van den. *Adam in Ballingschap*. Amsterdam, 1664.

Waddington, Raymond B. "Appearance and Reality in Satan's Disguises." *Texas Studies in Literature and Language* 4 (1962): 390–98.

Waldock, A. J. A. *"Paradise Lost" and Its Critics*. Cambridge: Cambridge University Press, 1947.

Waller, Edmund. "The Battle of the Summer Islands." In *The Poems of Edmund Waller*, vol. 1, 66–74. Ed. G. Thorn Drury. London: George Routledge, 1893.

Walton, Brian. *S. S. Biblia polyglotta*. 6 vols. London, 1654–57.

Walton, Izaac. *The Compleat Angler*. In *The Compleat Walton*, 1–198. Ed. Geoffrey Keynes. London: Nonesuch, 1929.

Ward, Robert. *Animadversions of Warre*. London, 1639.

Warton, Joseph. *An Essay on the Writings and Genius of Pope*. 2 vols. London, 1756–82.

———. "Notes." In *The Works of Virgil: In Latin and English*. 4 vols. London, 1753.

———. *The Adventurer*. October 23, 1753, 181–86.

Warton, Thomas. *Observations on the Fairy Queen*, 2 vols. 2nd ed. London and Oxford, 1762.

———. *Poems upon Several Occasions by John Milton: English, Italian, and Latin, with Translations*. 2nd ed. London, 1791.

Webster, John. *Displaying of Witchcraft*. London, 1677.

Werblowsky, R. J. Zwi. *Lucifer and Prometheus: A Study of Milton's Satan*. London: Routledge and Kegan Paul, 1952.

West, Robert H. *Milton and the Angels*. Athens: University of Georgia Press, 1955.

Whaler, James. "Animal Simile in *Paradise Lost*." *PMLA* 47 (1932): 534–53.

———. "Compounding and Distribution of Similes in *Paradise Lost*." *Modern Philology* 28 (1931): 313–27.

———. *Counterpoint and Symbol: An Inquiry into the Rhythm of Milton's Epic Style*. Copenhagen: Rosenkilde and Bagger, 1956.

Whately, William. *A Bride-bush; or, A Direction for Married Persons*. London, 1619.

Whiting, George Wesley. "'And without Thorn the Rose.'" *Review of English Studies*, n.s., 10 (1959): 60–62.

———. *Milton's Literary Milieu*. Chapel Hill: University of North Carolina Press, 1939.

Whitney, Geoffrey. *A Choice of Emblemes*. Leyden, 1586.

Whittaker, E. T. Introduction to *Sir Isaac Newton's Opticks*. 4th ed. New York: Dover, 1931.

Wierus (Weyer), Johann. *De Lamiis*. Franckfort am Mayn, 1582.

Wilding, Michael. *Milton's "Paradise Lost."* Sydney: Sydney University Press, 1969.

Willet, Andrew. *Hexapla in Genesin*. Cambridge: Cambridge University Press, 1605.

Willey, Basil. *The Seventeenth Century Background*. London: Chatto and Windus, 1934.

Williams, Arnold. "Milton and the Renaissance Commentaries on Genesis." *Modern Philology* 37 (1940): 263–78.

———. *The Common Expositor: An Account of the Commentaries on Genesis 1527–1633*. Chapel Hill: University of North Carolina Press, 1948.

Williams, Charles. *The English Poetic Mind*. Oxford: Clarendon, 1932.

Wind, Edgar. *Pagan Mysteries in the Renaissance*. London: Faber and Faber, 1958.

Wimsatt, W. K., Jr. *The Verbal Icon: Studies in the Meaning of Poetry*. Lexington: University Press of Kentucky, 1954.

Woodhouse, A. S. P. "Pattern in *Paradise Lost*." *University of Toronto Quarterly* 22 (1952): 109–27.

Wordsworth, William. "Preface." In *Poems*, vol. 1, vii–xlii. London: Longman, Hurst, Rees, Orme, and Brown, 1815.

———. *The Letters of William and Dorothy Wordsworth*. 8 vols. Oxford: Clarendon Press, 1935–39. 2nd ed. arranged and edited by Ernest De Selincourt. Oxford: Clarendon Press, 1966–88.

Wright, B. A. *Milton's Poems*. New York: E. P. Dutton, 1956.

———. *Milton's "Paradise Lost."* New York: Barnes and Noble, 1962.

———. "A Note on Milton's Diction." In *Th' Upright Heart and Pure: Essays on John Milton Commemorating the Tercentenary of the Publication of Paradise Lost*, 143–49. Ed. Amadeus P. Fiore. Pittsburgh: Duquesne University Press, 1967.

———. "Note on *Paradise Lost*, IV.310." *Notes and Queries* 203 (1958): 341.

———. "'Shade' for 'Tree' in Milton's Poetry." *Notes and Queries* 203 (1958): 205–08.

———. "Stressing of the Preposition 'without' in the Verse of *Paradise Lost*." *Notes and Queries* 203 (1958): 202–03.

York Plays. Ed. Lucy Toulmin Smith. Oxford: Clarendon, 1885.

Young, Edward. *Night Thoughts*. Ed. Stephen Cornford. Cambridge: Cambridge University Press, 1989.

Index